Crime and Criminology

JAY LIVINGSTON

Montclair State College

Prentice Hall
Englewood Cliffs, New Jersey 07632

Library of Congress Cataloging-in-Publication Data

Livingston, Jay.
   Crime and criminology / Jay Livingston.
      p.   cm.
   Includes bibliographical references and index.
   ISBN 0-13-192782-5
   1. Criminology. 2. Crime--United States.   I. Title.
HV6025.L537 1992
364--dc20   91-27015
                                                  CIP

Acquisitions editor: Nancy Roberts
Editor-in-chief: Charlyce Jones Owen
Cover art: *Straphangers 5 Lex*, 1949, by August Mosca. Courtesy of Grand Central Art Galleries.
Marketing manager: Roland Hernandez
Editorial/production supervision: Mary Kathryn L. Bsales

Copy editor: Eleanor Ode Walter
Designer: Levavi & Levavi/Amy Rosen
Cover design: Circa 86
Prepress buyer: Kelly Behr
Manufacturing buyer: Mary Ann Gloriande
Supplements editor: Sharon Chambliss
Editorial assistant: Pat Naturale

Credits—Photos: ONE: The Bettmann Archives; TWO: Laimute E. Druskis; THREE: United Nations; FOUR: Teri Leigh Stratford; FIVE: Weston Kemp; SIX: AP/Wide World Photos; SEVEN: Pitkin/Baker; EIGHT: AP/Wide World Photos; NINE: N.Y. Convention and Visitors Bureau; TEN: National Library of Medicine; ELEVEN: Eugene Gordon; TWELVE: UPI/Bettmann Newsphotos; THIRTEEN: Eugene Gordon; FOURTEEN: Stan Wakefield; FIFTEEN: Laimute E. Druskis; SIXTEEN: Charles Gatewood; SEVENTEEN: Laimute E. Druskis: p. 448–RESPECT Words & Music by Otis Redding, Copyright © 1965 East Memphis Music & Time Music. Copyright assigned to Irving Music, Inc. (BWI) 1982. All rights reserved. International Copyright Secured.

© 1992 by Prentice-Hall, Inc.
A Simon & Schuster Company
Englewood Cliffs, New Jersey 07632

Printed in the United States of America
10 9 8 7 6 5 4 3 2 1

ISBN   0-13-192782-5

Prentice-Hall International (UK) Limited, *London*
Prentice-Hall of Australia Pty. Limited, *Sydney*
Prentice-Hall Canada Inc., *Toronto*
Prentice-Hall Hispanoamericana, S.A., *Mexico*
Prentice-Hall of India Private Limited, *New Delhi*
Prentice-Hall of Japan, Inc., *Tokyo*
Simon & Schuster Asia Pte. Ltd., *Singapore*
Editora Prentice-Hall do Brasil, Ltda., *Rio de Janeiro*

Contents

6 *VIOLENT CRIMES, PART II: WOMEN AND CHILDREN*   *192*

PART THREE   THEORIES OF CRIME

PART FOUR   **THE CRIMINAL JUSTICE SYSTEM**

13   SOMETHING BLUE: THE POLICE   *427*

14 *COURTS AND RIGHTS*   *468*

15 *REHABILITATION*   *515*

Preface

ANOTHER CRIMINOLOGY TEXT?

"So why don't *you* write one?"

Some colleagues and I were sitting around a hotel room in Baltimore one evening at a sociology convention. I was running through my usual list of complaints about criminology textbooks, for several years of teaching the subject had sharpened my ability to point out what was wrong in these books. I had assigned one or two that I thought dealt with the subject in a serious way, presenting research findings as they related to each topic. But my students had consistently found these books frustratingly dull and inconclusive. I had to admit, the writing often sounded like a social science "review of literature"—e.g., "Schav (1977) found this, but Kugel and Cholent (1981) found that, while Knaidlach (1982) using a different measure found something else." I also have looked at books that might have appealed to the students but which I rejected as oversimplifying complicated issues. Too many of them gave scant attention to some central but difficult issues like race and social class. Books that did devote more than two pages to these topics tended to be ideologically one-sided and tendentious. What was a teacher to do?

Some of the others in the room added their own complaints about textbooks in the courses they taught. But someone finally asked me: "So why don't *you* write one?" The question wasn't meant as a challenge but rather as a suggestion, even as encouragement.

Several years later, you are now holding the results. During those years, I learned something about crime and criminology and about writing textbooks. I have also changed in my sympathy and respect for the authors of other textbooks. Every book, certainly this one, has its flaws—its errors and omissions. The errors are the result of the author's own limitations and perhaps the limitations of criminology itself. The omissions are the result of the necessity of making choices, choices about what to include and what to leave out. One criminologist who read earlier drafts of this book suggested that the introduction include an explanation of hypothesis-testing and mathematical modeling. Another wanted more thorough treatment of certain sociological theories. Still another suggested cutting back the material on the criminal justice system. And there were others. Some of these suggestions I incorporated, others I did not. In these decisions, I am grateful for the advice of my editors, who said on more than one occasion, "It's *your* book."

Throughout the writing of this book, I tried to keep three main goals in mind: first, to treat the various topics seriously, trying to answer the kinds of questions that students might ask; second, to address these questions with systematic evidence from actual research; and third, to present this material in a way that kept it interesting.

AN OVERVIEW OF THE BOOK

Part One. In the introductory chapter I try to make the case for evidence-based thinking about crime, for criminology differs from everyday talk about crime not so much in its ideas but in its use of evidence to test those ideas. Chapter Two asks the question, "Why is crime a problem?" and looks at crime as a political issue during the last quarter century. Chapter Three describes some of the difficulties of counting crime as well as the results of different methods of counting. It also gives some data on long-range trends in crime (mostly in the United States)—especially the puzzling decline in urban crime in the late 19th century—and it offers two competing explanations of those trends. Chapter Four presents evidence on the relation of crime to four demographic variables—age, race, sex, and social class—and tries to show why different sources of information (self-reports and arrests) give different answers.

Part Two. The first three chapters of this section examine in more detail the crimes usually known as "Index crimes" (though aggravated assault appears mostly in the category of family violence). Evidence from descriptive research—quotations from interviews with typical criminals—gives something of the flavor of ordinary street crime. The quantitative evidence should help in evaluating different explanations of these crimes. The next two chapters take a similar approach to organized crime and white-collar crime, two topics where, unfortunately, criminology must usually make do with case studies rather than quantitative data.

Part Three. Criminological theory is the topic that, from the student's perspective, carries the greatest potential for drugery. I have done my best here to present the classic statements on crime in a way that makes them as vital to students as they have been to criminologists. The order of presentation for both the biological/psychological and the sociological theories is for the most part chronological. In an earlier draft, I tried to place these ideas into categories (structural/cultural/process), but too many of the theories crossed these boundaries.

Part Four. Doing something about crime is usually the specific province of the criminal justice system—the police, the courts, and the prisons. In each of these sections, I try to focus on the effect these institutions have on crime. Of course, some side issues were too interesting or too important to leave out. Chapter Thirteen, therefore, besides discussing the police as crime-fighters, also has some historical material on the police as well as a discussion of police misconduct. Chapter Fourteen outlines the reasons for our adversarial court systems and for some of the due-process protections (those notorious "technicalities") that derive from the Constitution. The final three chapters are about prison, though they contain almost nothing about the internal dynamics, the sociology and psychology, of prison life. Instead, I focus on the question of how (if at all) prisons serve as an antidote to crime. To what extent and at what cost does the criminal justice system rehabilitate, deter, or incapacitate criminals?

ACKNOWLEDGMENTS

I came by most of the ideas and information in this book in the course of years of teaching criminology. To all those people—students, colleagues, friends—who asked questions, offered ideas, or just listened as I tried to sort my thoughts; to them, though they are far too numerous to list here, I owe the largest debt of gratitude. I have also benefited from the advice of the reviewers who read earlier drafts of the manuscript: Mitchell Chamlin, University of Oklahoma; Richard J. Lundman, Ohio State University; Sarah L. Boggs, University of Missouri-St. Louis; Richard Vandiver, University of Montana; Lawrence Rosen, Temple University; and Russell Craig, Ashland University. Comments on various sections of the manuscript and discussion of specific issues came from colleagues, friends, and others in the field: Candace Clark, David Dodd, Sylvia J. Ginnot, Jennifer Hunt, Roger Lane, S. A. Livingston, Peter Reuter, Wesley Skogan, and Amy Srebnick.

Thanks also to Bill Webber and Nancy Roberts, editors at Prentice Hall, for their encouragement, to Katy Bsales and the rest of the Prentice Hall production staff, and to the Word Perfect Corporation, without whose software I probably could never have completed this manuscript.

Finally, a very special thanks to my wife, Joan Tedeschi, for her love and support throughout the entire project.

J. L.

Introduction

CHAPTER 1

ON SCIENTIFIC THINKING AND OTHER MATTERS, OR WHAT DO I KNOW THAT A 16-YEAR-OLD DOESN'T KNOW?

ONE EVENING, ON THE WAY FROM THE ELEVATOR TO MY APARTMENT, I FELL INTO A conversation with my neighbor's son, a bright kid of 15 or 16. He asked me what I was teaching, and when I said, "criminology," he asked what that was about. By this time, we were at the doors of our respective apartments and I wanted to say something quick yet impressive.

"Well, we try to figure out the reasons for the increase in crime," I said.

"That's easy," he said, and suddenly I found myself wondering what I had missed. How could questions I had been puzzling about for the last several years have an easy answer—an answer that had eluded me yet was obvious to this teenager?

"It is?" I asked.

"Sure," he said, "the decline in morality."

At the time, I was at a loss as to how to respond. I couldn't tell him that he was wrong, for he might well have been right. Still, I knew that there was something wrong with his answer, but what? I was thankful that my key was already in the lock and that I could avoid answering by merely stepping into my apartment, which is exactly what I did.

I had a similar experience one semester when I began my criminology course by asking students to write down questions for the final exam: "Ask the kinds of questions that you would like to be able to answer after taking a course in criminology." The most popular question, in various wordings, was, "Why is there so much crime?"* I then asked students to answer the question. At first they balked—after all, answering questions was the teacher's job—but when I insisted, they came up with answers. Among other factors they mentioned were poverty, unemployment, drugs, peer pressure, the breakdown of the family, the lenience of the courts, and the decline in morality.

At this point I realized that the students' answers were strikingly similar to the leading theories in criminology. I was facing the same problem my neighbor had raised, only worse, for this time I could not avoid it: If everybody already knows the answers to "What are the reasons for crime?," then what do I have left to teach them for the rest of the semester?

Evidence

Only much later did I realize what the real problem was. It was not in people's answers to questions about crime. It was in my definition of the subject I

---

* The runner-up was "What is criminology?" I disallowed this question as lacking substance. Would these students in their other courses really thirst to know, "What is American history?" or, "What is accounting?"

teach. Criminology is not really about figuring out the reasons for crime. Most people, it turns out, offer answers very similar to those offered by criminologists who devote their working lives to these matters. Instead, what *criminology* is all about is finding out what we know about those questions and answers. What is the **evidence**, and how can we refine our ideas to make them more consistent with that evidence? The evidence is important because it allows us to test ideas to see to what extent they are true . . . or false. Most of the time, of course, the evidence is not so conclusive that it demonstrates an idea as absolutely true or absolutely false. Instead, social scientists usually speak in terms of whether the evidence *supports* the idea.

To put it another way, what differentiates criminology (or any social science) from everyday conversation is that science tries to anticipate one question: What if people disagree? Suppose I had said to my neighbor, "You say that the cause of crime is the decline in morality. My other neighbor says that morality has nothing to do with it. How can I know that you're right and he's wrong?"

Logic and Common Sense

"It's obvious," my neighbor might have said. "Everybody knows that the level of morality has been going down. And if people are less moral, then they're going to commit more crime."

At first this argument sounds persuasive. It certainly seems to me that morality is at a lower point than it was when I was younger. My neighbor's second statement about the morality-crime connection is also perfectly logical. The only trouble is that he has still not provided any evidence. He has offered common sense or common knowledge, and he has offered logic. But he has not offered any evidence. In everyday discussions, common sense, common knowledge, and logical deductions provide most of the support for people's arguments. But social science requires evidence to make sure that common sense and logic are actually right; for sometimes, what is logical, or what everybody "knows," turns out to be wrong.

The Fire Sermon

Each semester, after the introductory class, I begin my criminology course with a quiz. Since it's only the second day of class, I don't expect anyone to know the answers, but I do ask students to make their best guesses. One of the first questions is this:

Which of the following accounts for more deaths in the United States each year?
a. fires
b. drownings
c. neither—they are about the same

Nearly everyone selects fires. Nobody actually knows, but most people are very sure of their choice. Then I ask for the reasons for this answer. Some students have trouble coming up with a reason. It just seemed obvious, like common sense. After a moment for further thought, usually someone will say that you see more fires on the news. Other students reason that everybody lives in a building and is therefore at risk for fires, but only those who spend time on the water can die by drowning. Along the same lines, some students reason that we live in buildings all year round but spend only the summer months near the water. Still others say that a single fire can kill several people at once, but drowning is more an individual matter.

Evidence—Systematic and Anecdotal

These are all good reasons, often good enough to convince the few people who originally selected the other choices. But these reasons, for the most part, are not evidence. Evidence refers not to what logically *should be* but to what actually *is*. To give another example, many people believe that instituting capital punishment in their state will reduce crime. "If you stood to lose your life," they reason, "wouldn't you be less likely to kill someone?" This again is logic, not evidence. The evidence on what actually happens when states pass death penalty laws does little to confirm this logic.[*]

But now suppose that during our death penalty discussion someone says, "I heard about this guy in some state where they'd just passed a death penalty for cop-killers. He had a gun when he was arrested and was going to shoot, but he didn't. He said later that he could see going to prison for 10 years for a robbery, but he wasn't going to risk losing his life for shooting a cop." Isn't this evidence that the death penalty works?

Yes, it is evidence. It refers to something that actually happened. But it is a special kind of evidence—what social scientists call **anecdotal** evidence. An anecdote is a story, usually about a single event. It provides an excellent illustration of some idea. The problem is not with the fact (the event did actually happen). The problem with anecdotal evidence is whether it represents things in general. Is this potential cop-killer typical of most other potential cop-killers, or is he a rare exception? Can we go from one instance to a large generalization about cop-killer laws?[*] Does the ratio of fires to

[*] See Chapter 16 for a fuller discussion of the death penalty as a deterrent to murder.

[*] The answer is no. The death penalty for cop-killing has had no general deterrent effect on the killing of police officers. (William C. Bailey and Ruth D. Peterson (1987), "Police Killings and Capital Punishment: The Post-Furman Period," *Criminology*, vol. 25, no. 1, pp. 1–25.)

drownings that you see on the news represent their true proportion in the real world?

Anecdotal evidence is useful for illustrating a point, but for providing information that would allow us to generalize, it is usually inadequate. Anecdotal evidence, like the preceding story may be interesting. But if you are thinking scientifically, you should not find it very convincing. Suppose, for example, that I said that the crime rate was going down, and when you asked me for evidence, I said, "Well, I have a friend who was mugged last year, but he wasn't mugged this year." Would you find this to be convincing or adequate evidence for a decline in the crime rate? Probably not. Instead, you would want more **systematic** evidence. By systematic, I mean evidence that is gathered according to fairly regular procedures so that anybody who used those procedures would arrive at similar results. Anecdotal data usually fail this test. If you, too, asked a friend about victimization this year and last year, both of us would be using the same procedure—asking a friend about victimization—but we would probably come up with different results.

The most obvious type of systematic evidence comes to us in the form of statistics, or **quantitative data**—numbers that tell us how much of something there is. But nonstatistical, **qualitative data** from intensive interviews or "participant observation" also may be systematic. Some of the best and most durable studies in social science have been qualitative studies based on systematic observation. These studies usually describe how something works—a town government, a criminal gang, a marriage, a mental hospital. The choice of evidence—quantitative or qualitative—depends on the question being asked. If we want to know how much, we need quantitative data; if we want to know how something works, we need qualitative data. In either case, we must be sure the evidence has been gathered systematically.

Of course, to rely on anecdotal evidence (telling stories) is much easier—easier to do and easier to understand. Some people even dismiss systematic quantitative evidence, saying, "Oh, you can prove anything with statistics." In fact, the reverse is true. If you accept anecdotal evidence as proof, you can prove anything with anecdotes; for no matter how implausible the proposition, you can find at least one story that supports it: "Smoking cigarettes makes you live longer. My grandfather smoked two packs a day and he lived to be 96."

Death by Water

Let's return from this digression to our question about fires and drownings. In class, much of the logical reasoning and most of the anecdotal evidence (stories that students have heard about) point to fire as the cause of more deaths. But the systematic evidence, gathered by various agencies and presented as quantitative data, gives a different answer. (see Table 1–1). Each

Table 1 ▪ Accidental Deaths

Year	Fires	Drownings
1975	6,071	8,000
1980	5,600	7,100
1981	5,067	6,277
1983	4,600	6,600
1985	4,900	5,300
1986	5,210	6,351
1987	5,028	6,353

Source: National Safety Council.

year, drowning accounts for about 25 percent *more* deaths than do fires, a fact that surprises nearly everyone.

Variables

Obtaining systematic evidence to test ideas about crime is much more complicated. Let's take my neighbor's idea that a decline in morality is responsible for the increase in crime. The task for the social scientist is to make this idea testable; that is, to state it so that we can get evidence to support or contradict it. To put the idea to any kind of scientific, systematic analysis, we have to separate it into its components. My neighbor was really making three assertions: (1) that morality has in fact declined, (2) that crime has in fact increased, and (3) that the decline in morality caused the increase in crime.

We have now translated the idea into a statement about the relationship between two **variables**. A variable is just what its name implies—something that can vary, that can have more than one category. Age is a commonly used variable. We can divide it into two categories (e.g., under 21, 21 and up), or we can divide it into many categories (age 1, 2, 3, 4, etc.).* In my neighbor's theory, the two variables are morality and crime.

Defining and Measuring Variables

Our first task is to find out whether morality has decreased. But you can quickly see that a term like *morality* is subject to many different definitions.

* Age need not always be a variable. For example, if we study only one age group—e.g., "people in their 30s"—without bothering to compare older 30s with younger 30s, then age in this study is not a *variable* since we have only one category.

My idea of morality may be different from yours. But that is not the principal problem. The problem is vagueness. In order to make the statement scientifically testable, we have to define morality so specifically that it can be measured. To say that morality has declined means that whatever morality is, there's less of it than there used to be. Whether the variable is something as vague as morality or as specific as a cause of death, as soon as we use concepts like "more" and "less," we are talking about quantity. And if we are saying that there are different quantities of something, then we ought to have some way of measuring those quantities. Of course, it takes some thought and ingenuity to figure out a way to define morality so that it is countable. But unless we do so, we have little hope of getting adequate evidence.

Social scientists, criminologists included, have spent much time trying to come up with ways of turning abstract concepts like social class, opportunity, peer pressure, anomie, sociopathy, or social attachment into measurable variables. Often the measurement depends on people's responses to a questionnaire. Some questions try to assess people's ideas—their **attitudes** or **beliefs**. For example, to measure morality, we might ask people how strongly they agree or disagree with a series of statements like "Sometimes telling a lie is unavoidable," or "With government the way it is today, you really can't blame people for cheating a little on their income taxes." Other questions ask about actual **behavior**. Our morality questionnaire might ask students whether during exams they have looked at the papers of others seated near them, and if so, how regularly. It is far beyond the scope of this introduction or this book to go into all the complexities of constructing a scale or index of morality. I certainly hope I never have to construct such a scale, for no matter which items I included and how I phrased the questions or counted the behavior, many people would object that I had left out something important. And they would probably be right. Still, although even the best-constructed scale is subject to criticism, these measures do provide evidence for the purposes of testing ideas.

In criminology, the second part of our task is usually the definition and measurement of crime. While crime is a less elusive variable than morality, it still raises questions—questions about which crimes to count and where to find statistics about them. The first half of Chapter 3 explores these problems in much more detail, so for now I will say only that any measure of crime, like any measure of morality, will have its imperfections. In fact, an important question for criminologists is, "How do we know how much crime there really is?" Or, put slightly differently, "How good are our measures of crime?" To noncriminologists, defining and measuring variables may seem "merely technical" and therefore of little interest. But that's the difference between criminology and everyday discussions of crime. Criminology is concerned with *evidence*, and criminologists want to know how good that evidence is.

Social Science Generalizations

The third part of the task—showing that a change in one variable causes a change in the other—is usually the most difficult part of social science. Even if the data show that 30 years ago morality was higher and crime was lower than they are today, that would not necessarily mean that one caused the other. Establishing a *causal* relationship between two variables is difficult, and it often involves sophisticated mathematical techniques. In some sections of this book, while discussing some actual research, I will try to describe some of the problems and methods of establishing a connection between variables. The difficulties are such that often social scientists do not even use the word *cause*. Even when they can show that the two variables are related, they will instead say, for example, that lower morality "is associated with" higher levels of crime.

Most of the conclusions and evidence in criminology (certainly most of those you will find in this book) concern groups, not individuals. Suppose that we constructed some measure of morality and found that indeed morality was higher 30 years ago than it is now. This statement is a generalization about the **difference between two groups**—Americans of 30 years ago and Americans today. (Keep in mind that I am not presenting any real evidence of such a change; this example is entirely hypothetical.) But this does not mean that *every* American in the 1960s was more moral than *every* American in the 1990s. In all generalizations, even ones we are fairly certain of (e.g., men are taller than women), there will be many exceptions, so we must be careful about using a fact about **group** differences to make predictions about **individuals**.

In applying generalizations to individual cases, social science uses the language of **probability**. We cannot say with certainty that if you smoke, you will develop lung or heart disease. We can say only that if you smoke, you will increase your probability of getting these diseases. Even if smoking increased that probability to 90 percent, you might still be among the 10 percent who remain healthy. Yet just as one anecdote does not prove a generalization, the negative example of the healthy smoker does not disprove the generalization. In this case, we know that 10 cases out of 100 will be just such negative examples.

As you read through this book, and more important, when you see news items about crime, I hope you will keep in mind these distinctions and try to ask the right questions about the evidence and the generalizations.

WHAT YOU WILL NOT FIND IN THIS BOOK

Because so much of criminology revolves around these generalizations about group differences and about probability, it often ignores the individual case, especially if that case is highly unusual. Everyday discussions of crime, on the other hand, often focus precisely on the highly unusual case—the one that is in the headlines today, the one that gives rise to best-selling books and TV miniseries. But, as I try to explain in the next chapter, criminology is not television. In this book, there will be no lengthy probing of the unusually depraved, ingenious, or unexpected crimes.

Nor will this book have much to say about the solution of particular crimes. It will contain very little about criminalistics or police science—dogged investigation, high-tech tests of bullets or blood, and Sherlock Holmes-like deduction—though these are precisely the elements that make for a good story on the screen or in novels. In fact, the image of crime we get from television, movies, and fiction is one of ingenious (or psychotic) criminals eventually caught by even more ingenious and heroic police (mixed in with much gunfire and tire-screeching). Certainly such cases exist, but most crimes involve fairly ordinary techniques on the part of both the criminal and the police (see Chapter 13).

This book lacks something else as well—an answer to the crime problem. You may find the absence of answers frustrating, but a moment's thought should rid you of such expectations. If there were an answer, certainly somebody would have discovered it by now and the problem would have been long since solved. (And if by some chance I were the only person with the answer, I could probably find other outlets for my unique knowledge, outlets more socially beneficial and more financially rewarding than writing a college textbook.)

In fact, perhaps it is misleading to talk about crime in terms of problems and answers, as if a complicated social issue were like one of those algebra problems whose answer could be found in the back of the book. To be sure, there are answers—ensure that every criminal is punished; eliminate poverty; provide opportunity; strengthen the family; improve education—but to translate an answer into a policy raises further questions, questions of economics, law, morality, and politics. So while this book may not have *the* answer, it does offer in the next chapter some questions and some evidence about the crime problem.

The Crime
Problem

CHAPTER 2

FEAR OF CRIME

WHY IS CRIME A PROBLEM?

Every year, the opinion polls ask people to name the most important problems facing the country. You can imagine some of the choices: inflation, unemployment, peace, the environment, AIDS, education, drugs, crime, abortion, and others. Every year, I ask my students the same question, and usually several select crime as one of the top three. My next question—the one that opens this chapter—sounds rather stupid, especially coming from someone who teaches criminology. But it's my job to ask questions whose answers seem to be obvious. "But why is crime a problem?" Often students will say that crime is a problem because there's so much of it. But "so much" of something is a problem only if that something is bad.

"Why is crime bad?" I ask. "What's wrong with crime?" This question sounds even more stupid, but I ask students to humor me and try to answer it. Often the first thing someone will say is, "People get hurt." True enough. Criminals sometimes injure or even kill their victims. But more than twice as many people are killed by automobile accidents than by murder. Faulty consumer products and home accidents injure more people than do crimes like assault and robbery. Accidents at work and job-related disease cause more death and physical harm than do murders, rapes, robberies and other street crimes. For example, in 1988, about 2,500 people were murdered by strangers. Even adding the 6,500 murder victims whose relationship to the murderer was unknown, this number is still less than the 12,000 people who died in work-related accidents.[1] People risk death, disease, and injury on the job every day; yet not very many people would identify highway safety or dangerous working conditions as one of the nation's most important problems.

What about the costs of crime? Yes, crime costs money. But the crimes that cost the most money (and do the most physical harm) are *not* "the crime problem." Ask people what crimes they think of as the crime problem, and they will probably mention murder, rape, robbery, burglary, and theft. The cost of these crimes, though, pales in comparison with the cost of the crimes they are not thinking of: white-collar crimes. Ways of defining and measuring the cost of white-collar crime vary. A quarter century ago, a congressional committee estimated the cost at $44 billion;[2] a Senate subcommittee on antitrust "estimated that faulty goods, monopolistic practices, and other violations annually cost consumers between $174 and $231 billion."[3] It is unlikely that the cost of white-collar crime has decreased since then. The fraud involved in the savings-and-loan collapse of recent years is estimated at $20 billion, and the bank failures resulting from the fraud may cost the country as much as $150 billion. Tax cheating by individuals and corporations costs $100 billion each year.[4] In any case, even the lowest of these estimates far exceeds the $15 billion lost to street crime in 1988.[5] Even in terms of individual stealing, the costly crimes are committed by people who hardly fit the image of the hardened criminal. Banks, stores, and other businesses lose far more to their own employees through theft and embezzlement than they lose to shoplifters and robbers.*[6]

Why, then, when people talk about the crime problem do they mean street crime, and not white-collar crime or employee theft? For one thing, street crime seems to have a greater psychological impact on its victims. Victims of rape and robbery may suffer psychological effects of the crime—depression, anxiety, phobias—even years after the crime occurred, and, unfortunately, the criminal justice process often does little to ease their suffering. The same can be true for the relatives of murder victims. Even victims of nonviolent crimes like burglary may feel violated. The important difference between street crime and white-collar crime is that with street crime, the victimization is sudden and direct. White-collar crime, by contrast, seldom brings the criminal face-to-face with the ultimate victim. In shoplifting and employee theft, the real victim is the consumer, since the store or the corporation can cover its losses by charging higher prices. Because the company spreads the cost over a large number of people, no one person's loss is very noticeable. Other businesses also can pass along the cost of their victimization in a nearly invisible way that does not arouse public outrage. Few people know just what portion of their insurance premiums goes to cover insurance fraud, or how much higher the interest on their savings accounts might be were it not for embezzlement; few people filling a prescription know the excess profit the drug company may be taking through illegal monopolistic practices. Yet even if people were aware of these extra costs, it is unlikely that they would see them as a grave social problem. Our response when we read about bribes, embezzlement, kickbacks and price-fixing may range from indifference to anger to admiration. But we probably do not rank these crimes as threats to society.

Even for crimes that cause physical harm, the more indirect the link between cause and effect, between criminal and victim, the weaker will be the public reaction. If air or water pollution from a chemical plant doubles cancer rates in a region, the cause-effect link is almost invisible—especially since it may take decades before the diseases appear. The same gradual victimization occurs in occupational diseases like black lung among coal miners, brown lung among cotton workers, or asbestosis among asbestos workers (and their families). These diseases may cause workers higher rates of disability, death, and financial loss than do crimes like robbery, burglary, and assault.[7] Companies in these industries might even have prevented much of this suffering; but instead, in the interest of making profits, they avoided spending money for safety measures. In some cases they may have suppressed evidence of the dangers of their products (see box).[8] Yet when

---

* The cost of responding to crime, currently about $60 billion, also is far higher than the amounts of money lost to street crime.

DRUG MAKER PLEADS GUILTY OVER LETHAL SIDE EFFECTS

Allentown, Pa, Dec. 13 (AP)—The SmithKline Beckman Corporation has pleaded guilty and two of its medical officials have pleaded no contest to charges of failing to report to the Food and Drug Administration the lethal side effects of the blood-pressure drug Selacryn.

In June the Philadelphia-based pharmaceutical giant and three officers were charged with 14 counts of failing to file reports with the drug agency of adverse reactions to Selacryn, and 20 counts of falsely labeling the drug with a statement that there was no known cause-and-effect between Selacryn and liver damage.

Doctors across the country have reported 36 deaths and at least 500 severe cases of liver and kidney damage linked to Selacryn.

people think of the crime problem, they think of street crime, not corporate crime.

Clearly, street crime can be psychologically damaging for some—though certainly not all—of its victims. But the victims of accidents at work or on the roads may also suffer aftereffects and become fearful in situations that recall the accident. The fear of crime, however, has come to affect nonvictims as well. It seems to have become pervasive in U.S. society. One study done in 1980 found that 40 percent of Americans were "highly fearful" of becoming victims of violent crime and that half of all households kept a gun for protection. The majority of city residents said that they were afraid to go out at night.[9] When so many people are afraid, the problem goes beyond individual fear. It changes the nature of social life for everyone. "Fear of crime," the authors of the study said, exaggerating perhaps a bit, "is slowly paralyzing American society."[10] Studies like this suggest a contrast between a low-crime society where people walk about at night, gather in public places, feel little fear and much goodwill toward others they meet, and a society where people sit armed behind locked doors and barred windows, suspicious and fearful of others. In the words of Charles Silberman, "Crime . . . undermines the social order itself by destroying the assumptions on which it is based."[11] The crime problem, then, is not a matter of money or physical harm; many things that we do not think of as serious problems (job-related risks, car accidents, white-collar crime) cause more physical harm and financial loss. What makes crime a problem is the damage it causes to social life because of fear. According to this view, America has undergone a transformation from an open society to a fearful one, and crime—street crime—has been the cause.

How Important Is Fear of Crime?

This idea about crime and fear sounds logical, but the matter may not be quite so simple. We must reduce this general idea to a few questions which

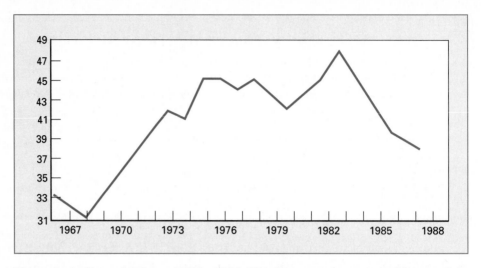

Figure 2–1 Fear of Crime, 1965–1988. "Is there any area around here—that is, within a mile—where you would be afraid to walk alone at night?" Percent answering "yes."

can then be tested against the available evidence. Has fear of crime been increasing? Has fear of crime changed American society? What is fear of crime? Is crime the cause of this fear? At first, some of the answers seem so obvious that asking the questions sounds at best naive, perhaps even stupid. But as we look more closely, we may find that what is obvious and logical may be difficult to prove, and may even be wrong.

There is little doubt that fear of crime has increased. For several years polls have asked people, "Are there any places within a mile of where you live where you'd be afraid to walk alone at night?" In 1967, about 31 percent of the population answered yes; by 1982, that figure had risen to 48 percent, though it has since fallen back to about 40 percent. (see Figure 2–1)[12] That finding is roughly consistent with those of other surveys. More concretely, increased sales of guns, private guard services, burglar alarms, and other protection devices attest to increases in fear. There is also ample anecdotal evidence in people's reminiscences about less fearful times when they could safely walk anywhere, day or night, sleep on fire escapes or in city parks; leave doors unlocked; and so on. Their routine behavior was different. In other words, fear is not just a feeling that people express in opinion polls; it changes the way they behave. Those who say they are more afraid are more likely to say that they have limited their behavior because of crime. Still, one–third of those who felt unsafe reported no such limiting of their activities.[13] These statistics suggest that while fear of crime has brought about some changes in American life, it has not "paralyzed American society."

Fear of Crime and the Urban Problem

On a larger scale, some people blame crime for the deterioration of cities. According to this view, crime drives from the city those who can afford to move, while those who cannot move are left to be victimized by the inner-city criminals. As the affluent leave, the cities become poorer; for those who remain, housing, schools, and other services deteriorate.

Most evidence confirms the pattern of migration from cities to suburbs and smaller towns, and the subsequent decline of city institutions. Census statistics on population and income, as well as other measures of urban well-being, paint the same bleak picture: Despite recent "gentrification" trends in a few areas where more affluent people have rehabilitated once-poor neighborhoods, the cities have been crumbling.

But is crime responsible for this change? If crime were the cause of the move to the suburbs, then the increase in crime would have to have happened first—or at least at the same time. But suburbanization began to accelerate in the late 1940s, immediately after World War II. Then, as now, people moved to the suburbs in search of better housing, more space, and better schools. During this period, urban crime rates were relatively low, perhaps at their lowest in the 20th century.[14] Since people started leaving the cities before crime rates soared, it is unlikely that crime caused the move to the suburbs. Even during the higher-crime years of the 1970s, surveys of people who had left the cities seldom found crime to be the most important factor. In a Portland, Oregon, study, only 5 percent of elderly people who had moved gave crime as a reason.[15] In another survey covering eight cities, only 3 percent of those who had moved gave crime as an important reason.[16] Even adding those who cited "deteriorating neighborhoods" or a "bad element moving in" (which may have been euphemisms for crime) raised this figure only to 10 percent.[17] The most important factor in moving to the suburbs seems to be the financial ability to do so. The higher people's income, the more likely they will move, regardless of their feelings about crime. If fear of crime were the basis for the decision to move, "movers" should be much more likely to say that crime had been a big problem in their old neighborhood. But in one study, when movers and "stayers" were asked how serious a problem crime was (or is) in their urban neighborhood, they gave similar responses. About 20 percent of each group rated crime as "a big problem." Table 2–1, based on a Chicago survey in the 1970s, shows the effects of income and perception of crime on people's decision to leave the city. (The figures are for whites only.)

Among poor and moderate-income whites, the problem of crime does not affect the decision to move. In the $10,000 to $20,000 income group, those who saw no problem in crime and those who saw a big problem were equally likely to move (46 percent and 47 percent, respectively). Only in the upper-income group did considering crime to be a big problem increase the like-

Table 2–1 ▪ **Effects of Income and Perception of Crime on People's Decision to Leave the City**

Current income and extent crime was a problem in original neighborhood	Percent who moved to the suburbs
Under $10,000	
Not a problem	38%
Some problem	20
Big problem	28
$10,000–$20,000	
Not a problem	47
Some problem	50
Big problem	46
Over $20,000	
Not a problem	47
Some problem	66
Big problem	67

Source: From Skogan and Maxfield, COPING WITH CRIME, p.248, copyright © 1981. Reprinted by permission of Sage Publications, Inc.

lihood of moving. Since the time this study was done, crime as a reason for moving has increased somewhat. In a 1980 Gallup poll, crime for the first time outranked overcrowding as a reason for leaving the city, and this perception was especially marked in large cities (1 million or more).[18] This change, along with the figures on who moves out, suggests a much more complicated and disheartening connection between crime and the deterioration of city neighborhoods. When middle-class and stable working-class people (i.e., those who can afford it) move to the suburbs, they leave behind the poor and the powerless—the people who are least able to resist crime in their neighborhood. The cycle seems to have started with the exodus from the inner city. This exodus led to an increase in crime, and crime then added pressure for further emigration.[19] Nevertheless, crime remains but one among several factors in the population shift from city to suburbs. Even if someone had waved a magic wand and reduced urban crime rates to match those of the suburbs, the miracle probably would have done little to change this historic demographic trend.

Who's Afraid?

Whatever the consequences of fear of crime, we must still ask, "What *causes* fear of crime?" The obvious answer is that crime causes fear of crime. Fear has increased because crime has increased; when crime goes down, fear will go down. This sounds logical. However, the connection between crime and fear may not be so direct or clear. Attempts to link fear specifically with crime often turn up puzzling results. The first such efforts were carried out as part of a Presidential Commission report on crime, published in 1967. The research on fear surveyed people in Washington, D.C., and used a measure of "exposure to crime," which included being a victim of a crime, a witness to a crime, or a close friend or relative of a victim. If crime creates fear, then those who had been exposed should have been more fearful than others. But the two groups showed no differences in levels of fear. It turned out that people who had been exposed to crime were no more fearful than those who had not been so exposed.[20] Does this mean that exposure to crime does not create fear of crime? Not quite. As later research showed, being victimized does make a person more fearful. But several other causes of fear made it more difficult to distinguish the effects of victimization alone.

To understand how criminologists discover such hidden effects, consider the following results from a later survey on the same question. Researchers asked a sample of people how safe they generally felt: very safe, moderately safe, moderately unsafe, or very unsafe. To simplify matters, Tables 2–2 through 2–4 reduce these categories to two—safe and unsafe, regardless of degree. The people also were asked whether they had experienced a "personal victimization" (rape, robbery, assault, or larceny with contact between offender and victim). Table 2–2 divides the sample into three groups: people who had no such victimization, people who had been victimized only once, and people who had been victimized twice or more. The survey polled 10,000 households in eight cities; the numbers in columns B and C are estimates (in thousands) for the entire population of these cities projected from this sample.

Table 2–2 shows no consistent effect of victimization. Among those who had been most victimized and those who had not been victimized at all, the proportion of people who felt unsafe was the same (45 percent—columns A and D), and those who had been victimized once were only slightly more likely than the others to feel unsafe. How can this be? How can crime—

Table 2–2 ■ Fear and Victimization

A Number of victimizations	B Number in category (1,000s)	C Number who felt unsafe (1,000s)	D Percent who felt unsafe
None	2,977	1,329	45%
One	180	90	50
Two or more	33	15	45

Source: Derived from Garofalo, *Journal of Research in Crime and Delinquency*, vol. 16, no. 1, copyright 1979. Reprinted by permission of Sage Publications, Inc.

Table 2–3 ■ Fear and Victimization

Males only

A Number of victimizations	B Number in category (1,000s)	C Number who felt unsafe (1,000s)	D Percent who felt unsafe
None	1,296	321	25%
One	96	32	34
Two or more	22	8	36
Total	1,413	361	

Source: Derived from Garofalo, *Journal of Research in Crime and Delinquency*, vol. 16, no. 1, copyright 1979. Reprinted by permission of Sage Publications, Inc.

direct, personal crime—have no consistent effect on fear? One possibility is that in this research, as in life, one of the things that often complicates matters is sex. To eliminate these complications we have to separate the men from the women, as shown in Tables 2–3 and 2–4.

Looking at men and women separately, we find what we expected: The more victimizations, the greater the percentage of people who say they feel unsafe. The victimized groups have an additional 10 percent (roughly) who say they feel afraid. What confused the issue in the unseparated data was the fact that women are both more likely to feel unsafe and *less* likely to have been victimized. Of the estimated 1,777,000 women, 95,000 (84,000 and 11,000) had been victimized—5.3 percent. Of the men, 118,000 of 1,413,000—or 8.3 percent—had been victimized. Yet, as you can see by comparing column D in both tables, much smaller percentages of men were fearful of crime.

Fear, then, depends not just on victimization but also on sex. Therefore, to eliminate sex as a source of confusion we have done what is called "con-

Table 2–4 ■ Fear and Victimization

Females only

A Number of victimizations	B Number in category (1,000s)	C Number who felt unsafe (1,000s)	D Percent who felt unsafe
None	1,682	1,008	60%
One	84	58	69
Two or more	11	7	67
Total	1,777	1,073	

Source: Derived from Garofalo, *Journal of Research in Crime and Delinquency*, vol. 16, no. 1, copyright 1979. Reprinted by permission of Sage Publications, Inc.

trolling for" the effects of sex. We control for a variable by holding it constant—that is, not letting it vary. When we looked only at men, sex ceased to be a variable. When we do look at sex as a variable, we see that it is quite an important one. To see this effect of sex, we control for victimization. We do this by looking at each level of victimization separately and comparing men with women at each level. For example, among those with no victimizations, 25 percent of the men but 60 percent of the women said they felt afraid. For people with one victimization, 34 percent of the men and 69 percent of the women were afraid. In both cases, women were more than twice as likely to say they were afraid.

There is still another factor in fear that we need to control for—age. Older people are less likely to be victims of crime but are more likely to feel unsafe. In Table 2–5 we have controlled for both sex and age. The percentage in each category represents the percent feeling unsafe; the number in parentheses represents the total number in that category. For instance, in the category of men 35 or older who had not been victimized, there were an estimated 742,920 such persons, and of those 32 percent said they felt unsafe. Table 2–5 is recreated from the original research report.

By comparing across different categories, we can at last see that in all sex and age groups, victimization does increase levels of fear, something that was not at all evident before we separated the data according to these categories. (But see the box on p. 20.)

Besides showing that victimization increases fear, these data tell us other interesting things. First, victimization was fairly rare. Only 5.7 percent of the total sample (and only 12.2 percent of the most victimized group—young males) had experienced a personal victimization. (Of the total, only 1.7 percent had been injured seriously enough to require medical attention.) Usu-

Table 2–5 ■ Fear of Crime (Proportion Responding "Somewhat Unsafe" or "Very Unsafe") by Total Number of Personal Victimizations During the 12 Months Preceding the Interview, by Sex and Age: Eight Impact Cities Aggregate, 1975

Number of victimizations	Males		Females	
	Under 35	35 or older	Under 35	35 or older
None	15%	32%	54%	64%
	(551,974)	(742,920)	(661,380)	(1,001,074)
One	22%	54%	63%	77%
	(61,404)	(34,753)	(48,183)	(35,887)
Two or more	26%	56%	64%	79%
	(15,930)	(6,181)	(8,196)	(3,021)

Source: Derived from Garofalo, Journal of Research in Crime and Delinquency, vol. 16, no. 1, copyright 1979. Reprinted by permission of Sage Publications, Inc.

Even when all the right factors are present, some cases just don't fit with social science knowledge. In the following incident, the victim is elderly, the robber is a stranger, and the crime involves physical injury and losses worth $3,000. Yet the victim's reaction does not seem to be one of fear.

L.I. GOLFER TEES OFF AFTER BEING STABBED

Mineola, L.I.—A 77-year old Long Island man was stabbed in the chest and hand Sunday by a robber, then went out to play golf before telling the police or seeking medical attention, the police said.

The golfer, Abe Zuckerman, was waiting in his car in front of his Mineola home about 6 a.m. Sunday when a man walked up and demanded his wallet. . . .

When the robber found the wallet to be empty, he grabbed Mr. Zuckerman's $3,000 Rolex watch. In the struggle that followed, Mr.

Zuckerman was stabbed in the chest and right hand. . . .

As the two men were fighting, Mr. Zuckerman's golfing partner drove up, saw what was happening and began blowing his car's horn until the assailant fled. . . .

The two men went to the golf course, played and then reported the robbery to the police.

Copyright © 1987 by The New York Times Company. Reprinted by permission.

ally, the more serious the crime, the more unsafe it makes the victim feel—though not always. One study of women victims found that a purse snatch increased fear nearly as much as a rape did.[21] The results also show that there is more to fear than just crime itself. Less than 6 percent of the people had actually been victimized by any of the crimes, yet nearly half said they felt unsafe because of crime. Clearly, they were not basing their fears on their own experience with crime.

Fear and Familiarity

Instead of the simple idea that fear of crime is caused by crime, perhaps we should think of fear as a person's reaction to an environment. According to this perspective, the causes of fear fall into three general categories: characteristics of the person, of the environment, and of the relation between the two. So far, we have seen how personal factors—such as having been a victim of a crime, being a woman, and being older—can contribute to feelings of vulnerability and fear. Certain characteristics of a person's relationship to the environment also may increase the feeling of apprehension. Something as simple as unfamiliarity can create fear. The Presidential Commission found that people felt safest in their own neighborhoods. Even among people who lived in high-crime areas, only about 20 percent of the people felt less safe in their own neighborhoods than they did when they were in other neighborhoods with less crime.[22] In another survey, only 7 percent of the people rated their own neighborhoods as more dangerous than average.[23] Polls over the last 20 years have usually found that while about 80 percent of the people think crime is increasing in the United States, less than half (sometimes less than one-fourth) think that crime is increasing in their neighborhood.[24] As another example, a journalist writing about New York City's subways observed that when people relate anecdotes of harrowing experiences on the subway, "they are invariably speaking of something that happened on another line, not their usual route. Their own line is fairly safe, they'll say."[25] It's as if people reasoned this way: Unfamiliar is unsafe, familiar is safe; my neighborhood is familiar to me, therefore it is safe—even though the unfamiliar places may in fact be safer. Crime is something that happens elsewhere.

It is not just the unfamiliarity of an environment that causes fear. Remember, between 40 and 50 percent of the population say they feel unsafe at night in their own neighborhoods. Nor is it the crime rate per se that makes people afraid. When you walk in a neighborhood—even your own—do you have any idea of the crime rate there? Do you know whether it has been increasing or decreasing? Even social scientists do not rely on statistical information in all their daily decisions. From time to time I read newspaper items detailing crime statistics; I usually clip and save these articles. But most of the time, as I walk down my street, I cannot recall whether my precinct reported increases or decreases, and I certainly cannot recall how many crimes there were or whether my precinct's statistics were higher or lower than those of other neighborhoods.

Reading the "Signs of Crime"[26]

If we don't know how much crime a neighborhood has, how do we arrive at our sense of safety or fear? Some interesting evidence on this topic comes from a 1977 study of four neighborhoods in Chicago.[27] All four had crime rates higher than the Chicago average. The researchers (Dan Lewis and Michael Maxfield) wanted to know about people's perceptions of typical predatory crimes (burglary, robbery, rape, assault). They asked people, "Where are the dangerous areas around here?" "How big a problem is each type of crime?" "How likely is it that you will be a victim?"

On the question of dangerous places, people generally had "a remarkably accurate picture of the crime problem they face," since they could identify the dangerous sections of their neighborhoods. But on the other questions, neighborhoods differed in some interesting ways. People in the Wicker Park section were the most likely to rate crime as a big problem; they also gave relatively high estimates of their own personal risk. However, the official crime rate in Wicker Park was lower than in two of the three other neighborhoods. The Woodlawn neighborhood was much the reverse, with a high incidence of crime yet lower levels of fear and concern. "Why," ask Lewis and Maxfield, "were the residents of Woodlawn seemingly unconcerned about the extraordinarily high rate of crime in their neighborhood? Why did the people in Wicker Park seem to live in fear when the rate of serious crime . . . was below that in Woodlawn?"

It might have been that Wicker Park had an older population, since we know that older people tend to be more fearful yet less victimized. But no, it was just the opposite. Woodlawn had more than twice the proportion of its population over 60 (22 percent vs. 8 percent in Wicker Park). Even with fewer older people and a crime rate 25 percent lower than that of Woodlawn, Wicker Park residents were more fearful. Why? A clue comes from some other questions the researchers asked—questions about problems in the neighborhood: teenagers hanging out in the street, vandalism, abandoned buildings, and drug use. The researchers grouped these under the heading of "incivility."* They are not predatory crimes, but they are, as other studies also have found, the kinds of things that make people feel uncomfortable and even afraid. More important, they are visible. Predatory-crime rates are merely numbers on file in some government agency; even predatory criminals, who, presumably, make some effort to be inconspicuous, are less visible than abandoned buildings and other signs of disorder. Imagine yourself walking through a city neighborhood where several buildings are boarded up and covered with graffiti; where groups of teenagers (looking more tough than preppy) are lounging around the streets, some of them offering you a variety of drugs as you pass. Would you feel much safer knowing that the local precinct recorded 25 percent less crime than the more pleasant-looking neighborhood you had walked through a few blocks back?

Not only were Wicker Park residents more afraid of crime, they were also more concerned about incivility. Wicker Park had both a large number of abandoned buildings (thanks to a recent wave of arson, allegedly for profit) and a proportion of teenagers that was the highest of any of the four neighborhoods, more than twice that of Woodlawn. Other studies have discovered this link between incivility and the perception of danger. In a Baltimore housing project, when residents were asked what was the most dangerous place, "they mentioned a place where young persons gathered to drink and play music, despite the fact that not a single crime had occurred there."[28] Vandalism, even when minor (and in some cases artistic), may have a similar effect. According to the subway journalist quoted earlier, "The first perception of subway crime came with the appearance of widespread graffiti in 1970. It was then that passengers took fright, and ridership . . . dropped rapidly. Passengers felt threatened."[29]

When we see graffiti or boarded-up buildings or loitering teenagers, we assume that less visible but more serious crimes must also be lurking. In-

---

* This study was done *before* the cocaine and crack boom of the late 1980s. Most of the drugs involved were marijuana, heroin, and, to a lesser extent, amphetamines. The study also predated "the homeless"—another feature of urban life that became more visible in the 1980s and would fall into the category of incivility.

civility, for most people, serves as a sign of crime. Yet the two need not always go hand in hand. A Newark, New Jersey, experiment in police tactics provides interesting data on incivility and crime. The city of Newark decided to put more police back on foot patrol, instead of cruising in cars. The purpose of the foot patrols was to maintain order, and officers were given fairly wide discretion in deciding what "order" meant in their particular area. In one case, it might mean controlling drunks and addicts by not letting them lie down on the sidewalks (sitting was o.k.), or drink on the main streets (side streets were o.k.), or bother people waiting for buses. Rowdy groups of teenagers might be dispersed, prostitutes kept to certain areas. Police enforced the rules with occasional street "sweeps," arresting all those who had not heeded the loudspeaker command to "break it up." In addition, the police tried to form closer ties to the residents. They opened a storefront office where people could come with questions and problems. Officers even went door to door, distributing a crime-prevention newsletter, asking residents about problems that might need police attention, and encouraging people to join neighborhood-watch groups.[30]

In one sense, the experiment worked: People felt safer and thought crime had been reduced; they also felt better about the police. On the other hand, actual crime rates did not go down. According to these figures, although people felt safer from predatory crime, they were in fact no safer than they had been before.[31] Obviously, people were taking their cues about crime from the orderliness of the neighborhood. Were they just fooling themselves?

Some social scientists argue that the people's instinctive reactions are right—that incivility or disorder does lead to real crime. For example, in an article called "Broken Windows," prominent criminologist James Q. Wilson and co-author George Kelling cite the Newark study and conclude that "disorder and crime are usually inextricably linked, in a kind of developmental sequence." They envision a scenario in which a stable neighborhood

can change, in a few years or even a few months, to an inhospitable and frightening jungle. A piece of property is abandoned, weeds grow up, a window is smashed. Adults stop scolding rowdy children; the children, emboldened, become more rowdy. Families move out, unattached adults move in. Teenagers gather in front of the corner store. The merchant asks them to move; they refuse. Fights occur. Litter accumulates. People start drinking in front of the grocery; in time, an inebriate slumps to the sidewalk and is allowed to sleep it off. Pedestrians are approached by panhandlers.

. . . Many residents will think that crime, especially violent crime, is on the rise. . . . They will use the streets less often. . . .

Such an area is vulnerable to criminal invasion. Though it is not inevitable, it is more likely that . . . cars will be stripped, drunks will be robbed, . . . prostitutes' customers will be robbed . . . perhaps violently. . . . Muggings will occur.[32]

Wilson and Kelling's logical scenario of disorder leading to serious crime suffers from only one major flaw: It runs afoul of the evidence of the Newark study they are discussing. Over the course of nearly a year, "community policing" had stemmed and reversed the tide of disorder; good citizens had come back to the streets rather than stay home behind locked doors. Yet rates of predatory crime had "not gone down—in fact may have gone up." Contrary to expectation, changes in "signs of crime" had no effect on actual predatory crime.[33]

What seems logical is not always the way the world is. While crime is usually most prevalent in neighborhoods of much incivility and disorder, changing the level of disorder may have little effect on crime. Of course, we should distinguish among the various types of disorder. As precursors of crime, unmended broken windows are not the same as a gang of teens, and the loitering of teenagers or winos is different from the presence of drugs. Even with drugs, the connection between disorder and crime may depend on the nature of the drug. Apparently, the traffic in marijuana, heroin, and other pre-crack drugs was far less devastating to neighborhoods than is the crack trade that began to flourish in the late 1980s.[34] In any case, it is visible disorder and incivility, rather than the volume of crime, that make people feel unsafe.[35]

The picture of fear in relation to crime and disorder* should now be a little clearer. The three are interrelated; where we find one, we usually find the other two. But which is causing which? We have gone from the simple idea that crime causes fear of crime (model A in Figure 2–2) to the realization that both disorder and crime cause fear (model B), with disorder probably being the more important. There is also Wilson's idea that disorder eventually causes crime, and both cause fear (model C).

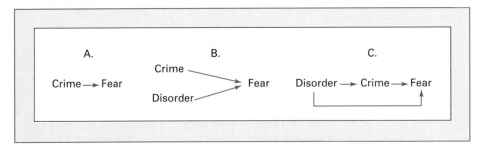

Figure 2–2 Models of Crime, Disorder, and Fear of Crime

---

* I am leaving out the individual characteristics of sex and age (about which we can do nothing).

Crime, Fear, and Community

Wilson's scenario, whatever its relevance (or lack of relevance) to the Newark study, does suggest an important factor that has been missing in our discussion so far: the general quality of the neighborhood, which provides the context for crime, disorder, and fear. Our images of "bad" and "good" neighborhoods include not only the physical environment but also the social one. At one extreme is the neighborhood people leave as soon as they can: many buildings are abandoned and vandalized; drug users and winos are in the streets; people do not know many of their neighbors; both crime rates and fear are high. At the other extreme is the kind of neighborhood where people know each other, have lived in the same place for many years, and take an active part in community life. They come to each other's aid, intervene or at least notify someone when they see someone or something suspicious, and feel safe in the streets and in their homes. Where crime and disorder are more frequent, residents also feel less attached to the community, more isolated, and more fearful.

Fear, in this picture, becomes a part of the relationship between the person and the general community, not merely an individual response to crime. The tighter integration of people in their communities probably helps to reduce fear and also may reduce disorder and crime. Unfortunately, Americans frequently have chosen to deal with the problem of neighborhood crime through individual rather than community efforts—usually by moving to a more pleasant area. This preference for individual solutions does little to improve community conditions. On the contrary, it may worsen them. Not only does it ensure that the poorest will be left in the high-crime areas, but the high rate of people moving out—even if others move in— makes stable attachments hard to maintain. As in Wilson's scenario of deterioration, when people are less involved, disorder may flourish; and the more disorder people see, the more they will want to move away. Once started, this cycle of deterioration is difficult to stop.

Crime is part of this general deterioration of a neighborhood already vulnerable because of its weak social integration. Strong community ties, on the other hand, may help a neighborhood resist urban decay. For example, the South Bronx section of New York City has suffered from deterioration that became the focus of national attention, with visits by presidential candidates and coverage by national television news. Yet in the midst of the South Bronx, an area called Belmont has remained stable and low in crime. Belmont is by no means an affluent neighborhood; it could be called working-class or lower-middle-class. But Belmont's residents have not moved out. People here know their neighbors more than do those in many wealthier urban areas. There is more of an active public life. People use the streets as a place to meet and talk. They are also more willing to take action when they see something suspicious happening. For example, an experiment done in a busy Manhattan neighborhood showed that a person could break into a car in broad daylight on a busy street, and seldom would anybody do anything to intervene. In Belmont, such an act would draw more attention and action. Criminals are more likely to be noticed, and if noticed, are more likely to be pursued.* Thus the strong sense of community, besides making Belmont a pleasant place to live, also serves to prevent crime.[36]

Creating Community

In the case of Belmont, residents were continuing a community that already existed. However, once a neighborhood has begun to disintegrate, reversing the process may prove more difficult. Interestingly enough, two of the Chicago neighborhoods studied by Lewis and Maxfield had been the sites of just such community-organizing efforts. One of these is Back of the Yards, named for its location behind the stockyards when the meat-packing industry was the chief employer in the area. This neighborhood served as the setting for Upton Sinclair's muckraking 1906 novel, *The Jungle*—an appropriate title at the time. The residents were poor, and they lived in slumlike conditions. Most were white Catholics, but the ethnic divisions among them (they were Polish, Irish, Lithuanian) made for a badly disorganized community. In the late 1930s, with the help of a young organizer named Saul Alinsky, Back of the Yards organized to pressure the city, landlords, merchants, and slaughterhouses for basic improvements—the sorts of things that today are guaranteed by law and frequently are taken for granted.[37] The Back of the Yards Council, which was formed at the time, was still the major neighborhood organization 40 years later when Lewis and Maxfield did their study on crime and fear. The stockyards had closed, and the area had changed. Now nearly 40 percent black and Hispanic, it was still a stable, working-class neighborhood. The average income was below the citywide average. The crime rate, while somewhat higher than the Chicago average, was the lowest of the four neighborhoods studied, and the people there were less fearful and less concerned about crime.[38]

Unfortunately, Back of the Yards may have been the exception rather than the rule. More recent efforts to organize community groups specifically to combat crime and disorder have not enjoyed the same kinds of success. Woodlawn provides a case in point. By 1960, it had become an impover-

---

* This attitude can, however, be carried to the point of brutal vigilantism tinged with racism. Three years after Belmont received attention as the nation's lowest-crime urban neighborhood, it was in the newspapers again. Belmont's population consists mostly of Italian-Americans and other "white ethnics," such as Albanians and Yugoslavians. In July 1986, two Puerto Ricans passing through the neighborhood "were attacked by eight white youths using a baseball bat and their teeth." One of the victims suffered skull and jaw fractures. (*New York Newsday*, July 30, 1986, p. 23.)

ished, black slum. Efforts of local clergymen to get the city to do something about the problems in the area had proven futile. So again Saul Alinsky was called in. And again, with much difficulty, the community slowly began to come together. The Woodlawn Organization (TWO) was formed to coordinate the activity of several smaller groups in the area; and after some successes against irresponsible landlords and dishonest merchants, Woodlawn successfully fought its powerful neighbor, the University of Chicago, over the university's plans to annex a large tract of land.[39] At the time of the fear study, the area was still impoverished but TWO was still functioning; and as we have seen, fear of crime was lower than one would expect. However, community efforts apparently had little effect on crime. Woodlawn's crime rate was the highest of the four neighborhoods studied, and in the years since the study, Woodlawn continued to deteriorate. The community organization became a weak, hollow shell.

In theory, then, community ties should reduce fear independently of other environmental factors (such as crime and disorder). In practice, as studies in other Chicago neighborhoods and Minneapolis have shown, these efforts are least successful in the neighborhoods that need them the most—areas of poverty, high crime, physical deterioration, and rapid population turnover. If the community organization programs are successful at all, it is in areas where residents already have some link to the community, where existing organizations add anti-crime and anti-disorder efforts to their agenda.[40]

Anti-Crime Design

Neither Back of the Yards nor TWO was designed specifically as a crime-prevention project; they were general community organizations. More recently, however, both in cities and suburbs, neighborhoods have started programs aimed at reducing crime. One such campaign in the 1970s in the Asylum Hill section of Hartford, Connecticut, shows the effects that citizen involvement can have on crime and fear.[41] This neighborhood had begun to decay, with buildings left unrepaired and the crime rate rising. A group of concerned citizens, urban planners, and criminologists drew up an anti-crime plan for this neighborhood. The plan called for three strategies: physical changes (closing some streets, altering traffic routes) to make the environment less friendly to criminals; a neighborhood police team to work more closely with the residents; and community organizations to involve the residents themselves in reducing crime. Residents were to take a more active part in reporting suspicious happenings, in patrolling their neighborhoods, and in planning the environmental and policing parts of the program. The results at the end of the first year were encouraging. Arrests for burglary and robbery had increased, while the rates for these crimes had decreased.

As you might expect, fear also had decreased. But why? Because there was less predatory crime? Because there were more police? Or simply because the residents had gotten involved in their community? As it turned out, the next two years provided an unforeseen experiment to answer this question, for during those years Hartford's budget became strained, and the city had to cut back on police expenditures. The extra police effort for this neighborhood was abandoned; by 1979, arrests for burglary and robbery had dropped to their old levels, and crime rates had returned to levels equivalent to those for the rest of Hartford. But people in Asylum Hill did not become more fearful. Levels of fear remained lower, and involvement in the community remained higher. Apparently, when citizens feel that they are involved with others in an effort to do something about crime, they feel less threatened and more secure. The more people take an active role in the life of their communities, the less they feel afraid, just as you would probably feel safer walking with a group of friends than you would when walking alone. Alone and isolated, people feel vulnerable. As part of a network of people, or especially as part of an organization to reduce neighborhood crime, they may feel more in control and more protected.

The experience of Sally Merry, an anthropologist doing research on crime and fear, nicely illustrates the theme of this chapter.[42] Initially, when she moved into a housing project in the high-crime neighborhood that was the setting for her research, she felt afraid—nervous and tense—especially when walking alone at night. She also felt uneasy about the local drunks, who would lounge around the streets and sometimes fight with each other. However, "after several months, I learned that they . . . did not pose a threat to my person, only to my sense of order and propriety." As she got to know the neighborhood and its people, her fear decreased to sensible caution: "After I became aware of the frequency of purse-snatching, I stopped carrying a purse."

Eventually, she became friendly with a group of black youths that some residents thought were responsible for much of the crime in the area. Once she got to know them, she writes, "I suddenly found that I did not consider the project dangerous at all, even at night, and resumed carrying a purse." The laundromat, which had before seemed like a dangerous place where kids hung out, now "seemed like a familiar, safe place."

After two-and-a-half years, she was robbed one night at the entrance to her house by "a young man, his hand held inside his jacket, either holding a gun or pretending to." Merry says that she was "shaken but not frightened" by the robbery and that afterward she was only more cautious, not more afraid.

But what is the moral of this story? On the one hand, it is optimistic. It shows that, in Merry's words, "familiarity with people and places overcame an initial sense of danger, and even the experience of victimization did not lead to a resurgence of fear."[43] On the other hand, her story may be so unusual as to be cause for pessimism. After all, Merry was an educated, middle-class person whose daily work as an anthropologist was to get to know the residents. But for people with fewer resources, people with other problems to occupy their time, creating familiarity and social integration may be a nearly impossible task.

THE MEDIA AND FEAR OF CRIME

For humans, as for all animals, the cues of the immediate environment may trigger a fear reaction. But unlike other animals, humans are affected by more distant and abstract kinds of information. In estimating danger, we use not only the first-hand information of our own senses and experiences, but also our general knowledge. This knowledge comes to us from other people and from less personal sources, such as newspapers, television, and the other mass media.* Tens of millions of Americans watch a single national evening news show; together the three major networks broadcast the news to as many as 100 million people. Even a daily newspaper may reach a large percentage of a city's population. This central position gives the media tremendous potential power. If people form their ideas on the basis of what they know, and if people get that knowledge mostly from the mass media, then the people who control the media have a great influence over those ideas. Consequently, a handful of editors may determine what millions of people will know about the world. This influence may be especially strong because people also tend to believe what they learn from the media—especially television. Television, much more than newspapers, serves as the chief source of news information for nearly two-thirds of Americans. In surveys, less than half the people say they rely on newspapers. And only 22 percent say that they believe the daily papers. By contrast, 53 percent believe that television news is for the most part telling the truth.[44] Even this figure may underestimate the impact of some television newscasts. For example, until his retirement, the person Americans found most "credible" was Walter Cronkite, a man who read the news each evening on television.

For some kinds of news, the media necessarily have a monopoly as our source of information. How else could we know about space shuttles or wars in distant countries or the general condition of the economy? Yet even closer to home, we may have to look to the media for our information. In large cities, people may be ignorant of a newsworthy event that took place in their own building unless or until they see it on the news.

---

* The word "media" is the plural of "medium"—something that mediates or comes between (literally, in the middle); in this case, the medium comes between an event and a person's experience of that event. Newspapers, radio, movies, TV, etc. are *mass* media; the identical program or paper reaches a mass of people.

Images and Realities

What part do the media play in the way we think about crime? We know that knowledge of crime and fear of crime arise from personal kinds of information—victimization experience, word of mouth, threatening aspects of the environment. Do the media also influence our fears and ideas about crime? One way of finding out is to compare people's ideas about crime with the reality of crime and with the portrayal of crime in the media. One of the first pieces of research on this question asked residents of Colorado to estimate the increase in crime in that state. The researcher also looked at changes in the official crime rate and at changes in the amount of crime reported in the newspapers. This was in 1951, when television was still something of a novelty, and most people got their news from the newspapers. It turned out that changes in the actual crime rate had no effect on people's perceptions, nor did changes in the crime rate affect the volume of crime reported in the press.[45] But increases in crime *news* did alter the public perception of actual crime.

That study was published nearly 40 years ago, but its general conclusions still stand. A more recent study which included television as well as newspapers found a similar distorting effect. This study, done in New Orleans, not only measured the volume of all crime and crime news but broke the crimes down by categories, using the FBI's seven Index offenses.* As you might expect, the media paid a disproportionate amount of attention to certain kinds of crime. For example, in the real world according to police records, murder was the least frequently committed of these crimes, accounting for 0.4 percent of all reported Index crimes. Yet on TV news, nearly half the crime stories concerned murder. The newspaper (*The New Orleans Times-Picayune*) did not vary quite so much from the actual proportion of murder, but in general all the media exaggerated violent crimes (murder, rape, and robbery) and ignored property crimes (auto theft, burglary, larceny), even though these occurred far more frequently.

To check on the public's perception of crime, the researchers conducted interviews by phone with New Orleans citizens. Like the news media, the public overestimated the frequency of violent crime. They ranked robbery as the most common crime, though police statistics showed it to be third. As for rape and murder, these crimes were the least frequently committed; together they made up only 1 percent of recorded Index crimes. Yet the public ranked them as third and fourth in frequency—ahead of auto theft, assault, and larceny.

Of all four profiles of crime—police records, newspapers, television, and public perception—no two were very much alike, though the public's ideas

---

* The seven Index offenses at the time were murder, rape, robbery, aggravated assault, burglary, larceny, and motor vehicle theft.

were closer to those of the media than to the police statistics.[46] Of course, people realize that TV news is not a perfect reflection of statistical reality. It is also true that the media do occasionally report on crime rates and not just individual crimes, though which kind of story carries more weight is still an open question. One review of studies on the effects of the media concluded that "the public is more influenced . . . by official counts than by media emphasis."[47] Nevertheless, the Colorado and New Orleans studies show that the media may create some distortion in the public mind.

Crime Waves—In the Streets and in the Media

These studies also suggest that fear of crime in general or of some specific crime can increase when the media influence public perception about crime. Could it be that a "crime wave" that grips a city with fear is nothing more than a sudden spurt of stories in the media?

Consider the following incident: A politician walking near his office is accosted by two men; one hits him on the head and grabs him around the neck while the other takes his valuables. It is a classic strongarm robbery, what today is called a mugging. This incident, however, occurred in London in 1862, and the term used was "garroting." The case of Hugh Pilkington, M.P., made the newspapers as one more event in a crime wave. For several months, this crime wave—the garroting panic of 1862—held the middle and upper classes of London in fear. As one newspaper put it, "the statistics on garroting in recent years would present a very frightful catalogue of outrages." In fact, the police statistics on "robberies with violence" (i.e., garroting) showed no such increase. They remained steady at about 2.5 per month. However, *after* the panic began, statistics showed a fivefold increase, but this increase was caused not by an actual increase in garroting but chiefly by the heightened sensitivities of the police and courts. Under pressure to do something about this crime, police and courts treated as garroting what before might have passed for a drunken fight or simple theft, and several "persons of bad character" and "ticket-of-leave" men (the equivalent of parolees) were arrested and tried for garroting.[48] Thus, although there was no real increase in garroting, a "wave" of crime stories in the media caused an increase both in public fear and in crime statistics.

Somewhat more recently, a team of researchers headed by Mary Baker happened upon a similar crime wave. They had originally set out to measure the effects, if any, of a new style of policing in Phoenix, Arizona. Consequently, in September 1979 and again in July 1980, they asked Phoenix citizens about their victimization experiences, their attitudes towards the police, and their feelings of safety. In the 10 months between the two surveys, however, something much more noticeable than police changes took place. The official crime rate in Phoenix went up dramatically, and the media made this increase big news. The newspapers carried more stories on crime statistics and more editorials on crime. Some papers ran headlines like "Crime Pays . . ." and began to keep running accounts of crime statistics ("35th armed robbery this month"). In short, Phoenix was experiencing a crime wave.

Or was it? Baker's victimization survey—though the sample was too small to be conclusive—showed no increase in crime, and in retrospect our best guess is that in fact no such increase occurred. Why then had police statistics gone up? For one thing, three police chiefs had resigned and the new administration changed the departmental rules for recording crime. Crimes previously classified as less than serious might now be counted as serious crimes*, or perhaps previously the police chose to ignore some of the crime reports phoned in to them. In any case, the increase in crime took place on paper, not in the streets.

At the same time that the police chiefs were stepping down, the major newspapers, probably by coincidence, had assigned new reporters to coverage of the police and crime. These reporters, new to the police beat, may have been more enthusiastic about finding and filing crime stories. Equally relevant, 1980 was an election year, and both papers were supporting a $40 million bond issue for new jails. This political position just may have influenced the editor's selection of news stories. After all, an editor who wants people to vote money for jails may want to convince them that crime is on a dangerous upswing.

The criminals of Phoenix in 1980, like the garroters of London in 1862, were no more active or numerous than they had been the year before, yet a chance combination of other forces created a "crime wave": first, a change in the police department created an increase in officially recorded crime; second, eager new reporters filed more crime stories than their predecessors; and third, the newspapers played up the crime wave as an argument for the jail bond issue.

The crime wave had a predictable effect on the public's perception. More people thought crime was increasing in Phoenix generally and even in their own neighborhoods. And the more people perceived an increase in crime, the more afraid they felt. Thus the media had—independently of actual crime—increased the fear of crime.[49]

Making Waves

Baker and her colleagues did not monitor the local TV news, but another study of a crime wave in New York City found that crime news in one medium soon gets picked up by the others. The New York crime wave, rather than starting as an increase in overall statistics, concerned a very specific kind of crime—crimes against the elderly. In mid-October 1976, *The New York*

---

* For more on the official definitions of "serious" crime, see Chapter 3.

Daily News gave prominent coverage to a couple of particularly grisly murders of elderly people. By the next week, both *The New York Post* and a local television station also increased the number of news items devoted to crimes against the elderly. The heightened media coverage continued for a few weeks. The mayor and the police chief made statements about the problem and their actions to combat it, and by mid-December, the number of these news items had returned to what it had been before. As you might expect, most New Yorkers thought that crime against the elderly had gone up, and according to surveys, half the people over age 50 felt more fearful of crime than they had felt the year before.

In this case, police statistics did show that crimes against the elderly had increased, but in most cases the increase was no more than that of any other sort of crime, and murders of elderly people had actually decreased by nearly 20 percent. In other words, the statistics did not square with the image spread by the media that vicious criminals had suddenly decided to start victimizing old people. Here was another crime wave that happened in the news, not in the streets. Consequently, when criminologist Mark Fishman decided to study this crime wave, he and his assistants went not to the streets or to the police but to the offices of the newspapers and a local TV station.[50]

How did murder and other crimes against the elderly become so newsworthy when there was no substantial increase in such crimes? To answer that question, Fishman first had to learn how any event becomes news. Let us take a hypothetical example: A man age 72 and his wife, 70, are walking near their apartment building. Two young men approach. One grabs the man from behind; the other holds the woman by the arm and threatens her with a knife. They demand the couple's money and take the man's wallet and the woman's pocketbook—a total of $85 in cash. Then they run off.

Is this news? Will it be in the papers or on TV? The answer is, it depends. If the crime occurred in a small town, where the local weekly prints the entire police blotter including traffic tickets, it certainly will be in the paper. Or if one of the victims happened to be a senator or another important person, it will be news. But what if we are in a large city where such incidents occur each day? Will it be news?

The answer again is, it depends. It depends ultimately on a person who is neither victim nor criminal nor police officer nor criminologist. It depends on the news editor. Remember, the news stories we see in the media represent a very small number of events selected from a very large number of events. When the announcer says at the end of the news program, "And that's the news today," we may think we have seen "what happened." But millions of things happen. Which of them is important? To understand how a crime (or any event, for that matter) becomes news, it is more useful to think of the 45 minutes of local news (60 minutes minus the commercials, titles, and credits) not as what happened, but as the outcome of decisions—decisions made by news editors as to what is and is not news.

How does a TV news editor decide whether our hypothetical crime is worth putting on the news tonight? Fishman, in his months of research, discovered one thing you might guess just by watching your local news: Editors like to have the news tell a story. Rather than presenting the news as a display of unrelated items, the editor will try to arrange the show so that the items fit into larger categories, or what Fishman calls "themes." Two fires in different parts of the city and having nothing in common will appear on the news one right after the other since both fit into the theme of fire. If a theme already exists, the editor tries to find items that fit with that theme. In the fall of 1976, even before the crime wave, the TV station had on hand a continuing series of stories on a special unit of the police department which had been set up to deal with crimes against the elderly. An item like our hypothetical robbery would have provided the perfect lead-in to one of these feature stories. If, on the other hand, the station had been running a feature on drugs or auto theft, the editors might well have ignored our elderly victims. The same event that was not news last month might be the first item on the news today.

A crime theme, however, is not a crime wave. For the theme of crime against the elderly to become a crime wave, several currents had to flow together. All the media—at least the two newspapers and one TV station under study—began to stress this theme. There was no conspiracy, no design. But news editors do pay attention to other media. The TV editor fed on the news. On arriving at work, he read the papers, watched the wire services, and listened to an all-news radio station. So when the *Daily News* began to run front-page stories about elderly murder victims, the TV editor sensed that similar items were now newsworthy. In other words, like you and me, the news editor found out what was news by looking at the media. Presumably, the editors at the *Daily News* and the *Post* also watched television, and perhaps when they in turn saw crime against the elderly on the TV news, they concluded that these crimes were important enough for continued emphasis. Before long, the TV and newspaper editors had unwittingly bounced the theme back and forth, each time amplifying it, until the number of such stories in the media was six times what it had been only a month before. It had become a crime wave.

Besides the interest of the various media, two other important elements were crucial to the creation of a crime wave: criminals and police. The media do not make news out of nothing. There must be actual incidents—no matter how rare—to report. In the case of crimes against the elderly, in a region of nearly 10 million people, there will be more than enough such incidents each day. Not all crimes are so common. For instance, while he was doing his research, Fishman noticed the beginnings of a "wave" of Mafia killings in the media. But the gangsters apparently did not provide more murders, and the "gangland war" theme died from lack of incidents.

At another time, New York City subway crime seemed to be drawing media attention. This theme, too, fizzled, though not for lack of incidents. Certainly enough subway crimes occur each day to fill a newscast. Why did the media lose interest? In part because the police department did not want the publicity: The transit police chief told the *Daily News* that there was no crime wave. Who was a reporter to contradict such an official statement?

Just as the police department can dampen media crime waves, it also can sustain or even create them. In the fall of 1976, the Senior Citizens Robbery Unit had been most cooperative with the TV station in creating their features on crimes against the elderly. In a more general way, the police department provides the media with their crime stories, whatever the topic. Newspapers may have reporters covering the police beat, which usually means the press room at police headquarters, but the media rely on the "police wire" for most of their stories. This is a wire service over which the department sends basic information on the two dozen or so stories it thinks will most interest the media. The police department, too, is making decisions about what crimes are news, selecting some items and rejecting others. According to Fishman, the police try to provide what the media want. If the media seem interested in crime against the elderly, the police wire will send out more of these stories. The TV, newspapers, and police, then, all pay close attention to each other, and through this tangle of mutual influence they can create in the public mind the impression of a real crime wave, even when the statistics show otherwise.

Nobody involved necessarily wishes to raise the level of public fear. The media want to inform readers or viewers, but they must also compete with each other for the largest share of this audience. They certainly do not want to miss out on a hot story. The police want to help the media and perhaps want to direct public attention to certain crime problems. In 1976 in New York City, this intertwining of cooperation and competition produced a crime wave which had little basis in reality. Nevertheless, the media changed the people's perception about crime and lowered their sense of security.

Prime Time Crime

Only some of the crimes you see on TV occur on the news shows. After the news is over, prime time begins. If the news distorts the picture of crime, stressing particularly unusual or lurid crimes, at least it is constrained by the available facts. Prime time fictional shows can give free rein to the imagination, and that imagination frequently turns to crime—an average of 10 crimes a night, with a heavy overrepresentation of murder and other violent crimes. These shows depart from statistical reality in other ways as well. For one thing, in fictional TV shows, criminals seldom get away with their crimes; they are either caught or killed. Second, it is not usually the police who solve the crime. Private investigators or other interested civilians are more likely to figure it out. The police—especially those in uniform—come off little better than Keystone Kops, maybe worse: One study found that in

13 percent of all fictional TV crimes, the criminal was a policeman. While some TV criminals are police officers, most are likely to be professionals and business people rather than the poor or unemployed.[51]

Do these shows influence our perception of reality? Most of us would probably say no. We know the difference between fiction and fact. But most of us would probably also deny being influenced by the fictions in advertisements. We know, for instance, that in the real world athletes do not argue loudly about the qualities of the beer they drink. And few people would say that seeing these athletes influenced their choice of beers. Nevertheless, advertisers continue to spend hundreds of millions of dollars each year. Either commercials do influence us or advertisers are tossing a lot of money down the drain.

To check commercial's effectiveness, advertisers can look at their sales. Measuring the influence of televised crime is a bit more complicated. For example, many people think that fictional violence in the media increases the amount of violence in society. Researchers have done thousands of studies on this topic, and their results frequently contradict each other. Even when studies find that violent behavior and watching violent television shows do go together, seldom can they determine which causes the other. Such a result might mean nothing more than that violent people enjoy watching violent TV, not that their favorite shows make them more violent as people. And even when studies can isolate televised violence as one cause of "aggressive behavior," the behavior measured is rarely serious enough to be called crime.[52]

Measuring the influence of television on people's perceptions also poses many problems, though there have been several empirical studies of this question. Generally, people who watch television a great deal overestimate the real-world levels of violent crime, killings by strangers, and numbers of police. The correlation exists, but it is not especially strong. Although TV has some influence on these perceptions, several other factors—socioeconomic status, sex, education—are stronger influences.[53]

Assessment of television shows as a cause of fear is complicated by a nearly insurmountable chicken-and-egg problem. Which comes first—watching TV or being fearful? It is true that heavy TV-viewers express more fear of crime than do infrequent viewers. We cannot conclude, though, that TV-watching causes fear. In the first place, when we control for other factors (like sex or age), the relationship decreases. But more important, this correlation might mean that fear causes TV-viewing, not that TV-viewing causes fear. People who are afraid to go out will stay home and watch television.

My own guess is that the media usually have little direct, lasting effect on fear. Even with media crime waves, the media have a built-in corrective tendency: The media's continual need for new themes may lead them to seize upon certain stories and create—in the media and in the public mind—a crime wave. But the same need for something new will eventually force such a crime wave to fizzle out. After two or three weeks, yet another robbery of an elderly person is no longer interesting news; unless there is something unusual about it, it will not sell papers or attract viewers. Thus, media crime waves seem to go through a natural life cycle: a few dramatic incidents; continued reporting of similar crimes; a well-publicized response by officials that something is being done; and finally a waning of media interest.

Compared with other sources of fear—personal vulnerability and victimization, environmental cues—the media probably don't make much difference. If local TV and newspapers reduced their crime levels by 50 percent or 75 percent, would people feel much safer in the streets? I doubt it.

CRIME, RACE, AND POLITICS

In the last 30 years, crime has become an important public issue. It has figured in political campaigns at every level of government, and the debate at times has seemed to appeal more to emotions than to reason. In the 1988 presidential campaign, for example, George Bush frequently brought up the case of Willie Horton. Horton, a convicted murderer, escaped while on furlough from a Massachusetts prison and eventually committed a horrible crime. Bush, of course, blamed his opponent, Michael Dukakis, who was governor of Massachusetts, and attacked him as being "soft" on crime. Apparently, the strategy worked, even though the federal prison system (for which the Reagan-Bush administration was ultimately responsible) had similar furlough programs and similar unfortunate cases.

Another issue that helped decide the 1988 election was the death penalty. Bush was for it; Dukakis against it. Candidates for the House and Senate, as well as city offices like mayor, have campaigned vigorously on their support of the death penalty as way of dealing with crime. Aside from the question of whether more executions will mean less crime, the death penalty in these campaigns was more a symbolic issue than a real one, primarily because for nearly all crimes that it might touch, the death penalty is a matter of state law. City mayors, U.S. senators and representatives, and even the president, have little direct power over it. In fact, if these candidates really wanted to execute more criminals, they would run not for these offices but for governor or state legislature.

The politics of crime which often dominates elections these days has its origins in the 1960s, and the debate then probably was no more or less cogent than it is today. For example, Richard Nixon, in his acceptance speech at the Republican convention in 1968, drew the most applause for his promise to appoint a new Attorney General.[54] Of course, every newly elected president appoints a new Attorney General (as he appoints new secretaries of Defense, State, and all other cabinet positions). What Nixon meant was that he was going to get tough on crime. Again, there was less to the issue than met the eye, for crime control is largely a matter for city police and state courts. Presidential policies have little direct effect on street crime. Like the death penalty, the crime issue was more symbolic than real, for crime had become an important symbol. The only question is, what is it a symbol of?

In the first part of this chapter, I went to great lengths to show that when people are asked about their fear of crime, they are responding to something much larger than crime itself. Fear of crime includes a general feeling of vulnerability that arises from personal characteristics or experience. The fear people associate with crime may also be triggered by a sense of unfamiliarity and differentness. As the Presidential Commission concluded, "fear of crimes of violence is . . . at bottom a fear of strangers."[55] Being among people who look different, behave differently, and perhaps speak a different language makes the world seem less predictable, less familiar and therefore more dangerous, regardless of the real risk of crime.

In the Chicago study, the neighborhood with the highest levels of fear (Wicker Park) was the one undergoing a change in the population from mostly white to a mixture of about 25 percent Hispanic and 15 percent black. The higher-crime but lower-fear neighborhood was ethnically homogeneous—almost all black.

The blending of fear of strangers and fear of crime has important consequences, for often those strangers are "strange" primarily because of the color of their skin. In the United States, the crime problem has become almost inextricably intertwined with the issues of race. In another chapter, I will take up the question of racial differences in committing crime. In this chapter, I want to look at how people react to crime, personally and politically. And racial differences are often an important factor in those reactions. To take one example that made national headlines a few years ago, in the Howard Beach section of Queens, New York, a group of white youths armed with baseball bats attacked three blacks who had wandered into the neighborhood when their car broke down. One of the blacks fled onto a roadway, where he was hit and killed by a passing car. Obviously, it was a racist crime. (Would the attack have occurred if the strangers had been white?) But more significant was the reaction of the community. When the mayor of New York, Ed Koch, spoke at a local church and deplored the incident, many people booed and shouted in protest. They objected that the mayor was ignoring the issue of black crime.

Seven years earlier and only a few miles away had occurred some less publicized events that resembled the Howard Beach incident. In Rosedale, a formerly all-white section of Queens, a few blacks had bought homes, and some of these houses had been hit by firebombings, rock-throwing, and other forms of intimidation. When *The New York Times* sent a reporter to cover the story, one of the white residents who approved of the bombings told him, "They've taken every nice area of the city and turned it into garbage . . . Wherever the blacks come, crime comes." The article continues,

> He spoke of a time when white women and children could walk the streets of Rosedale and other nearby communities alone at night. It doesn't seem to matter to him . . . that homes in the neighboring communities . . . , all overwhelmingly black, are every bit as well kept up as those in Rosedale. . . .
>
> It also doesn't seem to matter that, in the words of [the] community affairs officer for the 105th Precinct, 'There is nothing to indicate that Rosedale has suffered a dramatic increase or decrease' in crime as blacks have moved in.[56]

This single anecdote exemplifies a trend found in more systematic surveys: "One traditional form of irrationality—racial prejudice—*is* related to fear"[57] (emphasis in original). The man from Rosedale might argue that his attitudes are not irrational, since statistics show that blacks do in fact commit proportionally more violent crimes. But racially prejudiced people generally are more fearful—even in their own all-white neighborhoods. As the survey researchers concluded, "The relationship between racial prejudice and fear is not due to sharpened perception of the truth about crime; rather the relation is due to the fact that racial prejudice is part of a general tendency to fear the unknown."[58]

What "Crime" Means

As the studies of fear of crime show, the idea of crime may mean different things to different people. The same is true of crime as a political issue. For example, in the 1960s, U.S. politics saw the rise of "law-and-order" candidates, people who promised to fight "crime in the streets." It may seem odd that "law and order" and "crime in the streets" could become controversial political issues. After all, nobody was against law and order, and nobody was for crime in the streets. But in the view of their critics, the "law and order" candidates were using these slogans as acceptable code words for anti-black feelings. Remember, this was the period of riots in black sections of many cities, beginning with the Watts district of Los Angeles in 1965. One view of the riots (or "urban disorders") saw them as symptoms of desperate people in desperate social conditions—unemployment, poor housing, and social inequality—and as a demand for social change. To dismiss the riots as merely crime, as a matter of law and order, was just one more way of maintaining a racially unjust society. In the critics' view, conservative politicians and their supporters, rather than say that they were against racial change, could say they were for law and order. Rather than say they were against blacks, they could say there were against crime in the streets.* If "crime" is in fact such a code word, then perhaps when people tell pollsters they are afraid of crime or consider crime a big problem, they are using "crime" as a more acceptable way of saying racial change, or, more bluntly, blacks.

Liberal and Conservative

To understand the reactions to the riots of the 1960s or to street crime today, we need to go beyond the issue of race, for these reactions illustrate a fundamental difference in political views—the split between liberal and conservative. Phrases like "crime in the streets" and "law and order" carry connotations far exceeding their literal meaning. They symbolize a broad set of largely conservative ideas and attitudes. Sometimes these ideas are conservative in the literal sense of conserving things as they are (or were) and rejecting what is new. For example, when James Q. Wilson, in the mid-1960s, polled Boston homeowners, the majority recalled their neighborhood of 20 years before as "composed of people pretty much like myself"; in other words, a safe and predictable environment where people respected "standards of right and seemly conduct in public places." Consequently, when they spoke of urban problems, "the issue that concerned more respondents than any other was variously stated—crime, violence, rebellious youth, public immorality, delinquency. . . . a concern for impropriety in public places."[59] Aside from their tendency to recall the past as less troublesome than it seemed at the time, note that these people were putting under the heading of "crime" many things that hardly fit with our picture of crime in the streets: "rowdy teenagers . . . lurid advertisements. . . ." Along the same lines, one survey of Baltimore residents found that people with more conservative attitudes—i.e., people who resisted social, and especially racial, change—were more likely to rank crime as the number one domestic problem.[60]

In the politics of crime, conservatism also means a more punitive approach. Conservatives favor more severe punishment as a way to reduce crime. They talk about "getting tough" on crime. Liberals are more likely to favor rehabilitation for those criminals who are caught. As for solutions, liberals often talk about "getting at the root causes" of crime, and for liberals, these root causes are in the environment. In the liberal view, people commit crimes because of social or economic pressures, and the way to reduce crime

---

* In the mid-1980s, South Africa provided us with a comfortably distant and more extreme version of similar events and interpretations. Black townships in South Africa became the sites of rioting, looting, attacks on police, arson, and even murder. Many observers attributed the violence to apartheid and the inequality, injustice, and oppression it forced on black people. The South African government, however, often chose to see the unrest as an issue of crime vs. law and order.

is to reduce those pressures. They look to better schools and more job opportunities as ways to reduce crime. The conservative view of the cause of crime is much simpler: it focuses on the individual and downplays the environment. People choose to commit crime largely because they can get away with it, and the only way to alter that choice is to increase the penalty for it.

This brief sketch of political views oversimplifies both conservative and liberal thought. I have intended these descriptions more as the ends of a continuum rather than as absolute categories. Any one person's own views will undoubtedly be a mixture of ideas. Many people who think of themselves as conservatives and want harsher penalties for crime still may acknowledge the importance of economic factors as causes of crime. Nevertheless, the categories may be useful for understanding views about crime.

Fear of Crime, Concern with Crime

It is important to distinguish these political reactions to crime from the personal reaction of fear. Voting for a "law-and-order" candidate is not quite the same thing as being afraid to walk alone at night. Some years ago, Frank Furstenberg pointed out this distinction between *concern* with crime and *fear* of crime. "Concern" refers to political attitudes, ideas about what is best for society; "fear" refers to personal feelings about safety. The two are different, and they have different causes. Sex and age are important factors in fear of crime, but these variables make almost no difference in political views about crime.[61] But what about victimization? As we have seen, victimization does increase levels of fear (though it does not seem as influential as sex or age). But does it also affect people's political views about crime? As an illustration, imagine that we have a roomful of people, and your task is to divide them into two groups. Your goal is to have two groups that are most different in the proportion of who want courts to be harsher on criminals. Obviously, if you just divided people randomly, you would probably have the same get-tough proportion in each group. And I have already told you that separating the men from the women or the old from the young will not give you two groups that differ much in their support for harsher courts. So to help you, I will let you use *one* of two other pieces of information: whether the person has been a victim of crime in the last year, or whether the person favors busing to achieve racial integration in the schools. In other words, your two groups can consist either of victims and non-victims or of pro-busing people and anti-busing people. Which grouping will produce a bigger difference on the question of harsher courts?

Your first logical impulse probably tells you that you will do better if you use victimization: More people who have been victimized will favor harsher courts; those who have not been victimized may feel less strong about harsher courts. But if you think about what you've read so far, you might

Table 2–6 ▪ Opinion on Courts by Victimization (Robbery or Burglary in Past Year)

	Nonvictims	*Victims*
Too harsh	4.1	4.2
About right	10.2	9.7
Not harsh enough	85.7	86.1

Source: James Allen Davis and Tom W. Smith (1988), *General Social Surveys, 1972–1988*, Chicago: National Opinion Research Center.

choose the attitude on busing: Like crime, busing resonates with themes of racial fear, community homogeneity, and general conservatism. Tables 2–6 and 2–7 show the results of a national survey on these questions conducted in 1988. (The tables show the responses of whites only.)

The most obvious result these tables show is the widespread perception that courts are too "soft." (Even among people who describe themselves as extremely liberal, 75 percent favor harsher courts.) But we are interested in the differences between the two tables. In Table 2–6, nearly identical proportions of victims and non-victims say they want harsher courts. Compare this result against the glib assertion that "a conservative is a liberal who has just been mugged," a cute phrasing for a plausible idea. But the evidence doesn't support it. Being a victim of burglary or robbery apparently makes no difference in a person's opinions on courts.

While opinions on courts are unaffected by victimization, they do seem related to attitudes on busing. The differences are not large—a gap of about eight percentage points in the "not harsh enough" category—but they are larger than the no-difference of Table 2–6. And pro-busing people are more than three times as likely to say that courts are too harsh. To put the matter in the language of statistics, busing (at least for city dwellers) is a better "predictor" of attitudes toward courts than is victimization.[62]

Not only are fear of crime and concern with crime conceptually different, but Furstenberg found in his research that they also were located in dif-

Table 2–7 ▪ Opinion on Courts by Opinion on Busing (To Achieve School Integration)

	Pro-busing	*Anti-busing*
Too harsh	8.1	2.2
About right	10.3	8.4
Not harsh enough	81.5	89.3

Source: James Allen Davis and Tom W. Smith (1988), *General Social Surveys, 1972–1988*, Chicago: National Opinion Research Center.

ferent places in society. Fear was more prevalent in high-crime neighborhoods than in low-crime areas, as you would expect. But people in high-crime areas were less likely to rank crime as an important political issue—i.e., something the government should do something about.[63] Why should fear and concern appear in different places? If you think about who lives in high-crime and low-crime areas, you might find one important reason: People in high-crime areas are usually poor and often are black; they have many important, immediate concerns—poverty, unemployment, housing, schools, race prejudice—that they would like the government to act on. But the difference in perception of crime between richer and poorer go beyond mere self-interest. Like opinions on busing, these opinions on crime seem to be part of a more general political orientation, not just a projection of personal concerns. For example, poor people and black people are much more likely than middle-class people and white people to be victims of crime. But they are less likely to want harsher courts. Blacks are six times more likely than whites to be murder victims, but they are much less likely to favor capital punishment.[64] More affluent people in low-crime areas may be concerned with unemployment (especially if it is their own) or inflation, but after that they might well list crime—especially if they use that term to cover not just crime but a variety of social changes.*

SUMMARY AND CONCLUSION

The crime problem is not primarily one of physical harm or economic cost. Our bodies and lives are much more at risk from everyday hazards like working and driving than from criminals, and the crimes about which people are most concerned are not those which cost the most money. What distinguishes street crime as a problem is its effect on society. Since the sharp increase of crime in the 1960s, people have become more fearful, their lives more constrained. Yet actual exposure to crime seems to be only a minor cause of this fear. Among personal characteristics, sex and age are more important. The social and physical environment also contribute to fear. Abandoned buildings or teenagers hanging out on the street and other forms of disorder are not intrinsically criminal, but people see them as signs of crime and occasions for a heightened sense of apprehension. Unfamiliarity is another important source of fear. People become more apprehensive in unfamiliar surroundings and amid unfamiliar people.

---

* In the years since Furstenberg's research, things may have changed. In recent polls, the poor are slightly more likely than the affluent to rank crime a national problem. Still, even among the lowest-income group, only 3 percent identified crime as the most important problem facing the country. (*Sourcebook—1988.*)

Beginning in the 1960s, crime became not just a social problem but a political issue as well. Inevitably, the politics of crime became entwined with issues of race relations. The debate often went beyond any rational consideration of what the government could do about crime. Conservatives were accused of racism, of using "law and order" and "crime in the streets" as code words for race—as though the rising crime rates could be reversed by not speaking about them. Liberals, who stressed the need to improve the social and economic conditions of the poor, were criticized for being "soft" on crime and for showing too little concern for the victims—as though hatred of criminals and sympathy for victims were policies for reducing crime.

Clear thinking on crime requires accurate information. Unfortunately, the most available sources of information, the mass media, seldom give an accurate picture of the dimensions of crime. In extreme cases, the media, by giving more coverage to certain kinds of stories, can create the impression that a crime wave is occurring when the actual incidence of crime remains unchanged.

The trouble with crime news is not so much its volume but the style of presentation. Except for the occasional report of official crime statistics and overcrowding in prisons, the media seldom show crime from a more sociological view. They present crime, in the words of James Q Wilson, "as composed of individual events that have no systematic relationship to each other."[65] For the media, crime is an individual act, not evidence of some larger set of social forces. Poverty, unemployment, neighborhood conditions, peer influence, lenient courts—these are all but invisible on TV crime shows. The cause of crime, especially on fictional shows, usually is either insanity or insatiable greed. Even in the news, the more a crime resembles that of fictional TV or movies, the more coverage it gets. As I write this, the papers in New York are full of "the zodiac murders" that could easily be a story line on the old TV series "Kojak;" the Bensonhurst murder could have been Spike Lee's movie "Do the Right Thing." The media seldom give us stories about changes in neighborhood safety or the percentage of robbers convicted and imprisoned. Wilson suggests that the media should "cover crime the way the sports pages cover the American League," with "box scores tracking burglars or robbers through the system."[66]

Wilson's baseball analogy is a good one. The summer I wrote the first draft of this chapter, my local baseball team ran a 30-second commercial encouraging viewers to watch the game on TV or go out to the stadium. The ad showed our team hitting home runs, making diving catches, sliding into third under the tag. They looked good—very good. Yet when I checked the standings at the end of the season, I found they had the second worst won-lost record in either league.

Crime news is like that ad. Choosing from all reported criminal events, the media fill a limited time or space with those stories that will most interest the public. From the media we learn little about the frequent, typical crimes that are more likely to affect us directly; nor do we see the everyday workings of the criminal justice system. Unfortunately, these ordinary events, while they do not make the news, do make up a large part of the crime problem in America today. In the next chapter, we will look at ways of keeping score.

NOTES

1. *The 1986 Information Please Almanac*, Boston: Houghton Mifflin, p. 753.

2. *The New York Times*, Jan. 2, 1977, sec. 3, p. 15.

3. Marshall Clinard and Peter Yeager (1980), *Corporate Crime*, New York: Free Press, p. 8.

4. *The New York Times*, June 1, 1986, p. A16.

5. Federal Bureau of Investigation (1989). *Uniform Crime Reports 1988*, Washington, DC. United States Government Printing Office.

6. *The New York Times*, Oct. 19, 1975, p. 6. Annette Kornblum (1990), "Some Customers Are Always Wrong," *The New York Times Magazine*, Part 2, *The Business World*, June 10, p. 56.

7. Jeffrey Reiman (1984), *The Rich Get Rich and the Poor Get Prison* (2nd ed.), New York: Wiley, p. 55.

8. Paul Brodeur (1985), "Annals of Law: The Asbestos Industry on Trial," *The New Yorker*, June 10, p. 79. Morton Mintz (1985), *At Any Cost: Corporate Greed, Women and the Dalkon Shield*, New York: Pantheon.

9. Research & Forecasts, Inc., with Andy Friedberg (1983), *America Afraid: How Fear of Crime Changes the Way We Live (The Figgie Report)*, New York: New American Library.

10. John Crothers Polloc and Arney Ellen Rosenblat (1982), "Fear of Crime: Sources and Responses," *USA Today*, January.

11. Charles Silberman (1978), *Criminal Violence, Criminal Justice*, New York: Random House, p. 12.

12. Timothy J. Flanagan and Maureen McLeod, eds. (1983), *Sourcebook of Criminal Justice Statistics—1982*. U.S. Department of Justice, Bureau of Justice Statistics. Washington, DC: U.S. Government Printing Office, p. 212. Timothy J. Flanagan and Maureen McLeod, eds. (1988), *Sourcebook of Criminal Justice Statistics—1987*. U.S. Department of Justice, Bureau of Justice Statistics. Washington, DC: U.S. Government Printing Office, p. 139. Timothy J. Flanagan and Kathleen Maguire, eds. (1990), *Sourcebook of Criminal Justice Statistics—1989*. U.S. Department of Justice, Bureau of Justice Statistics. Washington, DC: U.S. Government Printing Office, p. 152–53.

13. Flanagan and McLeod, eds. (1983), *Sourcebook—1982*, pp. 220–22.

14. Ted Robert Gurr (1981), "Historical Trends in Violent Crime: A Critical Review of the Evidence," in Michael Tonry and Norval Morris, eds., *Crime and Justice, an Annual Review*, vol. 8, pp. 295–352.

15. M. A. Rifai (1976), "Older American Crime Prevention Research Project." Portland, OR: Multomak County Division of Public Safety.

16. Wesley G. Skogan and Michael G. Maxfield (1981), *Coping with Crime*, Beverly Hills, CA: Sage, p. 242.

17. Ibid.

18. *The New York Times*, May 16, 1981, p. 81, "Fear of Crime Leads in Survey on Reasons to Leave Big Cities" (John Herbers).

19. Wesley Skogan (1990), *Disorder and Decline: Crime and the Spiral of Decay in American Neighborhoods*. New York: Free Press. Leo Schuerman and Solomon Kobrin (1986), "Community Carers in Crime," in Albert J. Reiss, Jr. and Michael Tonry, eds. (1986), *Communities and Crime*, Chicago: University of Chicago Press, pp. 67–100.

20. The President's Commission on Law Enforcement and Administration of Justice (1968), *The Challenge of Crime in a Free Society*, Washington, DC: U.S. Government Printing Office, pp. 164–65.

21. In Skogan and Maxfield, *Coping*, p. 62.

22. The President's Commission, *The Challenge of Crime . . .* , op. cit.

23. James Garofalo (1979), "Victimization and the Fear of Crime," *Journal of Research in Crime and Delinquency*, vol. 16, no. 1, p. 86.

24. Data from the ABC News Poll, in Edmund F. McGarrel and Timothy J. Flanagan, eds. (1985), *Sourcebook of Criminal Justice Statistics—1984*, U.S. Department of Justice, Bureau of Justice Statistics, Washington, DC: U.S. Government Printing Office, p. 168. Flanagan and Maguire (1990), *Sourcebook—1989*, op. cit., p. 141.

25. Paul Theroux (1982), "Subway Odyssey," *The New York Times Magazine*, Jan. 31, p. 23.

26. The phrase comes from Arthur L. Stinchcombe, Rebecca Adams, Carole A. Heimer, Kim Land Scheppele, Tom W. Smith, D. Garth Taylor (1980), *Crime and Punishment—Changing Attitudes in America*, San Francisco: Jossey-Bass.

27. Dan A. Lewis and Michael G. Maxfield (1980), "Fear in the Neighborhoods: An Investigation of the Impact of Crime," *Journal of Research in Crime and Delinquency*, vol. 17, no. 2, pp. 160–89.

28. Research by Susan Estrich, cited in James Q. Wilson and George L. Kelling (1982), "Broken Windows," *The Atlantic Monthly*, March p. 32.

29. Theroux, op. cit., p. 71.

30. Skogan (1990), op. cit., pp. 111–13.

31. Wilson and Kelling, op. cit., p. 29.

32. Ibid., p. 32.

33. Ibid., p. 29.

34. Wesley Skogan, personal communication.

35. Tim Hope and Michael Hough (1988), "Area, Crime, and Incivility: A Profile from the British Crime Survey," in T. Hope and M. Shaw, eds. (1988), *Communities and Crime Reduction* London: Her Majesty's Stationery Office, pp. 30–47, cited in Skogan (1990), p. 77.

36. Harold Takooshian and Herzel Bodinger (1979), "Street Crime in 18 American Cities; A National Field Experiment," paper delivered at the American Sociological Association, Boston, MA. *The New York Times*, Sept. 14, 1983, p. B1, "Bronx Neighborhood: One Big Family" (Christopher Wellisz).

37. Saul Alinsky (1946), *Reveille for Radicals*, Chicago: University of Chicago Press.

38. Lewis and Maxfield, op. cit.

39. Charles Silberman (1965), *Crisis in Black and White*, New York: Random House.

40. Skogan, op. cit., pp. 125–57.

41. Brian Hollander, Francis X. Hartman, Linda R. Brown, Robert Wiles (1980), *Reducing Residential Crime and Fear: The Hartford Neighborhood Crime Prevention Program*. Washington, DC: U.S. Department of Justice, Law Enforcement Assistance Administration, National Institute of Law Enforcement and Criminal Justice. Floyd Fowler and Thomas W. Maguire (1982), *Neighborhood Crime, Fear, and Social Control: A Second Look at the Hartford Program*, Washington, DC: U.S. Government Printing Office.

42. Sally Engle Merry (1981), *Urban Danger*, Philadelphia: Temple University Press.

43. Ibid., pp. 28–29.

44. The Roper Organization (1983), "Trends in Attitudes Toward Television and Other Media: A Twenty-four Year Review," New York: Television Information Office.

45. James Davis (1952), "Crime News in Colorado Newspapers," *American Journal of Sociology*, vol. 58, 325–30.

46. Joseph Sheley and Cindy D. Ashkins (1981), "Crime, Crime News, and Crime Views," *Public Opinion Quarterly*, vol. 45, pp. 492–506.

47. James Garofalo (1981), "Crime and the Mass Media: A Selective Review of Research," *Journal of Research in Crime and Delinquency*, vol. 18, no. 2, pp. 319–50.

48. Jennifer Davis, "The London Garroting Panic of 1862: A Moral Panic and the Creation of a Criminal Class in Mid-Victorian England," in V.A.C. Gatrell, Bruce Lenman, and Geoffrey Parker, eds. (1980), *Crime and the Law: The Social History of Crime in Western Europe Since 1500*, London: Europa Publications, pp. 190–213.

49. Mary Holland Baker, Barbara C. Nienstedt, Ronald S. Everett, Richard McCleary (1983), "The Impact of a Crime Wave: Perceptions, Fear, and Confidence in the Police," *Law and Society Review*, vol. 17, no. 2, pp. 319–35.

50. Mark Fishman (1978), "Crime Waves as Ideology," *Social Problems*, vol. 25, no. 5.

51. Research by S. Robert and Linda S. Lichter, reported in *The New York Times*, "Who Breaks the Law on TV?" March 6, 1983, sec. 2, p. 35 (Richard Lacayo).

52. The literature on this topic is quite large and controversial. See James A. Garofalo (1981), "Crime and the Mass Media: A Selective Review of Research," *Journal of Research in Crime and Delinquency*, vol. 18, no. 2, pp. 319–50.

53. Ibid., pp. 336–38.

54. *The New York Times*, Aug. 9, 1968, p. 1.

55. Presidential Commission, *The Challenge of Crime . . .* , op. cit., p. 52.

56. *The New York Times*, Sept. 9, 1979, sec. 4, p. 5, "Rosedale Is Black, White, and Seething" (Don Wycliffe).

57. Stinchcombe, et al., op. cit., p. 65.

58. Ibid., p. 66.

59. James Q. Wilson (1967), *Thinking About Crime*, New York: Basic Books, p. 196.

60. Frank Furstenberg (1971), "Public Reaction to Crime in the Streets,." *American Scholar*, vol. 40, no. 4, pp. 601–10.

61. *Sourcebook—1987*, p. 143.

62. D. Garth Taylor, Kim Land Scheppele, and Arthur L. Stinchcombe (1979), "Salience of Crime and Support for Harsher Criminal Sanctions," *Social Problems*, vol. 26, no. 4, pp. 413–24.

63. Furstenberg, op. cit.

64. Flanagan and McLeod, eds., *Sourcebook—1987*, pp. 143, 161, 340.

65. James Q. Wilson (1983), untitled article in *The New York Times*, July 17, sec. 4, p. 6.

66. Ibid.

The Numbers Game: Counting Crime

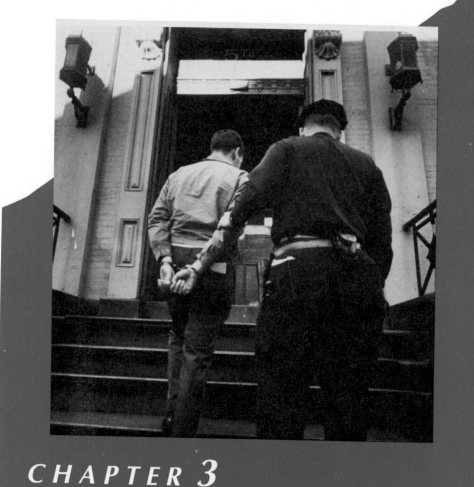

CHAPTER 3

SO MUCH CRIME

I SOMETIMES BEGIN MY COURSE IN CRIMINOLOGY BY ASKING STUDENTS WHAT THEY WANT to know about crime or what questions they would like to be able to answer after having taken a course in criminology. Often, the first question is, "Why is there so much crime?" I usually answer with another question: "How much crime is there?"

This is a puzzling question. In everyday speech, we often talk about problems like crime or air pollution or poverty as if they were things whose size was obvious and could be easily measured. But when we try to think of specific dimensions (instead of "so much"), we realize how vague our thinking is.

Sometimes when I ask, "How much crime is there?" a student will reply, "Too much." But this response raises the same kinds of questions. "How much is too much?" Or to put it another way, "How much crime would *not* be too much?" Occasionally a student will say that "any crime is too much—especially if it happens to me." This kind of answer usually gets a laugh, and the student has a point. From the standpoint of the individual, even one crime is too much. But from the standpoint of the society, if that one crime were the only one committed in the entire country, would we really say that there was too much crime because *any* crime was too much? We need to be able to distinguish between one crime and "so much."

The question "Why is there so much crime?" carries with it an assumption, the assumption that there is in fact a great deal of crime. But is this assumption correct? "How do you know that there's so much crime?" I ask. Typical answers are, "You always see it on the news," or "It's all around," or "My uncle's house was robbed last month." Of course, it doesn't take long for students to realize that these answers aren't very convincing. This "anecdotal evidence" tells only that there is *some* crime, not whether the overall amount is great or small.

The point of this exercise (besides to let students know that they will have to do some thinking during the semester) is that before we even start to answer important questions about crime, we will have to figure out some way of counting it. In the preceding chapter, I argued that personal experience, television, and newspapers may give us an impression of crime that has more to do with personal feelings than with accurate measurement. The mass media may be very good for letting us know what crime is like, but generally they do not tell us about the amount of crime and whether it is increasing or decreasing. To repeat Wilson's baseball analogy, we need more than just the videotaped highlights; we need some way of keeping score.

Of course, the media do sometimes give the score. At least once a year, newspapers print items sounding much like the following:

Crime Fell by 4 percent Last Year

AUG. 26—According to FBI figures released today, serious crimes in the United States decreased 4 percent from the previous year. Police reports showed a decrease in most major crimes. Violent crime, however, declined by only 1 percent. . . .

At first glance, the story seems fairly obvious. It gives the score, and the score looks pretty good. But read the item again. Are you sure you know what all the words mean? What does the FBI have to do with these figures? What are "police reports?" And just what constitutes a "serious crime" or a "violent crime"?

Suppose that during that year, a government employee was caught and convicted of selling secrets to the Soviet Union. Is that a "serious crime"? Or suppose that a politician was caught for extorting $200,000 in kickbacks from companies that received city contracts. Is that a "serious crime"? Or suppose that you went to the parking lot only to discover that some people had taken sledge hammers and reduced your new car to scrap metal. Is that a "serious crime"? Is it a "violent crime"? Or suppose that a drug dealer was arrested for selling heroin and cocaine with a street value of $500,000. Is that a "serious crime"?

The answer to all these questions is "no."

None of these crimes would have been counted in the tally referred to in the newspaper article. That story is based on something called the Index to serious crime. The Index was devised in 1929, and for over 60 years it has been the official measure of crime in America. When criminologists speak of *official* crime rates, it is the Uniform Crime Reports (UCR) Index they are referring to. Originally, the Index contained seven crimes: murder, rape, robbery, aggravated assault, burglary, larceny, and motor vehicle theft. In 1982, arson was added to the list. The FBI gathers information on these crimes from local police departments. This tally, along with a mountain of other information, is published each year in a volume called *Crime in the United States*, also known as the Uniform Crime Reports (or UCR). The hypothetical news item above, about serious crime in the United States, was referring to the UCR Index crimes: those eight crimes and no others— no drug deals, no vandalism, no extortion, no bribes.*

---

* In some ways the UCR Index of crime is analogous to the Dow Jones Index for the stock market. Of the thousands and thousands of stocks on the New York Stock Exchange, the Dow includes only 30. When stock brokers say that "the market" was up 6 points, they are referring to an average based on these 30 stocks.

CONSTRUCTING A CRIME INDEX

Clearly, these omissions are serious drawbacks. Statements about "crime"—meaning this official crime rate—will necessarily be somewhat misleading. So why not count these other crimes? In order to understand why the UCR Index leaves out what seem like some fairly serious crimes, perhaps we should start from scratch. Let's suppose that the country does not have any method of counting crime and that it is now our job to create one. What shall we count, and how shall we count it? To begin with, do we want our final total to include *all* crime? Should we count every violation of every criminal statute—every drunk-and-disorderly violation, every playground or barroom shoving match, every joint of marijuana? I doubt it. What we want is not a count of all crime, but some tally that will indicate how much serious crime there is—that is, an *index* (or indicator) of *serious* crime.

Besides seriousness, two other factors should influence our decision about counting crime. First, we want our count to be accurate; second, we want the information to be fairly convenient to get. Unfortunately, accuracy and convenience do not always go hand in hand. For the sake of convenience, we will have to find our statistics where records of crime are kept. But as a general rule, the further our source is from the actual crime, the less accurate the count will be. For example, it would be very convenient to look at the prison population and see what crimes they have been convicted of. But data on prisoners will not give a very accurate picture of crime. Between the crime itself and prison lies a series of steps—arrest, conviction, sentence—and at each step, many cases drop out of the system. Records from prisons, courts, and arrests do have the advantage of convenience: They already exist. We do not have to create any new methods; all we have to do is count. In fact, historians interested in counting crime from bygone eras must often rely on these sources for their statistics. But it's easy to see that prison, courts, and even arrests miss the great bulk of crime—all those crimes for which no one was arrested.

But how else can we know how much crime has occurred? Where can we go for information about crimes? The obvious answer is the police. Arrest statistics may miss too much crime, but the police have other information that will be much more useful: citizens' reports of crimes. Let's assume for a minute that when a crime is committed, somebody calls the cops. Therefore, to count burglaries, robberies, etc., we can go to police records to see how many people called the cops for each type of crime.

Making Crime Reporting Uniform

Now that we have decided to limit ourselves to serious crime and to use police reports, we face a further problem of definition—that of uniformity.

We want our definitions of crime to be uniform for all parts of the country. Because different states have different criminal laws, we cannot base our definitions on legal definitions. In one state, breaking into a car to steal something may be prosecuted as burglary; in another state, the same act may be called larceny.[1] Relying on legal definitions also creates problems in counting because several laws will apply to a single act. For example, suppose a man runs up to woman, grabs her purse, pushes her away, and runs off. In one state, he can be charged with all of the following crimes: robbery, attempted robbery, assault, larceny. In another state, the possible charges might be different. But which one or ones shall we include in our count of crime in America?

Obviously, we need a set of definitions that will be independent from the laws. And in fact, the UCR provides such definitions. The legal processing of crimes may vary from one locality to another, but the reporting of crime statistics will be the same for all police departments. That is why the system is called Uniform Crime Reports: It is a uniform way of reporting crime.

We now have a uniform system for the police to report the crimes they discover, but we still haven't decided which crimes to include. We want to leave out trivial offenses and include the more serious crimes, and we also want our count to be accurate. In some cases, the more serious the crime, the more accurate our information will be. For example, police statistics for murder—a very serious crime—are probably more accurate than for any other crime. But sometimes seriousness and accuracy may conflict with each other. In some serious crimes, nobody calls the police. For example, if I sell you a kilo of heroin that you then divide and sell to other customers, we are both committing crimes that many people would consider serious.[2] But who's going to call the police? With nonpredatory or "victimless" crimes (drug trafficking, prostitution, illegal gambling, etc.), the only count we have is arrests. Unfortunately, the number of arrests will reflect not the level of crime, but the level of police activity. Therefore, if we want our index to be an accurate reflection of crime, we had better leave out the kinds of crime— even serious crime—where nobody calls the cops.

In the interests of accuracy, we should also leave out crimes that seldom get discovered. Most white-collar crime comes to light not because a victim calls the cops but because some agency decides to investigate. These crimes may be quite serious. Suppose, for instance, that a defense contractor, instead of testing the computer chips in the components it builds, sends in made-up test data or none at all. The company keeps the money it would have spent on tests, but its lack of testing puts the military and the country at risk. Certainly, this is a serious crime, as are other kinds of fraud. But should we count these crimes on our scoresheet that will give us an idea of how much crime occurs each year? If we do, our count will lose accuracy, since it is unlikely that the crime will be discovered. (And if the government does discover it, how many other similar crimes are going undiscovered?) Even if the crime is discovered, how many crimes should we put on our index of serious crimes—one for each person involved? One for each shipment? One for each computer chip?

The FBI's Index Crimes

You can see by now that even deciding which crimes to count and how to count them are not such easy matters. There are good reasons behind the UCR's omissions. Still, when you see news items about crime statistics, you should remember just what kinds of crime are being included and excluded. And you also should be aware that the excluded crimes involve much more money than do those on the Index. The losses to white-collar crime far exceed the losses to the street crimes in the Index. Table 3–1 lists and defines the eight Index crimes.

The first four crimes listed—murder, rape, robbery, and aggravated assault—are called "violent" crimes or "crimes against the person." The latter term is probably more accurate, since in these crimes the criminal confronts the victim directly. In the "crimes against property"—burglary, larceny, motor vehicle theft, and arson—the property, not the person, is the object

Table 3–1 ▪ The UCR Index Crimes

Murder	The willful killing of one person by another without legal justification.
Rape	The carnal knowledge of a female against her will. (Attempts are included.)
Robbery	Taking or attempting to take anything of value from a person by force or threat of force. (Purse-snatching is not included.)
Aggravated assault	Inflicting serious bodily injury on a person. Attempts with a weapon are included, even if no injury occurs, (e.g., a gunshot that misses).
Burglary	Unlawful entry of a structure (building) with the intent to commit a felony or theft. The use of force to gain entry is not required. (Attempts are included.)
Larceny	The unlawful taking of property other than motor vehicles, without force or threat of force to the person. (Included are pocket-picking, purse-snatching, bicycle theft, thefts from motor vehicles, theft of motor-vehicle parts, shoplifting.)
Motor vehicle theft	Theft or attempted theft of a motor vehicle.
Arson	The intentional damaging by fire of a building, vehicle, etc. (Attempts are included. Fires of unknown origin are excluded.)

of the criminal's action. This violent vs. property classification contains some contradictions. If a man walks into a bank, hands the teller a threatening note, and walks out with a sack of money, it is a robbery, (i.e., a "violent" crime). *All* robberies are classified as violent crimes, even if no actual violence occurs and even if the criminal's object is to get money, not to do violence to someone. On the other hand, all burglaries, no matter how much breaking is involved along with the entering, are classified as property crimes, not violent crimes.

Computing Crime Rates

Since we want to use crime statistics to compare different times and places, merely counting the crimes is not quite enough. For example, in 1976, according to the UCR, there were 18,780 murders in the United States; in 1985, there were 18,976, a slight increase. The change in the absolute number of murders is misleading, though, because there were more people in the United States in 1985 than there were in 1976. In order to compare the two years, we must make the number of murders relative to the number of people. That is, we must convert the number to a *rate* of murders *per* population. A rate is a fraction with a given denominator. In percentages—the most commonly used rate—the denominator is 100, but because the number of crimes is small compared to the population, percentages would be too difficult to interpret. We could say that in 1976, 0.0088 percent of the population was murdered, but that number hardly seems meaningful. Instead, the UCR uses 100,000 as its denominator. To convert the number to a rate per 100,000, we divide the number of murders by the number of people in the United States (which gives the rate per person), and then multiply by 100,000 to get the rate per 100,000 persons.

$$\frac{\text{Murders in 1976}}{\text{Population in 1976}} = \frac{18{,}780}{214{,}659{,}000} \times 100{,}000 = 8.8$$

$$\frac{\text{Murders in 1985}}{\text{Population in 1985}} = \frac{18{,}976}{238{,}740{,}000} \times 100{,}000 = 7.9$$

Although more people were murdered in 1985, the murder *rate* declined from 8.8 per 100,000 to 7.9 per 100,000.

The UCR uses this same general formula for all its Index-crime rates:

$$\frac{\text{Crimes known to the police}}{\text{Population}} \times 100{,}000 = \text{Crime rate}$$

Using the same formula, we can compare the rates of motor vehicle theft in Boston and Houston in 1987:

	Boston	Houston
Motor vehicle theft known to the police	16,698	30,425
Population	579,921	1,725,421
Rate per 100,000	2,879.4	1,763.3

Source: UCR, 1988.

Houston had nearly twice as many thefts, but Boston's *rate* of motor vehicle theft is about 40 percent higher.

Table 3–2 shows the UCR rates of Index crimes for 1989.*

Table 3–2 ■ Index Crime Rates, 1989

Murder	8.7
Rape	38.1
Robbery	233.0
Aggravated assault	383.4
Burglary	1,276.3
Larceny	3,171.3
Motor vehicle theft	630.4
Violent crime	663.1
Property crime	5,077.9
Crime index total	5,741.0

Source: UCR, 1989.

Crime: What to Count?

No system of counting crime is perfect, and although the UCR solves some of the problems of counting crime, it contains some major flaws. First, there is the problem of seriousness. As we have already seen, the Index definition of serious crime leaves out many crimes that most people think are serious: white-collar crimes, embezzlement, drug crimes, kidnapping, all federal crimes (e.g., counterfeiting, skyjacking), and others. But even for the serious crimes the Index does include, it does not distinguish between levels of seriousness within each type of crime.

Four robbers enter a store, beat the owner with their guns, and take $20,000; the victim calls the police. Score one robbery on the UCR.

* Because of technical problems, the FBI does not compute a national rate for arson and frequently omits arson from its totals.

One boy threatens to punch another unless the victim gives up his lunch money. The victim calls the police. Score one robbery on the UCR.

(In the first example, although both aggravated assault and robbery occurred, the UCR's rule for counting violent crimes is one victim, one crime, listed under the most serious—in this case, robbery.*)

Normally, I would not bother to mention this problem. I would expect that for purposes of comparing one time or place with another, seriousness would not be important. The proportion of more and less serious robberies should not be too different from one time or place to another. But at least one study of robbery has found that measuring robberies by seriousness gives different results from merely counting them. From one year to the next, the number of robberies increased, but the overall seriousness of robbery decreased.[3] Did robbery get better or worse? From the victim's point of view, robbery had gotten worse, since more people had been victimized. But this did not mean that the robbers were doing better. In fact, their net income was down.

Population: Who—or What—to Count?

The numerator of the UCR crime rates tells us only how many crimes, not how serious these crimes are. The denominator in UCR rates also can be misleading. To take an obvious example, the rate for rape is computed by dividing the number of rapes by the population of the country, even though the UCR's definition of rape puts only women at risk. If the rate were computed as rapes per 100,000 *women*, it would be about twice what appears in the UCR.

Another denominator problem arises when we try to compare crime rates between cities. The problem is not that some cities have large populations while others have smaller populations; using crime *rates*, with their common denominator (100,000), solves this problem. Instead, the problem lies in the way that the population is counted. For example, each year when the UCR is published, one city which usually turns up with extraordinarily high crime rates is Atlantic City, New Jersey. Why? Your first impulse in answering this question is to think of the numerator—crimes committed. In the last 15 years, Atlantic City has built its economy on gambling, and no doubt this kind of economy brings crime. Gamblers with ready cash in their hotel rooms or pockets attract more burglary and larceny (pocket-picking). These crimes increase the numerator. But remember, a rate is a fraction (crime divided by population), and there are two ways to raise the value of a fraction: Keep the numerator high, or keep the denominator low. Atlantic

---

* The UCR ranks murder the most serious, followed in order by rape, robbery, and aggravated assault.

City's high crime rate derives just as much from peculiarities in the de-nominator—the number of people in the population. Who is counted in the population? Answer: only the resident population. If you go to Atlantic City, get your pocket picked, and report it to the police, you call the local police. Score one in the numerator for Atlantic City larceny. But do you get counted in the Atlantic City population? No. Score zero in the denominator. The same problem will occur in other cities with large nonresident populations. Commuters, tourists, migrant workers, and others all may contribute to the crime rate as victims (numerator) but not as population (denominator). Therefore, the city will have an inflated crime rate.

The UCR crime rates, based on crimes per population, can be misleading in yet another way. Look at Figure 3–1, which shows rates of motor vehicle theft as reported in the UCR. Between 1968 and 1978, the rate went from about 390 to nearly 460 per 100,000 people, a 15 percent increase. In only two years out of ten did the rate decrease.

What the UCR rate tells us is the proportion of Americans who had cars stolen. But is this the only way to measure auto theft? Why should we use the population as our denominator if what's being taken is cars? Let me make up an extreme example: Suppose that at a particular school we wanted to compare auto theft rates in 1930 and 1990. In both years the school had a population of 1,000 students. In 1930, there were five auto thefts; in 1990, there were 10. The auto theft rate has doubled—from five per thousand to 10 per thousand (or from 500 per 100,000 to 1,000 per 100,000). In which year would you feel more secure about the safety of your car?

If you thought about that question for more than a second, you probably wanted one other very important bit of information: How many cars were there in each year? To judge whether car theft had gotten worse or better,

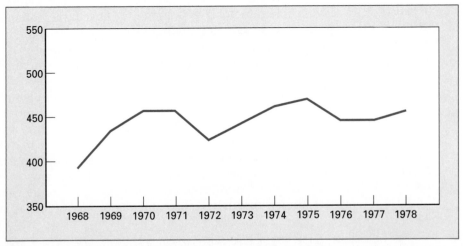

Figure 3–1 Motor Vehicle Thefts per 100,000 Population, 1968–1978

you would want to know not what *proportion of students* lost cars, but what *proportion of cars* got stolen. Suppose that in 1930, only 50 students owned cars, but that in 1990, that figure had risen to 500. Now the picture changes. Instead of increasing, the rate has gone from five per 50 cars (100 per 1,000) to 10 per 500 cars (20 per 1,000)—an 80 percent decrease.

	Students		**Cars**	
	1930	**1990**	**1930**	**1990**
Thefts	5	10	5	10
Population	1,000	1,000	50	500
Rate per 1,000	5	10	50	20

For my hypothetical example, I invented some extreme numbers. What would happen if we looked at some real data on auto theft? Figure 3–2 shows the same UCR rates as Figure 3–1, but it also shows rates of motor vehicle theft figured on the basis of the number of registered vehicles. As you can see, in each year, the rate based on registrations is higher than the UCR rate, since there are fewer vehicles than people (a lower denominator gives a higher rate). But more important, the changes in rates go in opposite directions. The UCR rate shows a more or less steady increase—overall, a 15 percent *increase*. The other graph shows a decrease—from nearly 760 per 100,000 vehicles to about 640 per 100,000—a 15 percent *decrease*. And the year-to-year changes show a decrease in seven out of ten years.

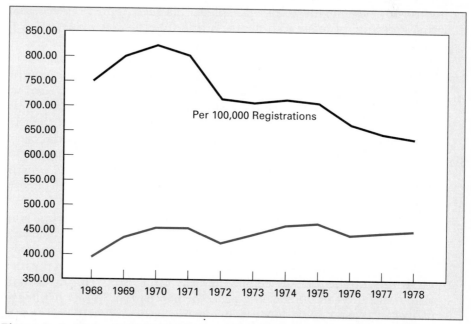

Figure 3–2 Motor Vehicle Thefts per 100,000 Population, 1968–1978

Do you find this discrepancy frustrating? Are you hoping that this paragraph will tell you which figure is "right" and whether auto theft "really" increased or "really" decreased? Sorry.

What Crime Rates Mean—and What They Don't Mean

I, too, find these statistics puzzling. But I think we are frustrated because we expect too much. We want a single statistic to tell us the entire story of auto theft. Perhaps, in some way we are not fully aware of, we even use overall crime statistics as an index of morality. We see the UCR as a melodrama. If crime goes down, the good guys are winning; if it goes up, the bad guys are winning. We assume that if crime goes up, something else bad also must have happened—we have become a less moral society, or there are more bad guys, or the system is not doing its job, or society is unjust.

But the two graphs tell us something more complicated: that the amount of theft depends not just on the number of bad people but on the amount of stealable property. More autos were stolen because there were more of them to steal; in fact, the thieves did not quite keep up with the increase in auto sales. In the language of business, car thieves were not "maintaining market share." Crime went up not just because we were less moral but also because we were more wealthy.

Let me give another made-up example—a college library. In the last couple of years, the cost of thefts at the library has increased alarmingly. The chief librarian looks at his accounts, shakes his head, and wonders about the moral decline in today's students. But is this the only explanation for the sad increase—that today's students are more criminal than were those of 10 years ago? Or has the seriousness of theft increased because in the last few years the library has been acquiring desirable electronic equipment? After all, if the library's inventory consists mostly of books, losses will not be so great (especially since the loss will not be discovered until somebody else wants the particular book). But if instead of a $20 book, the thief can now make off with a VCR (which is also easier to resell), crime becomes a costlier item. Dollar losses have increased, but does that mean that the student body is less moral, or that the campus security has become less attentive, or that some other evil has worsened? Probably not. It just means that there was more opportunity for crime.

The lesson on larceny in the library may apply to broader crime statistics as well. For example, during the 1970s, UCR burglary rates per 100,000 population increased by about 40 percent. But as with motor vehicle theft, factors besides the "badness" of the society can explain some of the increase. First, the number of households (like the number of vehicles available for auto theft) increased faster than did the population. In fact, while the rate of burglaries per population was increasing in the 1970s, the rate per household was decreasing slightly. Second, more of those houses were easily burglarized because nobody was home. And third, those households contained more stealable and valuable items—expensive cameras, color TVs, tape recorders, etc. What would the statistics look like if we didn't measure burglaries per population, but instead looked at what proportion of our property was stolen? Did the increase in burglary keep up with the increase in stealable wealth? Unfortunately, there are too few statistics on this question to allow a definitive answer. But it does appear that the increase in consumer goods contributes to increases in crime rates.[4]

More people working instead of staying home, greater wealth—these changes are not clearly bad, yet they play an important role in crime. Perhaps this line of thinking does not extend to violent crimes like robbery or murder. But with property crimes, which make up 90 percent of all Index crime, the message behind the statistics is a complicated one. In short, I am arguing that when we see crime statistics like those in the UCR, we should interpret them cautiously and narrowly, rather than treating them as an index of other evils.

THE UCR IN THE REAL WORLD

All of the flaws in the UCR crime rates mentioned so far are inherent in the way these statistics are computed. That is, even before it is put into operation, the UCR has several shortcomings in the way it defines and counts crime. In addition, the actual process of gathering these crime statistics has its own types of inaccuracy.

Let's take burglary as an example. In 1985, the UCR statistics showed 2,984,434 burglaries—a rate of about 1,260 per 100,000 people. Does this mean that exactly 2,984,434 burglaries occurred in the United States? Of course not. For a crime to appear in the UCR total, a citizen must report it to the police, and the police must record it in the figures they send along to the FBI. That is why the FBI labels their UCR crime statistics "crimes known to the police." If the victim does not call the police, or if the police for some reason choose not to record it, the crime will not become part of the official statistics.

Unreported Crime—The Dark Figure

Have you ever been the victim of a crime? Did anybody ever steal something out of your car, or take your handbag when you weren't paying attention, or steal your bicycle? Or did you ever find that someone had gone into your room and stolen your stereo or something else? If so, did you report the crime to the police? If you did not report the crime, what were your reasons?

Did you believe that nothing could be done, or that your loss was not great enough to bother the police about? (These are the reasons behind most non-reporting.) Or did you report it to someone else—your landlord or campus security? In any case, if you did not report the crime to the police— and many people victimized by these crimes do not—then the statistics on larceny or burglary in your area and in the nation will be incorrect.

From the beginning, people interested in crime have realized that the figures in the UCR must be inaccurate. They knew that many crimes went unreported. But how many? Nobody knew; nobody even had a way of making a good guess. Criminologists referred to this unknown quantity as the "dark figure" of crime.

Knowing more about the dark figure is crucial to keeping score on crime, especially since people often take crime rates as a measure of police effectiveness. Usually we think that lower crime rates reflect good police work, while higher crime rates mean that the police have been less effective. But if we are using UCR data (crimes known to the police), we must be very careful about making that interpretation. In fact, higher *official* crime rates might be a sign of better police work, not worse.

How can better police make for higher crime rates? Remember, the most common reason for not reporting a crime is that "nothing could be done." In other words, people have resigned themselves to thinking that the police can't help. But if the police become more effective and if victims now have more confidence that the police can do something about a crime, people may be more likely to call the police. In other words, because the police improve, the official crime rate (based on *reported* crime) may increase. Similarly, if the police gain a reputation for ineffectiveness, rates of reported crime may decrease. For example, a New Jersey police chief, referring to a decrease in the official rate of crime in his state, said, "An interesting statistic that I have a great difficulty accepting: Crime in New Jersey is down 11 percent. I believe that people are no longer reporting crime at the level they once did."[5]

How does the chief know? The answer is that he doesn't. But how could he find out? How might we throw some light on this dark figure? How might we find out how many crimes really occurred beyond those reported to the police?

Other Sources of Crime Statistics

If we can't rely on information from citizens' reports, we must move back one step closer to the crime itself; we must go either to the victims or to the criminals. And that's just what criminologists have done. They have developed two types of tools for estimating crime: the **victimization survey**, where people are interviewed about the crimes committed against them, and the **self-report study**, where people are asked about crimes they themselves have committed.

These solutions are obvious, but they are also inconvenient. The advantage of using crimes known to the police was that the information already existed; all the FBI had to do was to get police departments to cooperate in categorizing and filing it. Getting valid information from victims or criminals is much more difficult and costly, primarily because surveys about crime require large samples. A sample of 1,000 or 2,000 people may be adequate for election polls or television ratings. But being a crime victim or criminal, unlike being a voter or TV viewer, is fairly rare, so we have to survey many people before we find enough victims or criminals to give us a clear picture.

Because of the effort and expense, most self-report surveys have focused on a local population rather than on a national sample. These studies are of little use in estimating the amount of crime in the United States. Also, even within a single locality, self-report researchers often have used a captive audience—usually high-school students—rather than using a random sample of the entire population. Self-report studies, therefore, tell us mostly about juvenile crime and delinquency. A few self-report studies have asked adult prison inmates (another nonrandom, captive audience) about their crimes. These studies, like those of juveniles, can be very useful for finding differences between people who commit crimes and those who do not, or between the most serious criminals and the less frequent offenders. But self-report surveys are of little help in estimating overall rates of crime.*

Victimization surveys, too, are inconvenient for many of the same reasons. So it was not until the mid-1960s that the first nationwide victimization surveys were done. In 1965, the National Opinion Research Center (NORC) surveyed 10,000 households and found that of all serious crime (all the Index crimes, except murder) only about half was reported to the police.[6] The NORC study provided a better view of the dark figure of crime, but since it was a one-time survey, it could not be used for assessing increases or decreases in crime. However, beginning in 1973, the U.S. Justice Department set up a regular victimization survey, known now as the National Crime Survey (NCS).

Every six months, the NCS conducts interviews with a national sample of 50,000 households comprising a total of about 100,000 people. Interviewers ask a variety of questions about crime, ranging from the very serious ("Were you knifed, shot at, or attacked?") to the not so serious ("Was anything stolen that is kept outside your home, such as a bicycle, a garden hose, or lawn furniture?"). (Both of these would qualify as Index crimes in

---

* In the last decade, the National Youth Survey has asked a nationwide sample of teenagers about their crimes, but the sample size (under 2,000) may be too small to give good estimates of the incidence of serious criminal behavior.

the UCR: The first is an aggravated assault; the second a larceny.) They also ask whether the crime was reported to the police, and how much loss and damage occurred. In "personal" crimes, where the victim sees the criminal, they also ask questions about the criminal (age, sex, etc.).

What does the NCS tell us about crime? First, the victimization survey turns up far more crime than appears in the UCR. For example, the 1988 UCR shows 910,092 aggravated assaults "known to the police." For the same crime, in the same year, the NCS estimates 1,741,000—nearly twice as many. For residential burglaries, the figures are (roughly) UCR 2 million, NCS 5.8 million.* The UCR and NCS are not directly comparable, but generally it's safe to say that the victimization survey finds two to three times as much crime as do official records.

Why are the numbers so different? The most important reason is that victims frequently do not report the crime to the police. According to the NCS, only about one crime in three gets reported. Of course, the rate varies from crime to crime. Generally, the more serious the crime, the more likely people are to report it. Victims of thefts where the loss is between $100 and $250 call the police about 45 percent of the time, while the reporting rate on auto theft or theft of property with value totaling $1,000 or more is near 70 percent. Victims of robbery without injury call the police slightly more than half the time; robbery victims who are injured report the crime 67 percent of time. However, consider the other side of these percentages. Theft of over $1,000 and robbery with injury sound like very serious crimes, but still nearly one victim in three chooses not to report these crimes to the police.

Victims give several reasons for not reporting crimes. Most frequently the victim felt that nothing could be done and that the matter was not important enough. These reasons apply more to property crimes, especially those where the loss was not great. When violent crimes go unreported, the reason is more likely to be that it was a private or personal matter. Often, the victim and attacker know each other or are related. Even when the crime is serious or when injury occurs—as in fights between acquaintances, spouse abuse, or marital rape—the victim may define the act as part of the relationship rather than as a criminal matter for the police and courts.

The non-reporting of crime is probably the point at which most crimes are "lost" from official statistics, which are based on "crimes known to the police." But there is another important link in the chain between the crime itself and its inclusion in the UCR tally: the police. In some cases, even if a citizen reports a crime, the police may choose to leave it out of their records.

---

* For the most recent National Crime Survey data, check your library for Bureau of Justice Statistics reports. These six- to 12-page reports give the basic victimization rates and rates of reporting crimes to the police. If your library does not receive these reports, look in the *Sourcebook of Criminal Justice Statistics*, a large, annual collection of data on many aspects of crime and the criminal justice system, also published by the Bureau of Justice Statistics.

Off the Record—The Police and Crime Statistics

Why do the police sometimes not record crimes? In some cases, the reason is that the police have standards and definitions of crime different from those of citizens. The act that provokes a citizen to call the police may not meet the legal criteria for a crime. In other cases, the police do not record the crime for reasons that closely resemble the reasons that citizens do not report crime: It was not important enough; nothing will come of it; it was a private matter. On the basis of these criteria, the officer who arrives on the scene may decide not to write up the crime even though the victim has called the police. In addition, sometimes the complainant (the person who calls the cops) may have had a change of heart about wanting the case pursued. In that event, the police almost never write up the crime. Or if the complainant gives the police a hard time, the officer may not bother to write up the crime.[7]

One other important element influences the police decision to record the crime: the presence of a suspect. If, when the police arrive at the scene, a suspect is there to be arrested, the crime usually gets written up. But when there is no suspect, the police are more likely to let the crime go unrecorded. One study found that police responding to misdemeanors (less serious crimes) failed to write up nearly half the crimes where they did not have a suspect. Even for felonies (more serious crimes), when there was no suspect, police would ignore one crime for every three they wrote up.[8]

One reason for dropping crimes without a suspect is that it means a lot of paperwork for "nothing" since the crime probably will not be solved, and police officers generally do not like paperwork.[9] But another reason is that no-suspect crimes, if recorded, will tarnish the two principal measures of police effectiveness: crime rates and "clearance rates" (the percentage of crimes solved). Police departments are sensitive to the image that these two stastistics portray. Police, and often citizens, see crime rates as a measure of how well the police are doing their job of protecting the city, and see clearance rates as a measure of how well they are doing their job of catching criminals.[10] Police departments want low crime rates and high clearance rates. Recording a crime where they can arrest someone does raise the crime rate, but it also raises the clearance rate; therefore, it shows that the police are doing their job of catching criminals. But every *unsolved* recorded crime raises the crime rate and lowers the clearance rate. Is it any wonder that the police would rather not record some of these unsolvable crimes?

Since non-recording of crime allows police to manipulate their department's image, crime statistics are a political matter. The amount of non-recording varies from city to city according to the police department's policy and according to the political climate surrounding the police department.

How much crime are the police keeping off the books? And how can we find out? Victimization surveys can tell us about citizens' non-reporting of crime. But studying police nonrecording is another matter. It is harder to shed light on this area of the "dark figure" of crime, though sometimes we can catch glimpses. For example: In 1950, New York City's rate of burglary (based on "crimes known to the police") increased by 1,300 percent. For every recorded burglary in 1949 there were 14 in 1950. It was not the burglars of New York who were responsible for this increase; it was the chief of police. And, of course, the huge increase had nothing to do with changes in the actual amount of burglary. What happened was that prior to 1950, most burglary reports had been removed from the records (a practice known in police lingo as "canning" or "referring the case to Detective Can"). However, the police chief, under pressure from the FBI, changed this policy; from then on, the great majority of reported burglaries went on the books.[11]

The history of official crime statistics is dotted with similar tales. To take another example, a national victimization survey in 1972 found that in almost all cities the ratio of victimization survey crime to police statistics was between 2:1 and 3:1. That is, for every 1,000 crimes the survey discovered, between 350 and 500 would be on the official statistics of the city's police department—except in Philadelphia. The ratio in Philadelphia was closer to 5:1. For every 1,000 victimization survey crimes, the police would have recorded only 200.[12] Were victims in Philadelphia so much less likely to call the police than were victims in Atlanta or Cleveland? Probably not. But why were the Philadelphia police so reluctant to record crime? Some observers think that this policy had something to do with local politics. The former chief of police had just been elected mayor, and had campaigned on a tough anti-crime platform (not so rare a position then among conservative politicians, as we saw in Chapter 2). Low crime rates would demonstrate his effectiveness. And sure enough, one way or another, Philadelphia's crime rate remained low.[13]

A similar low crime rate occurred in Washington, D.C., shortly after the election of Richard Nixon in 1972. Nixon had campaigned strongly against crime. Given the structure of American government, the only city that a president can directly affect is Washington. So Washington, the demonstration city for the "war on crime," showed decreases in crime. However, the decreases occurred mostly on paper, not on the streets.[14]

More recently, FBI investigations discovered that the Chicago police "unfounded" an unusually high proportion of reported crimes. When a citizen's report turns out to be invalid, the case is "unfounded" and removed from the crime tally; for example, if a stolen car turns out to have been merely borrowed by a relative who forgot to inform the owner, the crime is unfounded. Most cities unfound 1 or 2 percent of reported crime. Chicago police were unfounding 20 percent.[15] The FBI then pressured the Chicago police department to start keeping the books more honestly. As a result, between 1982 and 1984, when most cities saw decreasing robbery rates, Chicago's official robbery rate rose 80 percent.

Clearly, we must be cautious about using the UCR official crime rates (crimes known to the police) in comparing cities. It would be nice to know if one city is really "safer" than another. But differences in police policy on recording crimes, differences in the type of population on which the rate is figured, and even differences in citizens' willingness to report crimes, make these official figures very suspect. Victimization surveys are not much help either. The NCS, even with its sample of 100,000 people nationwide, is not large enough to allow accurate comparisons between cities. Even as a measure of crime in the country as a whole, the NCS has its flaws.

How Accurate Are Victimization Surveys?

It is clear that the UCR severely undercounts crime. But how accurate is the NCS? There are two points of view on this question. Some criminologists argue that the NCS gives an inflated picture of crime. Others argue that the amount of crime reported in the NCS, while much larger than that in the UCR, still *under*counts the actual amount of crime.

To argue that the NCS overcounts crime—i.e., that it counts more crime than actually occurred—is to argue that it includes crimes that never really happened. How can this be? Why would people report nonexistent crimes to the NCS interviewers?

First, there is the memory factor. The NCS interviewers call every six months and ask about only those crimes that have occurred since their last visit. But people's minds do not have exact calendars built in. An unusual event may stand out in our minds; even though it happened 10 months ago, we may remember it "as though it were yesterday." Some crimes may be this kind of memorable event.

A greater problem exists for the less serious crimes reported to NCS interviewers. Some of these may not be crimes, at least not as the respondents describe them. In one study, researchers carefully reviewed all incidents gathered by a victimization survey. In nearly one-third of the cases, the information provided failed to meet the legal definition of crime.[16]

In contrast to those who think that victimization surveys exaggerate the amount of crime, most criminologists think that victimization surveys give a low estimate of the amount of crime. The memory problem, they say, is not that people remember crimes too well, but that they forget them. Also, some victims may not tell an interviewer about a crime for the same reasons that they don't call the police: It was a private matter; they don't want to take the time; or (in the case of rape or assault) they are embarrassed. Even when people report a crime to the police they may still, for some reason, omit it later in a victimization interview.[17]

There may also be systematic differences in the way people of different social classes respond to a survey. For example, according to the NCS figures, people with at least some college education are assaulted nearly twice as often as people who never got past eighth grade.[18] Is there really more interpersonal violence among the better-educated? More likely, middle-class people remember and report many of the kinds of assault that lower-class people either forget or ignore. Thus, the NCS rate for aggravated assault, while nearly double the official rate, still underestimates the actual amount of serious violence.

Official Data and Survey Data—A Comparison

Now that you know about the two major sources for counting crime in the United States, you may be tempted to ask "Which one is right; which one tells us how much crime there really is?" And you probably also lean toward the NCS as being more accurate. Perhaps you even agree with those who dismiss the UCR altogether as hopelessly inaccurate. After all, if there are so many ways a crime can disappear before it gets into the UCR, then not only is the total wrong, but even year-to-year changes will reflect changes in the behavior of victims and police, not changes in actual crime.

I think such a view is wrong. After all, our goal is not to select the single best measure of crime; our goal is to get as complete a picture of crime as we can. Toward that goal, we should recognize first that both the UCR and the victimization survey have inaccuracies. Second, and perhaps more important, the two counts of crime are measuring different things. It's not just that the NCS measures only crimes against households and persons while the UCR includes commercial crime as well. Even within the same category of crime, say household burglary, the two crime tallies have important differences. In 1988, the two tallies for residential burglary differed by 3.8 million. But most of the burglaries left out of the UCR were those that citizens or police did not define as "serious." If you come home and find that someone has jimmied the lock, ransacked the house, and taken most of your valuable property, you will probably call the police. But if you left the door unlocked, and the neighbor's kid walked in, knocked over the fishbowl and took a soccer ball and a pocket calculator, you might prefer to settle it with the boy's parents. You would probably not call the police about it. However, you would remember it when you are interviewed by the National Crime Survey.

The NCS includes every violation of the law that the interviewees can recall. The UCR (at least in theory) contains only those crimes about which the victim was upset enough to call the cops. The NCS measures crimes that happened. The UCR measures crimes that people think the police ought to do something about. The NCS measure is "objective" in the sense that it is more detached from how people feel about the crime. The UCR Index in this sense is more "subjective," since it depends on the feelings and behavior of the victim.

Some criminologists argue that it is precisely this subjectivity that may make the UCR the better measure of "serious" crime. The UCR contains crimes that are defined as serious not by some abstract, distant set of rules but by the people directly involved. There is one easy way to discover the criteria an ordinary person uses for deciding seriousness: Does he or she call the police? It turns out that most people share these same informal criteria: If a crime does not involve losses of high value, bodily injury (or the serious threat of bodily injury), victimization by a stranger, or breaking and entering, then most people do not think of it as serious. The police, too, seem to share this definition of "serious" crime, even though it differs from the official UCR Index definition. So while the NCS may come closer to estimating the total amount of crime according to abstract, legal definitions, the UCR contains only those crimes that citizens thought were serious enough to report and that the police thought were serious enough to record. In this way, the UCR shows us the size of the *crime problem*.[19]

Of course, if the official crime rates go up, we still cannot be sure which has changed—the amount of serious crime or people's subjective judgments. This problem is especially important in comparisons between different places or times. It may be that, as the police chief implied, people have become so resigned to crime that they no longer report it to the police as often as they did in the past. However, what evidence there is on this question does not bear him out. The NCS began in 1973, and since that time, the percentage of victims who report crimes to the police has been remarkably stable (see Table 3–3). The reporting rates also tell us that police statistics on frequently reported crimes (e.g., auto theft) should be more accurate than their statistics on larceny. However, even a seemingly small change can have some effect. For example, suppose that the reporting rate for larcenies increases from 25 percent to 27 percent, with no change in the actual amount of larceny and no change in the real or reported rates

Table 3–3 ■ **Rates of Reporting Victimizations to the Police**

	1973	1976	1979	1982	1985	1988
All crimes	32%	35%	33%	36%	36%	36%
Rape	46	49	45	48	48	48
Robbery	52	53	51	53	61	45
Burglary	47	48	48	49	50	51
Household larceny	25	27	25	27	27	26
Personal larceny with contact	33	36	36	33	33	35
Motor vehicle theft	68	69	67	72	71	73

Source: "Criminal Victimization 1988," U.S. Department of Justice, Bureau of Justice Statistics, Washington, DC: U.S. Government Printing Office.

for other Index crimes. Since larceny accounts for over half of all Index crimes, the total rate of reported crime (the UCR) will rise by 4 percent.

Rereading the Headlines

Let's return to the typical headline about an increase or decrease in the rate of serious crime. Consciously or not, people often read this statistic as a barometer that tells us how well we are doing in the fight against crime. And since it comes with the authority of the FBI, people may also tend to accept it as accurate. Of course, having read this far, you now know better. The FBI may be scrupulously honest, but it is only the last step in the process by which a crime becomes a statistic. Along the way from the event to the statistic, many crimes will disappear.

The accuracy of official crime statistics depends most on the victims and on the police. Ironically, these two groups that are so crucial to our knowledge of crime are the greatest source of error in crime statistics. Both the victim, in deciding whether to report a crime, and the police, in deciding whether to record it, have many things on their minds. Unfortunately, one of the things they probably are *not* thinking about is the accuracy of crime statistics.

Victimization surveys like the National Crime Survey are our other major source of information on the amount of crime. But the NCS has its own limitations. It omits commercial crimes; it includes many crimes which most people would regard as trivial; and it depends on the memory and cooperativeness of victims. Nevertheless, trends in the NCS have generally mirrored trends in official UCR rates.

Before jumping to conclusions from this year's UCR figures, there are other things we want to know. Do victimization figures from the NCS resemble the UCR trends? Do the trends in the most accurately reported crimes (murder and auto theft) parallel those in the other crimes? Even if the answer to these questions is "yes," we should be cautious about small changes in crime rates from one year to another. It is only when we look at longer trends that we can be more confident in statements about how crime is changing.

COMPARED WITH WHAT?

Let's go back to the original question: How much crime is there? Obviously, to answer this question objectively, we must count crime; and so far, this chapter has examined the different techniques for counting crime. Each method has its own strengths and its own types of inaccuracy, and each comes up with different numbers. It's frustrating. We ask a simple question, and instead of a simple answer, we get several answers that rarely are in agreement, and all are in some way inaccurate.

However, even if we could arrive at a perfect, accurate count, we still would not have an answer to a more difficult and perhaps more important question. Suppose we know that last year in the United States there were exactly 20,000 murders, a rate of about 8 per 100,000. Is that a lot or a little?

When I ask students this question in class, they have two typical responses. Some take the absolutist position I mentioned at the beginning of this chapter: Even one murder is a lot (especially if you yourself happen to be the victim). This answer is not very useful; it does not distinguish between one murder and 20,000. Any crime is "too much." Other students look at the question in relative rather than absolute terms. They answer my question with a question: Compared with what?

Excellent question. The answer is that criminologists, like anyone else, make two kinds of comparisons. Historical (or "time-series") studies compare levels of crime at different times in the same place. When the newspaper headline says "Crime in United States Down 4 percent," it is comparing the United States this year with the United States last year. Other historical studies, as we shall see, cover much longer periods of time.

Besides comparing current crime rates with those in the past, we might also want to see how the United States compares with other countries. Whether we are using crime rates as part of some index of the quality of life, or whether we are trying to see what other factors correlate with differences in crime rates, it probably makes sense to compare ourselves with countries that are similar in many other respects. For a few specific purposes, we might compare the United States with, say, Vietnam, which is a communist, nonindustrial, and very poor country. But generally, we will want to compare the United States with countries whose society, economy, and political system resemble our own—the "Western industrialized" countries. These include the countries of Western Europe (Great Britain, France, Germany, Italy, the Scandinavian countries, etc.), Canada, Australia, and Japan.

Comparisons among countries are not easy to make. All of the problems that plague crime statistics within a single country become multiplied. Countries will differ in their definitions of crime, the willingness of citizens to report crime, the diligence of the police in recording crime, and other factors that affect official crime rates. Comparisons based on victimization surveys also may be misleading. To begin with, most European crime surveys are one-shot surveys confined to one or two cities. There are few regular, nationwide surveys like our National Crime Survey. Second, the questions asked in these surveys may not always be comparable from one country to another, though a few studies have been designed explicitly for comparative purposes.

U.S.A.—We're Number One

Because of all these difficulties, criminologists often look at those crimes where differences in definition and reporting will be minimal and where statistics will be most accurate. The most obvious candidate for such a crime is murder, especially since data on this crime come not only from the police but also from public health agencies that record "cause of death." Table 3–4 shows the murder rates from around 1980 for a few countries (including some in Eastern Europe).

These figures immediately raise the question of why the U.S. murder rate is so much higher than that of other countries. The answer is complicated and a matter of some debate, which I would like to leave for another chapter. For example, many people point to the easy availability of guns in the United States, but guns constitute only part of the answer. Even if all gun murders were removed from the U.S. total, our murder rate would be more than twice that of most European countries.

These murder rates raise a different question: Is the murder rate a good indicator of the overall level of crime? We know that the murder rate is the most accurate of any of the crimes we might use for comparing countries. But will a country with a high murder rate also have high rates of burglary or auto theft? There is good reason to think not. First of all, murder constitutes a very small part of the overall crime rate. In the United States, murder's share of the total crime Index is less than two-tenths of 1 percent. In addition, murder differs from the bulk of Index crime in that it usually has no economic motive. In this way it resembles aggravated assault and perhaps rape: It shows a willingness to use extreme force in interpersonal matters. But this motive probably plays a less important part in the robberies, burglaries, larcenies, and auto theft that account for over 90 percent of all Index crime.

Therefore, while the United States clearly has more murders than do other Western industrialized countries, if we want to know about crime in general, we still should look at the other crimes, even though the data will not provide

Table 3–4 ▪ Murder Rates in Selected Countries

United States (1979)	9.9	Austria (1982)	1.5
Japan (1981)	1.0	Czechoslovakia (1979)	1.1
France (1981)	1.0	Greece (1981)	0.8
West Germany (1982)	1.2	Hungary (1982)	2.4
Ireland (1980)	0.7	Australia (1980)	1.9
Yugoslavia (1981)	2.3	Holland (1982)	0.8
England/Wales (1981)	0.4	Italy (1979)	1.6

Source: United Nations Demographic Yearbook, 1983.

Table 3–5 ■ Crime Rates, 1980

	United States	*West Germany*
Murder	10.2	1.7
Rape	36.4	11.2
Robbery	245.5	39.3
Aggravated assault	290.6	93.0
Burglary and larceny	4,824.43	698.0
Motor vehicle theft	494.6	353.0

Source: Reprinted with permission from Journal of Criminal Justice, Vol. 10, Teske and Arnold, Comparisons of Criminal Statistics of the U.S. and the Federal Republic of Germany. Copyright 1982, Pergamon Press PLC.

as clear a conclusion. Table 3–5 compares 1980 rates of "Index" crime in the United States with those in West Germany. The researchers tried to overcome differences in definitions, though in one case they had to combine two property crimes (burglary and larceny-theft).

The United States has higher rates for every category of crime, with very large differences in violent crimes. Our property crime rates are "only" about 35 percent higher than those of West Germany, but our rates of violent crime are 200–500 percent higher. Comparisons with other industrialized countries give roughly similar results. These statistics come from police sources, but where there are victimization surveys to make comparison possible, similar patterns turn up. Our NCS figures, compared to a national survey in Australia, for example, show that we have 300 percent more robbery but only about 25 percent more motor vehicle theft.[20]

In short, compared with other Western industrialized countries, the United States has generally higher rates of crime, and much higher rates of violent crime.

DON'T KNOW MUCH ABOUT HISTORY?

Besides comparing our crime rates with those of other countries, we also judge the current levels of crime by comparison with earlier periods in our own history. Have we always had so much crime? Has crime increased steadily since the founding of the republic so that the farther back in our history we go, the less crime we will find? Or does crime fluctuate from one period to another? If it does, how can we explain those fluctuations?

Of course, most people do not analyze the broad sweep of history. Their historical comparisons tend to be impressionistic and unsystematic and

Table 3–6 ■ Selected Crime Rates, 1955, 1960, 1975

	1955	*1960*	*1975*
Murder	4.7	5.1	9.6
Robbery	60.6	60.1	218.6
Burglary	423.0	508.6	1,525.9

Source: UCR 1955, Edmund F. McGarrel and Timothy J. Flanagan, eds. (1985) *Sourcebook of Criminal Justice Statistics—1984*, U.S. Department of Justice, Bureau of Justice Statistics, Washington, DC, U.S. Government Printing Office.

probably are limited to the fairly recent past, perhaps only as far back as personal recollection will take them. For this reason, and perhaps because we tend to remember the past as better than it actually was, it seems that many people think that crime has never been worse than it is now. There is a widespread impression that America's high crime rates are rather recent and unprecedented, a product of the most recent one or two generations. People can remember times when they felt safer, when merchants did not have to put iron grates over their store windows, when people could safely sleep in the city parks or on fire escapes in the summer.

These perceptions are reflected in more systematic kinds of evidence. Police statistics from the UCR show a dramatic increase (see Table 3–6). Remember, these are official statistics and therefore subject to changes in police recording practices. In any case, crime rates changed little during the 1950s. But in the 1960s, crime grew quite rapidly. The murder rate—our most accurate figure—nearly doubled. And between 1960 and 1971, the robbery rate tripled. Nor is this just a matter of increased reporting and recording. In 1965, the official rate of robbery of individuals (as opposed to businesses) was about 65 per 100,000. A national victimization survey that year estimated that there were an additional 30 unreported robberies per 100,000 people. The total of all robberies—reported plus unreported—was no more than 95 to 100 per 100,000. By 1973, reported robberies alone came to 180 per 100,000, and a victimization survey estimated an additional 500 unreported robberies per 100,000.[21]

Since then, crime rates, depending on the source of statistics, have either increased or remained fairly stable. Police statistics (UCR) show an increase in the late 1970s, with some tapering off after 1980. Victimization survey data (NCS) show little overall change—if anything a slight downward trend, as the graph for robbery shows (see Figure 3–3). The graph for burglary presents something of a puzzle (see Figure 3–4). From 1973 to 1981, official rates of burglary increased by 35 percent while rates found by the victimization survey remained about the same. For motor vehicle theft, the two sources of statistics show roughly parallel trends, at least after 1978 (see

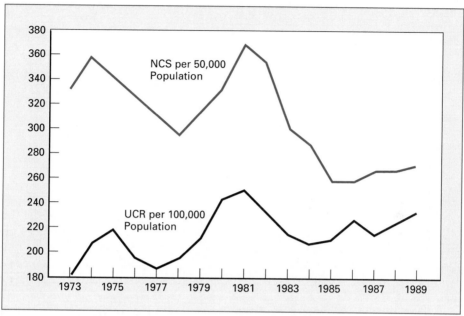

Figure 3–3 Robbery Rates from UCR and NCS, 1973–1989

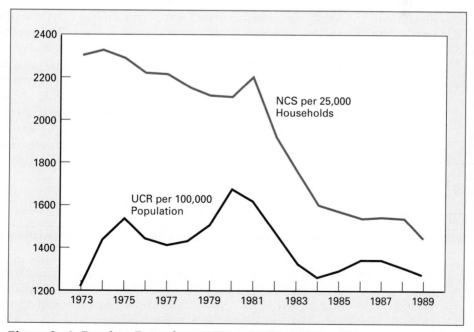

Figure 3–4 Burglary Rates from UCR and NCS, 1973–1989

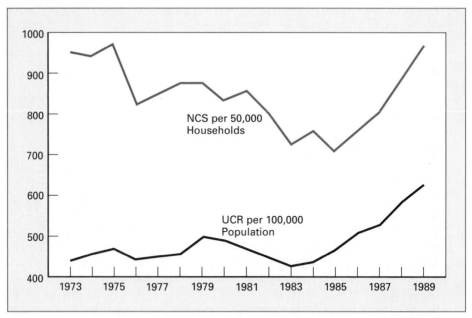

Figure 3–5 Motor Vehicle Theft Rates from UCR and NCS, 1973–1989

Figure 3–5). This result is reassuring, for aside from murder (a crime not included in the NCS), motor vehicle theft is the crime for which UCR figures are most accurate. (Remember that for both burglary and auto theft, the NCS figures its rates on the basis of the number of households. One possible reason for part of the discrepancy between UCR and NCS trends may be that the number of households was increasing more rapidly than was the number of crimes.)

By any measure, crime rates in the 1980s and early 1990s are much higher than those of the 1940s and 1950s. The question, though, is whether we should take crime rates from the 1940s and 1950s as our standard for comparison.

CRIME IN U.S. HISTORY

Much thinking about crime today seems to be based on the assumption that current crime rates are not only unacceptable, but that they also are unusual and unprecedented. Crime and violence have remained at high levels for nearly two decades now, but this persistence has done little to alter the popular notion that these rates are abnormal and downright un-American. The assumption behind this thinking is that America has always been a peaceful and law-abiding country, but that somehow things began to fall apart in the 1960s. Therefore, if only we can find the right solution, we can return to the "normal" levels of crime that characterized the 1950s.

However, some critics paint a much less flattering picture of American history. In their view, America has a long tradition of violence and crime, stretching back perhaps to the founding of the republic. In their view, the unusual and puzzling part of this half century is not the current high rate of crime but rather the period of peace and order in the 1950s. Seen from this perspective, the rise in crime during the 1960s was just a return to America's normal high level of crime. Much of the evidence for this view concerns more or less organized violence: massacres of Native Americans, election riots, race riots, and labor-management battles. European countries, too, have had similar sorts of conflict—with the exception, of course, of the slaughtering of Native Americans as whites extended their dominion from Atlantic to Pacific. But America's urban riots and labor strife have generally involved more violence.[22] To take probably the bloodiest example, the New York Draft Riot of 1863 lasted three days and left at least 300 dead (estimates ranged as high as 1,200). It started as an attack on draft headquarters, but the mob subsequently burned some mansions, attacked the police, and "increasingly turned its fury against blacks, burning, stomping, clubbing, hanging, shooting."[23] And that was only the first day.

Even if we acknowledge a history of collective violence, these riots and battles hardly resemble the street crime that concerns us today. It's not that this violence happened so long ago; riots like these may still occur. As recently as the late 1960s, ghetto riots erupted in several cities. But what of the more individual kinds of crime—not the mass violence and looting but the ordinary burglaries, robberies, and murders? Are these also part of America's legacy?

This is a harder question to answer, since the historical record usually documents only the more spectacular, newsworthy events. Ideally, we would like some sort of statistical count of crime from previous eras, but such an index would be hard to reconstruct. Telling stories from the past is much easier. For example, those who argue that violence is "as American as cherry pie" sometimes point to the crime and violence that marked the frontier towns of the West—the cattle rustlers, the famous bank robbers like Jesse James, the gunfighters, and the vigilantes.[24] Much of this evidence on crime is highly anecdotal, more a basis for making Western movies than for estimating the actual amount of crime. But the vigilantes are another matter. Even if we do not know the actual amount of crime, the existence of vigilantism tells us how people at the time viewed things: Apparently, they felt that crime had gotten out of hand and that the legitimate government could not control it.

How Wild Was the West?

Vigilantism may be a desperate expression of concern about crime. But what kind of crime were the citizens on the frontier concerned about? Did crime and justice really resemble what we see in cowboy movies? One answer comes from Roger McGrath's historical study of two notoriously rough mining towns—Bodie and Aurora—that flourished briefly in the 1870s in the rugged mountains near the California-Nevada border. These were boom towns. News of the discovery of silver or gold nearby would attract all sorts of men eager for quick fortune. A town would flourish for a few years, its population growing from a few hundred to around 5,000; then nearly as suddenly the boom would end, and the community would fade from boom town to ghost town.

Because of this pattern, a town like Bodie at its most booming had all the characteristics that should make for high crime rates: The population consisted largely of single men, with varying amounts of cash, no deep ties to the community, and a social life that centered around liquor, gambling, and prostitutes. Bodie even had racial minorities (Mexicans and Chinese) and hard drugs (opium). For law enforcement the town had only a constable, who doubled as jailer, and his deputies. Crime rarely resulted in arrest, much less in conviction and sentencing. Under these conditions, crime should have been widespread. But was it?

In trying to reconstruct a full picture of crime in Bodie during the five years of its heyday, McGrath read carefully through the newspapers and court documents for reports of crime. Even with a population of 5,000, Bodie was small enough that most crimes would come to light. His results appear in Table 3–7, which gives both the absolute number of crimes known to McGrath in the years 1878 to 1882 and the rate per 100,000. For example, during this five-year period there were 21 robberies. That makes for an average of 4.2 per year. Since the population was 5,000, we multiply by 20

Table 3–7 ■ Crime Rates—The Frontier and Today

	Bodie Number of Crimes	*1878–1882 Rate*	*United States 1989 Rate*	*Sparks, NV, 1989 Rate*	*Denver, 1989 Rate*
Robbery	21	84.0	233.0	137.4	256.2
Burglary	32	132.0	1,276.3	1,186.2	2,078.5
Rape	0	0.0	38.1	95.7	65.7
Murder	31	116.0	8.9	8.7	11.1

Source: Roger McGrath (1984), "Gunfighters, Highwaymen, and Vigilantes: Violence on the Frontier," the Regents of the University of California.

to get the annual rate per 100,000. For comparison, I have included more recent rates for the United States as a whole, for a small Nevada city, and for a large Western city, Denver.

Two things stand out in these figures: Compared with the United States today, Bodie had far more murder and far less of the other crimes. The robbery rate is less than half that for the United States as a whole, and about one-fourth that of urban Denver (and still less than the rate of many other cities today).

Why was Bodie's crime rate, except for murder, so low? Perhaps even the criminals had a certain code of honor. Apparently, they did not victimize women. In five years, there were no known rapes. And, according to McGrath, it was not just a matter of women not reporting the crime. "For the women of Bodie, including the prostitutes of Bonanza Street, the threat of rape or robbery was virtually nonexistent."[25]

A similar code may have extended to other persons as well. For example, today most robbery victims (about two of every three) are individuals rather than businesses. But in Bodie, in half the robberies, the criminals took money not from individuals but from commercial enterprises. In other words, as you've probably already guessed if you've seen a Western or two, they robbed the stagecoach, taking the strongbox and usually leaving the passengers alone.

Another factor may have been the relatively small amount of stealable property. Few of Bodie's residents owned the kind of goods taken in today's burglaries and larcenies—TVs, VCRs, jewelry, furs, etc. They didn't have silverware; they had silver mines, which are a bit harder to steal. Ranches in the area did have cattle, and individuals owned horses, but contrary to what we see in Western movies, Bodie's boom years saw only six horse thefts and no cattle rustling. In fact, the items most frequently stolen were firewood and blankets. It gets cold up in those mountains.

A frontier code of ethics and the lack of easily transferred property may have helped reduce Bodie's crime rate, but what about the high murder rate? In McGrath's view, the major cause of the low rates of stealing and the major cause of the high rate of murder are the same: Everyone had guns. Bodie had two banks, but nobody ever tried to rob them, perhaps because even the tellers were armed. Citizens, too, seemed willing to shoot in order to defend their own property. But while guns may have prevented some crimes, they also made ordinary conflicts much more deadly. Fights that erupted in the gambling halls and saloons could easily end in gunfire. True, the limited technology of the time reduced the accuracy of the weapons, and the unlimited liquor frequently reduced the accuracy of the shooters; nevertheless, bullets found their mark often enough to give Bodie a murder rate several times that of the most murderous cities in America today.

Are America's high crime rates today our inheritance from the frontier? The typical murder today certainly isn't much different from those in Bodie and Aurora. Perhaps the people in Bodie, Aurora, and other Western towns passed their frontier mentality on to subsequent generations. Back then, for the towns' residents this kind of violence was an accepted fact of life, and some criminologists see this attitude, this acceptance of violence, as a cause of high murder rates today. They speak of a "subculture of violence" flourishing in certain sectors of American society.[26]

The idea that current crime is part of our "frontier legacy" may sound good at first; it may even have some validity. However, violent traditions do not always survive. Australia, for example, also had a violent frontier in the 19th century—guns and cattle and cowboys—but today its levels of crime and violence are similar to those of Western Europe. Even in Bodie and Aurora, the evidence should make us look more critically at the violent-traditions idea. Bodie's low rates of non-homicide crimes seem to argue against the "frontier legacy" as an explanation for crime in general. The lawlessness and violence in the Wild West—at least in Bodie and Aurora—were confined largely to personal fights.

It would be hard to trace a continuous thread linking barroom brawls and shootouts in Bodie in 1880 to mugging or burglary in New York in 1991. If we are looking for historical sources for today's crime, perhaps the search should start nearer to the scene of the crime. After all, street crime today—the burglaries and robberies and thefts—is largely an urban and suburban problem. So we might do better to look at the history of crime in the cities rather than on the frontier. If we're looking for roots, we ought to start right under the tree rather than 2,000 miles away out in the Sierra Nevada.

Meanwhile, Back in the East

While towns like Bodie changed as people came West seeking their fortunes in mines and cattle ranches, cities back East were changing in quite a different way. These changes, too, were expected to have serious consequences for crime. History textbooks usually group these changes into three broad categories: industrialization, urbanization, and immigration.

In 1830, most Americans worked on farms or in small-scale enterprises that employed only a few people. The word "factory" still meant a shop run by someone who bought and sold (a "factor"). However, as the century wore on, this meaning and the way of life that went with it eventually gave way to steam-driven, mass-production factories.[27] These changes were most visible in Eastern cities like Boston, where, by 1870, 44 percent of the population was employed in manufacturing.

Accompanying the change in work was another demographic upheaval—urbanization. What had been a nation of small towns and villages was becoming a nation of cities. The country itself was growing. A typical decade in the 19th century might see the total population increase by 35 percent.

But the urban population, in a typical 10-year period, would increase by 60 percent, and by as much as 90 to 100 percent in some decades. In 1820, less than 10 percent of the American people lived in cities; a century later, over half the population lived in cities.[28] In some areas the change was even more extreme. In Massachusetts, the urban proportion of the population went from 19 percent in 1835 to 79 percent by the turn of the century.[29] The cities swelled with people, many of them immigrants—from Germany and Ireland in the first part of the century, from Russia and Southern Europe in the last decades. In many U.S. cities in the late 19th century, one-third to one-half of the population was foreign-born.[30]

People today (criminologists included) would take changes like these as cause for concern, as did many citizens over a century ago. By the mid-19th century, cities were already thought of as sites of disorder and riot, a breeding ground for what came to be called "the dangerous classes."* Many middle-class people feared that these demographic trends—industrialization, urbanization, immigration—would cause even further increases in crime. After all, many of the newcomers to the cities were young, single men. Whether they came from American farms or from Europe, they found themselves freed from traditional community ties and restraints, working in inhuman and dehumanizing factories, frequently living in impoverished slums, and not yet assimilated into American culture. Such men might easily turn to crime and violence. But did they?

As nearly as we can tell, urban crime did not increase during the late 19th century; it decreased. Of course, assembling evidence on 19th-century crime rates presents historians with difficult problems. Statistics on homicide will be the most accurate, though they may not necessarily be a good measure of crime in general. For other crimes, court records can give only a part of the picture, since we cannot know how many crimes never made it to court. Arrests provide a better measure, but police records from a hundred years ago may have been thrown out or destroyed by fire or water.

Fortunately, one of the cities whose police records still exist is Boston, a city whose history should be most useful for studying the effects of social change. It was the center of the textile industry, and it was a major port. Consequently, it grew rapidly, swelling with large numbers of immigrants— first the Irish in the 1840s and 1850s, then later in the century the Italians. Certainly, if any city should show the effects of industrialization, immigration, and urbanization, it is Boston.

To trace crime rates in Boston, historian Theodore Ferdinand went back through police files, grouping the records of arrests into three-year periods from 1850 to 1950. He counted every arrest for crimes that correspond to today's Index crimes and converted these arrests to an annual rate per

---

* Today, few people use this phrase. We are more likely to hear of "the inner-city underclass." The two concepts, then and now, are certainly similar in the reaction of "respectable" people, if not in the behavior of the urban poor.

100,000. His results for murder, robbery, burglary, and "all major crimes" appear in Figures 3–6 through 3–9.

The graph for murder is certainly the most accurate, and the graph for all major crimes, though inaccurate, gives the broadest picture. Both show a similar trend. Crime rises sharply in the 1850s and in the period just after the Civil War. The effect of the Civil War is not unique. Wars deplete the number of young men in the civilian population, so during wars, crime rates—and especially murder rates—go down. When Johnny comes marching home, crime rates go back up. In countries that fought in the two world wars, for example, post-war murder rates were generally *higher* than pre-war rates.[31] In Ferdinand's graphs, the World War I period shows little change in the murder rate, but then the United States entered the war for only two years, 1916 to 1917. The World War II period shows the expected decrease. The change is not as dramatic as that of the Civil War, probably because the Civil War took a greater proportion of young men out of the civilian population.

Interestingly, the graphs show no consistent increase of crime during economic crises. The panics of 1873 and 1893 do not cause great swings

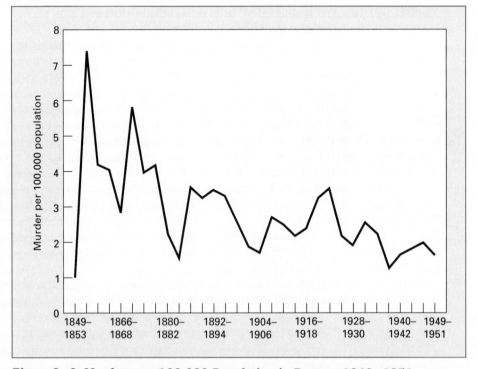

Figure 3–6 Murders per 100,000 Population in Boston, 1849–1951
Source: Theordore N. Ferdinand (1967), "The Criminal Patterns of Boston since 1846," American Journal of Sociology, *vol. 73, pp. 84–89.*

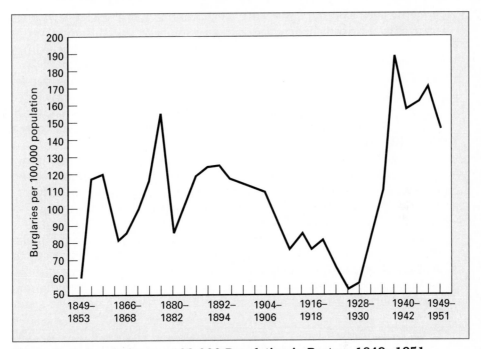

Figure 3—7 Burglaries per 100,000 Population in Boston, 1849—1951
Source: Theordore N. Ferdinand (1967), "The Criminal Patterns of Boston since 1846," American Journal of Sociology, *vol. 73, pp. 84—89.*

in crime rates. The Great Depression of the early 1930s seems to have brought increases in burglary and robbery in Boston, but nationwide crime rates showed no such changes. The most striking feature of Ferdinand's data is the overall trend across most of the 100-year period. From roughly 1875 through 1950, crime decreases. The graphs raise two important questions: First, do they reflect a real change in crime, or just a change in arrests? Second, if the downward trend is real, what caused it?

The question of accuracy is a serious one, since arrest statistics depend not just on the amount of crime but on the attitude and behavior of victims and police. For example, most of those crimes that make up Figure 3—9 ("all major crimes") are larcenies and assaults, crimes which are less serious and therefore more susceptible to changes in people's willingness to call the police and the willingness of the police to make an arrest. Is it possible that the decline is caused not by a real decrease in the amount of crime but by a decrease in citizens and police doing something when a crime occurs? Did Boston's residents become more tolerant of less serious offenses?

The answer appears to be "no." Of course, there are no victimization surveys or other independent measures of crime. Historians can, however, make good guesses about changes in attitudes towards crime, and their studies point to the same conclusion. City people in the 19th century were growing less tolerant of all sorts of lawbreaking. Evidence for this conclusion comes from records of arrests for less serious crimes. Although Ferdinand's graphs do not show it, at the same time that arrests for major crimes were decreasing, court cases involving "disorder" increased greatly.[32] That is to say, the criminal justice system was turning its attention to drunkenness and disturbing the peace rather than theft and burglary. Why? Probably because thieves and burglars were no longer as much of a threat. With these criminals more under control, people were calling on the police to deal with disorder—the kinds of rowdiness that people decades earlier took for granted. (Apparently a similar change took place in London earlier in the century. At the same time that many Londoners were demanding more action against disorder, they also called for less brutal punishment for major crimes.[33]) Both these changes in public opinion suggest that major predatory crimes were decreasing.

In the 1830s and 1840s, the city was a much rougher, riotous place. No police force existed, only a town "night watch," which served mostly to warn of fires. It would not enter some of the more dangerous neighborhoods. Periodic mob violence was a fact of life. Youth gangs regularly fought with each other and attacked other citizens as well. Some gangs also specialized

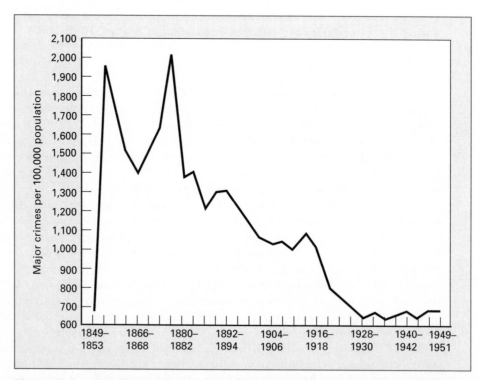

Figure 3–8 All Major Crimes per 100,000 Population in Boston, 1848–1951
Source: Theordore N. Ferdinand (1967), "The Criminal Patterns of Boston since 1846," American Journal of Sociology, *vol. 73, pp. 84–89.*

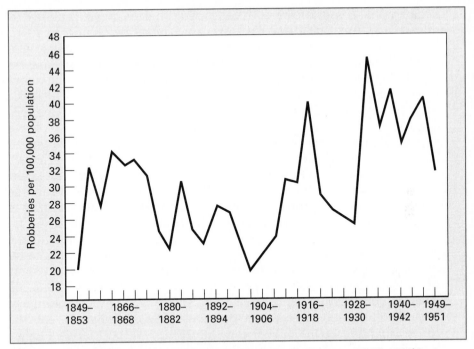

Figure 3–9 Robberies per 100,000 Population in Boston, 1849–1951
Source: Theordore N. Ferdinand (1967), "The Criminal Patterns of Boston since 1846," American Journal of Sociology, *vol. 73, pp. 84–89.*

in theft and robbery. In Philadelphia, youth gangs became part of volunteer fire companies, and some of the worst battles occurred between rival fire brigades. One company might even deliberately set a fire to ambush another group with bricks, stones, and even guns.[34] However, by the 1870s, the city had changed substantially. A police force had been established, and people called on police to intervene in brawls, to deal with drunkenness, to prevent riots—in short, to keep order.

Thus, the city was gradually becoming less criminal, as the decrease in arrests for major crimes shows. But more than that, it also was becoming less tolerant of disorder; hence the increase in less serious court cases. A similar trend might occur in cities today if serious, predatory crime were to decline. In that case, we would probably see an increase in arrests and even jail terms for "quality of life" offenses that today go all but ignored.

Explaining the Past—The Triumph of Morality?

Why didn't the great social changes of the 19th century create greater chaos and crime? Why did crime in fact decrease? There are two leading explanations, both with some relevance for today's crime problem. The first one is more conservative: it emphasizes individual morality. It argues that the demographic trends of the 19th century did indeed create pressure toward more crime, but that these pressures were offset by other forces—in particular by people's participation in various moralistic and religious movements. The second explanation is more liberal, holding that larger social and economic forces are the major source of the change in crime rates. This explanation argues that contrary to what most of us think, the process of industrialization itself was a force for reducing crime and making life more orderly.

In explaining the decrease in crime in the late 19th century, a prominent, conservative criminologist, James Q. Wilson, points to the variety of programs that flourished in the 19th century: traditional churches; the Sunday school movement, which meant all-day lessons in both Bible and self-restraint; the Young Men's Christian Association; the temperance movement—these and other growing organizations all shared "a desire to alter and strengthen human character."[35] The effects of the temperance movement were especially evident. Between 1830 and 1850, per capita alcohol consumption declined from 7 to 10 gallons per year to about 2 gallons per year. This decrease probably contributed to the orderliness of life, though its effect on predatory crime is not clear. Still, Wilson argues, the importance of the temperance movement lay not just in its campaign for sobriety but in its general fostering of self-restraint. It may be hard for us today to get a sense of what temperance meant. It was not a bunch of women with umbrellas smashing bottles on saloon shelves. It was a widespread movement for self-improvement. Today, self-improvement usually comes packaged in an ideology of individualism, or as the title of a 1980s self-improvement best-seller put it, "looking out for #1."

By contrast, temperance and other self-improvement programs of a century ago stressed that self-improvement came not through standing out but through fitting in, not through individualism but through conformity—conformity to what we now call "middle-class morality." Today, this phrase carries a connotation of boring conventionality. But a century ago, the middle class was much smaller than it is today, and neither middle-class morality nor middle-class status was taken for granted; they had to be achieved. Nor did alcohol have the same social meaning that it has today. Instead, it was, though in a milder way, analogous to heroin today—a vice associated in people's minds with the disreputable and violent urban lower class. Temperance—abstaining from drink—signaled that a person was striving for or had achieved middle-class status.[36]

Young men who in earlier eras might have devoted their energies to the saloons and the streets instead became caught up in the trend toward self-improvement through self-restraint and social conformity, and crime rates declined. In the 20th century, as Wilson sees it, this morality that emphasized the community came to be replaced by a morality that emphasized the individual. An ethic of self-restraint gave way to an ethic of self-expression. The value placed on self-expression appeared first among intellectuals in the 1920s, and it subsequently affected the way "experts" in popular magazines advised parents on child-rearing. They began to emphasize the child's happiness and personality rather than his or her moral character. "Permissive" child-rearing and the new "fun morality"[37] did not take hold immediately. The hardships of the Depression and World War II delayed these changes, Wilson says. But amid the affluence and youth culture of the 1960s, they became an additional factor contributing to the steep rise in crime to levels which have persisted now for over 20 years.[38]

Strictness vs. permissiveness, self-restraint vs. self-indulgence, temperance vs. mood-altering substances, church organizations vs. individual nonchurch-going; it all has a familiar and contemporary ring to it, a sort of Jerry Falwell view of crime and history. However, there are some problems with Wilson's theory. To begin with, if it were the new morality that caused crime to increase, then we should expect to find the most crime among those groups that most adopted this permissive, individual-centered morality—i.e., the elite and then the middle class. But they are not the ones committing most street crime.

In addition, the timing of the changes in culture doesn't always match up with changes in crime. For example, religious revivalism was still strong in the 1830s and 1840s; it was also in these decades that Americans greatly reduced their alcohol consumption. From Wilson's theory, we should expect crime to decrease in this period. But, contrary to what Wilson's argument would predict, these were decades of high levels of crime and violence. Also, as the temperance movement gathered strength and rolled toward its greatest triumph—Prohibition—crime and violence should have decreased. But they did not. The temperance movement began to win passage of county and state prohibition laws in the early 1900s. National Prohibition was passed in 1917. So we should expect decreasing crime roughly from the turn of the century to 1930, a few years before Repeal. But if anything, crime increased during these years. Murder rates (again, our most accurate indicator) rose nationally from about 1 per 100,000 in 1900 to more than 4 per 100,000 in 1910 to nearly 9 per 100,000 in 1930, a rate higher than today's murder rate.[39]

Explaining the Past—The Impact of the Industrial City

The other explanation for the decline of crime in the late 1800s clashes with our commonly held notions about industrialization, cities, and the causes of crime. In this view, the Industrial Revolution may have caused much hardship and disruption in people's lives, but in the long run it exerted a "civilizing" influence. To quote historian Roger Lane, the chief proponent of this idea, "The regularity, cooperation, and interdependence demanded by life and especially work in the city literally 'civilized' its inhabitants."[40]

If Lane is correct, then violent crime should have decreased not just in

America but in other countries undergoing industrialization and urbanization. And indeed, that is what happened. The decline of criminal violence in the 19th century was not unique to American cities. A similar pattern occurred in England, despite the absence of widespread religious revivalism, temperance, or similar social movements. In England, this process—the decline in crime and the onset of industrialization-urbanization—began a generation or two earlier than in the United States, but the pattern was the same. This historical trend to lower crime rates may seem surprising since it seems to contradict the negative image we have of the early industrial city—the crowded and huddled masses of people living in slums and shantytowns. However, while industrialization may cause much human misery, it also seems to bring a decrease in violence. Historians have found this pattern in cities as culturally and geographically diverse as Stockholm and Calcutta.[41] In our time, it is the cities in Third World countries that have been undergoing expansion and industrialization. The trend in violence in these cities is hard to assess, especially in countries torn by war and political violence. At the very least, we can say that there is no consistent increase in murder rates as these cities grow.

Although Lane's ideas on the decline of violence may have general application, his research that inspired these ideas was quite detailed and specific—a study of causes of death in 19th-century Philadelphia. Lane was particularly interested in death by murder, by suicide, and by accident. He found, as you can already guess, that murder rates declined during this period. At the same time, death by accident also decreased, but suicide rates increased. Lane attributes all three trends to industrialization and the ways it reshaped the way people lived.

Lane contrasts the structure of earlier forms of work with work in the newer, industrialized sectors of the economy. Both factories and office bureaucracies require the coordination of many people. To accomplish this coordination, businesses imposed the kind of structures workers today often take for granted: scheduling, whistles and bells that told workers when to start and stop, and foremen or supervisors to make sure that everything ran according to schedule, according to plan. By contrast, the pace of agricultural work on the small farms of the 19th century was determined by the season—long slack periods alternating with periods that demanded long, hard working hours. One person's work was not closely linked to or dependent on another's. Factories required close coordination and synchronization among workers; farms did not. Farm workers could interrupt their work for diversion or excitement; factory workers could not.

This less restrained work style characterized not just farming but also the pre-industrial production in the cities. Most enterprises employed only a few workers, and the hours and pace of work depended on how much there was to do, not on the clock. Lane's conclusion from all this is that nonindustrial work, both rural and urban, permitted a greater amount of spontaneity, impulsiveness, and even recklessness. These qualities—at home, at work, and at play—often led to accidents and to interpersonal violence. And sometimes the accidents and violence were fatal.

As the century wore on, especially after the Civil War, factories and their regimen of discipline and control came to dominate the work life of more and more people, even children. And for those children who did not work, there was the childhood equivalent of the factory: the school (which even today still emphasizes scheduling, bells, and restraint of movement). As a result of this transition to a fully industrial society, over the course of the decades deaths by recklessness and violence toward others gradually decreased; deaths by suicide (i.e., violence directed inward) increased.

None of this should blind us to the harsh conditions in which many people lived in the late 19th century. Especially for immigrants, the industrial city meant low-paying factories and crowded tenement housing; living and working conditions frequently were hazardous to health. But we are concerned here with crime and violence. Yes, there was urban violence; but as most historians agree, it decreased over time. More significantly, the violence tended to occur more among those not yet affected by the Industrial Revolution. Even among those violent youths with the volunteer fire companies in the 1840s and 1850s, "most came from traditional crafts, such as tailoring, shoemaking, and construction, rather than from more innovative, discipline-oriented enterprises carried on in factories."[42] Later in the century, rates of violent crime were highest among the one ethnic group excluded from the industrial economy: blacks. In the 1890s nearly half of Philadelphia's workers worked in manufacturing and industry; but only 8 percent of blacks had that kind of job.[43] Accordingly, blacks also had higher rates of violence.

That Was Then; This Is Now

What can this analysis of crime in the Industrial Revolution tell us about crime a hundred years later here in the "post-industrial" age? For one thing, it can tell us how we got here. From the historical perspective outlined here, the mugging, rapes, and murders in today's cities are a legacy of the past. The Industrial Revolution over a century ago was not just a revolution in the organization of production; it also brought about a revolution in personality. The hard-drinking, free-swinging, and wild-shooting men, whether in the saloons of Bodie or the streets of Philadelphia, gave way to the regular 9-to-5 employees of today's factories and offices. The transition was gradual and in many ways painful. For those who were left out, however, things were even worse.

How did the Industrial Revolution affect those who never made it inside the factory gates? The results are most visible in the case of blacks, if only because records of crime and death have always taken note of race and because we know that blacks were systematically kept out of the industrial labor force. Over the years, patterns of both work and violence changed among whites, but not among blacks. In 1850 in Philadelphia, the black murder rate was not much higher than that of the Irish; in the 1890s, it was about the same as that of the Italians. These white groups, however, eventually became integrated into the industrial world and the more regulated existence it imposed. Outright discrimination prevented blacks from entering this world. Consequently, through the 20th century the gap between black and white murder rates increased. There was a brief hopeful period in the 1940s and 1950s, when factories began to hire larger numbers of blacks. But soon, as America entered the post-industrial age, this sector of the economy began its long decline, and as it faded, so did the chance for blacks to follow the path taken by white immigrant groups.

Lane ends his book rather pessimistically: "The essential problem for blacks in the modern city has been . . . the lack of the kind of employment that not only sustained but *socialized* the white immigrant groups of the 19th and early 20th centuries"[44] [emphasis added]. Even schools can no longer socialize youngsters to middle-class norms of restraint since it is not at all clear to students that such socialization will lead to a decent job:

> The virtues of orderly or middle-class behavior are not self-evident to young people exposed to modern excitements and expectations. In the absence of employment that demands these virtues, the attempt to impose them is inevitably resented as irrelevant, even tyrannical, and thus doomed to failure.[45]

SUMMARY AND CONCLUSION

A news item about this year's crime rate has little meaning without some comparison. Usually, news reports confine that comparison to the last year or two. In this section, I have tried to provide a broader global and historical framework. Comparisons with other countries and with other historical periods are necessarily inexact, but the following conclusions are probably valid.

1. Rates of economic crime in the Wild West were relatively low. Rates of interpersonal violence, including deadly violence, were quite high.
2. Compared with today, the 19th and early 20th centuries had higher levels of collective violence—riots, labor wars, gang wars. These forms of violence also occurred in Europe but probably with less death and bloodshed than in the United States.

3. Cities in the first half of the 19th century were more disorderly and violent than they are today.
4. Starting about 1870, crime rates began a long, slow decline, except for an increase in murder during the 1920s and, perhaps, a rise in urban, economic crime during the Depression of the 1930s.
5. Crime remained low through the 1940s and 1950s, rose sharply for a decade beginning in the early 1960s, and leveled off in the 1970s and 1980s.
6. Wars decrease crime, especially violent crime, to the extent that they remove young men from the civilian population. Crime rates rise when "the boys" come home.
7. Economic depressions, panics, and recessions appear to have no general, consistent effect on crime rates. Economic crises may increase crime in certain areas among certain populations.
8. U.S. rates of crime, especially violent crime, have always been higher than those of other Western industrialized countries.

Finally, I have sketched three general ideas that attempt to explain some of these facts about crime and relate them to current rates of crime. First, the "frontier" theory sees levels of crime and violence in the United States today as a legacy of our frontier traditions. The frontier way of life emphasized independence, action, masculinity, and a disdain for the inhibiting niceties of the law. This mentality, coupled with the easy availability of guns, made for high rates of violence—both then and now.

Two other theories attempt to explain the decline in crime rates in the late 19th century, despite demographic changes that might have led to an increase in crime. The more conservative theory argues that self-improvement movements emphasizing moral uplift and social conformity counteracted the disruptive effects of urbanization and industrialization. The more liberal theory sees industrialization as a "civilizing" force that eventually imposed a more orderly, less violent way of living on those who worked in factories and large-scale organizations.

Each of these last two theories fits with a perspective on crime today. If crime results from a morality that emphasizes the individual over social institutions, then proposals on crime should aim at establishing more respect for social institutions—not just the police and the law, but family, church, government, school, and work. If, on the other hand, crime is more related to the kinds of work available, then government policy should try to extend decent, respectable jobs to those people now excluded from the industrial labor market.

Of course, the national economy and individual morality are only two factors that might be connected with crime. The next chapter discusses four others—four "demographic variables" that have traditionally been of interest to criminologists: sex, race, age, and social class.

NOTES

1. Victoria W. Scheider and Brian Wiersema (1990), "Limits and Use of the Uniform Crime Reports," in Doris Layton MacKenzie, Phyllis Jo Baunach, and Roy R. Roberg, eds. (1990), *Measuring Crime: Large-Scale, Long-Range Efforts*, Albany, NY: State University of New York Press, pp. 21–48.

2. U.S. Department of Justice, Bureau of Justice Statistics (1983), *Report to the Nation on Crime and Justice: The Data*, Washington, DC: U.S. Government Printing Office, pp. 4–5.

3. Andre Normandeau (1969), "Trends in Robbery as Reflected by Different Indexes," in Thorsten Sellin and Marvin Wolfgang, eds. (1969), *Delinquency: Selected Studies*, New York: Wiley.

4. Lawrence E. Cohen, Marcus Felson, and Kenneth C. Land (1980), "Property Crime Rates in the United States: A Macrodynamic Analysis, 1947–1977; With Ex-Ante Forecasts for the Mid-1980s," *American Journal of Sociology*, vol. 86, pp. 588–607.

5. *The New York Times*, Oct. 10, 1983, sec. IV, p. 6.

6. Philip H. Ennis (1967), *Criminal Victimization in the United States: A Report of a National Survey*, President's Commission of Law Enforcement and the Administration of Justice, Field Surveys II, Washington, DC: U.S. Government Printing Office.

7. Donald J. Black (1970), "The Production of Crime Rates," *American Sociological Review*, vol. 35, pp. 733–48.

8. Ibid.

9. Wesley G. Skogan (1975), "Measurement Problems in Official and Survey Crime Rates," *Journal of Criminal Justice*, vol. 3, pp. 17–32.

10. Peter K. Manning (1977), *Police Work: The Social Organization of Policing*, Cambridge, MA: MIT Press, pp. 18–19.

11. Institute of Public Management (1952), *Crime Records in Police Management: New York City, New York*, excerpted in Marvin E. Wolfgang, Leonard Savitz, and Norman Johnson (1970), *The Sociology of Crime and Delinquency* (2nd ed.), New York: Wiley, pp. 114–16.

12. James A. Inciardi (1978), *Reflections on Crime: An Introduction to Criminology and Criminal Justice*, New York: Holt, Rinehart, and Winston, p. 81.

13. For a comparison of Philadelphia, San Francisco, and Chicago on this matter, see Wesley G. Skogan and Michael G. Maxfield (1981), *Coping with Crime: Individual and Neighborhood Reactions*, Beverly Hills, CA: Sage, p. 29. For a British comparison, see Richard F. Sparks, Hazel G. Genn, and David J. Dodd (1977), *Surveying Victims: A Study of the Measurement of Criminal Victimization, Perceptions of Crime, and Attitudes to Criminal Justice*, London: Wiley, p. 157.

14. Harold Pepinsky (1976), "The Growth of Crime in the United States," *Annals of the American Academy of Political and Social Sciences*.

15. *The New York Times*, May 2, 1983, p. A20. R. Block and C.R. Block (1980), "Decisions and Data: The Transformation of Robbery Incidents into Official Robbery Statistics," *Journal of Criminal Law and Criminology*, vol. 71, pp. 622–36.

16. Ennis, op. cit.

17. Richard F. Sparks (1981), "Surveys of Victimization—An Optimistic Assessment," in *Crime and Justice: An Annual Review of Research*, vol. 3, pp. 26.

18. Sparks, op. cit., p. 33.

19. Walter R. Gove, Michael Hughes, and Michael Gerken (1985), "Are Uniform Crime Reports a Valid Indicator of the Index Crimes? An Affirmative Answer with Minor Qualifications," *Criminology*, vol. 23, no. 3, pp. 451–502.

20. John Braithwaite and David Biles (1984), "Victims and Offenders: The Australian Experience," in Richard Block, ed., *Victimization and Fear of Crime: World Perspectives*, Washington, DC: U.S. Government Printing Office, pp. 3–10.

21. Philip H. Ennis (1967), *Criminal Victimization in the United States: A Report of a National Survey*, Washington, DC: U.S. Government Printing Office. Edmund F. McGarrel and Timothy J. Flanagan, eds. (1985), *Sourcebook of Criminal Justice Statistics—1984*, U.S. Department of Justice, Bureau of Justice Statistics, Washington, DC: U.S. Government Printing Office, pp. 288, 380.

22. Charles Silberman (1974), *Criminal Violence, Criminal Justice*, New York: Random House, p. 28.

23. Richard Hofstadter and Michael Wallace, eds. (1970), *American Violence*, New York: Random House, p. 212.

24. Silberman, op. cit., pp. 21–47.

25. Roger McGrath (1984), *Gunfighters, Highwaymen, and Vigilantes: Violence on the Frontier*, Berkeley, CA: The Regents of the University of California.

26. Marvin Wolfgang and Franco Ferracuti (1976), *The Subculture of Violence: Towards an Integrated Theory in Criminology*, London: Tavistock.

27. Ray Ginger (1975), *America, People on the Move*, Boston, MA: Allyn & Bacon, p. 282.

28. David Ward (1971), *Cities and Immigrants*, New York: Oxford University Press, p. 6.

29. Roger Lane (1980), "Police and Crime in Nineteenth-Century America," in Michael Tonry and Norval Morris, eds., *Crime and Justice: An Annual Review*, vol. 2, Chicago: University of Chicago Press, pp. 1–52.

30. Ward, op. cit., p. 76.

31. Dane Archer and Rosemary Gartner (1984), *Violence and Crime in Cross-National Perspective*, New Haven, CT: Yale University Press.

32. Lane, op. cit.

33. Wilbur E. Miller (1977), *Cops and Bobbies*, Chicago: University of Chicago Press, p. 6.

34. David R. Johnson (1979), *Policing the Urban Underworld*, Temple University Press, pp. 30, 87.

35. James Q. Wilson (1985), *Thinking About Crime* (2nd ed.), New York: Vintage, p. 229.

36. Joseph N. Gusfield (1963), *Symbolic Crusade*, Urbana, IL: University of Illinois Press.

37. Martha Wolfenstein (1951), "The Emergence of Fun Morality," *Journal of Social Issues*, vol. 7, pp. 15–25.

38. Wilson, op. cit., p. 237.

39. U.S. Department of Justice, *Report to the Nation . . .* , op. cit., p. 10.

40. Lane (1980), op. cit.

41. Ted Robert Gurr, Peter N. Grabosky, and Richard C. Hula (1977), *The Politics of Crime and Conflict: A Comparative History of Four Cities*, Beverly Hills, CA: Sage.

42. Laurie, "Fire Companies and Gangs in Southwark," quoted in Lane, op. cit, p. 182.

43. W. E. B. DuBois, *The Philadelphia Negro, A Social Study*, New York: 1899, cited in Roger Lane (1979) *Violent Death in the City: Suicide, Accident, and Murder in Nineteenth-Century Philadelphia*, Cambridge, MA: Harvard University Press, p. 132.

44. Lane, op. cit.

45. Ibid.

Who Commits Crimes?

CHAPTER 4

WHO COMMITS CRIMES?

This is not quite the big question. That question, the one most people ask, is *why* do people commit crimes—and how can we get them to stop. However, although *why* may be the most natural question to ask, it may also be the most difficult and least rewarding to answer. We probably get a better picture of crime if we ask the other "reporter's" questions: Who, what, when, where, how? These questions provide the evidence on which to build explanations. If we can answer these questions, we will find that we have gone a long way toward answering *why*.

Explanations and theories of crime—the answers to those "why" questions—are necessary, but first we have to discover just what the facts are that need to be explained. It makes little sense to spin out an elaborate explanation of why poor people commit more crime if in fact it turns out that middle-class people commit just as much crime as do lower-class people. And, as we shall see, discovering the facts—finding out who commits crimes—can be a much more challenging task than coming up with explanations for those facts.

When we ask *who* commits crimes, we are usually thinking about categories of people, not individuals (unless, of course, we are playing "Clue"). The categories most frequently investigated by criminologists are the traditional "demographic variables": sex, race, age, and social class. The results of these investigations can be quickly summarized: Crime rates are higher among males rather than females; blacks and Hispanics rather than whites; younger (late teens) rather than older people; and those from the lower end of the social ladder.

However, behind these fairly simple conclusions lies a tangle of controversies and problems. In some cases, people disagree over the reasons these differences exist. For example, although nearly all criminologists acknowledge sex differences in crime, not all agree on the reasons for these differences or on the size of the differences. In other cases, there is even dispute over the facts, as when some criminologists argue that the link between social class and crime is a myth. In the area of race, too, there is much controversy over just how great the differences are and how they can be explained. Is race really the crucial factor in black-white differences in crime, or is it more a matter of economics?

Therefore, although I have already given some general answers to the question of who commits crime, I am going to describe in greater detail the controversies and problems of the research. It is important to understand not only what we know about crime but also how we know it. The research problems may seem merely technical, but often the way a research study is set up can greatly influence the conclusions it reaches. The more you know about the specific problems and solutions in criminology research, the better you will be able to evaluate the ideas about crime that you hear. Often, both sides of a controversy have seemingly good evidence. But this does not mean that you should shrug your shoulders and mutter in disgust that "you can prove anything with statistics." It does mean that if you read, for instance, that feminism has led to a "new female criminal"; or that blacks have higher crime rates only because of police and court bias; or that there is no connection between poverty and crime; or any other such statement, you should be able to ask at least some basic questions about the evidence on which that statement is based.

CRIME AND SEX

It's a Man's World

Of all the demographic variables, the one where there is the most agreement as to the basic differences is sex. Everybody knows that men commit far more crimes than do women. You probably believe this, too. But how do you know? And how could you convince someone who insisted that women commit as much crime as do men? You might refer to your own experience. Maybe most of the people you know who got into trouble with the law are male. And nearly all the criminals you see in the news are male. But this kind of evidence is highly selective. To be conclusive, the data should be more comprehensive and more systematic.

Information about Criminals—Official Sources

One of the most frequently used sources of information on criminals is the FBI's Uniform Crime Reports. Besides estimating the amount of crime ("crimes known to the police"), the UCR also contains information on "persons arrested for crime." As with crime-rate data, local police departments keep statistics on the people they arrest, both for Index offenses and non-Index offenses. The FBI then combines these statistics to form a table such as Table 4–1. The overall male-female arrest ratio is nearly 5 to 1. Among serious (Index) crimes, the ratio is about 3 to 1 for property crimes, and nearly 8 to 1 for violent crimes. Even for larceny, the Index crime where sex differences are smallest, men still outnumber women by 2 to 1. The only crimes for which women were arrested more frequently than men were prostitution and running away from home.*

---

* Running away is a "status offense"—an act which is against the law only if committed by someone of juvenile status. The category includes truancy, "incorrigibility," and drinking, among others. The only such offense tabulated by the FBI is "runaways."

Table 4–1 ▪ Arrests, Distribution by Sex, 1989

	Number of arrests	*Percent male*	*Percent female*
Murder	17,975	88.1	11.9
Rape	30,544	98.8	1.2
Robbery	133,830	91.4	8.6
Aggravated assault	354,735	86.6	13.4
Burglary	356,757	91.3	8.7
Larceny	1,254,220	69.6	30.4
Motor vehicle theft	182,810	89.8	10.2
Arson	14,667	86.4	13.6
All other	8,915,797	82.7	17.3

Source: UCR, 1989.

However, remember that these numbers tell us only who was *arrested*, and obviously not everyone who commits a crime gets arrested. In fact, only about one in five reported Index crimes results in an arrest. This "clearance rate" (the percentage of reported crimes for which an arrest is made) varies from crime to crime. For murder, it is about 70 percent, while for burglary, it is only about 15 percent. Since less than half of all crimes even get reported to the police, the persons arrested make up an even smaller percentage of the crime-committing population than the clearance rate leads us to believe. Therefore it is important to know whether the persons arrested accurately reflect the entire group of lawbreakers.

What if, for some reason, female criminals were more successful at avoiding arrest? It might be that the police are more "chivalrous" toward the women and girls they arrest than toward men. Where the police might make an official arrest of a male, they might deal with the female offender more informally, perhaps letting her off with a warning.[1]

In other words, conclusions about criminals based on only those who get arrested may present a distorted picture. Since the number of arrests is only a small fraction of crimes committed, the question of who is *not* arrested becomes very important. For every robbery where an arrest is made, there are about seven uncleared robberies, i.e., robberies where the UCR knows nothing about the robber. For property crimes like burglary and theft, the ratio is even higher. Of course, the differences in male and female arrest rates are so large that they almost certainly reflect differences in actual behavior. Still, it would be nice if we could double-check by getting different sources of data on the same question.

Other Measures of Crime—Victimization Surveys

If police arrests are at best incomplete and perhaps biased, how can we find out who commits crimes? Generally, criminologists have followed two strategies. The first of these is the victimization survey. Just as these surveys offer an alternative to police reports as a measure of the amount of crime, they can also provide information about offenders. The National Crime Survey, besides asking questions about the victims themselves, also includes questions about the offenders. Of course, victims can provide such information only for crimes where they actually see the offender. These do include the more serious crimes—assaults, robberies, rapes—but they still constitute only about 16 percent of all victimizations.

Nevertheless, for these violent crimes, the results of victimization surveys strongly resemble those based on arrests. For example, the UCR for 1988 shows that of the 111,344 people arrested for robbery, about 8.5 percent were female. The National Crime Survey gives an estimate of victim identifications in nearly 1 million robberies. According to these victims' reports, about 7 percent of the robbers were female. The victimization survey, which counts both unreported and unsolved crimes, obviously turns up a greater amount of robbery than police arrests, but in both sources of data, the proportion of women robbers is quite small.

Self-Report Studies

Victimization surveys may be useful for finding out who commits crimes against the person, but how can we determine the proportion of women committing burglary, auto theft, larceny, or other property crimes? Outside of arrest data, the most commonly used technique is the self-report study. This is just what the name implies: a study in which people are asked to report on the crimes they themselves have committed.

Obviously, this method has its problems, though not necessarily the ones that first come to mind. That is, most people are remarkably willing to tell an interviewer about the crimes they have committed. In fact, one of the results that surprised researchers who conducted early self-report studies was the amount of crime people would admit to. Just about everyone, it turns out, has committed crimes which, from a strict point of view, could have landed them behind bars. Even among adult women, 83 percent admitted to at least one grand larceny (and this was in the 1940s, a period of relatively low crime rates).[2]

Since then, several self-report studies have discovered much crime by females. Most of these studies conclude that while males still commit more crimes than females, the differences between the sexes are not as great as arrest data suggest. One typical study of juvenile delinquency asked boys and girls for self-reports on 36 delinquent acts. The results showed a male-female ratio "considerably smaller . . . than the official arrest ratio," and a "considerable uniformity between males and females." The ratio for self-reported robberies in this study was about 5.5 to 1, considerably smaller than the 12-to-1 ratio in the UCR.[3]

Self-Reports and Arrests—Explaining the Differences

We started off with a question: How great are male-female differences in crime? But now we have two answers:

The differences are large if we measure crime by the number of arrests;
The differences are small if we measure crime by self-reports.

What's going on here? If self-reports are accurate, then arrest figures showing crime as an overwhelmingly male world are giving us a distorted and exaggerated picture. On the other hand, if arrests are more accurate, how can we explain the results of the self-report studies?

To answer these questions, we need to take a closer look at these two sources of data. Understanding the difference between arrests and self-reports will clarify our picture not only of male-female differences but of other variables as well. As we shall see later in this chapter, the same discrepancies occur with variables like race and social class: Data on persons arrested show significant differences (white vs. black, middle class vs. lower class); research using self-reports finds little or no difference.

Arrests as a "Carnival Mirror"

One explanation for the discrepancy between arrests and self-reports uses the analogy of the "carnival mirror."[4] The logic goes as follows: Self-reports give a fairly accurate profile of the criminal population. However, the criminal justice system is biased. The statistics it produces create a distorted image, magnifying certain parts (men, blacks, the poor) and diminishing others (women, whites, the wealthy). The criminal justice system, dominated by white, middle-class males, is shot through with "chivalry and paternalism." Both of these terms refer to the idea that women are "the weaker sex." Chivalry requires that women be treated in special, protective ways. Paternalism carries the idea further: Based on the parent-child relationship, it implies that the woman must not only be protected but also guided, since, like a child, she does not always know what is good for herself. The chivalrous or paternalistic point of view sees women as less threatening; the criminal justice system need not take such strong action against them. Like children, if they break the law they do not need to be punished to protect society; rather, they should be "helped" for their own good, not arrested on criminal charges. Therefore, arrest statistics diminish the true proportion of female criminals.[5] These attitudes act at every stage of the criminal process to keep female offenders out of the system and therefore out of official counts of who commits crimes. Chivalry, in this view, is the most important factor in determining what happens when a woman commits a crime. "Victims or observers of female violators are unwilling to take action against the offender, because she is a woman. Police are much less willing to make on-the-spot arrests or to 'book' and hold women for court action."[6]

Arrests as a "Coarse Net"

Not all criminologists would agree with this explanation. They offer a different model of the criminal justice system, one which sees it not as a distorting carnival mirror but rather as a "coarse net." The small fry swim through without being counted; only the big fish get caught. Big fish, in this case, means those who either commit crimes more frequently or commit the more serious crimes—or both. Women do commit crimes, but their crimes are less serious and they commit them less frequently. Therefore, they do not appear in arrest statistics. The big fish are predominantly male.

Supporters of the coarse-net theory tend to accept arrest data as giving a fairly accurate picture of the *serious* offender.[7] They do not dismiss self-reports as hopelessly inaccurate (though inaccuracies do occur). But they do caution about the generalizations that can be made from self-report studies. The question to keep in mind about research based on self-reports is this: Whose crimes and what kinds of crimes are being investigated?

The answer, generally speaking, is that self-report studies are very useful for discovering the less serious kinds of misbehavior of young people. But for finding out about serious crime, self-report studies have severe limitations. To begin with, most self-report studies have surveyed juveniles rather than adults. It is true that juveniles (those under 18) account for a disproportionate amount of serious crime, but leaving out adults means omitting well over half of the criminal population.

Typically, researchers will interview a few hundred youths, asking them about a variety of misbehavior. Some of these "delinquent acts" are serious crimes like robbery and burglary; some are less serious or nonpredatory crimes (minor theft or vandalism, drug use); some are "status offenses," i.e., acts which are offenses only if committed by someone of juvenile status (e.g., drinking, truancy); and some are not crimes at all (disobeying parents). Obviously, this kind of survey will produce a large amount of "delinquency," especially if the kids are asked if they have ever committed the offense—even once in the last three years. For example, here are the results for the crime of "entering" (roughly equivalent to burglary) from a national sample of 847 juveniles: 42 percent of the boys and 33 percent of the girls said they had committed this crime at least once in the last three years.[8] This gives a male-female ratio of 1.3 to 1, not a very large difference. In contrast, the UCR figures on youths arrested for burglary show a male-female ratio of 12 to 1.

Probably, most of the "entering" in this self-report study was not very serious, and the "enterers" were not making a career of it. They committed so few crimes that in most cases they probably did not get caught; or if they did get caught, the "entering" was so minor that the police may have let them go with a warning. On the other hand, most of the people *arrested* for burglary are probably "real" criminals—i.e., those who commit serious burglary often enough that they eventually get arrested. And these burglars are overwhelmingly male.

Seriousness and Self-Reports

When self-report studies do try to distinguish between levels of seriousness, they usually find what you would expect: The more serious the crime, the greater the differences between males and females. Table 4–2 shows some results from a self-report survey taken in two high schools in a city in the Midwest. For the sake of simplicity, I have left out several of the 36 "delinquent acts" which might not quite fit the pattern: drugs (where there may be some disagreement as to seriousness), and offenses involving cars, which regardless of seriousness remain a masculine domain. The table shows two obvious things: First, the more serious the crime, the fewer people of either sex who have committed it; second, the more serious the crime, the greater the difference between males and females.

Self-report studies, then, tell us that nearly all kids break the law, though boys do so somewhat more frequently than do girls. Most of these violations, however, are relatively minor or infrequent—standard teenage misbehavior. It is useful information to have, especially in comparing the youths of dif-

Table 4–2 ■ Percent Engaging in Act One or More Times

Offense	Male	Female	Ratio (male/female)
Disturbing the peace	71.6%	68.9%	1.04
Theft (under $2)	66.5	58.2	1.14
Theft ($2 to $50)	33.9	26.0	1.30
Theft (over $50)	12.7	4.6	2.76
Burglary (unoccupied)	16.5	3.7	4.46
Robbery	5.0	0.9	5.55

Source: Derived from Cemkovich and Giordano (1979).

ferent generations. But it is still not the sort of "real crime" people are most worried about.

Serious Crime: Self-Reports and Victimizations

In drawing conclusions about the more serious crimes and criminals, even among juveniles, self-report studies have major limitations. First, the more serious offenders tend to underreport their crimes. Second, self-report studies may inadvertently exclude the most serious juvenile offenders. Instead of being at home or school to be interviewed, they may be out on the streets or even locked up in some juvenile jail. Finally, and perhaps most important, because serious crime and serious criminals are relatively rare, the size of the total sample must be fairly large in order to get reliable information. For widely practiced behavior, a small sample serves quite well. Thanks to scientific sampling methods, pre-election polls can estimate the preferences of 35 million voters by polling only 2,000 people. National television ratings for over 70 million TV sets are based on a sample of about 1,200.[9] These small samples work because nearly everyone watches TV, and most people vote. For infrequent events, like serious crime, researchers need much larger samples. The National Crime Survey goes to 50,000 households (representing 100,000 household members), but even with this large sample, some categories of crime occur so rarely that the information is not reliable. For example, suppose we wanted to know about women who commit serious, violent crimes, e.g, robberies where the victim was injured. Among all 100,000 potential victims, the number of such victimizations annually would probably be 10 or less—too small a number to be reliable.[10]

So can we really expect a random sample of 850 juveniles to tell us much about serious crime and criminals? In fact, just such a national survey found identical rates of self-reported robbery for boys and girls: 0 percent.[11] A later self-report survey of 3,000 high school seniors found that 4.4 percent of boys and 1.1 percent of girls said they had committed a robbery in the past year.[12] These data support the idea that males commit more crime than females, but for measuring the true extent of juvenile robbery, this is hardly an informative statistic.

Feminism and the New Female Criminal

Although women commit relatively little street crime, the subject of female crime has provoked interesting debates, both theoretical and factual. The theoretical questions concern the explanations for the low crime rate among women. As for debate over the facts, we have already looked at the amount and seriousness of female crime. However, there is one more important question left to answer: Has female crime changed over the course of recent history? After all, if the causes of crime are social, if different groups of people have different crime rates because of their position in society, then when that position changes, their crime rate should also change.

In the particular case of women, undoubtedly their role in society has changed. In the decades following World War II, more women have taken jobs and gotten college degrees. They have, on the average, been waiting longer before marrying and having children. In addition, the women's movement has probably changed the way in which many women think about themselves. I do not want to imply that the age of sex equality is upon us. Most women still marry and have children; they still face significant barriers in "nontraditional" roles; and although more of them are working, their salaries remain well below those of men. Nevertheless, the change is undeniable. The question is whether these changes have also made for changes in women's crime.

A New Female Criminal?

In the mid-1970s, the question of female crime began to receive public attention, with articles in popular magazines like *Psychology Today* and *Newsweek*. Then in 1975, a criminologist, Freda Adler, published a book with the title *Sisters in Crime: The Rise of the New Female Criminal.* Adler saw the social changes in women's roles not as a small and gradual improvement, but as "a rising tide of female assertiveness" that "has been sweeping over the barriers which have protected male prerogatives and eroding the traditional differences which once nicely defined gender roles."[13] Part of this tidal change included a change in female crime.

> In the same way that women are demanding equal opportunity in fields of legitimate endeavor, a similar number of determined women are forcing their way into the world of major crimes. . . . It is this segment of women who are pushing into—and succeeding at—crimes which were formerly committed by males only. Females . . . are now being found not only robbing banks single-handedly, but also committing assorted armed robberies, muggings, loansharking operations, extortion, murders, and a wide variety of other aggressive, violence-oriented crimes which previously involved only men.[14]

Was such a change actually occurring?

Much of the evidence Adler used in her book was anecdotal—stories gathered from cops and criminals. The more systematic evidence consisted of comparing the percentage increase in arrests of men and women. Take the crime of robbery as an example: Between 1960 and 1973, arrests of men increased by 160 percent, but arrests of women increased by 287 percent. Undoubtedly, this is a big increase in arrests of women for robbery. But in what sense is it really larger than the increase in male arrests? Men's and

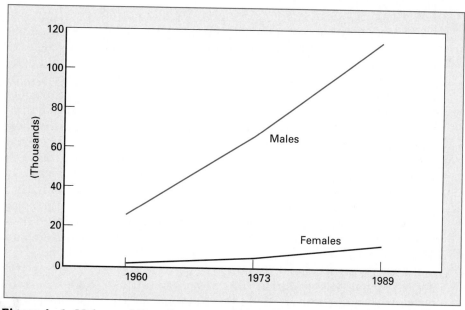

Figure 4–1 Males and Females Arrested for Robbery—1960, 1973, 1989

women's rates of robbery are so different to begin with that such percentage-increase comparisons may be misleading.

Putting the actual numbers on a graph may give a clearer picture (see Figure 4–1). In 1960, approximately 25,000 men were arrested for robbery; in 1973, the number was about 65,000—the 160 percent increase mentioned previously. For women, the corresponding numbers were roughly 1,200 robbery arrests in 1960 and 4,600 in 1973—a 287 percent increase. In Figure 4–1, I have added the data from 1989. In the period from 1973 to 1989, the percentage increase was twice as large for women as for men—roughly a 132 percent increase for women vs. a 75 percent increase for men.

Two things are clear from the graph: (1) Women still make up a small fraction of robbers; and (2) In terms of absolute numbers, women have not closed the "robbery gap." Since robbery by both sexes was increasing, it seems unlikely that the women's movement was the cause. More probably, the increase in robbery by women was part of a general upswing in crime and violence that occurred in the 1960s. And the causes of that general upswing are still a matter of debate.

"She Could Steal, But She Could Not Rob"

Some other pieces of evidence also suggest that Adler was overstating the case. In the first place, the crimes for which sex differences narrowed were *not* crimes of violence. They were property and non-Index crimes: larceny, fraud, and embezzlement. As with nonpredatory crimes like drug offenses and prostitution, arrest statistics for these three crimes—especially fraud—can be very misleading. Changes in arrest rates may reflect not changes in the actual occurrence of the crime, but rather changes in the willingness of police or victims to take official action. But even if arrest figures for these crimes were accurate, the increase in embezzlement merely shows that more women were working: The more female employees there are, the more employee theft they will commit.[15] The larceny committed by females remains predominantly shoplifting, which has always been women's crime of choice. It hardly suggests a change in female aggression or assertiveness.

As for more serious predatory crime, the women who do commit these crimes are not independent, financially successful, or in any other way "liberated." For the most part, they are drug-dependent and poor, and they turn to crime because they have been recruited by boyfriends or husbands as part of a team.[16]

Finally, apart from arrest statistics, we have evidence from a self-report study, comparing juveniles in 1972 with those in 1967. In contrast to official data, these self-report studies showed no increase in crime for either boys or girls. Boys, in fact, reported less crime in 1972 than those in 1967. The teenage girls of 1972 reported more drug and alcohol use than the girls of 1967, but less larceny, vandalism, and burglary.[17]

Since then, although women have continued to make some gains toward equality in education, employment, and income, their levels of crime have shown no further increase. And teenagers of both sexes today are probably less criminal than those of the early 1970s. In short, it appears that the new female criminal is really the old female criminal.

Summing Up

I have gone to great lengths here to establish the unsurprising fact that women commit far less street crime than do men. This sex difference occurs not just in the United States, but in every other society that keeps data on crime and violence. In some countries, male-female ratios for serious crimes may be less than in the United States. In many other countries, the ratio is even greater. Along the way to proving the obvious, I have also tried to show the strengths and weaknesses of two major sources of information on who commits crimes—arrests and self-report studies.

These two sources give somewhat different pictures of the male-female crime ratio, largely because they measure different things. Arrests give a profile of the most serious and frequent offenders; they may also reflect chivalry or paternalism on the part of the police. That is, gender as well as the crime itself may influence police perceptions of how serious the criminal is and whether to make an official arrest. Self-reports usually give a picture of less serious lawbreaking, and for these lesser offenses, male-female ratios are more nearly equal. Self-report studies that focus on serious and frequent crime give a picture that resembles that of arrests.

SOCIAL CLASS

The differences between arrest data and self-report data do not end with sex. They figure prominently in the debate over crime and social class, one of the enduring major controversies in criminology. At first it seems like a simple question—Do people with less money commit more crime?—with an equally obvious answer: yes. For decades, many sociologists took social class as their starting point. Their theories may have differed as to exactly why social class was an important factor, but they agreed that poorer people commit more crime.

The public probably agrees. Public opinion polls that ask about causes of crime do not specifically include social class as a choice. But people usually cite unemployment as a cause of crime more frequently than anything else.* Poverty is also sometimes mentioned, though not as frequently as non-economic causes like "the decline of the family" and "lenient courts."[18] In any case, many people think that economic factors are an important cause of crime. After all, everybody knows that the dangerous neighborhoods in a city are those where the poor people live, and that wealthier neighborhoods are relatively safe.

Of course, this idea must still be tested against the evidence so that we can see whether what is "obvious," or "what everybody knows," is also true. In this case, exploring the evidence is especially important since some people believe that lack of money is *not* a cause of crime. And the dispute is not merely an academic, ivory-tower discussion among social scientists. Politicians take positions on it, and their statements appear in the media. For example, in the 1980s, Mayor Ed Koch of New York dismissed the idea of a connection between social class and crime. "Are you saying that because people don't have an education and are poor they are going to turn to crime? I don't believe that."[19] President Reagan, soon after taking office, offered similar ideas on this question: "It's obvious that prosperity doesn't decrease crime—just as it's obvious that deprivation and want don't necessarily cause crime."[20]

---

* In the late 1980s, drugs became the most frequently mentioned cause of crime.

Ideology, Facts, and Policies

It's fairly easy to see why the economic causes of crime have become a political issue, with "liberals" facing "conservatives." There are really two questions involved: (1) Should the government give direct help to those suffering economic hardship? and (2) Does economic hardship cause crime? The first question is not factual but moral, a matter of political philosophy. Liberals generally favor direct government action to reduce the economic burdens of unemployment and poverty: extended unemployment benefits, job-training programs, food stamps, family income supports, and other forms of welfare. The conservative view, on the other hand, calls for less direct intervention by the government. In this view, it is *not* the government's role to ease the economic hardships that individuals may suffer.

But the second question—Does economic hardship cause crime?—is factual. Unfortunately, however, despite stacks of research reports there is still no simple and conclusive answer. Therefore, each side states as fact the answer that best fits with its general outlook. Liberals insist that poverty and unemployment cause crime; conservatives disagree. Apparently, a person's attitude on government determines his or her perception of what causes crime, although there is no logical connection between the two. In fact, each side might be wiser to hedge its bets. Liberals might say, "It is a good thing in itself to eliminate poverty, inequality, and unemployment through government action, even though it will not reduce crime." Or conservatives might say, "It is wrong and economically unsound for the government to support low-income individuals, even though we realize that this withdrawal of support may increase crime."

But of course, each side sees its approach as being best in all respects. Liberals propose social and economic programs as a solution for both crime and economic want. Conservatives deny any connection between economic need and crime. In its place they emphasize two other ideas: first, that criminals commit crimes because they are bad people; and second, that criminals commit crimes because they can get away with it. President Reagan, in his speech on crime, went on to say that people commit crimes "because they believe no one will stop them." Mayor Koch's explanation for crime was that you had a better chance for profit at crime "than you do at the racetrack." James Q. Wilson, the criminologist the mayor cited as the source for his theories of crime, put it equally bluntly: "Wicked people exist. Nothing avails except to set them apart from innocent people."[21] In other words, giving them job training, jobs, and money will not make them less criminal.

Who Is Right?—Why There Is No Simple Answer

If the question of social class as a cause of crime is a factual one, why can't we just get the relevant facts and settle it once and for all? Why do social scientists still argue about whether poverty, unemployment, and lack of money cause crime?

Part of the problem lies in the word "cause." In matters of human behavior, it is very difficult to establish definite cause-and-effect relationships. Even in the "harder" social sciences like economics, there is disagreement as to the causal connections among such factors as federal deficits, interest rates, unemployment, inflation, etc. Similar uncertainty haunts even laboratory sciences. In medicine, for example, the tobacco industry still claims that there is still no proof that smoking *causes* cancer, and in a sense they are right. All that the anti-smoking people can accurately say is that smoking *increases the risk* of cancer.

Therefore, instead of talking about "causes," we use words like "factor" or "source" (e.g., poverty is a "source of crime"). This is a more modest proposition, but in order to prove it we must still show that there is a *correlation* between social class and crime.* Finding this correlation may sound simple; just measure a sample of people on each of the two variables— social class and criminality. However, when it comes down to the actual definition and measurement of these variables, what looked simple becomes much more complicated. The principal reason for the disagreement over the connection between crime and social class is that different studies define and measure these items differently. Unemployment is not the same as poverty, and both are different from social class.

Defining Terms—Social Class

What is *social class*? What exactly do we mean when we refer to "the lower class" or "the middle class?" When we use terms like this, we are drawing a picture of a society with a limited number of social groups. The members of each group have certain things in common, things which make them different from the other groups. "Class" also implies that most people will remain in their group; only a few will cross the boundaries into another class. Most of us don't usually give the matter of social class much systematic thought. When we do, we probably use a straight hierarchical model—

---

* Technically, a correlation means that if we know something about a person's score on one variable, we can better predict (or guess) his or her score on the second variable. For example, if you are trying to guess the height of each person in a list of names, it will help in your guessing if each person's weight is also listed. The greater the weight, the greater the height you will predict. You will still make some mistakes, but overall the degree of error will be less. Your guesses will be more accurate because height and weight generally are *correlated*: the more of one, the more of the other.

The question with crime and social class comes down to this: If we know something about the economic position of individuals or neighborhoods, will we be better able to predict their criminality? In this case, the correlation we expect is "negative" or "inverse"—i.e., the more of one, the less of the other: the higher the social class, the less crime, and vice versa.

upper, middle, lower. Unfortunately, one large problem with this model is that a very large part of the population (at least in America) classifies itself as middle-class, including the janitor earning $15,000 a year and the lawyer making $150,000 a year.[22] This model makes the upper class so small in numbers as to be negligible, and it reserves the label "lower class" for those in dire poverty. Also, if everybody is middle class, then class does not vary from one person to another. It is no longer a variable.

Of course, we know that not everybody belongs to the same social class. We know that the lawyer and janitor differ from each other in some important ways. But what refinements can we make in the upper/middle/lower model so that it fits with our perceptions? Some people will add the concept of "working class," meaning those in "blue-collar" work. These jobs require manual skills rather than the "communication skills" needed for white-collar jobs—e.g., driving a truck rather than selling insurance. Some sociologists continue to use this model, putting the working class somewhere between the lower class and the middle class.

Another way of making class a more useful variable is to make distinctions within each class. So instead of just referring to people as middle-class, we may distinguish between "lower-middle-class" and "upper-middle-class" (with "middle-middle-class" presumably falling somewhere in between), and similarly for the lower and upper classes. Now instead of three classes or four, we may have six or even nine, and we are moving away from the idea of a class as a group of people with its own interests. Instead, we have something more like "status," or what sociologists refer to as "socio-economic status" (SES). This concept is probably closer to what most Americans have in mind when they think of class. It seems to fit better with the way people see themselves and others in the society.

But now that we have a model of status, how do we measure SES to see just where everybody is? Obviously money is important. When people try to assess their own or others' social class (or SES), money is probably the most important factor.[23] In fact, it seems that for everyday purposes, the whole idea of class is being replaced with the simple idea of money. Nowadays, politicians and other public speakers seem reluctant to talk about "lower-class" people or neighborhoods. Instead, they use phrases like "lower-income groups."

Money is important in determining SES, but, as the saying goes, money isn't everything. Education also counts toward a person's social standing, as does occupation—how a person makes that money (a Supreme Court justice is of higher status than a sales representative, who may make twice the justice's salary). Ideally, we would use all of these in determining SES, or we could use each one separately to see which made the most difference in crime. As a practical matter, however, researchers must frequently make do with less.

Separating the Men from the Boys

Like the research on sex and crime, research on social class often tries to find a correlation by measuring each individual's crime and social class. Most of this research has studied juveniles, and this focus creates a technical problem: how to measure social class. It makes little sense to measure a 15-year-old's income, education, or occupation, so researchers usually define the juvenile's SES as that of the parents. Since juveniles may not know their parents' income or education, many of these studies ask only for father's (or parents') occupation. Not only is this single measure less accurate, but it may be misleading: The socioeconomic status of the parent may not necessarily be relevant to the child's social life.

Studies that do look at adult criminals face a different and more theoretical problem: What is causing what. Suppose it turns out that criminals place far down on the SES scale, that they have little education or income, and work only sporadically at low-paying, low-status jobs.[24] This strong correlation has two plausible explanations, one more part of the liberal ideology, the other more conservative. The liberal explanation is that those who cannot get a decent education or good jobs will be more likely to turn to crime. The conservative explanation (see Mayor Koch and criminologist Wilson quoted earlier in the chapter) reverses this causal relationship: People who choose to commit crimes are "wicked people" who do not bother to stay in school and will not stick with a regular 9-to-5 job.

Which comes first, the crime or the low SES? Studying juveniles, whatever its other drawbacks, at least has the advantage of diminishing this problem. The child's delinquency is unlikely to have much impact on the parents' education or income.

Measuring Crime: Arrests

Whatever the difficulties in measuring social class or SES, they are nowhere near as controversial as the other half of the problem: measuring crime. Remember, we are trying to test the "obvious" idea that crime is more widespread among poorer people. For a long time, the evidence supporting this idea came from "official" figures—police records of crimes reported and persons arrested. One of the most influential and frequently cited studies of delinquency is Marvin Wolfgang's follow-up of all boys born in 1945 who lived in Philadelphia from age 10 to age 18—about 10,000 boys in all. As his measure of how much crime a boy had committed by age 18, Wolfgang went to the city's police files. And, as you would expect, he found that boys from the lower half of the income ladder had far more arrests than did boys from the upper half.* The differences were even greater when Wolfgang and his researchers looked not just at the number of arrests but at the severity of the crime, based on the amount of injury and damage. On the whole, the crimes of lower-SES boys were three to four times more severe than those of higher-SES boys.[25] Many other studies in the United States and other countries have reached this same, unsurprising conclusion.[26]

But as with gender and crime, arrests may not give a true picture of who is committing crimes. In Wolfgang's study, it might be possible that the middle-class boys committed as much crime as the others, but merely got picked up by the police less often. After all, if the police operate on the assumption that poorer neighborhoods have more crime, they will patrol those neighborhoods more heavily. They will, therefore, be more likely to come upon boys loitering or getting into other kinds of illegal behavior. It also may be possible that when the police pick up a boy in these neighborhoods, whether for mischief or a more serious crime, they will be more likely to make an official arrest. On the other hand, for a similar crime involving a "good" (i.e., middle-class) boy, they might just give him a warning and send him home—especially if in the past they have found that middle-class parents are more likely to make trouble for the cop (e.g., by filing a complaint) when their kids are arrested.[27] Middle-class parents also may be better able to prevent arrest by paying for the property that their children damage or steal.

Undoubtedly, police have a great deal of discretion in deciding whether to make an arrest, and there are many reasons police *might* discriminate against poorer people. Still, we must look for evidence that police actually *do* discriminate. One well-known study found that youths who look or act "tough" in their run-ins with the police are much more likely to be arrested than are those who act properly respectful—despite the seriousness of the crime.[28] (And we assume that this tough behavior and appearance will be more common among lower-class boys.) But not all research agrees that the police do in fact discriminate against poorer people. The severity of the crime and the person's past record may play a larger part in the decision.

To sum up: We begin with the question of whether there are class differences in criminality. When we look at arrest statistics, we find the lower class overrepresented, especially in the more serious and violent crimes. We then ask whether that overrepresentation results from a real difference in crime or just from police bias in who gets arrested. From the available evidence, we cannot conclude definitely that police bias is distorting the arrest figures.

---

* Wolfgang could not directly measure economic status. Instead, as a measure of each boy's SES, Wolfgang used the average income of the "census tract" (or geographical area) in which the boy lived.

Other Measures of Crime—Victimization Surveys

If arrest statistics are questionable, we must look to other sources of information on the connection between social class and crime. Unfortunately, victimization surveys are of little help here. Interviewers will ask the victim of a violent crime for some information about the criminal: What race was he or she, what sex, approximately how old? But they cannot very well ask "What would you estimate his annual income to be?" or "What are her parents' occupations?"

What victimization surveys can tell us is the geographic and social location of crime. These results give generally the same picture as arrests. For crimes of violence and for burglary, there is a negative relationship between income and crime: The poorer a family is, the more likely it is to be victimized. For these and some other crimes as well, the sharpest difference, at least for violent crime, seems to be between those at the very bottom of the income ladder and the next highest group (see Figures 4–2,

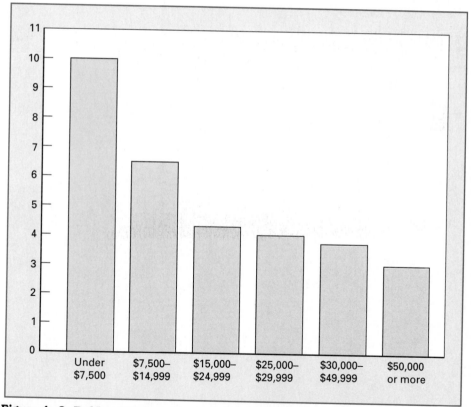

Figure 4–2 Robbery by Income, 1988; Victimizations per 1000
Source: National Crime Survey, 1988.

4–3). Victimization surveys also confirm the idea that more crime occurs in central cities than in suburbs or outlying areas (see Figures 4–4, 4–5, 4–6).

The facts about where crime occurs lead to two conclusions: first, that criminals frequently commit their crimes close to home; and second, that there are greater numbers of these criminals in poor, urban neighborhoods. (The only other possible explanation is that wealthier people come to poor neighborhoods to rob and steal, a proposition which seems very unlikely.) In short, victimization surveys, like arrest data, do provide some evidence that crime is related to social class.

Another type of evidence comes from observational studies. Rather than interview strangers about crime and criminals, the researchers themselves spend long periods of time in a neighborhood, getting to know the people. The result is frequently a rich understanding of a single area and the people in it. But this kind of observation, unfortunately, seldom allows for systematic comparisons between social classes. Fortunately, there is one exception,

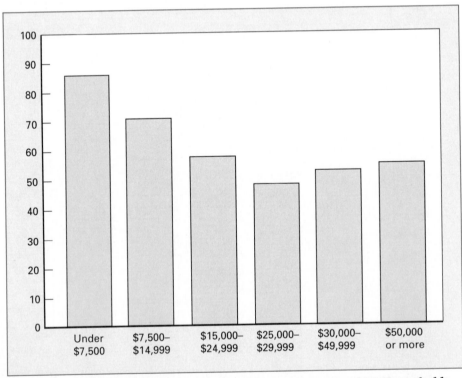

Figure 4–3 Burglary by Income, 1988; Victimizations per 1000 Households
Source: National Crime Survey, 1988.

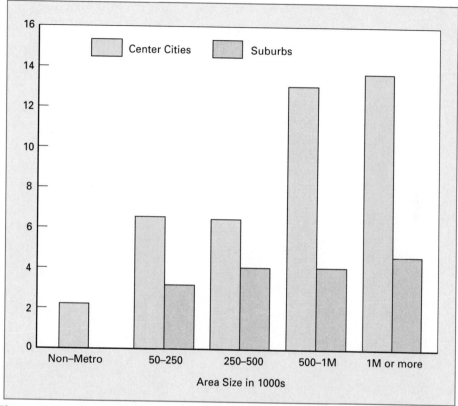

Figure 4—4 Robbery by Type of Locality, 1988; Victimizations per 1000

a study in which a team of researchers hung around with teenage gangs in different neighborhoods. The field-workers kept count of the kinds of crime the gang members committed, and the results were clear: SES mattered. Lower-class gangs were more criminal than were middle-class gangs. Even within the lower class, the lowest–SES level youths stole twice as often as the lower-class kids just above them.[29]

Self-Reports

In 1978, America's leading sociology journal published an article entitled "The Myth of Social Class and Criminality."[30] The authors (Charles Tittle and his colleagues) argued that although many people—social scientists included—believed that lower-class people committed more crime, this idea was a myth. It was a convenient belief that had no basis in fact.

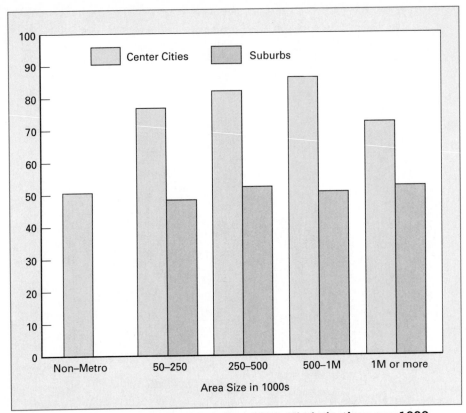

**Figure 4–5 Burglary by Type of Locality, 1988; Victimizations per 1000
Households**

If the evidence from arrests and victimization surveys all pointed to a
connection between social class and crime, how could the authors dismiss
such a connection as a myth? First, they pointed out that most of the evidence for a class-crime connection was based on arrests, and that even in
these studies the differences between SES groups were not so large. Second
and more important, they looked at several studies that measured crime by
using self-reports. In many cases, self-report studies have found that SES
is not a factor in crime, at least not in juvenile crime. High-SES youths
report committing as much crime as those of low SES. Even in the self-
report studies that do show poorer people committing more crime, the differences between social classes are much smaller than those found in studies based on arrests.

These self-report studies, however, have their limitations. For example,
most of them look only at juvenile crime, leaving out the crimes of adults.
Also, as we have already seen in connection with gender and crime, self-
reports and arrests are really measuring different things. Self-reports tell

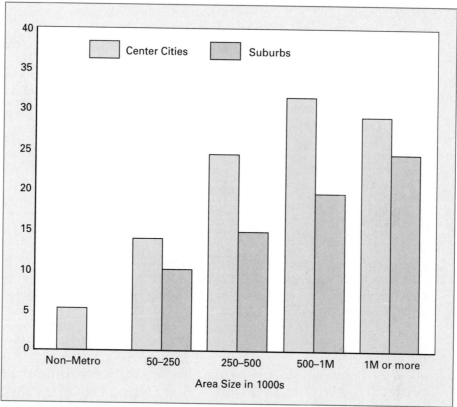

Figure 4–6 Motor Vehicle Theft by Type of Locality, 1988; Victimizations per 1000 Households

us who is committing the garden-variety teenage misbehavior; arrests, for the most part, tell us who is committing serious crimes or committing a variety of crimes quite frequently.

Recently, some self-report studies have tried to remedy these previous shortcomings. They have tried to get information on the more serious offenders and offenses. Unfortunately, the results of these recent studies are no more conclusive than the earlier ones. Some of them find no significant class differences, even among the most serious offenders.[31] For example, a recent national survey of youth was able to identify a small group of "serious career offenders"—the worst 3 percent of the entire sample. As we would expect, these tougher kids were more likely to come from cities than from suburbs or rural areas. However, on the average, their socioeconomic status was roughly the same as that of the least criminal youth.[32] Even a study which included youths in reform schools and other detention centers found no differences in social class. Youths serving time were no more likely to come from poor backgrounds than were noncriminal youths.[33]

At the same time, other surveys using the same methods have found that among the most criminal kids—those self-reporting 200 or more offenses per year or 55 or more Index offenses—more come from the lower class than from the middle class or working class.[34]

It can be frustrating to go through so many contradictory studies without being able to find conclusive evidence for what seems like an obvious idea— that poor people commit more crime. Yet in 1990, 12 years after his "Myth" article, Tittle once again concluded,

> Research published since 1978, using both official and self-reported data, suggests again . . . that there is no pervasive relationship between individual SES and delinquency.[35]

Class and Underclass

One of the problems might be in the definitions of social class or SES. It might be that it is only at the very bottom of the social ladder that we find more crime, so that studies using broad categories like lower class and middle class will not detect this difference.[36]

In the 1980s, some writers began talking about the "underclass." The term has no precise definition (but then neither does middle class or lower class). It refers to the lowest part of the lower class. In the United States, about 25 million people have so little money that they fall beneath the government's "poverty line." For most of these people, poverty is cyclical; their incomes may rise above the poverty line or fall back below it depending on a variety of factors (employment or loss of a job, marriage or divorce, illness in the family, etc.). But about 25 percent of Americans in poverty remain permanently outside the society of the employed. Some lack job skills or motivation, others are elderly or disabled, still others are single mothers.[37] Those in the underclass seem to care little for entering the mainstream of conventional society and its institutions—work, education, conventional family. In this way, they differ from other people in poverty. Perhaps if we revised our model of social class or SES to differentiate this underclass from the lower class, we would find the correlation that has proven so elusive. In fact, more recent self-report studies have shown that crime—especially violent crime—is most prevalent among the "disreputable poor."[38]

Individual and Neighborhood

Another possibility is that we've been approaching the problem in the wrong way. Remember, one of the reasons we intuitively think that crime and class are related is our sense that lower-class neighborhoods are more dangerous. But most of the studies we have looked at have emphasized the *individual's* social class and not that of the neighborhood (reread the quote from Tittle three paragraphs back). These studies that search for a correlation between an individual's SES and his or her crime seem to assume that a person's decision to violate the law is somehow based on how one stands in relation to some large, vague thing called American society. Perhaps this assumption does not make much sense, especially for studying juvenile crime. After all, which is likely to have more effect on whether a teenager commits crimes—parents' occupations or the kind of kids in the neighborhood? Common sense (and much research) tells us the answer: The peer group has more effect than the parents' social status.[39]

Some recent studies have turned away from individual-based measurements of social class. Instead of measuring the social class of each youth's family, they measure the class of the area where he or she lives.* Fewer studies have taken this approach, but these few give more consistent results than do the individual-based studies. Youths from lower-class areas are more criminal than those from middle-class areas.[40] This is no surprise. But poor adolescents who live in middle-class areas are less likely to commit crimes than are similar kids who live in poor neighborhoods. Even within the same lower-class neighborhood, the children of welfare families may be no more criminal than those of working families.[41] So apparently, it is not just the individual's or family's lack of money. As sociologists have long noted, there seems to be something about the area, not just its individual members, that shapes people's behavior.

This fact lends some support to one part of the conservative view of crime outlined at the start of this section. Conservatives argue that economic want is not a cause of crime. The evidence on lower-class areas and individuals suggests that these kids steal not just for lack of money, and certainly not to buy necessities for their families, but rather because they live in areas where crime is more accepted, at least among youth. It's a matter of attitudes, not finances. Of course, what the conservative argument cannot explain is why these attitudes are more prevalent in poorer neighborhoods.

Whose Status?

Even if economic need is not necessarily the prime factor in juvenile crime, there may still be an important relationship between social status and crime. However, to demonstrate this relationship may require a slight revision in our model of social class or SES. In nearly all studies on the crime-class connection, SES was measured as the parents' income or occupation. These measures may tell us something about the level of material comfort

---

* As I pointed out in the previous footnote, although Wolfgang used his income measure as an indicator of *individual* SES, it really was a measure of *neighborhood* income.

in the child's home, but in terms of social standing, it tells us only where children have come from, not where they are now or where they are going. If crime is a response to low status, perhaps in studying juvenile crime we should measure status not by where parents stand in the wider society, but by where juveniles stand in their own world.[42] For the adolescent, the place for measuring status is not the world of work and income; it is the world of school.

Unfortunately, as obvious as this idea might seem, few researchers have tried to test it. It would require new ways of measuring status, for adolescent society offers several ways to gain status in school: grades, sports, activities, physical attractiveness—not just having money. The "clique" structure in some schools may also make for difficulties in comparing all students on a single status scale. Still, when we are trying to predict who will become a delinquent, we do much better by looking at the adolescent's own academic ranking in school rather than at parents' SES. The kids who are least successful in school, rather than those whose parents are poorest, are the most likely to be delinquent. Even in Wolfgang's cohort study, which exaggerated the importance of SES and race, the factor that correlated most with crime was school performance.[43]

Summing Up

What can we conclude from all this?

1. Research confirms one bit of common sense knowledge: Lower-class neighborhoods have more crime than do middle-class neighborhoods.
2. This difference is greater for violent crime than for property crime.
3. Among individuals (as opposed to neighborhoods), lower-class people are more likely to be arrested than middle-class people.
4. Self-reported crime differs only slightly from one socioeconomic level to another. Differences are greater for very serious and very frequent offenders.
5. The greatest difference seems to be between those at the very bottom of the social scale and those at the next highest level.
6. For juveniles, the SES of the family is not as influential as the general social class of the neighborhood.
7. For juveniles, the SES of the family is probably not as important as the youth's own status in school.

As I said at the beginning of this section, many theories of crime have given economic factors and social class a central place in explaining crime. Considering this emphasis, the evidence on social class is disappointing. Some criminologists think that the correlation between crime and social class, if it exists at all, is very weak.[44] That is, differences between classes are small, and within each class, there is a great deal of individual variation. Perhaps this is indeed an instance where what "everyone knows" is wrong or at least unsupported by systematic evidence. For myself, I am not so convinced, and I have tried to offer reasons for the failure of researchers to find the crime-class connection. Certainly the data on victimization point to class differences, especially for violent crime. It may be that the important differences occur more for adults than for juveniles.

I have omitted here a discussion of some crucial issues. For example, this section is *not*, strictly speaking, about economics and crime. It is about social class. It does not address the economic questions of whether crime pays and whether people commit crime because it pays. Those questions will be dealt with in other chapters. For the most part, I have also left the explanations for the facts on class and crime for the chapters on theory. However, I hope that when you read those chapters you will keep in mind the tentative nature of the evidence.

RACE

Of all the demographic factors that might be associated with crime, the most controversial is race. As Charles Silberman put it in 1978, "It is impossible to talk honestly about the role of race in American life without offending and angering both whites and blacks—and Hispanic browns and Native American reds as well. The truth is too terrible, on all sides."[45] The terrible truth, in his view, consists of two interrelated parts: black violent crime and white racism. The "terrible truth" on one side is that blacks do in fact have higher rates of violent crime; on the other, it is that white racism still exists and has been an important cause of that crime. Not everybody agrees with Silberman. Some people deny the existence of one point or the other; some people deny the connection between the two.

In the following pages, I will try to present the relevant ideas and evidence on these questions, much as for any other. However, I also realize that the first part of Silberman's statement is not in dispute: The topic of race is a volatile one, and some readers will doubtless take exception to what I say.

Race and Biology

One reason that this topic causes such heated debate is the whole notion of race itself. Too often people have failed to distinguish between **race** and **culture**. Both terms imply a set of characteristics which distinguish one group from another. But while culture is learned, race is inherited. Racial characteristics are passed genetically from one generation to the next. The individual and the social environment have no power to change them. Physical characteristics obviously are transmitted this way. Nobody disputes this—it is a matter of biology. What is at issue, in part, is whether *behavioral, personality,* or *moral* characteristics also have an inherited, biological component, and whether such components differ from one race to another. In other words, are some races *biologically* more predisposed to crime?

Earlier in this century, even educated people spoke of the Scots as being a "thrifty race" or the Japanese as a "clever race." This casual use of the term "race" can be misleading, even dangerous. In the first place, identifying the Scots as racially different from the English stretches the idea of race quite a bit and raises an important question: How many different races are there, and what are the criteria for establishing some group as a race? It turns out that scientists do not agree on any single answer to these questions. In fact, because of the difficulty in defining race in a precise way, social scientists often broaden the phrase to "race and ethnicity" or "racial and ethnic groups." But more important, to say that the Scots are a thrifty "race" implies the biogenetic transmission of what is obviously a cultural or personality trait (thriftiness).

Some evidence does support the idea that certain general personality tendencies may be biologically inherited, though these findings remain a focus of dispute among scientists.* However, even if children may inherit some social traits from parents, there is a second issue implied in the discussion of race and crime: that criminality is one such trait, and that different races have a different inherited propensity to commit crime. If criminality or violence were truly a racial characteristic, then criminality, like straight hair, might be greater among some races than others. By analogy, straight-haired "races" may, with much effort and expenditure on permanents and curlers, succeed in having curly hair, but their basic tendency toward straight hair will not be changed; it is inherent in their race. Similarly, if criminality were racial, the more criminal races would always need more external forces to control their crime. The implications of this idea are extremely ominous. Since crime is a moral issue, the existence of inherent biological and racial differences would mean that one race is morally superior to another.

Because of these kinds of implications, discussions of race and even scientific research on racial differences can become explosive, especially when the topic includes moral qualities like intelligence or crime. In 1985, James Q. Wilson and Richard Herrnstein published a book suggesting that there might be a racial basis for black-white crime differences in the United States. They could not trace a direct link: "There is no evidence to suggest the existence of a 'crime gene' in the same sense that we may know there is a gene that produces red hair."[46] Instead, they say that certain inherited

---

* For a fuller discussion, see the Chapter 10 on biological theories of crime.

factors may predispose a person to crime, and that races differ on these factors. One of these factors is intelligence, as measured by IQ. They say first that lower IQ makes a person more likely to be criminal, and second that blacks on the average have lower IQ scores than whites. Both of these propositions touch very sensitive areas in social science. The IQ-crime connection implies that the causes of crime lie within the individual, not in society. The race-IQ connection implies that blacks are not as intelligent as whites.

The evidence on these topics is almost as controversial as the ideas themselves. In a debate too long and complex to outline here, social scientists have raised questions about the IQ tests themselves. Are the tests biased in favor of middle-class whites? Do IQ tests measure innate intellectual capacity, or can IQ be affected by environmental factors? The evidence, for what it's worth, has shown that delinquents score, on the average, 6 to 10 points lower on IQ tests than do nondelinquents, and that the mean IQ score for blacks is slightly lower than the mean IQ score for whites.[47] Wilson and Herrnstein, do not, however, claim that these group differences are racially inherited.[48] Even so, their ideas are extremely controversial, and it should be clear why. Remember, it was a theory of racial superiority that provided the "scientific" grounds for the horrors of Nazism.

Despite Wilson and Herrnstein's tentative suggestions, I find it unlikely that the tendency toward crime or violence is a racial characteristic in the biogenetic sense. It is true that in the United States blacks have higher rates of violent crime than do whites. But if this had something to do with their African biological, genetic heritage, then we should expect to find even higher rates of violence in black African countries. Yet these countries have rates of murder, rape, and robbery well below those of American whites.[49] Even if Wilson and Herrnstein were right, genetic theories would still be useless for explaining important questions about *changes* in crime rates. For example, the alarming increase in black crime in the 1960s cannot have arisen from racially inherited factors, since the genetic composition of a population does not change over such a short period.

Race and Ethnicity

Although crime is probably not a racial factor in the literal, biological sense, we must still be concerned about the differences in crime rates among different racial and ethnic groups. In nearly every society with more than one racial or ethnic group, there will usually be corresponding differences in crime rates. The history of the United States, with its successive waves of immigration from various countries, provides a good example. Generally speaking, the most recent immigrant group has occupied the lowest place in the society and has had the reputation as the most criminal. Go back to the mid-19th century and you will find statements about the violence and

criminality of the "Irish race" that closely resemble some of the racist remarks made about blacks a hundred years later. When Irish railroad workers
in Jersey City rioted, seeking wages owed them by the Erie Railroad, a local
newspaper referred to them as "animals . . . a mongrel mass of ignorance
and crime."[50] Move ahead 50 years to the turn of the century, when groups
from Southern and Eastern Europe constituted the bulk of the crime problem. In 1902, when Jewish women took to the streets to protest the price
of kosher meat, some observers referred to them as a "pack of wolves"—the
same kind of language used to describe black rioters three generations
later.[51]

One function of this kind of racial remark is to focus attention on the
criminals—to locate the cause within them rather than in social forces.
They are of a different race, a different kind of people altogether, almost a
different species—animals.

Other countries, too, have their ethnic groups. In England, people of Irish
descent have long contributed in disproportionate numbers to statistics on
crime and violence, though the Irish Republic from which they or their
ancestors came has one of the lowest crime rates in the industrialized
world.[52] In Israel, there are differences among Jewish ethnic groups. Jews
of European descent have lower rates of crime and delinquency than do
Jews from North Africa and Asia.[53]

Race and Crime in America

In the United States, the discussion of crime and race (or ethnic groups)
has had one principal focus: black street crime. Sometimes disguised by
code words, and sometimes out in the open, the topic has provoked bitter
controversy among social scientists, politicians, and the public at large. One
of the first questions to answer, then, is whether blacks are in fact more
criminal than whites.

For a long time, most of the data showing blacks as overrepresented in
crime came from UCR information on arrests. Table 4–3 comes from the
1988 UCR, and shows the percentage of arrestees from each race. (Percentages do not quite add to 100 percent because I have left out Native
Americans and Asians, who account for less than 2 percent of crime.) The
U.S. population is about 82 percent white, 12 percent black, and 5 percent
Hispanic.*[54]

Although blacks make up only 12 percent of the population, they account
for one-third of all Index crime arrests. Their arrests for violent crimes are
even more disproportionate: 47.1 percent. And three out of every five ar-

---

* In tables on race such as this one, the UCR counts Hispanics as white; they account for
about 12% of the arrests for each crime.

Table 4–3 ▪ **Arrests, Distribution by Race, 1988**

	Number of arrests	*Percent white*	*Percent black*
Murder	16,090	45.0	53.5
Rape	28,036	52.7	45.8
Robbery	110,427	36.3	62.6
Aggravated assault	302,311	57.6	40.7
Burglary	329,812	67.0	31.3
Larceny	1,157,150	65.6	32.2
Motor vehicle theft	151,719	58.7	39.5
Arson	14,374	73.5	25.0
Total violent	456,864	51.7	46.8
Total property	1,653,055	65.3	32.6
All other	7,957,528	70.2	28.0

Source: UCR, 1988.

rested robbers were black. This is a huge difference. If we compute the robbery arrest rate for each race, we get a rate of about 24 per 100,000 whites, and nearly 300 per 100,000 blacks. In other words, given an equal number of each race, 12 times as many blacks will have been arrested for robbery.

Since these data tell us only about criminals who were *arrested*, we must ask whether we would find the same racial disproportion among *all* criminals. If police are prejudiced, and if their prejudice influences their decision to make an arrest, or if police departments deploy more officers in black neighborhoods, then arrest statistics on race will be misleading. Some people argue that arrest data reflect police racism, not black crime. However, arrest statistics for one crime—murder—may be fairly useful. A relatively high proportion of murders result in arrest (70 percent), and the police probably do not allow prejudice to influence their decision in making homicide arrests. In any case, roughly half of all people arrested for murder are black. This means that relative to their numbers in the population, blacks are arrested for murder seven times as often as are whites.

For the other crimes, we should check the arrest data against information from other sources—victimization surveys and self-reports. Victimization surveys can tell us only about crimes against the person (what the UCR calls "violent" crime), where the victim sees the criminal. For robbery, the data from victims' reports resemble to some extent those from arrests. While blacks account for over 60 percent of all robbery arrests, identifications from victimization surveys put the figure at about 50 percent.[55] The difference may reflect police bias (the "carnival mirror" explanation). But it might also mean that blacks, compared with white robbers, black robbers are more likely to be serious or frequent offenders (the "coarse net" explanation).

Self-report studies—the other source of information about who commits crimes—give less clear-cut evidence. The more recent studies generally do find blacks self-reporting more crime than whites, especially violent crime, but the differences are not as wide as those from arrest data. Of course, self-report studies have shortcomings, too: Most of them survey only juveniles; their sampling method sometimes misses the most serious criminals; and serious offenders as well as blacks are more likely to omit more of their crimes from their self-reports.[56] Still, some self-report studies—even those that include serious criminals—find little difference between whites and blacks.[57] Nevertheless, the bulk of the evidence from all three types of sources—arrests, victimization surveys, self-reports—points to the same conclusion: Blacks commit a disproportionate amount of crime, especially violent crime. Moreover, the more serious the category of criminal, the greater the proportion of blacks. That is, among those who commit only one or two offenses, black-white differences are small. But the population of the most serious and frequent offenders will be disproportionately black.

Explaining Black Crime

How to explain this greater involvement of blacks in crime? In the opening part of this section, I dealt with the biological explanation—the one that holds that blacks have a biogenetic tendency toward crime and violence. At present, this idea seems improbable.

A second explanation emphasizes the economic position of blacks in U.S. society. According to this argument, black crime is not so much a question of race as it is a matter of economic inequality. It only looks like a racial question because blacks are so disproportionately poor. Crime, so this argument goes, has its roots in poverty, unemployment, and economic inequality; since a greater percentage of blacks live in conditions of economic hardship than do whites, blacks have higher rates of crime.[58]

One way of testing this idea is to compare black crime rates with those of another group equally poor and equally the victim of racial discrimination. Although no group will be exactly like blacks in all ways except race, Hispanics come close. Blacks and Hispanics have roughly the same average income (in both cases, median family income is about 40 percent lower than that of whites). And Hispanics are also the victims of racial discrimination. If discrimination and poverty are the most important factors in crime, then blacks and Hispanics should have roughly equivalent rates of committing crime. But look at Table 4–4, adapted from a study of youth crime in Los Angeles. Even allowing for differences in the amount of discrimination faced by the two groups, even allowing for the possible distortion of data based on arrests, the differences are too large to be dismissed. The proportion of

Table 4–4 ▪ Arrest Rates (per 100,000) of Juveniles in Los Angeles, 1980

	Whites	Hispanics	Blacks
Murder	15	103	292
Robbery	250	918	5,500

Source: Peter Greenwood, et al. (1983), *Youth Crime and Juvenile Justice in California*, Santa Monica, CA: RAND.

black youths arrested for murder is nearly triple that of Hispanics; the robbery ratio is five times as high.

The economic or social-class explanation may be adequate for explaining black-white differences in property crime. Blacks make up 12 percent of the population, and they comprise 30 percent of those arrested for property crimes. This degree of overrepresentation is about what we would expect just from economic factors. It is close to the crime rates of other groups (whites or Hispanics) at similar economic levels. But violent crime is another matter. Here, the differences between blacks and whites, even between blacks and Hispanics, are too large to fit with the social-class explanation. Even controlling for other demographic variables, black rates of murder, rape, and robbery are still much higher than those of other groups.

Cultural Explanations

Given the limitations of biology, economics, and social class in explaining the high rates of black violence, some criminologists have looked for an explanation in the social and cultural ways of blacks in the United States. The "subculture of violence" theory, for example, says that not all social groups regard violence in the same way. Some groups are more willing to accept violence as a way of dealing with interpersonal matters. Among groups that share this attitude, criminal violence will be higher. Certain white groups (e.g., some of the poorer people in the South) participate in this subculture of violence, but it is even more widespread among blacks.[59]

A second cultural explanation focuses on the family. Especially controversial has been the idea that black "family structure" contributes to crime. Since far more blacks than whites are raised in single-parent homes (nearly 50 percent for blacks vs. 15 percent for whites),[60] perhaps single-parent families are more likely to produce violent children. Or perhaps there is something about the way black parents interact with their children that causes the increased tendency toward violence. These are very popular ideas. Many people see the family as the principal source of criminal or law-abiding behavior. But what is the evidence? To see if the family is a cause of black criminal violence, we must ask two questions: (1) Do certain family patterns (single parents, abusiveness) produce violence? and (2) If so, are these patterns more widespread among blacks?

These are very important questions, and they go to the heart of a widely held, common sense notion about crime—namely, that the "breakdown of the family" is responsible for high rates of crime. You would expect that by now we would have much high-quality, conclusive research on these questions. The first question, especially the broken-homes aspect of it, has provoked a great deal of research. Unfortunately, it is far from conclusive. It appears that the broken home in itself does not contribute to delinquency.[61] Even authors like Wilson and Herrnstein, who are predisposed to find a link between family and crime, must conclude that "when we look for evidence for a direct connection between broken or abusive homes and subsequent criminality, we find that it is less clear-cut than we had supposed."[62] If there is anything about the family that makes for more delinquency, it is in the consistency of parental supervision, not the structure of the family.[63] On the second question, that of black-white differences in child-rearing, there is little systematic research. To quote Wilson and Herrnstein again, "It is astonishing how little we know about the consequences of being raised in a black family, intact or broken."[64] In other words, if there is a connection between specific black family patterns and crime, nobody has yet proven it.

The Family Reconsidered

We started with two important facts: First, blacks have much higher rates of illegitimacy and female-headed households; second, blacks have much higher rates of crime. How can we explain the connection between the two? So far, we have tried the common sense explanation that the "breakdown of the family" is an important cause of crime; blacks have more broken homes, therefore they have more crime. Yet when we looked for evidence, we found that the broken-homes idea does not go very far toward explaining crime rates. Other research shows something that parents, especially parents of delinquents, often believe: Whatever the influence the family may have, it is not nearly so great as the influence of the peer group and other forces outside the home.[65]

Surely, though, the data on family breakup and crime cannot be just coincidence. The problem is that in the search for an explanation, we have been looking in the wrong place and asking the wrong question. We have been looking inside the home and asking a psychological question: "How does the absence of a father in the home affect a child's delinquency?" Instead, we should be looking outside the home and asking a more sociological question: "How does the absence of many fathers in a *neighborhood* affect the rate of juvenile crime in that neighborhood?"

In any neighborhood, but especially in lower-class neighborhoods, kids get into trouble. The statistics on larceny, burglary, and auto theft are fairly clear on this. But neighborhoods with a high percentage of working men will have less juvenile crime, largely for two reasons. First, there are more men around to keep kids in line. Employed men have a greater stake in their homes and their neighborhood. They will not let neighborhood kids get away with so much. Also, stronger communities make for less crime, and two-parent households can more easily form ties with formal and informal community groups. Single mothers do not have time for such luxuries.[66]

Second, employed men provide a link to the job market. For the older teenager, a steady job at a decent wage can be an attractive alternative to an uncertain and risky income from crime. It's not a question of an employed father providing a good "role model" for a son; the connection between employed fathers and less criminal sons is far more concrete than this vague psychological notion. Getting jobs at this level is still largely a matter of personal contacts—knowing somebody who knows somebody. In a neighborhood where men are unemployed or employed in dead-end, low-paying, or temporary jobs, teenagers will see little reason to mature out of crime. Instead, they may turn to more profitable and more serious kinds of crime. A few may be recruited by adults and move on to dealing drugs or stealing cars for "chop shops." Others will add robbery to their repertoire.[67]

This explanation, looking beyond the individual home, places the female-headed household in a secondary role. The primary factor here is male unemployment. The female-headed household does not derive from a separate black culture; it is a result of male unemployment.[68] Women are less willing to marry a man who brings home little money, and unemployed men find it difficult to remain in a home where they cannot fulfill their role as breadwinner.[69] So it is neither unemployment itself, nor the female-headed household itself, that makes for higher crime. Instead, in this model, the combination of these two factors—high male unemployment leading to single-parent households—creates *community* conditions for higher crime.

White Racism, Black Crime

The explanation I have just described has an advantage over the other two cultural explanations—the theories based on the "subculture of violence" or "black family patterns." These explanations ignore the social context within which a subculture or family is formed. That cultural and historical context, however, is the focus of one final type of the cultural explanation—the "white racism" theory mentioned at opening of this section. If blacks have uniquely high rates of violence—even in comparison with other groups that have endured poverty and discrimination—then in explaining that violence we must look to the unique history of blacks in the United States.

Probably the best version of this theory is Charles Silberman's chapter, "Beware the Day They Change Their Minds."[70] Silberman shows how the black experience in the United States was like that of no other ethnic group. Slavery and racism consistently kept blacks from moving up the social scale. An Irish immigrant in the 1850s might move from less-skilled labor and unsteady employment to more highly skilled and regular jobs, and his son might even move into a white-collar position. But this kind of occupational mobility remained out of the reach of blacks. Even when blacks were able to enter better-paying jobs—on the railroads, for example—their gains were short-lived. Another wave of white immigrants would arrive from Europe and displace them.[71] In addition to this economic burden, blacks also bore the psychological burdens of racism—"humiliation, insult, and embarrassment as a daily diet."[72] Even into the latter half of the 20th century, a Southern black who failed to be properly servile was literally risking his life.

Given this history, says Silberman, "what is remarkable is not how much, but how little black violence there has always been." For three centuries, blacks had developed a system of controls, mechanisms that kept anger in check or channeled it into activities that did not threaten the wider society. Some of these activities, like "the dozens" (a sort of "rap" contest based on insults), were harmless; others, like violent crime, could be deadly. But white America was willing to tolerate relatively high rates of black crime— so long as that crime remained confined to the black community.

Beginning in the 1960s, things began to change. Blacks began to challenge white domination. In politics, the new black consciousness took the form of freedom rides, boycotts, voter registration, marches, and demonstrations. It was a courageous and even heroic effort. But the challenge to traditional lines of authority had a nastier underside. The 1960s was a period of general economic prosperity, but once again this prosperity largely bypassed blacks. The promise of civil rights contrasted with the realities of ghetto life, and black neighborhoods in many cities became the sites of rioting. Besides the sporadic, collective violence of riots, violent street crime as well became more and more a fact of life, and like the televised riots, street crime affected the wider society. Black crime began to spill over its usual boundaries, no longer a matter of young blacks victimizing young blacks. It seemed that black criminals were more often victimizing older, middle-class, and even white victims.

Black crime was breaking out because the old controls were breaking down. In part, this breakdown was caused by the large number of youths— the result of the baby boom. In part, it was a result of the new, more defiant black consciousness. And in part it was, ironically, a result of blacks' success in the battle against segregation. When middle-class blacks had been unable to move out of the ghetto, they provided a force for stability and control. But as laws against segregated housing were passed and enforced, middle-class and even stable working-class blacks began to move out. Left in the ghettoes were those who lacked the resources either to move or to exert

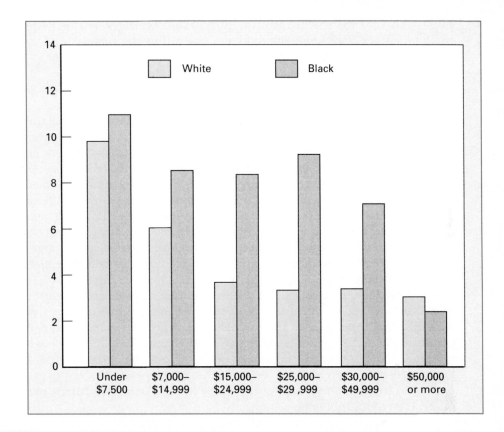

In the graph above, at each level of income, blacks are more likely than whites to be victims of robbery. But the graph also shows that as white income increases into the middle range, victimization drops considerably. Since most robbers commit their crimes close to home, the graph reflects the much higher participation in robbery of people living in areas near or below the "poverty line." Whites with greater incomes are able to move away from high-crime areas.

For middle-income blacks, however, no similar decrease occurs. One possible, though unlikely, explanation is that middle-income blacks are nearly as likely as low-income blacks to commit robbery—i.e., blacks who become richer do not become any less criminal. The more likely explanation is that the graph reflects the segregation that still prevails in the American housing market. For blacks in the United States, even those with above-average incomes can not so easily move away from high-crime neighborhoods.

Figure 4–7 Robbery by Income and Race, 1988; Victimizations per 1000
Source: National Crime Survey, 1988. (The victimization rates for Blacks in the $50,000 or more category are based on fairly small samples and may not be reliable.)

much control over the burgeoning population of angry youths. The "bad nigger," long a staple of black folklore, was out of the closet.*[73]

Summing Up and a Personal Note

In many countries around the world, the population is composed of different racial and ethnic groups. These groups do not always coexist in peace. Each day, it seems, the world news brings us reports of regions where conflict between ethnic (or religious) groups has flared into violence and death— Northern Ireland, India, Azerbaijan, Armenia, South Africa, to name a few. Conflict may be especially likely where different groups have different degrees of economic success and political power. In the United States, the most serious racial and ethnic divisions have been between blacks and whites. Although open, organized violence has been relatively rare, race remains a volatile and persistent issue. One of the most controversial parts of the issue is crime.

Our three major sources of evidence—police arrests, victimization surveys, and self-report studies—all show that in the United States, blacks commit a disproportionate amount of crime, especially violent crime. Blacks constitute about 12 percent of the U.S. population. We might expect blacks to commit twice that percentage of crime, given their overrepresentation among the poor. Indeed, blacks commit roughly 25 to 30 percent of property crime. But blacks account for over 40 percent of all violent crime, and nearly 60 percent of all robberies.

There are several possible explanations for these troubling data. Biological explanations—that blacks have some biogenetic tendency toward crime and violence—seem unlikely. Even the idea that blacks have lower than average IQ and therefore higher rates of crime has come in for a great deal of criticism. In any case, these theories cannot explain short-term changes in crime, such as the rapid increase of black crime in the 1960s.

Some explanations look to family patterns as the source of crime and violence. There may be some validity to this popular notion. However, the evidence is far from clear either that specific family patterns breed crime and violence or that black families follow these crime-causing patterns.

Finally, cultural explanations look to traditions and ways of life as the principal factor in crime. Some criminologists have argued that blacks participate in a "subculture of violence" that condones or even demands violent behavior. Other, more liberal cultural theories see the violence in black cul-

---

* Needless to say, not all social scientists agree with this theory. To quote the noted "futurist" Herman Kahn, "This 'suppressed rage' idea is crap." Blacks rioted, says Kahn, because "they have no idea of what moral standards are." (Kahn's statement, by the way, echoes almost verbatim what well-established people said about Jewish, Irish, and Slavic rioters at earlier times in history.)

ture as an understandable response to the conditions that blacks find themselves in. For two centuries, the function of black culture was not to evoke
violence but to inhibit it or channel it into behavior that did not threaten
white society. Beginning in the 1960s, this control began to break down.
Both types of cultural explanation are difficult to evaluate. Translating their
central concepts into measurable variables seems an impossible task. It is
far easier to *describe* subcultural norms or historical injustice than to measure them for purposes of comparison. For the moment, we should probably
look upon these theories as plausible but not proven.

When an issue is as politically charged as that of race and crime, most
people will choose their explanations not on the basis of evidence but on
the basis of their general political view. Unfortunately, discussions over
explanations too often turn into arguments about who is to "blame." Conservative critics will argue that historical explanations seek to blame white
racism or society and to exonerate blacks for their crimes. Liberal critics
will argue that theories based on individual deficiencies (low IQ) or family
patterns (illegitimacy, father-absent homes) "blame the victim" and ignore
the more serious problems of inequality and injustice.

Today, discussions of race often become discussions of crime. But crime
is only part of the problem, and criminology by itself can offer little to resolve
it. We would be kidding ourselves if we thought that the problem of black
crime and violence was separate from the more general problem of the position of blacks in U.S. society. Black-white difference in crime and violence
are of a piece with differences in employment, income, physical and mental
health, housing, and education. Race is, as Gunnar Myrdal called it in his
1950 volume, "an American dilemma"; perhaps it is *the* American dilemma.
DeToqueville, that most perceptive of observers of the American scene, predicted the dilemma in 1830, 120 years before Myrdal (and 30 years before
the end of slavery). A Presidential Commission (the Kerner Commission)
reminded us again in 1968 that "our nation is moving toward two societies,
one black, one white—separate and unequal."[74] Since then, change has
been slow and not entirely positive.

I wish that I could have ended this section on a more optimistic and more
conclusive note. This is the area in criminology which I personally find the
most distressing—not just the high levels of black violence, but also the
lack of convincing explanations, the tendency of discussion to degenerate
into battles over blame, and the absence of workable solutions.

AGE

The principal question of this chapter is this: Who commits crimes? To
answer it, criminologists try to find variables that are correlated with crime.

As we have seen, it's not always easy to figure out just what the facts are. Different ways of asking questions and different ways of measuring each variable can produce different results. Even when researchers agree on the facts, they may disagree strongly on the explanation for those facts. Race, sex, social class and economic hardship, historical forces like urbanization—all these variables have been at the center of criminological disputes.

There is one variable, however, on which criminologists seem to agree—at least on some of the basic facts. That variable is age. One basic fact is that street crime is largely a young man's game. Look at Figure 4–8, derived from UCR information on people arrested for Index crimes in 1988. It shows the arrest rate per 100,000 for each age group.

The graph makes some things obvious. First, arrest rates for property crime are far higher than arrest rates for violent crime. Second, property crime arrest rates rise sharply in the mid-teen years, then decline nearly as sharply in the late teens. Look at the property crime arrest rate for 15-, 16-, and 17-year olds. Of every 100,000 of these mid-teenagers, nearly 3,000 were arrested. That is three times higher than the rate for 25- to 29-year-olds. Third, violent crime follows a slightly different pattern: It rises more slowly, peaks at a later age (18, compared with 17 for property crime), and declines very gradually.

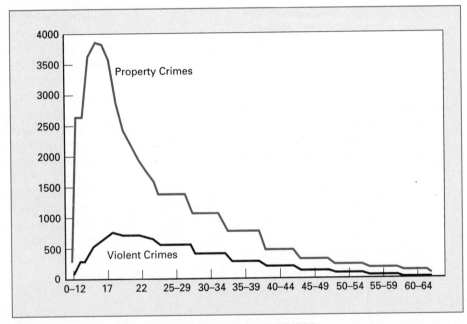

Figure 4–8 Arrests by Age, 1988; Rates per 100,000
Note: The UCR groups 13- and 14-year-olds together. It also groups ages above 24 into 5-year groups, giving the graph its slightly misleading, step-wise appearance.
Source: Uniform Crime Reports Reporting Program, FBI (1990), Age-Specific Arrest Rates and Race-Specific Arrest Rates for Selected Offenses 1965–1988, Washington, DC: U.S. Department of Justice.

Of course, these figures tell us only who got arrested. Remember, for every 100 Index crimes, only 50 become "crimes known to the police" (I am giving a high estimate here), and of these, only about 10 result in arrests. It might be that teenagers just aren't very good at committing crimes and therefore get caught more often. Would we get a similar graph if we could somehow find out the ages of all people committing Index crimes, not just those who got arrested? As nearly as we can tell from self-report studies and victimization surveys, the answer is yes.[75] But younger criminals seem somewhat *less* likely than older criminals to get arrested for a crime they commit, which means that their contribution to crime is even greater than Figure 4–8 shows. So we can use arrest data as a conservative estimate of age differences in crime.

Explaining the High-Crime Years

There are several reasons for this pattern of age and crime. To begin with, young children do not have much ability to commit serious crime. Some 10-year-olds may steal, but their victims are likely to be other 10-year-olds, and the cost of the crimes will be low; these crimes will not turn up in statistics on arrests, crimes known to the police, or victimization surveys.

It is in the early teenage years that kids begin to have the capacity for serious crime. This is also the time when parental influence over children diminishes; our society expects 15-year-olds to be less dependent on their parents than are 10-year-olds. Consequently, the influence of peers increases. Finding acceptance in this or that crowd may depend on intangible qualities like "personality," but teenagers may also feel pressured to have the right kinds of clothes, records, sneakers, drugs, and other things that can be bought—or stolen. Boys face the additional pressure to establish their manhood, and some of the ways of demonstrating their masculinity— stealing, fighting, joyriding, vandalism—may violate the law. In addition, many teenagers who break the law may have relatively little to risk. The punishments for crime are less severe for juveniles. More important, while adults risk losing jobs or families, teenagers have no such attachments.

As youths mature into their late teens—and especially as they leave school—these pressures toward crime all decrease. Youths no longer need to try to prove that they are men; responsibilities like jobs and families are adequate testimony of adult status. Jobs and families also constitute investments that the person might not want to put at risk; therefore, the cost of getting caught is higher. As youths move into the adult world and out of the age-segregated world of school, peer pressure is less intense. There are even changes in attitudes and feelings about the very act of committing a crime. While a young man may find it exciting, the older man of 25 to 30 is more likely to feel worry and anxiety rather than exhilaration.

While each theory places its primary emphasis on a different factor, each acknowledges that young people—especially young men—are the problem and that as these youths get older, they grow out of crime. This pattern seems to be universal. If you graphed the age of persons arrested in other countries or in the United States in earlier historical periods, you would get a curve that closely resembles Figure 4–8: a sharp rise in early youth, followed by a decline. The peak might come at a younger or older age, but the general trend would be similar, with the highest rates occurring in the late teens and early 20s.[76]

Birth Rates and Crime Rates

In the United States, nearly half the arrests for Index crimes involve people age 15 to 25. From this simple fact follow some obvious conclusions: The more 15- to 25-year-olds, the more crime; the greater the proportion of 15- to 25-year-olds in the population, the higher the crime rate. And since 15-year-olds do not suddenly appear full-grown, we can anticipate changes in crime by looking at the number of babies born. For this reason, the increase in crime rates in the 1960s should not have come as such an unexpected shock.

World War II had a tremendous impact on the United States. Economically, government spending for the military helped boost the nation out of the Great Depression. Socially, however, the war brought disruption to many people's lives. Men went into the service, and women went to work. Consequently, many people postponed marriage and children. The end of the war also brought important changes. Soldiers were gradually demobilized back into civilian society. Economic prosperity continued, and government programs encouraged home-buying. One notable result of it all was that birth rates began to rise. In 1940, the birth rate (the number of births relative to the total population) was about 19.4 per 1,000. In 1946, this rate began a sharp increase and remained high for a decade. In 1957, the rate began to decline, though it did not reach the pre–World War II level until the mid-1960s. This period of high birth rates, roughly 1947 to 1960, was the "baby boom (see Figure 4–9)."

The social effects of the baby boom should have been easy to foresee. After all, if you see a jump in the birth rate in 1947, you don't have to be too much of a genius to figure out that by the early 1950s, there will be an increased demand for tricycles, or that by 1957 elementary schools will be crowded unless new ones are built. Nevertheless, some of these predictable changes took many people by surprise.

You also might have predicted that in the 1960s crime rates would rise and that they would remain high until the last of the baby boomers began to ease into their late 20s. Had you made such a prediction, you would have been right—partly. Indeed, crime rates rose, but the increase far exceeded what birth rates would have led you to expect. By 1970, the proportion of

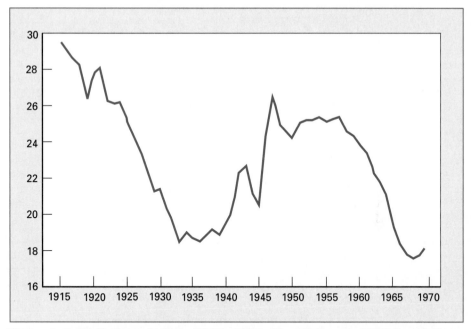

Figure 4–9 Birth Rates in U.S., 1915–1970; Live Births per 1000 Population
Source: U.S. National Center for Health Statistics, Vital Statistics for the United States, 1968, Vol. I.
Monthly Vital Statistics Report, March 4, 1971 Vol. 19, No. 12.

15- to 25-year-olds in the population had increased by about 40 percent. But crime rates had increased by 100 to 200 percent. Not only were there more young people, but they were committing a lot more crime.

Figure 4–10 illustrates this change by showing changes in the arrest *rates* of different age groups for the years 1961 to 1985. By giving rates per age group, the graphs control for the size of the different birth cohorts. The year 1961 is important because that is the year just before the children at the leading edge of the baby boom came into the high-crime ages. The graph of arrests of people under 18 shows that the increase in arrests per 100,000 begins in 1962, when the 1947 cohort was turning 15. In 1960, for every 100,000 teenagers, about 3,700 were arrested. By 1975, that rate had more than doubled to nearly 8,000. Not only were there more teenagers, and not only were teenagers a larger part of the population, but as the graph shows, a greater proportion of those kids were committing crimes and getting arrested.

Figure 4–10 shows a similar increase for 18- to 20-year-olds. But the upswing starts slightly later—in 1965, just as the first baby boomers were turning 18. The line for 21- to 24-year-olds shows a decrease from 1961 to 1966. Then the baby boomers enter this age group, and arrest rates climb.

We can get a similar picture by comparing two cohort studies done by Marvin Wolfgang. Wolfgang's first cohort consisted of every boy who lived

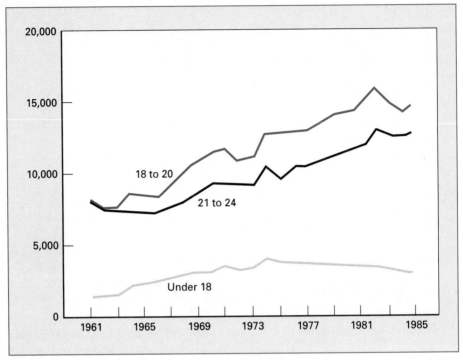

Figure 4–10. Arrests per 100,000 Age-Eligible Population
Source: Report to the Nation on Crime and Justice, Second Edition.

in Philadelphia between his 10th and 18th birthdays and who was born in 1945. The year is important, since it comes just before the baby boom. In the second study, Wolfgang followed a second cohort—those born in 1958, a high–birth rate year near the end of the baby boom. The 1958 cohort was, of course, larger—about 30 percent larger—but it also committed 50 percent more crime. Moreover, the *rate* of crime (which controls for the different sizes of the groups) was much higher in the 1958 cohort. They had a rate of violent crime three times that of the 1945 cohort.[77]

Crime and the Baby Boom—Explanations

Why did crime increase so steeply in the 1960s? Why were the teenagers of the baby boom so much more criminal than were those of previous generations? Like other "why" questions, these have no single answer that all criminologists agree on. I cannot tell you which answer is right and which is wrong. All I can do is to outline some of the more prominent explanations.

Deterrence—The View From the Right

One explanation sees the increase in crime as one element in a set of social changes occurring in the United States in the 1960s, the period when the baby boomers were entering their teens. "It all began in about 1963. That was the year, to overdramatize a bit, that a decade began to fall apart."[78] Teenage unemployment was rising; more people were using heroin. More unwed mothers were having babies and going on welfare. And all these trends occurred most strikingly in poor, urban neighborhoods, especially black neighborhoods. It was the start of what 20 years later came to be called the "underclass."

The conservative explanation for much of this "falling apart" emphasizes deterrence; it attributes the falling apart to rational choices people made based on the attractiveness of the alternatives. Welfare payments made unemployment more attractive than working; hence the increase in the welfare rolls. Crime, too, became more attractive. Changes in the courts made it easier for people to get away with crime. Supreme Court rulings made it harder to arrest and convict criminals. A smaller percentage of crimes resulted in arrest, and of those people arrested, a smaller percentage went to prison. For juveniles, courts were even more lenient. From the conservative "deterrence" perspective, these policies were "incentives to fail." Kids were committing crimes because "there was no reason not to."[79]*

The most important factors in this explanation are the policies of the government and courts, rather than anything specific about the baby boom itself. However, keep in mind one additional set of facts. The crime increase occurred not just in the United States but in most other countries involved in World War II. Countries with different systems of justice and different systems of welfare also experienced the same pattern: a high post-war birth rate followed 15 to 20 years later by disproportional increases in crime. For example, in England, in the 12-year period 1948 to 1960, robbery rose by 73 percent. But in the next 12 years, it rose by 277 percent. In France, the rate of theft *decreased* in the 1950s by over 50 percent; in the 1960s, it increased by 60 percent.[80]† This pattern suggests that something about high birth rates in themselves, regardless of government policy, creates pressure for crime.

---

* For a more thorough assessment of the impact of changes in criminal law, see Chapter 14. For more on the deterrence question, see Chapter 16.

† The notable exception is Japan, where beginning about 1950 crime rates decreased steadily for nearly three decades.

Demographic Overload—Barbarians at the Gate

There are two other explanations for the link between birth rates and crime rates. One emphasizes social and psychological factors; the other focuses on economic matters. Both start with the reminder that what is important is the birth *rate*—that is, the number of babies born compared with the number of adults.

The social-psychological model views the child-adult ratio as operating much like the student-faculty ratio in a school. When the student-faculty ratio gets too large, things can get out of hand. Similarly in the wider society, the important task of adults is to control children by teaching them to be good members of their society. This process is called socialization, and without it, there would be chaos. Babies, after all, come into the world utterly indifferent to the rules of society. Parents may think of an individual birth as a blessed event, but to demographer Norman Ryder, it is part of a "perennial invasion of barbarians who must somehow be civilized." When the "invading army" is small relative to the "defending army" of adults, then the task of socializing these children runs fairly smoothly. But when a baby boom sends in a relatively large invading army, the result is **demographic overload**, and the breakdown of the socialization process. During the baby boom, "the increase of the magnitude of the socialization tasks in the United States . . . was completely outside the bounds of previous experience."[81] Instead of adults socializing and controlling younger members of society, youths looked more to each other, to their own youth culture, for their cues as to what to think and how to act.

The decade of the 1960s, during which the 15- to 24-year-old age group increased by 50 percent, marked the full flourishing of "youth culture." This culture was too broad and diverse to summarize in a single sentence, but at least in part—the part we are concerned with here—it was disdainful of "straight" behavior and tolerant of deviance. This "subterranean tradition"[82] had existed in the past, but it had been kept underground by the large ratio of responsible adults. But in the 1960s, the sheer number of youth allowed it to emerge and become a visible force in U.S. culture. Although few youths actually believed that street crime was right and good, the youth culture's generally tolerant attitude towards deviance allowed a larger place for predatory crime.

Big Cohort, Small Prospects

A second explanation for the increased crime of the baby-boom generation is fundamentally economic. In place of vague concepts like socialization and culture, this explanation emphasizes the very concrete factors of jobs and income, and the very simple notion of supply and demand—in this case the supply and demand of labor. Imagine going to a job interview at a firm that has five openings. In the waiting room, you find four other people who have applied for the jobs. Now imagine going to the same interview and finding 10 other hopeful applicants. It's not hard to guess which room will produce more disappointed people.

Birth cohorts are like those waiting rooms. Some have more people than others. People born in the 1930s were members of a small birth cohort. They were lucky. As they looked toward and then entered their years in the labor market (the late 1940s and early 1950s), the economy was expanding. The demand for labor increased, but labor was in short supply. Since there were fewer young people relative to older people, young adults did not have to compete as much for jobs. Consequently, unemployment was low, wages were good, and people advanced fairly quickly up the career ladder. Of course, they were not yet making as much money as the older workers were, but their relative position was pretty good.

People born to those large birth cohorts of the late 1940s and early 1950s faced a reversed labor market. As they reached working age, they crowded the labor market. The growth in job seekers outpaced the growth in available jobs. This discrepancy made for higher unemployment and lower wages. And since the adults of the previous generation were now occupying the higher jobs, advancement for the younger group was slower. Relative to older workers, young people in the 1960s and 1970s were doing far worse than the young people of the 1940s and 1950s.

This picture conflicts somewhat with the image of baby boomers as the successful "yuppies" of the 1980s, indulging themselves in all sorts of consumer goods. The discrepancy comes first from the difference between the broad statistical reality and anecdotal evidence. With so many people in an age cohort, there are bound to be enough success stories to keep the media busy. Stories about clever young entrepreneurs inventing Apple computers or Trivial Pursuit games and selling them to the other members of their generation make more pleasant reading than grim statistics about teenage or adult unemployment. However, even for the middle-class baby boomers, affluence was not all that it seemed. Many of them accumulated the money to spend on computers and cars by delaying or forgoing entirely two much more expensive items—houses and children—that their parents been able to afford while enjoying the luxury of a one-earner household.

The yuppies were only one end of the economic scale. At the lower end, the less affluent members of the baby-boom generation faced far less enviable decisions. For them, the choice was not between houses and BMWs; it was between unemployment and low-paying jobs. For women, it was often a question of having an illegitimate child or marrying a man with meager economic prospects. Logically, under these circumstances unemployment, divorce, and illegitimacy become reasonable economic choices. The psychological result is depression, bitterness, and resentment, which will build up and emerge in the form of higher rates of mental illness, suicide, and crime.[83] As the last cohorts of the baby-boom generation turn 25 and age out of their high-crime years, crime rates should start to fall. Birth rates began to decline in 1957, and by 1967 they were at about their pre-boom level. This means that crime rates should have begun to decline in 1982, and that by 1992 they should be well below the high levels of the 1970s. The evidence on crime rates has not yet confirmed this optimistic prediction. Beginning in 1981, official crime rates (the UCR's crimes known to the police) declined for three years, an apparent fulfillment of the demographic promise of lower crime. But beginning in 1985, crime rates began to rise again.

If the crime rate does not exactly parallel the birth rate, it may be because other factors (the economy, the criminal justice system, the weather, etc.) play a more important role.[84] It may also be that we have looked at the birth rate for the nation as a whole rather than the birth rate in those areas that are likely to produce greater amounts of crime. What would happen if we looked at birth rates among the urban poor? Here birth rates remained high well after national rates began to decline. So if we are expecting long-term reductions in crime because of a smaller 15- to 25-year-old age group, we might have to wait until well into the 1990s.[85]

SUMMARY AND CONCLUSION

I have tried in this chapter to present evidence and, to a lesser extent, explanations on four variables—sex, race, social class, and age—and their relationship to crime. These are not the only variables that might be related to crime. I have mentioned in passing, here and elsewhere in this book, differences between urban, suburban, and rural areas and between different sections of the country. Crime also varies with temperature, month of the year, day of the week, time of day, and perhaps even the phases of the moon.

However, to answer the question "Who commits crimes?" criminologists have traditionally focused their research on the demographic variables of sex, race, social class, and age. The results, though not always in agreement, show that criminals, at least street criminals (those who commit Index crimes), are usually young men, somewhat more likely to come from the lower end of the economic ladder, and, in the United States, disproportionately black. These last two factors (class and race) are more strongly related to violent crime than to property crime.

Our information on crime comes from three major sources, each with its own particular strengths and inaccuracies: police arrests, self-reports, and victimization surveys. These also tell us something about the victims of crime: The demographic profile of victims of crime closely resembles the profile of the perpetrators (with the obvious exception that the victims of rape are female). The bulk of lawbreakers commit their crimes close to home, in their own geographic and demographic areas. For crimes against the person, what the UCR calls "violent" crime, the similarity between criminal and victim is even more striking. Both the perpetrators and the victims of street crime are those people who are in the street, and young men are much more likely to be in streets. Often, those who commit assault and robbery have themselves been victims of these crimes.

Putting together the information on these variables, we get a picture something like this: As children in all social classes grow into their early teens, many get involved in minor offenses. A smaller number, most of whom are boys, will commit more serious property offenses like burglary and auto theft. In the lower class, a small number will also commit violent crimes, including robbery. As they near age 18, most of these kids, especially those in the middle class, will give up crime. In the lower class and the working class, a minority of youths will continue to commit crimes, and an even smaller number of them (especially in the black lower class) will commit violent crimes as well. They will become the "career" criminals who commit a variety of crimes and commit them frequently.

Of course, this is a very general picture, and there are many variations and many exceptions. Even though most youths who get involved in crime soon go relatively straight, enough of them remain in the game to sustain high levels of violence and crime. The next chapters offer a somewhat more detailed account of these crimes.

NOTES

1. Gail Armstrong (1977), "Females Under the Law—'Protected' but Unequal," *Crime and Delinquency*, vol. 23, pp. 109–20. Meda Chesney-Lind (1977), "Judicial Paternalism and the Female Status Offender," *Crime and Delinquency*, vol. 23, pp. 121–30.

2. James Wallerstein and Clement J. Wyle (1947), "Our Law-Abiding Lawbreakers," *National Probation*, March, pp. 107–12.

3. Stephen A. Cernkovich and Peggy C. Giordano (1979), "A Comparative Analysis of Male and Female Delinquency," *The Sociological Quarterly*, vol. 20, no. 1, pp. 131–45.

4. Jeffrey Reiman (1984), *The Rich Get Richer and the Poor Get Prison* (2nd ed.), New York: Wiley.

5. Elizabeth Moulds (1980), "Chivalry and Paternalism: Disparities of Treatment in the Criminal Justice System," in Susan K. Datesman and Frank R. Scarpitti, eds., *Women, Crime, and Justice*, New York: Oxford University Press, pp. 277–99.

6. Walter Reckless and Barbara Kay (1967), *The Female Offender: Report to the U.S. President's Commission on Law Enforcement and the Administration of Justice*, quoted in Datesman and Scarpitti, op. cit, p. 279.

7. Michael J. Hindelang, Travis Hirschi, and Joseph G. Weis (1979), "Correlates of Delinquency: The Illusion of Discrepancy Between Self-Report and Official Measures," *American Sociological Review*, vol. 44, p. 995–1014.

8. Jay R. Williams and Martin Gold (1972), "From Delinquent Behavior to Official Delinquency," *Social Problems*, vol. 20, pp. 209–29.

9. Todd Gitlin (1985), *Inside Prime Time*, New York: Pantheon, p. 49.

10. Bureau of Justice Statistics (1989), *Criminal Victimization in the United States, 1987*, Washington, DC: U.S. Department of Justice, p. 46.

11. Williams and Gold, op. cit.

12. Jerold G. Bachman, Lloyd D. Johnston, and Patrick M. O'Malley (1986), *Monitoring the Future 1986*, Ann Arbor, MI: Institute for Social Research. Reprinted in Katherine M. Jamieson and Timothy J. Flanagan, eds. (1989), *Sourcebook of Criminal Justice Statistics—1988*, U.S. Department of Justice, Bureau of Justice Statistics, Washington, DC: U.S. Government Printing Office, p. 341.

13. Freda Adler (1975), *Sisters in Crime: The Rise of the New Female Criminal*, New York: McGraw-Hill, p. 1.

14. Ibid., pp. 13–14.

15. Rita J. Simon (1975), *Women and Crime*, Lexington, MA: Lexington Books.

16. Leon E. Pettiway (1987), "Participation in Crime Partnerships by Female Drug Users: The Effects of Domestic Arrangements, Drug Use, and Criminal Involvement," *Criminology*, vol. 25, no. 3, pp. 741–66.

17. Martin Gold and David Reimer (1975), "Changing Patterns of Delinquent Behavior Among Americans 13 Through 16 Years Old: 1967–1972," *Crime and Delinquency Literature*, pp. 483–517, cited in Datesman and Scarpitti, op. cit., p. 47.

18. Timothy Flanagan and Maureen McLeod, eds. (1983), *Sourcebook of Criminal Justice Statistics—1982*, U.S. Department of Justice, Bureau of Justice Statistics, Washington, DC: U.S. Government Printing Office. Timothy Flanagan and Katherine Jamieson, eds. (1989), *Sourcebook of Criminal Justice Statistics—1988*, U.S. Department of Justice, Bureau of Justice Statistics, Washington, DC: U.S. Government Printing Office.

19. *The New York Times*, Feb. 15, 1985, p. B2.

20. *The New York Times*, Sept. 29, 1981, p. 18.

21. James Q. Wilson (1975), *Thinking About Crime*, New York: Basic Books, p. 235.

22. R. W. Hodge and D. J. Treiman (1968), "Class Identification in the United States," *American Journal of Sociology*, vol. 73, no. 5.

23. Richard P. Coleman and Lee Rainwater with Kent A. McClelland (1978), *Social Standing in America: New Dimensions of Class*, New York: Basic Books, p. 29.

24. Terence P. Thornberry and R. L. Christenson (1984), "Unemployment and Criminal Involvement: An Investigation of Reciprocal Causal Structure," *American Sociological Review*, vol. 49, pp. 398–411.

25. Paul E. Tracy, Marvin E. Wolfgang, and Robert M. Figlio (1985), *Delinquency in Two Birth Cohorts—Executive Summary*, Washington, DC: U.S. Department of Justice, p. 7.

26. For a review and listing of this literature, see John Braithwaite (1979), *Inequality, Crime, and Public Policy*, London: Routledge and Kegan Paul, pp. 23–63.

27. D. H. Bayley and H. Mendelsohn (1969), *Minorities and the Police*, New York: Free Press.

28. Irving Piliavin and Scott Briar (1964), "Police Encounters With Juveniles," *American Journal of Sociology*, vol. 70, pp. 206–14.

29. Walter B. Miller (1967), "Theft Behavior in City Gangs," in M. W. Klein, ed., *Juvenile Gangs in Contest: Theory, Research, and Action*, Englewood Cliffs, NJ: Prentice-Hall.

30. Charles Tittle, Wayne Villemez, and Douglas Smith (1978), "The Myth of Social Class and Criminality: An Empirical Assessment of the Empirical Evidence," *American Sociological Review*, vol. 43, pp. 643–56.

31. Stephen A. Cernkovich, Peggy C. Giordano, and Meredith Pugh (1983), "Chronic Offenders: The Missing Cases in Self-Report Delinquency Research," paper presented at the American Society of Criminology.

32. Delbert S. Elliott, Franklyn W. Dunford, and David Huizinga (1983), "The Identification and Prediction of Career Offenders Utilizing Self-Reported and Official Data," Boulder, CO; unpublished manuscript. Delbert Elliott and David Huizinga (1983), "Social Class and Delinquent Behavior in a National Youth Panel," *Criminology*, vol. 21, pp. 149–47.

33. Cernkovich et al., op. cit.

34. Delbert S. Elliott and Suzanne S. Ageton (1980), "Reconciling Race and Class Differences in Self-Reported and Official Estimates of Delinquency," *American Sociological Review*, vol. 45, no. 1, pp. 95–110.

35. Charles R. Tittle and Robert F. Meier (1990), "Specifying the SES/Delinquency Relationship," *Criminology*, vol. 28, no. 2, pp. 271–99.

36. Donald Clelland and Timothy J. Carter (1980), "The New Myth of Class and Crime," *Criminology*, vol. 18, pp. 319–36.

37. Ken Auletta (1981), "A Reporter at Large: The Underclass," *The New Yorker*, Nov. 16, p. 95.

38. David Brownfield (1986), "Social Class and Violent Behavior," *Criminology*, vol. 24, no. 3, pp. 421–38.

39. Delbert S. Elliott, David Huizinga, and Suzanne S. Ageton, *Explaining Delinquency and Drug Use*, Beverly Hills, CA: Sage, pp. 88–89.

40. Braithwaite, op. cit., p. 51. Brownfield, op. cit., pp. 434–35.

41. Paul A. Strasburg (1978), *Violent Delinquents: A Report to the Ford Foundation from the Vera Institute of Justice*, New York: Monarch. Also Travis Hirschi, "Crime and the Family," in James Q. Wilson, ed. (1983), *Crime and Public Policy*, pp. 53–68. Joseph G. Weis, op. cit., pp. 89–90.

42. Rodney Stark (1979), "Whose Status Counts?," *American Sociological Review*, vol. 44, pp. 668–69.

43. Gary F. Jensen (1976), "Race, Achievement, and Delinquency," *American Journal of Sociology*, vol. 82, pp. 379–87.

44. Joseph G. Weis (1987), "Social Class and Crime," in Michael R. Gottfredson and Travis Hirschi, eds. (1987), *Positive Criminology*, Newbury Park, CA: pp. 71–90.

45. Charles Silberman (1978), *Criminal Justice, Criminal Violence*, New York: Random House, pp. 117–18.

46. James Q. Wilson and Richard J. Herrnstein (1985), *Crime and Human Nature*, New York: Simon and Schuster, p. 468.

47. Travis Hirschi and Michael J. Hindelang (1977), "Intelligence and Delinquency: A Revisionist Review," *American Journal of Sociology*, vol. 42, pp. 571–87. Wilson and Herrnstein, op. cit.

48. Ibid., pp. 459–86.

49. Dane Archer and Rosemary Gartner (1984), *Violence and Crime in Cross-National Perspective*, New Haven, CT: Yale University Press.

50. Herbert Gutman (1977), "As for the '02 Kosher Food Rioters . . . ," *The New York Times*, July 21, p. A23.

51. Ibid.

52. Wilson and Herrnstein, op. cit., p. 459.

53. S. Shoham (1966), *Crime and Social Deviation*, Chicago: Henry Regery, cited in Wilson and Herrnstein, loc. cit.

54. Andrew Hacker (1983), *U/S: A Statistical Portrait of the American People*, New York: Penguin Books.

55. U.S. Department of Justice, Bureau of Justice Statistics (1989), *Criminal Victimization in the United States, 1988*.

56. Michael J. Hindelang (1978), "Race and Involvement in Common Law Personal Crimes," *American Journal of Sociology*, vol. 43, pp. 93–109. Delbert S. Elliott and Suzanne S. Ageton (1980), "Reconciling Race and Class Differences in Self-Reported and Official Estimates of Delinquency," *American Journal of Sociology*, vol. 45, pp. 95–110.

57. Cernkovich and Giordano, op. cit.

58. See Reiman, op. cit., p. 79.

59. Marvin E. Wolfgang and Franco Ferracuti (1967), *The Subculture of Violence: Towards an Integrated Theory in Criminology*, Beverly Hills, CA: Sage.

60. Hacker, op. cit, p. 94.

61. John H. Laub and Robert J. Sampson (1988), "Unraveling Families and Delinquency: A Reanalysis of the Glueck's Data," *Criminology*, vol. 26, no. 3, p. 355–80.

62. Wilson and Herrnstein, op. cit., p. 261.

63. Laub and Sampson, op. cit.

64. Wilson and Herrnstein, op. cit, p. 479.

65. Jeffery Fagan and Sandra Wexler (1987), "Family Origins of Violent Delinquents," *Criminology*, vol. 25, no. 3, pp. 643–69.

66. Robert J. Sampson (1986), "Crime in Cities: The Effects of Formal and Informal Social Control," in Albert J. Reiss, Jr. and Michael Tonry, eds. (1986), *Communities and Crime*, a special issue of *Crime and Justice, an Annual Review*, vol. 8, pp. 271–311.

67. Robert J. Sampson (1984), "Urban Black Violence: The Effect of Male Joblessness and Family Disruption,"*American Journal of Sociology*, vol. 93, no. 2, pp. 348–82. Mercer Sullivan (1983), "Youth Crime: New York's Two Varieties," *New York Affairs*, vol. 8, pp. 31–48. Also see David Greenberg (1977), "Delinquency and the Age Structure of Society," *Contemporary Crises*, pp. 189–223, which makes a similar argument.

68. William Julius Wilson (1987), *The Truly Disadvantaged*, Chicago: University of Chicago Press.

69. Elliot Liebow (1967), *Tally's Corner*, Boston: Little, Brown.

70. Silberman, op. cit., pp. 117–65.

71. Ibid., p. 129.

72. Ibid., p. 133.

73. Silberman, op. cit., p. 157. Nicholas Lemann (1986), "The Origins of the Underclass," *The Atlantic Monthly*, June, pp. 31–55; July, pp. 54–68.

74. The National Advisory Commission on Civil Disorders (1968), *Report of the National Advisory Commission on Civil Disorders (The Kerner Commission Report)*, New York: Bantam, p. 1.

75. Michael J. Hindelang (1981), "Variations in Sex-Race-Age–Specific Incidence Rates of Offending," *American Sociological Review*, vol. 46, pp. 461–74. Robert M. O'Brien (1985), *Crime and Victimization Data*, Beverly Hills, CA: Sage, pp. 92–96.

76. Travis Hirschi and Michael R. Gottfredson (1983), "Age and the Explanation of Crime," *American Journal of Sociology*, vol. 89, pp. 552–84.

77. Tracy, Wolfgang, and Figlio, op. cit., p. 7.

78. James Q. Wilson (1975), *Thinking About Crime*, p. 5.

79. Charles Murray (1981), *Losing Ground: American Social Policy, 1950–1980*, New York: Basic Books, pp. 166–72.

80. Archer and Gartner, op. cit.

81. Quoted in Wilson (1975), *Thinking About Crime*, p. 13–14.

82. David Matza (1961), "Sub-Terranean Traditions of Youths," *Annals of the American Academy of Political and Social Science*, vol. 378, p. 116.

83. Richard A. Easterlin (1980), *Birth and Fortune: The Impact of Numbers on Personal Welfare*, New York: Basic Books.

84. Alfred Blumstein, Jacquelme Cohen, and Richard Rosenfeld (1986), "Effects of Demography and Criminality on Crime Rates," paper given at the American Sociological Association.

85. Silberman, op. cit., p. 36.

Violent Crimes, Part I: Heavy Dudes

CHAPTER 5

MURKER

PICK A CRIME, ANY CRIME—A CRIME YOU'D LIKE TO KNOW MORE ABOUT, A CRIME THAT'S interesting or important, or a crime you are afraid of. If you are like most of the people I've asked, the crime that first came to mind was murder.

Certainly murder is more serious than other crimes. It also gets the most publicity in the media. In the realm of fiction, few other crimes are worth bothering with. Television shows rarely depict burglaries or auto thefts, but it is practically impossible to get through a night of prime time without someone getting killed. In movies, burglary and robbery appear, if at all, as material for comedy. Only murder deserves serious treatment.

Media coverage of real crime gives a similar picture. Of all crime stories on TV news, about half are murders. Moreover, when news editors select real murders for TV news, they choose the unusual cases that most resemble the murders of fiction. A really celebrated murder case may give rise not just to news reports but to a book (or even several). Many of these "true stories" of murder probe for deep psychological twists in "the mind of the murderer"; other stories contain a moral about wayward youth or pathological greed or love gone wrong. Or else the accounts create the fear that *nobody* is safe. We see the statistics from the FBI—a murder committed every 25 minutes. We think of the murders on TV, and we wonder: Will we be next?

Yet despite the images in the media and perhaps in our minds, murder, relative to other crimes, is a rare event. It accounts for two-tenths of 1 percent of all crimes on the FBI's Index of serious crime. Even rarer are the kinds of homicide that make for good TV stories. Instead, the more frequent, typical murders are hardly the stuff of high drama. The motives and methods in most homicides are utterly predictable and commonplace. As for fear, murder is one crime it is fairly easy to avoid. If you stay out of arguments with people who have been drinking and have weapons; if, in case you do get into such an argument, you back down before push comes to shove; and if you pursue a career in something other than drug dealing or organized crime; then you will greatly reduce your chances of being murdered.

PRIMARY HOMICIDE

Below are two examples of what criminologists call "primary homicide"— deaths that result from a more or less spontaneous fight between people

MURDER—BODIE, NEVADA, 1880

William Page had been drinking and dancing for several hours at a dance house on King Street. About 2 a.m., he and his dance partner were bumped by Pat Keogh and his partner. Page responded by making a "threatening remark."

Keogh "made some insulting remark and used an opprobrious epithet." Page reached for his gun but was too slow. Keogh outdrew him and shot him through the temple. Page fell to the floor dead.

Source: Roger McGrath (1984), *Gunfighters, Highwaymen and Vigilantes: Violence on the Frontier,* Berkeley, CA: The Regents of the University of California.

MURDER—NEWARK, NEW JERSEY, 1988

Man Held in Shotgun Slaying of Girlfriend

A Newark man allegedly shot and killed his girlfriend in their apartment . . . following a domestic quarrel, police said.

Karimeerz Majek, 42, was arrested as he attempted to flee the apartment. . . . [He] was later charged with homicide and possession of a dangerous weapon.

The victim, Danuta Wolak, 44, was found dead on the bedroom floor with a gunshot wound in the neck and the chest.

Witnesses told police the couple had been arguing when they heard shots.

Source: The Star Ledger (Newark), Feb. 3, 1988, p. 28.

who know each other.* Although primary homicides make much less exciting news than planned murders do, they account for the largest share of murder even during times (such as the late 1980s and early 1990s in the United States) when other kinds of murders are on the rise.

In 1986, of all murders where the circumstances were known,† nearly half stemmed from arguments. Another quarter were committed under the

---

* I am using the term *murder* here in a criminological sense, not a legal one. Laws, though they may vary from one jurisdiction to another, often make fine distinctions among different degrees of murder and manslaughter, distinctions which do not concern us here. My use of the term murder corresponds to the *Uniform Crime Reports* category of "murder and non-negligent homicide." This definition includes most willful killings; it excludes involuntary manslaughter (accidents) and "justifiable homicide."

† Much of this information comes from the *Uniform Crime Reports*—a compilation of police reports on murders and people arrested for murder. For many crimes, these official statistics are questionable (see Chapter 3). But for murder, especially primary homicides, the accuracy of reporting and the high clearance rate (70 to 75 percent) make the data more trustworthy than for most other crimes.

Table 5–1 ▪ Murder 1988 Victim/
Offender Relationship by Race (average
per 100 Murders)

	Race of offender	
Race of victim	White	Black
White	44	6
Black	3	45

Source: UCR, 1988.

Table 5–2 ▪ Murder 1988 Victim/
Offender Relationship by Sex (average per
100 Murders)

	Sex of offender	
Sex of victim	Male	Female
Male	64	11
Female	23	2

Source: UCR, 1988.

influence of alcohol or drugs. The data also show a remarkable similarity between murderers and their victims. For example, 91 percent of all murders involving whites or blacks are *intra*racial (whites killing whites, blacks killing blacks) (see Table 5–1). Also, out of 100 murders, about 87 are committed by men, 64 of these against other men (see Table 5–2).‡ These statistics confirm the picture of murder as something that occurs between people who inhabit the same geographic and social space. The data on victim-offender relationships add to this picture. About 16 percent of murders take place between members of the same family; another 40 percent between friends, neighbors, and acquaintances. Only 13 percent of murders occur between strangers. (In 30 percent of the cases, the police did not know the relationship between murderer and victim.)

The next sections of this chapter will offer three sociological perspectives on murder. The **interactionist** approach analyzes the sequence of events that lead up to the killing. It looks for the necessary elements which turn some incidents of friction into a murder. The **cultural** approach focuses

‡ Tables 5–1 and 5–2 do not include those murders where the race of either the victim or the offender is "unknown" or "other" (about 4 % of all murders) or where the sex of either the victim or the offender is unknown (about 1 % of all cases).

not on individual incidents but on homicide rates. It sees different rates as a function of the culture (values and norms) of different groups. The **structural** approach explains differences in homicide rates as a function of elements of the social structure, particularly economic and social inequality.

The Interactionist Perspective: The Murder Scenario

Why should people kill those they know? The murderers we see on television are usually motivated either by insatiable greed or by a nearly psychotic mental warp. They plan carefully so that their crimes are insoluble without the intervention of a heroically clever cop (or private investigator). In the real world, however, homicides result from motives like anger, and they are rarely planned in advance. They occur as the culmination of an argument or fight. The deadly intent, if there is any, usually develops during the course of the interaction. If the circumstances had changed—if the other person had responded differently, if the onlookers had intervened, if the weapon at hand had been less deadly—the end result would probably not have been fatal. Alcohol, too, can make conflicts more violent and perhaps more deadly. In nearly two-thirds of all murders, either the murderer or the victim or (most frequently) both had been drinking.[1] There is some debate over why alcohol is related to murder and other violent crime. Presumably, though, alcohol reduces inhibitions and makes people less attentive to the long-range consequences of their behavior.

The sequence of escalation usually begins with some point of difference which quickly leads to argument, confrontation, and fight. Often, the victim or witnesses play an important role in the outcome. Usually the sequence begins when one person (A) does or says something that offends or upsets the other (B). Of course, murder is not B's immediate response. Instead, B needs to confirm the meaning of A's action or to give A a chance to stop. If A continues, it is one more step toward the murder. Many murders of children represent an extreme version of this pattern.

> The victim [a 5-week-old boy] . . . started crying early in the morning. The offender, the boy's father, ordered [the boy] to stop crying. [The boy's] crying, however, only heightened in intensity. The . . . persistent crying may have been oriented not toward challenging his father's authority, but toward acquiring food or a change of diapers. Whatever the motive for crying, *the child's father defined it as purposive and offensive.*[2] [emphasis added]

In most cases, this vicious cycle of child abuse stops short of death. Nevertheless, about 4 percent of all murder victims are under 5 years of age, and almost all of them are killed by parents.

Sometimes it is the victim who either starts the fight or plays a crucial part in escalating the conflict. In fact, about one murder in four is "victim precipitated."[3]

> During a lovers' quarrel, the male hit his mistress and threw a can of kerosene at her. She retaliated by throwing the liquid on him and then tossed a lighted match in his direction. He died from the burns.[4]

> A man, his wife, and two neighbors were sitting in the living room drinking wine. The man started calling his wife abusive names. She told him to "shut up." Nevertheless, he continued. Finally, she shouted, "I said shut up. If you don't shut up and stop it, I'm going to kill you and I mean it."[5]

Note that the latter murder took place in front of bystanders—not unusual in primary homicides. One study from a California city (pop. 350,000) found that 70 percent of all homicides occurred in the presence of others. In most of these cases, the "audience" actively encouraged the murderer and sometimes even supplied a weapon. In the other cases, they merely did nothing to stop the offender.[6] There were no murders in this study where bystanders tried to stop the fight. Presumably, bystanders did intervene in some fights, with the result that these incidents did not end in death. So apparently *any* intervention was sufficient to prevent an argument from turning into a murder. This is one more bit of evidence contradicting the idea that murder begins with the murderer's unwavering intent. Even where they announce their intent ("I'm going to kill you and I mean it"), potential murderers may still be deterred by the intervention of other people.[7]

On the other hand, bystanders may push the person toward murder, rather than away from it.

> The offender and his friend were sitting in a booth at a tavern drinking beer. The offender's friend told him that the offender's girlfriend was "playing" with another man at the other end of the bar. The offender looked at them and asked his friend if he thought something was going on. The friend responded, "I wouldn't let that guy fool around with [her] like that if she was mine." The offender agreed, and suggested to his friend that his girlfriend and the [man—the eventual victim] be shot for their actions. His friend said that only the [man] should be shot, not the girlfriend.[8]

This incident illustrates one other general aspect of murder (and assault), especially cases involving lovers and spouses. Although the law would regard this shooting as a crime, the offender felt that he was acting not just out of personal anger, but out of a sense of general principle. Like the woman who retaliated against her husband's verbal abuse, this man was seeking to control actions which he thought were wrong. These murders—and they are typical—occur as the last step in a sequence of attempts to control the actions of another person, to make that person behave properly. The prospective murderer interprets the other's action as a devastating and unjustified attack on the self. The murderer's response, therefore, is one of humiliation which is then transformed into rage coupled with a sense of righteousness. The murderer feels that in order to restore the self, to right the wrongs inflicted, he or she must do something. Sometimes the enraged person sees a way out or chooses some inanimate object (like the furniture) as the target of rage. But in other cases, the murderer takes action against the source of humiliation to remove that person forever, to "blow him away."[9] The offenders feel that their act is justified or even necessary—that they are enforcing some right, redressing some grievance. As one legal scholar puts it, "Most intentional homicide in modern society may be classified as social control, specifically as self-help, even if it is handled by legal officials as crime."[10] In the words of criminologist Jack Katz, the murder is an act of "righteous slaughter."[11]

The Cultural Perspective: Attitudes and Actions

It is important to note that these ideas about right and wrong are not merely individual. In the barroom incident, both the offender and his friend believed that they were acting on general principles that most other people would recognize. These widely shared ideas about proper behavior are part of a society's *culture*. Since even murderers base their behavior on these shared ideas, some sociologists have theorized that culture deserves a central place in explaining murder. Some groups have values (ideas about what is right and good) and norms (rules for everyday interaction) which promote violence. Cultural theories see murder as the outcome of attitudes toward violence—attitudes that are shared among the members of some social group that is more tolerant of violence and more likely to see violence as a legitimate, though perhaps unfortunate, response in certain situations. Certainly in the above incident, the murderer and his friend felt that the circumstances justified and even required violence. But cultural theories go beyond individual incidents. They also explain something most of us know or at least suspect: Some social groups have higher murder *rates*.

The United States has the highest murder rate of any industrialized country. Some Third World countries have higher rates—the murder rate in Mexico, for example, is several times that of the United States—but most industrialized countries have rates well below 3 per 100,000 people. For the last 30 years the U.S. murder rate usually has been more than twice that figure, ranging between 5 and 10 per 100,000. The murder rate in the United States in this century has rarely, perhaps never, been as low as 3 per 100,000.[12] For those people most at risk—young men—the differences between the United States and other countries are even greater. Homicide rates for men age 15 to 24 in most European countries are generally between 1 per 100,000 and 2 per 100,000. Canada's rate is about 3 per 100,000;

Japan's is 0.5. In the United States the rate is 21.9 per 100,000—about 15 times higher than European rates.[13]

According to cultural theories, these differences persist because in the United States, compared with other industrialized countries, typical attitudes are more tolerant of aggression and violence, including deadly violence. Americans socialize their children into these ways of thinking and acting. "American society," to quote one typical statement, "makes relatively little collective effort to discourage physical aggression among young males."[14] The images in the media reflect the same set of attitudes. In legitimate movie theaters and on network television, violence, but not sex, may be shown in graphic detail and great quantity. In the summer that I am writing this, a district attorney in Florida brought criminal obscenity charges against a rap group (2 Live Crew) because of the sexual content of their songs; in Alabama, the government took similar action against a store that sold 2 Live Crew records.* Another DA in Ohio brought similar charges against a museum which exhibited—in a special section open only to adults—some photos with a homosexual theme (only one showed actual sexual contact) and a few others which showed "partially nude" children. At the same time, the movies bringing in big box-office receipts—with no interference from the government—include *Die Hard II* (264 deaths, including one in which Bruce Willis stabs an icicle through a man's eye socket and into the brain), *Robocop 2* (81 deaths), *Another 48 Hours* (20 deaths), and *Total Recall* (74 deaths, including one by falling which leaves the hero, Arnold Schwarzenegger, holding the victim's severed arms).[15] Cultural theorists take this sort of thing as evidence about American attitudes toward violence. Where attitudes are more accepting of violence, the logic goes, violence will be more frequent and more serious. The tolerance for violence also underlies the American reluctance to limit the manufacture, importation, ownership, or sale of guns. Thus violence, when it does erupt, is more likely to have fatal consequences.

The theory can be used to explain not only the difference between U.S. murder rates and those of other industrialized countries, but differences among various geographic and social sectors of American society. In fact, the best known cultural theory attributed such differences to the existence of a "subculture of violence" within the larger U.S. society.[16] One variation of this idea (known as the "Gastil-Hackney" thesis, after two of its proponents) begins with the observation that U.S. murder rates are higher than those of other industrialized countries and that within the United States, murder rates have always been highest in the South. It follows then that

---

* I suspect that it is probably not so much the sexuality of the lyrics which roused the DAs to action but rather the attitude about sex that they reflect.

high homicide rates in the United States today are related primarily to the persistence of Southern cultural traditions developed before the Civil War and subsequently spreading over much of the country.[17]

During the last two decades, as more Northerners have migrated to the South and regional differences of all kinds have generally decreased, the murder gap between the South and other regions has narrowed.

Figure 5–1 again raises the issue of guns, for the regions with the highest rates of gun ownership, the South and the West, also have the highest rates of murder. But cultural theorists see gun ownership more as a symptom of the underlying attitude toward deadly violence than as a cause of high murder rates. Even if every gun murder were removed from the statistics, the U.S. murder rate would still be double that of most European countries. In the same way, Southern murder rates (and gun ownership) are higher because of Southern culture and its attitudes toward guns and violence (see box, p. 157).[18] Similar arguments can be made about the social class and racial difference in homicide rates. According to the subculture of violence theory, the ideas and attitudes that promote violence are more prevalent in the urban lower class, especially among blacks.

The major criticism of the theory of the subculture of violence is empirical. To find out whether groups with higher rates of murder really have different

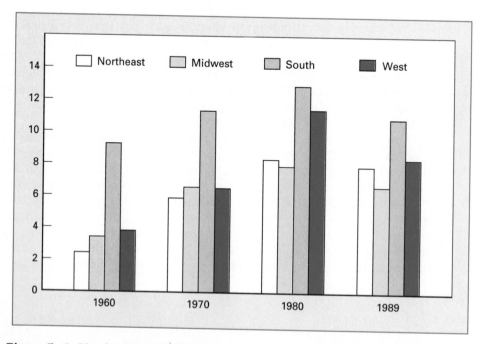

Figure 5–1 Murder Rates by Region
Source: UCR, 1960, 1970, 1980, 1989.

DO SOUTHERN TRADITIONS INCLUDE A "SUBCULTURE OF VIOLENCE"?

The fierce 'rough-and-tumble' fighting in the Southern backcountry that began at least as early as the mid-eighteenth century and flourished through the antebellum period offers a particularly disturbing example. . . . In 1774, Philip Fithian, the tutor at Robert Carter III's grand household in Tidewater Virginia, wrote in his journal:

The cause of the battles I have not yet known; I suppose either that they are lovers, and one has in jest or reality some way supplanted the other; or has in a merry called him a *Lubber*, or a *thick-skull*, or a *buckskin*, or a *Scotsman*, or

perhaps one has mislaid the other's hat, or knocked a peach out of his hand, or offered a dram without wiping the mouth of the bottle; all these, and ten thousand more quite as trifling and ridiculous, are thought and accepted as just causes of immediate quarrels, in which every diabolical stratagem for mastery is allowed and practiced, of bruising, kicking, scratching, pinching, biting, butting, tripping, throttling, gouging, cursing, dismembering, howling, etc.

Source: John F. Kesson (1990), *Rudeness and Civility: Manners in Nineteenth-Century Urban America,* New York: Hill and Wang, pp. 142-43.

values and norms, we must measure these norms separately (so as not to make the mistake of using murder rates as evidence of such norms). Usually, sociologists measure norms and values by asking people to respond to multiple-choice questionnaire items. For example, in surveys asking people to rate the severity of various crimes, Southerners give lower severity scores to homicide and rape than do people from other sections of the country. Poorer, less educated, and black Southerners are especially likely to rank these crimes as less severe than their Northern or Midwestern or Western counterparts.[19] All this supports the subculture of violence theory. However, there is little evidence showing that Southerners or blacks or lower-class people are actually pro-violence in their attitudes and ideas. Furthermore, measuring attitudes is difficult, and frequently people's behavior does not match their stated attitudes. And most studies show that there is *no* group of people that actually supports violence. More interesting, these questionnaire studies also find very little difference in attitudes between men who have committed violent crimes and those who have not.[20]

The Structuralist Perspective: Murder and Inequality

The "structuralist" approach seeks to explain the same data as do cultural theories—differences in murder rates within different sectors of the society. But instead of placing primary emphasis on the shared ideas, it tries to link murder rates to elements of the social structure—economic and racial inequality, poverty, and population crowding. From the structuralist point of view, murder rates are higher in the South not because the South has its own violence-prone culture, but because Southern states have high levels of poverty and inequality.

Structuralist theories have one advantage over the cultural theories: Structural variables are much easier to measure than are attitudes and values. Critics can justifiably question whether a person's responses to questionnaire choices really reflect a complex set of ideas in that person's mind. There is far less disagreement on measurements that indicate poverty—variables like low income, low education, substandard housing, and high rates of infant mortality. And all these items correlate strongly with murder rates. In the United States, states and cities with higher levels of poverty also have higher levels of murder—regardless of geographic location.[21]

Some structural theories question whether poverty is the crucial factor in homicide rates. After all, some of the poorer industrialized countries in the world (e.g., Ireland) have very low murder rates. Instead, what matters is economic standing relative to other people—not poverty but inequality. Some research has shown that in cities where the income gap between the poor and the rich is greater, rates of murder are higher.[22]

Though some critics have questioned the data, let us assume for the moment that the structural idea is valid—i.e., that murder rates are higher where there is either more poverty or less equality or both. We must still ask why poorer or less equal people are more murderous. In the chapter on historical trends in crime (Chapter 3), I outlined one explanation: Industrialization has a moderating effect on recklessness and violence; it imposes a more orderly way of living. Those who are left out of the industrial sector—e.g., today's urban "underclass"—are unaffected by this process and retain higher levels of violence.[23]

A second approach resembles Robert Merton's theory of **anomie**.* This explanation assumes first that much inequality is structural rather than individual; that is, that people find themselves at the bottom of the social ladder not because of their individual talents but because of the narrower opportunities open to them. Second, in a country based on the ideal of equality for all, those who are victims of structurally based inequality will react with frustration and anger. Since race is even less changeable than the conditions one is born into, these feelings will be especially acute where the inequality is based on race. Thus, the greater black-white economic differences, the greater the difference in murder rates between the races.[24]

There is another way of linking poverty or inequality with murder. Recall that murderers are often responding to what they perceive as an insult. They feel that the other person has violated some socially recognized

---

* See Chapter 11 for a fuller discussion of this idea.

"right."* The argument may start over some trivial matter, but the minor affront becomes a matter of "honor"—a threat to the person's entire identity. But how do we maintain a sense of identity or self-worth? Middle-class people may have careers, jobs, families, and houses to give them a sense that they are "somebody." Among the poor, however, many people do not have a job, while others may have a job so menial it cannot serve as a source of respect, and so poorly paid it does not allow a person to support a family. Poor people, therefore, may have to stake their identities entirely on their performance in interpersonal relationships. A man's self, his "honor," may be all that he has. An insult or a challenge, therefore, can loom as a much more serious threat. And when other people are around to remind the man of the challenge to his honor, the outcome can be deadly.[25]

"Guns Don't Kill People"—Or Do They?

Most fights, of course, do not end in death. What then distinguishes the merely injurious fight from the fatal one? One obvious factor is the presence of a weapon. The deadlier the weapon, the more likely the fight will result in death. The difference between a knife and a gun may be the difference between aggravated assault and murder.

Not everyone agrees that weapons are important. You may have seen bumper stickers that say, "Guns don't kill people, people kill people." Even some criminologists maintain that "if a firearm were not immediately present . . . the offender would select some other weapon to achieve the same destructive goal."[26] The evidence, though open to different interpretations, provides little support for this view. Instead, it points to the importance of guns.

To begin with, the UCR provides data on the type of weapon used in homicides, as shown in Table 5–3.

Table 5–3 ▪ Murder: Type of Weapon Used

Guns	62%
Knives, etc.	18
Personal weapons (fists, feet, etc.)	6
Unknown	14

Source: UCR, 1989.

---

* Some social scientists see important sex differences on this matter: In personal relationships men tend to think in terms of their "rights" while women think in terms of their responsibilities. Men, therefore, are more likely to kill (or get killed) defending their rights. See Carol Gilligan (1982), *In a Different Voice: Psychological Theory and Women's Development*, Cambridge, MA: Harvard University Press.

Obviously, guns—three-quarters of them handguns—account for the largest number of murders. One possible conclusion you might draw from this table is that "people kill people"; that is, when people want to kill someone, they go out and get a gun. The intention comes first and determines the choice of weapons. This interpretation evokes a picture of a person bent on murder, selecting the most efficient weapon—a gun. If he can't get a gun, he settles for a knife. This picture may fit a few murders, but for most homicides, there is a more probable interpretation: The presence of a gun can transform an assault into a homicide. It is the weapon, not the intent, that makes the difference.

This lack of deadly intent is often clear from the scenarios of individual homicides. It also is reflected in the demographic data on murder and other violent crimes. The social and geographic location of robbery differs from that of murder. (In robbery, victims and criminals are usually strangers, and rates are highest in the cities of the Northeast, lowest in the South.) Patterns of murder do, however, closely follow those of aggravated assault. Where murder rates are high, rates of aggravated assault also are high, for to a great extent, they are the same crime. The typical murder is an aggravated assault—one that becomes a bit too aggravated.

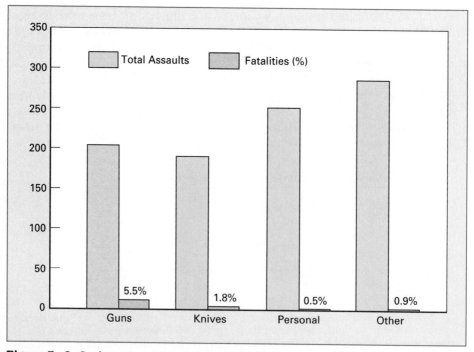

Figure 5–2 Serious Assaults and Fatalities by Weapon, 1988
Source: UCR, 1989.

Both murder and aggravated assault begin as an attack arising from some interpersonal dispute. What determines whether that attack will become an aggravated assault or a murder? Figure 5–2 shows the importance of the choice of weapons. (Note: the graph does not include "simple assault"; it includes only attacks which result in serious injury or death.)

Nearly 6 percent of attacks with guns ended in death. We can probably discount the data on serious attacks with personal weapons—i.e., fists and feet—where 0.5 percent ended in death. In most cases, the assailant probably realized the difference between an armed assault and an assault with a weapon. But gun attacks were three times deadlier than knife attacks (1.8 percent).* There may also be important differences not just between guns and other weapons but also between deadly guns and less deadly guns. Many law enforcement officials think that the increase in murder in the late 1980s was at least in part attributable to the change in weapons. In terms of range, accuracy, and the seriousness of the wounds it creates, a .357 Magnum is much deadlier than a "Saturday night special" (a cheap .22 caliber handgun), and an Uzi is much deadlier than a shotgun. The statistical impact of these newer additions to America's home arsenals is probably not so much on primary homicides but on other types of killing.

FELONY MURDERS

Most murders fall into the category of "primary homicide." In the United States, primary homicides make up over four-fifths of all murders. In other industrialized societies the percentage is even higher. The remaining 20 percent of homicides are "felony murders." Though far fewer in number, these felony murders are the kinds of crimes more likely to receive attention in the media: murders occurring in the course of another felony such as robbery or rape; mass murders and serial murders; murders between rival gangs; and planned murders meant to accomplish some rational goal (the "gangland rub-out" is a classic example). When murder rates increased dramatically in the 1960s (along with rates of other crimes), the proportion of felony murders also increased. Consequently, the clearance rate for murder dropped. In 1960, when most murders were primary homicides, police cleared 92.3 percent of all murders. By the mid-1970s, that rate had dropped to 79 percent. The proportion of felony homicides remained stable for nearly

---

* These figures overstate the deadliness of non-gun attacks. Unarmed attacks or knife attacks are less likely to be reported to the police. These unreported crimes make the denominator of the fraction artificially low and therefore make the value of the fraction artificially high. Other studies, even those based on police statistics, have estimated that compared with knife attacks, gun attacks were five times more likely to result in death.

a decade but rose again in the late 1980s, and the clearance rate fell to 70 percent.[27]

Robbery Murder

The most frequent form of felony murder happens during a robbery, where the robber kills the victim. Of every 1,000 robberies in the United States, between 3 and 4 end in death.* In a very few of these cases, the robbers begin the crime with the full intent of murdering the victim. The robber who robs a drug dealer of cash and inventory may think (often correctly) that unless he kills the victim, the victim will later kill him.

> Two men sat in the back seat of a car with a drug dealer and shot him and his girlfriend to death, subsequently taking money and drugs from them. One of the offenders had owed money to the male victim, and the latter, on a round of collections earlier that evening, had threatened the offender if he did not pay.[28]

Most of the time, however, as in primary homicides, the criminals do not begin the robbery with the intention of killing the victim. And the factors that turn a robbery into a felony murder are the same factors that turn an argument into a primary homicide: the deadliness of the weapons, the presence of other people, and the sequence of interaction between murderer and victim.

If robbers do not intend to kill their victims, why do they still carry guns—especially since many states now have harsher penalties for crimes committed with guns? One obvious reason is that a gun is a great "equalizer." The robber who goes after a big "score" that is likely to be well defended needs a weapon that will overcome the resistance. In smaller robberies as well, robbers use weapons for control, because in a robbery, the criminals must control the actions of the victims. Usually, the mere threat of force is sufficient for this purpose, and the deadlier the weapon, the more effective the threat. However, if the victims do not cooperate, then the robbers may use actual force. In non-gun robberies victims are more likely to resist, and therefore are more likely to be injured. (Even in gun robberies, the gun is more frequently used to strike than to shoot.) But if the victim does resist and the robber has a gun, then the injury will be more severe, perhaps even fatal.

> The victim, a 24-year-old man, and his woman friend were walking down the street. Two men grabbed both of them, knocking the woman down and snatching

---

* I have based this estimate on UCR data—robberies reported to the police. If unreported robberies were included, the proportion of murders would be closer to 2 per 1,000 robberies.

her purse. The victim broke away from one man and ran toward the other, who shot him in the chest.

While a holdup was in progress in a private home, a man came to the door. One of the holdup men pulled the door open all the way and told the man to 'freeze.' The man ran and was shot in the back of the head.[29]

Even cooperative robbery victims may be murdered. In over half of all robbery murders, victims do not resist; in some cases, they may even be tied up or otherwise immobilized before being shot.[30] However, even in these cases, the robbers often do not start with the intent to kill their victims. Instead, they make that decision some time during the course of the robbery. Here again, guns may make the difference between life and death since a gunshot can be deadlier than a stab wound. Moreover, the impulsive decision to kill a victim may depend on the psychological and technical ease of doing so. And it is far easier to shoot someone from a safe distance than it is to kill with weapons that require actual contact with the victim.[31]

As in primary homicides, other people involved in the robbery can play a crucial role—especially with younger, more opportunistic criminals. The highly professional minority of robbers carry guns solely for "instrumental" purposes—as a means toward their goal of accomplishing the robbery. They prefer not to shoot and will do so only if it is necessary.[32] Even some career robbers who brutalize or kill helpless victims may have a rational motive nevertheless. For one thing, there is little honor, and in fact much danger, among thieves. "A reputation for violence, perhaps sustained by 'irrational' brutality against the robbery victim, could be valuable for offenders who are interested in not becoming their colleagues' secondary victims."[33]

Most robbers, however, seem to have more complicated motives, both instrumental and "expressive." They want the money, though the amounts involved are often small. But they also seem to be seeking some psychological gain. Some robbers mention the sense of power and vengeance they feel during their crimes. The robber may also want to appear "tough" in the eyes of his fellow robbers, not afraid to use his gun. "Group members often say, 'Go ahead, shoot' to another member who has the weapon."[34] The larger the group of robbers, therefore, the more likely it is that violence will occur.[35] And when the robbers have guns, especially very powerful guns, the violence is more likely to end in death.

In Cold Blood: Planned Murder

Some murders, including some which also involve robbery, are instrumental—performed with the express purpose of killing the victim. Often both victim and murderer are part of the criminal underworld. Drug dealers are especially vulnerable to robbery murder. Because they may be carrying large amounts of cash or drugs, dealers make attractive targets for robbery. And as I mentioned previously, robbers may be tempted to kill in these robberies since the drug dealer, if allowed to live, might soon take revenge on the robbers.[36]

Sometimes the murders occur in disputes between rival criminal organizations. These assassinations and executions increase when organized crime becomes somewhat *disorganized*. Disputes over territory or over control of new forms of crime may make for a series of murders. During Prohibition in the 1920s, murder rates increased, in part because of competition in a new criminal enterprise—illegal liquor. Similarly in the late 1980s, the new commerce in cocaine and crack gave rise to increases in murder in cities where rival drug-dealing organizations competed for shares of the market. (Still, the murder rate in Miami during this period, though one of the highest in the country, was only one-third of what it had been in the 1920s, another period when Miami was a wide-open town.[37]) Recently in Los Angeles, two large gang-like groups (the Crips and the Bloods) have been struggling for control of the drug market within the black population. This economic motive has heightened traditional gang rivalry, which, combined with the availability of Uzis and other semiautomatic military assault rifles and the participation of younger (and therefore less prudent) gang members, has resulted in a large number of "drive-by" killings, including some where non-gang members have also been killed.

Other "gangland" murders are intended as a way to punish a person within the organization and to deter others. These organizations may have their own members do the killing or they may hire independent contractors—"hit men"—to do the job. These killers are usually no strangers to violence.

> As young as I was (about 16 or 17) and with sellin' drugs like I was . . . I went on a couple of things with [my older partners]. . . . After they dug the nerve that I had . . . they took an' offered me a couple jobs. I had been known to shoot already.[38]

Like soldiers, hit men learn to distance themselves psychologically from the people they kill.

Mass Murder

One final category of murder—mass murder—deserves mention here, not necessarily because it happens frequently, but because when it occurs or is discovered, it receives so much attention in the press. Mass murderers are those who kill several victims, either all at once or over a period of months or even years. Some mass murders resemble the felony murder. They occur in connection with some other crime and have some instrumental motive.

Wars between criminal gangs may lead to mass murder, as in the St. Valentine's Day massacre of 1929. Other criminals commit multiple killings as a way to escape prosecution for other crimes. They kill witnesses or accomplices who might testify against them.[39]

Still, the most frequent type of mass murder is not the gangland war or the work of a psychotic gunman. It is the family killing, where one member of a family kills several of his* relatives.[40] Often, these killings are exaggerated responses to the emotions and pressures that can occur in families. The teenage child who feels wronged takes revenge against his parents and perhaps everyone else in the house. The rejected husband, angry with his wife over the divorce, returns to kill her and her children.† In other cases, the dominant emotion seems to be not anger but hopelessness. A father who has suffered some setback assumes that his wife and children will share his despair; in order to spare them the pain of his humiliation, he kills them in what one psychiatrist has called "suicide by proxy."[41] In the end, he also may kill himself. A 1985 Iowa case, which achieved national headlines, combined elements of both revenge and suicide by proxy. A farmer whose farm was falling into bankruptcy and foreclosure took a shotgun and killed his banker, his wife, his neighbor, and himself.[42]

Finally, there are the multiple murders of strangers. Unlike the crime-related killings or family slayings, these murders involve victims chosen almost at random; they happened to be in the wrong place at the wrong time. In some cases, the murders occur all at the same time. For example, in 1984, James Huberty, despondent over losing yet another job, armed himself with a rifle, a shotgun, and a pistol, walked into a San Diego McDonald's and opened fire. He killed 21 people and wounded 19. In a somewhat similar example in 1966 at the University of Texas, Charles Whitman, an ex-Marine and A-student, turned his anger and despair into deadly violence at specific others and at people in general. One night, he killed his wife and his mother. The next day, he went to the campus, climbed a water tower and opened fire on the people below, killing 14 and wounding 30 more.[43]

Mass murderers like Huberty and Whitman do not repeat their crimes. Either they kill themselves or are killed or captured by the police. However, there is another type of murderer—the "serial murderer"—who kills one or

---

* Nearly all mass murderers are male. Of the 42 mass murderers Levin and Fox discovered in their research, only one was female: a woman who burned down her house with her children inside.

† In the Greek tragedy of Medea, it is the wife who kills the children as a way of gaining vengeance against the husband who has left her for another woman. Later poets have also warned of "the fury of a woman scorned." Such a view of the battle of the sexes does not square with statistical realities. Rejected males are far more murderous than their female counterparts. The misperception by Euripedes and the other poets is not hard to explain: They were not criminologists, and they were men.

two victims at a time but repeats the crime several times over a period of months or even years. Often, there is an obvious element of sexual sadism involved. The killers derive sexual excitement and release by torturing and killing their victims. Serial murder seems to feed on itself. Each murder that the killer gets away with makes the next one that much easier to do. The murderer will have fewer doubts and fears of getting caught. In the case of sadistic murderers, their crimes seem to grow more and more vicious, as though they needed increasingly cruel scenarios for their sexual pleasure.[44]

Serial murderers often escape detection for a relatively long period of time. Their crimes are difficult for the police to solve because either the murderer, the victim, or both move at the fringes of society. Serial murderers who drift about the country occasionally killing people are especially difficult to identify since the police in any one case will be unable to recognize a pattern. Even the serial killers who stay in one place may be hard to catch. They often choose as victims people who have few stable relationships—skid-row winos, runaway children, prostitutes. Not many people will be able to trace the victim's whereabouts just before he or she disappeared. Moreover, since serial killers select strangers as victims, the people the police usually question—relatives, friends, underworld competitors—seldom produce any leads.

Popular analyses of murders—the kind that appear in best-selling books or on TV—tend to focus on the individual crime and the way in which the police finally solved the case. The killers in these stories are of the type that is fairly rare—the middle-class family murderer or the mass murderer. The explanation for murder in these cases usually focuses on the tangled psychology of the killer's mind. A classic example of this genre is *Helter Skelter*, an account of the crimes, capture, and trial of the Charles Manson "family."

As fascinating as these accounts may be, they seldom help us to arrive at any general statements about murder or even about mass murder, except perhaps that these murderers rarely conform to our image of mass murderers as looking like some sort of fiend. In their appearance and in their manner, they are usually indistinguishable from other people. Besides, even if we could find traits common among mass murderers, this information would have very little predictive value. Whatever those traits are (e.g., male, between ages 20 and 40, troubled childhood, etc.), for every killer they described, there would be millions of non-killers to which the same descriptions could apply.

Psychological concepts are even less useful in explaining the primary homicides that make up the bulk of murder statistics. People who commit murder are not easily distinguishable from those who commit other street crimes. If anything, murderers are less "criminal" than burglars or robbers. That is, they are less involved in other crimes, and when released they are less likely than other criminals to be returned to prison on a new conviction. The recidivism rate among homicide offenders is about 22 percent, while for those of convicted of robbery it is 35 percent, and for burglary offenders 43 percent. And when homicide offenders are returned to prison, it is usually *not* for a violent crime; instead they are returned for theft, or drug possession, or parole violations.[45]

Summing Up

Not all murders are alike. In this section, I have tried to describe a few types of murder. The most frequent, accounting for up to four-fifths of all murders in the United States, is the primary homicide—a killing which evolves out of an argument. Most other homicides are classified as felony murders. These include rape murders and robbery murders, planned "hits" by criminal organizations, and mass murders.

Individual murderers—especially the rarer types like mass murderers—can make for fascinating psychological studies. However, for purposes of prediction, there is no way to distinguish precisely between murderers and non-murderers. Instead, criminologists usually ask questions not about murderers but about murder rates. Why does the United States have such a high murder rate compared with other industrialized nations? Why does the South have a higher murder rate than other sections of the country have? Why do men, blacks, and poor people kill at higher rates than women, whites, and non-poor people?

Sociological approaches to murder fall roughly into three types: interactionist, cultural, and structural. Interactionist ideas stress the scenario of murder, particularly the ways in which the participants interpret each other's actions—interpretations that turn an ordinary dispute into a matter of life and death. These explanations focus on the sequence of interaction leading to murder. They look at contributing factors like the availability of deadly weapons, the influence of alcohol, the behavior of the victim, and the intervention of bystanders.

Cultural theories, notably the "subculture of violence" theory, explain murder as an exaggerated version of culturally approved behavior. In cultures which tolerate and even demand violence in certain situations, violence will be more frequent and more deadly.

Structural theories see violence, especially murder, as a product of social and economic inequality. In a society whose ideology stresses equality but whose social structure creates great inequality, the underprivileged will feel a kind of diffuse hostility. They might more rationally direct this anger into some sort of collective effort to change or overthrow the system, but they lack the resources and organization for such action. Instead, their hostility takes the form of occasional angry outbursts at the nearest available source of frustration.

What, If Anything, Is to Be Done?

It is hard to imagine how any of these theories might lead to policies that would lower homicide rates. Certainly the government cannot legislate sub-cultural norms out of existence, nor can it change the ways in which people interact. As for the material factors involved (i.e., liquor, weapons), govern-ments have tried to control them. But restrictions on alcohol and guns, besides being controversial political issues, have not had overwhelming suc-cess in reducing murder. Governmental policy can, theoretically, change the economic structure. Changes in taxation and government spending could greatly reduce economic inequality and even possibly bring the urban underclass more into the mainstream of economic life. Politically, however, such change is extremely unlikely. In fact, during the 1980s, governmental economic policies (of one of the most popular administrations in U.S. his-tory) actually increased the gap between rich and poor.

You may have noticed that in all this discussion of murder I have said nothing about the effects of the police or courts—and for good reason. There is little they can do to affect murder rates. They can only intervene after the fact. Punishment—even capital punishment—has no effect on murder rates.* Furthermore, since most captured murderers never kill again, even after being released, locking them up for longer periods of time will not reduce the overall rate of murder.

ROBBERY

I sometimes ask students the following question: "If you wanted to know how dangerous a country or city or neighborhood was, and you could look at statistics on only one crime, which one would you choose?" Most often, students pick murder, probably because the crime is serious and the sta-tistics on it are the most accurate. Not me. I would choose robbery. Murder is rare, as crimes go, though not as rare as we would like. And since most murder victims know their killers, avoiding murder is not too difficult. Prop-erty crimes like burglary and auto theft occur more frequently, and I am much more likely to be a victim of these crimes than of robbery. But I imag-ine that for victims these crimes are more matters of expense and incon-venience and anger, rather than fear.

Robbery is the crime that most resembles our image of the crime problem

---

* See Chapter 16 for a fuller discussion of the death penalty as a deterrent.

or of "street crime." It is unexpected, sudden, and sometimes terrifying. It is committed mostly by strangers, and unlike murder, it cannot be easily avoided: Robbery victims, unlike murder victims, seldom contribute to the sequence of steps that leads to the crime. Property crime rates may measure a population's dishonesty in ways of getting money. Murder rates can tell us about people's willingness to use violence to settle personal scores. But robbery rates, despite the inaccuracies of statistics, provide a measure of people's willingness to use violence on strangers to get money. And for some reason, I find that most frightening.

Robbery also conforms to our ideas about the social location of crime. European cities may have as much burglary as U.S. cities of similar size. But U.S. cities have far higher rates of robbery. When we consider just the United States, we often think of crime as most prevalent in the cities—especially industrial cities of the North—and in the poorer, inner-city neighborhoods of these cities. The crime that best fits this image is robbery. Cities have higher rates than suburbs; and poor, inner-city neighborhoods have the highest rates of all. With nonviolent property crimes, city-suburb differences are not so great.

The geographic distribution of robbery is also closer to what we would expect. Murder rates are highest in the South, and burglary and larceny rates are highest in the West. The Northeast, however, leads in robbery with a rate nearly 40 percent above that of the nation as a whole. Of the 20 cities with the highest robbery rates, seven are Northern, industrial cities like Newark and Chicago. New York City's robbery rate is nearly 400 percent above the national rate.[46] Even allowing for all the inaccuracies of crime statistics, these differences are impressive.

What Is Robbery?

Robbery means the taking of something from a person by force or the threat of force. This definition includes everything from sixth-graders extorting lunch money from their classmates to the multimillion dollar heist of an armored car. What all robberies share—by definition of the word *robbery*—is that the criminal confronts the victim. That is why the FBI's *Uniform Crime Reports* classifies robbery as a "violent" crime—i.e., a crime against the person—whether or not the criminal actually uses that force.* Without force or threat, it isn't a robbery (see box).

---

* Purse-snatches, in the FBI's categories, are larcenies, not robberies. This classification is not just a ploy to reduce the number of robberies. It follows a certain logic. The purse-snatcher, unlike a robber, does not confront the victim (even though the purse-snatch may involve some force). To the FBI a purse-snatch is a heavy-handed version of pocket-picking.

This item will be especially interesting to those who remember Woody Allen's bank robbery in his film Take the Money and Run.

UNCONVINCING SUSPECT IN HOLDUP ATTEMPT ACQUITTED

By Morris Kaplan

A man who walked into a Brooklyn bank and handed a woman teller a note reading "Give me all the money you have," has been acquitted of attempted holdup charges because he failed to frighten the teller.

Federal Judge Jack B. Weinstein . . . ruled that the use of intimidation was "a crucial element" that the government had to prove to win a conviction. He added . . . that the teller's conduct indicated "a singular lack of fear or intimidation."

The defendant [named Brown] did not dispute the fact that he handed the note to the teller last June 11 in the Manufacturers Hanover Trust Company branch at 1014 Gates Avenue in the Bedford-Stuyvesant section.

The teller, Mrs. Catherine G. Murphy, noting that both Mr. Brown's hands were empty after he had given her the note, responded: "You have got to be kidding."

"No," he replied.

At this point, Mrs. Murphy turned to a teller next to her and said: "Look what I've got," showing the note. She also tripped an alarm, alerting the police and summoned a bank guard.

The defendant stood at the counter, neither speaking nor moving for a while . . . and then walked to a table in the center of the room.

A picture by the bank's automatic cameras showed him relaxed in white shirt and slacks, lounging against a table, "observing the scene with detached amusement.". . .

On the witness stand, Mrs. Murphy was asked by Simon Chrein, a Legal Aid Society lawyer, "Were you afraid my client might do something to you if you didn't give him the money?"

"No, I wasn't," she answered. . .

Source: Copyright © 1970 by *The New York Times Company.* Reprinted by permission.

Types of Robbery, Types of Robber

In 1989, the UCR counted about 500,000 robberies known to the police. The UCR broke these down by categories as shown in Table 5–4. According to these figures, about one-third of these robberies were commercial robberies. The other two-thirds were of individuals, either on the street or at home. (The true percentage of individual robberies is probably higher since many individual robbery victims do not report the crime to the police.)

These different targets of robbery correspond very roughly to a dimension that might be called "professionalism," a dimension based on the size of the payoff and the ease of committing the crime. At one end are the most **professional**—robbers who will overcome all sorts of difficulties if the "score" is large enough. And large scores usually are businesses, not individuals on the street. At the other end are the **opportunists**. In opportunistic robberies, the robber is responding to an apparently easy opportunity that

Table 5–4 ■ Robbery—Percent Distribution, 1989

Street/highway	54.9%
Commercial house	11.8
Gas station	2.8
Convenience store	6.3
Residence	9.8
Bank	1.4
Miscellaneous	12.9

Source: UCR, 1989.

crops up, even though the payoff may be very low. For these robbers, an attractive target is likely to be an individual alone in a public place like a street.

The professional-opportunistic dimension comprises other factors besides payoff and convenience. The most obvious is planning. Planning and payoff logically go together since people or institutions with large amounts of money are likely to take precautions to guard it. Robbers seeking a big score must plan carefully. They must decide which target to hit—and when. Among bank robbers, for instance, the opportunists do little planning and get little money. They hand a note to the teller and walk out with whatever the teller gives them—rarely more than three or four thousand dollars, often only a few hundred—or even nothing. Professional bank robbers, though, are interested in more than the contents of a single till. They want to know when the bank will be holding a substantial amount of accessible cash. And they find out.

> There's quite a few mills around here, so I sat down and bought some beers for a couple of guys who work in mills, and just in conversation . . . I asked them when does this group get paid. . . . So they told me. So I figured, well, a lot of these guys cash their cheques here [a local bank] and more do on Thursdays than on Fridays, so sure enough I went down . . . the following week on Thursday.[47]

Robbers also may need to know in advance about security systems, guards, police patrol schedules, and escape routes. The plan may require special material—guns, masks or other special clothes, and a getaway car (preferably stolen so it would not be traceable to one of the robbers).

Professional robbery requires a fairly exact division of labor. Each member of the team has a special role to play, and the team may rehearse once or twice before the actual performance to make sure each player knows his part. In a bank robbery, one robber may be assigned to control the customers while another forces the bank manager to get the money; a third member will act as lookout. There may be a fourth member as driver, though gangs now make the driver go into the bank with them.

> In the old days, they used to leave the driver of a bank car outside, and most times they'd come out and the car would be gone! Now, you take the driver with you and he's the first one out.[48]

Aside from this planning, bank robbers do not much resemble the romanticized criminals of Hollywood movies like *Bonnie and Clyde*. Robbery teams today are not long-term gangs. They get together for one big job or perhaps a short series of robberies; then they split up. Nor is there necessarily honor among these thieves. The fainthearted "wheelman" in the above quotation is only one example of general problems of loyalty. The norms of the criminal world say that the team member who is caught should not tell on his partners. But robbers today recognize that this norm is more an ideal than a reality. They know that the police and prosecutors can pressure the robber to give up his partners. So most robbers expect that if one of the gang gets caught, the others are likely to be arrested as well.[49] Worse things could happen, and do. Some of the robbers who participated in the multimillion dollar robbery of the Lufthansa Terminal at JFK Airport in 1978 were murdered by their greedier partners.[50] Professional robbers may also go after smaller scores than six-figure or million-dollar targets. Supermarkets and payroll offices may yield tens of thousands of dollars, depending on the time of the day, and they are usually less well defended than banks and armored cars.

Below the large-score professional jobs come all the smaller commercial robberies—gas stations, liquor stores, convenience stores, and taxicabs. The more professional robbers reject such targets because the payoff is too low and the possibility of trouble too great.

> I would rather walk into a bank any day with all their cameras and security officers and . . . alarms. . . . I would rather go facing the cameras and the FBI than rob a gas station. Not only will the guy in the gas station buck on you, but he will pull a gun and shoot somebody.[51]

For most robbers, however, the danger of these smaller robberies is offset by their convenience. A single robber can do the job unassisted and without much planning: Just wait till there is nobody around, show a weapon, and demand the money—hardly the level of skill and planning implied by the word "professional."* Criminologists, therefore, have looked for other terms to describe these stickup artists: "habitual" robbers, "career" robbers, "experienced" robbers.[52] All these terms imply a certain level of skill, frequency

---

* Robbers themselves do not use the word "professional." They are more likely to use the word "good." A criminal would say, "He's a good stickup man," not "He's a professional robber."

of crime, and general involvement with the criminal world—something between the professional and the impulsive opportunist. There are also "intensive" robbers—those who commit a large number of crimes in a short
time span.[53] The payoff in each robbery is fairly low, so these robbers will
have to do several robberies in order to get enough money. And since they
do not take professional precautions like wearing a mask or using a stolen
car or a stolen license plate, they can be identified more easily. As a result,
these "intensive" robbers soon get caught and go to prison.

The professional-opportunistic dimension clearly is useful for distinguishing types of robberies—the well-planned bank heist, the convenience
store stickup, the street mugging. It also seems logical to apply these distinctions to the robbers themselves—we assume that professional robberies
are committed by professional robbers. In reality, however, this distinction
often breaks down. Except for the most skilled professionals, criminals do
not limit themselves to one type of crime. People who commit professional
robberies also may commit opportunistic robberies as well as a host of other
crimes—selling drugs, dealing stolen goods, pimping, and perhaps engaging in burglary or auto theft.[54] In other words, by looking at planning,
payoff, and other factors, we can easily classify robberies, but we are much
less certain about classifying the robbers who have committed them. I recall
interviewing a robber who described at length the planning and organization that went into one of his big scores. It was a professional job, well-
planned and highly profitable. Yet a few months later, this same man had
been eating in a luncheonette, sitting near the cash register, when another
customer paid her bill. When this "professional" robber saw all those green
bills in the till, he jumped up, grabbed a knife from behind the counter,
threatened the counterman, took the money, and ran. Of course, the victim
ran out and hollered for the police, who easily caught the robber, which is
why the setting for our interview was the state prison.*

Mugging—*The* Crime in the Streets

Over half of all robberies are muggings—robberies of individuals in a street
or other public place or the entrance of a building. Compared with more
professional robbers, muggers are usually younger, more likely to work in

---

* Conklin implies that professionals commit unplanned, impulsive robberies only when they
are drunk. However, since robbers are drunk quite a bit of the time, their impulsive crimes
are probably not such a rarity. See John E. Conklin (1972), *Robbery and the Criminal Justice
System*, Philadelphia: J.B. Lippincott, pp. 65, 97. Laurie Taylor says of English robbers, "It
isn't a case of two kinds of professional criminals—the small-time and the big-time. Only the
opportunities which are available fit into these two categories. The criminals move between
them." Laurie Taylor (1985), *In the Underworld*, London: Unwin Paperbacks, p. 39, quoted
in Katz, note 9, p. 204.

groups, more likely to come from the lowest social class, and more likely to be black.[55] Most muggers are at the opportunistic end of the scale. They focus on the ease of committing the crime rather than the size of the payoff, and their planning of the crime may be minimal or nonexistent.

> You don't plan anything. . . . You're just standing there. . . . It's like, let's take the box [radio] or buy some herb. Some guys are still doing school-yard jobs. They take $2 or $3 from kids around the school.[56]

Muggers do not even need a weapon—just one person to grab the victim, another to take the money. These weaponless "strongarm" robberies account for about 40 percent of all muggings today.[57]

Despite their impulsiveness, muggers may make some choices in order to get the largest payoff for their efforts. They may try to judge from a potential victim's looks how much money he or she might be carrying. Or they may follow people coming out of a store, a bank, or a check-cashing agency, on the assumption that shopping and banking indicate cash on hand. Muggers may even use moral criteria in choosing their victims. They

> have predispositions for or against mugging women (generally against); for or against mugging old people (generally against); for or against mugging whites rather than blacks (generally for); and for mugging the rich rather than the poor (always the rich).[58]

But frequently, despite these preferences, they wind up robbing whoever is most available and most vulnerable.

> One thing I could never do—I could never rip off a female. I could never snatch a pocketbook, even though I was a dope fiend. One day my package didn't come through; my connection didn't show. I had no choice. Went out there looking for something, and it so happens that a pocketbook was the best thing that came along.[59]

If the payoff is small, muggers may have to commit two or three muggings before they get enough cash for their immediate needs, enough to have a good time for a day or two—what they call "getting over."

Money

All robbers commit their crimes for the money, but obviously the financial motives of muggers differ from those of older robbers. Younger, more opportunistic robbers tend to use their money for spur-of-the-moment pleasures—clothing or records, drugs or fast food. Professional robbers tend to be older, and their needs are different. They may have regular expenses like rent or even family expenses. They also are more likely to use the money to support a drug habit (rather than just buying drugs for kicks). Professional robbers sometimes intend to use the money from a big score to get out of crime altogether—to get start-up capital for a legitimate business.[60] However, they almost never carry out these plans. Instead, they celebrate: They buy themselves a few nice things; they drink and they spend money on women; they lend money to friends. And in a few days or weeks or perhaps months, the money is gone.

> Since we were spending money so fast we had to pull jobs at least once a week. We'd spend $200 a day [this was in the 1960s] buying everything we wanted. You spend money like this because in the back of your mind you know that you can always get more just by pulling another job.[61]

Even the few who say they want to leave crime usually abandon their good intentions.

> When I start out I say, "Well, man, I need about $15,000 to get on my feet." That's what I'll say.
>
> So I start out and I'll work and I'll save; I don't spend any money, I don't party, I don't do anything but steal—until I get that amount of money in my bank account, and then I quit; I throw away my tools and I just say, "Now I've forgotten how. I'll never crack another safe."
>
> I'll sit around a few days . . . and I'll be ready to . . . go to work, get a job.
>
> And believe me, I've had some good jobs offered to me, but I just never take them. I don't know why.
>
> So I'll get off and I'll start partying and it doesn't take me very long to spend that money.*[62]

Violence

Robbery, by definition, combines two elements: the taking of property and the use or threat of violence. The previous section sketched differences among robbers' motives regarding money. However, what makes robbery of special concern is the question of violence. In recent years, the "violent offender" has come to occupy a place of special attention in the media, in criminological research, and in the criminal justice system. Jurisdictions with overburdened courts and prisons may choose to focus on "the violent offender" by devoting valuable court time and prison space disproportionately to robbers. At the heart of this strategy is the idea that robbers are different from mere thieves.

---

* The man quoted here is obviously a burglar, not a robber. Still, his statement is typical of robbers as well.

Violence: Expressive and Instrumental

Are robbers different from other criminals? Are they violent people? Some evidence suggests that the answer is yes, robbers are the most "hardened" of criminals. For example, people arrested for robbery are worse bail risks than are people arrested for other crimes. They are more likely to commit further crimes while on bail than are murderers, rapists, or property criminals.[63] In addition, criminals themselves often regard robbery as different from other illegal ways of getting money. Nearly all career criminals do commit a variety of crimes, but most limit themselves to property crimes. A burglar, even a fairly skilled burglar, might also sell drugs, pass bad checks, steal cars, and shoplift. But he will draw the line at robbery. Robbers, on the other hand, commit all these crimes and robbery as well. They even commit more of the other crimes than they do robberies. But it is the robberies which distinguish them from the other criminals.[64] Apparently, even for career criminals, it takes something special to be able to go up to somebody and forcefully demand money.

To say that robbers are violent people implies that robbers are *essentially* different, that their robbery results from some internal impulse toward violence and power. No doubt this generalization applies to some robbers. But just as robbers have different views of money—the amount needed and their motives for seeking it—the same may be true of violence. Robbers differ in their use of violence and in their motives for using it.

It is useful here to distinguish between **instrumental** violence and **expressive** violence. These two terms—instrumental and expressive—refer to the motives or purposes behind an action. Instrumental action serves to accomplish some ulterior, rational purpose (like getting money)—it is a means toward some goal. Expressive action is a goal in itself—it serves to express some inner psychological state. For example, if I am driving 90 mph in order to get to the emergency room, my lawbreaking is instrumental. Many others would do the same even if they did not like speeding. But if I am driving 90 mph just because I really like going fast, it is expressive. Only those with similar tastes, only similar kinds of people, would do likewise. When we speak of robbers as violent people, then we are implying that their violence is expressive.

Headlines about "senseless," or "excessive," or "sadistic" violence are referring to this kind of noninstrumental violence that goes beyond what is necessary to get the victim's property. Of course, any crime probably combines both expressive and instrumental motives, and it is difficult to know just how much of the violence in robbery is expressive. However, we can make some guesses. Of every 100 victims in noncommercial robberies, about 33 are injured, five of them seriously enough to require medical care.[65] One researcher concluded, "In a high proportion of these crimes, the attack that caused the injury was not instrumental to the robbery, but rather was a distinct act."[66] These robbers who injure their victims are good candidates for the label "violent people," and they are likely to commit other violent crimes like assault.[67] We can see expressive violence in one other fact about robbery: Injury is more likely in robberies committed by three or more offenders.[68] If violence were instrumental, then groups of robbers should be *less* likely to resort to actual force. Instead, their violence seems aimed towards noninstrumental goals, perhaps the need to appear tough in the presence of their peers.

Professional robbers, of course, look down on such unnecessary violence.

> When you're out on a heist, you're out to get the dough and keep out of trouble. Halloween's the night for scaring people.[69]

Professionals see the actual use of force as something they would rather avoid. That's why they carry guns. As a general rule, the deadlier the weapon, the less likely it will actually be used to attack. The threat is sufficient.[70] And even if the robber does use the gun, he is much more likely to hit with it rather than shoot it.[71] Unarmed robbers, on the other hand, use actual attacks twice as often as they merely threaten.

There are two arguments against the idea that robbers are essentially different or that they are basically violent people. First, on the issue of violence: While victims may see an act of violence as excessive, the robber may see it as rational and instrumental. Second, the idea that robbers are violent people assumes that violent motives come first, that they are part of the person's original psychological makeup and are the cause of his violent crimes. But it may also be the other way round: Expressive, violent motives may be the *result* of doing robberies rather than the cause.

The simplest explanation of the violence in robbery is that it is essential to the job. In this one important way, the robber's job is similar to a police officer's. Both jobs involve the control of other people. Both jobs require force—actual or potential—to get people to do something they don't want to do, and to do it quickly.* Robbers have only a few minutes to get the money and run, and force is an excellent way to make victims comply immediately. In other words, the violence is instrumental. It is part of the job, not necessarily part of the person performing that job. To appreciate this distinction, consider professional football players. The violence in their work is instrumental; if they could not use force effectively, they would be lousy football players. We understand that the violence we see on Sunday is part of the job, not necessarily part of the person—off the field they may

---

* See Chapter 13 for a fuller discussion of the police role.

be quite gentle.*) Here is a professional bank robber describing the opening seconds of a bank robbery.

> Sometimes we select the strongest person—the manager especially or another teller which [sic] is very big—a six-footer, or something like that, you know. And we won't say a word, we just walk up to him and smash him right across the face, you know, and we get him down. And once he's down the people, the girls especially, they look at him and they say, "My God—big Mike, he's been smashed down like that—I'd better lay down too, and stay quiet." You know—it's sort of like psychology, to obey us immediately.[72]

To the people in the bank, the violence appears to erupt from the uncontrollable urges of a dangerous person. But in reality, the robber is deliberately creating this image. From the robber's own viewpoint, the violence is purely instrumental.

> We made him know that we are brutal, subhuman bastards. . . . We project that image.[73]

Street muggers, too, usually see their violence as instrumental.

> I didn't go with the intention of hurting him—because I figured he was smart enough to give up the money. But what he did when I had him in the hallway: He screamed. And I got uptight, you know. And me being uptight, I used the knife. And other times people I went to rob, they gave me a hard time. To get the money that I wanted to get I had to stab them.[74]

In the cases just quoted, the victims resisted. But what about the seemingly senseless use of violence when the victim does not resist? Isn't such violence purely expressive? Undoubtedly, some of it is—but not all of it. For example, sometimes muggers attack the victim *after* the mugging has been completed. These attacks may look senseless, but to the robber, they are quite instrumental.

> You push them down hard so that they don't get right up and yell, but we're gone. We're fast.[75]

Sometimes a mugger attacks before demanding the money. Again, from the victim's viewpoint such violence is irrational ("I would have given him the money. . . ."). But how does the mugger know this in advance? Here is a

---

* The difference is most striking among those who play the more violent positions. For example, defensive tackle Merlin Olsen, as seen in old Ram game films, certainly looks violent. But compare that picture with his subsequent screen career as a gentle priest or flower salesman. The violence, like the gentleness, is part of the role, not the person.

Though old-style bank robbers have been largely replaced by note-passers, professional bank robberies do still sometimes occur.

THREE ARMED MEN ROB BANK IN LEXINGTON

Lexington—Three armed men wearing masks robbed a Lexington bank early yesterday, forcing some employees to lie face down at gunpoint and then escaping with an undetermined amount of money, police officials said.

According to police reports, the men were armed with shotguns or rifles when they robbed the Depositors Trust Bank on Hartwell Avenue just before the bank's 8:30 a.m. opening. They apparently had gained entry during the night by sawing a hole in the roof, police said.

"Someone outside the bank called us around 8:30 a.m.," Capt. James Kilmartin said. "We got there within 5 minutes and they had already fled through the front door.

"It was almost a relief, because God knows what would have happened to the employees inside if we had a confrontation with them."

About a half-dozen employees were forced to lie face down while the three men emptied one of the bank's vaults, which was on a timing device and opened automatically, police said.

"From what we've heard, they were fairly aggressive with the employees," Kilmartin said. "The employees were really shaken up by the whole thing."

As a ploy to scare them, the thieves attached an electrical device—a black box with a flashing light—on one of the employees and pretended it was a bomb. State bomb experts later determined it was not an explosive, police said. . . .

Source: Suzette Parmeley, July 21, 1990, reprinted with courtesy of The Boston Globe.

---

mugger whose previous attempt had been foiled when he failed to control the victim.

> The second time I said, "I'm not gonna fumble up the job. And I'm not gonna let him scream either." . . . This time I didn't even tell him he was getting held up. . . . I just hit him, you know, to make sure he knew I meant business. I hit him with the pistol.[76]

Violence: Psychological Trait or Acquired Taste?

If what seems like expressive violence also can include instrumental motives, the reverse also is true. Instrumental violence may take on expressive qualities. The robber who sees his methods largely as instrumental may nevertheless come to enjoy them. He may get to like the power, control, and violence for themselves, not just because they are necessary tools. The taste for violence, then, is not necessarily inborn; it is acquired—perhaps too easily acquired—in the course of one's work. It is acquired by both professional robbers and opportunistic muggers (and perhaps even by legitimate users of violence like football players and police officers).

You're a pretty big man standing there with your gun. Makes you feel oh—kinda important—big, somebody people don't mess with.[77]

Sometimes we would get somebody and they would have nothing. And a lot of times . . . we would get mad, so mad that we wanna hurt the person that has nothing. You're saying: "I'm going through all this for nothing." That's how a lot of times, you know, things happen.[78]

Does this taste for power and violence mean that the robber is a different sort of animal from other criminals? This is the standard psychological view. It assumes that the robber begins with a personality that needs violence and power; he then seeks out robbery as a way of gratifying those needs. By contrast, the sociological view I am sketching here argues that the "need" or liking for violence is acquired on the job. It does not take an unusual personality type to learn to like these feelings or to engage in cruel and senseless violence. For example, we are horrified at the mugger who laughs about the suffering he has inflicted on a victim:

We were goofing around and bragging: "Eh, man, we got this guy. We kicked the s--- out of him." We started goofing on the guy's head, calling him rockhead. . . . I don't know if he had a steel plate or something; that bottle bounced off his head like it didn't even phase him.[79]

You and I could never deliberately inflict that kind of suffering on a person, let alone find it something to enjoy and laugh about. Or could we? Many colleges have fraternities, whose members tend to be nice, middle-class kids who think of themselves as neither criminals nor sadists. These fraternities usually have what they call "hazing" and "initiation," rituals which sometimes involve the inflicting of extreme psychological and even physical suffering.* Frequently, those doing the torture laugh and apparently enjoy the proceedings. They may still laugh about it weeks later—something like the mugger quoted above. Apparently, many people, given the right setting and social support, can commit sadistic acts. Muggers are no exception.

Muggers do not start out viewing crime as a way to satisfy their need for power. They enter into their first mugging with the same feeling that most people would—fear.

Q: How did you feel about doing this?
R6: Fear. Cold-blooded fear.

---

* This collegiate brutality is so common that it becomes newsworthy only in two extremes: when it kills someone, or when a fraternity decides *not* to use it. See "Fraternity Bans Hazing," *The New York Times*, July 30, 1987, p. A20.

R12: Only thing, I was scared. That's all. Other than that I don't know other feelings that I can remember.[80]

If left to their own devices, most of them probably would not go through with it. But the more experienced members of the group teach them. So the novice mugger learns not only how to commit the crime, but also to enjoy it—especially if he continues to be successful. In fact, the mugger acquires a set of attitudes completely different from those he started with; he moves from a sense of fear in taking someone else's money to a sense of entitlement. With each successful mugging, he reinforces the idea that the victim's money is rightfully his.

Like I tell him: "Give it up!" He says: "No." He's giving me, you know, trouble. I'm gonna feel like he has a whole lot of nerve. Dig it. I'm gonna get violent. I would get extremely violent. I felt like it was my right; it was my due.*[81]

This is the combination that can make mugging so dangerous for victims. Young street muggers go into the crime almost impulsively. They work in groups, where no one wants to appear unmanly in front of his colleagues. And over the course of many successful muggings, they have acquired a sense of entitlement. This is the formula for the excessive, senseless violence that sometimes accompanies robbery. Even among older robbers and those who prefer commercial targets, the potential for violence (seemingly irrational violence) is always present. For the career robber—the stickup artist—robbery and its potential or actual violence are not just a matter of getting some quick cash. Beyond that, each robbery is an enactment of the robber's self, his sense of who he is. To resist even in the slightest way is to threaten that self. And that self, that identity is that of the hardened criminal, the "badass" or "bad nigger" or, in the phrase of criminologist Jack Katz, the "hard man."

The robber makes a commitment to this identity even in the face of the grave risks and powerful emotions that fill each robbery—risks and emotions that the robber must conquer. Katz, therefore, sees robbery not as a matter of work and payoff but as something more cosmic.

In stickups, as in other fields in which a difficult spiritual commitment must be made, many are called but few are chosen. A large number of adolescents in low-income ghettoes try stickups, doing one or a few and then stopping; only a small

* One final cop-robber comparison: Police officers who engage in petty corruption may acquire a similar attitude of entitlement to others' property. They may come to feel that the merchant who demands that cops actually pay for merchandise has some nerve. And cops, like the muggers, find ways to convince the merchant to adopt their point of view. There are two important differences: (1) Muggers threaten and use violence; cops harass by using their power of law enforcement and (2) the mugger's victim is victimized only once; the merchant finds that the cops keep coming back.

percentage continue into their late 20s and 30s, becoming the relatively few heavies who commit scores or even hundreds of robberies for each year they spend out of jail. . . .

The practical constraints on making a career of stickups are such that one *cannot* simply adopt violence as an instrumental device to be enacted or dropped as situational contingencies dictate. It is practically impossible to make a career of stickups just by making a calculated show of a disposition to be "bad"; you must live the commitment to deviance. You must really mean it.

The commitment according to which violence with robberies makes sense to the offenders is the commitment to be a hard man—a person whose will, once manifested, must prevail, regardless of practical calculations of physical self-interest. Fatal violence in robberies is far less often a reaction of panic or a rationally self-serving act than a commitment to the transcendence of a hard will.*[82]

ROBBERY AND SOCIETY

Bank robbery and street mugging represent two obviously different forms of robbery. The robbers, too, differ from each other. Their typical profiles would show differences in age and race, differences in their use of violence, differences in how they spend their money, and probably differences in career paths. There is another interesting difference between these two types of crime: While street mugging has changed little over the course of the last few centuries, bank robbery has undergone a continuous and rapid evolution. The bank robber of a generation or two ago, like the family doctor who makes house calls, is practically an endangered species. I am not being frivolous in comparing doctors and robbers. The comparison can be very useful for understanding how and why crimes change. It redirects our focus from the individual practitioner to the more general sources of change. In the practice of robbery, just as in the practice of medicine, change arises not so much from individual motivations as from changes in technology and society.

The Decline and Rise of Bank Robbery

Table 5–5 shows the number of bank robberies in the United States over a 50-year period. You don't have to be a statistician to see that these numbers show some big changes—from 609 in 1932 to only 24 in 1943, and then a huge increase beginning in the 1950s.

---

* In this paragraph, Katz is seeking to explain fatal violence, but his analysis applies equally well to nonfatal violence.

Table 5–5 ■ **Number of Bank Robberies in the United States, 1932–1984**

Year	Number of robberies
1932	609
1937	129
1943	24
1950	81
1959	346
1963	658
1976	4,565
1984	6,800

Source: Derived from James A. Inciardi (1975), *Careers in Crime*, Chicago: Rand McNally, p. 97. UCR, 1984.

How can we explain these changes? There is a popular and simple idea that since crime is bad, it is caused by bad people (or as one criminologist put it, "wicked people exist"). Changes in crime, therefore, reflect the number of bad people or their level of activity. This is a logical and morally reassuring idea. But the numbers given in Table 5–5 show how inadequate it is. Can the population of wicked people decrease by 94 percent or increase by 1,000 percent in the space of only a few years?

A fuller explanation would emphasize not just people but the social context as well. Yes, some people are more wicked than others, more willing to commit crimes. But the pressures and opportunities pushing and pulling them toward particular types of crime also contribute to changes in the overall amount of bank robbery. Behind the numbers are some important developments—changes in banks, changes in criminal techniques, and changes in law enforcement. These changes in turn have transformed the number of robbers and their typical profile.

Until the 1930s, there were relatively few banks in the United States, and banking was greatly centralized. A bank would keep its money in one place, not spread out over a number of branch offices. Consequently, banks made an attractive target for professional robbers. With enough organization, planning, and weapons, they could overcome the bank's defenses. Since the take from a robbery was likely to be high, robbers could build up a nice nest egg without risking too many robberies. In addition, the only law enforcement was at the local level, and it was frequently ineffective (those movies like *Bonnie and Clyde* are accurate when they show the robbers escaping to safety by crossing a state line). Robbers, therefore, often worked in gangs and moved from place to place.

In the 1930s, two important things happened. First, the Depression reduced the number of banks. Between the stock market crash of 1929 and

Roosevelt's inauguration in 1933, 5,500 banks (nearly 23 percent of all banks in the United States) had failed.[83] Second, and probably more important, bank robbery became a federal crime, and the FBI under J. Edgar Hoover began an effective war against bank robbers. Fewer banks and more cops greatly reduced the opportunity for successful bank robbery. In addition, as bank robbers got caught and went to prison, the population of bank robbers became severely depleted. After a few decades, though, as the numbers show, bank robbery eventually made a comeback. But the robberies and the robbers were of a different sort. The opportunities had changed, and so had the people willing to take them.

The post-war period of the late 1940s and the 1950s was the era of suburbanization. As the population shifted from cities to suburbs, businesses followed, banks included. In the 1930s, a city might have a half-dozen different banks, all of them downtown. In the 1950s, each of those banks would spawn branch offices in all the surrounding suburbs. The new banks themselves were different. In the 1930s, banks tried hard to foster the image that money there was safe. Banks dramatized their security measures—armed guards, alarms, tellers behind iron bars, etc. It was an understandable strategy, since during the Depression, many people had lost their life savings by putting all their money in a bank.

In the 1950s, with government-insured deposits, banks no longer needed to maintain the tough-but-safe image. In order to attract customers, banks began to soften their image. The austere banker and bank faded into history, replaced with "friendly" banking. The new banks were designed to be especially friendly to the automobile-based life of the suburbs, so it was now quite easy to drive up, transact business, and drive away—easy for customers, and easy for robbers. Interior decor also played a part. Down came the iron bars, in favor of friendly counters. Of course these changes, too, were friendly not just for customers but also for robbers. "The lower the counter, the better I like it," said one robber. "You just hop over and hop back."[84]

Banks were not defenseless. By keeping less money on hand and keeping larger amounts in new, time-lock safes, they could prevent large losses. So while the number of bank robberies increased, the average take in a robbery decreased. The big-score bank heist gradually became a thing of the past. More and more robberies were solo, low-profit jobs—a robber handing a teller a note and walking out with a few thousand dollars or less. Today, the take might be less than $1,000, and if the teller, protected now by bulletproof glass, refuses, the robber might walk out empty-handed.

Bank defense measures have also ensured that robbers eventually will be caught. Banks have cameras that make identification easier. Some banks have put time-delayed dye bombs in money sacks so that the robber who walks out of the bank with a bag of money may find himself on the street a minute later covered with bright red dye. Note-passers can get away with a few crimes, but since their take per robbery is so small, they must continue to commit crimes. As a result, most bank robbers today eventually get caught and go to prison. And here is another change from the golden age of bank robbery. Prison does not solve the problem. In the 1930s, when the FBI put several professional bank robbers out of business, bank robbery nearly disappeared. However, sending today's casual bank robbers up the river has done nothing to decrease the number of bank robberies. Because the crime requires so little skill and because the robber usually can get away with the first few crimes, there are always others willing to get into the game.

Highway Robbery

While changes in banking, technology, and law enforcement altered the profile and numbers of bank robbers, some other types of robbery have been most affected by changes in transportation. Over the centuries, "highway robbery" has taken various forms. In England in the 1700s, "footpads" lurked along the major roads between towns. It is important to keep in mind the small scale of those cities. Today, the journey from central London to Hampstead is merely a passage through a city, from one section to another. In the 17th and 18th centuries, the road led through unpopulated stretches, ideal for highway robbers like Dick Turpin. Government policies also affected robbery rates, though in unintended ways. England's 18th-century "enclosure laws," which forced large numbers of people off the land, probably served to swell the ranks of highwaymen—despite the extensive use of the death penalty for robbery and other crimes. In time, the city populations expanded greatly, the government improved road surfaces, and the new railroads provided safer, swifter passage. As a result, opportunities for highway robbery decreased. In the United States, stagecoach robbery flourished in the West during the early 1800s but faded with the expansion of the railroads. The early railroads also fell victim to train robbers like Jesse James and the Younger Gang. But train robbery also decreased as railroads fortified their baggage cars and heavily armed their security men.

By the 19th century, the robbery problem was no longer on the highways but in the urban streets. In contrast to other types of robbery, street robbery has changed little over the centuries—probably because the targets are still the same. Banks may have changed in numbers, location, security systems, and amounts of cash on hand, but people in the streets have undergone no similar transformation. As for the methods of street robbers, guns and knives have been available for centuries. The most frequent form of street robbery is still the unarmed mugging. A century ago, it was called "garroting," since the criminal usually placed his arm around the throat of the victim, a technique which remains popular among muggers today.[85] The criminals, however, may be of a different sort. In 18th- and 19th-century New York or London, garroters were probably men in their 20s and 30s who were part of a large criminal subculture. Today's muggers are frequently teenagers with no extensive commitment to a criminal underworld.

Some changes in robbery depend less on technology than on social structure. Think, for example, of the bandit-hero, the Robin Hood–like robber who is admired, sheltered, and aided by the common people. This type of banditry seems to arise in particular social conditions: It is usually rural, arising where a relatively poor, peasant-like population works on land owned by distant and wealthy persons. Some writers believe that train-robbing and bank-robbing gangs flourished in the American West not just because trains and banks were relatively defenseless, but because the general population condoned the robbers and even helped them avoid capture. Bandits like Jesse James took on the aura of folk heroes, and ordinary people may have been honored to offer them a temporary hideout if they were being chased by the law. Why did people not despise them as evil criminals? Probably because of the robbers' targets. Farmers and ranchers in the West often resented the railroads, which had bilked the settlers out of their land, set unfair rates, and obtained vast amounts of land from the government only to resell it at much higher prices.

Later, in the Depression, banks acquired a similarly unpopular reputation for foreclosing on mortgages and taking people's farms and homes. People with little left to lose might disapprove of robbery, but they also might admire the person who could turn the tables on the bank. Banks were seen as institutions that took people's property. Robbers were people who took the bank's property.

Many countries have similar legendary figures—"social bandits," as one historian has called them. It is important to understand that these Robin Hoods, whatever their individual virtues or vices, are produced by particular kinds of economic structures.

> Social banditry is universally found, wherever societies are based on agriculture . . . and consist largely of peasants and landless laborers ruled, oppressed, and exploited by someone else—lords, towns, governments, lawyers, or even banks.[86]

SUMMARY AND CONCLUSION

Robbery comes in various forms, from the opportunistic mugging that might net only a few dollars to the highly planned and profitable robbery of institutions like banks. Although the FBI classifies robbery as violent crime (i.e., a crime against the person), in fact it combines elements of both property and violent crime. It consists of the taking of property from a person by force or threat of force. The element of force, whether threatened or actual, suggests that robbers are psychologically different from other criminals, who have no qualms about taking other people's money but wish to avoid violent confrontations. However, in looking at robbers and robbery, it is useful to try to distinguish between expressive violence and instrumental violence. Though any violent crime contains elements of both, expressive violence seems to be more characteristic of younger, opportunistic robbers, while the violence of older, more professional robbers is more likely to be instrumental. Even older, career robbers may become committed to the identity of "hard man," an identity based on willingness to use violence.

The demographics of robbery conform to popular notions about violent crime. Robbery is most common in the cities, especially those of the industrial Northeast. Robbers are almost entirely men, usually from working-class and lower-class areas. Blacks have exceptionally high rates of committing robbery. Since the majority of robberies are committed by opportunistic criminals who stay in their own neighborhoods, the profile of victims closely resembles that of the robbers—men rather than women, poorer rather than middle-class, and black rather than white—though in all cases, the differences are not as great among victims as among robbers.

Historically, robbery has been shaped by the broad forces in the society at large. In commercial robbery, there has been a steady evolution, with banks, transportation companies, and other businesses taking various defensive measures, and different types of robbers adapting to the new targets. Bank robbery, for example, has changed from a crime committed by teams of well-organized professional criminals to a crime committed almost entirely by casual, unskilled criminals.

The picture of bank robbery today also describes the bulk of the robbery problem today. Though the courts have sent more and more robbers to prison, this policy has made hardly a dent in the rate of robbery. Apparently, for every robber removed from the population, another stands ready to enter the field. In earlier generations, juvenile criminals who committed property crimes would, as they grew older, leave the streets for unskilled or semis-killed jobs in industry. Today, more of those juveniles graduate instead into robbery, especially the less skilled and potentially more violent robberies like muggings and convenience-store holdups.

NOTES

1. Marvin Wolfgang (1958), *Patterns in Criminal Homicide*, Philadelphia: University of Pennsylvania Press.

2. David F. Luckenbill (1977), "Criminal Homicide as a Situated Transaction," *Social Problems*, vol. 25, no. 2, p. 180.

3. Marvin Wolfgang (1958), op. cit.

4. Ibid.

5. Luckenbill, op. cit.

6. Ibid.

7. Richard B. Felson, Stephen A. Ribner, and Meryl S. Siegel (1984), "Age and the Effect of Third Parties During Criminal Violence," *Sociology and Social Research*, vol. 86, no. 4, pp. 452–62.

8. Luckenbill, op. cit.

9. Jack Katz (1988), *Seductions of Crime: Moral and Sensual Attractions in Doing Evil*, New York: Basic Books, pp. 12–51.

10. Donald J. Black (1983), "Crime as Social Control," *American Sociological Review*, vol. 48, no. 1, pp. 34–45 (quote on p. 36).

11. Jack Katz, op. cit.

12. James A. Inciardi (1978), *Reflections on Crime*, New York: Holt, Rinehart, Winston, p. 51.

13. The data from 1987, the National Center for Health Statistics, cited in *The New York Times*, June 27, 1990, p. A10 (Elisabeth Rosenthal, "U.S. Is by Far the Homicide Capital of the Industrialized Nations").

14. Christopher Jencks (1987), "Genes & Crime," *The New York Review of Books*, vol. 34, no. 2, pp. 33–40.

15. Vincent Canby (1990), "Now at a Theater Near You: A Skyrocketing Body Count," *The New York Times*, July 16, 1990, pp. C11, 13.

16. Marvin E. Wolfgang and Franco Ferracuti (1967), *The Subculture of Violence: Towards an Integrated Theory in Criminology*, New York: Barnes and Noble.

17. Raymond D. Gastil (1971), "Homicide and a Regional Culture of Violence," *American Sociological Review*, vol. 36, pp. 412–27.

18. Ibid.

19. Marvin E. Wolfgang, Robert M. Figlio, Paul E. Tracy, and Simon I. Singer (1985), *The National Survey of Crime Severity*, Washington, DC: U.S. Government Printing Office, pp. 52–73.

20. Sandra J. Ball-Rokeach (1975), "Values and Violence: A Test of the Subculture of Violence Thesis," *American Sociological Review*, vol. 38, no. 6, pp. 736–49. Howard Erlanger (1974), "The Empirical Status of the Subculture of Violence Thesis," *Social Problems*, vol. 22, no. 2, pp. 280–92.

21. Colin Loftin and Robert Nash Parker (1985), "An Errors-in-Variable Model of the Effect of Poverty on Urban Homicide Rates," *Criminology*, vol. 23, no. 2, pp. 269–87. Colin Loftin and Robert H. Hill (1974), "Regional Subculture and Homicide: An Empirical Examination of the Gastil-Hackney Thesis," *American Sociological Review*, vol. 39, pp. 714–24.

22. Judith R. Blau and Peter M. Blau (1982), "The Cost of Inequality: Metropolitan Structure and Violent Crime," *American Sociological Review*, vol. 47, pp. 114–29.

23. Roger Lane (1986), *Roots of Violence in Black Philadelphia*, Cambridge, MA: Harvard University Press.

24. Blau and Blau, op. cit.

25. Richard J. Gelles (1972), *The Violent Home: A Study of Physical Aggression Between Husbands and Wives*, Beverly Hills, CA: Sage.

26. Wolfgang (1958), op. cit. See also James D. Wright, Peter H. Rossi, and Kathleen Daly (1983), *Under the Gun: Weapons, Crime, and Violence in America*, New York: Aldine.

27. UCR, 1987.

28. Katz, op. cit., p. 182.

29. Mary Lorenz Dietz (1983), *Killing for Profit: The Social Organization of Felony Homicide*, Chicago: Nelson-Hall, p. 69–70.

30. Cook, op. cit., pp. 72, 75. Dietz, op. cit., p. 212. Katz, op. cit., p. 186.

31. Philip J. Cook (1983), "The Influence of Gun Availability on Violent Crime Patterns," in Michael Tonry and Norval Morris, eds., *Crime and Justice: An Annual Review*, Chicago: University of Chicago Press, pp. 49–90.

32. Peter Letkeman (1973), *Crime as Work*, Englewood Cliffs, NJ: Prentice-Hall.

33. Ibid., p. 183.

34. Dietz, op. cit., pp. 157–59.

35. Cook, op. cit., p. 73.

36. Dietz, op. cit., p. 65.

37. William Wilbanks (1984), *Murder in Miami: An Analysis of Homicide Patterns and Trends in Dade County (Miami) Florida, 1917–1983*, Lanham, MD: University Press of America.

38. Dietz, op. cit., p. 175.

39. Jack Levin and James Alan Fox (1985), *Mass Murder: America's Growing Menace*, New York: Plenum, pp. 123–38.

40. Ibid., p. 100.

41. Shervert H. Frazier (1975), "Violence and Social Impact," cited in Levin and Fox, op. cit., p. 100.

42. *The New York Times*, Dec. 10, 1985, sec. I, p. 18.

43. Levin and Fox, op. cit., pp. 16, 63.

44. Ibid., p. 143.

45. John F. Wallerstedt (1984), "Returning to Prison," *Bureau of Justice Statistics Special Report*, Washington, DC: U.S. Department of Justice.

46. UCR, 1986.

47. Letkeman, op. cit., p. 96.

48. Ibid., p. 112.

49. Ibid., p. 125.

50. Nicholas Pileggi (1985), *Wiseguy: Life in a Mafia Family*, New York: Simon & Schuster.

51. John Allen (1977), *Assault With a Deadly Weapon: The Autobiography of a Street Criminal*, New York: McGraw-Hill, p. 52.

52. George B. Vold (1979), *Theoretical Criminology*, (2nd ed., prepared by Thomas J. Bernard), New York: Oxford, p. 345. Letkeman, op. cit., p. 28. W.J. Einstadter (1969), "The Social Organization of Armed Robbery," *Social Problems*, vol. 17, no. 1, pp. 64–83.

53. Sylvie Bellot (1985), "Les Auteurs de Vols à Main Armée à Montréal: Une Typologie Empirique," *Criminologie*, vol. 18, no. 2, pp. 35–45.

54. For an excellent example, see Allen, op. cit., passim.

55. Conklin, op. cit., p. 82.

56. Nicholas Pileggi (1981), "Meet the Muggers," *New York*, Mar. 9, p. 32.

57. Caroline Wolf Harlow (1987), "Robbery Victims," *Bureau of Justice Statistics Special Report*, Washington, DC: U.S. Department of Justice.

58. Robert Lejeune (1977), "The Management of a Mugging," *Urban Life*, vol. 6, no. 2, p. 135.

59. Ibid., p. 136.

60. Einstadter, op. cit.

61. James Carr (1975), *Bad*, New York: Herman Graf Associates, p. 38, quoted in Katz, op. cit., p. 216.

62. Bruce Jackson (1972), *Outside the Law: A Thief's Primer*, New Brunswick, NJ: Transaction Books, p. 114. Conklin (1977, p. 65) notes a similar pattern.

63. Wayne H. Thomas (1976), *Bail Reform in America*, Berkely, CA: University of California Press, Chapter 20.

64. Jan M. Chaiken and Marcia R. Chaiken (1982), *Varieties of Criminal Behavior*, Santa Monica, CA: Rand.

65. Harlow, op. cit., Table 14.

66. Philip J. Cook (1983), "Gun Availability and Violent Crime," in Michael Tonry and Norval Morris, eds. (1983), *Crime and Justice: An Annual Review*, Chicago: University of Chicago Press, pp. 49–89, p. 73.

67. Ibid. Chaiken and Chaiken, op. cit., p. 27. Allen, op. cit.

68. Cook, op. cit.

69. Everett DeBaun (1950), "The Heist: The Theory and Practice of Armed Robbery," *Harper's Magazine* (February).

70. Harlow, op. cit., Table 12.

71. Richard Block (1977), *Violent Crime: Environment, Interaction, and Death*, Lexington, MA: D.C. Heath.

72. Letkeman, op. cit., p. 110.

73. Ibid., p. 105.

74. Lejeune, op. cit., p. 144.

75. Nicholas Pileggi (1981), op. cit., p. 32.

76. Lejeune, op. cit., p. 142.

77. Einstadter, op. cit.

78. Lejeune, p. 145.

79. Ibid., p. 133.

80. Ibid., p. 129.

81. Ibid., p. 144.

82. Katz, op. cit., pp. 187, 193.

83. William Manchester (1973), *The Glory and the Dream: A Narrative History of America,* New York: Bantam, pp. 72–73.

84. Letkeman, op. cit., p. 94.

85. Jennifer Davis (1980), "The London Garroting Panic of 1862: A Moral Panic and the Creation of a Criminal Class in Mid-Victorian England," in V.A.C. Gatrell, Bruce Lenman, and Geoffrey Parker, eds., *Crime and the Law: The Social History of Crime in Western Europe Since 1500,* London: Europa Publications, pp. 190–213. Nicholas Pileggi (1981), op. cit.

86. Eric Hobsbawm (1969), *Bandits,* New York: Dell, p. 15.

Violent Crimes, Part II: Women and Children

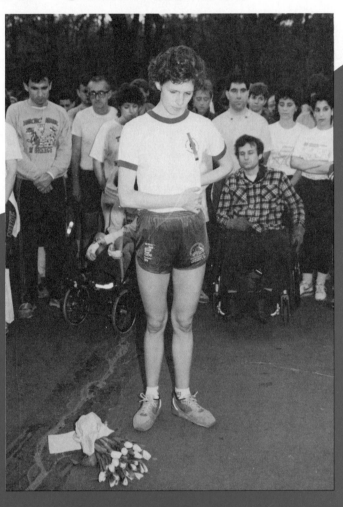

CHAPTER 6

RAPE

THE ISSUE OF RAPE BRINGS OUT THE MOST CONTRADICTORY REACTIONS. ON THE ONE hand, people generally regard it as an extremely serious crime, even when the victim suffers no other physical injury,[1] and the laws on rape reflect this judgment. The crime carries very severe penalties. In fact, of all executions between 1930 and 1965, 12 percent were for rape.[2] On the other hand, because rape is a sexual crime, it can evoke in grown men the kind of sniggering humor usually found among seventh-grade boys. The "jokes" are often based on the idea that rape is not really such a serious matter. For example, in 1979, commenting on the "marital exemption" (an exemption which made it legal for husbands to rape their wives), a California state senator said, "If you can't rape your wife, who can you rape?"[3] He was speaking to a group of women lobbyists.

But rape *is* serious. Rape victims suffer considerable psychological harm. The effects of rape—which can include extreme fears, sleep disturbances, and various sexual symptoms—last months and even years, in what psychiatrists call "post-traumatic stress disorder."[4] Of course, not all rape victims react in the same way. The degree of violence and cruelty during the rape, the relationship between rapist and victim, the victim's general psychological health, her previous victimization (or lack thereof), her general expectations about male-female relationships, and the support she receives from others—all these factors can affect the victim's reaction.[5] Unfortunately, we do not know with any certainty the proportion of victims who suffer severe, moderate, or mild symptoms, for rape remains a largely hidden crime. Until recently, even criminology textbooks tended to give this serious crime relatively brief coverage.[6] Textbooks neglected rape, not necessarily because the authors were insensitive males, but because the evidence on rape was so insubstantial and so questionable.

How Much Rape?

Criminologists have long suspected that statistics on rape were among the least accurate. Worse yet, the reasons for the inaccuracies were far more troubling than were reasons for inaccuracy in other crimes. Larceny victims and robbery victims may fail to report these crimes, and police may choose not to record them. But their reasons are frequently that the crime was not serious enough or that nothing could be done to catch the offender. Rape is different. The rate of non-reporting (about 50 percent) is roughly equivalent to that of robbery victims or victims of $500 theft. But rape victims rarely dismiss the crime as trivial. Instead, their reasons for not reporting the crime are first, that it was a "private or personal matter"; and second, that they fear reprisal from the man who victimized them. These reasons are given more often for rape than for any other crime.[7]

Because rape victims often do not call the police (and perhaps because police do not record some of those crimes that are reported), we know that police data omit many rapes. Victimization surveys, as well, probably undercount rapes. The same reasons that keep a woman from reporting a rape to the police—shame, embarrassment, fear of letting others know, the desire to avoid further questions—may also keep her from reporting the crime to a survey interviewer. These inaccuracies make the statistics on rape a very low estimate. Even so, the numbers sometimes can be puzzling.

The definition of rape includes both completed rapes and attempts, and in 1986, for example, the UCR recorded about 90,000 rapes—72,000 completed rapes, 18,000 attempts—known to the police. The same year, the National Crime Survey estimated that there were 130,000 rapes, a number about 50 percent higher than the police statistics as we might expect. But 65 percent of the rapes counted in the victimization survey were attempts; 35 percent were completed rapes. That is, the survey estimated a total of 46,000 completed rapes—considerably *less* than the 72,000 completed rapes reported to the police. Either the survey's sample is too small to give an accurate estimate of rape, or else many women who report rape to the police choose not to reveal the crime to survey interviewers. Both explanations may be valid.

In any case, both the police reports and the survey estimates are questionable—especially for "nonstranger" rapes, where victim and rapist know each other. Surveys of college women have found that 20 to 25 percent had been the victims of rape or attempted rape.[8] Most of these probably were committed not by strangers lurking in the bushes but by male students. These "date rapes" may not match our image of rape as a brutal and bloody attack. The victim may feel too ashamed to report the crime, or she may not even define it as a crime. "I didn't think it was rape," said one victim of date rape at a college, "I just thought I'd been bad." One of the first systematic studies of rape found that in half the cases the victim and rapist had had a prior relationship.[9] According to the National Crime Survey, in about 40 percent of rapes, the victim knew the rapist. The true proportion of non-stranger rapes probably is much higher, since women raped by husbands, other relatives, dates, or lovers are less likely, even in victimization interviews, to report the crime than are women raped by strangers. But whether stranger or acquaintance, if a man uses threat or physical force to have sex with a woman against her will, it's rape.

Marital rape—where a man forces his wife to have sex—also should fall into this definition. However, in many states a husband's rape of his wife is not a crime. Since 1977, 13 states have abolished the marital exemption entirely; the other states still retain some form of marital exemption (for example, in many states, the exemption applies only to married couples living together, not to cases where one spouse has filed for divorce or has moved out).[10] Even so, wives who have been raped by their husbands are especially likely not to report the rape to a crime-survey interviewer or to the police. As a result, both police statistics and victimizations surveys undercount marital rape.

The Social Distribution of Rape

Rape is a violent crime, and the social map of rape resembles that of murder, perhaps because both crimes arise from a willingness to use violence in interpersonal relations. The UCR's minimal 90,000 rapes annually yields a rate of 37.5 per 100,000 *persons* (the rate per 100,000 *women* would be nearly twice this figure). The U.S. rape rate is much higher than that of other industrialized countries. In Great Britain, for example, the rate is closer to 10 per 100,000. If you remember the figures on murder, these differences should come as no surprise. Within the United States, the West and South have higher rape rates than do the Midwest and Northeast.* Poorer people are victimized more frequently than are middle-class people; blacks more than whites. Because in most rapes the criminal and victim inhabit the same social space and often know each other, these differences hold true for rapists as well.

Race and Rape

The topic of race and rape deserves further comment here. Blacks comprise only 12 percent of the population, yet about 50 percent of those arrested for rape in 1988 were black; a victimization survey that year estimated the proportion at 30 percent. The explanations for this high rate are similar to explanations for high rates of murder among blacks. The "structuralist" position emphasizes social and economic inequality; "cultural" explanations emphasize different subcultural views about relations between the sexes. The overrepresentation of blacks as rapists also raises the question of interracial rape.

In most rapes, as in most murders, victim and criminal are of the same race. However, while less than 8 percent of all murders are interracial, 22 percent of rapes cross racial lines. These interracial rapes are the most explosive part of this topic, especially since most of them involve black rapists and white victims. However, we should remember that for most of the history of this country and the world, the most frequent form of interracial rape probably was white men raping nonwhite women.[11] Still, it is the image

---

* There are some interesting variations. For example, the states of Oregon and Washington have fairly low rates of murder and aggravated assault but their rates of reported rape are among the highest in the country.

of a black man raping a white woman that has been the source of so many myths and fears. It has also been the source of many deaths—whether by lynching or by legal means. Until well into the 20th century, rape laws, especially in the South, were used in a highly discriminatory way to execute blacks convicted of raping white women.[12] In the South from 1930 to 1965, 43 whites were executed for rape. For blacks the number was 398—more than nine times as many.[13]

Today, according to victimization surveys, black-white rape is far more frequent than white-black rape. Table 6–1 shows the number for each category of inter- or intraracial rape. The numbers in the table are the actual numbers of victims in each category interviewed by the National Crime Survey over a 10-year period.

As the table shows, white rapists nearly always select white victims. However, about 55 percent of black rapists (229 of 417) rape white women. On the face of it, it looks as though blacks are much more eager to commit intraracial rape. Some sociologists accept this interpretation of the statistics, and find support for it in interviews with individual rapists.

> Reflecting in part the standards of sexual desirability set by the dominant white society, a number of black rapists indicated they had been curious about white women. Blocked by racial barriers from legitimate sexual relations with white women, they raped to gain access to them. They described raping white women as 'the ultimate experience' and 'high status among my friends. It gave me a feeling of status, power, macho.' For another man, raping a white woman had a special appeal because it violated a 'known taboo,' making it more dangerous, and thus more exciting, to him than raping a black woman.[14]

There is a simpler, if less sexy, explanation for the seemingly high proportion of black rapists who victimize white women: In the U.S. population, potential white victims far outnumber potential black victims. In other

Table 6–1 ■ Race of Victim by Race of Offender for Rapes Reported to NCS Interviewers (1973–1982)

	Race of offender		
Race of victim	White	Black	Total
White	698	229	927
Black	17	188	205
Total	715	417	1,132

Robert M. O'Brien (1987), "The Interracial Nature of Violent Crimes: A Re-examination," *American Journal of Sociology*, vol. 92 no. 4, pp. 817–35.

words, the interracial pattern could be the outcome of random processes in a population that is 88 percent nonblack.

To visualize such a random process, imagine a room with 88 whites and 12 blacks, all walking around blindfolded. People will bump into each other. What race will be most of the people that blacks bump into? Statistically, we would expect that nearly 80 percent of blacks' bumping "victims" will be white. Obviously, the cause of this seemingly high percentage of interracial bumping is randomness, not the "special appeal" of bumping into whites. This statistical reasoning does not deny that such an appeal exists; it only shows that we do not need recourse to such motives in order to explain the proportion of black-white rape.

Of course, the real world is not a room of people walking about randomly. In fact, the world of U.S. cities is a fairly segregated one. Still, even taking into account the amount of segregation, the proportion of black-white rapes is about the same as the chances of a black having any other sort of interaction with a white.[15]

Explaining Rape

Rape is both a violent and a sexual crime, committed almost exclusively by men and almost always against women. Rape is most likely to occur among men whose feelings of sexuality and aggression are closely intertwined.

There is some question as to why these two types of feeling should be linked at all. Some sociobiologists argue that rape is a result of evolution. Rape, in their view, is a "reproductive strategy" for those males who could not otherwise attract a mate. They point out that rape occurs not only among humans but also among apes and in other species ranging from bullfrog to bluebird. Thus rape, the linking of sex and aggression, is a way of ensuring genetic survival, and evolution, over millions of years, has programmed rape into human nature.[16] Needless to say, many people have criticized this idea.[17]

Even if the biological argument were correct, it still would be of little use in explaining the wide variation in rape among different human societies. For example, among the Minangkabau in West Sumatra rape is all but unknown.[18] Among the Yanomamo of Brazil, rape occurs frequently. Yet there is no reason to think that there are important biological or genetic differences between the two societies. The question is not why rape exists at all but rather why rape is more frequent among some societies, groups, or individuals.

For many years, theories of rape were dominated by psychological ideas. Most researchers were psychologists, who saw rape as a sexual perversion. In keeping with psychological explanations of other sexual perversions, theories of rape looked to general personality factors or traumatic childhood experiences as the cause of rapists' behavior. Unfortunately, psychological studies rarely gave consistent results; researchers have had to conclude that rapists come in a variety of psychological types—aggressive or insecure, abused or not, alcoholic or sober.[19]

In the 1970s, thanks largely to the resurgence of feminism, social scientists began rethinking theories of rape. One of the most important books in this period was Susan Brownmiller's legal and historical account of rape, *Against Our Will*. Brownmiller argued that rape was a social and political issue and not just a sexual one. Rape established and maintained the power differential between the sexes. Even though most men did not commit rape and even though most women were not raped, rape was basic to men's legal, social, and political domination over women. Through rape and the threat of rape, men created a system that forced women into permanent subjugation, dependent on men for protection from men.[20] Rape was not a sexual oddity of a relatively few psychological deviates. It was part of a society-wide protection racket.

During this same period, theories about individual rapists were following a parallel change in direction. Psychiatrists and psychologists came to view rapists' motives as not entirely sexual, perhaps not sexual at all. While this psychiatric view still saw rapists as suffering from some "psychological dysfunction," it also held that rape was a "pseudo-sexual" act. The rapist's real motivation was not sex but power and aggression.

Psychiatrists discounted the sexual motive because many of the rapists they interviewed did not need to rape in order to get sex. They had active sex lives, either with their wives or other consenting women.*[21] Other evidence of nonsexual motives for rape came from the rapists' own statements about their crimes. Typical of "revenge" rape is the case of the man who went to collect some money from another man and found the man's wife home alone. They started to argue about the money. Then,

> I grabbed her and started beating the hell out of her. Then I committed the act. I knew what I was doing. I was mad. I could have stopped but I didn't. I did it to get even with her and her husband.[22]

For some rapists, rape was a way to assert strength and dominance and to deny feelings of inadequacy. For others, rape was a means of expressing anger.[23]

> Rape was a feeling of total dominance. Before the rapes, I would always get a feeling of power and anger. I would degrade women so I could feel there was a person of less worth than me.[24]

---

* This is hardly convincing evidence. After all, married men who regularly have sex with their wives may also have affairs or visit prostitutes. Are their motives "pseudo-sexual?"

Some rapists did see their acts as sexual; they used force or threat only as a means to obtain sexual intercourse. For the other rapists, the threat or actual violence was an end in itself.

The "Normality" of Rape

If we view rape as a crime committed by depraved individuals, then our explanations will focus on psychological factors—the twisted mind of the rapist. Undoubtedly, some rapists fit this picture. They are warped by unusual, unique histories; they provide excellent examples for psychological explanations showing how childhood experiences shape later behavior. However, in many ways psychological approaches are not especially useful. Standard measures of personality (the Rorschach ink-blot test, the Minnesota Multiphasic Personality Inventory, and others) find no consistent differences between rapists and non-rapists.[25] Even if there were a psychological "profile" of the rapist, it would have little predictive value. It might fit many rapists, but it would also fit far more non-rapists as well. Moreover, psychological explanations tend to distract attention from the normality of rape. By normality, I mean three related things. First, many rapes are committed by men who are normal (i.e., not noticeably different psychologically from those around them). Second, rape is normal in the same way that traffic accidents are normal: The crime occurs with regular frequency, and rates of rape vary predictably according to demographic factors. Third, while most rapes appear to violate general social "norms" (everyday ideas about proper behavior), in fact the norms regarding forced sex are not so clear as we might hope or think they are.

Rape and Inequality

The demographic facts of rape have led social scientists to offer the same kinds of explanations they apply to murder rates. Structural explanations see rape as a product of inequality. We have already seen the structuralist argument that economic and social inequality lead to increased aggression and violence among those on the short end of the inequality. However, while structural factors—poverty and economic inequality—are correlated with rates of murder and robbery, their connection to rape is less clear. Some studies find a correlation; others do not.[26]

Of course, rape is a sexual crime, and some sociologists argue that structural explanations for rape should include not just economic and racial inequality but sexual inequality as well. Where women have little power, they can be more easily victimized. The anthropological evidence on rape in small-scale, pre-industrial societies provides the best clue to the general conditions that give rise to rape. For example, in some simple, pre-industrial tribes or societies women have a place roughly equal to that of men. They have an important part in religious rituals, and they take part in decisions both in the family and in the society. This equality between men and women characterizes the societies where rape is all but unknown. In other societies, men dominate most aspects of life, with women living a subservient and even segregated existence. This inequality, especially in violent societies, makes for high rates of rape. High-rape societies are those where men are violent, where men have far more power than women, and where men are socially distant from women.[27]

The most extreme illustrations for these ideas come not from strange "primitive" tribes visited by anthropologists, but from accounts of soldiers—including European or American soldiers—in war. Combat soldiers often come to take for granted the kinds of behavior that would bring reactions of horror in the civilian world—things like individual rape, gang rape, sexual torture, and rape-murder.[28] One American GI told how seven men from his company had gang-raped a Vietnamese girl: "I know the guys and I know basically they're not really bad people, you know? . . . It was just part of the everyday routine."[29] In this case, the victim was not even from an enemy village.

War—especially war between nations—exaggerates all the conditions found in high-rape societies: violence, segregation, and inequality. For combat soldiers, violence is not just a part of life, it is the center of daily life. Also, soldiers live in an all-male environment segregated from women. This social distance allows them to dehumanize others, to treat them as objects. The social distance is even greater when the soldier comes from a different culture, when rapist and victim cannot even understand each other's language. Finally, the power difference is absolute—conquering male soldier and conquered female civilian.

In civilian life in complex societies, the relationship between rape and sexual inequality is less clear. Some societies may have great sexual inequality but little rape. In these societies, women, though powerless and dependent, are nevertheless protected by a strict code of male morality. This protection, however, may extend only to women of the upper classes. (Of course, getting reliable data is a problem, since rapes of women from the powerless classes are much less likely be part of the record.) The South of the plantation era featured both sides of this chivalrous ideal. The rape of white women—especially those of the land-owning class—was probably quite rare. The rape of black women (slaves) was much more frequent, though such rape usually was not even considered a crime.[30] In the United States today, states vary in the degree of sexual equality, as indicated by measures of income, political position, and legal measures (e.g., an equal rights amendment). Yet the correlation between sexual inequality in a state and its rate of rape is fairly small.[31]

Rape Culture and Rape Myths

The other leading sociological view of rape is a cultural approach, similar to the "subculture of violence" argument. Rape, in this view, occurs where cultural ideas condone it, where men (and even women) think that forced sex is legitimate. Some groups of young men consider gang rape as just one more adventurous form of delinquent activity. Participants think of these gang rapes not as loathsome, perverted crimes but as socially approved behavior. They may even avoid using the word *rape* to refer to their actions.[32] Similarly, in date rape, neither rapist nor victim may think of this form of forced sex as rape. And, as mentioned previously, in some states forced sex between husband and wife is not legally rape.

As these examples suggest, permissive ideas about forced sex are not confined to black or lower-class subcultures of violence. These ideas—what have been called "rape myths"—exist to varying degrees throughout American society. Even the lone rapist can find in the general culture a set of ideas that legitimize rape. Besides defining rape so as to exclude date rape and other forms of the crime, these myths usually shift the blame for the rape from the man to the woman. They include the idea that most women who are raped are promiscuous or "bad" women. Another rape myth holds that some women want to be raped and can even enjoy it.* Belief in these myths is not limited to men.[33] One survey asked college students, "If a woman were raped and nobody knew about it, would she enjoy the experience?" Thirty-two percent of the men answered yes, but so did 27 percent of the women. (When women were asked if they themselves would enjoy being raped, 98 percent said no.)[34]

Other myths serve to discredit the rape victim. The "cry rape" myth holds that many charges of rape are false; i.e., that women falsely accuse men of rape (so goes this myth), either because they do not want to admit to having consented to sex or because they are seeking revenge on a man. Other myths seek to shift the blame for the crime from the rapist to the victim. One such myth is the idea that any healthy woman could successfully resist a man if she really wanted to (the obvious corollary is that if a woman was raped, she must have wanted it). Another variation of the blame-the-victim theme is the idea that women provoke rape by the way they dress or act. Consider the following letter from a convicted robber-rapist, who nevertheless thinks of his crimes as the fault of the woman.

* Every once in a while, some public figure will voice the idea that "if you're going to be raped, you may as well lie back and enjoy it." The statement usually provokes a public outcry, especially from women. The speaker, surprised by the anger that his statement arouses, then claims either that it was "just a joke" or that he was speaking metaphorically. One of the most recent public figures to make the lie-back-and-enjoy-it "joke" was Clayton Williams in his 1990 campaign for governorship of Texas. He lost.

I was more the victim in this case, this person came to the door, dressed with a towel wrapped around them. I told the person to go and get some clothes on, she went into her bedroom . . . but she put the clothes on so I could see her. I was in the other room watching her more or less so she couldn't do nothing funny, and when she started putting on clothes, there she was right in front of my eyes.[35]

It is not only rapists or the uneducated who believe this idea. In 1977, a Wisconsin judge said that a 15-year-old boy who had raped a girl in the stairwell of the high school was "react[ing] normally" to the general sexual permissiveness of the society and the provocative clothing women wore.[36]

In 1984, four men were convicted in a gang rape in a bar in New Bedford, Massachusetts.* The victim had stopped in at a bar to buy some cigarettes and have a drink. There was some testimony that she may have flirted with some of the men. When she tried to leave the bar, the men picked her up, put her on the pool table and raped her. The jury found the men guilty, but a crowd of 10,000 to 15,000 people marched to protest the convictions, and a local priest had this to say: "The girl is to blame. She led them on."[37]

Rape and Pornography

Some feminists contend that rape culture extends to the most conventional ideas and practices, even traditional child-rearing. By socializing boys and girls to adopt the "correct" sex-role behavior (aggressive for boys, passive for girls), even solidly law-abiding Americans contribute to rape culture. Another widespread element of rape culture is the male tendency to view women as sexual objects. Of course, sometimes men do relate to women as real people. But the sexual-object view is widespread, and more important, this attitude seems to bring very little disapproval. In fact, there is a multimillion–dollar pornography industry thriving on this tendency for men to dehumanize women into mere sexual objects.

If rape actions derive from rape ideas, then it seems logical that anything that promotes rape culture will increase the amount of rape. As one anti-pornography slogan puts it, "Pornography is the theory, and rape the practice."[38] But does exposure to the theory turn people into practitioners? Does pornography lead to rape? Of course, rape is not the only issue in the pornography controversy. The debate ranges over a variety of legal and social issues—from the First Amendment (freedom of speech and freedom of the press) all the way to the general decline of morality. These are interesting and important topics. But for the purposes of this book, I am going to stick to one narrow topic—the connection between pornography and rape—and to one limited but important perspective: What is the evidence?

---

* This incident was the basis for the fictional movie *The Accused*.

In 1970, a Presidential Commission which spent two years and $2 million studying the issue of pornography did base their conclusion on the available evidence: "Empirical research . . . has found no reliable evidence to date that exposure to explicit sexual materials plays a significant role in the causation of delinquent or criminal sexual behavior among youth or adults."[39] Unfortunately, people—even those who eventually decide what kinds of movies and books will be available to us—do not necessarily decide on the basis of evidence. Especially on controversial issues, they may offer variations of the old slogan, "My mind's made up; don't confuse me with facts." For example, the facts uncovered by research did not convince President Nixon, who rejected the conclusions of the Commission. Nor did Charles Keating,* the commission member appointed by President Nixon, wish to be bothered with facts.

> Credit the American public with enough common sense to know that one who wallows in filth is going to get dirty. This is intuitive knowledge. Those who spend millions of dollars to tell us otherwise must be malicious or misguided, or both.[40]

Sixteen years later, another governmental commission investigated pornography. The Attorney General's Commission on Pornography (also known as the Meese Commission, after Attorney General Edwin Meese) spent much less time and money in their research than did the first commission. But this time, the Meese Commission concluded that exposure to pornography did increase sex crimes. But this conclusion about a pornography-rape connection went far beyond the available evidence.

The basic idea behind much of the research is that exposure to pornography changes men's attitudes and also their behavior. The evidence usually comes from experiments carried out in college psychology laboratories. Experimenters ask students to watch pornographic movies and then fill out questionnaires. How strongly do they agree or disagree with various statements about rape, violence, women, men, etc.? How long a prison sentence would they recommend for a convicted rapist? In one set of these experiments, students given massive doses of pornography (eight six-minute films once a week for six weeks) showed less support for the women's rights movement; they also recommended rape sentences about half as severe as students who had not seen the movies (five years vs. 10 years). These attitude changes occurred with both males and females.[41] So apparently, watching 48 "loops" in 40 days can erode feminist attitudes.

As for behavior, *some* pornography *sometimes* increased aggression toward women. The trouble is that this "aggression toward women" was a far

---

* This is the same Charles Keating who gained a certain amount of unwanted fame in 1990 as the director of savings and loans whose failure cost the government billions of dollars. Before the banks' collapse, Mr. Keating had contributed generously to five U.S. senators, who then urged government actions favorable to these banks.

cry from rape. Men who volunteered for the experiment thought that they were in an experiment to help another person learn by administering a shock or loud noise when the person gave an incorrect answer. This other person (actually a confederate of the experimenter) had previously insulted the subject. Result: The men who had been insulted and who had been exposed to violent pornography were more likely to select higher levels of shock or noise.

Is this result evidence that exposure to violent pornography increases rape? Did the "victim" resist or even ask the subject to lower the shock? Could the subject see how his action affected the victim? To equate this behavior with rape requires a large leap of imagination, and the social scientists who conducted the experiments were careful not to jump to conclusions. The Meese Commission, however, felt no such inhibitions: "Finding a link between aggressive behavior toward women and unlawful sexual violence requires assumptions not found exclusively in the experimental evidence. We see no reason, however, not to make these assumptions.[42]

The evidence coming from outside the experimental laboratory also leads us to question the idea that pornography causes rape. In the late 1960s, Denmark legalized pornography, and consumption of pornography quickly increased. Sales of hard-core magazines rose from 20,000 in 1966 to 1,600,000 in 1968 before leveling off.[43] What effects would the "Danish pornography wave" have? Some people predicted that sex crimes would increase, but others thought that easily available pornography might cause sex crimes to decrease. They reasoned that men who might previously have played out their sexual fantasies in criminal acts could now gain safer satisfaction via pornography and masturbation. As you might expect, researchers and policy makers paid close attention to reports of sex crimes.

Although the statistics on the various sex crimes may have some inaccuracies, the results were fairly clear. The amount of rape in Denmark did not increase; it remained level. And other sex crimes such as peeping and sex crimes against small children decreased.[44] While there is some disagreement among social scientists, the data from other countries also fail to show a connection between liberalized pornography policies and rates of rape.[45] Japan, for example, has a flourishing pornography trade. Japanese law prevents pictures from showing pubic hair or genitals, a policy which makes Japanese pornography less sexually explicit than that of America or Europe. On the other hand, Japanese pornography includes far more bondage and rape, and the victim in these sadistic scenes is frequently a high-school girl. Moreover, the Japanese appear not to condemn these messages. Men read these books and magazines openly on the subways and commuter trains.[46] If violent pornography causes rape, or if the propagation, acceptance, and consumption of rape myths causes rape, then Japan should have an extraordinarily high rate of rape. Yet Japan's rate of rape has remained extremely low—less than one-quarter of the rate for Germany or Great Britain, and one-fourteenth the rate for the United States.[47]*

In any case, new tests of the pornography-rape connection should be coming soon, for in the last few years, the VCR has greatly expended the consumption of pornography throughout the industrialized world. So far, however, there has been no dramatic increase in the rate of rape. Since 1983, U.S. police statistics show an increase, while victimization surveys show a decrease.

Rape and the Legal System

As researchers have found in other areas, it is not so easy to trace direct links from messages in the media to people's ideas and then to people's behavior. It seems unlikely that belief in rape myths will cause a person to go out and commit an extremely serious crime, one carrying very harsh penalties. However, while the connection between ideas and behavior remains tenuous, there is one area where people's ideas and assumptions about rape may make an important difference: the decisions they make in dealing with rape cases. Belief in rape myths may be the source of some of the more unfortunate reactions by both the victim and those around her. Imagine a husband who believes in the rape myths reacting to the rape of his wife: Was she "asking for it"? Or leading on her attacker? Why didn't she successfully resist? Did she enjoy it? This blaming the victim will be even worse if the woman herself reacts with shame.[48] Rape myth attitudes and assumptions also may affect the response to rape cases by people in the legal system—police officers, judges, prosecutors, defense attorneys, and jurors.

Traditional sexist ideas seem to underlie many of the legal curiosities involved in rape cases. The marital exemption—extended in some states to include "cohabitors" as well—is a good example. The assumption behind these laws seems to be that a woman who consents to marry or live with a man is to be regarded as his permanent sexual property. If he uses force (even brutal force) in order to use his wife sexually, it may not be nice, but it's still legitimate in the eyes of the law.

---

* It is possible that some of the difference might be a result of differences in the willingness of victims to report rape. Perhaps in Japan, because of the position of women in society and because of the cultural importance of shame, rape victims will be less likely to call the police. There is no way we can be certain. Still, the 14-to-1 difference is too large to ignore.

Victims, Police, and Attorneys

Recently, films and television shows have dramatized the plight of rape victims, showing the further indignity and insult which they suffer in the criminal justice system. The victims' humiliation occurs largely because people in the criminal justice system, like those in the world outside, act on the basis of rape myths.

The most aggressive use of these myths comes from the defense attorney. When the rapist is a stranger, the defense usually bases its case on mistaken identification. But when the victim knows the defendant, the defense is usually "consent," i.e., that the woman consented to have sex with the man. In using the consent defense, attorneys try to play on every rape myth. The defense lawyer's job is to defend his or her client, and that means discrediting any damaging testimony. The most damaging testimony usually comes from the victim, and one way of discrediting testimony is to discredit the victim/witness herself. One defense tactic is the use of the "good girls don't get raped" myth. Until recently, defense attorneys would use the victim's prior sexual history to establish that she was not a "good girl." The defense would ask the victim about her sex life: Had she slept with men and how often? If she was married, had she ever had sex with someone other than her husband? This line of defense implied that a woman who has willingly had nonmarital sex in the past was not a "good girl," and that therefore she must have been a willing partner in this instance as well. This defense became so notorious that in recent years many states have changed their laws so that rape victims no longer have to testify about their sexual history. Nevertheless, the attorney, trying to play on the jurors' acceptance of rape myths, will try to establish or at least suggest that the victim enticed the man, or consented to sex, or "cried rape" to get revenge—or all three. These lines of reasoning might be useless for other crimes. In a robbery, for instance, the victim's having given money to people in the past could hardly be used as evidence of consent to giving the accused robber all her money.

Rape victims sometimes feel victimized by the people who are supposed to be on their side—the police and prosecutors. These feelings arise mainly from two facts about the system. First and most obvious, the system is a largely male world; most police, lawyers, and judges are men, and frequently they may act on the basis of rape myths. Whether deliberately or inadvertently, they blame the victim. Second and more important, the people who work in the system have goals and concerns that are different from those of the victim. The victim seeks support, comfort, reassurance, and advice. The police and prosecutors, though they may have concern for the victims of crime, see their primary role as catching and convicting criminals. Sometimes these two roles—comforter and crime-fighter—coincide. Police officers, for example, often treat the rape victim with admirable gentleness and understanding. It is the humane thing to do. It also is the best way to get the evidence they need.

However, the crime-fighting role sometimes may conflict with the role of comforter. As crime-fighters, police and prosecutors also must decide whether a case is strong enough to pursue. They know that successful prosecution depends on being able to counter the rape myth arguments that the defense lawyer is likely to make. Evidence of forced sex provides one element for this decision—but not the only one. Officials also seek a general moral assessment of the victim: Is she a prostitute? Was she drinking? Does she use drugs? Has she ever attempted suicide? Does she have a psychiatric history? Is she on welfare? Did she know the offender? Did she agree to go somewhere with him? Does she have an extensive prior sexual history?[49] Prosecutors and police officers know that every "yes" to these questions further weakens the chances for convicting the rapist. In addition, police tend to be cynical about most things.[50] They have seen too many false accusations, too many rapists acquitted in court, too many cases where victims later decide not to testify—experiences which extend police cynicism to rape cases as well. As one officer said regarding rape cases, "After six years on the force, I believe no one."[51]

Since police officers want a case that will stand up in court, they may ask a victim to repeat her story several times, searching for inconsistencies. All these questions can make the victim feel that it is she who is on trial; she must prove her moral character. She may even get the feeling that she is there to serve the police rather than vice versa. She must convince the police that her case is not a waste of their time.

Prosecutors, too, may appear unsympathetic toward the victim. But prosecutors' attitudes, like those of the police, arise from the goals built into the job. In pre-trial interviews with the victim, prosecutors, anticipating that the defense attorney will try to construct a consent defense, ask the questions they think the defense will ask. These questions, implying that the victim is not a "good girl" and that she consented to sex, seem to place the burden on the victim. She must show that she will be a convincing witness—articulate, not too fat or unattractive, not on welfare, and with no sexual history. She also should have physically resisted the rapist. If the victim's story is at all weak, the prosecutor may pressure her to drop the charges or agree to lower charges. Prosecutors at this point are not necessarily interested in comforting the victim; they are not even so much interested in winning trials. They are interested in not losing. Therefore, they tend to drop all but the strongest cases. "Don't get me wrong. I'm prepared to go all the way if that's what you want," a district attorney typically told the victim after a preliminary court hearing, "But downtown [i.e., at a trial] it will be like this but five times worse."[52] With this kind of advice, the rape victim may feel that even the DA is not on her side.

Summing Up and Conclusion

Rape is both a violent and a sexual crime, committed almost exclusively by men and almost always against women. Our knowledge of rape is uncertain because so many victims do not report the crime to the police or to victimization survey interviewers. Especially underreported are rapes where the rapist is an acquaintance or relative of the victim. The available data show that the social distribution of rape somewhat resembles that of other violent crimes.

Public attitudes toward rape are strangely ambivalent. On the one hand, people generally consider rape an extremely serious crime. On the other, there is a widespread acceptance of rape myths—ideas about rape that place the blame upon the victim rather than the rapist. The relation between "rape culture" ideas and rape itself is not clear. For example, though pornography embodies many of the assumptions of rape culture, there is little evidence that it increases the amount of rape. Rape myths do have an influence on the treatment of rape in the criminal justice system—in the behavior of police, prosecutors, defense lawyers, and sometimes judges and jurors.

In the last 15 years, laws and criminal justice policies regarding rape have begun to change. Some states have rewritten their laws to differentiate between several degrees of rape. Before, when anyone convicted of any type of rape faced severe punishment, the victims, police, and prosecutors were unlikely to pursue the less aggravated cases like date rape. Now that there are different penalties for varying degrees of seriousness, the people involved may be more willing to pursue the case. Other changes in some states have protected the victim from being questioned about her sexual history, eliminated the requirement of corroborating evidence of force or coercion, and eliminated or restricted the marital exemption.

Besides these changes in the criminal justice system, other social changes may affect rates of rape in the near future: trends in economic and social equality between the sexes, changes in the availability of pornography, and changes in public awareness about marital rape and date rape. Criminologists interested in rape will be trying to determine what effects these changes will have on the actual incidence of rape, the amount of reported rape, and the outcome of rape cases in the criminal justice system.

DOMESTIC VIOLENCE

If you had picked up a criminology textbook 15 or 20 years ago, probably you would not have seen a category for domestic violence. Textbooks might have noted the rather high percentage of murders by husbands and wives, but generally criminologists devoted little effort to studying crime in the family. Their neglect of family violence was not surprising. It merely reflected the relatively minor place that domestic crime—wife beating, child abuse, and incest—occupied in the criminal justice system.

In the 1960s, family violence began to come out of the closet. It is not clear exactly what caused the "rediscovery" of child abuse in the 1960s, wife beating in the 1970s, and sexual child abuse in the 1980s. We still do not know whether the amount of domestic violence actually increased during these decades or whether it was the rate of reporting that increased. Nevertheless, these were years of tremendous changes at several levels—changes in public awareness of domestic violence as a social problem, changes in social science knowledge, and changes in the policies of the criminal justice system.

Is Domestic Violence a Crime?

Even when people are aware of domestic violence, they often think of it as special—different somehow from other crimes. Domestic violence also receives special treatment from those who make and enforce the laws. Legislators, police, and courts have often been reluctant to intrude—to send the long arm of criminal law into the family. Of course, laws have always limited what family members may do to each other. Law and custom usually have also given extensive power within the family to the man. "Patriarchy"— the notion that the man is the ruler of his family—has long been a part of our Judeo-Christian heritage. In biblical times, a man had rights over his wife and children much as he had rights over his other "property," rights which extended to physical violence and even decisions of life and death.[53] Later centuries paid similar tribute to patriarchy. For example, just as the biblical law spelled out the conditions under which a man could kill members of his family, the "rule of thumb" of English common law defined the limits of proper wife beating: For that purpose a man could use a stick no bigger around than his thumb. Modern society is less patriarchal, yet most people (officials included) see wife beating as different from other assaults. As for child beating, the great majority of Americans still approve of spanking and other forms of violence; though, as with the rule of thumb, Americans distinguish between legitimate and illegitimate instruments for these purposes.

WIFE BEATING*

Changes in Attitudes

In the early 1970s, wife beating began to draw more public attention in the United States. Not only did the media carry more stories about battered women, but concerned groups created women's shelters for the victims of abuse and at the same time urged changes in criminal justice policy. This was not the first such campaign in U.S. history. As early as the 1830s, the temperance movement had made wife abuse a prominent theme in the campaign against alcohol. Fifty years later, temperance organizations like the Women's Christian Temperance Union (WCTU) joined forces with feminists in the attack against domestic violence.[54] By 1870, according to one historian, wife beating was generally considered disreputable, and in most states it was illegal.[55] However, the issue gradually disappeared from public sight, only to be rediscovered a century later in the 1970s.

The new social consciousness was rooted in social change. As in the 1870s, wife beating was a major issue for a growing women's movement a hundred years later. In addition, women in the 1960s and 1970s were moving out of their traditional roles. They were delaying marriage and child-bearing—that is, spending more years not being wives and mothers. They were getting more education, and they were taking paid jobs outside the home. At the same time, divorce rates were also increasing. So whether by desire or by default, women were becoming more independent, and this new independence contributed to the new emphasis on wife beating as a serious crime.

Changes in Knowledge

While the laws had long made wife beating a crime, enforcement of the law was another matter. In practice, the criminal justice system treated just about any spouse abuse short of death as a domestic matter rather than a criminal one. Criminologists, too, largely ignored wife abuse as a topic for research, perhaps because they shared the same assumption that it was a domestic matter, or perhaps because research on wife beating is especially difficult. For any crime, it's hard enough to get the most basic data—how much of it there is and who commits it—but this problem is even more

* I am using the terms "wife" and "spouse" here beyond their narrow legal meaning. The terms as used here should be understood to include "boyfriend-girlfriend" relationships as well.

difficult when the crime is wife abuse. The usual sources of information—police reports and victimization surveys—have some obvious shortcomings. Official police statistics are suspect, since abused women frequently do not call the police. They may feel too ashamed, or they may fear retaliation from their husbands. Some victims may define the beating as a private matter rather than as a crime to be reported to the police. Then, even when victims do call the police, the officers may fail to write up the incident as a crime, preferring to handle the matter informally. Consequently, police data on wife abuse have been essentially worthless.

Victimization surveys, for similar reasons, also miss a great deal of domestic violence. These surveys ask about "criminal acts." Therefore they contain only those incidents which the victim herself both defined as a crime and was willing to report to an interviewer. A woman who felt that marital violence was "normal" or at least not criminal would not be counted in any of the statistics on wife abuse. The National Crime Survey estimate of 260,000 to 400,000 wife beating incidents per year is probably far too low.[56]

More recently, social scientists have tried to estimate the amount of family violence through the equivalent of self-report studies. In 1975, a team of social scientists interviewed a national sample of 2,143 families. Interviewers asked people how often they used various ways of dealing with family conflict. There were 20 items, beginning with "We discuss the issue calmly." Number 16 referred to "slapping or spanking"; number 20 was the actual use of a knife or gun. Because of the sample size, we must regard the results with caution. A sample of 2,143 may be adequate for common behaviors (like choosing between two presidential candidates), but it is far too small to give reliable estimates of rare behavior. Nevertheless, 3.8 percent of the couples reported serious violence, a figure which translates to nearly 2 million instances in the United States *each year*,[57] though a similar survey taken 10 years later showed a slight decrease in spouse abuse.[58] Other researchers have estimated that 20 to 25 percent of U.S. women have been abused at least once in their lives. That's 12 to 15 million women.[59]

Who Abuses?

We must be especially cautious about analyzing the evidence on who commits spouse abuse. The source of the sample, the phrasing of the questions, and the definitions of "violence" or "abuse" all can make for radically different results. For example, most people assume that spouse abuse usually involves a man beating a woman. Yet some researchers claim that there is as much husband abuse as there is wife abuse.[60] On the self-report survey items "threaten with a gun or knife" and "using a gun or knife," similar numbers of men and women (seven or eight out of the 2,143) answered yes. On the other hand, police statistics on murder confirm the idea that violence in the home, like violence elsewhere, is much more a male phenomenon.

In 1986, about 800 women in the United States killed their husbands or boyfriends; for men killing wives or girlfriends, the number was more than 1,400.[61] The evidence on serious but nonfatal assaults gives a similar picture: Severe marital violence usually is the work of men.

In most ways, the demographic breakdown on wife abusers resembles that for other violent crimes. They are male and young, the highest rates occurring among those age 20 to 35. The data on social class and race are not so clear, though they seem to follow the pattern of other violent crimes. Higher rates occur among poorer people and among blacks. The 1975 survey found that serious marital violence was five times more likely in poor families than in families with above-average incomes.[62] However, other researchers have found wife battering to be nearly as frequent in the middle class as in the lower class.[63] At this point, we just do not have enough good data to be certain which estimates are closer to the truth. But we can say, at a minimum, that above-average income does not always mean immunity from abuse.

Explanations

Although each violent family is violent after its own fashion, two themes stand out in wife abuse. One is jealousy.[64] The abusive man often seems motivated by the most patriarchal kinds of ideas. He sees his wife as his property, and when she appears to be involved with another man, his jealousy can turn to violence—even deadly violence.[65] The woman's infidelity may be real or it may be only imagined; in either case, the man is using violence to enforce his view that the woman is his property.* But jealousy is one special version of the more general theme in wife abuse: male dominance. Often the actual detail that sets an incident in motion—dinner not ready on time, some dust on the floor—is so trivial that we must suspect that the violence is about something other than good housekeeping. Instead, as the ensuing argument usually makes clear, the real issue is power. The man's goal is the establishment of his own dominance and the humiliation and degradation of the woman.[66]

Wife battering is associated with other factors—alcohol, drugs, lack of money, social isolation, and stress from things like unemployment or illness. Yet some critics are reluctant to label these factors as "causes." According to these critics, to focus on these factors as causes diverts attention from the real cause: the wife beater himself. In this view, "Men batter because they can; that is, because no one has told batterers that they must stop."[67] As with other arguments over causes of crime, the conflict between

---

* The notorious "double standard" is often at work here. The man who uses violence to punish his wife's real or imagined adultery may feel no compunctions about his own infidelities.

these approaches should be more apparent than real. They are going after two different issues—cause and blame. To determine cause and correlation is a matter of social science; to assign blame is a matter of politics and morality. Keeping these issues separate is important. For example, suppose that research identifies alcohol and the stresses of poverty as sources of wife abuse. These results mean only that men who drink or endure economic stress are more likely to beat their wives, and that where we find more alcohol and more unemployment, we also will find higher levels of wife beating. But these findings do not absolve the abusive man of blame.

Why Do They Stay?

For most crime victims, the crime is a one-time, isolated event. For victims of wife battering, however, the crime can happen again and again. Media stories of wife abuse often depict women who are assaulted repeatedly by their husbands. A Texas study found that of men who beat their wives, nearly half did so three times a year or more.[68] The National Crime Survey estimates that about one-third of the victims of domestic violence are assaulted again within six months.[69] Extending the follow-up period to a year or two or more would make this percentage even higher. These findings, like the media stories, raise a question: Why don't the women just leave? In fact, many do. Nearly half of all victims of wife battering are in their 20s, especially their early 20s. The higher the age group, the lower the rate of victimization. This means that "older" women (i.e., those over 30) either have done something to end the violence or have left.[70]

Still, many women do stay—hundreds of thousands each year. Why do they stay? Although some critics complain that merely asking this question tends to blame the victim rather than the batterer,[71] it is still a question that needs to be answered. To begin with, many women stay because they want the relationship to continue, though without the violence. They believe that a peaceful future is possible. After all, most batterers do not constantly beat their wives. Instead, the abuse seems to follow a cycle. After battering his wife, the man becomes contrite; he offers apologies, gifts, sweet talk, and the promise never to do it again. The man is no longer an abusive monster; instead he is once again the person to whom the woman was originally attracted. The couple is reconciled, and in some cases that is the end of the violence. In many instances, however, the relationship reverts to its old pattern, with conflicts over jealousy or dominance.

Finding things no better than before, the woman may try to leave. This gesture threatens to undermine completely the man's domination and possession of her. Separation, actual or threatened, is the most dangerous point in the cycle, the time of greatest risk of extreme violence and even homicide. Some men threaten that if the woman does anything—goes to the police, seeks help, or leaves—they will commit even more violence upon her, her children, or anything else she holds dear.[72] Since the man already has demonstrated that he is capable of violence, the woman must take his threat seriously. Threat, then, is a second reason that women don't leave.

Even without threat, there are social and economic pressures that make leaving difficult. A social stigma still attaches to the label "abused wife," and some women feel ashamed to leave—ashamed to admit that they did not have a proper, respectable marriage and that they married a wife beater. In addition, many women lack the money to leave. The lack of an adequate income may make leaving seem impossible, especially for the woman with children. How will she live, and where will she go? How will she house and feed her children? Women's shelters are a fairly recent innovation, and some women may still not know about them. And even if a woman knows that shelters exist, she may not be able to get into one. Women's shelters in the United States have room for perhaps as few as 50,000 women, though some estimates put the figure at 150,000. Yet each year, over half a million women are severely and repeatedly battered.[73]

Changes in Policy

Of all changes regarding spouse abuse, none is perhaps more noticeable or more important than changes in criminal justice policy. Previously, police and courts dismissed domestic violence as something more for social work agencies or informal intervention. More recently, they have begun to treat wife beating as a crime—arresting and prosecuting the batterer much like any other criminal. But even today, only 1 or 2 percent of serious spouse abuse cases come to court.

We might ask why the old policy existed for so long and why spouse abuse, so frequent a crime in society, is still so rarely found in court.* How can police and prosecutors look at a woman who has been beaten, bludgeoned, or knifed, and not treat the perpetrator as a violent criminal?

Part of the answer, but only part, is that criminal justice workers are usually men, and they share traditional sexist attitudes towards women. More important, probably, is their attitude toward their own work. Police and prosecutors tend to measure their work in terms of cases won and lost, and in any crime, the closer the relationship between criminal and victim, the harder it is to get a conviction. Wife beating cases have been especially likely to end short of a conviction. Often, the victim herself wants the charges dropped. By the time the case first comes to court, she is no longer angry, and the man is very apologetic. She finds the court appearances inconvenient, and if she depends on the man's income, she may be especially reluctant to see him sent to jail.

---

* The surveys by Gelles and Strauss (see note 73, p. 172) found over 800 incidents of marital violence, 250 of them involving serious violence. Only five of these went to court.

The police know this scenario all too well. Consequently, many police officers called to the scene of a domestic dispute choose to deal with the matter informally. They may try to talk to the couple, or they may tell the man to leave for several hours until tempers have cooled. In the old days, police even dispensed their own immediate justice. A New York cop who patrolled an immigrant neighborhood at the turn of the century recalls,

> In a neighborhood like that, there are a great number of family quarrels and the policeman had to be the judge and the jury. . . . Arresting a drunken wife beater wouldn't help the family. The wage-earner would be in jail, the children would be without food and the wife would come pleading to the court to discharge her husband so that the family wouldn't starve. . . . Whenever a drunken man beat up his wife, I beat the man up myself and gave him a taste of his own medicine.[74]

In the last 10 years or so, police departments and prosecutor's offices have begun to take formal action against wife beaters. In part, city agencies were responding to pressure from women's groups. In part they were protecting themselves against lawsuits by women who have asked for protection, not gotten it, and then suffered further serious injury.* Finally, courts and police departments were basing their new policies on social science evidence. For example, data from the National Crime Survey showed that women who call the police are less likely to be assaulted again than are those who do not call.[75] However, the evidence for the new policies came almost entirely from a single study. In this study, a 16-month project involving the Minneapolis police, formal intervention worked—at least it worked better than did informal methods of dealing with domestic violence. The most effective policy for deterring further assaults was arrest. Arrest worked better than informal mediation; it worked better than an enforced eight-hour cooling-off separation. Although a similar study a few years later failed to get similar results, the Minneapolis evidence, coupled with legal pressures and changed attitudes, made for changes in policy. Today, nearly half of all city police departments have guidelines encouraging or even requiring arrests for domestic assault.[76] However, police do not always follow these guidelines, preferring to rely on their own judgment as how best to handle the situation. Even in cities with an arrest policy, less than one in five domestic calls results in arrest.[77] And the other 50 percent of all cities still leave these cases entirely up to the officer's discretion.[78]

---

* A Connecticut woman filed suit against 24 police officers. She had left her husband, who then found her, stabbed her repeatedly, and kicked her in the head, leaving her scarred and partially paralyzed. Over a period of months preceding this attack, she had made repeated requests to the police for protection from her husband. Her suit claimed that the police had not treated the complaints seriously. In 1985, a jury found in her favor and awarded her $2.3 million. Connecticut now has a law requiring police to make an arrest in all cases of domestic assault.

Even when the police do make an arrest, wife battering cases seldom get as far as a verdict in criminal court. Most of these cases disappear because the victim refuses to cooperate. Women have good reason for dropping charges. Women who want to keep their husbands seldom wish to continue the prosecution. Those who have decided to leave may want to avoid the inconvenience and unpleasantness of testifying several times in court. Some women also may fear retaliation from their abusers. Little wonder that prosecutors have been reluctant to pursue domestic cases.

In the last decade, many district attorneys' offices have changed the way they handle wife beating, though as with police departments, policies vary widely. Some DAs merely try to weed out the cases they are likely to lose because of victim noncooperation. For example, they may accept only those cases where the victim has filed for separation or divorce. Other more aggressive policies aim at overcoming the victim's reluctance to follow through with the prosecution. To prevent the abusive man from threatening the woman, prosecutors can make separation a condition of bail, they can get a "stay-away order" from civil court, or they can threaten the man with felony prosecution for tampering with witnesses. Victim assistance programs can give financial aid. For victims who continue to live with their abusers, prosecutors may suggest that the woman inform the local police of her situation to ensure that they respond quickly should she need help.[79]

The prosecutor has one other card to play: bringing charges even when the victim is reluctant to cooperate. Remember that in criminal cases, it is the state that brings charges, not the victim. She is merely a witness, and the prosecutor can call on her to testify like any other witness. By taking the decision to prosecute out of the victim's hands, the district attorney hopes to protect the woman against pressure from the abuser. She can tell the man truthfully that the decision to pursue the case is not hers; it is the DA's.

There is still the problem of what to do after conviction. Many victims do not wish to see their husbands or boyfriends jailed, especially if they depend on the man for financial as well as emotional support. Domestic violence offenders therefore are often given non-incarcerative sentences, such as probation contingent on their going to an abuse-counseling program.[80]

CHILD ABUSE

In 1984 over 1 million cases of child abuse were reported to the American Humane Association.[81] If there were ever a statistic where the cliché "tip of the iceberg" applied, this is it. Reported attacks in the family represent only a small portion of the total. The great bulk of domestic violence lies beneath the surface. Every so often, a case of family child abuse gains public attention through the media, though usually only when the child dies. Unfortunately, as with other media coverage of crime, these stories do not even attempt to answer some of the most important questions about child abuse—the kinds of questions we ask about any crime before we start to construct explanations: How much of it is there? Is it increasing or decreasing? Are there any systematic similarities among offenders or among victims?

With child abuse, these questions are very difficult to answer. There may even be substantial disagreement among the public and among experts over basic definitions. Just what is child abuse? The extreme cases—the ones that get media publicity, the ones where children are scalded, tortured, or killed—clearly qualify as abuse by anyone's definition. But what about spankings, paddlings, whippings, and other physical punishments? What is acceptable discipline, and what is abuse? Each society has its own definition of acceptability. Many of the standard child-rearing techniques of our 17th-century Puritan forebears or even Americans of a century ago today would be condemned as severe child abuse.[82] Yet while most Americans no longer approve of severe whippings and beatings, no objective standard or even any clear consensus exists on where to draw the line between discipline, punishment, and abuse. Sweden, by contrast, has adopted a simple solution to the definition problem. There, the law forbids both teachers and parents from hitting children. Of course, such a law never could be passed in America, where most people approve of at least some form of child beating. Ninety percent of U.S. parents report spanking their children, in many cases even children of high-school age.[83] Most states in the United States permit teachers to hit students, and all states allow parents to hit their children. The only question is at what point the beating becomes "abuse."

For purposes of criminology, the most likely strategy would be to define child abuse as an incident of aggravated assault where a child is the victim. Aggravated assault is defined as an assault that is likely to cause serious physical harm. This excludes "psychological abuse," a category that would involve far too much disagreement over definition and which in any case would not fall into the area of criminal behavior. It also excludes negligence, even though child neglect has always caused more harm than has child abuse. Even today, children suffer more from malnourishment, unhealthy living conditions, lack of supervision, and other forms of neglect than from direct physical abuse. Parents may carelessly leave poisonous materials where children can get them, and though this is not a good thing, it hardly qualifies as violent criminal behavior. Nor does buying a child a skateboard—even though more children are injured each year in skateboard accidents than by direct violent acts.[84]

How Much Child Abuse?

Even more than with wife abuse, the usual sources of statistics on crime are useless for child abuse. Police reports depend on a victim calling the cops—something which is fairly rare in all sorts of family violence, especially when the victim is a child. Only when the abuse results in death can we trust police statistics to be accurate. The National Crime Survey, our other national source of crime statistics, limits questions to household members age 12 and over. It does not even ask about assaults against younger children. Even for older children who are included, the survey will miss many cases of abuse because the person interviewed may wish to keep the abuse secret even from an interviewer.

Much of the data on child abuse come from other sources—social service agencies, hospitals, and doctors. In fact, the "rediscovery" of child abuse in the 1960s came about largely thanks to the efforts of pediatric radiologists, doctors who specialize in X-rays of children. Instead of accepting parents' statements about accidents or falls, the pediatric radiologists began to suspect that certain fractures and blood clots were the results of beatings or other deliberate assaults by the parents. Social workers, pediatricians, and emergency room doctors and nurses quickly became more sensitized to the possibilities of child abuse, and the number of reported incidents rose rapidly. Still, hospitals and social agencies were not accurate sources for answering the question of how much child abuse there is. They could provide valuable information on the families in which abuse occurred, or the circumstances which led to abuse. But the number of cases they saw were only a small percentage of the real number. Who could guess how many cases, some perhaps not quite as severe, remained hidden?

The national self-report survey of 2,143 families estimated that in the United States each year, 4 percent of children are victims of abuse. Abuse, in this study, was defined as kicking, biting, punching, attacking with an object, threatening with or using a knife or gun. That means more than 2 million children are abused each year.[85] In a single year, the study estimated, 50,000 parents use knives or guns against children. Put another way, these figures mean that nearly half a million American children will be the victims of a knife or gun attack during their childhoods.*

Who Commits Child Abuse?

As with other types of violence, child abuse is more likely to occur among poor people, though the official statistics may exaggerate this difference.

---

* As with the estimates of spouse abuse from the same survey, the relatively small sample makes generalizing less precise. The actual incidence might be much higher than the numbers cited here, or it might be much lower.

Doctors are more willing to define a case as child abuse when the parents are poor or black rather than middle-class and white.[86] From our knowledge of other violent crimes, we might expect males and blacks to have higher rates of child abuse. The available data, however, paint a different picture. Abusers are more frequently women, probably because women spend far more time with children than do men. Also, black-white differences are smaller for child abuse than for other violent crimes. According to most research, blacks are no more likely than whites of similar income to commit child abuse, even though other forms of violence are more frequent in the black community. Some observers credit the black family structure for this lack of high rates of child abuse. The isolated nuclear family, typical among whites, places a great strain on all relationships within it—strains that can erupt in violence. Black family structure, however, is more extended or open. The basic family unit may include grandparents, aunts, and uncles. This means that the child has more caretakers, and the mother has more support. Therefore, the intensity of strain is diffused among several people, not focused into a single parent-child relationship.[87]

Why Child Abuse?

The explanations for child abuse are often the same as the explanations for spouse abuse. Stress theories, for example, hold that when adults experience stress or oppressive conditions in the outside world, they may respond by becoming violent in the home. The target may be the child, the spouse, or both.[88] The "cycle of violence" theory (abused children grow up to be abusive adults) also applies to any sort of family violence, perhaps even more to child abuse than to wife abuse.

These theories assume that child abuse is an irrational, emotional response to current or past conditions: The parent takes out his or her own anger and frustration on the child. Yet child abuse is not a completely irrational act. Like many other violent crimes, child abuse begins as an attempt to control someone else's behavior. However, unlike other violent crimes, the control of children is something we expect and even demand. Most people even approve of parents using some level of force in exercising this control. Of course, not everybody shares the same ideas as to what level of force constitutes abuse. Little wonder, also, that some parents sometimes go beyond the line drawn by official institutions.

Child abuse, then, is not just a matter of emotions. It also involves a *cognitive* element—a matter of what parents know and how they think about children. "Parents who abuse their children seem . . . less able to take into account their children's perspectives, to see their children as separate from themselves and having needs independent of the parent's needs."[89] The parent may not realize the limited extent to which children—especially young children—can control their own behavior. The child just may not be old enough to follow the parent's order, but the parent interprets the child's behavior as willful disobedience.[90] In addition, once parents do cross the line, there is often little to prevent their continued crossing of it. As one expert says, "People abuse family members because they can. There are rewards to be gained for being abusive: the immediate reward of getting someone to stop doing something; of inflicting pain on someone as revenge; of controlling behavior; of having power."[91] Parents may abuse children first because they do not know any better, and second because they do know that they can get away with it.

These cognitive theories seem to provide the basis for the handling of child abuse in the criminal justice system. Courts seem to operate on two assumptions: first, that the family should be preserved; and second, that court intervention can improve abusive parents. Sentences for child abuse, therefore, aim at *changing* abusive parents rather than punishing them. The courts prescribe counseling and other social services rather than prison. Courts, probably wisely, try to avoid sending children into the foster-care bureaucracy and childhood in a series of foster homes. Only in cases of extreme and repeated abuse will a court order the child removed or the parent sent to prison.[92]

Sexual Child Abuse

There is one form of child abuse where courts take a much more punitive policy: sexual abuse of children. This does not mean that all child molesters go to prison—far from it. More than 90 percent of the cases are dropped[93]— not because the courts take them lightly, but because they take sexual child abuse so seriously.

Sexual abuse of children differs from physical abuse in several ways. Though statistics on both are only slightly more than "best guesses," the estimates of sexual abuse are far lower than those for physical abuse. For example, for the year 1983, the U.S. Department of Health and Human Services estimated 72,000 cases of sexual child abuse.[94] Also, while the amount of physical child abuse probably has changed over the course of the last century, the incidence of sexual child abuse and incest probably has remained fairly constant.[95]

There are other important differences. In most cases of sexual abuse, the child suffers no other physical injury. Indeed, most cases involve only fondling rather than intercourse.[96] Also, while physical abusers are more often women than men, sexual abuse is nearly always committed by males.* With

---

* In the 1980s, the most celebrated prosecution for child sexual abuse—at the McMartin School in California—involved women. This case was unusual also in that some of the victims suffered physical trauma.

physical abuse, the abuser nearly always is the child's parent. Sexual abuse, while committed mostly by fathers or stepfathers, also is committed by other relatives, people known to the parents and child (neighbors, baby-sitters), and even strangers. Finally, it seems that social class is not such an important factor in sexual abuse. Sexual abusers, on average, have higher incomes than do physical abusers.[97]

The Difficulty of Prosecution

Why are so many cases of sexual abuse not successfully prosecuted? Before the "rediscovery" of sexual child abuse in the early 1980s, many people preferred to believe that sexual child abuse—especially incest—was a rare phenomenon. Even if a young child told his or her mother about the incest, the child might not have been believed. In some cases, the mother might almost deliberately have avoided seeing the obvious. More often, the mother was ill, disabled, or utterly dominated by her incestuous husband.[98] Even if the mother went to court, the prosecutor might dismiss the accusation as false. After all, the conventional psychiatric wisdom of the time held that many children imagined incestuous scenes. Psychiatrists hearing even an adult's recollection of sexual victimization were likely to treat it as fantasy rather than reality. Along the path from abuse to prosecution, every adult— mother, doctor, district attorney—was reluctant to believe the child's story. Many of these obstacles to prosecution still exist.

Even if prosecutors do want to pursue sexual abuse and incest cases, they run into several problems. A successful case must rest on evidence and on testimony from witnesses. In sexual child abuse cases, both of these sources may be shaky. Most reported sexual abuse cases do not involve actual intercourse, so there may be no physical evidence of sexual contact.[99] As for witnesses, the only witness will usually be the victim—a child. Child victim-witnesses present two problems. First, since the victim will have to testify at interviews and hearings, and at the trial itself, prosecutors (and parents) may be reluctant to subject the child to this process. Second, children may not make believable witnesses. When the accused is a parent or another close figure, the child—out of fear of reprisal or of abandonment, or out of love—may be reluctant to damage that person and may waver in testifying. To help prosecutors avoid this problem, some people have proposed that children be allowed to testify via closed-circuit TV. This method would remove the child from the courtroom, away from the defendant.* The

---

* This practice would seem to conflict with the Constitution, which guarantees the accused the right "to be confronted with the witnesses against him." It's hard to be confronted with someone who is nowhere to be seen. Nevertheless, in 1990, in a close decision, the Supreme Court ruled that the rights of the accused in some cases must take a back seat to the "compelling state interest" of prosecuting those accused of these crimes.

accused also has the right to cross-examine witnesses, and children may find such questioning even more upsetting. Even without traumatizing the child, a defense lawyer may be able to make his or her testimony seem confused and contradictory. The testimony of young children may be especially vulnerable, since young children often lack both the understanding to know exactly what was happening and the vocabulary to describe it.

All these problems may make it difficult to prove beyond a reasonable doubt that a crime occurred and that the accused committed it. A good thing, too. For with the increased prosecution of sexual child abuse has come an increase in false accusations. Just as it is possible for a defense lawyer to confuse a child's testimony, it also is possible for parents, prosecutors, and "experts," in many hours alone with the child, to shape the child's testimony. The child may be more interested in pleasing these people than in telling the truth. The adults, by suggestion, by persistence, and by subtly rewarding the child for certain types of statements, can shape the child's testimony—even to the point where the child will make up things that are not true. The false accusation is especially troubling given the awesome power of the state against the defendant and the serious and stigmatizing nature of the charges. In the McMartin case, prosecutors originally accused several of the school's teachers of sexual abuse. Eventually, for lack of evidence, they dropped all charges against everybody except the school's director and her son. Nevertheless, the arrests, the lawyers' fees, and the stigma of accusation ruined the lives of several teachers who probably were innocent.*

LOOSE ENDS AND A FINAL WORD

This chapter and the previous one have been about individual violent crimes—murder, robbery, rape, and domestic violence. I have omitted collective forms of violence—gang fights, racial and ethnic violence, labor violence, and lynching. Riots, too, are sometimes labeled as violence, which is a bit misleading.† Rioters—whether poor townsfolk demanding lower food

---

* Perhaps the greatest use of false accusations occurs not in criminal but in civil cases—bitterly contested custody battles. One parent may accuse the other of abusing the child. The accusing parent may even hire "experts" who are skilled at eliciting stories of sexual abuse from children—even perhaps when no such abuse has in fact occurred. (Ellen Hopkins (1988), "Fathers on Trial," *New York*, Jan. 11, pp. 42–29.)

† Since the 1960s, the term "violence" has become stretched to the point of losing its specific meaning; instead it has come to mean anything the speaker does not like. It is now commonplace, in discussions and arguments about violence, for one person to interrupt with a phrase like, "No, the *real* violence is the malnutrition that still exists. . . ." Other candidates I have heard declared as the *real* violence include racism, sexism, inadequate health care, pollution, pornography, communism, and capitalism. These things may be bad, depending on your point of view, but they are not in themselves violence.

prices, angry ghetto-dwellers, or exuberant college kids—do most of their damage to property, not to persons. Collective violence seems much less mysterious than individual violence. It emerges from conflict between groups, each with its political agenda. The political conflict may arise over concrete economic issues like wages, or it may concern vague issues of status and respect. In either case, collective violence is pretty obviously "the furthering of politics by other means."*

Individual violence often is no different. Murder and aggravated assault usually begin as disputes over seemingly trivial items, disputes which escalate into conflicts over "rights." Even rapists may feel that their crimes are in some way justified, and they may derive these justifications from ideas in the wider culture. The criminal, from his own point of view, is only trying to get the other person to act properly—to do something that she or he ought to be doing, or to stop doing something that ought not be done. Other forms of control—mediation, legal intervention—do not seem to be available, and violence appears as the immediate solution. It is the furthering of interpersonal politics by other means. The main difference between individual and collective violence seems to be the number of people who agree with the violent person's perspective. Relatively few people will accord full legitimacy to the goals or methods of the individual assailant or murderer. Certainly the state will not.

There is another important topic I have not explored here in any depth—the biological, evolutionary link with violence. The sociobiological view of human violence begins with the one outstanding demographic fact about violent crime: It is committed overwhelmingly by men. Sociobiologists see this aggressiveness in men as a legacy of evolution—a mechanism to determine whose genes are transmitted for survival in subsequent generations. From this perspective, those murders and assaults that develop out of arguments resemble aggressive encounters between males of many other species. Add the violence over issues of territory and the "crimes of passion," and the difference between humans and "lower" species seems to disappear. The violent man's justification in terms of his "rights" begins to look like a thin veneer for the real reasons, reasons that exist in species from birds to baboons: dominance and sexual access to females.[100]

Of course, the sociobiological perspective does not directly address questions of different rates of violence. All human societies have roughly the same biogenetic heritage. Yet some of those societies have much higher rates of violence. Nor do biological theories suggest any policies that might reduce violence. Some critics of the "subculture of violence" theory complain that it does not point to any policy alternatives, for how can government policies change a widespread culture? But if changing culture is extremely difficult, changing evolution is impossible.

---

* The quote is from Klausewitz's definition of that ultimate form of collective violence—war.

With other explanations of violence, it is easier to use our knowledge to point toward directions in policy. In fact, the trouble is not in coming up with ideas but in devising realistic policies. For example, if we know that violent crime occurs more frequently where people are poor, unemployed, and uneducated, then it seems reasonable to expect that policies aimed at improving those conditions will reduce violence. At the very least, such changes will not increase violence. However, to date nobody has come up with politically and economically acceptable solutions to these problems. Similarly, we know that murder rates rise during disputes over the control of illegal markets—alcohol in the 1920s, drugs today. Yet it was not until the cocaine/crack crisis of the late 1980s that policymakers even began to think about reducing murder by legalizing drugs, for obviously decriminalization entails many problems, both practical and political. Instead, lawmakers chose to increase penalties for drug-related violent crimes, just as a decade before they had increased penalties for other violent crimes. To some limited extent the criminal justice system can reduce violence through the arrest and imprisonment of violent criminals. Yet "get-tough" proposals, too, run into political and economic problems: Do we want to be such a heavily policed and punitive society? And do we want to spend the billions of dollars required to build more prisons and to hire more police, lawyers, judges, and guards?

NOTES

1. Marvin E. Wolfgang, Robert M. Figlio, Paul E. Tracy, and Simon I. Singer (1985), *The National Survey of Crime Severity*, Washington, DC: U.S. Department of Justice, Bureau of Justice Statistics, United States Government Printing Office, p. vii.

2. Edmund F. McGarrel and Timothy J. Flanagan, eds. (1985), *Sourcebook of Criminal Justice Statistics—1984*, Washington, DC: U.S. Department of Justice, Bureau of Justice Statistics, United States Government Printing Office, p. 693.

3. State Senator Bob Wilson, quoted in Diana E.H. Russell (1982), *Rape in Marriage*, New York: Macmillan, p. 18.

4. Ann Wolbert Burgess and Lynda Lytle Holmstrom (1985), "Rape Trauma Syndrome and Post-Traumatic Stress Response," in Ann Wolbert Burgess, ed. (1985), *Rape and Sexual Assault: A Research Handbook*, New York: Garland, pp. 46–61.

5. Ibid. Also, Joyce E. Williams and Karen A. Holmes (1981), *The Second Assault: Rape and Public Attitudes*, Westport, CT: Greenwood Press.

6. Gail Wisan (1979), "The Treatment of Rape in Criminology Textbooks," *Victimology*, vol. 4, no. 1, pp. 86–99.

7. U.S. Department of Justice, Bureau of Justice Statistics (1983), *Report to the Nation on Crime and Justice: The Data*, Washington, DC: U.S. Government Printing Office, p. 25.

8. R. Lance Shotland and Lynne Goodstein (1983), "Just Because She Doesn't Want to Doesn't Mean It's Rape: An Experimentally Based Causal Model of the Perception of Rape in a Dating Situation," *Social Psychology Quarterly*, vol. 46, pp. 220–32.

9. Menachem Amir (1971), *Patterns in Forcible Rape*, Chicago: University of Chicago Press.

10. National Center on Women and Family Law (1987), "Marital Rape Exemption," New York: National Center on Women and Family Law.

11. Susan Brownmiller (1975), *Against Our Will: Men, Women, and Rape*, New York: Simon & Schuster.

12. Marvin E. Wolfgang and M. Riedel (1975), "Rape, Race, and the Death Penalty in Georgia," *American Journal of Orthopsychiatry*, vol. 45, pp. 658–67.

13. McGarrell and Flanagan, eds., op. cit.

14. Diana Scully and Joseph Marolla (1985), "'Riding the Bull at Gilley's': Convicted Rapists Describe the Rewards of Rape," *Social Problems*, vol. 32, no. 3, pp. 251–63 (quote on p. 259). See also Gary D. LaFree (1982), "Male Power and Female Victimization: Toward a Theory of Interracial Rape," *American Journal of Sociology*, vol. 88, pp. 311–28.

15. Robert M. O'Brien, (1987), "The Interracial Nature of Violent Crimes: A Reexamination," *American Journal of Sociology*, vol. 92, no. 4.

16. Randy Thornhill and Nancy Wilmsen Thornhill (1983), "Human Rape: An Evolutionary Analysis," *Ethology and Sociobiology*, vol. 4, pp. 137–73.

17. Suzanne R. Sunday and Ethel Tobach, eds. (1985), *Violence Against Women: A Critique of the Sociobiology of Rape*, New York: Gordian Press.

18. Peggy Reeves Sanday (1986), "Rape and the Silencing of the Feminine," in Sylvana Tomaselli and Roy Porter, eds. (1986), *Rape*, Oxford, UK: Basil Blackwell, pp. 84–101.

19. Raymond A. Knight, Ruth Rosenberg, and Beth A. Schneider (1985), "Classification of Sexual Offenders: Perspectives, Methods and Validation," in Burgess, ed., op. cit, pp. 222–93.

20. Brownmiller, op. cit.

21. A. Nicholas Groth (1979), *Men Who Rape: The Psychology of the Offender*, New York: Plenum.

22. Scully and Marolla, op. cit., p. 256.

23. Groth, op. cit. For a summary, see Knight, Rosenberg, and Schneider, op. cit.

24. Scully and Marolla, op. cit.

25. Richard T. Rada (1978), *Clinical Aspects of the Rapist*, New York: Grune and Stratton. For other references, see Neil Malamuth (1981), "Rape Proclivity Among Males," in Arnie Cann, Lawrence G. Calhoun, James W. Selby, and H. Elizabeth King, eds. (1981), "Rape: A Contemporary Overview and Analysis," *Journal of Social Issues*, vol. 37, no. 4, pp. 138–57.

26. Larry Baron and Murray A. Strauss (1987), "Four Theories of Rape: A Macrosociological Analysis," *Social Problems*, vol. 34, no. 5, pp. 467–89. Judith R. Blau and Peter M. Blau (1982), "The Cost of Inequality: Metropolitan Structure and Violent Crime," *American Sociological Review*, vol. 47, pp. 114–29.

27. Peggy Reeves Sanday (1981), "The Socio-Cultural Context of Rape: A Cross-Cultural Study," in Cann, et al., eds., pp. 5–27.

28. Brownmiller, op. cit., pp. 31–113.

29. Ibid., p. 111.

30. Ibid., pp. 153–73.

31. Larry Baron and Murray A. Strauss (1984), "Sexual Stratification, Pornography, and Rape," in Neil M. Malamuth and Edward Donnerstein, eds. (1984), *Pornography and Sexual Aggression*, Orlando, FL: Academic Press, pp. 185–209 (which found no correlation). Baron and Strauss (1987), "Four Theories of Rape," op. cit. (which found correlation of 0.23).

32. Scully and Marolla, op. cit., p. 260.

33. Martha R. Bart (1980), "Cultural Myths and Supports for Rape," *Journal of Personality and Social Psychology*, vol. 38, pp. 217–30.

34. Neil M. Malamuth, S. Haber, and Seymour Feshbach (1980), "Testing Hypotheses Regarding Rape: Exposure to Violence, Sex Differences, and the 'Normality' of Rapists," *Journal of Research in Personality*, vol. 14, pp. 121–37.

35. Lee Sussman and Sally Bordwell (1981), *The Rapist File*, New York: Chelsea House, p. 198.

36. *The New York Times*, June 15, 1977, p. A17.

37. *The Boston Globe*, Mar. 24, 1984, p. 18, cited in Valerie P. Hans and Neil Vidmar (1986), *Judging the Jury*, New York: Plenum, p. 203.

38. Robin Morgan (1978), *Going Too Far*, New York: Vintage.

39. The President's Commission on Obscenity and Pornography (1970), *The Report of the Commission on Obscenity and Pornography*, New York: Bantam, p. 169.

40. Charles Keating, quoted in Clive Barnes (1970), "Special Introduction," in Ibid., p. ix.

41. Dolf Zillman and Jennings Bryant (1984), "Effects of Massive Exposure to Pornography," in Malamuth and Donnerstein, eds., op. cit., pp. 115–38.

42. Attorney General's Commission on Pornography (1986), *Final Report*, quoted in Larry Baron (1987), "Immoral, Inviolate or Inconclusive?" *Society*, vol. 24, no. 5, pp. 6–12.

43. Richard Ben-Veniste (1970), "Pornography and Sex-Crime: The Danish Experience," in *Technical Report of the Commission on Obscenity and Pornography, Vol. VII—Erotica and Antisocial Behavior*, Washington, DC: United States Government Printing Office, pp. 245–62.

44. Ben-Veniste, op. cit. Also Berl Kutchinsky (1987), "Deception and Propaganda," *Society*, vol. 24, no. 5, pp. 21–24.

45. John H. Court (1984), "Sex and Violence: A Ripple Effect," in Neil Malamuth and Edward Donnerstein, eds. (1984), *Pornography and Sexual Aggression*, Orlando, FL: Academic Press, pp. 143–72.

46. James Fallows (1986), "The Japanese Are Different From You and Me," *The Atlantic*, vol. 258, no. 3 (September), pp. 35–41.

47. Paul R. Abramson and Haruo Hayashi (1984), "Pornography in Japan," in Malamuth and Donnerstein, op. cit., pp. 173–83.

48. Thereas S. Foley (1985), "Family Response to Rape and Sexual Assault," in Burgess, ed., op. cit., pp. 159–88.

49. Lynda Lytle Holmstrom and Ann W. Burgess (1978), *The Victim of Rape: Institutional Reactions*, New York: Wiley, pp. 30–61.

50. Jerome Skolnick (1975), *Justice Without Trial: Law Enforcement in a Democratic Society*, (2nd ed.), New York: Wiley.

51. Holmstrom and Burgess, op. cit., p. 49.

52. Ibid., p. 137.

53. Rafael Patai (1959), *Sex and Family in the Bible and the Middle East*, Garden City, NY: Doubleday, p. 133.

54. Linda Gordon (1988), *Heroes of Their Own Lives: The Politics and History of Family Violence*, New York: Viking, p. 254.

55. Ibid., p. 255.

56. Patsy A. Klaus and Michael R. Rand (1984), "Family Violence," *Bureau of Justice Statistics Special Report*, Also Patrick A. Langan and Christopher A. Innes (1986), "Preventing Domestic Violence Against Women," *Bureau of Justice Statistics Special Report*.

57. Murray A. Strauss, Richard J. Gelles, and Suzanne K. Steinmetz (1980), *Behind Closed Doors: Violence in American Families*, New York: Doubleday.

58. Murray A. Strauss and Richard Gelles (1986), "Societal Change and Changes in Family Violence from 1975 to 1985 As Revealed by Two National Surveys," *Journal of Marriage and the Family*, vol. 48, pp. 465–79.

59. Evan Stark and Anne Flitcraft (1987), "Violence Among Intimates: An Epidemiological Review," in B.B. Van Hasselt, R.L. Morrison, A.S. Bellack, and M. Strauss, eds. (1987), *Handbook of Family Violence*, New York: Plenum, pp. 293–317.

60. R. A. McNeely (1988), "In the Battle of the Sexes, Who's More Violent?" *New York Newsday*, June 2, 1988.

61. UCR, 1986, p. 11.

62. Strauss, et al., op. cit.

63. Stark and Flitcraft, op. cit., p. 308.

64. Lenore E.A. Walker (1986), "Psychological Causes of Family Violence," in Mary Lystad, ed. (1986), *Violence in the Home: Interdisciplinary Perspectives*, New York: Brunner/Mazel, pp. 71–97.

65. Martin Daly and Margo Wilson (1988), *Homicide*, Hawthorne, NY: Aldine de Gruyter, pp. 196–213.

66. Walker, op. cit., p. 85.

67. Gail A Goolkasian (1986), "Confronting Domestic Violence: The Role of Criminal Court Judges," Washington, DC: National Institute of Justice, p. 2.

68. Strauss, Gelles, and Steinmetz, op. cit.

69. Langam and Innes, op. cit.

70. Martin D. Schwartz (1986), "Age and Spousal Assault Victimization," paper presented at the American Sociological Association.

71. Goolkasian, op. cit., p. 3.

72. Walker, op. cit., p. 85.

73. Richard J. Gelles and Murray A. Strauss (1988), *Intimate Violence*, New York: Simon & Schuster, p. 180.

74. Cornelius Willemse (1931), *Behind the Green Lights*, New York: A.A. Knopf, in Michael Feldberg (1985), "Police Discretion and Family Disturbances: Some Historical and Contemporary Reflections," in Eli H. Newberger and Richard Bourne, eds. (1985), *Unhappy Families*, Littleton, MA: PSG Publishing, pp. 121–29.

75. Patrick A. Langan and Christopher A. Innes (1986), "Preventing Domestic Violence Against Women," Bureau of Justice Statistics Special Report, Washington, DC.

76. Lawrence W. Sherman and Richard A. Berk (1984), "Deterrent Effects of Arrest for Domestic Assault," *American Journal of Sociology*, vol. 49, no. 2, pp. 261–72. Franklin W. Dunford, David Holzinga, and Delbert S. Elliott (1990), "The Role of Arrest in Domestic Assault: The Omaha Police Experiment," *Criminology*, vol. 28, no. 2, pp. 183–206.

77. Kathleen J. Ferraro (1989), "Policing Woman Battering," *Social Problems*, vol. 26, no. 1, pp. 61–74.

78. *The New York Times*, Jan. 27, 1986, p. A13 ("More Police Seeking Arrests in Instances of Domestic Assault," reporting a study by the Crime Control Institute of Washington).

79. Lisa G. Lerman (1986), "Prosecution of Wife Beaters: Institutional Obstacles and Innovations," in Lystad, ed., op. cit., pp. 250–95.

80. Ibid.

81. Gelles and Strauss (1988), op. cit., p. 73.

82. Gordon (1988), op. cit., p. 180.

83. Suzanne K. Steinmetz (1986), "The Violent Family," in Mary Lystad, ed. (1986), *Violence in the Home: Interdisciplinary Perspectives*, New York: Brunner/Mazel, pp. 51–67.

84. Richard Bourne (1985), "Family Violence: Legal and Ethical Issues," in Newberger and Bourne, eds., op. cit., pp. 93–46.

85. Strauss, Gelles, and Steinmetz (1980), op. cit.

86. Robert Hampton and Eli Newberger (1985), "Child Abuse Incidence and Reporting by Hospitals: Significance of Severity, Class, and Race," *American Journal of Public Health*, vol. 75, no. 1, pp. 56–60. Patrick Turbett and Richard O'Toole (1980), "Physicians' Recognition of Child Abuse," paper delivered at the American Sociological Association. Also Richard J. Gelles (1985), "Family Violence: What We Know and Can Do," in Newberger and Bourne, eds., op. cit., pp. 1–8.

87. Gelles and Strauss (1988), op. cit., p. 86. See also Carol Stack (1974), *All Our Kin: Strategies for Survival in a Black Community*, New York: Harper & Row.

88. David Gil (1986), "Sociocultural Aspects of Domestic Violence," in Lystad, ed., op. cit., pp. 124–49.

89. Carolyn M. Newberger (1985), "Parents and Practitioners as Developmental Theorists," in Newberger and Bourne, eds., op. cit., pp. 131–44. Quote on p. 133.

90. Ibid.

91. Gelles (1985), op. cit., p. 6.

92. Gelles and Strauss (1988), op. cit., p. 174.

93. Debra Whitcomb (1985), "Prosecution of Child Sexual Abuse: Innovations in Practice," National Institute of Justice, Research in Brief, Washington, DC: United States Government Printing Office.

94. U.S. Department of Health and Human Services, National Center on Child Abuse and Neglect (1984), *National Study on Child Neglect and Abuse Reporting*, Denver: American Humane Association. Cited in Whitcomb, op. cit.

95. Gordon, op. cit., p. 210.

96. Diana E.H. Russell (1986), *The Secret Trauma: Incest in the Lives of Girls and Women*, New York: Basic Books, pp. 96–99.

97. David Finkelhor (1985), "Sexual Abuse and Physical Abuse: Some Critical Differences," in Newberger and Bourne, eds., op. cit., pp. 21–30.

98. Judith Herman (1985), "Father-Daughter Incest," in Burgess, ed., op. cit., pp. 83–96.

99. Ibid.

100. Daly and Wilson, op. cit., Chapters 6–9.

Property Crime

CHAPTER 7

BURGLARY

WHEN CRIMINOLOGISTS WANT TO FOCUS ON "REAL" STREET CRIME, THEY OFTEN PICK robbery and burglary as the crimes to investigate. Robbery obviously qualifies as real crime. It is a "violent" crime (even when the violence is only threatened), usually committed by a stranger. *Burglary*—the unlawful entry into a building, an apartment, or other structure—is a "property" crime. It involves no confrontation between victim and criminal. Burglars even take great precaution to avoid running into their victims. Yet burglary victims, like the victims of violent crime, often say they feel personally "violated"— as though the house were an extension of the body. Burglary, like robbery, can increase people's feelings of vulnerability, for despite the person/property distinction, these two crimes have important similarities: Someone unknown, probably a stranger, unexpectedly violates the victim's personal territory in order to take valuable property.

The original laws defining burglary—as opposed to theft—were meant to protect the sanctity of the home. Since the 1700s, people have taken this sanctity for granted. We have all heard that "a man's home is his castle" (a phrase coined, by the way, in an argument for protecting homes not against burglars but against the government). Yet the concept of the home probably evolved gradually as society changed. In medieval times, people were less proprietary and private about their houses. The houses themselves were not separate living spaces apart from the outside world. The houses of the wealthy might contain several families, both kin and servants; peasant quarters might house pigs and cows and other animals we now think of as belonging outside the house. For merchants and craftsmen, houses were workplaces as well as dwellings. The distinction between inside and outside—especially during the daytime—was not so great, and people seemed to have conceived of this inside/outside distinction more in terms of the town than the individual house.[1] In fact the word itself derives from *burg* (town); in medieval England, *burgh-breche* was a breaking of the city walls. So while taking another person's property had long been against the law, it was not until the 1500s that burglary in English law began to focus on housebreaking.[2] Under such burglary laws, even if the offender did not take anything (or even if the state could not prove that there was theft), the unlawful entry itself was a crime. As society became more individualized and privatized, the home began to take on the qualities that we now take for granted. The home became a specialized living space, a protected haven closely identified with the self.

Residential Burglaries

Not all burglaries are alike. For example, they can be classified according to the type of target—residential or commercial (i.e., homes or businesses). Residential burglaries are far more frequent, if only because homes far outnumber businesses. The FBI's *Uniform Crime Reports* (UCR) for 1989 shows about 1 million commercial burglaries and 2 million residential burglaries reported to the police. Of course, many burglaries go unreported. The National Crime Survey (NCS) for that same year estimated 5.8 million residential burglaries, almost three times the UCR figure. This number means that 6.2 percent of the nearly 90 million households in the United States were victimized by burglary in a single year.[3] Of course, victimization surveys turn up many burglaries that are less serious. In fact, of the 5.8 million NCS burglaries, 1.2 million (21 percent) were unsuccessful attempts.

The victimization survey also discovered something interesting about the social distribution of burglary. Since colonial times, the individual solution to the crime problem has been to move away from it—at least for those who can afford to. The solution works well for violent crime, as victimization statistics demonstrate: the wealthier a person is, the less likely he or she is to be victimized by violent crime. But look at Figure 7–1. Burglary rates

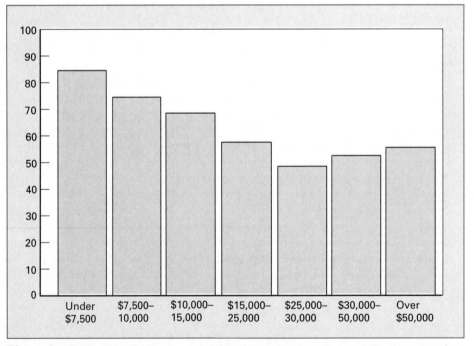

Figure 7–1 Burglary by Income, 1988; Victimizations per 1,000 Households
Source: National Crime Survey, 1988.

are highest among the poorest groups, and decrease among middle-income groups. But then the graph levels off and turns back upward; the risk of burglary for upper-income homes is greater than for middle-income homes.

Even this simple graph tells us some important things about burglary and burglars. In burglary (as in robbery and perhaps in noncriminal work as well), there is often a trade-off between the ease of the job and the size of the payoff. Burglaries run from the most opportunistic to the highly professional. Opportunists focus on convenience; professional focus on payoff. The left end of the graph in Figure 7–1 reflects opportunists who pick targets close to home. The right end of the graph reflects the professionals, who go where the money is.

Easy Come—The Opportunists

The media—fictional TV programs and the news as well—convey an image of burglary as a high-payoff crime committed by fairly skilled criminals. In reality, as the graph shows, most burglaries are not very glamorous or spectacular events. Remember, over 20 percent of burglaries are unsuccessful attempts. The burglars do not even manage to break in. Of successful burglaries, many do not involve forced entry. The burglar enters through an unlocked door or window.[4] Most burglars, therefore, are not the determined and skilled professionals we might imagine. They are "door-shakers" making midmorning rounds of hotels or apartment buildings.[5] Or they are neighborhood opportunists who can be deterred by securely locked doors and windows. If they find someone at home, they usually run away. Nor are their crimes very profitable. Most burglary victims estimate their net losses as less than $250 (and even that figure is higher than the sum that the stolen property will ultimately bring to the burglar). Most victims of these small-scale burglaries do not even bother to call the police.*[6]

So the typical burglary is the kind of crime you are unlikely to see on TV: Two or three boys, age 15 to 18, wandering in their own low-income neighborhood, find a house or apartment with nobody home; they go in through an open door or window and take a television or tape recorder or something else they can sell quickly, probably to people they know.[7] Many older burglars as well may prefer to operate in this opportunistic way. They are constantly sizing up their immediate surroundings for possible targets, and when an opportunity looks ripe, they strike. One study of adult burglars in England found that half of them worked largely on impulse. "Spur of the moment," as one of them put it. "I saw the open window and took a chance."[8]

---

* Burglary victims who do call the police are likely to have suffered heavier losses. The average loss in *reported* burglaries, according to the UCR, was over $1,000.

Although the no-force walk-in is the most frequent type of burglary, more determined burglars use other methods. At a somewhat more sophisticated level are the burglars who are "kicking it in"—giving the door a sharp kick "just next to the latch. Burglars assert that most doors of both houses and business establishments are so poorly made that a kick-in will usually spring the door open."[9] Less sophisticated burglars will use a crowbar or simply batter at a door until it breaks. Like the burglars who merely walk in, kick-in burglars have little expertise and do not plan their crimes very extensively. Yet, as haphazard and unglamorous as these simple burglaries may seem, from the burglar's point of view they do have certain advantages. The burglars are familiar with the neighborhood, so they know the easier targets and the better routes of escape. Also, since possession of burglar's tools is itself a crime, burglars who do not use crowbars, "loids,"* lock-picks, or other tools are reducing one more risk.

On the other hand, opportunistic burglary has some obvious disadvantages. The payoff of any one score is usually small, so opportunistic burglars will have to commit a fairly large number of crimes. This combination of high frequency and lack of skill or sophistication is a sure formula for getting caught. Juveniles or first offenders may receive probation, but because their skills for legitimate jobs are usually no greater than their burglary skills, they often continue to commit burglary as well as other types of theft or drug crimes. Eventually, they wind up in prison.[10]

The "Good" Burglar

These low-end, opportunistic crimes—walk-ins and kick-ins—account for the majority of burglaries. Slightly higher up the scale are the more professional burglars, less numerous but more committed to their work. I should note here that burglars themselves, like robbers, rarely use the word "professional" in this sense, just as they do not use the word "opportunist." Instead, they speak of the "good" burglar[11] or the "better" burglar or—since these criminals commit other crimes besides burglary—the "better thief."

> Say we're talking to some females or to some people we know that is straight. . . . They knows we're burglars but don't know what kind. . . . So we say 'professional'—means we got skills, know our s---, 'cause they understand the word. . . . Whereas if we'd say 'good burglar,' that they wouldn't understand. . . . More than anything you hear 'good people'—means the guy is trustworthy but can mean he's into crime for a living. . . . Burglars mainly say a guy is good or decent or is half-assed.[12]

---

* A "loid" is a strip of celluloid that can be used to open a simple door catch.

A former burglar and fence makes the following distinction between "better" thieves and others he worked with:

> Your better thief is choosey about what he takes. He ain't gonna carry a f---ing sofa or TV out of a house. The run-of-the-mill burglar and the shoplifter, your common thief, will pretty much take what he runs across.[13]

The same man, like the burglar quoted just before, also distinguishes between "good" burglars and those somewhat less professional, whom he calls "decent" burglars. For the common thieves, he uses a variety of words: "penny ante," "bottom-barrel," "ordinary" thief or, more simply, "asshole."

Good burglars, as the fence says, are more selective about what they steal. They prefer valuables like jewelry and silverware rather than bulky goods like televisions. Good burglars also tend to be older, and even if they use simple methods of entry, they may range farther from their own neighborhoods in search of larger payoffs. Professional burglars plan their crimes more carefully and use more sophisticated methods of entry. They are also more likely to be part of a well-developed criminal subculture—a group of people who share a set of ideas (norms, values, beliefs) which differ from those commonly held in the wider society. Another dimension for differentiating the more opportunistic from the more professional is commitment. Opportunists might see crime as something to do for kicks and a few dollars, but they are not fully committed to a life of crime. Criminals in the "good burglar" subculture, on the other hand, see crime as a way of life. This professional subculture is also marked by a greater specialization or "division of labor." Good burglars may even specialize in the type of loot they prefer: Some specialize in jewels, others in furs, still others in antiques. Division of labor extends to the job itself. Low-skill burglaries usually have a minimal division of labor—one person to act as lookout, one or two to go into the house. More sophisticated burglars may team up to combine different skills and roles in addition to just keeping watch: monitoring police calls, disarming burglar alarms, or opening safes.

A Little Help from Their Friends

The criminal subculture extends beyond its central core of professional criminals, and the division of labor goes beyond the burglary itself. Professional burglars, whether they work in teams or alone, are usually connected with a loosely organized support system of other people. "Fingermen," for example, provide information about lucrative targets. Fingermen do not have to be criminals themselves (nor do they have to be men). All that is required is the right information and a willingness to share it with a burglar. Night watchmen, window cleaners, deliverymen, prostitutes, bartenders, as well as other thieves or ex-thieves may, for a percent of the profits, pass along tips about possible "scores."[14] Even the more respected members of the community may act as fingermen.

> We always got a lot of tips on places to clip—like from a bartender, an insurance man, a salesman, maybe a guy that drives a delivery truck. But more from lawyers than anybody. See, your lawyers handle a lot of wills. And many times they know the house and the people exceptionally well. It's too bad, really, that people trust a lawyer that way. Your older people especially talk to their lawyers, open up an awful lot to them. Which they shouldn't, but they do.[15]

After a successful score, burglars need to get rid of the jewels, furs, art, or other valuables. Some burglars try to sell the items themselves, offering them to people at the bars where they drink. But what if a burglar has stolen several suits in a commercial burglary, or expensive jewelry, or furs—items that are less easy to sell? The burglar needs to get rid of the stolen merchandise quickly since it constitutes incriminating evidence if the police make an arrest. For this reason, the good burglar probably will know at least one "fence"—a person who trades regularly in stolen goods. Fences offer burglars a safe and reliable outlet. Fences may pay only from 10 percent to 50 percent of the item's value, but the money probably is better and surer than what the burglar could get trying to sell the merchandise himself.

Finally, the burglar's network includes those he can turn to in case of misfortune. These are people at the criminal justice end of the system—bail bondsmen, criminal lawyers, and perhaps even corrupt police, prosecutors, or judges.[16] As one burglar sums it up,

> To make it, really make it, now, as a burglar—not this penny-ante s---. . . . You need someone on the inside to give you information, say, a lawyer, or have a contact with somebody that works in a security agency or a place that sells burglar alarms. . . . Need a good partner unless you can hack working alone, which freaking few can do; a lawyer to get you off and help line you up with the right people; the right kind of fence unless you're going strictly after cash which is getting harder and harder to do; and a good woman to stand by you but not get in your way.[17]

Career Paths in Burglary

There are two principal paths into these networks. In a city neighborhood with a criminal tradition, a boy can serve something like an apprenticeship with an older, more experienced burglar. "[I] grew up with a lot of thieves, learnt off them,"[18] is a typical statement. Of course, other criminals do not accept the newcomer automatically. The apprentice may have to demonstrate his toughness and reliability and his willingness to break the law.[19] Through this apprenticeship, he can acquire the basic techniques of burglary and a generally more "professional" outlook on crime. More important, he can also meet the other people who provide the services and information professional criminals may need. Other young criminals lack these neighborhood connections. For them, the link to more experienced criminals occurs in another logical, inevitable place: prison. In prison, the young criminal can make connections, learn criminal techniques, and acquire the criminal world view.

> In the adult penitentiaries you would be meeting guys who were a whole lot better. . . . With the better criminal, you don't hear that much talking, that much bragging. But, in a way, I learned how to crack a safe . . . from hearing different ones talking about it. Main thing I got from the safecrackers was that crime was a business. I learnt that crime is a business.[20]

Commercial Burglaries

Burglars also steal not just from houses but from businesses. Commercial burglaries in 1988, according to police reports, numbered about 1 million, with an average loss of nearly $1,000.* Like residential burglaries, commercial jobs range from the highly profitable, highly planned, and technically sophisticated down to the spontaneous and simple. Teenagers may break into local factories and take what goods are around.[21] Older criminals, too, using simple methods may also pick commercial targets.

> Smash a window and if I hear an alarm run.[22]

Even opportunistic burglars have good reasons to prefer commercial targets over residences. Some burglars find it less troubling personally to steal from businesses than from individuals—especially when the burglar realizes that the victims are ordinary people like him.

> In one house, I found photos of people. . . . It didn't seem right [to steal].[23]

For opportunistic burglars, the size of the score is always an uncertainty, but many think that commercial targets are more profitable than residences—and less risky. They are more likely to find something of value and less likely to run into people. And if the worst does happen, burglars who steal from businesses and factories can expect to receive more lenient sentences than can burglars who break into houses.[24]

---

* The National Crime Survey does not survey businesses. These figures on commercial burglary come from police records compiled in the FBI's *Uniform Crime Reports*. As with residential burglaries, victims of smaller commercial crimes are less likely to call the police. Therefore, the actual cost per burglary is probably lower, while the actual number of burglaries is probably higher.

Naturally, businesses that have a lot to steal will take greater preventive measures, so burglars in search of these larger scores may have to develop more sophisticated methods. Some burglars may be deterred by alarms; other burglars will learn techniques that "beat" the alarms.[25] Once inside, some burglars may content themselves with the cash they can take from easy targets—the cash register, juke box, and game machines. But burglars aiming for big commercial scores will have to learn how to open safes.

Even safecracking is not as glamorous as you might think. Few safe-crackers these days can delicately feel their way through the combination to a lock. Besides, many safes yield to much simpler methods. Some safes can be "peeled"—a technique similar to peeling open a sardine can. The safecracker uses wedges and then a heavy bar to pry open a hole between the door and door jamb, peeling the metal back until he can put his hand through the hole. Another method, "punching," attacks the lock directly. The burglar knocks off the dial with a hammer and then uses a long steel punch to knock in the spindle until the tumblers fall. If all goes well, he can then turn the handle and open the door.[26]

> Actually, anybody with any kind of knowledge can crack an old type safe, the old square boxes. They're easy to punch or can peel. . . . And many of the new square boxes you buy even today are tin cans. They're fire protection, not protection from the good safeman.[27]

Some burglars who beat safes use explosives. This technique requires a good deal of knowledge and skill: how to make nitroglycerine from available chemicals, transport it to the job, load it into the safe, and detonate it. Blowing a safe is a complicated process. Use too little nitroglycerine and you will "bulge" the safe, leaving it unopenable. Use too much and you may literally burn the money or blow out a window, either decreasing the profit or increasing the risk.[28]

The burglar who wants to learn how to blow safes, therefore, must become part of the criminal subculture. Some of the necessary information useful for safecracking is available from open, legitimate sources.

> *How did you learn to make the stuff [nitroglycerine]?*
> Oh, I'd hear about it—the thing that I actually studied was the *Encyclopaedia Britannica*—they've got a very good run-down on it.[29]

But generally, there is no substitute for experience—one's own or someone else's.

> *Did you know right away what had gone wrong on the first safe?*
> Well, we went back to a couple of safeblowers we knew and we talked this over with them, and they explained to us exactly what we had done wrong.
> *So next time you used less grease [safeblower slang for nitroglycerine]?*
> So we used less grease and less grease as we went along until we found that

we could blow a safe and just have the door open instead of havin' it flyin' right off its hinges and across the hall![30]

Here again we see a criminal subculture—a group of people who share a set of values and a way of life different from that of the dominant society. In fact, within the broader criminal subculture, those few people who specialize in safeblowing seem to have their own subculture. They know each other and recognize each other's work. They share information about methods, though they also believe that each safecracker develops his own particular style. And style is important. A safecracker can gain status in this subculture, not necessarily by the amount of money he takes but by the artfulness of his technique.

There is an ironic twist in this subculture. Usually subcultures form as a source of protection for their members. But the burglars' subculture also may work to the disadvantage of its members and even lead to arrest. Since members of the subculture must cooperate in various aspects of their work, they will know about each other's crimes. The police, then, can pressure one criminal to divulge important information. When the police arrest a burglar, they may offer him a lighter sentence in return for information about other burglars, fences, or even (though rarely) corrupt officials. The police also may make deals with the fence. They will allow the fence to operate safely; in return the fence will occasionally inform on burglars or provide general information from the criminal grapevine.[31] In this way, the police also may come to have a fairly good knowledge about the criminal world. Individual criminal styles become known not just to other burglars but to police specialists as well.

> Let's say four or five safes have been blown, the police can look at the jobs and it's just as if they've left their fingerprints—they know immediately who did it just by how it's done.[32]

More important, the safecracker's need to gain recognition in the eyes of his peers can easily lead to his undoing.

> Conversation . . . would be the biggest factor. . . . Seems like nobody is able to keep this to himself so you get in a big crowd, a whole bunch of you, and you're yakkin', and pretty soon it gets to be common knowledge and all the safecrackers all over town know who did just about every score, you see? And, well, this is alright if you was only talkin' amongst yourselves, but you get girlfriends and wives and other guys that aren't safecrackers and pretty soon—I think it's just a matter of time before it gets back to the police.[33]

Preventing Burglary

For individuals, preventing burglary is largely a matter of "target-hardening"—making the house or apartment harder to break into. The best deterrent is having people at home, though better locks, guard dogs, or alarms may also help. Of course, such measures may have less effect on the overall burglary rate, since the burglar will merely keep looking for an easier target.

Reducing burglary rates would seem to be a job for the criminal justice system. Yet it is difficult to devise effective strategies against burglary. Prevention by police patrols seems an obvious answer, but a moment's reflection will show that this is probably not a very effective policy. Police patrols, whether on foot or in cars, are unlikely to deter a burglar. Most of these patrols—especially cars—go down the street, while most burglars prefer to make their entrances from places that cannot be seen from the main street. The following quote from a black burglar illustrates how burglars—even black burglars in white neighborhoods—feel they have little to fear from police.

> As long as we stay off the main drag, we're safe. It's the service entrances, the fire escapes. We know about back doors. Most people never question a black man walking through a service entrance. They kind of go together. That was Whitey's idea, you know, sending us in the back door.[34]

In any case, the burglar can always wait till the police go by. Then, once the burglars get inside, police patrol becomes irrelevant. Burglars, therefore, rarely even bother to get much information beforehand about police patrols.[35] Even citizen patrols and neighborhood crime-watch programs rarely take much of a bite out of burglary.[36]

Some policies aim at catching more burglars, especially the career criminals who commit so many crimes, and sending them to prison. This strategy, too, will have a very limited effect. To begin with, catching burglars is difficult. Police figures give the official clearance rate as 14 percent, and some independent studies estimate the real clearance rate as closer to 4 percent.[37] This low rate should hardly surprise us: Burglary victims do not see the burglar, and there are rarely other witnesses. In addition, by the time the victims arrive home and call the police, the burglars are long gone. For the same reason, if the police do pick up a suspect, it may be difficult to get enough evidence for a conviction. And even if a burglar is convicted, there is still the matter of sentencing. Not that judges have a soft spot in their hearts for burglars; but with prisons already overcrowded, and with some states requiring mandatory sentences for drug crimes, judges prefer to save the available valuable prison space for people convicted of violent crimes. Judges, therefore, may be lenient with burglars. Those caught for commercial burglaries or those with shorter records may receive light sentences or probation. Career burglars or those who have burglarized homes may serve some time, but far less than what the law allows. In 1986, the average sentence length for convicted burglars was more than six years, but the estimated average of actual time served was between one and one-half and two and one-half years.[38]

Some people think that even if the courts did lock up more burglars, it would do little to decrease burglary. Much burglary is committed by teen-agers who do it as part of growing up. Getting a few professional burglars off the street will have little effect on the succeeding waves of adolescents coming of age in poor neighborhoods. To these opportunists, people at home or securely locked doors are probably a much surer deterrent than is the arm of the law.

LARCENY

Larceny is the most basic of property crimes: taking something that belongs to someone else. The crime is also known as theft or, more simply, stealing. It is the crime you are most likely to be familiar with, either as victim or perhaps as perpetrator. If your bicycle has been stolen, or if your pocket has been picked, or if someone took a lawn chair from your back yard, you have been the victim of larceny. And if you have ever shoplifted, or if you have ever walked off with a book or umbrella you found in a classroom, then you have committed larceny.

Of the seven Index crimes that the FBI uses for comparison (arson is omitted), over half are larcenies.(see Figure 7–2). For example, in 1989, the

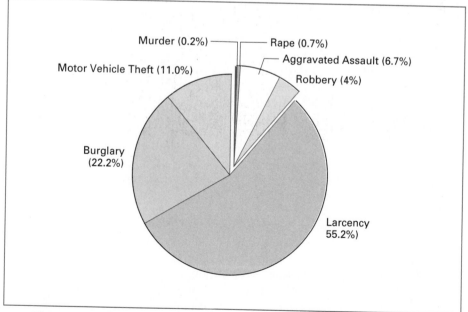

Figure 7–2 Percentage Distribution of Index Crimes, 1988

police recorded a total of about 14 million Index crimes; of these, 7.7 million (about 55 percent) were larcenies. Another 20 million larcenies never became official statistics because the victims did not bother to call the police.[39] These unreported crimes are usually less serious—thefts where victims feel it is just not worth the bother to report the crime, especially since they think the police will be unable to catch the thief or recover the stolen property.

Explaining Larceny—Supply and Demand

How can we explain these 27 million or more thefts? Most explanations assume that crime rates are simply a function of the number of "bad guys" in the population. But larceny is largely an economic crime, and from the economic point of view, "bad guy" explanations give only half the picture—the supply side, i.e., the supply of criminals and their "services." These explanations neglect the demand side. Of course, it sounds odd to speak of a "demand" for theft; perhaps "opportunity" is more accurate. But just as legitimate jobs providing legitimate opportunities represent a demand for legitimate labor, so too opportunities for crime represent a demand for criminal labor. And just as the demand for legitimate labor is reflected in the pay, so too the demand for crime is reflected in the profitability of that crime. The full economic picture of crime, then, would have to include changes in opportunity or profitability (i.e., the "demand"), independent of the supply of bad people.

Take for example the two forms of larceny that have grown the fastest in recent years (say, since 1985): thefts of auto parts and accessories, and thefts of other things from automobiles. To explain this increase, most people (including most law enforcement officials) point to the supply side: The spread of drugs (largely cocaine and crack) increased the number of criminals; more drug users needing more money to pay for more drugs meant more larceny. For these and other opportunistic criminals, automobiles on city streets provided an easy target. The following excerpt from a news item exemplifies this supply-side explanation of car break-ins in New York City.

> They have risen steadily since [1983]—in large part, the police say, because drug addicts can sell a car radio on the street, no questions asked, for the $10 or $20 it takes to buy a few vials of crack.[40]

Sometimes, however, auto break-ins have increased when drug use was *not* on the rise. For example, in 1980, nearly all of the increase in the Los Angeles crime rate was attributable to this type of larceny.[41] Drugs were an unlikely cause of this change, for the increase occurred well before the crack crisis. Nor had theft from automobiles suddenly become easier. It has always been a fairly simple matter for a thief to smash the window of the car and take whatever is inside. Instead, the explanation probably lay on the "demand" side, particularly in the value of what thieves might steal. The fashion trend in luxury cars was moving away from Cadillacs and toward BMWs and Mercedes, and the German imports came equipped with expensive, high-quality sound systems. For the potential thief, an AM radio that picked up mostly static interference hardly provided a tempting target. But a $600 Blaupunkt was quite a different proposition, as the Los Angeles crime statistics showed. Nationwide figures reflected a similar trend, as shown in Table 7–1. The value of the average theft of auto accessories, which had decreased in 1979, shot up suddenly by 75 percent in two years.

The trend in the quality of highway sound continued, and so did the trend in theft. Soon, Chevrolets and Hondas were sporting stereos equal to those of the BMWs of a few years earlier. The high-quality radios, tape decks, and CD players also opened up a new source of profit for opportunist thieves. Equally important, a market in used car stereos arose, allowing thieves to convert the electronic gear into quick cash. Without this market, the new wave in larceny might have leveled off. Instead, the market and the crime both grew.

A similar pattern occurred in another form of larceny—chain snatching, which in some cities increased greatly in the 1970s. As with breaking car windows, the increase had little to do with the new criminal populations or new techniques: Tearing a chain from someone's neck does not require sophisticated criminal skills. The most likely cause of this trend in crime was international economics. In the late 1970s, the price of gold on international markets rose from about $350 an ounce to nearly $800 an ounce. This price translated to similar increases at the retail level, where many jewelers were willing to pay people cash for gold—and no questions asked about its origins. Unfortunately, crimes do not go out of fashion as quickly as they come in. The price of gold eventually fell, but chain snatching remained part of the urban scene.

Both these cases—car stereo theft and chain-snatching—involve a sim-

Table 7–1 ■ Average Value of Auto Accessories Theft

Year	Value
1976	$134
1977	128
1978	139
1979	109
1980	172
1981	192

Source: National Automobile Theft Bureau (1987), *Annual Report*, Palos Hills, IL: p. 4.

ilar interplay of criminal and legitimate elements: Changes in the legitimate world increase the profitability of an easily committed crime. Criminals then take advantage of the new opportunities. Finally, a regular market for stolen merchandise is created by people who straddle these two worlds.

Snitches and Boosters

With these and other types of larceny, we must distinguish among various types of crime and types of criminals. Not all thieves are alike. They differ in their levels of professionalism and in their motivation. At the low end is the casual, opportunistic thief—the person who steals relatively infrequently, taking things for personal use rather than resale. At the other end is the professional thief for whom theft is a regular source of income. In the jargon of shoplifting, these two ends of the spectrum are represented by the "snitch" and the "booster."[42] Snitches are opportunists. They do not think of themselves as thieves and may have no intention of stealing when they enter the store. Yet the temptation of free merchandise, combined with a variety of "neutralizing"[43] justifications, may help them overcome their inhibitions. Some snitches steal out of need: They are poor people who simply cannot afford all the necessities of life.* More often, however, opportunistic shoplifting is a matter of convenience rather than necessity. The shoplifter could pay for the item but finds it more convenient not to. These snitches can come from all socioeconomic levels, even the highest. Every so often, the media will report on a case of shoplifting by a government official or celebrity or perhaps a member of some wealthy family.

Similar to these opportunistic shoplifters are the juveniles, though juveniles often have motives beyond simply wanting to get something for nothing. These youths may shoplift for excitement or to impress friends with their daring and skill.[44] A colleague of mine told me that the teenagers who hung out at his local shopping mall had a "200 club": To be a member, a kid had to have shoplifted an item worth at least $200. These were middle-class or even upper-middle-class kids. And they were not necessarily unusual. Surveys of high-school seniors find that nearly 30 percent have shoplifted in the last year, and nearly 10 percent have done it three times or more in that period.[45] Most of the time, these shoplifters do not try to convert their swag into cash, or if they do, they sell the items to friends or acquaintances, probably for a tiny percentage of the item's value.

Youths commit a substantial number of other thefts as well. In fact, 15-, 16-, and 17-year-olds, while making up perhaps 7 percent of the U.S. population, account for about 18 percent of all larceny arrests.[46] Accord-

---

* Not surprisingly, supermarkets and other food stores in low-income neighborhoods experience far more shoplifting losses than do those in better-off areas.

ingly, as the proportion of teenagers in the population decreases, we should find some predictable trends—especially in the area of opportunistic larceny for personal use. Bicycle theft, for example, should be especially sensitive to changes in the age structure of the population. Fewer young teenagers means both fewer kids who want to steal bicycles and fewer kids with bicycles to steal. As the baby boom children aged out of their teens between 1975 and 1986, the overall number of reported larcenies in the United States increased by 67 percent. But the number of bicycle thefts *decreased* from about 70,000 to about 48,000.[47] The smaller proportion of teenagers was only part of the decrease. The teenagers of the 1980s were not only fewer in number; they were also less criminal than the baby boomers who preceded them. From 1975 to 1986, the percentage of high school seniors who said they shoplifted dropped from 35.1 percent to 27.9 percent; the three-times-or-more proportion fell from 14.3 percent to 8.9 percent.[48]

Besides these young and opportunistic thieves, more serious, professional criminals, "boosters," also contribute to the larceny statistics. With theft, as with other crimes, several factors distinguish the more professional criminals from the opportunistic. Professionals use theft as a regular source of income. Therefore, their crimes often involve more planning and more sophisticated techniques. Professional shoplifters, for example, may have specially designed clothes or packages with compartments for hiding stolen items. Professionals also focus on the resale value of the item, not on how easily it can be taken or whether they personally want it.

Professionals also have a different self-concept. They think of themselves as criminals; opportunists do not. For this reason, the opportunistic shoplifter, when caught, may experience a social-psychological crisis. Perhaps by "neutralization" or by mentally compartmentalizing the shoplifting, he or she might have been able to keep the shoplifting from conflicting with a basically noncriminal self-concept. Other people, not knowing about the thefts, would confirm this good-citizen identity. Thus, the casual shoplifter could maintain a self-concept as a good, law-abiding person. Once caught, however, the snitch is forced to face a fact which utterly contradicts this self-concept. And the experience can be temporarily devastating.

> 'This is a nightmare,' said one woman pilferer who had been formally charged with stealing an expensive handbag. 'It can't be happening to me! Why, oh why, can't I wake up and find that it isn't so,' she cried later as she waited at a store exit, accompanied by a city and a store policeman, for the city police van to arrive. 'Whatever will I do? Please make it go away,' she pleaded with the officer. 'I'll be disgraced forever. I can never look anyone in the face again.'[49]

For professionals, by contrast, being caught is not likely to produce such a social and psychological crisis. They see arrest more as a technical problem to be solved than as a completely disorienting experience.

Good Fences

Professional and casual thieves differ not just by their behavior when they are caught, but when they are successful, too. A serious thief must have some way of converting stolen items into cash. Casual thieves sell their loot to friends or to local tradespeople. For the professional thief, however, these outlets are too irregular and uncertain a way of doing business. Most likely, he will take his swag to a "fence," someone who buys and sells stolen goods.* Fences, much like retailers of legitimate goods, provide a crucial link between suppliers (in this case thieves) and consumers. In fact, because fences create a market for stolen goods, law enforcement people have long thought that if fences could somehow be put out of business, property crime would decrease dramatically.[50] With no reliable outlet for their goods, thieves and burglars would soon find their work unprofitable and move into other lines of work. As Patrick Colquhoun put it nearly two centuries ago, "Nothing can be more just than the old observation, 'that if there were no receivers there would be no thieves.' "[51] (Note that even when Colquhoun wrote this in 1796, he acknowledged that it was already an "old observation.")

Since many people think fences are so pivotal in property crime, why doesn't the criminal justice system put them out of business? One part of the problem is that with fencing, as with theft, a large part of the market consists of small-time nonprofessionals. As a study of fencing in San Diego concluded, "Receivers of stolen property include a myriad of occasional receivers: the bartender at the neighborhood tavern, the gas station operator, the car salesman, the secondhand dealer, and the Sunday shopper at the swapmart."[52] Just as the arrest of occasional shoplifters will not take much of a bite out of the larceny rate, the arrest of these casual receivers, even if the arrest leads to conviction and imprisonment, will hardly affect the market for stolen goods.

Law enforcement is much more likely to focus on the professional fences, who provide an outlet for professional thieves and who handle stolen merchandise on a much larger scale. Yet, despite the efforts of police and prosecutors, most fences manage to stay in business, operating at the intersection of legitimate and illegitimate worlds. That is, fencing is often only a part of an otherwise legitimate business. Consider the theft of car stereos—a form of larceny which has grown dramatically in the last 10 or 15 years. As noted, the increase occurred in part because of the increase in value of these stereos. The thieves, for the most part, are young males who need to get a little cash quickly to spend on pleasures of the moment— drugs, food, liquor, movies, etc. Stealing the stereo is simple enough. But then who can they sell it to? The most likely buyer is a store that sells car stereos and other car accessories. It certainly makes economic sense for the

---

* In official language, fences are called "receivers," for the crime they commit is officially known as "receiving stolen goods."

store owner to fence the merchandise. He or she pays the thieves a fraction of the dealer's usual cost, allowing for either greater profit or very attractive prices for customers. Without such stores to provide a regular market for stolen stereos, it is doubtful that the wave of this type of larceny would have continued for so long.

At the other end of the spectrum, financially speaking, are the fences for expensive items like jewelry and furs. Here, too, the fencing operation is often only part of a legitimate business. A jewelry store, for example, can sell items stolen from private homes or from other stores (see box). Especially safe from prosecution is the jeweler who deals not only in finished pieces of jewelry but who also buys and sells the actual gemstones. Once he removes the stones from their settings, they become very difficult to identify. Then, in trading with other dealers, he can easily include the stolen gems among those bought from legitimate sources.

A crucial element in fence's success seems to be the legitimate front. Even fences who deal in a wider variety of merchandise will have a legitimate front that can cover for this variety. For example, one of the widest-read and entertaining scholarly works on fences was Carl Klockars's case study of a fence, a man who ran a store that sold everything—clothes, luggage, electric appliances, toys, perfume, etc.[53] The fence, to whom Klockars gave the pseudonym "Vincent Swaggi," provided an outlet for all sorts of property crime—burglary, shoplifting, employee theft. Burglars came to Vincent's store early in the morning, as did deliverymen who stole packages from their own trucks. Shoplifters came later in the day.

> Around half-past one, the boosters [shoplifters] start comin' in. Most of 'em work just a couple of hours a day. All of 'em work lunch time. That's when everything's so busy, customers shopping their lunch hours. . . . Things get so rushed the security guards don't know what they're doin'. . . . If I had a department store I'd keep a skeleton crew all day except for lunch hour. Then I'd flood the store with security.[54]

Note in the following news item the elements typical of larceny: The store is losing its merchandise to an employee, not a shoplifter, the thief gets only about 10% of the retail value, and the fences are people who also have legitimate jewelry businesses.

Several years ago, a Tiffany's employee, Joel d'Anjou, systematically stole more than 150 pieces of jewelry from the store's Schlumberger Collection. Mr. d'Anjou, a slightly built,

24-year-old clerk who wore expensive clothing and $250 shoes, sold the jewelry over a period of months [to jewelers] on 47th Street, a few blocks south of Tiffany's.

After he was arrested, he told the police he had been paid $25,000 for items that, according to Tiffany's, had a retail value of $250,000.

Source: Copyright © 1983 by *The New York Times* Company. Reprinted by permission.

It is common knowledge around town that Vincent sells stolen merchandise, and Vincent does nothing to change that image. It's good for business.

> See, most people figure all of the stuff in my store is hot, which you know it ain't. . . . People figurin' they're gonna get something for nothing. You think I'm gonna tell 'em it ain't hot? Not on your life. . . . If they figure it's hot, you can't keep 'em away from it.[55]

Staying Free

If everyone, including police and prosecutors, knows that Vincent is a fence, how does he stay out of prison? To begin with, there exists an uneasy but symbiotic relationship among the three sides in this game—thief, fence, and law enforcement. Vincent, for example, counts among his regular customers several police officers, detectives, insurance adjusters, even a judge or two. Besides offering bargain prices to law enforcement people, the fence may also "take care of" them with outright bribes and payoffs. As a fence (not Vincent) puts it,

> You can't be a dealer . . . without the police knowing and being taken care of. You can't operate without their cooperation. One way or another, they have to give you some slack, really a license to steal.[56]

Other fence-justice relationships may be more complicated. Fencing is a "victimless" crime. Neither buyer nor seller is going to complain to the police. But this also means that both buyer and seller know about each other's crimes. The police, therefore, can put pressure on a fence to inform on thieves. It's a convenient exchange: The fence gets a continued license to operate; the police get information that will make their arrest records look good.

> Makes the detective look good and the chief, too, 'cause in the public's mind they're solving all those crimes. It's all bullsh---. What they do is get the fence to snitch on a few burglars or a couple of dopers. And the ones the fence is turning in are usually . . . the penny-ante thieves. . . . They will end up admitting crimes they didn't even do.[57]

Police can also pressure thieves to inform on fences. Yet even though the police can get information on the fence, arresting and convicting him may be another matter. The lack of a complainant makes the state's job more

difficult. In addition, in order for the state to convict a fence, it must prove
that the goods were stolen and that they were in his possession. Fences can
make such proof hard to establish. They can avoid possession by using a
"drop" (some storage place that they do not own) until they are ready to sell
the merchandise. As for the requirement that the fence knew (or could reasonably be expected to know) that the goods were stolen,[58] here, too, fences
have some effective maneuvers. Vincent explains:

> Look, you got a store, I got a store. Some shine [thief] takes a load of mer-
> chandise from you and sells it to me. Even if detectives find out it's me that's got
> it, how you gonna know it's yours? Say it's suits, Botany suits. How are you
> gonna know they're yours? I got Botanys, you got Botanys, every store in town's
> got Botanys. . . .
>
> Now of course, if you got suits nobody else is supposed to have, say Sears or
> Macy's, then you just cut the labels off and you own 'em. And there ain't a thing
> nobody can do once you got those labels off.

Vincent also uses his legitimate dealings to provide "proof" that can cover
his illegitimate dealings.

> Suppose some detectives come in and say somethin' I got ain't legit. . . .
> Chances are I got a bill for it. [How?] Look, how many things you think I buy
> legitimate, with bills, each year? Hundreds! I gotta keep all those bills, you know,
> for Uncle Sam. So two months ago I bought 75 suits at auction. You know what
> that bill says, "One Lot of Suits Sold to Vincent Swaggi, Paid in Full." It don't
> matter what those detectives have on their warrant then. Those suits are mine.
>
> I do that with bills a lot. Like a while ago I had a guy bringin' me electric razors
> and hot combs. Every day or so he'd bring me a dozen of each. So what did I do?
> I bought two dozen legitimate from the supplier he was workin' for. Now, if there's
> a backup, I'm covered.[59]

In order to prove that the fence bought the goods and knew they were stolen,
police may have to rely on the testimony of an informer, usually the person
who stole the goods. The trouble is that burglars and thieves do not make
good witnesses. They may be very valuable to the government for information, but for convicting fences, they leave much to be desired. How much
faith will a jury place in the word of a thief, who probably has a long record
of arrests, convictions, and prison terms? To quote Vincent again,

> See, that's my rule in court. . . . Swaggi's rule is always go after the informant.
> He's probably a rat bastard and the cops ain't gonna take no chances puttin' him
> on the stand.[60]

The Sting

In recent years, the police have introduced some variations in the strategy of setting a thief to catch a fence and vice versa. The police have themselves set up "sting" operations, where undercover cops pose as fences to attract criminals eager to sell stolen goods. They rent a warehouse, put out the word that they are in business, and wait for the thieves to come. The police secretly videotape each deal, and when they have accumulated enough evidence on enough criminals, they start making arrests.

These "buy-and-bust" operations have provided some interesting information. For example, they confirm popular ideas about the kinds of items thieves look for: The most frequently fenced items are cars, electronic goods, credit cards, jewelry, and silverware. But the police also found that thieves, given a potential market, will steal just about anything. Stings have been offered everything from a 250-lb. lion to nerve gas stolen from a government arsenal. Sting operations have proven highly effective in catching thieves and burglars—even (or perhaps especially) career criminals. A single operation will usually net between 100 and 300 criminals, most with prior arrests. Because the witnesses are police and because the evidence is on videotape, these sting arrests are far more likely than others to result in conviction. One Detroit sting, for example, recovered $3.3 million of stolen property and arrested 176 people. In court, only 8 percent of the cases were dismissed (compared with nearly 50 percent under ordinary conditions—see Chapter 14, on courts). The other 92 percent, with no reduction in charges, all pleaded guilty.

For the police and courts, who are interested in catching crooks, the operation was highly successful. But for ordinary citizens interested in the safety of their property, the results were less clear: Although 162 of Detroit's serious burglars and thieves wound up behind bars, rates of property crime did not go down. Sting operations in several other cities have produced similar results: many arrests and convictions, much stolen property recovered, and no reduction in crime.

Other stings have taken Colquhoun's advice to heart and aimed at fences rather than thieves. Anti-fencing stings involve a slight change in the script. Police pose as thieves with loot for sale in order to catch fences. These "sell-and-bust" operations turn out much like the buy-and-bust stings. The police arrest fences and the courts convict them, but rates of property crime remain unchanged.[61]

The inability of police to reduce theft, even using these undercover methods, brings us back to the idea that rates of property crime are more than just a matter of the number of bad people in the population. These rates also indicate the profitability of property crime. Police strategies are designed to affect chiefly the supply side by removing thieves from the population. These tactics have failed to lower crime rates probably because they can reach only a very small proportion of those who steal. At the opportunistic end of the scale, the millions of teenagers who swipe things are unlikely to be much affected by stings or any other type of police effort. "Target-hardening" measures such as car alarms or store detectives or better bicycle locks may deter some opportunistic theft, or they may just displace the theft to easier targets. In any case, most of these young, opportunistic thieves will "age out" of property crime, just as the preteens coming behind them will age into it, though the criminality of each generation may be different. We don't really know why teenagers of the late 1980s were less criminal than those of a decade earlier.* At the other end of the scale, police may be able to arrest and convict career criminals, but if the market for stolen goods continues to provide a demand for the services of criminals, other enterprising thieves apparently move in to take up the slack. In fact, some observers think that sting operations, in creating a market for just about anything thieves bring in, may actually amplify theft rather than reduce it.[62]

MOTOR VEHICLE THEFT

The American love affair with the automobile began around the turn of the century and has continued unflaggingly ever since. Today, there are over 180 million private motor vehicles registered in the United States, an average of more than two vehicles for every three people in the country (including babies).[63] In 1985, 12 percent of all consumer spending went toward buying and maintaining these vehicles—a total of $320 billion (about 12 times as much as consumer spending on all other forms of transportation).[64]

The invention of the auto also meant the creation of a new crime—auto theft. As the horse gradually gave way to the auto, the horse thief came to be replaced by the auto thief. And in the early years, stealing an automobile was not much more difficult than stealing a horse. No need to worry about locked doors; there were no car doors, at least not until after the turn of the century. Nor did thieves have to worry about having a key to start the motor; just turn the crank in front and go. Nor was there any system of registration or serial numbers that would allow victims to identify their cars. It was not until the 1920s that states began to use the certificate of title to keep track of a car's ownership.[65]

---

* For some speculation on the criminality of the baby boomers, see the section on age in Chapter 4.

Counting Vehicle Thefts

In 1989, the number of reported motor vehicle thefts in the United States was 1,564,800. Of all the Index crimes, except perhaps murder, the motor vehicle theft count is the most accurate—especially if we consider only the completed thefts.* People whose cars are stolen call the police—and for obvious reasons. In any type of crime, the greater the loss, the more likely people are to report it, and a car is a costly item. In addition, car-theft victims want to have an official police report in order to file an insurance claim or in case the police find the car. So while the reporting rate for most other crimes is about 50 percent, the reporting rate for completed auto theft is nearly 90 percent (attempts are reported only about 35 percent of the time).[66]

The real problem in computing motor vehicle theft rates is not the accuracy of the numerator of the fraction, but the choice of a denominator. The UCR computes the rate per 100,000 population. The National Crime Survey gives a rate based on the number of households. Yet basing the auto theft rate on population or households may be misleading—especially for comparing times and places that may differ widely in the number of cars available to steal. Insurance companies compute the rate a third way. When they estimate risks, they use a rate based on the number of registered vehicles. These different ways of computing rates can lead to different results, as shown in Table 7–2. In the time period shown in the table, police reports show a large increase in motor vehicle theft, the national victimization survey shows a fairly large decrease, and the National Auto Theft Bureau (an arm of the insurance industry) shows a moderate decrease.

Understanding these differences is important in thinking clearly about the causes and prevention of auto theft. Obviously, auto theft rates depend on the number of people willing to steal cars. But the rates are just as clearly a matter of opportunity. The more opportunity (i.e., the more households to steal from, the more cars to steal) the more theft.

Joyriding

The oldest and most common type of car theft is joyriding. Typically, two to four people—usually boys, usually teenagers—will steal a car, drive it around for a while, and then abandon it, sometimes not far from where they took it. The motives and explanation for the crime are transparent. It's a classic instance of anomie theory (see Chapter 11): Unequally distributed opportunities do not allow some people to achieve socially induced goals; some of these people then take illegitimate means to attain these goals.

---

* The UCR definition of motor vehicle theft includes attempts as well as completed thefts. Attempts account for about 15 percent of all reported auto thefts.

Table 7–2 ■ **Motor Vehicle Theft Change in Rates, 1973–1985 (Per 100,000 Registered Vehicles)**

Source of Information	1973	1985	Percent Change
Uniform Crime Reports (per 100,000 population)	442.6	462.0	+4.4%
National Crime Survey (per 1,000 households)	19.2	14.2	−26.0
National Auto Theft Bureau (per 100,000 vehicles)	771.7	622.6	−12.5

Sources: Sourcebook—1987, derived from NATB, 1988

In this case, the goal is driving. Undoubtedly, this goal is socially induced. Detroit and Madison Avenue spend billions of dollars each year to convey the message that a car is the most desirable thing in the world. The automobile is a symbol of independence, excitement, sex, and power. This not-too-subtle message may be especially alluring to the teenage boy eager to latch on to symbols of adult status. The effects can be read in the statistics on theft rates for different cars. Late-model Firebirds, Camaros, and other sporty cars have theft rates several times the national average (see Table 7–3). Your Chevy wagon, especially if it's a few years old, is much less likely to be an object of envy for potential joyriders. At the same time, younger teenagers often lack legitimate means to this culturally valued goal: Economics denies many teenagers the ability to own a car; parents may deny them the use of a car; and laws deny them the right to drive a car. With legitimate paths closed, several hundred thousand American teenagers each year resort to illegitimate means to motor machismo: They steal a car. Little

Table 7–3 ■ **Theft for One Year for Cars Manufactured in a Single Year (per 1,000)**

Pontiac Firebird	30.1
Chevrolet Camaro	26.0
Chevrolet Monte Carlo	20.3
Toyota MR2	19.2
Buick Regal	14.8
Mitsubishi Starion	14.6
Ferrari Mondial	13.6
Mitsubishi Mirage	12.8
Pontiac Fiero	12.7
Olds Cutlass Supreme	11.7

Source: National Auto Theft Bureau, National Highway Traffic Safety Administration, National Crime Information Center, and Motor Vehicle Manufacturers Association.

wonder that auto theft—especially joyriding—increased when the children of the baby boom reached their early teens.

There is a second type of opportunistic car theft: short-term transportation. The thieves steal a car not for the thrill of driving, but in order to get from one place to another. Most thefts of this type are probably committed by teenagers who feel that there is no other convenient way of making the trip. Or a person may just need to leave some place and hit the road.

> In other, more serious cases, the thief may drive to another city or state and steal yet another car to continue his journey; he often leaves a trail of incidents in which he purchases gasoline and leaves the station without paying.[67]

From Joyriding to Professional Theft

Although we cannot be certain of the exact proportion of motor vehicle theft attributable to the opportunists, the best indicator we have is the percentage of stolen cars that are recovered. When professionals steal a car, it's gone for good. When opportunists steal a car, it is more likely to be recovered. In fact, the National Crime Survey estimates that in about one car theft in 12, the offenders themselves return the car to the owner.[68] In the 1960s, over four-fifths of all stolen cars were recovered. By the early 1980s, that figure had dropped to about 53 percent.[69]* And clearance rates fell from 25 percent to 15 percent. These statistics almost certainly reflect a change in the type of auto theft—from joyriding to professional crime.

Several factors caused this transition. Demographic change undoubtedly played a part. Auto theft, perhaps more than other crimes, may have been sensitive to changes in the age structure of the population. The end of the baby boom, the year when birth rates started to decline, was 1957. Seventeen years later, the last of the baby boomers were finally passing out of their joyriding years. Second, opportunistic criminals by definition are those who commit a crime because it is easy. Up until the 1960s, stealing a car was very easy. A substantial number of people left their cars unlocked, often with the keys in the ignition. Locked cars were not much more of a problem. With equipment no more sophisticated than a coat hanger, any teenager could get into the car of his choice. Once inside the car, the thief could start the motor by crossing the ignition wires, which were within easy reach under the dashboard.†

---

* Not all recovered cars are stolen by joyriders. In a few cases, professional criminals will steal a car for use in a robbery or burglary, then abandon it.

† This knowledge was part of teen culture. I grew up in a very low-crime suburb, and most of my upper-middle-class friends would discuss how to "hot-wire" a car, though I suspect that few of them used this knowledge to actually steal one.

As auto theft rates increased, car manufacturers, car owners, and insurance companies all took steps to deter the casual car thief. Insurers pressured car owners to lock their cars, and manufacturers made locks more difficult to open without a key. They also began to install various kinds of steering-wheel locks so that even if a thief managed to start the engine, the car would still be undrivable. The previously loose ignition wires were now encased in the steering column. All this "target-hardening" served to deter the purely opportunistic spur-of-the-moment thief. For the rest, it simply meant a few more sophisticated tools—a "slim jim" instead of a coat hanger, a special tool to remove the ignition switch from the steering column, and screwdriver to start the ignition.

But the most important factor in the transition to professional auto theft was the creation of a market. It was a question of demand and supply. Prior to the 1960s, demand for stolen cars was low. The person who stole a car could not do much with it besides drive it around for a while. He could not sell it as he might other stolen goods, for cars were easily traced. They had serial numbers, and they had to be registered with the state, with the appropriate license plates. A car couldn't be kept out of sight, like a television in the living room, nor could it be sold to a pawn shop, like stolen jewelry or furs.

The Marketplace: Demand and Supply

The late 1960s saw the expansion of two markets for auto theft: "new" cars for resale, and auto parts. The demand for stolen cars increased, and suppliers (i.e., thieves) increased their output accordingly. The resale market also demanded a slightly different type of thief. Selling a stolen car to a consumer requires techniques and personal connections beyond those of the joyrider. It requires first of all that the car not be damaged during the theft, so professional thieves for this market need special skills and equipment. The resale market also requires someone who can provide registration papers and someone who can find customers. Existing criminal organizations meet both these needs. Their other criminal dealings—loansharking, gambling, higher-level fencing—bring them into a network of people who don't mind buying merchandise of questionable origin. Of course, even many otherwise legitimate people might be unable to resist the offer of a nearly new Cadillac at half price. Criminal organizations can also obtain the necessary documents either by bribing people within the motor vehicle bureaucracy, by hiring skilled forgers, or by a method known as the "salvage switch." "Salvage" cars are those which have been "totaled"; that is, the cost of repair would be higher than the car's book value. In the salvage switch, the criminals buy (cheaply) a salvage car of the same make and model as the stolen one. They do not want the car itself; they want the title and the vehicle identification number, which they then switch to the stolen car.

The business of theft and resale was so organized and the thieves so professional that they adopted the "just in time" system of supply long before it became fashionable in other industries. Rather than stealing cars randomly or on spec, thieves would wait for an order from a dealer. Usually, they can find and steal a nearly new model to order (e.g., a dark green four-door Cadillac) more quickly than one can be supplied legitimately by Detroit—often in a matter of days. Some thieves keep a log of available cars. A thief might note that a late-model Buick Riviera is parked regularly in a particular lot. He records this information so that when he gets an order for such a car, he can consult his log and know where and when to find it.[70]

While the market for stolen cars already existed to some extent before 1970, it was relatively small and confined mostly to the Northeast.* Since then, it has expanded, even to include overseas outlets, where cars stolen in the United States are unlikely to be discovered. Consequently, major port cities have been experiencing increasing thefts of these high-priced cars, which are often shipped to foreign countries. The advent of "containerization" has made it easier for criminals to export stolen cars. A 40-foot container, which can hold two cars, can be loaded and sealed anywhere in the country and then sent by truck or rail to a port. From there, the container, still sealed, can be loaded onto a ship and sent anywhere in the world (though Europe and the Middle east seem to be the most popular destinations). Although there is no way of knowing precisely how large this industry is, U.S. Customs estimates that about 200,000 stolen vehicles (15 percent of all vehicles stolen in the United States) are exported each year.[71]

Chop Shops

While the market for cut-rate luxury cars was expanding, another market for stolen cars was developing even more rapidly: the market for auto parts. It expanded on the supply side because thieves came to realize that parts were worth something. But other changes contributed to the demand side of the equation—changes in the noncriminal world. Americans were keeping their cars longer, fixing the old car rather than buying a new one. Cars were becoming more complicated; parts that a mechanic might once have repaired now had to be replaced. In addition, legitimate parts became harder to get. For economic reasons, legitimate dealers cut back on their inventories, preferring to order parts from Detroit as the need arose. So repair

---

* When I first started looking at the UCR in the mid-1970s, I noticed that some cities with low rates for all other Index crimes had among the highest rates of motor vehicle theft—cities like Boston, Brockton, and Worcester, Massachusetts, and Providence, Rhode Island. Could New England teenagers be so fond of joyriding? I confess, it took me a while to figure out what was going on.

shops calling a dealer for some part might find they had to wait two weeks.* As a result, the price of parts increased—so much so that the resale value of a used or even new car broken down for parts was often *more* than that of the car itself.

The market in parts provided an enormous advantage to those with criminal inclinations. Stealing a car had always been fairly easy, but state requirements about documents made for difficulties in selling it. On the other hand, it was fairly easy to sell stolen car parts. License and registration papers might be necessary for a 1980 Chevy, but not for a 1980 Chevy transmission or door panel. The potential market in stolen parts was nearly all there—the potential supply of stolen cars and the potential demand for stolen parts. All that was missing was someone to match the supply and the demand—that is, someone who would reduce the stolen car into parts. So in time, at this central point in the market there emerged a new type of business—the "chop shop."

A chop shop is essentially a fence operation; it buys and sells stolen goods. The only difference is that after it buys a stolen car, the chop shop quickly breaks it down into component parts.† Like other kinds of fences, the chop shop owner often trades in legitimate merchandise as well, thus providing a cover for the illegal side of his business. As with other forms of fencing, several others may be in the know. The employees who do the actual "chopping" and the buyers of the shop's reasonably priced parts probably know or at least suspect what's going on, and they are all part of the network that sustains the crime. However, the people who benefit the most—the chop shop owners—take the least risk. A few owners steal cars themselves, but most pay others—usually teenagers—to do this more exposed and riskier part of the work. The actual thief might get a few hundred dollars for a car whose parts will bring the chop shop anywhere from $500 to $2,500, depending on their condition.[72]

Other Vehicles

Although cars make up the bulk of stolen vehicles, there has been a growing market in "off-road vehicles"—tractors, bulldozers, farm machinery. The thief may find it somewhat more difficult to drive off in one of these big pieces of equipment, and there may be fewer potential buyers. But for the

---

* To speed up the search, repair shops and salvage yards now have a network, called "the long line," for matching up those who need some part with those who have that part. Of course, illegitimate suppliers can also subscribe to the "long line" and offer the needed part faster than the legitimate competition. (National Auto Theft Bureau (1987), *Annual Report*, p. 24.

† Jewel thieves or fences take similar precautions, removing valuable gems from their settings and thus making identification nearly impossible.

thief who can solve these problems, off-road vehicles make attractive targets. First, most off-road machinery does not require registration or title documents, and manufacturers do not have a uniform system of identification numbers. Once stolen, a tractor or log-skidder may be hard to identify, and the victim may have a difficult time proving ownership. Second, these pieces of industrial equipment are obviously much more expensive than cars. You may not know what a log-skidder is (I don't), but whatever it is, it costs upwards of $100,000. A good bulldozer may be worth as much as half a dozen new Cadillacs. The value of all *on-road* vehicles stolen in 1987 was about $6.4 billion. That year, the value of all *off-road* vehicles (not including farm equipment) was $1 billion.[73]

Insurance Fraud

Of the nearly 1.3 million reported motor vehicle thefts each year, perhaps as many as 190,000 have not really been stolen. Instead, the owner is filing a false report for purposes of making an insurance claim. Who are these fraud artists? Some of them are people who deliberately set out to maximize their profits through fraud. They buy a popular car, making a low down payment, export the car for sale overseas, and then report it stolen. In most "owner give-ups," however, the owners committing insurance fraud are not professional criminals. Instead, they are car owners who for one reason or another want the insurance money more than they want their cars. In New York City in 1988, for example, an investigation of insurance fraud resulted in the arrests of 30 people, among them executives, a respiratory therapist, a carpenter, a student, a secretary, and a homemaker. People like these turn to fraud for a variety of reasons. Some need cash, others have run into payment problems, some just want to avoid the hassle of selling an unwanted car. In some cases, the owner is stuck with a "lemon"; tired of trying to get the car repaired, he or she arranges to give up the car, report it stolen, and file an insurance claim for a car in good condition. Some owners will add claims for a set of golf clubs or a fur coat that supposedly had been in the trunk of the stolen car.

These one-time defrauders may rationalize their act with the argument that unlike real auto theft, their scheme doesn't really hurt anyone. Of course, on the insurance company's bottom line, a claim paid is a claim paid, whether the theft was real or fraudulent. And the insurer, through higher rates, passes its costs on to consumers. Still, most of these people probably do not think of themselves as criminals. And since they do not belong to groups that serve to reinforce their "neutralizations," they may be easily deterred. For example, to reduce fraud, the Houston police instituted two small changes: They refused to take auto-theft reports by phone, so the victim had to file the claim face-to-face with a police officer; police reminded victims that if the report proved false, he or she could be charged with theft. Theft reports dropped by 10 percent.[74] (Actually, proving false claims beyond a reasonable doubt is very difficult, a fact unknown to most of the one-time, nonprofessional criminals.)

Insurance fraud still leaves room for professional criminals, who act as middlemen. For a fee, they take the car and assure the owner that it will not be seen again. The middleman then hires a disposer to get rid of the car. Lakes and rivers are popular disposal sites since even if the car is eventually found, the water may have corroded it beyond recognition. Says one Florida official,

> We have a 55-foot deep canal around here that gets filled up with cars at least once a year. The cars are stacked so high that a diver can stand on the top one, and he will be out of the water from the waist up.[75]

SUMMARY AND CONCLUSION

Burglary, larceny, and motor vehicle theft account for nearly 90 percent of the "serious" crimes on the FBI's Index of crimes reported to the police, and about 85 percent of all crimes reported in victimization surveys. The crimes vary from the trivial to the very serious. Because the motivation in property crime is largely economic, I have tried to look at rates for these crimes both in terms of the criminals (the "supply" of criminal labor) and the opportunities for profit (the "demand"). Increases in property crime reflect, at least in part, an increase in the opportunity for profitable stealing. Opportunity has three important components: the amount of stealable property; the ease of stealing it; and the existence of a market for converting the stolen property to cash. The first two elements depend almost entirely on the actions of law-abiding people. If more of them stock their houses with more VCRs and jewelry, and if more of them leave those houses empty during the day, they are creating more opportunities for burglary. The third element— the market for stolen goods—often depends upon people who straddle the criminal and noncriminal world. They are the "fences" whose legitimate business provides a cover for traffic in stolen goods. Ultimately, the market must also be provided by consumers who are eager to take advantage of low prices, regardless of their suspicions (or knowledge) about the origins of the merchandise. Remember, some of Vincent Swaggi's best customers were police officers.

On the other side of the equation are those who commit the crimes. They range from the opportunistic to the professional. While the professionals— highly skilled, selective, profit-oriented—make for more interesting stories, the bulk of property crimes are committed by criminals toward the opportunistic end of the scale. They spend little time in planning and make little money from their crimes. Many are younger people who commit property crimes but who quit in their late teens. Of those who remain in crime, a few become more professional in their attitudes and methods. Most, however, do not. They continue in their minimally planned, low-profit crimes and eventually wind up in prison.

Controlling property crime has proven a difficult task. Some strategies—such as "target hardening" or moving far from poor neighborhoods—may be effective for the individual. Good locks and other security devices may be enough to deter the casual criminal. But these strategies are unlikely to change the overall rate of crime in the society. Unfortunately, the policies available to the criminal justice system also seem to have only a modest effect, if any, on rates of property crime. "Sting" operations that aim at career thieves or at fences have been successful at arresting and even convicting these targets, but have had no demonstrable effect on the rate of crime.

NOTES

1. Georges Duby, ed. (1988), *A History of Private Life, Vol. II: Revelations of the Medieval World* (tr. Arthur Goldhammer), Cambridge, MA: The Belknap Press of Harvard University Press.

2. J. W. Cecil Turner, ed. (1962), *Kenny's Outline of Criminal Law*, Cambridge, UK: Cambridge University Press, pp. 244–48.

3. National Crime Survey, 1988

4. *Report to the Nation on Crime and Justice (2nd ed.)* (1988), U.S. Department of Justice, Bureau of Justice Statistics, p. 3.

5. Nicholas Pileggi (1968), "1968 Has Been the Year of the Burglar," *The New York Times Magazine*, Nov. 17, p. 79.

6. *Criminal Victimization in the United States, 1987*, National Crime Survey, United States Department of Justice, Bureau of Justice Statistics, pp. 74, 92.

7. Carl E. Pope (1977), *Crime-Specific Analysis: An Empirical Examination of Burglary Offender Characteristics*, Washington, DC: Department of Justice.

8. Dermot Walsh (1986), *Heavy Business: Commercial Burglary and Robbery*, London: Routledge and Kegan Paul, p. 45.

9. Peter Letkeman (1973), *Crime as Work*, Englewood Cliffs, NJ: Prentice-Hall, p. 52.

10. Pope, op. cit.

11. Neal Shover (1972), "Structures and Careers in Burglary," *Journal of Criminal Law, Criminology, and Police Science*, vol. 63, no. 4, pp. 540–49.

12. Darrell J. Steffensmeier (1986), *The Fence: In the Shadow of Two Worlds*, Totowa, NJ: Rowman and Littlefield, pp. 48–49n, also pp. 57–58n.

13. Ibid., p. 26.

14. Shover, op. cit. Also Bruce Jackson (1969), *Outside the Law: A Thief's Primer*, New York: Macmillan, pp. 121–22, 138.

15. Steffensmeier, op. cit., p. 47.

16. Jackson, op. cit., p. 133. Also Steffensmeier, op. cit., pp. 154–56.

17. Steffensmeier, p. 56n.

18. Walsh, op. cit., p. 17.

19. Shover, op. cit. Also Richard A. Cloward and Lloyd E. Ohlin (1960), *Delinquency and Opportunity: A Theory of Delinquent Gangs*, New York: Free Press.

20. Steffensmeier, op. cit., p. 43.

21. Mercer Sullivan (1983), "Youth Crime: New York's Two Varieties," *New York Affairs*, vol. 8, pp. 31–48.

22. Walsh, op. cit., p. 26.

23. Ibid., p. 42.

24. Ibid.

25. Letkeman, op. cit., p. 56.

26. Ibid., pp. 77–78.

27. Steffensmeier, op. cit., p. 49.

28. Letkeman, op. cit., pp. 49–89.

29. Ibid., p. 60.

30. Ibid., p. 72.

31. Steffensmeier, op. cit., pp. 148–51.

32. Letkeman, op. cit., p. 84.

33. Ibid., p. 86.

34. Pileggi, op. cit., p. 80.

35. Repetto, op. cit., p. 74.

36. Dan A. Lewis, Jane A. Grant, and Dennis P. Rosenbaum (1988), *Social Construction of Reform: Crime Prevention and Community Organization*, New Brunswick, NJ: Transaction Books.

37. Repetto, op. cit., p. 74. Peter W. Greenwood (1970), *An Analysis of the Apprehension Activities of the New York City Police Department*, New York: Rand Institute.

38. "Felony Sentences in State Courts, 1986," *Bureau of Justice Statistics Bulletin*, February 1989. "Time Served in Prison and on Parole, 1984," *Bureau of Justice Statistics Special Report*, December, 1987, Washington, DC: U.S. Government Printing Office.

39. U.S. Department of Justice (1989), *Criminal Victimization in the United States, 1987*, Washington, DC: Bureau of Justice Statistics.

40. *The New York Times*, July 3, 1989, sec. 4, p. 14 (Sam Roberts, "Parked Car, No Radio: Where the City Is Losing Control").

41. *The New Yorker*, Dec. 21, 1981, p. 34.

42. Mary Owen Cameron (1964), *The Booster and the Snitch*, New York: Free Press.

43. Gresham M. Sykes and David Matza (1957), "Techniques of Neutralization: A Theory of Delinquency," *American Sociological Review*, vol. 22, pp. 664–70.

44. Jack Katz (1988), *Seductions of Crime: Moral and Sensual Attractions in Doing Evil*, New York: Basic Books.

45. Timothy J. Flanagan and Katherine M. Jamieson, eds. (1987), *Sourcebook of Criminal Justice Statistics—1987*, U.S. Department of Justice, Bureau of Justice Statistics, Washington, DC: U.S. Government Printing Office, p. 265.

46. Federal Bureau of Investigation (1988), *Crime in the United States: Uniform Crime Reports 1987*, Washington, DC: U.S. Government Printing Office.

47. UCR data, in *Sourcebook—1987*, p. 344.

48. Ibid.

49. Cameron, op. cit., p. 164.

50. Marilyn E. Walsh (1977), *The Fence: A New Look at the World of Property Theft*, Westport, CT: Greenwood Press.

51. Patrick Colquhoun (1796), *A Treatise on the Police of the Metropolis*, quoted in Carl B. Klockars (1974), *The Professional Fence*, New York: Free Press, p. 164.

52. S. Pennell (1979), "Fencing Activity and Police Strategy," *Police Chief*, September., pp. 71–75.

53. Klockars, op. cit.

54. Ibid., p. 73.

55. Ibid., p. 79.

56. Steffensmeier, op. cit., p. 147.

57. Ibid., p. 149.

58. Klockars, op. cit., p. 80.

59. Ibid., p. 82.

60. Ibid., p. 99.

61. Gary Marx (1988), *Under Cover: Police Surveillance in America*, Berkeley, CA: University of California Press, pp. 108–28.

62. Ibid., p. 126.

63. National Automobile Theft Bureau (1988), *Annual Report*, Palos Hills, IL, p. 9.

64. U.S. Bureau of the Census (1986), *Statistical Abstract of the United States: 1987*, Washington, DC: U.S. Government Printing Office, table 710. Cited in Caroline Wolf Harlow

(1988), "Motor Vehicle Theft," *Bureau of Justice Statistics Special Report*, Washington, DC: U.S. Government Printing Office.

65. National Auto Theft Bureau (1987), *Annual Report*, Palos Hills, IL, pp. 9–12.

66. National Crime Survey, 1986.

67. Charles H. McGaghy, Peggy C. Giordano, and Trudy Knicely Henson (1977), "Auto Theft: Offender and Offense Characteristics," *Criminology*, vol. 15, no. 3, pp. 367–85, quote on p. 379.

68. Harlow, op. cit., p. 3.

69. National Auto Theft Bureau (1988), *Annual Report*, p. 5.

70. National Auto Theft Bureau (1987), *Annual Report*, p. 24.

71. Ibid., p. 16.

72. Ibid., p. 24.

73. Ibid., p. 44.

74. Ibid., p. 29.

75. Ibid.

Organized Crime

CHAPTER **8**

WHAT IS ORGANIZED CRIME? MOST TOPICS IN THIS BOOK HAVE NOT BEGUN WITH definitions. They would have been unnecessary and, for the most part, irrelevant. It's pretty clear what stealing and burglary and murder are. Of course, for any crime there will be cases at the fringes. Is abortion murder? Is it murder for a doctor, following a patient's living will, to pull the plug on a life-sustaining machine? But these are legal curiosities, more relevant for lawyers than for criminologists. For most homicides, our everyday concept is sufficient. Similarly for robbery or burglary, most acts that fit the legal definition also correspond to the everyday notion of these crimes.

Not so with organized crime. Legal definitions of organized crime are often so vague that they could include almost anything. They usually stress that organized crime is a "pattern" of crime (usually defined as two or more criminal acts) committed by more than one person. But these criteria are far too loose. Many crimes are "organized" since they involve the coordination of two or more people. Many criminals also commit more than one crime. The legal criteria therefore do not allow us to distinguish the Mafia from a group of kids who commit a few break-ins or a stock brokerage that violates some minor securities regulations. A good sociological definition should be able to make these distinctions.

One obvious difference between a Mafia family and a burglary gang is permanence. The true criminal organization is institutionalized, not just organized. It exists above and beyond the participation of any single member or group of members. It has different positions that will be filled if someone leaves—just like a baseball team. The Yankees are still the Yankees even though the names in the starting lineup may be completely different from the roster of only a few years ago. So, too, in criminal organizations, individual members may leave, but the organization goes on. For example, what is called the "Gambino" family is headed by a man named Gotti, and the "Genovese" family may no longer have any Genoveses in it (at least not in the top positions). However, permanence cannot be the only criterion, since legitimate businesses, too, are institutionalized. We want our good definition of organized crime to distinguish the Genovese family from General Motors.

Current laws do not make such a distinction. The most important statute in this area is a federal law known as RICO (Racketeer Influenced and Corrupt Organizations). Under RICO, an organization that has engaged in a "pattern" of criminal acts (two or more crimes in a 10-year period) is subject to harsh penalties. The law was designed to make it easier for the government to prosecute organized crime. Yet the law has also been used in various civil and criminal cases against companies like Shearson/American Express, Lloyd's of London, E.F. Hutton, and General Motors. RICO has been the basis of cases against anti-abortion protesters, and it has been used by at least one woman in a divorce case.[1] Apparently, the respectability of these organizations and individuals makes little difference to prosecutors or judges armed with RICO. Yet most people would prefer a definition that can separate white-collar crime from organized crime.

Distinguishing the gangsters from the stock brokers is harder than it seems at first—as the history of RICO shows. For example, the financial firm of Drexel, Burnham, Lambert pleaded guilty to violations of the RICO law, but we do not really think of the firm as a corrupt organization, nor do we think of their executives and other employees as racketeers. One possible difference between a crime family and a stock brokerage is that for the criminal organization, crime is its primary means of income. Merrill, Lynch brokers may have violated SEC regulations, but the company still makes most of its money legally. Yet even this distinction is of little use in classifying legal businesses that are dominated by organized crime. For example, in the New York City area, most private garbage collectors belong to a cartel—an association of businesses. The cartel divides up the territory and allocates sections to each member. Members do not compete against each other, so each member can charge higher prices in his sector. As a result, the cartel makes substantial excess profits, of which it pays a small percentage to the local Mafia.[2] Is the cartel part of organized crime? Most New Yorkers (including those in law enforcement) would say yes. Few people, on the other hand, consider Texaco or Shell Oil to be part of organized crime. Yet for many years, the oil industry in the United States was dominated by a similar cartel arrangement with the similar effect of high corporate profits at the expense of the consumer.[3]

Besides the size and permanence of the organization and its reliance on crime for income, the most significant and troubling aspect of organized crime is its use of violence. The large oil companies may have conspired to divide up the market and fix prices; they may even have used their financial power to drive competitors out of business; but they did not use violence to create and enforce their cartel. The garbage cartel is another matter (see

---

I live in New York City. Sounds from the street reverberate up the buildings, and in the summer, with the storm windows out and the windows open, the noise becomes inescapable. The city has regulations about noise. In residential neighborhoods, for example, garbage trucks, with their loud grinding, may not pick up until 7 a.m. But the summer I began to write this section, the garbage trucks collecting from the grocery store downstairs were coming at 5:30 every morning, and sometimes earlier. Sleep was impossible. I mentioned the problem to the store owner.

"What time are they coming?" he asked. I told him. He said, "They shouldn't come till 7. I'll look into it."

Nothing changed in the next several days, and when I saw the owner again, I told him so. "I called the trucking guy up," he said. "He told me to mind my own f____ing business. When I said I'd switch to another company that *would* pick up later, he says to me, 'Do you want to get murdered?'"

box). On Long Island, for example, a single garbage hauler tried to compete against the cartel, offering lower bids and better service. At first, the cartel director encouraged him to join and share in the benefits of the cartel, but the independent hauler refused. Eventually, some of his trucks were sabotaged. When government prosecutors began investigating the cartel, he cooperated by providing information. Then, a year or so later, with the close scrutiny of the investigation past, he was murdered.[4] Of course, actual violence is the exception, not the rule. But the threat is always there, even when the gangsters make no explicit statements or even suggestions. The person who borrows money from a loan shark in a criminal organization knows that violence, while unlikely, is still a possible risk of not repaying.

To summarize: Organized crime involves large, long-standing organizations with diversified roles for its members; a criminal organization derives much of its income from crime; and it relies on violence, real or potential, to accomplish its goals. Some criminologists add a fourth element: corruption. Certainly, organized crime usually goes hand-in-hand with the corruption of government and police. But some criminal organizations do not participate in such corruption. For example, biker gangs may derive much income from drug deals without paying off politicians or police. In any case, any definition will have flaws, and I am offering this one not as a perfect system for classifying all possible cases but as a help in understanding similarities and differences among criminal groups.

MAFIA OR MYTH?

The media often use "organized crime" and "Mafia" interchangeably, along with a variety of other terms: the underworld, gangland, the syndicate, the mob, racketeers, and La Cosa Nostra. Whether the story is tragedy (*The Godfather*), comedy (*Married to the Mob*), or history (John Gotti on the evening news), the media convey the impression that organized crime *is* the Mafia. In the definition I am using, organized crime includes not only the Mafia but other criminal organizations as well. Indeed, there are many such organizations. What remains a matter of debate is the relative importance of the Mafia compared with these other organizations. The media, even when they recognize the existence of other criminal groups, still portray the Mafia as the largest, most powerful, most highly organized, and wealthiest criminal organization. In this picture, other criminal organizations are either dependent on the Mafia or exist only with its consent. They do not compete with the Mafia.

Opposed to this view are the critics who claim that the Mafia is a myth, an invention of our principal sources of information about the Mafia—law enforcement and the media. These critics question both the accuracy and the motives of these sources. Far from being neutral and disinterested, the media and law enforcement derive much benefit from the "myth of the Mafia." By building up the enemy as a single, giant criminal conspiracy, the police, FBI, prosecutors, and other law enforcement agencies make their job look all the more important. For law enforcement, the Mafia myth is good public relations, affecting not just their image but also perhaps the size of next year's budget. Law enforcement agencies may therefore color the way they depict their work. After all, it is one thing to put out a statement that you have arrested Joey Cazzo the bookmaker; it's another to arrest Joey Cazzo, "a gambler with ties to organized crime," and quite another to nab Joey ("The Shark") Cazzo "a high-ranking member of the Nocciolo crime family."

The media get hooked into myth in two ways. First, they are totally dependent on the police and prosecutors for their information. If a federal prosecutor tells reporters that Joey ("The Shark") Cazzo is a captain in some crime family, reporters usually have no independent way of verifying this claim. Second, the media, too, prefer big news. A story about a "Godfather" far outweighs a story about ordinary criminals. And a story about a "boss of all bosses" is bigger news than a story about a gang leader.[5]

If information from law enforcement and media is tainted, the other source of information—testimony from former members of the Mafia—is even less credible. These people usually come from fairly low in the ranks and often do not have accurate information about goings-on elsewhere in the organization. They also may not be the most truthful of souls and may, for a variety of reasons, embellish or even invent stories. They may want to inflate their own importance or the importance of their former colleagues. They may be trying to tell the story the way they think the authorities want to hear it. Or they may themselves be paying more attention to the myth than to the reality.

The critics of the "Mafia myth" see in it an even less savory motive—racism. They point out the blatant anti-Italian message contained in Mafia reporting. Some of these critics are obviously self-serving. Joe Colombo, himself head of a New York crime family, formed the Italian-American Civil Rights League and, in his role as its chairman, complained openly to the press about the anti-Italian bias. Referring to a New York legislature report on crime, he said, "This book lists *only* Italians. Is it *possible* in New York that only *Italians* have committed crimes? . . . If you know any Italian that's in jail, his records get stamped 'O.C.' for organized crime. O.C. means only for Italian people. They do the last day of their sentencin'. I got one to two-and-a-half for checking the wrong box on a form."*[6] Granted that Colombo may have been a gangster, but he also may have been right about the anti-Italian slant of Mafia journalism and law enforcement.

---

* In applying for a real estate license, he concealed his arrest record and was subsequently convicted of perjury.

The public, too, plays a part in the propagation of the myth. We find it more interesting to read about things that resemble the movies. And according to some critics, we find it more comforting to think of our crime problems as coming not from our own society but from some alien force. Communism has long been a favorite candidate for this role. Currently it is Latin American drug cartels. But the idea of the Mafia serves a similar purpose. Journalist Murray Kempton expressed this view: "We believe in the Mafia because, without it, we would have to accept the fact that crime can be American and thus a taint of our blood and our fault."[7]

In the view of the Mafia-myth critics, then, everyone has suspect motives. Law enforcement and the media use the myth to enhance their organizations. The public uses the myth as a source of fascination and moral comfort.

Of course, even people with impure motives may be telling the truth. So the critics also challenge the factual basis of the Mafia myth. They charge that the purveyors of the Mafia myth have ignored many facts, while exaggerating the importance of others. Certainly, some criminals are Italian, but most Italians, even those who commit crimes, are not part of any organization. Certainly, some criminal organizations are largely Italian. But they are not the only such organizations, and they are not all-powerful. Often the evidence turns up instances where the supposedly all-powerful Mafia cannot get things done. For example, wiretaps on two high-ranking Mafiosi in New Jersey found Sam ("The Plumber") de Cavalcante constantly grumbling about his inability to control his own agents, and Angelo (Gyp) De Carlo spending much time worrying about very small sums of money.

Evil empire or the gang that couldn't shoot straight? These contrasting views of the Mafia and organized crime raise some questions that I will try to answer in this section. How do criminal organizations make their money? Does the Mafia control these illegal operations? Does it control criminal infiltration of legitimate organizations? What is the relationship between the Mafia and other criminal organizations?

A BIT OF HISTORY

In 1890, David Hennessy, the police chief of New Orleans, was murdered. Before he died, he was heard to say, "The dagos shot me." New Orleans, whose population was 240,000, had 10,000 to 15,000 Italian-born inhabitants, most of them from Sicily, and Hennessy's murder was the occasion for much anti-Italian sentiment. The newspapers began to carry stories referring to a secret Italian organization so powerful that, according to one news story, it constituted a government unto itself. The organization was called the *Mafia*. Eventually, a number of Italians were tried for the crime, but the jury acquitted all of them.* When news of the verdicts came out, a lynch mob invaded the prison where the men were still being kept, and killed them.

The story came to national attention, bringing with it a debate over the existence of the Mafia. *The New York Tribune* said that the Mafia existed not just in New Orleans but in most large cities nationwide. Denying the existence of any Mafia, either in Sicily or in the United States, were the Italian-language newspapers and community leaders.[8] This may have been the first such debate, but it was certainly not the last. For the next hundred years, this same question would crop up periodically, with journalists, law enforcement figures, prominent Italian-Americans, and academics arguing about the nature, extent, and even existence of the Mafia. At one extreme are those who argue that the Mafia is a tightly controlled and organized national organization with orders emanating from a central commission.[9] At the other extreme are those who argue that the Mafia is largely the creation of the media and law enforcement, who weave a small amount of evidence into an improbable web of connections. In this skeptical view, Americans have a weakness for stories about secret, powerful, broad-based conspiracies. These theories, often tinged with racism or xenophobia, provide convenient explanations for the country's failings or difficulties.[10]

Criminal Gangs

Even in 1890, criminal gangs were hardly a new feature of U.S. cities. Earlier in the century, New York had the Plug Uglies, the Dead Rabbits, and the Bowery Boys—street gangs who committed mostly small-time thefts and fought each other over turf. Gangs like this have continued to the present day, though the prevalence of gangs varies from city to city and from one historical period to another.[11] Especially for young men, gangs provide an alternative to the recognized social institutions. It is from the gang, rather than from work or family, that these young men derive a sense of self. Usually, the gangs are very loosely organized, and their crime—like their non-criminal activity—is oriented less toward economic profit than toward social matters. Sometimes the gangs become more serious about crime, more profit-oriented, and more vicious. In the 1800s, for example, New York also had waterfront gangs like the Charlton Street Gang and the Short Tails, who specialized in theft and robbery of cargoes on ships coming in to the city, and who used violence, including murder, to accomplish their goals.[12]

These variants still exist today. The Westies, for example, an ethnic gang based in an old West Side neighborhood called Hell's Kitchen, sound like

---

* Historians disagree over the reason for the verdict. Some say that the gangsters threatened the jury. Others maintain that the evidence was too flimsy.

the gangs depicted in "West Side Story." Indeed, gangs like the "Sharks" and the "Jets" still exist in New York and other cities. But the Westies, until a series of criminal convictions in the late 1980s slowed them down, were committing a variety of profit-oriented crimes ranging from hijacking to contract murder.[13]

Gangs interested in high profits usually are better organized. They use violence in attempts to monopolize illegal enterprises like gambling or (more recently) drugs, and to gain control of legitimate businesses. In fact, at the time of the New Orleans shooting in 1890, two rival gangs had been fighting over control of the Italian sections of the docks, where fruit was unloaded. Today, though the weapons, drugs, and businesses have changed, this pattern of ethnic gangs still persists. Today, similar gangs have arisen in the Southeast Asian communities of California, the Russian immigrant neighborhood in New York, and perhaps in other communities of recent immigrants as well.[14] The major structural difference involves the link between gangs and politicians. In the 19th century, the political "machines" that dominated city politics were often allied with neighborhood street gangs, and the gangs were active on election day—voting several times and sometimes intimidating other voters. As machine politics has faded, so have the political connections of gangs.

The Mafia in Italy and America

The Mafia shares many of the characteristics of other ethnic criminal gangs and organizations. However, in its historical development, its internal organization, its scope, and its position in the illegal world, the Mafia is different.

The rise of the Mafia in America is a product of historical forces. The waves of immigration from Italy, beginning in the late 19th century, obviously played an important role. Then as now, immigrant communities gave rise to their own criminal gangs, gangs which often specialize in extorting their own countrymen. The gangsters may start by providing government-like services—settling disputes within the community or helping immigrants in dealings with city agencies.* The gang owes much of its power—for both good and evil—to the unwillingness or inability of people in the community to go to the authorities. Perhaps the immigrants do not speak English, or perhaps they feel (often rightly) that the American bureaucrats or the police will not understand them or will not give them adequate protection. The gangster steps in to fill this governmental role. But, just as governments levy taxes, the gangs extort regular payments from the merchants of the community.

---

* The movie *The Godfather II* provided good illustration of this in the scene where the young Don Corleone helps a poor woman in a dispute over her rent.

This mistrust of official institutions ran particularly high among Italian immigrants, who were mostly from the south of Italy, especially Sicily. Many Mediterranean cultures emphasize that a man does not turn to the government for help; instead, he takes action personally to defend his honor. In Sicily especially, with its history of repeated foreign domination, people were alienated from official governments. One historian quotes Palermo's police chief Antonio Cutrera:

> Long domination by succeeding invaders had produced people who were suspicious, diffident, intolerant, and above all, enemies of government—any government—and of all law enforcement. Thus, disrespect for laws, hatred of authority, and contempt for all those who had dealings with authorities characterized Sicilians.[15]*

Not only was government distant and untrustworthy, but so was the economy. Most agricultural production took place on plantation-like estates called *latifundia*, whose owners were largely absentees and whose workers were little better off than slaves. Under such conditions, peasants might well turn to anyone, even criminals, who offered them any semblance of protection against exploitation by government and landowners. Not surprisingly then, the Mafia arose not in the cities but in the agricultural sections in western Sicily.† Mafiosi emerged from the peasantry but distinguished themselves from the rest by their ability and willingness to use violence. They portrayed themselves as protectors of the peasants, but soon protection became a protection racket, and their Robin Hood—like altruism came to be mixed with heavy portions of self-interest. They used their reputation for violence more for their own purposes, even as agents for landowners and eventually as landowners themselves. Their power spread, and different Mafia groups came to dominate different territories or different industries in the cities. Mafia figures also became influential in local poli-

---

* In the novel *The Leopard*, set in the mid–19th century, the central figure, an aging Sicilian prince, explains why Sicilians will be unlikely to participate in the new unified Italy in its march towards modern government and economy. He speaks of "a long hegemony of rulers who were not of our religion and who did not speak our language . . . Byzantine tax gatherers, . . . Berber emirs, . . . Spanish viceroys." After describing the harsh conditions of nature on the island, the Prince continues,

> This violence of landscape, this cruelty of climate, this continual tension in everything . . . all those rulers who landed by main force from every direction, who were at once obeyed, soon detested, and always misunderstood, their only expressions works of art we couldn't understand and taxes which we understood all too well and which they spent elsewhere: all these things have formed our character, which is thus conditioned by events outside our control as well as by a terrifying insularity of mind. (Giuseppe di Lampedusa (1960, orig. 1958), *The Leopard*, New York: Pantheon, pp. 204, 208.)

† Eastern Sicily apparently did not experience the same rise of Mafia. In the early 1900s, the eastern cities of Messina and Syracuse had rates of murder and robbery that were only one-third those of Palermo in the west.

tics, using their money and power to corrupt incumbent officials and to elect new officials they could control.[16]

Naples and Calabria, the other two regions of heavy emigration to the United States, had similar customs and similar criminal organizations. The Camorra of Naples was more centrally controlled and tightly organized than the Sicilian Mafia. Like the Mafia, though, it operated on both the legitimate and illegal levels. It extorted money from small businesses both legal and illegal (waiters and porters as well as prostitutes and thieves). The Camorra also held influence among politicians and businessmen.[17]

It is a matter of some debate whether the Mafia leaders who came to power in the United States had also been gangsters in Italy. Most of them probably had not.[18] However, the sociologically important point is that when the Sicilians emigrated to the United States, they brought with them a set of assumptions and expectations about government and nongovernmental institutions. This culture allowed for a home-grown mafia to spring up in the United States. It may have been different in both personnel and structure from Italian criminal organizations, but it was a mafia nevertheless.

In the early 1900s, criminals in Italian-American communities began extorting money from Italian shopkeepers, workers, and professionals by sending threatening notes:

> This is the second time that I have warned you. Sunday at ten o'clock in the morning, at the corner of Second Street and Third Avenue, bring three hundred dollars without fail. Otherwise we will set fire to you and blow you up with a bomb.[19]

The notes were signed "Mano Nera," or Black Hand. Black Hand extortion continued for more than a decade, and spread to many cities and even to small towns. However, although their methods and signatures may have been the same, this was not necessarily evidence for the existence of a large, criminal conspiracy. In fact, most Black Hand crimes were the work of individuals or small gangs. The Federal government stepped in around 1915 and began to enforce laws against using the mails to defraud, and the Black Hand gangs faded.[20]

Prohibition and the Roaring Twenties

Historical accident played an important role in the next evolutionary stage of the Mafia. Just when Black Hand groups were looking for new sources of money, Prohibition came along, opening up large-scale criminal opportunities. Before 1920, the typical arrangement between gangsters and politicians left politicians at the top. The local ward leader may have owed many of his votes to the cooperation of the gangs, but they in turn counted on him for protection from the police. (The politicians and police were predominantly Irish, the gangsters Jewish and Italian.)[21]

Prohibition reversed this relationship. The reversal was an unintended consequence of the vigorous reforms brought in with the triumph over liquor. For many of those who backed Prohibition, the issue was not clean living but clean government. The machine politics that dominated most cities had been revealed to be corrupt, and the source of that corruption was often the saloon. In the minds of reformers, all these elements were linked: the corrupt machine, the ward boss, the saloons, and the crooks. By getting rid of the saloons, reformers would kick the support out from under the corrupt political machines.*

The irony, of course, is that Prohibition had the opposite effect. By creating a source of tremendous wealth for criminal organizations, Prohibition enhanced the power of criminals. It even gave them a certain respectability in the eyes of the public; illegal alcohol linked the bootleggers with the non-gangster drinkers. Suppliers and consumers alike participated in evading the liquor laws. In a similar irony, the replacement of corrupt political machines with relatively honest city government sometimes transformed the criminal underworld from an orderly, controlled operation into an anarchic and bloody battlefield.

Chicago provides a good illustration of these processes. Chicago is important in itself, of course—if only because it was the base of operations of the most famous gangster in U.S. history, Al Capone. In the decades before Prohibition, Chicago had its gangs, and different gangs dominated different parts of the city. With the protection of the politicians in their respective wards, the gangs ran various illegal enterprises. After 1920, the most important source of profits was the importation, manufacture, and distribution of alcohol. Johnny Torrio, a master strategist among gangsters, created a system of cooperation among gang leaders in various parts of the city—on the North Side, Dion O'Banion; on the South Side, smaller groups like Ragen's Colts (they began as a baseball team), the "Terrible Gennas" (six brothers), and the O'Donells. Torrio's own territory included some of the South Side and the West Side, extending as far as suburbs like Cicero. In controlling this small enterprise Torrio had help from a young man he had recruited from New York—Al Capone.

The arrangements proceeded fairly peacefully under the corrupt administration of Mayor Big Bill Thompson. But in 1923 a reform candidate, William Dever, unseated Thompson. The new mayor and his chief of police refused to continue the old *modus vivendi* with the mobsters. In one raid, Torrio himself was arrested. Whatever other effects the gangbusting may

---

* There may have been an element of ethnic or religious politics involved as well; the reformers were largely Protestant while the urban populations had become increasingly Catholic—first Irish, then Italian.

have had, it demonstrated to other gangsters that Torrio was vulnerable. It was then that Chicago began to see the gang warfare that has become legendary. O'Banion was murdered in 1924 in his flower shop. Both Capone and Torrio were victims of attempted murder, probably by people from the organization of O'Banion's successor Hymie Weiss. Weiss himself was killed in 1926 and eventually Bugs Moran took control of the O'Banion group. There was more violence over control of bootleg liquor, and there was violence during elections. In three years, gangsters killed over 200 of their competitors; police killed another 160. The gangland wars culminated in the famous St. Valentine's Day massacre of 1929, where men from Capone's organization murdered seven members of Bugs Moran's group. Soon, Capone solidified his control over the entire Chicago area, and the number of mob-related killings dropped. In 1931, Capone was jailed for income tax violations, but the organization he had built continued to control Chicago's underworld. Thus, one of the most violent and largest criminal organizations was shaped by one of the country's most idealistic programs—Prohibition.

After the St. Valentine's Day massacre and with the repeal of Prohibition in 1933, organized crime ceased to command the kind of public attention it had gotten in the 1920s. Interest dwindled partly because of a lack of characters as colorful or willing to talk to the press as Capone had been; partly because (thanks to Repeal) far fewer people were involved in mob-controlled services; and partly because law enforcement, especially the FBI under J. Edgar Hoover, channeled its efforts in other directions.

The Mafia in the Age of Television

Organized crime returned to the spotlight reluctantly in 1950, when Sen. Estes Kefauver presided over hearings of a special Senate committee. The hearings took the committee to a number of cities and lasted several months. Most of the 600 witnesses who testified were law enforcement officials, but the roster also included bookmakers, pimps, "enforcers," and others connected to organized crime. The star of the show was Frank Costello. The committee and the media built up Costello as the crime boss of the entire country, which was a considerable exaggeration. The Kefauver hearings gained special prominence because they were televised. Television was just becoming a prominent medium, and the possibility of seeing real live gangsters proved an unbeatable attraction (even though all that viewers could see of Costello, who objected to the cameras, were his hands).

Television gave the Kefauver Committee a wide audience for its ideas about the nature of organized crime. The committee promulgated the view that organized crime was more centralized than had been thought previously, with the Mafia as the hub of the organization. Back in the days of the New Orleans lynchings, there had been several mafias, small associations of criminals who engaged in extortion and racketeering. But now, the word had taken on a new meaning.

> There is a sinister criminal organization known as the Mafia operating throughout the country with ties in other nations. . . . The Mafia is the direct descendant of a criminal organization of the same name originating in the island of Sicily. In this country, the Mafia has also been known as the Black Hand and the Unione Siciliano [sic]. . . . The Mafia is a loose-knit organization specializing in the sale and distribution of narcotics, the conduct of various enterprises, prostitution, and other rackets based on extortion and violence. The Mafia is the binder which ties together the two major criminal syndicates [one in Chicago, the other in New York] as well as numerous other criminal groups throughout the country.[22]

As we have seen, the actual history of the Mafia is not quite the direct line that the committee portrays. The committee makes it sound as if the progression from Sicilian Mafia to Black Hand to American Mafia was merely a change in name and place—something like the Washington Senators becoming the Texas Rangers. In fact, few American gangsters, even in the early years, had been connected with Sicilian mafias, and the Black Hand existed as many small, independent extortion operations rather than as franchises of a single, large organization. The Unione Siciliana was originally an above-board fraternal organization. In New York in the 1920s, gangsters who had come to power in the Unione forced members to operate stills producing "bathtub gin" in their homes. The police appropriated the name to refer to the combination of the various Italian crime groups in New York.[23]

The Kefauver hearings ended in 1951, giving way in the media to Senator Joe McCarthy's hearings. In the public eye, the menace of the Mafia conspiracy was replaced by the menace of the Communist conspiracy. The next brief flurry of publicity about a nationwide Mafia came in 1957. In Apalachin, New York, a small upstate town, approximately 60 men had gathered at the home of Joseph Barbara, a soft-drink bottler. None of the men was carrying a gun or was wanted by police. They owned legitimate businesses. Their number included

> a Man of the Year from Buffalo, a manufacturer of bleach, a grocery clerk . . . . the Eastern distributor for a national brand of whiskey, a bandleader, a Boston cheese purveyor, a trucking tycoon, and even a Manhattan hearse salesman.[24]

Yet when a curious state trooper pulled up in the driveway, the men bolted for the woods. They were soon rounded up but refused to answer police questions, for which refusal they were indicted and convicted. The convictions were overturned on appeal, the court ruling that the police had no probable cause to make the arrest in the first place.

But what did the Apalachin conference mean? To the most conspiracy-minded, it was evidence of a nationwide criminal organization. Although most of the Barbara guests were from New York, New Jersey, and Pennsylvania, a few had come from as far away as Florida, Texas, Colorado, and Cuba.[25] These men, many known to authorities as being involved in organized crime, may have been making decisions about underworld business. Or the "convention" may have been a mostly social gathering. At any rate, if this was a meeting of a structured organization rather than a reunion of people who happened to be in the same line of (illegal) work, it remained unclear what that structure was and what kinds of business decisions were to have been made.

Six years later, another Senate committee, this one headed by Sen. John McClellan, tried to clarify things, though many people dispute the accuracy of the picture the committee painted. The star witness of these hearings was Joe Valachi, a government informer who had been serving a sentence in a federal prison. Valachi was only a low-level member of one New York crime family; his testimony was inconsistent and at times vague; some of his testimony—e.g., his tale of a nationwide coup in which 40 high-ranking Mafiosi were killed in a three-day period—turned out to be simply wrong; but the committee and the media generally accepted his story as the truth. He told of a secret ceremony, of oaths he had taken while holding burning scraps of paper, of the "kiss of death." It was Valachi who introduced the country to the term *La Cosa Nostra* (literally, "our thing"). And it was Valachi who put terms like *capo* and *consigliere* in the public glossary and added new meanings to words like *family, lieutenant,* and *soldier*. Only *The Godfather* (the novel and movies) has had more of an impact on public conceptions of the Mafia.*

HOW IS ORGANIZED CRIME ORGANIZED?

The basic unit of the organization is the gang, known as a "family" or *borgata*. According to law enforcement officials, there are 24 families active in the United States, five of them in the New York area. Other cities have only one. Disputes between families are handled by a "commission" made up of high-ranking members of a few of the families. Most descriptions of the structure of a Mafia family agree that there are certain hierarchical relationships designated by the various titles. At the top are the "boss" (also known as the "don"), "underboss," and *consigliere* or adviser. At the next

---

* *The Godfather* had an impact on the Mafiosi as well. One undercover detective reported that "They had a lot of things taught to them through the movie. They try to live up to it. The movie was telling them how" (quoted in Abadinsky, p. 318).

level are those with the title of "capo" (short for *caporegima*), also known as captains or lieutenants (some models put lieutenants in a separate rank below capos). Below them are the *soldati* or soldiers (sometimes called "buttons"). Each family controls the number of these "made" members. According to the FBI, the total number of members is about 2,000 nationwide, a number that has remained basically unchanged since the 1930s.[26] In addition, many nonmembers work with or for the family.

What is a matter of some dispute is the nature of the relationships among these various roles. What does a boss or a capo or a soldier *do*? According to some models of the crime family, these positions function much like those in a legitimate business organization. The president (boss) makes decisions regarding the general strategy and direction of the company; the underboss acts as a sort of general operations manager. The capos are like division managers, while the soldiers, in cooperation with nonfamily employees, produce the actual product or service. This is the **bureaucratic** model, and it is the one favored by law enforcement. A good example comes from the opening paragraph of a Presidential Commission Task Force report:

> [Organized crime] involves thousands of criminals working with structures as complex as those of any large corporations, subject to laws more rigidly enforced than those of legitimate governments. The actions are not impulsive but rather the result of intricate conspiracies carried on over many years and aimed at gaining control over whole fields of activity to amass huge profits.[27]

The image is of a corporation with several ongoing businesses, staffed with bureaucrats.

The problem with the bureaucratic model is that it makes things seem more organized than they really are. In reality, most organized crime businesses have a much looser, decentralized structure than the chain-of-command model suggests. How could it be otherwise? True business bureaucracies depend on routinized procedures, a large flow of information, and elaborate record-keeping. Illegal businesses, because of their vulnerability to law enforcement, must minimize all these elements. The less predictable and routine they are, the less everyone knows; the fewer the records that might become evidence, then the safer the operation is. But if illegal businesses cannot be run like legitimate corporations, then perhaps the popular image of organized crime dominating these businesses is also exaggerated or just plain wrong. This image, often mirrored in the mass media, portrays the Mafia as a tightly run organization that dominates many forms of crime. However, the economic realities of crime make this kind of organization and domination unlikely. The difference between image and reality will become clearer if we look more closely at some of these crimes.

UNORGANIZED CRIME

Bookmaking

Part of the conventional wisdom about the Mafia is that it controls vice. That is, most bookmakers, loan sharks, prostitutes, and other providers of illegal goods and services either belong to the Mafia or work for members of the Mafia. Nonmembers in these businesses must pay money to the Mafia and must accept orders from the Mafia. In return, the Mafia will use its resources to provide protection from law enforcement. Arrests will be rare, convictions even rarer, and serious sentences rarer still. This picture of Mafia control is considered to be especially true in the area of illegal gambling—both numbers and bookmaking. Consequently, gambling is supposed to be the major source of Mafia income. A typical version of this idea can be found in the testimony of Vincent Teresa, before a U.S. Senate subcommittee in 1971. Teresa was a criminal who worked with the Mafia in New England, though he never became an actual member of the Mafia.

> There is no bookmaker that can do business by himself; he couldn't survive. The mob would turn him over to the police, give him a few beatings, or even kill him if he's real stubborn. He has to go with them, because they run everything.
> Gambling is the single most important activity for organized crime. They control it all over the country and all over the world.[28]

(Teresa was including legal casino gambling in Las Vegas and Europe, but the turf he knew firsthand was illegal bookmaking in New England.)

Some scholars echo Teresa's views. According to criminologist Donald Cressey,

> In most large American cities, the opportunity to gamble is provided by Cosa Nostra. Members of this organization do not themselves own and operate all the illegal betting and lottery enterprises, but those they do not own they control, or provide with essential services.[29]

But does the Mafia control illegal gambling? Both economic logic and the available evidence cast doubt on this widely held assumption. From the economic point of view, any industry—legal or illegal—will be difficult to control if it is decentralized (i.e., made up of many independent entrepreneurs). If one element in the business is centralized, then the organization that can control that element can also control the business. For example, for several decades, bookmakers derived most of their income from gambling on horse racing. They were subject to control from a single crime group because there was one element in the system that was centralized: information. The law prevented racetracks from broadcasting the races, and racetracks could not have public telephones. Bookies, therefore, had to get their information from a telegraph service, an illegal monopoly run by Moe Annenberg. A bookmaker who wanted to go into business had to have the wire service. Whoever controlled the wire controlled access to bookmaking.

Corruption, an essential part of most illegal business, was also centralized. Horse race bettors found it more convenient to have a place to go—a "horse room" or "wire room" where they could bet, hang out, and hear the call of the race. (The 1973 movie *The Sting* depicts a fairly elegant version of a 1920s horse room.) Horse rooms were easy targets for raids, so bookmakers needed to pay off the police. The corruption often extended all the way through a city police department right to the top, and often to top politicians as well. Only a large organization (the Mafia) could buy such protection.

In the 1960s, both information and police corruption became more decentralized. More and more of the bookmakers' business came from gambling on football, baseball, and basketball—sports where information flowed freely over radio and television. Many bookmakers dealt exclusively by phone, so they no longer needed elaborate and semi-public places like the horse rooms that required protection from the police. At the same time, many city police departments were undergoing anti-corruption reforms, which often had the effect of reducing or at least decentralizing corruption. A small-time bookie had only to pay off the local cops, if he had to pay anyone at all. In addition, as predatory crime burgeoned in the 1960s, police and courts paid less attention to illegal gambling, so bookmakers had even fewer worries about payoffs. In this new atmosphere, the two sources of control—the wire and big payoffs, which had allowed organized crime to dominate illegal betting—were things of the past. These changes should have made it more difficult for the Mafia or anyone else to maintain a monopoly on bookmaking.*

There is a further economic reason to question the idea that gambling is a Mafia monopoly. A monopoly must be a continuous, permanent enterprise, large and centralized. Such a structure may work in the legitimate world, but illegal businesses are different. If the police do make a raid, they can seize the operation's assets and arrest the employees. In the underworld, therefore, a large, centralized operation is potentially a liability.

The economic conditions of bookmaking would seem to make it an un-

---

* While horse rooms may have passed into history, some cities still have a latter-day counterpart: the after-hours gambling club, where patrons may drink and play casino gambling games (craps, roulette, blackjack). These clubs, except for those with an exclusively Chinese clientele, probably are a Mafia monopoly.

likely candidate as a Mafia monopoly. But what is the evidence? On the one hand, there is Vincent Teresa's statement. But some researchers have sought more diverse types of evidence: the books and betting slips seized from police raids, conversations from wiretaps, and interviews with both arrested and unarrested informants. This evidence shows that in most cities, the bookmaking industry consists of many small enterprises with a high rate of turnover. Some of the bookmakers are connected to the Mafia; others belong to other criminal organizations; but many are just independent entrepreneurs operating completely apart from any organized crime.

New York City offers an interesting example, since while most cities have only one Mafia family, New York has five. According to the conventional wisdom, these five families have divided the city among themselves so that each has exclusive control over the various illegal operations in its territory. Presumably, this control should extend to bookmakers. Yet the evidence suggests otherwise. For one thing, if the Mafia controlled bookmaking, it would do what any other monopoly tries to do when it gains control of an industry: It would reduce competition and raise consumer prices. But prices have not gone up.

In bookmaking, the bettor is the consumer, and the "price" of making a bet takes the form of odds. The bookmaker makes his profit because the bettor must give odds of 11–10. That is, the bettor puts up $11 to the bookmaker's $10. Or, as some bettors think of it, there is a 10 percent surcharge on losing bets. If bookmaking were a monopoly, it could raise the surcharge to 15 percent or even 20 percent. In fact, some bookmakers have tried conspiring to change the standard odds to give themselves more profit. The result was a rapid loss in business to bookmakers who offered competitive prices.[30]

One other bit of evidence suggests that bookmaking is not a monopoly but rather a market of small, competing entrepreneurs. That evidence is the variability of the betting "line." In football betting, for example, bookmakers establish a "point spread" or "line" on each game as a way of equalizing the teams. In the Giants–Cowboys game, the line might be Giants minus 4. If you bet the Giants, you start with a four-point deficit. The Giants must win by more than four points. Conversely, if you bet the Cowboys, you get the Cowboys plus four points. If the Giants win 20–17, Giant bettors lose; Cowboy bettors win. If the final difference is 4 points (e.g., 31–27), it's a tie, and no money changes hands. If bookmaking were a controlled monopoly, all bookmakers would have the same line. But as any bettor knows, different bookies will have different lines on the same game. One bookie may have the Giants at minus 4 while another has the same game at Giants $-3\frac{1}{2}$ and still another Giants at $-4\frac{1}{2}$. Also, each bookmaker will adjust the line according to the flow of money. If a bookie has the Giants at -4 and most of his customers are betting the Giants, he may raise the line to $4\frac{1}{2}$ so that the next customer might be more tempted to bet the Cowboys, now that they are getting an extra half-point (with a final score of Giants 21, Cowboys 17, the Cowboy bettor still wins). No monopoly would be so responsive to shifts in consumer demand.*

There is one low-risk way that the Mafia might control bookmaking—extortion. The principal quality of bookmaking that makes it susceptible to Mafia domination is its illegality. People who make their money illegally make good targets for extortion, since they are less likely to go the police for protection. However, social science studies have found little evidence for extortion. For example, an economist who studied illegal enterprises in New York concludes that while there is some Mafia extortion of bookmakers, "it is neither systematic nor unavoidable. Such extortion yields only modest sums to the Mafia members."[31]†

It may be that in some cities, the Mafia does make an effort to control bookmaking by extorting money from bookmakers. In Boston, the territory Vincent Teresa knew best, the Mafia did manage to control most illegal gambling. As a result, Boston bettors had to give 6–5 odds.[32] In most cities, however, the bookmaking market is classic free enterprise. Some Mafia members run bookmaking operations, but they do not dominate the business, and the occasional attempts to raise prices have failed against the free market competition of bookmakers who continued to offer the usual odds.[33]

The Numbers

A second type of gambling often thought to bring untold riches to the Mafia is the numbers. Today, many states run their own lotteries, but until the 1970s, the only available lotteries were the illegal "numbers rackets." In the game's most common form, the bettor selects a three-digit number and places the bet with a collector. The collector gathers the bets, turns them

---

* By moving the line, a bookmaker runs the risk of being "middled." Suppose he starts by offering the Giants at $-3\frac{1}{2}$, and all his callers bet the Giants. Now he raises his line to the Giants at $-4\frac{1}{2}$, and the next batch of callers all bet the Cowboys. If the Giants win 21–17, the bookmaker will lose all bets. No monopoly, certainly not the Mafia, would expose itself to such risk.

† The organization of prostitution closely resembles that of bookmaking. At one time, it may have been centralized and dominated by a few criminal groups. Earlier in this century, prostitution was centered in brothels. Racketeers may even have moved prostitutes from one city to another—what was called the "white slave" trade. Independent brothels, like wire rooms, could be extorted. But in the latter half of the century, brothels gave way to call girls and streetwalkers, which, like telephone-based bookmakers, provided too decentralized a target for extortion. Organized crime groups lost interest in prostitution, even brothels (and their 1960s version, "massage parlors"). In Philadelphia, for example, in the 1970s, "an FBI informant opened three brothels in the central vice district. At no time did he have to 'get permission' from any other organization. In fact, the only people who called upon him for tribute were the police." (Gary N. Potter and Philip Jenkins, (1985), *The City and the Syndicate: Organizing Crime in Philadelphia*, Lexington, MA: Ginn Press, p. 8.)

over to a pickup man, who in turn gives them to a middle-level manager called a controller. The controller is the link to the central "bank." That afternoon, the day's number is determined by some random process, and winners are paid off at odds usually between 500-1 and 600-1. Popular, heavily bet numbers get even lower odds, sometimes as low as 350-1. Different banks offer different odds, and a bank may change its odds.

Obviously, the numbers game requires a larger organization than does bookmaking. It is also more difficult to hide. While bookmakers operate by phone, numbers runners collect bets in person. The size and visibility of the numbers game should make it a much more likely candidate for domination by a single criminal organization. In the 1930s, a single gangster, Dutch Schulz, did gain control of the numbers in New York City. A wave of anti-corruption reform had hit New York politics, and the police had raided several numbers banks in Harlem. Schulz seized upon the banks' temporary weakness and, largely through threat, took over these formerly independent numbers banks. According to one historian, the numbers yielded Schultz $20 million a year.[34]

As with other forms of gambling, the numbers game has since become decentralized. In a large city like New York, 50 or more numbers banks may be operating at any one time. Even a single neighborhood may have three or four numbers banks that compete with each other. Some of the banks are Mafia-run, but many are not. Instead, they are neighborhood industries. Banks in black neighborhoods are run by blacks, those in Hispanic neighborhoods by Hispanics. No single group dominates or controls the industry.

The numbers game is decentralized even within each bank, with those at the bottom of the pyramid (the collectors) getting the largest share of the money bet. Of each dollar he brings in, the collector keeps 25 cents. He also takes a 10 percent tip from the payoff when one of his customers has a "hit." Moreover, collectors exercise their own entrepreneurial options. The collector may decide to offer higher odds in order to attract customers.* The collector may also decide to book the small bets himself rather than turn them in to the bank. If by chance a 25-cent bet hits, he will have to pay out only $135 (25 cents at 600-1, minus the collector's 10 percent tip). If the controller finds out that a collector is holding back too much money (say, more than 10 percent of the total wagers), he may fire the collector. But the collector in turn may also move to another bank. Obviously, if a single group (like the Mafia) were controlling things, collectors could have no such independence.

How much does the bank make? If it pays out at 600-1, then of every $1,000 coming in, it should pay out, on average, $600 to winning bettors,

---

* Even if his bank pays out at 550-1, the collector may offer 600-1, making up the difference out of his own pocket. If a customer hits, say for $1, the collector must pay the extra $50, but the 10 percent tip ($60) keeps him from taking a loss.

$250 to collectors, and $100 to controllers. That leaves $50, or 5 percent of the total amount bet, as the bank's gross. The average numbers bank in New York in the 1970s was taking in about $7,000 a day, or about $2.2 million per year. The 5 percent gross works out to $110,000 annually, out of which the bank must pay for its operating costs (rent, clerks' salaries, police payoffs, etc).[35]

How does this reality square with the image of the numbers racket as a huge profit center dominated by a relatively small, central group of Mafia mobsters? The system as it really works features a diversity of banks, often competing in the same geographic area. And the competition can be serious. For example, one Cuban numbers organization in New York was, according to the FBI, using profits from drug smuggling to increase payoff odds in order to attract numbers bettors.[36] Although numbers banks are more permanent than bookmaking offices, some of them go out of business (too many hits by customers, a raid by the police), and new ones may enter the field. The system also pays a high percentage of the income to the lowest level personnel, the collectors, who also have a great deal of discretion. All of this suggests that the numbers business is a relatively free market, not one dominated by any one organization, such as the Mafia.

Loansharks

The classic movie *On the Waterfront* depicts a corrupt union that runs the docks, a union dominated by organized crime. Longshoremen who wish to continue to get work must borrow money at high interest rates from the union-connected loanshark, a thoroughly detestable character. In another movie, *Rocky*, the hero's physical and moral self-improvement seem all the more noble because the place where he begins is so contemptible: He is a bone-breaker for a loanshark (though, of course, our Rocky cannot bring himself to use actual violence against debtors).

Popular conceptions of the loanshark resemble these media images. The term itself summons up images of horror. After all, we usually think of sharks as vicious creatures who prey upon the innocent. And once the shark sets out to get his prey, the victim rarely escapes. Bloodshed is the rule. This picture of the loanshark has several notable elements. The loanshark:

> charges usuriously high interest rates
> preys upon innocent victims
> uses violence to collect debts
> uses loans as a means to take over legitimate businesses
> is closely tied to the Mafia.

How accurate is this picture?

The first element—usury—is certainly true. While bank loans are figured on an annual interest rate (say 15 percent per year), and credit card companies charge a monthly rate on unpaid balances ($1\frac{1}{2}$ to 2 percent per month), loansharks figure interest on a per-week basis. A typical rate is 3 percent a week, or more than 150 percent a year, though the interest rate depends on the size and repayment terms. The larger the loan, the less the interest. Very small loans go at the standard rate of "six for five." Borrow $100 today, pay back $120 next week. The $20 weekly interest works out to an annual interest rate of over 1,000 percent! The terms of a $1,000 loan typically will be 12 weekly payments of $100. A loan on these terms is called a "knockdown" loan, since the payments steadily reduce the principal. The other type of loan is the "vig" loan*: The borrower pays a specified rate of interest, or vig, each week (typically 2 to 3 percent), and the repayment of the principal varies according to each situation. If I take a $5,000 vig loan at two "points" a week, I must pay the loanshark $100 each week. In addition, we will have worked out some schedule for repayment of the $5,000. Very large loans might go for as little as 1 percent a week. In any case, whether the annual interest is 1,000 percent or "only" 50 to 100 percent, it is far higher than what banks and finance companies may legally charge.

If the interest rates are so high, why would anyone borrow from a loanshark? The answer sometimes suggested in the media is that the loanshark somehow forces the client to take the loan. In reality, such victimization is extremely rare. The nearest version of this is the loanshark who hangs around card games or other gambling settings, ready to lend money to the gambler who has lost his capital and wants to continue playing. I suppose the moral thing for the loanshark to do would be to advise the gambler to quit before he loses any more. But dispensing wisdom is not the loanshark's role, and besides, few gamblers in that situation would heed the advice.

This example of the gambler illustrates some of the reasons borrowers go to a loanshark rather than to legitimate lenders. A borrower may need the money quickly, or wish the loan to remain secret. Some borrowers need the money for purposes no bank would approve. Drug dealers may need money to finance a large deal. A numbers bank that undergoes a few heavily played hits may need money to stay in business. So might a bookmaker whose customers have had a run of good luck.

Even legitimate businesses or individuals may find that banks will not lend to them. Perhaps they already have a loan outstanding at the bank, or they cannot put up enough collateral, or the loan looks too risky for a bank to approve. Or they may need the money quickly and for only a few weeks. Furriers, for example, have little income during the summer. If they need a few thousand dollars to buy pelts in the fall, their cash reserves will be too low. Other small businesses may have similar cash-flow problems.

---

* "Vig" is short for "vigorish." No linguists have yet figured out the source of this term.

Loanshark customers, then, come because they need the money, not because anyone is forcing them. In this sense, they come just as voluntarily as do the customers of banks and finance companies. As for the extortionary interest, a loan shark charges high rates because he is taking a greater risk. Some of his clients are criminals, perhaps even unsuccessful criminals whose schemes have already gone sour (a losing bookmaker or gambler, a fence who is stuck with merchandise he cannot sell). His customers may be arrested and have their assets seized (or stolen by the police), greatly reducing their ability to pay. And if the criminal is convicted and imprisoned, the chances of repayment become extremely remote. Even the loanshark's noncriminal borrowers are high-risk customers, people whom Chase Manhattan and Household Finance wouldn't touch.

The most unsettling aspect of loansharking, however, is not the usurious interest (which may be understandable) but the potential violence. The media often portray threat and violence as the most frequent outcome when borrowers are late in paying. The reality is more complicated. Yes, violence and threat are part of the understood terms of a loanshark loan; actual violence, on the other hand, is rare. To understand both parts of this equation, consider the transaction from the loanshark's point of view. His clients are not reputable people, and the terms of the loan are neither legal nor officially recorded. If the borrower does not repay, what can the loanshark do? Against the risk of nonpayment, loansharks often demand some sort of collateral, but often the resale value of the collateral is much less than the amount of the loan.[37] If the client does not pay, the loanshark cannot file a lawsuit in court; he simply has no legal means to get his money back. Under these conditions, what else but violence does the loanshark have to make sure he doesn't lose his money?

Nevertheless, violence is by far the exception rather than the rule. In my own research on compulsive gamblers, I met scores of men who had taken loans from "shylocks"; a man might have loans from two or more loansharks, an arrangement which usually left him deeper in debt and unable to keep up payments. "I owed more in vig than I was making each week," said one man who was only slightly worse off than many others. Many of these men had received continual reminders from the loansharks; a few had been threatened, but none of them had actually been beaten up.[38] Peter Reuter, an economist who studied gambling and loansharking in New York, found a similar pattern.

> Violence is, in most cases, a very late stage of the collection process. Harassment is the most common first stage. The borrower is called with increasing frequency. Threats become more explicit and are made increasingly at night and at the borrower's home. It appears that the typical process of harassment may extend for a reasonable length of time, not less than a month in most operations.[39]

Some loansharks are more prone to violence than others, and they are the ones the public is most likely to learn about. After all, only when a borrower is severely beaten are the police likely to find out about the loansharking. The anecdotal evidence in the media also suggests that debtors who cannot pay may even be murdered. This seems unlikely, since it is so unwise economically. Dead men make no payments. If murder occurs at all, it would be only when the borrower is trying to defraud the loanshark— that is, taking a large loan with no intention of repaying it.

Because loansharking is illegal and because it depends ultimately on violence, many people, including many in law enforcement, believe that it is controlled by the Mafia. There may be logical reasons for this belief. To begin with, it is the kind of enterprise the Mafia would find attractive: It requires neither hard work, nor skill, nor intelligence. The only requirements are cash and access to violence. In addition, if successful loansharking depends ultimately on violence or threat of violence, then the group whose threats are most credible will be most successful. And that group is the Mafia.

Despite these considerations, loansharking, like bookmaking and numbers, is probably a decentralized market rather than one that is centrally controlled. To be sure, many loansharks are Mafia members or have Mafia connections, which can put them at an advantage. "To be able truthfully to tell a loanshark customer that 'this is Fat Tony's money' is a considerable asset."[40] ("Fat Tony" Salerno was head of the Genovese crime family in New York.) But what is to prevent other lenders from entering the market? For example, suppose that I am a businessman with cash on hand, and another businessman I know needs money quickly. What is to prevent me from lending him my money at 3 percent a week? (I might even tell him that the loan is backed by the mob.) Through referrals in the network of people in our business, I might get other borrowers. In fact, Reuter's research found non-Mafia loansharks who started in just this way. If threat or violence became necessary, they could always hire enforcers on a free-lance basis.

So while the Mafia is active in loansharking, the market may also have many independent lenders. Unfortunately, since loansharking is one of the crimes least likely to become known to the police, the available evidence is quite limited. A study of organized crime in Philadelphia found the loansharking market to be made up of many independent lenders with no monopoly by the Mafia or anyone else.[41] Loansharking in other cities probably resembles this disorganized structure.

Finally, there is the idea, also popularly disseminated, that Mafia loansharks use loans as a way of taking over legitimate businesses. In fact, such takeovers are rare, and it is not hard to imagine the reasons why. Why would a loanshark want to take over someone else's business? Running a business is hard work. When a Mafia loanshark takes over a business, it is for one of three reasons: (1) to sell off its assets and get cash; (2) to use it in a bankruptcy scam (see p. 292); or (3) to use it as a legitimate front for other illegal activity.

Drugs

Here is one area where even the mythology of the Mafia is divided. In a famous scene in *The Godfather*, the Don (Marlon Brando) takes a principled position against drugs. As long as he remains in control, the family will not traffic in drugs. Other Mafiosi want to take advantage of the easy profits to be made in drugs. This ambivalence existed in reality as well. Some Mafia leaders gave orders that their members stay out of the drug business, though their reasons may have been more practical than principled. In any case, the restriction seems to have been more often broken than observed.[42] For decades, police and media have portrayed organized crime and the Mafia as deeply involved in the drug trade. Appealing to the morality of those who might be tempted to bet on a number or a football game, officials would remind the public that organized crime used the proceeds of illegal gambling to finance their drug operations. The "French Connection" case, made famous by the 1972 film, furthered the idea that the Mafia controlled the importation of heroin. The case that perhaps settled the question, at least in the media, was the 1987 "Pizza Connection" trial, which centered on a former head of the Sicilian Mafia who used his American contacts to import heroin and cocaine into the United States. All the defendants in the trial were of Italian origin, mostly Sicilian, and the case took its name from the pizzerias the drug smugglers frequently used as a cover for phone conversations, meetings, and money laundering. These media events, both fiction and news, offered a model of the drug distribution business as a sort of pyramid. The lowest and most visible levels—the small-scale distributors and street dealers—were for the most part blacks and Hispanics. The few at the top, the importers, made the big money—and those importers were the Mafia. However, in the late 1980s, as cocaine replaced heroin as the country's most feared drug, law enforcement began to downplay the role of the Mafia and concentrate instead on another large conspiracy—the Medellin cartel, a group of drug producers based in Colombia.

The reality of drug importation and distribution differs somewhat from the image of a business controlled at the top by a small, immensely powerful group. As with other illegal businesses, Mafia people may be involved in importing these drugs, but certainly they are not the only ones. Nor does the Mafia control the market. The large shipments of drugs into the United States come from Latin American organizations, which seem to be doing quite well without the assistance of older American crime groups. In addition, much of the cocaine and marijuana coming from South America is imported by many independent entrepreneurs and small partnerships. The main reason organized crime does not dominate the market is that smuggling drugs does not require very much organization. Some importers smuggle drugs in large quantities—thousands of kilos of cocaine aboard cargo ships. These operations obviously require a larger organization to coordinate the purchasing, loading, shipping, unloading, and storage of these large shipments. But these large shippers are a fairly recent addition to the drug scene. For smaller-scale smuggling—less than a ton per shipment—just about anyone can become a cocaine importer. The operation has three stages: buying the drugs in South America, bringing the drugs into the United States, and selling the drugs. The only stage that requires organization is the middle step—smuggling. The first step—connecting with a source—is a matter of "networking" through the distribution chain. Some would-be dealers actively look for ways to link up with sources. A low-level dealer or even a nondealing drug user seeks out a large dealer who is willing to take him as a temporary partner. For others who become dealers, the opportunity arises almost by chance. Bartenders, waiters, even people in more upscale occupations like real estate brokers or lawyers may find their social or business paths intersecting with high-level dealers willing to cut them in.[43] Another type of networking occurs in prison. Other prisoners can offer information (who to meet, what bars to hang out in) valuable for making contacts with large dealers and even suppliers in Latin America.[44] As for the third stage—selling the drugs—if a person has been using drugs or selling in small quantities, he will have little trouble finding buyers for his inventory.

It is the second part of the process—smuggling drugs into the country—that may require some degree of organization. The dealer must find someone willing to transport the drugs to the United States. Since cocaine is so expensive, even a $100,000 purchase weighs only 5 kilos (11 pounds),* takes up little space, can easily be carried on small airplanes or pleasure boats, and has a street value several times the initial cost.[45] A pilot approached by a drug dealer may well be tempted by the offer of $10,000 for a round-trip flight south of the border. However, the pressure can be unnerving, especially when things do not go precisely according to plan. As one dealer explained, "They burn out so fast I have to replace them every six months to a year."[46] Marijuana is much bulkier than cocaine and may require specially rigged boats or planes. Or the importers may send the drugs on a commercial ship that lies offshore and downloads its cargo in smaller quantities to pleasure craft, which then run the drugs into the mainland. This method also is used for larger shipments of cocaine.

For a single criminal organization like the Mafia to control drug trafficking, it would have to control at least one part of the business—either sources, smuggling routes, or distribution networks. For cocaine and marijuana, all three elements are decentralized. On the other hand, if a drug comes from more limited sources and requires longer supply lines, it may be more susceptible to control by a single group. Until the 1970s, the market in heroin fit this description. The geography of heroin kept smaller entre-

* At 1990 prices.

preneurs out of the market. The poppies were grown in the Middle East (Iran, Afghanistan, Turkey), converted to heroin in Mediterranean ports like Marseille, and shipped to the United States in large commercial ships. Because the distance was much too far for importation by small aircraft or pleasure boats, and because the Mafia controlled corruption on the New York docks, the Mafia could control the heroin market. Then in the 1970s, global politics (i.e., the war in Vietnam) opened up Southeast Asia as a source of heroin. Increased U.S. presence in the region allowed growers and dealers to establish links to American distributors.[47] The long distance between Indochina and the United States still meant that drug traffic could be dominated by large crime groups, but these new groups were Asian (Chinese and Vietnamese) or even African (Nigerian) rather than American or European.

OTHER CRIMES, OTHER RACKETS

I have gone into detail in the foregoing sections in order to cast doubt on one widespread image or model of the Mafia. In this model, the Mafia is a giant corporation that dominates the various businesses of "vice"—gambling, loansharking, prostitution, and drugs. As we have seen here, there is much in the way of both logic and evidence to question these two assumptions. In fact, it appears that while Mafia members may be involved in these rackets, usually they do not control them. The supply side of the market in illegal goods and service consists of many independent enterprises. In some cases, the criminal enterprises may be quite large, with dozens of employees and gross incomes of millions of dollars. Yet no one enterprise or organization controls the market.

Crime, Business, and Labor

In addition to the sale of illegal goods and services, organized crime groups sometimes are involved in predatory crimes like theft and robbery. Most street crime, of course, is highly decentralized. Thieves, burglars, and robbers operate in small, temporary groups, and their income from crime is too low and too irregular to interest criminal organizations. Therefore, when these organizations are involved in street crime, they are more likely to direct or control the actual predators rather than to be out on the streets committing the actual crimes. The term "ring" frequently crops up in these kinds of operations: a car-theft ring, a burglary ring, a hijacking ring. Rings bring in money on a regular basis. Car thieves, for example, sometimes are professional criminals closely tied to the organization. But they are just as likely to be teenagers who get a few hundred dollars per car. The criminal organizations take care of the final disposition of the car—exporting it, selling it in this country (complete with forged documents), or breaking it down into parts for repair shops—for a profit of thousands of dollars per car.

Occasionally, the Mafia or other organized crime groups will be involved in a single theft or burglary. But that single crime will have a very large payoff. For example, the best-seller *Wiseguy* shows the involvement of Mafia (and non-Mafia) criminals in the robbery of the Lufthansa terminal at JFK airport, a single crime that netted several million dollars. Truck hijacking or theft of shipping containers, which can be worth hundreds of thousands of dollars, also may be part of organized crime activities. The Mafia also may get involved in large-scale theft where the proceeds cannot be immediately converted to cash—items like stock certificates, bonds, and other securities stolen from financial firms.

To some people, the most damaging Mafia activities are not these predatory crimes, nor even the provision of illegal goods and services. The most threatening and insidious projects are those that involve legitimate business and labor organizations. Loansharking and drug importing are serious and illegal; large-scale robbery and theft obviously are serious crimes. But while these crimes may attack society, they do not undermine it. In other organized crime activity, however, the interweaving of legal and illegal becomes much more complicated. Indeed, the most problematic part of organized crime is its involvement in the legitimate world. It is here that the Mafia distinguishes itself from other criminal groups; no other criminal organization has entered into legitimate business on a similar scale. Various Mafia groups own several individual companies. In some cases, like garbage collection and concrete production in New York, the Mafia controls an entire industry through a cartel. Through rigged bidding and suppression of competition, the companies (and organized crime) make millions of dollars in excess profits. Similarly with labor, the Mafia runs several union locals and in some cases controls the entire national union.

Frequently we hear officials warning us that organized crime has "infiltrated" or "taken over" legitimate businesses. Why is this bad? What is the harm if, say, a soap company is run by someone "with ties to organized crime?" Doesn't it still have to sell soap?

Law enforcement officials usually give two answers to this question. The first is that the profits of the company may go to finance illegal operations like drug smuggling (though usually the officials warn of the reverse—that the Mafia will use its profits from drugs and gambling to take over legitimate businesses). The second answer is that the Mafia uses the legitimate enterprise as a front. The front can serve as a legitimate cover for money that was really made illegally—a fairly simple form of "money laundering." It can also provide the appearance of employment for people who otherwise have no way of explaining the source of their income.

There are other reasons to fear criminals in legitimate business. Most important, criminals in business are more likely to engage in illegal business practices like the "bankruptcy scam." In this scenario, criminals will establish a corporation and buy out a legitimate company, paying only part of the purchase price in cash. The rest is to be paid off in mortgage-like installments. They then order merchandise from the company's regular suppliers, who are probably unaware of the change in ownership. The crooks then sell off all the company assets (including the new supplies) and transfer the cash from these sales to another corporation, also controlled by the criminal organization. The company then goes bankrupt, leaving its suppliers unpaid. The company and its good name have been destroyed. The suppliers have taken severe losses they can never recover. And the money winds up largely in the pockets of organized crime. In one variation of this scam, before the company declares bankruptcy a mysterious fire destroys its books and records and perhaps its buildings, which are, of course, insured.

Another criminal practice involves substituting inferior goods or services. Hauling companies in an organized crime cartel are more likely to violate environmental laws. In some cases, trucks hauling toxic wastes have simply discharges their toxic contents into ordinary city sewers or at the side of a road.[48] In the meat business, companies connected to the Mafia have used rotting or diseased meat in ground beef, frankfurters, and sausage. They have even used horse meat in place of beef.*[49] Diseased meat is potentially harmful to consumers, as are the chemicals suppliers may use to mask its smell. That's why the government inspects meat. However, to avoid the inconvenience of having meat rejected, criminal companies bribe inspectors. Here is another common area for organized crime: corruption. Since organized crime operations—especially the fully illegal ones—require that law enforcers look the other way, bribery of police and other public officials is an important part of organized crime. At higher levels, they may bribe officials who decide which companies get government contracts.

Ignoring regulations, bribing officials, and using cheap ingredients are ways to beat the competition. When the Mafia becomes involved in legitimate business, it also seeks to eliminate competition altogether. Businesses run by organized crime may use violence (actual or threatened) as a method for accomplishing this goal. For example, in the 1970s, an organized crime outfit took over a not very successful detergent company. The soap was not very good, and the company tried to market it as a low-price, supermarket

---

* In one case a wiretap recorded a conversation between a meat supplier and a meat buyer, who was trying unsuccessfully to get information from the supplier so that they could both avoid trouble. The buyer finally put the question about the meat this way: "Does it moo?"

"Well," said the supplier, "some of it moos and some of it don't moo."

In this case, inspectors turned up meat that the laboratory could not positively identify but suspected was kangaroo meat from Australia.

house brand. By threatening stores with labor problems if they didn't go along, the Mafia people managed to get their inferior soap into most of the New York markets. Only A&P refused to go along, since the soap did not pass A&P's quality control tests. Soon, A&P stores and warehouses became the targets of a series of fires and explosions. Store managers were beaten, and two managers were murdered.

The Justice Department stepped in, and while no one was convicted, the continual pressure of grand jury subpoenas and indictments convinced the mobsters to quit. However, the soap remained in other stores. Only when the FDA, some years later, ruled the soap "corrosive" to the skin did it disappear from the shelves.[50]

Of course, usually the Mafia does not have to go so far in carrying out its violence. Remember, the other supermarket chains gave in and stocked the inferior soap. In a similar way, the Mafia can use violence to gain control of a union. Once it has control, further actual violence seldom is necessary as the threat is usually sufficient to elicit compliance.

What is so bad about organized crime controlling a union? The same answers apply here as for the question about Mafia firms in the legitimate marketplace. The Mafia can use the union for purposes of money launder- ing, or it can provide the cover of employment for people who make their money illegally. The main problem is similar to the threat from Mafia-con- trolled businesses: The union will be run for the purpose of enriching the criminals who run it, rather than for the rank-and-file membership. Union leaders can use their positions to extort bribes from businesses which must deal with unions. A builder may find that unless he pays off certain people, he will have labor problems. Every non–work day on his building costs him money, so he will save money by paying the bribe. The bribe, of course, stays in the pockets of the criminals; it does not go to any purpose that might benefit the rank and file.

Some bribes are detrimental to union members themselves. In these cases, the bribe does not ensure that the work goes on. Instead, the corrupt union leaders write a "sweetheart contract"—one which allows the employer to violate the usual contract terms by either paying lower wages, hiring nonunion workers, or ignoring various rules. The union leaders who take the bribes benefit, and the employer benefits. But the workers themselves wind up working under less pleasant, more dangerous conditions, and for less money.

Finally, where criminals run a union, they may steal the union's money. It's usually not as simple and obvious as embezzlement, but the effect is the same. The most notorious and large-scale examples come from the Teamsters Union. Through members' dues and employer payments, the union has amassed large funds—well over $10 billion—to pay for each teamster's pension when he or she retires. In the meantime, the pension fund money must be invested. Much of the Teamster pension fund "in- vestments" turn out to be risky loans, often to Mafia associates. If the borrower goes bankrupt, the union loses out, but someone has profited. At the same time, while Mafia figures easily tap into the pension funds, some retired union members have had great trouble getting the union to pay out their pensions.[51]

"A Government for Wiseguys"[52]

In many of these ventures, the Mafia itself is still not running the actual business. Instead, it sanctions the illegal work of others and in return gets a share of the profits. The picture of the Mafia we get here is not a business bureaucracy, but a loose network of **patron-client** relationships, an authority structure.[53] Those below pay tribute to those above. This structure, rather than that of a corporation, is something like a (nondemocratic) government. The government licenses operations, and in return each level must pay a percentage or fee (like a tax or licensing fee) to the level above. The garbage company owner pays money to the cartel organizer, who in turn pays money to a Mafia member, who in turn passes some of that money to his "capo" (or captain, a patron higher up in the authority structure). The capo may not really care what kind of business his soldati are running, as long as they pay him his share. It may be a business cartel or a labor union, a hijacking ring or stock fraud. But some of the profits go upward through the organization. In return, those who pay the tax or tribute receive the equivalent of a franchise. They operate their business with the backing of the Mafia, which provides any necessary protection.

Thinking of the Mafia as a licensing structure of power rather than as a bureaucratic organization points to what may be the Mafia's unique and most important function—not business but arbitration. The Mafia, unlike any other criminal organization, functions as a court for settling disputes in the underworld. In illegal business, competition among different organizations can lead to conflict. And when there is no established way of resolving conflict, the result can easily be violence—as the experience of the 1920s and 1930s showed. What seems to have emerged from the gangland wars of that era is not so much the elimination of non-Italian, non-Mafia criminal organizations. Non-Italian gangsters (mostly Jewish and Irish) continued to run illegal businesses. But the Mafia came to occupy a central place in settling conflict. It became a sort of government.

A government—an official government—almost by definition has a monopoly on the legitimate use of force. Consequently, government acts as the ultimate settler of disputes, and the authority of the courts in settling disputes rests finally on the government's monopoly of force. Similarly, what distinguishes the Mafia from other criminal organizations is its reputation for being able to command great force. It does not necessarily have a monopoly on heavy persuasion but it does have the reputation of being the most effective. The Mafia earned this reputation in the 1920s during Prohibition, when Italian gangs won out over their rivals largely because of their greater willingness or ability to use violence. That reputation continues to this day. Thus, while the Mafia may not have a total monopoly on violence in the criminal world, it has carved out a large enough chunk of the market that it has come to function as a kind of government. After all, somebody has to fulfill this role, since parties in these disputes cannot turn to the usual sources to resolve their differences. For example, if a legitimate liquor supplier has trouble collecting payment from a bar owner, the supplier can sue in court for the unpaid balance, or he can recover the liquor and sue for the expense of shipping. But what if the supplier is a thief and the liquor is stolen? What recourse does the supplier have?

Because the Mafia arbitrates disputes, a Mafia member can provide a second service for the criminal who pays it tribute: If a dispute arises, he has representation. To have the backing of a Mafia member in such a dispute is an invaluable advantage. Only Mafia members may participate in settling disputes. Nonmembers must be represented by a member. The higher the rank of the person backing you, the better off you are. Remember, the Mafia is not a bureaucracy run according to rules. The "rules"—to the extent that they exist at all—are ideals like respect, honor, loyalty, and secrecy: qualities which have more to do with personal relationships than with a highly specified set of procedures. The basic principles of the organization are personalistic rather than bureaucratic; it is a government of men, not of laws.

At the simplest level, a disputant with no Mafia backing has no chance in a dispute with a Mafia member. An independent loanshark or bookmaker, for example, who is owed money by a member of the Mafia (or someone fronting for a Mafioso) has no way of collecting if the Mafioso decides not to pay.[54] The illegal entrepreneur has two ways of avoiding this problem—either screen customers carefully, or make a connection with a member of the Mafia who will represent him if the dispute must be arbitrated.

When disputes arise between Mafia members or between people who are represented by members, things can become more complicated, as the following example shows.

> Michael Hellerman was a successful, young (Jewish) stock manipulator. He maintained a long-term relationship with Johnny (Dio) Dioguardi, a major mafioso in the Lucchese family, whose main source of income seems to have been labor racketeering.
>
> Hellerman had been involved in an unsuccessful swindle that had lost money for two minor mafiosi, Fusco and Burke, members of the Colombo family. He now began a new one and offered to let them share in the proceeds so as to compensate them for the former failure. The swindle required that Hellerman control all the sales of a certain stock. The other party, Stein, who had initiated the deal, now tried to cheat Hellerman through some undisclosed sales. Hellerman found out about this and confronted one of Stein's associates at a meeting in Miami.

Stein arranged for Fusco and Burke to be informed that he was being backed by a Mafioso of the Bonnano family, Evola. Stein, in the course of negotiations about arranging an adjudication, insulted Fusco. Fusco obtained permission from his own boss, Aloi, and Stein's mentor, to give Stein a beating for failure to show respect.

A meeting was arranged involving all the principals and their mentors. The other participants had not believed that Hellerman would be able to obtain Dioguardi's explicit help and had arranged that Hellerman would end up as the loser, being required to compensate everyone else. When Dio actually turned up at the meeting, Hellerman moved from being the least protected to the most protected, since Dio was the most senior of the Mafiosi present.

Dio ordered Stein to work out an acceptable arrangement with Hellerman; this yielded a total of $78,000 to be divided by the numerous parties. The division was extremely complicated. Hellerman ended up as the prime individual beneficiary, with $15,000. However, Dio, who had risked no money and invested minimal time, also received $7,500. Aloi and his associates, who had invested a great deal more time, received only about $1,500 each.[55]

This incident illustrates several points. First, not all scams work; Hellerman's original swindle had lost money. Second, notice the lack of honor among thieves. Stein tried to cheat Hellerman. One partner cheating another is a constant problem in illegal enterprises, as is the cheating of employers by employees. Third, the use of violence (especially against other Mafia members or associates) has to be cleared with a superior. This seems to be a general rule in the Mafia. Fourth, what mattered ultimately was not so much the facts of the case but the status of the representatives involved. Fifth, the high-ranking Mafioso winds up with nearly 10 percent of the money, all because of his position, not his effort.*

Finally, the incident shows that the dispute-settling mechanism works not just within a Mafia family but between different families, and that members of one family respect the rank designations of other families. Johnny Dio, because of his position in the Lucchese family, outranks the lower-level members of the Colombo family. In this sense, and probably only in this sense, is the Mafia a coordinated network of families. This coordination occurs primarily in the settling of disputes, usually between families, but occasionally within families.

SUMMARY AND CONCLUSION

While most crime is socially organized in some degree, the term *organized crime* refers to large-scale criminal organizations—especially those which

---

* Johnny Dio was involved in rackets ranging from corrupt unions to kosher meat and was widely believed to have been the one who, in a famous incident in the 1950s, blinded journalist Victor Riesel by throwing acid in his face. Hellerman eventually became a government witness and testified against Dio, who received a long prison sentence.

rely on violence, threatened or actual, to make money through crime. Organized crime often goes hand-in-hand with the corruption of public officials. Nevertheless, precise, useful definitions of organized crime have proven elusive in both criminology and law enforcement. The principal law defining organized crime (the Racketeer Influenced and Corrupt Organizations Act, or RICO) is so broad that it has been used in criminal and civil actions that have nothing to do with what most people think of as organized crime.

In America, criminal organizations often have arisen in immigrant communities. Groups that start by providing real services for their fellow immigrants may end up extorting them. Protection can turn into a protection racket. Criminal organizations still make money by meeting the demand for illegal goods and services. However, the supply side of the market in illegal drugs, gambling, loans, and sex consists of a large number of small-scale entrepreneurs. Even the largest suppliers do not control the market in vice.

The Mafia is probably the largest and longest-lived criminal organization. Like members of other criminal organizations, Mafia members often make their money from vice. In addition, the various Mafia groups, probably more than other criminal organizations, make a great deal of their money from their influence in more legitimate organizations—unions and businesses. By manipulating the legitimate functions of these organizations (strikes and contract negotiations, bids for private and government contracts, investment of pension-fund money, filings for bankruptcy, etc.), the Mafia-backed groups derive income far in excess of what an unrigged market and honest business practices would bring.

The degree of organization within the Mafia is a matter of much debate and uncertainty, as is its connection (past and present) with criminal organizations in Italy. Law enforcement people often portray the Mafia as a highly organized national and international conspiracy. Other observers see each Mafia "family" as a loose arrangement in which members independently seek out criminal opportunities and pay a portion of the profits to those above them in the organization. The organization in return provides backing, should any disputes arise. In fact, it probably would be more accurate to think of the Mafia not as an arrangement for committing certain types of crime, but rather as an arrangement for regulating relations among people who do commit those crimes.

NOTES

1. Russell Mokhiber (1985), "Triple Damages," *The New York Times*, Sept. 14, p. 23. *New York Newsday*, Jan. 18, 1990, p. 3 ("Suit II: Nancy Capasso Asks $70M," Paul Moses).

2. Peter Reuter (1987), *Racketeering in Legitimate Industries: A Study in the Economics of Intimidation*, Santa Monica, CA: The RAND Corporation.

3. John M. Blair (1976), *The Control of Oil*, New York: Random House. James William Coleman (1989), *The Criminal Elite: The Sociology of White Collar Crime* (2nd ed.), New York: St. Martin's, pp. 22–30.

4. *The New York Times*, Aug. 11, 1989, p. B1.

5. Jack Newfield (1979), "The Myth of Godfather Journalism,"*The Village Voice*, July 23, p. 1, 11–12. Peter Reuter and Jonathan B. Rubinstein (1978), "Fact, Fancy, and Organized Crime," *The Public Interest*, vol. 53, pp. 45–67.

6. Tom Buckley (1971), "The Mafia Tries a New Tune," *Harper's Magazine*, August.

7. Murray Kempton (1963), " 'Che Cosa?' Means 'What's That?' " *The New Republic*, Oct. 12.

8. Humbert S. Nelli (1976), *The Business of Crime: Italians and Syndicate Crime in the United States*, New York: Oxford, pp. 47–69.

9. Donald R. Cressey (1969), *Theft of a Nation: The Structure and Operations of Organized Crime in America*, New York: Harper & Row.

10. Dwight Smith (1975), *The Mafia Mystique*, New York: Basic Books.

11. Irving A. Spergel (1990), "Youth Gangs: Continuity and Change," in Michael Tonry and Norval Morris, eds. (1990), *Crime and Justice: A Review of Research*, Chicago: University of Chicago Press, pp. 171–275.

12. Edward Crapsey (1872), *The Nether Side of New York: or Vice, Crime and Poverty of the Great Metropolis*, New York: n.p., excerpted in Wayne Molquin with Charles Van Doren, ed. (1976), *The American Way of Crime: A Documentary History*, New York: Prager, pp. 17–21.

13. *The New York Times*, Nov. 11, 1987.

14. *The New York Times*, Aug. 24, 1986, sec. 4, p. 6.

15. Nelli, op. cit., p. 3.

16. Ibid., p. 13.

17. Ibid., pp. 14–23.

18. Ibid., p. 136.

19. Ibid., p. 80.

20. Ibid., pp. 69–100.

21. *Kefauver Crime Report* (1951), New York: Arco, p. 2. Quoted in Howard Abadinsky (1985), *Organized Crime*, (2nd ed.), Chicago: Nelson Hall, p. 89.

22. *Kefauver Crime Report* (1951), p. 2. Quoted in ibid. p. 312.

23. Nelli, op. cit., pp. 199–210.

24. Nicholas Pileggi (1966), "The Lying, Thieving, Murdering, Upper-Middle-Class, Respectable Clerk," *Esquire*, January. Reprinted in Molquin with Van Doren, op. cit., pp. 286–91.

25. Nelli, op. cit., p. 261.

26. Abadinsky, op. cit., p. 20.

27. President's Commission on Law Enforcement and the Administration of Justice (1967), *Task Force Report: Organized Crime*, Washington, DC: U.S. Government Printing Office, p. 1. Quoted in Peter Reuter (1983), *Disorganized Crime: The Economics of the Visible Hand*, Cambridge, MA: MIT Press, p. 3.

28. U.S. Congress, Senate Permanent Subcommittee on Investigations of the Committee on Government Operations (1971), 92nd Cong., 1st Sess., Washington, DC, part III, pp. 772–838. Reprinted as "Vincent Teresa on a Life in Crime," in Molquin with Van Doren, op. cit., pp. 332–41.

29. Cressey, op. cit., p. 75.

30. Reuter, *Disorganized Crime*, pp. 43–44.

31. Ibid., p. 42.

32. Gerald O'Neill and Dick Lehr (1989), *The Underboss: The Rise and Fall of a Mafia Family*, New York: St. Martin's.

33. For information on New York, see Reuter, *Disorganized Crime*. For Philadelphia, see Gary N. Potter and Philip Jenkins (1985), *The City and the Syndicate: Organizing Crime in Philadelphia*, Lexington, MA: Ginn Press.

34. Nelli, op. cit., p. 228.

35. Reuter, *Disorganized Crime*, pp. 62–67.

36. *The New York Times*, Feb. 1, 1986, "470 Betting Places Raided."

37. Reuter, *Disorganized Crime*, p. 98.

38. Jay Livingston (1974), *Compulsive Gamblers: Observations on Action and Abstinence*, New York: Harper & Row.

39. Reuter, *Disorganized Crime*, p. 100.

40. Ibid., p. 149.

41. Potter and Jenkins, op. cit., p. 78.

42. Peter Maas (1968), *The Valachi Papers*, New York: Bantam, pp. 245–46.

43. Patricia A. Adler (1985), *Wheeling and Dealing*, New York: Columbia University Press.

44. Peter Reuter and John Haaga (1989), *The Organization of High-Level Drug Markets: An Exploratory Study*, Santa Monica, CA: The RAND Corporation, pp. 35–39.

45. Joseph B. Treaster (1990), "More Drugs in Ship Containers Flood Ports," *The New York Times*, April 29, 1990, p. 1.

46. Adler, op. cit.

47. Alfred W. McCoy (1973), *The Politics of Heroin in Southeast Asia*, New York: Harper & Row.

48. Alan A. Block and Frank R. Scarpitti (1985), *Poisoning for Profit: The Mafia and Toxic Waste in America*, New York: William Morrow.

49. Kwitny, op. cit., pp. 1–46 (quote on p. 18).

50. Ibid., pp. 274–76.

51. Ibid.

52. The phrase comes from Henry Hill, the informant in Nicholas Pileggi (1985), *Wiseguy: A Life in the Mafia*, New York: Simon & Schuster.

53. Robert P. Rhodes (1984), *Organized Crime: Crime Control vs. Civil Liberties*, New York: Random House, p. 7. Also, Joseph Albini (1971), *American Mafia: Genesis of a Legend*, New York: Appleton-Century-Crofts.

54. Reuter, *Disorganized Crime*, p. 105.

55. Ibid., pp. 163–64.

White-Collar Crime

CHAPTER 9

EVERY SO OFTEN, A BIT OF SOCIOLOGICAL LANGUAGE CROSSES OVER INTO GENERAL USE. Despite criticism of sociology for its needless use of "jargon"—new and clumsy words that make the obvious seem obscure—sociological terms like *lifestyle* and *role model* are now part of language. But of all the terms originating in sociology, none has passed into greater currency than *white-collar crime*. The phrase was coined by Edwin Sutherland and first used in his presidential address to the American Sociological Society in 1939.* Sutherland was chiding his colleagues for focusing their criminological theorizing and research almost exclusively on the crimes of the poor. This focus, he said, not only led them to ignore a great deal of crime, but it also led them to construct bad theories. These theories—reflecting ideas which are still popular—attributed crime to individual or social defects like poverty, low intelligence, psychological problems, or broken families. But, asked Sutherland, how useful were these theories if they could not apply to white-collar crimes?[1]

Sutherland mentioned several crimes and topics which remain on the research agenda for white-collar crime: bribery in government and business, unnecessary treatment in medicine, embezzlement, tax fraud, insider trading, and political corruption. These crimes, as Sutherland pointed out, are far more costly than are the street crimes of the poor. The high cost of white-collar crime contradicts our usual assumption that people in respectable positions in society are somehow more moral than are those who live at the margins of society. But it takes only a moment of consideration to realize that the wealthier and more powerful the people, the more serious are the crimes they can commit. The "robber barons"—the 19th-century giants of the railroads, banks, and other enterprises—were perhaps the most glaring examples of upperworld criminal greed, though the savings-and-loan debacle of the late 20th century may come to rival them. Only people with access to large amounts of money—especially if they have the support and approval of government—could do so much financial damage. The respectability that comes with wealth and government backing also serves as a buffer against efforts to control white-collar crime. Sutherland, writing over 50 years ago, pointed out these problems in the control of white-collar crime. Not only do the wealthy and powerful influence the writing of the very laws that are intended to control their sins, but their status and respectability protect them from harsh penalties when they do violate these laws.[2]

In the years following Sutherland's landmark article, white-collar crime remained relatively ignored among criminologists and sociologists. Instead, most theory and research continued to center on juvenile delinquency and

---

* Clearly, white-collar crime was a concept waiting to be born and christened, and Sutherland, the father of white-collar crime, seems to have chosen precisely the right name. The term passed quickly and broadly into general use. The French now have *crime en col blanc*; the Italians, *criminalità in colletti bianchi*; and the Germans, *weisse-kragen-kriminalitat*. (John Braithwaite (1985), "White-Collar Crime," *Annual Review of Sociology*, vol. 11, p. 3.)

street crime. Perhaps this inattention to white-collar crime reflected the temper of the times, for in the two decades following World War II, the large institutions of business and government in the United States enjoyed a position of popular confidence and respect. The only noticeable dark spot in the picture occurred in 1961, when several vice presidents of GE, Westinghouse, and other manufacturers of electrical equipment were convicted and imprisoned for price fixing. Even this case probably did little to shift the public trust in big business. Only government prosecutors seemed to be complaining that the rules were being broken. The public could not find any victims to feel sorry for. And the executives on trial had not been taking any money for themselves.

However, beginning in the late 1960s the political climate began to shift. Public reactions to the Vietnam War and then Watergate signaled the increasing suspicion and even resentment of the government. Business, too, suffered a loss of public confidence[3] as consumer activists and environmentalists began to document unsafe car design, the indiscriminate use of chemicals, the marketing of unsafe products, and other business shortcomings (see Figure 9–1). The stories involved some of the largest corporations—GM, Ford, Firestone, Union Carbide, Eli Lilly, A. H. Robbins—and the misdeeds did more than add a few dollars to corporate profits. They cost human lives.

A few criminologists, too, began to turn their attention to white-collar crime, though their output was small—so much so that two criminologists

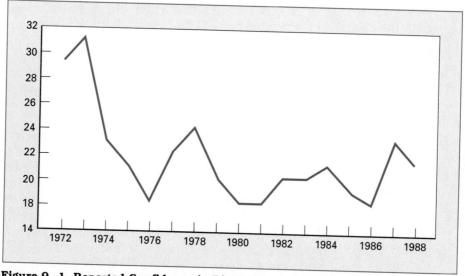

Figure 9–1 Reported Confidence in Big Business. Percent Reporting a Great Deal of Confidence.
Source: The Harris Survey, reprinted in Sourcebook—1987.

putting together a book of readings on the subject in 1977, commented that "social scientists have been relatively inactive in their investigation of white-collar crime. . . . The challenge offered by white-collar crime . . . has continued to be unanswered."[4] It has now been a half-century since Sutherland's landmark article, and still few theories of white-collar crime have emerged in social science. As late as 1989, Sutherland's long-time collaborator Donald Cressey, criticized white-collar-crime studies for their "Poverty of Theory."[5] Today, we have many more case studies (often the work of investigative journalists), and we have studies and suggestions (usually from lawyers) about the tactics of law enforcement and regulatory agencies. But satisfying explanations of white-collar crime remain elusive.

DEFINING WHITE-COLLAR CRIME

According to Sutherland's original definition, white-collar crime is "a crime committed by a person of respectability and high social status in the course of his occupation."[6] This definition distinguishes upperworld crime from street crime, but it still includes a diverse multitude of sins. For example, in Sutherland's definition, the bank teller who embezzles and the bank president who launders drug money are both white-collar criminals. But obviously, their crimes differ in some important ways. Criminologists have tried to refine the definition to distinguish between these different types of crime. In sorting white-collar crimes into different categories, criminologists have looked at several aspects of the crime. Who is the victim—the public (as in consumer fraud) or the organization itself (as in embezzlement)? Who benefits directly from the crime—the individual or the organization? Does the individual criminal act more independently or more as a member of the organization? Is the crime the central part of the company's business (like fraudulent land sales) or is it only one part of an otherwise legitimate business (tax evasion, bribery)?

Some crimes that Sutherland might have classified as white-collar crime seem to resemble street crime. Employee theft, for example, is not much different from shoplifting. Some criminologists have created the category of **occupational crime**, meaning crimes that people commit at work. In most occupational crime, the employee victimizes the employer; embezzlement is an obvious example. Other crimes committed at work by "respectable" people —tax evasion, insurance fraud, credit-card fraud, check kiting— qualify, by Sutherland's definition, as white-collar crime. But these crimes, too, hardly seem worthy of a separate category. They do not require white-collar occupations. In fact, they seem to have more in common with ordinary forms of stealing: They require little organization, planning, or coordination, and they do not involve the abuse of a position of trust or power. Nor are they limited to respectable and high-status people. Blue-collar workers, too, can steal from an employer, get a phony repair bill for auto insurance, or cheat on their income taxes. The demographic profile for these crimes also resembles that of street crime. The people most likely to commit them are men between the ages of 17 and 30.[7]

Closer to most popular conceptions of white-collar crime is the **swindle**,[8] for which a position of some responsibility in business or government is a necessity. Even so, many of these crimes are fairly simple. They require only setting up a business as a front—a means of making money through fraud and deceit. Examples include bankruptcy scams* and elaborate confidence games. The criminal misrepresents either himself or his business in order to get people to hand over their money. Ponzi swindlers are often so persuasive that their victims can scarcely believe that such a kind and generous person could have been stealing all their savings. People involved in a pyramid scheme often cannot believe that the scheme could be illegal.† Equally persuasive, though they operate almost entirely by phone, are salesmen in "boiler room" sales rackets. They convince people to put their money into investments—penny stocks, real estate, art, coins—which turn out to be nearly worthless.[9]

Individuals are not the only victims of fraudulent schemes. Bankruptcy frauds victimize other businesses, as do other forms of cheating or **chiseling**, where bills are inflated or goods or services are not provided in full. Some forms of chiseling—like Medicaid fraud, where doctors file false bills or perform many unnecessary procedures—victimize the government.

In all of these cases, the criminals set out with the express purpose of getting money through fraud. In **corporate crime**, corporations that are by and large legitimate break some laws as part of their operations. Price fixing, bribery, commercial espionage, misrepresentation of goods, and the violation of safety regulations all fall into this category. While some of the criminals are fairly small-scale, this type of white-collar crime sometimes involves large, well-known corporations.[10]

---

* These are described in Chapter 8.

† In a Ponzi scheme, the swindler poses as an investment broker and promises a temptingly high return. Investors who put in $50,000 may find themselves receiving a dividend of $2,000 after only two months—an annual rate of 24 percent! Word spreads, more investors get in on the good deal, and for a while, the dividends keep coming. The only problem is that there is no real investment. The swindler is paying the early investors' dividends out of the money received from new investors. When the swindler has brought in enough capital, he disappears with the money.

Pyramid schemes operate on a similar principle, except that the organizers take a straight fee; newcomers pay the early entrants directly, and the early entrants must drum up the business themselves. The principle is basically that of the chain letter. In the late 1980s one such scheme (called Airplane), operating largely in Los Angeles and New York, required entrants to pay $1,500 with the promise of an eventual return of $8,000 if they brought in others to fill up the airplane and move themselves up to "co-pilot."

How Much White-Collar Crime Is There?

The problems associated with counting street crime are nothing compared with the difficulty measuring white-collar crime. Defining the crimes is difficult, and getting an accurate count is impossible. Unlike street crimes, white-collar crimes often have no direct victim who will call the cops. Suppose, for example, that a businessman bribes a city official in order to get a contract, and then inflates his bid to cover the cost of the bribe and give himself a handsome profit. Neither of the parties involved is likely to make the crime known. And the real victims—the taxpayers—are unlikely to know that they have been ripped off. Often, even a direct victim might not realize that a crime has occurred. If a patient suffers harmful side effects from a drug, she probably will not know whether the drug company had suppressed data concerning the drug's harmfulness. She may call her doctor, but she is unlikely to call the police. Even for crimes that do come to light, counting is a problem. Suppose that the drug company suppressed the data from two different tests of its drug, that doctors then prescribed the drug to 250,000 patients, and that 500 of these patients suffered harmful side effects. How many crimes shall we count? Or if a corporation violates 14 safety regulations in three of its factories over the course of 18 months, but no workers suffer harm as a result, how many crimes should be counted?

A few criminologists have used the FBI's *Uniform Crime Reports* as sources of data on white-collar crime.[11] The UCR has information on fraud, forgery, and embezzlement—often thought of as white-collar crimes. The UCR tally, however, comes not from "crimes known to the police" (i.e., crimes where the victim called the police) but from arrests. It is unlikely that these numbers reflect much of the reality of white-collar crime. For example, the arrest data in the 1987 UCR show that 9,700 people were arrested that year for embezzlement. By contrast, 15,000 were arrested for murder. If we took these arrests as an indicator of the true amount of these crimes, we would think that murder occurred 50 percent *more* frequently than embezzlement—that is, for every two embezzlers, there were three murderers. The UCR also shows that for fraud, as measured by arrests, Southern states had a rate 600 percent higher than that of Western states. Should we conclude that Southerners are really seven times more fraudulent than people in the West? Obviously, these statistics on white-collar crime tell us not about the true amount or distribution of fraud, forgery, or embezzlement, but about the willingness of police to arrest and charge persons for these crimes. Like the tallies for gambling, prostitution, and other forms of "vice," the official count of white-collar crime—i.e., arrests reported in the UCR—depends mainly on what the police do, not on what criminals do. More important, these crimes are usually not sophisticated or corporate-level crime but individual or small-scale: Most forgery turns out to be nothing more than writing bad checks, and fraud often means the use of a stolen credit card.[12]

Other estimates of white-collar crime have used the self-report method. Unfortunately, most of these studies have looked only at occupational crime. Most company executives, when sent self-report surveys about corporate crime, do not bother to respond.[13] Field experiments, where investigators pose as customers, also can provide an idea of the extent of white-collar crime, especially consumer fraud. These experiments find a disappointingly high proportion of stores that give short weight, taxi drivers who overcharge, and garages that make unnecessary repairs or inflate prices when an insurance company is paying. Similar studies find that many city inspectors who enforce health, safety, and other types of regulations will take a bribe if one is offered. In most of these cases, the sampling and methods leave much to be desired, and they serve less to measure the actual amount of white-collar crime than to alert us that it is far more common than we might think.

One other source of information on corporate crime is the official records of the various inspection agencies that monitor certain industries for health and safety violations. These records, however, are subject to the selective bias of the inspectors. Probably most corporate misdeeds never come to light. Even so, despite all the companies whose crimes escape detection or prosecution, the numbers are astonishing. The most complete records are those of the U.S. Mine Safety and Health Administration, which is required by law to inspect mines four times each year. The agency records about 140,000 violations annually.[14] Little wonder that miners have one of the highest rates of work-related death; much higher, for example, than that of the police.

As for nonsafety violations, Sutherland, in his pioneering work in the 1940s, examined the 70 largest corporations in the United States over a 50-year period. Nearly all the companies (98 percent) had two or more violations, and the total number of violations came to 980—an average of 14 per company. The majority of these violations—mostly for things such as restraint of trade, unfair labor practices, and false advertising—had occurred in the last 10 years Sutherland examined (1932 to 1941), not because the companies had been more honest in the past, but because the government had not been as interested in prosecuting corporate wrongdoing. "Of the 70 corporations, 30 were either illegal in their origins or began illegal activity immediately after their origin, and eight additional corporations should probably be added to this 30."[15] Thirty-five years later, a study of the nation's 477 largest manufacturing corporations found that nearly half had committed at least one "serious or moderate"* violation. One hundred twenty of these firms had multiple violations.[16] And these are only the violations that resulted in some government action. Presumably, they represent only a fraction of the true number of violations. Some industries were

---

* This category excluded minor violations such as those concerning record keeping.

more law-breaking than others. Oil refining, for example, had a dispropor-tionate share of the violations, financial as well as environmental. Motor vehicle and pharmaceutical manufacturers also had far more than their share of the total violations.[17]

EXPLAINING WHITE-COLLAR CRIME

Most theories of crime focus on the individual. From Beccaria in the 18th century right up to the present, most theories of crime try to show how different factors—biological, psychological, economic, or social—affect the individual's decision to commit a crime. Not so with theories of white-collar crime. Until very recently, theory and research about the individual was noticeably absent in the study of white-collar crime. Few criminologists bothered to investigate the characteristics of individual white-collar crim-inals. Instead, these explanations have assumed that white-collar criminals are psychologically and biologically no different from white-collar workers who do *not* violate the law. And in fact, the few psychological studies of white-collar criminals find them to be quite normal.[18] In searching for ex-planations of white-collar crime, especially corporate crime, criminologists have turned their attention to institutional forces, both external and in-ternal. External forces include the pressures and opportunities of the mar-ket; internal forces refer mostly to the "culture" of a particular company or organization.

Some external pressures permeate the entire society. Emphasis on com-petition and the profit motive predominate in U.S. businesses. In addition, as Merton suggested in his classic 1938 essay, American culture places a higher value on goal attainment than on strict adherence to proper pro-cedures, a value which may get the job done but which also produces more crime.*[19] Of course, these aspects of American culture affect all businesses. Studies that try to show the effect of external forces, therefore, usually focus on factors that vary from one business to another. For example, by using these ideas we might test the hypothesis that corporate crime will be less frequent in nonprofit organizations (like colleges or universities) or govern-ment agencies, where the profit motive is unimportant, than in for-profit corporations.

---

* For a fuller discussion of Merton, see Chapter 11.

External Forces—The Market

Even among profit-oriented businesses, external factors may influence corporate crime. For example, we would expect that violations would be more frequent when business is bad. In fact, some research finds that firms in depressed industries and firms with declining profits are more likely to violate antitrust laws.[20] Of course, fixing prices is easier in some industries than in others. Therefore, another factor that might be related to price fixing and other antitrust violations is **market concentration**—the degree to which the market is concentrated in the hands of a few producers. Criminologists assume that despite all the patriotic statements from business executives and politicians about the virtues of free enterprise, those who run the business would rather not leave such an important matter as profit to the uncertainties of a free market. As Adam Smith, the father of free enterprise economics, wrote nearly 300 years ago,

> People of the same trade seldom meet together . . . but the conversation ends in a conspiracy against the public or in some contrivance to raise prices.

In an industry consisting of many sellers, antitrust violations seem unlikely since the conspiracy, if it is to be effective, must involve so many participants. Where an industry is highly concentrated, with a few large firms dominating the market, collusion to reduce competition becomes more possible. The electric price fixing case, for example, required the collusion of only a few manufacturers. Despite this intuitive and anecdotal evidence, actual research into antitrust violations has not been able to provide systematic evidence for this relation between market concentration and price fixing.[21]

Market concentration can create pressures for other crimes apart from antitrust violations. When a few manufacturers dominate the market, they can squeeze distributors, who in turn resort to shady practices in order to make a profit. For example, two studies from the 1970s illustrated the way in which automobile dealers, who were in a truly competitive market, were squeezed by Detroit. The manufacturers, through the use of sales quotas, bonuses, and threats of cutting off the low-sales dealerships, pressured dealers to sell cars at low prices. The dealer could scarcely take his business elsewhere; a Chevy dealer could not quickly switch to Ford. And if he did, he would probably find himself under similar pressures. So to avoid losses, dealers engaged in service and repair fraud: phony labor charges, unnecessary repairs, used parts billed as new, etc. Sometimes the victim of repair fraud was the manufacturer (if the car was under warranty). But manufacturers, by paying only set rates for each repair or by offering rewards to

OVERCHARGES FOUND ON EXTENDED CAR-REPAIR DEALS
BY BARRY MEIER

Automobile dealers in New York State are overcharging consumers more than $25 million a year by selling them extended-service contracts at prices substantially above those suggested by car manufacturers, State Attorney General Robert Abrams says. . . .

In a study covering the sale of more than 900 service contracts offered by major auto makers, the state investigators found that dealers sold the contracts for an average of $265 above the manufacturer's suggested retail price. Some dealers charged up to six times that price, which already includes a sizable dealer profit, the study found.

Source: Copyright © 1990 by *The New York Times,* Company. Reprinted by permission.

dealers who underspent their warranty budget, could protect themselves. Usually the victim was the car owner.[22] Pressures on dealers have probably not changed much in subsequent decades (see box).

Internal Forces—Corporate Culture

The other major explanation of white-collar crime is cultural theory. The earliest version is Sutherland's own theory of "differential association,"* which he saw as an explanation for both street crime and white-collar crime. Sutherland stressed the learning aspect of crime—that both criminal techniques and criminal ideas were learned from other people. Other theorists extended this principle of differential association, explaining different crime rates by looking at the values and norms of different cultures or subcultures. Applied to white-collar crime, particularly corporate crime, these theories suggest that an organization, like different groups or subcultures in society, develops a particular "corporate culture." Some of these cultures may be more tolerant of crime. In fact, the employees may find themselves under great pressure to participate in various forms of unethical or even criminal behavior.

The case for cultural explanations seems much more applicable to corporate crime than to street crime. The culture of a small group, a neighborhood, or a social class may affect more aspects of a person's life, but the demands of that culture are far less compelling. These groups are more open, and group members may be exposed to the values and norms of other, more law-abiding cultures. The person who wishes to avoid the demands, especially the law-breaking demands, of such a culture will have little difficulty, psychologically or socially. Corporations, by contrast, are a more

* See Chapter 11.

closed environment. They have clearer boundaries, and within those boundaries the organization exerts far more control. One business expert has compared the executive levels of the corporation to a monastery or the army—the sameness of people one meets socially, the emphasis on loyalty, and the great demands on the executive's time.[23] Even if the area of the employee's life that the corporation touches is more limited,* the leeway for individual choice in that area is much narrower. Those who resist corporate pressures for unethical or illegal behavior may be kept from promotion or given less attractive assignments. "Whistle blowers" may find themselves demoted or even fired. There is another difference between corporate culture and subcultures in the wider society. Because corporate culture exists in a more structured environment, those at the top can exert more direct control over it. As several researchers have found, the highest levels of management, particularly the CEO, set the tone of corporate culture, including its tolerance for breaking the law.[24] Therefore, compared with the less structured subculture of a neighborhood or social class, corporate culture is easier to change—*if* the managers want to change it.

While the general culture of the organization may be the most important aspect in corporate crime, it provides a difficult target for law enforcement agencies. After all, you can't prosecute a cultural atmosphere; you can prosecute only specific acts by specific people. Usually, top executives are able to use the structure of the organization to keep themselves insulated from any legal responsibility. Typically, they pressure middle-level managers for results with no word as to whether the results must be achieved ethically and legally. In such a climate, employees understand that results are more important than methods, and this message easily travels down through the levels of management. At the same time, corporate structure often prevents "bad news" from traveling up. If test results show a product to be ineffective or unsafe; if bribes have been paid to clients or government officials; or if managers have colluded with other corporations to fix prices—this sort of information may never reach the top levels of a company's management.

Two American executives I interviewed explained that they had held the position of 'vice-president responsible for going to jail' and I was told of this position existing in a third company. Lines of accountability had been drawn in the organization such that if there were a problem and someone's head had to go on the chopping block, it would be that of the 'vice-president responsible for going to jail.'[25]

---

* Of course, organizations often seek to extend their control over their employees beyond the boundaries of work life. For decades, corporations have subtly pressured their white-collar male employees to marry (and to marry the "right" sort of woman), to join the "right" club, or to participate in the "right" types of leisure activities. More recent and far less subtle is the increasing use of lie-detector tests and urinalysis to probe into the formerly private spheres of employees' lives.

CONTROLLING WHITE-COLLAR CRIME

In the last decade or so, the prosecution of white-collar crime has become more visible. Nearly every week, it seems, the financial section of the newspaper carries word of some new investigation, grand jury indictment, or trial. Of course, the misdeeds of the rich and famous have always provided the media with good headlines, and perhaps these stories reflect the ambitions of prosecutors who want to bring newsworthy cases.[26] Even so, the sales of newspapers and the TV ratings, along with more systematic surveys, tell us that the public takes a generally punitive position on white-collar crime.[27] We may even hear complaints that the prisons for white-collar criminals are not dismal enough. Yet despite the desires of both the public and law enforcement officials, those who commit white-collar crimes—especially corporate crime—rarely wind up behind bars. To understand something about the control of white-collar crime, it might be best to start with a single example.

The Pinto

The history of the Pinto—a small car produced by Ford—illustrates several of the difficulties in using traditional criminal laws to punish corporate crime. In the late 1960s, the top executives at Ford, after much internal debate, decided to build a subcompact car to compete with the Volkswagen Beetle and the small Japanese cars, which were just beginning to enter the American market. The Ford executive most instrumental in this decision was a man who earlier in the decade had scored a huge success with the Mustang. His name was Lee Iacocca, and the Pinto, like the Mustang before it, came to be known at Ford as "Lee's car." Iacocca stressed to Ford engineers that the car must be kept under 2,000 pounds and under $2,000 dollars. He also wanted the car in the showrooms by the fall of 1971, a deadline which made it impossible for Ford to retool in order to take care of defects that might turn up. Both the accelerated production schedule and the market objectives (economy, size, style, performance) left no room for attention to safety. But, as one Pinto engineer later said, "Safety wasn't a popular subject around Ford in those days. With Lee it was taboo." Iacocca himself was fond of saying, "Safety doesn't sell."[28]

The chief safety defect in the Pinto was the position of the gas tank. A rear-end collision at over 30 mph would buckle the tank. It would be punctured by the differential-housing bolts, and gasoline would flow into the passenger compartment. The car would become almost a fire bomb, awaiting any post-collision spark to set it off. Several Pinto passengers were badly burned or even killed in rear-end collisions. Some of the victims (or their families) filed lawsuits against Ford, and in most of these cases, the plaintiffs and Ford settled out of court.

None of this should have taken Iacocca or his staff by surprise. The company had reports from tests which showed the vulnerability of the gas tank. Engineering reports also suggested that the danger could be substantially reduced by design changes that would add about $11 to the price of the car. Ford managers decided not to make the changes. They based their decision in part on a "cost-benefit analysis." They estimated the number of rear-end crashes that Pintos would be involved in and the consequent deaths and serious injuries. For each death, they expected pay out about $200,000 compensation in civil lawsuits, most of which would be settled out of court. Nonfatal injuries would cost less—an average of $67,000. They multiplied these costs by the estimated number of accidents. The total— that is, the amount they expected the gas tank to cost the company in compensation—came to about $50 million. On the other hand, to spend $11 on each of the 12.5 million Pinto cars and trucks would cost the company $137 million. So it made economic sense *not* to spend the $11 per car, *not* to save perhaps hundreds of people each year from death or injury from burning.[29]

The facts of Ford's cost-conscious policies emerged in a suit filed by a Pinto victim who chose not to settle out of court. Eventually, he won a multimillion dollar judgment against Ford. Three months later—that is, seven years after Ford started putting the unsafe cars on the market—the company announced a recall of the Pinto for fuel-tank modification.[30]

Still, all the action on the Pinto had taken place in civil courts. Nobody had accused Ford of committing any crime. However, in August 1978, two months before Ford's recall notice actually went out, a Pinto carrying three girls was rear-ended by a van near Elkhart, Indiana. The girls were burned to death. The local prosecutor brought criminal charges of murder (reckless homicide) against Ford. The case pitted a small-town prosecutor against a team of the best lawyers Ford could buy. Ford even hired a sociologist (at $1,000 a day) to help them with jury selection. Ford won a motion for a "change of venue," to move the trial to another jurisdiction. When they found out who the judge there would be, Ford hired the judge's friend and former partner as a member of their legal team. The issues in the case were complicated, and on various legal grounds, Ford moved to keep some crucial evidence out of court. The judge agreed, and in the end, the jury found Ford not guilty.[31]

Prosecution and Its Alternatives

It is important to note that all the successful efforts to get Ford to do something about its explosive car took place in civil rather than criminal court. In fact, the Pinto case illustrates several of the difficulties of bringing the criminal law to bear on corporate misdeeds. Corporate crime is different from street crime; not only are the crimes and the people who commit them different, but so is the official response. Street crime is largely the province of the criminal justice system—police, courts, prisons, and probation— agencies whose chief weapon is the criminal law. Corporate crimes and misdeeds are much more likely come under the control of noncriminal agencies—civil courts and government regulatory agencies like the Federal Trade Commission or the Securities and Exchange Commission. In addition, the penalties for corporate crime rarely involve incarceration. Corporations and their executives may have to pay fines, recall products, or change the way they do business. But seldom do they go to prison.

Bringing corporate criminals to justice is no simple matter. To begin with, the crime itself often goes undetected. In bribery and illegal political contributions, in money laundering, insider trading, and price fixing, the criminals are the only ones who know about the crime. The victims—other investors, the public, the taxpayers—have no way of knowing that their reduced government services or higher taxes, their lower profits or higher prices, are the result of a criminal conspiracy. If a business competitor does complain to the Department of Justice about a conspiracy, the antitrust officials are usually suspicious of the complainant's motives and are unlikely to take action.*[32] Even in cases like the Pinto, asbestos, or the Dalkon shield (see box at the end of this chapter)—instances where corporate decisions cause physical harm or even death—the individuals who suffer will usually not realize that they are victims of corporate wrongdoing. Only later, when someone else (usually a lawyer, sometimes a government agency) begins to see a pattern, will questions of corporate criminal liability emerge.

Criminal Laws and Corporate Crimes

Suppose that a government agency does find of evidence of corporate crime; for example, that a drug company is marketing an unsafe drug. What should the government do? Our first response would probably be to turn the matter over for criminal prosecution and to try to win convictions against the chief executives of the corporation. Surely, such a prosecution would have a deterrent effect. Many people (criminologists included) think that while prison may not do much to deter street criminals, even the possibility of a prison term may scare white-collar criminals into doing the right thing.[33] Yet despite the desire of both public and prosecutors to see white-collar criminals punished, a very small proportion of corporate criminals ever see the inside of a prison.

---

* Complaints from disgruntled insiders are more likely to bring action, probably because the insiders can also provide concrete evidence.

The first problem is the law. An action can be a crime only if there is a law against it. Laws are made by legislators, and legislators are open to influence. And large, wealthy corporations or entire industries can wield a great deal of influence. For example, when Congress, in response to public pressure, drafted the Motor Vehicle Safety Act in the mid-1960s, it originally included criminal penalties for manufacturers who willfully marketed unsafe cars. The automobile industry used its influence to have this provision removed.[34] More recently, in 1990 the U.S. Justice Department, after a long study, proposed much larger fines for corporations convicted of white-collar crime. A business lobbying group met with White House officials, and the next day the Justice Department withdrew its support for the stiffer penalties.[35] Tax law is another area where corporations, business lobbying groups, and some powerful individuals have been able to get the tax code changed so that they can avoid taxes without breaking the law. Local governments, especially, often give tax breaks to big business, usually with the justification that these generous tax policies will attract or keep the industries which provide jobs. Not just with taxes but for most types of laws, the ability of corporations to influence legislation and prosecution is probably even greater at the state and local levels (see box).

New laws specific to corporate crime are often necessary because ordinary criminal laws are difficult to apply to corporations. Criminal laws derive mostly from individual crimes. They are designed to allow for the prosecution of a single criminal (or small group of criminals) whose crimes have a direct victim. These laws are not well designed for prosecuting people who, as employees in corporations, play a limited part in a complicated process that eventually causes some sort of harm. Murder statutes, for example, fit cases where one person directly kills another. But what about a death that results from an accident and from a series of decisions taken by a variety of people working for a corporation? The usual legal concepts of murder may be inadequate for these cases.* In addition, many of the due-process regulations that protect individual defendants also protect corporations, and corporate lawyers make excellent use of these protections.

Prosecuting Corporate Crime

The clumsiness of traditional criminal law is only one factor that makes it difficult to bring corporate criminals to justice. Laws written specifically to control corporate crime also may be difficult to apply. In prosecutions of

---

* A similar problem plagues sociological explanations of corporate crime. Some criminologists maintain that the whole concept of corporate crime is misguided. Corporations, they say, cannot act; only people can act. (See Donald R. Cressey (1989), "The Poverty of Theory in Corporate Crime Research," in William S. Laufer and Freda Adler, eds. (1989), *Advances in Criminological Theory*, Vol. 1, New Brunswick, NJ: Transaction Publishers, pp. 31–55.)

This is an excerpt from an article on politics in Alabama.

No Alabama prosecutor has ever initiated any comprehensive sting operation in Birmingham or Montgomery, the major transfer points of political money.

State Senator Charles D. Bishop . . . says no systematic cleanup can occur until there is a governor willing to stanch the unregulated flow of corporate money into the Legislature.

"I don't know whether you want to call it corrupt money or not, because we have a very gray line in this state," Bishop said. "What is corrupt? It's legal in Alabama, for instance, if there is a bill on the floor to address an envelope [to me], and I'm walking out of the Sen-

ate floor, and one of these people can walk up to me and hand me a check for $10,000 and say to me: 'Senator, now this is for your next campaign. This is not for anything to do with trying to sway your vote on the bill.' And I can simply say, 'Well, look, I'm going to tell you, I'm going to take your money and I appreciate it, but this has nothing to do with the way I vote because I was going to vote for the bill before you gave this check.' That's legal in Alabama. It's rotten."

Source: Howell Raines (1990), "Alabama Bound," *The New York Times Magazine,* June 3, p. 42.

---

corporate economic crimes, both the laws and the business transactions are complicated. Prosecutors must spend a great deal of time interviewing a variety of people in and out of the company; and since these people will have had different positions and had access to different information, they may give conflicting accounts. Prosecutors also must devote hundreds of hours to combing through large piles of documents, a paper trail which the company may have created for the express purpose of hiding its wrongdoing. Then, the prosecutors may have a difficult time explaining to a jury of ordinary citizens just which transactions in the mountain of documents violated which laws—and proving it beyond a reasonable doubt. In the savings-and-loan crisis, for example, many of the executives whose banks failed (leaving taxpayers to foot the bill for the insured deposits) had engaged in phony appraisals of real estate values, loans to family and friends, kickbacks, and other wrongdoing. But, as the head of the fraud division in the Justice Department said, "There is a difficult dividing line between what is mismanagement and what is criminal fraud. Merely proving someone is acting imprudently is not enough to get a conviction."[36]

Often, while it's clear that something wrong has been done, proving exactly who did what remains a very difficult task. As with organized crime, the people at the top who are most responsible for the wrongdoing are farthest from the incriminating evidence. They give general goals and leave the details to subordinates. The actual payment of bribes, collusion with competitors, fudging of finances, etc., occurs further down the corporate line, sometimes at the factory level, sometimes among lower executives like the "vice presidents responsible for going to jail."

In another strategy, a corporation may contract out its dirty work. A large pharmaceutical company needing safety data on a new drug will contract the job to a testing company known for its loose standards, rather than pressure its own scientists. The testing company knows that future contracts may depend on telling the client what it wants to hear and producing those results—even with falsified data. If thousands of people suffer serious side effects, the pharmaceutical giant will claim total innocence.[37]

Prosecution or Regulation?

Because of the difficulties in bringing criminal prosecutions against corporate criminals, the control of corporate wrongdoing falls largely to **regulatory agencies**. At various times in U.S. history, Congress has established an agency to regulate a particular industry. Sometimes the legislators were responding to pressures from interest groups, sometimes to a more general need. For example, over a century ago, Congress set up the Interstate Commerce Commission (ICC) mainly in response to farmers and merchants, who had no other effective way to fight the high shipping fees that the railroads charged them. The Securities and Exchange Commission (SEC) was created in the depths of the Depression in order to prevent another stock market crash. The federal bureaucracy includes many other such regulatory agencies, some smaller and less noteworthy than others. In the area of corporate wrongdoing, the Federal Trade Commission (FTC), the Food and Drug Administration (FDA), the Occupational Safety and Health Administration (OSHA) and the Environmental Protection Agency (EPA) are among those with potentially important roles.

These agencies can create rules and regulations that industries must follow. Often, the congressional act that creates the agency gives it a general direction and establishes the scope of its actions but leaves the specific methods up to the agency itself. Of course, if a regulatory agency adopts an unpopular policy, Congress can pass a law to change it. Agencies may require companies to provide various types of information—about their financial dealings, about the contents of the goods they produce, about the specific safety precautions in their workplaces, and so on. Agencies can also undertake more thorough investigations when they suspect a violation. When regulators do uncover violations, they have a number of options. The most extreme is to turn the matter over to the Justice Department for criminal prosecution. The problem with prosecution, as we have seen, is that it requires extraordinary amounts of time and may not be successful.

Agencies also may seek civil fines against corporations, but the maximum penalties allowed are so small as to have no real deterrent effect, nor do they seem to square with most ideas of justice. For example, in the early 1970s, Firestone began selling a steel-belted radial tire called the "500." The problem with the tire was tread separation. After only a few thousand miles of use—sometimes less—the tread would become distorted, the tire would bulge, and in some cases it would blow out. Firestone's own testing had revealed the defect, but the company marketed the tire anyway and for years thwarted the efforts of the National Highway Traffic Safety Administration (NHTSA) to stop the production and sale of the tire. Under the 1966 law that created the NHTSA, there simply were no criminal penalties that could apply. The NHTSA had really only two ways to get Firestone to remove its dangerous 500s from the roads: It could create bad publicity by releasing its own information about the tires, and it could go to court to force Firestone to recall the tire. The maximum fine the agency could have imposed was $50,000, a trifling sum for a corporation that had made millions of dollars from its tires. The NHTSA eventually did get Firestone to recall the tires in 1980, and Firestone did pay the $50,000 fine. By that time, millions of consumers had paid good money for defective tires—tires that caused thousands of accidents, including at least 34 fatalities.[38]

Deterrence or Compliance?

Besides seeking criminal or civil penalties, regulatory agencies also may take **administrative** actions at an administrative hearing before a judge. Administrative courses of action often begin with an official **warning**. Agencies can seek an **injunction** requiring that the corporation halt its illegal practice immediately, pending further court decisions. Or they may try to force the company to issue a **recall** of its unsafe product. A fairly common administrative device is the **consent decree**, whereby the officers of a corporation do not admit any guilt, but they do agree not to commit further violations. Such an alternative is much less threatening to the corporation and its executives. For the general public, it also may be less satisfying morally. How would we react to news that the directors of a company that had cheated others out of hundreds of thousands of dollars were punished with nothing more than having to sign a statement that they wouldn't do it again? On the other hand, these noncriminal sanctions may be much quicker and more effective in reducing white-collar crime. The path of criminal prosecution is long and expensive, and the outcome is never certain. Especially if the case involves physical and not just financial harm, the regulators may be more interested in ensuring public safety than in punishing the guilty. The recall of a faulty product may seem too light a punishment for a corporation that has put the public at risk. On the other hand, the recall may save more lives than would a prolonged criminal case. Regulators, therefore, may face a choice: to seek justice or to save lives.[39] Often they choose the path of compliance rather than that of punishment. Of course, as the Firestone case and the Dalkon Shield case show, (see box) if a company wants to "stonewall," both courts and regulatory agencies may find it very difficult to change.

THE DALKON SHIELD

Beginning in the late 1960s the A.H. Robins company marketed an intrauterine contraceptive device (IUD) called the Dalkon Shield. Within the first two years of production, Robins learned of several drawbacks to their IUD. More than one-fourth of the women who used it suffered bleeding and severe cramps. About 5 percent became pregnant while wearing the Shield, and of those who did, more than half suffered miscarriages. Others delivered stillborn babies with serious birth defects. But the most dangerous side effect of the Shield was pelvic inflammatory disease, an infection which can cause chronic pain, sterility, hemorrhaging and other severe medical problems, or even worse. Eighteen Shield users in the United States died. So did many hundreds more outside the United States, where Robins vigorously marketed the Shield, especially in Third World countries. Yet Robins continued to market the device, ignoring or covering up warnings of its harm, until the FDA, in 1974, requested that Robins take the product off the market. Nevertheless, Robins continued to maintain that its IUD was safe "when properly used," and made no effort to alert women who might still be wearing the Dalkon Shield. Six years later, it finally urged doctors to remove existing Shields from their patients, and in 1984 it issued a full recall.

Following are excerpts from a statement read in February 1984 by Judge Miles W. Lord, Chief U.S. District Judge for Minnesota, to three officers of A.H. Robins. Judge Lord had heard much of the evidence in the court cases involving the Dalkon Shield, and his statement details some of the techniques corporations can use to avoid or minimize criminal and civil penalties: the diffusion of knowledge and responsibility, the legal decay, and the special out-of-court settlements to prevent victims from sharing their knowledge. The Robins officers were E. Claiborne Robins, Jr., president and CEO; Carl D. Lunsford, senior vice president for research and development, and William A. Forrest, Jr., vice president and general counsel.

You, Dr. Lunsford, as director of the company's most sensitive and important subdivision, have violated every ethical precept to which every doctor under your supervision must pledge as he gives the oath of Hippocrates and assumes the mantle of one who would help and cure and nurture unto the physical needs of the populace.

You, Mr. Forrest, are a lawyer—one who, upon finding his client in trouble, should counsel and guide him along a course which will comport with the legal, moral, and ethical principles which must bind us all. You have not brought honor to your profession, Mr. Forrest.

Gentlemen, the results of these activities and attitudes on your part have been catastrophic. Today as you sit here attempting once more to extricate yourselves from the legal consequences of your acts, none of you has faced up to the fact that more than nine thousand women have made claims that they gave up part of their womanhood so that your company might prosper. It is alleged that others gave their lives so you might so prosper. And there stand behind them legions more who have been injured but who have not sought relief in the courts of this land. . . .

If one poor young man were, by some act of his—without authority or consent—to inflict such damage upon one woman, he would be jailed for a good portion of the rest of his life. And yet your company, without warning to women, invaded their bodies by the millions and caused them injuries by the thousands. And when the time came for these women to make their claims against your company, you attacked their characters. You inquired into their sexual practices and into the identity of their sex partners. You exposed these women—and ruined families and reputations and careers—in order to intimidate those who would raise their voices against you. You introduced issues that had no relationship whatsoever to the fact that you planted in the bodies of these women instruments of death, of mutilation, of disease. . . .

Under your direction, your company has . . . continued to allow women, tens of thousands of them, to wear this device—a deadly depth charge in their wombs, ready to explode at any time. Your attorney, Mr. Alexander Slaughter, denies that tens of thousands of these devices are still in the bodies of women. But I submit to you that Mr. Slaughter has no more basis for his denial than the plaintiffs have for stating it as truth, because we simply do not know how many women are still wearing these devices, and your company is not willing to find out. The only conceivable reasons you have not recalled this product are that it would hurt your balance sheet and alert women who already have been harmed that you may be liable for their injuries. You have taken the bottom line as your guiding beacon, and the low road as your route. . . .

The policy of delay and obfuscation practiced by your lawyers in courts throughout this country has made it possible for you and your insurance company, Aetna Casualty and Surety Company, to delay the payment of these claims for such a long period that the interest you earn in the interim covers the cost of these cases. You, in essence, pay nothing out of your pocket to settle these cases. What other corporate officials could possibly learn a lesson from this? The only lesson could be that it pays to delay compensating victims and to intimidate, harass, and shame the injured parties.

Mr. Robins, Mr. Forrest, Dr. Lunsford: You gentlemen have consistently denied any knowledge of the deeds of the company you control. Mr. Robins, I have read your deposition. Many times you state that your management style was such as to delegate work and responsibility to other employees in matters involving the most important aspects of this nation's health. Judge Frank Theis, who presided over the discovery of these cases during the multidistrict litigation proceedings, noted this phenomenon in a recent opinion. He wrote, 'The project manager for Dalkon Shield ex-

plains that a particular question should have gone to the medical department, the medical department representative explains that the question was really the bailiwick of the quality-control department, and the quality-control department representative explains that the project manager was the one with the authority to make a decision on that question.' Under these circumstances, Judge Theis noted, 'it is not at all unusual for the hard questions posed in Dalkon Shield cases to be unanswerable by anyone from Robins.'

Your company seeks to segment and fragment the litigation of these cases nationwide. The courts of this country are now burdened with more than three thousand Dalkon Shield cases. The sheer number of claims and the dilatory tactics used by your company's attorneys clog court calendars and consume vast amounts of judicial and jury time. Your company settles those cases in which it finds itself in an uncomfortable position, a handy device for avoiding any proceeding which would give continuity or cohesiveness to the nationwide problem. The decision as to which cases to try rests almost solely at the whim and discretion of the A.H. Robins Company. In order that no plaintiff or group of plaintiffs might assert a sustained assault upon your system of evasion and avoidance, you time after time demand that able lawyers who have knowledge of the facts must, as a price of settling their cases, agree to never again take a Dalkon Shield case nor to help any less experienced lawyers with their cases against your company.

Minnesota lawyers have filed cases in this jurisdiction for women from throughout the United States. The cases of these women have waited on the calendar of the court for as many as three years. . . . Yet your company's attorneys persist in asking that these cases be transferred to other jurisdictions and to other judges unfamiliar with the cases, there to wait at the bottom of the calendars for additional months and years before they have their day in court. Another of your callous legal tactics is to force women of little means to withstand the onslaught of your well-financed, nationwide team of attorneys, and to default if they cannot keep pace. You target your worst tactics for the meek and the poor. . . .

Please, in the name of humanity, lift your eyes above the bottom line. You, the men in charge, must surely have hearts and souls and consciences. If the thought of facing up to your transgression is unbearable to you, you might do as Roger Tuttle did and confess to your Maker, beg forgiveness, and mend your ways.

Please, gentlemen, give consideration to tracing down the victims and sparing them the agony that will surely be theirs.

Judge Lord's statement did not have its intended effect. Instead, Robins filed to have the judge's remarks removed from the record, claiming that "The company believes it has acted responsibly in the handling of the Dalkon Shield." Robins hired President Reagan's former Attorney General, Griffin Bell, to represent it. Some months later, a panel of the federal circuit court ordered Judge Lord's statement stricken from the record.

Source: Stuart L. Hills, ed. (1987), Corporate Violence: Injury for Death and Profit, *Savage, MD:* Rowman & Littlefield, pp. 41–46.

SUMMARY AND CONCLUSION

The category of white-collar crime is a fairly recent one in criminology, dating back only to Sutherland's coinage of that term in 1940. It includes a variety of crimes—from small-scale individual crimes like embezzlement, to deliberate business fraud, to corporate crime like antitrust conspiracy. It is impossible to know the true extent of white-collar crime, though certainly it costs several times more than street crime. We probably will never know just how much of the $300 billion lost in the savings-and-loan collapse was criminal fraud and how much was merely poor judgment.

Explanations of white-collar crime should distinguish between the different levels of crime. The white-collar crimes committed largely by individuals acting alone (embezzlement and certain types of fraud) resemble other types of theft and probably do not require special theories. Corporate crimes are different—both in the way they are committed and in the types of people who commit them. Theories of corporate crime take two general approaches. Some emphasize the external conditions that make it more attractive for even relatively affluent people to commit crimes in their work. The general profit orientation and competitiveness of business in America, the threat of declining profits or even losses, the ease of fixing prices when a few firms dominate a market, the impersonality and diffusion of responsibility in large firms—all these can affect corporate decisions to violate the law. The other type of explanation focuses on the internal dynamics of the corporation and the ways in which employees learn both the methods of violating regulations and the justifications for doing so.

The problems involved in controlling white-collar crime are even more frustrating than are those connected with street crime. The criminal justice system may have no effective means for lowering rates of burglary, robbery, or murder, but at least it usually can punish the individual street criminals it does pursue. With white-collar crime, especially corporate crime, the situation may be reversed. That is, law enforcement agencies often have a difficult time dispensing justice, even in those cases where they have "caught" the criminal corporation. On the other hand, the increasingly powerful role of regulatory agencies probably has, over the long run, reduced corporate illegal behavior. Regulators, therefore, are more likely to seek compliance on the part of corporate offenders rather than to seek justice in the form of some penalty proportionate to the offense.

NOTES

1. Edwin Sutherland (1940), "White-Collar Criminality," *American Sociological Review*, vol. 5, pp. 1–12, reprinted in Gilbert Geis and Robert F. Meier (1977), *White-Collar Crime: Offenses in Business, Politics, and the Professions*, New York: Free Press, pp. 38–49.

2. Ibid., p. 45.

3. Louis Harris (1988), *The Harris Survey*, Orlando, FL: Media Services, Inc., reprinted in *Sourcebook, 1987*, p. 129.

4. Geis and Meier, op. cit., p. ix.

5. Donald R. Cressey (1989), "The Poverty of Theory in Corporate Crime Research," in William S. Laufer and Freda Adler, eds. (1989), *Advances in Criminological Theory, Vol. 1*, New Brunswick, NJ: Transaction Publishers, pp. 31–55.

6. Edwin Sutherland (1949), *White-Collar Crime*, New York: Dryden, p. 9.

7. Travis Hirschi and Michael Gottfredson (1987), "Causes of White-Collar Crime," *Criminology*, vol. 25, no. 4, pp. 949–74.

8. This and some of the following categories are taken from Mark Moore (1980), "Notes Toward a National Strategy to Deal with White Collar Crime," in Herbert Edelhertz and Charles Rogovin, eds. (1980), *A National Strategy for Containing White Collar Crime*, Lexington, MA: Lexington Books, p. 32–44.

9. Marlys Harris (1989), "You May Already Be a Victim of Investment Fraud," *Money*, vol. 18, no. 8, August, pp. 74–91.

10. Marshall Clinard and Richard Quinney, eds. (1973), *Criminal Behavior Systems: A Typology*, New York: Holt, Rinehart, and Winston, pp. 206–23. Herbert Edelhertz (1970), *The Nature, Impact, and Prosecution of White-Collar Crime*, U.S. Department of Justice, Law Enforcement Assistance Administration, Washington, DC: U.S. Government Printing Office.

11. Hirschi and Gottfredson (1987), op. cit.

12. Darrel J. Steffensmeier (1989), "On the Causes of 'White-Collar' Crime: An Assessment of Hirschi and Gottfredson's Claims," *Criminology*, vol. 27, pp. 345–58. Kathleen Daly (1989), "Gender Varieties of White-Collar Crime," *Criminology*, vol. 27, no. 4, pp. 769–93.

13. John Braithwaite (1985), "White Collar Crime," *Annual Review of Sociology*, vol. 11, pp. 1–25.

14. Ibid.

15. Edwin Sutherland (no original date), "Crime of Corporations," in Albert Cohen, Albert Lindesmith, and Karl Schuessler, eds. (1956), *The Sutherland Papers*, Bloomington, IN: Indiana University Press, pp. 78–96.

16. Marshall B. Clinard and Peter C. Yeager (1980), *Corporate Crime*, New York: Free Press, p. 118.

17. Ibid., pp. 118–20.

18. James William Coleman (1989), *The Criminal Elite: The Sociology of White Collar Crime*, New York: St. Martin's, pp. 200–204.

19. Robert Merton (1938), "Social Structure and Anomie," *American Sociological Review*, vol. 3, pp. 672–82.

20. Coleman, op. cit., p. 230–31.

21. Clinard and Yeager (1980), op. cit., pp. 31–34.

22. Harvey Farberman (1975), "A Criminogenic Market Structure: The Automobile Industry," *Sociological Quarterly*, vol. 16, pp. 438–57. William N. Leonard and Marvin Glenn Weber (1970), "Automakers and Dealers: A Study of Criminogenic Market Forces," *Law and Society Review*, vol. 4, no. 3, pp. 407–24.

23. Peter F. Drucker (1972), *Concept of the Corporation*, New York: John Day. Cited in Coleman, op. cit., p. 222.

24. Braithwaite, op. cit., pp. 1–25. John Conklin (1977), "Illegal but Not Criminal," *Business Crime in America*, Englewood Cliffs, NJ: Prentice-Hall, ch. 5.

25. John Braithwaite (1985), *Corporate Crime in the Pharmaceutical Industry*, London: Routledge and Kegan Paul, p. 308.

26. Jack Katz (1980), "The Social Movement Against White-Collar Crime," in Egon Bittner and Sheldon Messinger, eds., *Criminology Review Yearbook*, vol. 2. Beverly Hills, CA: Sage.

27. Francis T. Cullen, Bruce G. Link, and Craig W. Planzi (1982), "The Seriousness of Crime Revisited: Have Attitudes Toward White-Collar Crime Changed?" *Criminology*, vol. 20, pp. 83–102.

28. Mark Dowie (1977), "Pinto Madness," *Mother Jones* (September/October), pp. 18–32. Reprinted in Stuart L. Hills, ed. (1987), *Corporate Violence: Injury and Death for Profit*, Savage, MD: Rowman & Littlefield.

29. Ibid., p. 21.

30. Russel Mokhiber (1988), *Corporate Crime and Violence: Big Business Power and the Abuse of the Public Trust*, San Francisco, CA: Sierra Club Books, pp. 373–82.

31. Ibid.

32. Donald W. Scott (1989), "Policing Corporate Collusion," *Criminology*, vol. 27, no. 3, pp. 559–87.

33. John Braithwaite and Gilbert Geis (1982), "On Theory and Action for Corporate Crime," *Crime and Delinquency*, vol. 28, pp. 292–314.

34. Downie, op. cit., p. 29.

35. *The New York Times*, April 29, 1990, p. 23.

36. David E. Rosenbaum (1990), "A Financial Disaster With Many Culprits," *The New York Times*, June 6, pp. D1, D4.

37. Braithwaite, *Corporate Crime in the Pharmaceutical Industry*, p. 308.

38. Mokhiber, op. cit., pp. 196–203.

39. Braithwaite (1985), *Corporate Crime in the Pharmaceutical Industry*, op. cit., p. 291.

Body and Soul:
Biological and
Psychological
Theories

CHAPTER **10**

THEORIES OF CRIME—AN INTRODUCTION

EVERYBODY HAS A THEORY ABOUT CRIME. EVEN BEFORE YOU HAD READ ONE WORD IN this book or any other book about crime, you had some ideas about the kinds of questions it was important to ask. You may even have had some notions about the answers to these questions—questions like, Why is there so much crime? Who commits crimes, and why? What influence does the peer group have? What is the connection between crime and the economic situation, family, psychology, age, race, or education of the criminal? Why do some countries have much less crime or much more crime than others? What can be done to reduce crime? What is an effective way of dealing with criminals?

These may seem like rather obvious questions to ask, even if the answers are far from obvious. However, although crime has existed for thousands of years, it was not until the 18th century that people began to think systematically about it. To be sure, philosophers as far back as the ancient Greeks had written about law. But they did not pay special attention to criminal law, and they ignored the questions about crime itself—its causes and cures.

People in centuries past left little written record of their theories of crime. However, even though we may not know exactly what people thought about crime, we do know what people did about crime. So perhaps by looking at their actions we can reconstruct the ideas that inspired those actions. For example, in medieval times, a criminal dispute might be settled through *trial by combat*, where the accused and accuser fought to the death. Presumably, whoever was right would win. In some cases, courts decided guilt on the basis of *trial by ordeal*, where the accused could prove his or her innocence by surviving some test. In one such test, the ordeal of cold water, a priest would sanctify a body of water, and the accused would be bound and lowered into the water. Sanctified water would not receive a guilty person; that is, a guilty person would be buoyed up by the water. Therefore, a person who floated was obviously guilty; a person who sank was innocent.[1]

Since the criminal justice process depended on supernatural signs of guilt or innocence, we can reasonably assume that people—at least those in authority—thought that crime was caused by supernatural forces. The criminal had fallen from grace with God or had been influenced by the devil. This theory was used to explain crimes associated with witchcraft, but probably other crimes as well. The emphasis on the spiritual nature of crime also served as a justification for torture. Torture was not just an effective way to get a confession; it also saved the soul. Because the soul was so much more important than the body, the body had to be purged, however painfully, in order to save the soul.[2]

Like the treatment of the accused, the punishment of the guilty in other times and places can also seem irrational and brutal to us. I will spare you detailed descriptions of these tortures and methods of execution. When I read about them, I have three different reactions. First, I am horrified and appalled at the cruelty of which people were capable.* Second, I imagine that perhaps there was some rational justification for the practices; perhaps people believed that public torture and execution might deter others from crime. But third, I am convinced that the cruelty must have been based on ideas that go beyond the merely rational, since the burning and dismemberment often continued long after the victim had died. Sometimes the actions seem so alien that it becomes difficult to imagine the ideas that lay behind them. For example, in medieval Europe, the same sorts of punishments also were inflicted on animals that had committed misdeeds. A pig that killed a child might be subjected to a trial, and if found guilty sentenced to hanging, dismemberment, or burning alive.[3]

The purpose of the punishment must have been something other than the prevention of crime. Certainly, retribution was part of it. The judges reserved the most horrible deaths for those crimes they thought most offensive. Perhaps another component was just a sort of sadistic curiosity, like that of the kid who pulls wings off a fly, to show what could be done to the body. Or perhaps by beheading offenders, or cutting out their internal organs, or burning them, the society was protecting itself against the return of the evil spirits of the dead. Certainly much about punishment was ritualistic and based on invisible forces like spirits, demons, the soul, and the hereafter. Behind all of it seemed to be a view that the person had committed a crime because of supernatural forces, especially possession by the devil. Remember that during medieval times and even later, many of the crimes for which people were tortured and executed were religious crimes like blasphemy, heresy, and witchcraft.

Beccaria and Classical Theory

In the 1700s, philosophy in general began to emphasize rationality and logic rather than mystery. The 18th century was the Age of Reason, the Enlightenment. The most influential thinkers on crime and justice shared this approach. In criminology, it came to be called "classical" theory. Probably the most famous writer of the classical school was Cesare Beccaria, an Italian who in 1764 published an essay called "On Crimes and Punishments." Many of Beccaria's ideas may seem unexceptional or obvious to us today, but we must remember that although the Middle Ages had waned, and the Renaissance had come and gone, some of the same brutalities persisted even in the Enlightenment of the 18th century. Beccaria was writing at a

---

* Of course, I should not be surprised, since I know that torture still goes on today, carried out by "educated" people in "modern" societies.

time in which a judge might find a person guilty on the flimsiest of evidence and impose a sentence of "breaking on the wheel"; a time when torture was used to extract confessions; a time when in England raucous crowds turned out to watch the public hanging of criminals, several at a time, whose crimes might have been nothing more serious than stealing a fish.[4] The time was ripe for just such an essay as Beccaria's. Here are some of its proposals:

> The only purpose of punishment should be the prevention of crime.
> In preventing crime, the severity of the punishment is not so important as the swiftness and certainty of punishment.
> Punishments should be proportional to the seriousness of the crime.
> Punishments should be just severe enough to offset the utility to be obtained by committing the crime.
> The penalty should depend on the nature of the crime, not on the nature or position of the offender. A penalty should be applied equally to anyone found guilty of that crime.[5]

The basis of Beccaria's ideas was a philosophy known as **utilitarianism**. Utilitarianism saw human behavior as a highly rational and calculated pursuit of pleasure and avoidance of pain. Society, however, had to stress the general good rather than individual pleasure. Therefore, for society to maintain itself, it had to find a way to "counterbalance the passions of the individual which oppose the general good."[6] The counterbalance was to be found in punishing people for crimes. Note here that in the utilitarian view, society punished a criminal not for purposes of retribution—not just because the criminal had done something wrong. Society punished the criminal because the punishment was useful in preventing crime. As the English utilitarian Jeremy Bentham argued, punishment was not a matter of what someone "deserved," but rather a matter of what was necessary. Unnecessary punishment was irrational and should be eliminated.

Beccaria's essay outlined an idea whose time apparently had come. European criminal procedures, though in need of change, already had become somewhat more rational. In fact, Beccaria probably had exaggerated the irrationality and atrocity of the courts of his day.[7] Nevertheless, his ideas found an immediate welcome in the courts of Europe, from Russia to England, and in the American colonies as well.*

Some of Beccaria's ideas were rejected or modified. He opposed the death penalty, and he favored corporal punishment for people convicted of violent crimes. He was utterly inflexible about fitting the penalty to the crime and not the criminal. That is, he allowed no room for altering a penalty just because the offender was insane or very young. Nevertheless, many of Bec-

---

* In 1770, John Adams, defending British soldiers accused in the Boston Massacre, opened his defense with a quote from Beccaria.

caria's ideas still are relevant, and some of the most influential criminolog-ical research in recent years represents a return to classical ideas. However, Beccaria was much more concerned with questions of justice than with questions of the causes of crime. It was not until a century after the pub-lication of Beccaria's essay that criminological theory began to explore ideas about why a person breaks the law. In the next section, we will explore this new type of theory, a theory which sees criminals not primarily as rational people making choices but as creatures who differ in the most basic ways from law-abiding people.

BIOLOGICAL AND PSYCHOLOGICAL THEORIES OF CRIME

In the mid-19th century, a new "science" of personality came to enjoy con-siderable popularity. It was called "phrenology," and it was based on the idea that different behaviors were controlled by different areas located at specific places in the brain. For example, if the "destructiveness" area were overdeveloped, then the person would be more aggressive. The more devel-oped an area was, the larger it would be. These larger areas of the brain would push out on the skull in particular places, causing slightly different skull shapes, depending on the aggressiveness or "amorousness" of the in-dividual. By examining the location of the bumps on a person's skull, the trained phrenologist could discover which areas were most developed. It was a hands-on method of personality assessment.

At the time, phrenology was just as scientific as anything else in medicine or psychiatry, and it was just as legitimate. Prisons, for example, did phren-ological analyses of inmates. But phrenology also was a popular science. Some phrenologists worked in road shows, as do tarot readers today. Others adopted a more distinguished manner, traveling from town to town giving lecture/demonstrations. After explaining the scientific basis of his work, the phrenologist would call a person from the audience up to the stage, carefully run his hands over the person's skull, and then give an account of the person's character. Before leaving town, the phrenologists might also do private readings—personality assessment coupled with advice. And then the next week, the town would get a hypnotist or a Shakespeare troupe or a lecture/slideshow on the mysterious East.[8] My point here is not to poke fun at phrenology or those who believed in it. I want merely to show the appeal of an idea that keeps cropping up in different forms: the idea that differences in character reveal themselves in the body.

This mind-body idea has appeared in several forms, both in scientific research and in more popular notions. The basic idea remains this: If people behave differently, then their minds must work differently, and therefore their physical makeup also must be different. If the behavior is extremely different, as is predatory crime, then the person may be so different in both mind and body as to be less than fully human. It may be more than just a figure of speech, therefore, when people refer to criminals as "animals." There is a certain logic to the label. If someone does something that we cannot imagine ourselves doing, the person must be a different order of being, not quite a human like us. Even a phrase like "cold-blooded killer" implies that the criminal's physiological responses are different from our own warm-blooded reactions, which in turn are not to be confused with those of "hot-blooded," impulsive types. Of course, few people really believe that blood temperature determines a person's temperament.* What some people may believe, however, is that criminals differ from the rest of us in some very basic and essential way.

Lombroso Discovers the Born Criminal

It was just such an idea that inspired the man sometimes called the "father of criminology," Cesare Lombroso. Lombroso was born in Italy in 1835 and studied medicine and psychiatry there (though keep in mind that at this time these were very ineffective and inexact sciences). In 1870, Lombroso had one of those "aha!" insights, when different notions and observations suddenly come together to create an idea. By that year, Darwin's theory of human evolution (published 11 years earlier) had become of interest in social sciences as well as biology, and doubtless Lombroso was familiar with it. At the same time, he was using his knowledge of anatomy in an attempt to differentiate physically between criminals and the insane. One day, Lombroso was doing a post-mortem examination of the skull of a notorious criminal and noticed that not only was it different from a normal skull, but that the differences resembled those of "primitive men and of inferior animals." In a flash, it all became clear. "At the sight of that skull, I seemed to see all at once . . . the nature of the criminal, who reproduces in civilized times characteristics not only of primitive savages, but of still lower types as far back as the carnivora."[9] Here was the basis for a new theory. The criminal was an **atavism**—that is, although he lived in the present time, he was biologically and physiologically a throwback to an earlier stage of evolution.

Lombroso's next step was to begin studying the heads of criminals in search of other such atavists, or what he called "born criminals." After much research he concluded that one-third of the criminal population consisted of these born criminals. Moreover, they could be distinguished by their facial

---

* Words can stay in use long after a theory is forgotten. Nobody still believes in the ancient notion that temperament is determined by a mix of four "humors," each corresponding to a body fluid—phlegm, black bile, yellow bile, and blood. Most people today do not know such a theory ever existed. Nevertheless, words like *phlegmatic, melancholic, bilious,* and *sanguine* remain part of the English language—if not in most daily speech, then at least on the SATs.

features: thick skull bones; protruding chin; low, sloping forehead; large ears; abundant and curly hair; thin beard. In his later research, Lombroso even claimed that specific types of criminals had different kinds of faces and bodies. For example, "thieves have mobile hands and face; small . . . frequently oblique eyes." Rapists "are of delicate structure and sometimes hunchbacked." Among murderers, "the nose, always large, is frequently aquiline or, rather, hooked; the jaws are strong . . . ," and so on.

Lombroso also mentioned aspects such as "laziness," which we would think of as social or psychological. The list continues with this mixture of physical, psychological, and social traits, which Lombroso saw as all part of the same basic underlying pattern of atavism:

> great agility; relative insensibility to pain; dullness of the sense of touch; . . . ability to recover quickly from wounds; . . . precocity as to sensual pleasures . . . absence of remorse; impulsiveness; . . . excitability; . . . improvidence, which sometimes appears as courage and again as recklessness changing to cowardice . . . great vanity; a passion for gambling and drinking; violent but fleeting passions; superstition; extraordinary sensitiveness with regard to one's own personality; . . . the custom of tattooing; the cruelty of their games; the excessive use of gestures.[10]

Lombroso reasoned as follows: (1) Criminals have these characteristics (e.g., impulsiveness, tattoos); so do savage peoples; (2) savage peoples are at a lower point in the evolutionary ladder; (3) therefore, criminals must also be evolutionary throwbacks. Criminals, at least these atavistic ones, were essentially savages who, through some accident of nature, happened to get born into 19th-century Italy.

At this point, you may be asking this: If Lombroso, with his ideas about criminal ears and jaws, is the "father of criminology," what can we expect of subsequent generations of criminologists? But Lombroso's importance lay not so much in the specifics of his theory of atavism. In fact, Lombroso's ideas were criticized as soon as they appeared, and by the time of his death (1909) few people believed in his ideas about atavism. We now know the basic error in Lombroso's theory: In terms of evolution, humans in 19th century Italy—criminals and noncriminals—were no more or less evolved than humans in other times and places that Lombroso may have read about.

Positivism

Lombroso's primary idea was not very fertile, but what remained was a general approach to studying crime—an approach called **positivism**. The essence of the positivist school of thought was the **empirical** search for the **causes** of criminal behavior. In both respects, their approach departed from that of Beccaria and the classical thinkers. Beccaria's classical theory may seem more reasonable to us today, especially compared with Lombroso. But Beccaria did no research to generate or to support his ideas. His work may have been logical, but it was not scientific in the modern sense. Beccaria's ideas also take a rather simple-minded view of the causes of behavior: that people calculate the pleasure and pain to be gotten from any particular act and then decide accordingly. In the view of the positivists, the causes were more complex and subtle. Nevertheless, if they could ever identify these causes, then they could predict criminal behavior. This may seem like an innocent enough idea, since the basis of any science lies in identifying causes and predicting results. But if that science deals with human behavior, then it casts doubt on our idea that we have **free will**; that is, that we can freely choose what we will do and what we will try to become in life.

The debate over free will and **determinism** was a long-standing issue in philosophy and religion, where some thinkers took the view that God determined or predestined the fate of people. In a similar way, the positivist approach raised questions of determinism, scientific rather than religious. Even though the positivists looked to worldly forces rather than to God, their ideas challenged everyday assumptions about free will. After all, if my behavior is the predictable, inevitable result of biological or social or economic causes, and if I have no power to alter those causes, then how much control do I have over my behavior? Do I really have free will? The positivists, then, far beyond Lombroso's wrongheaded ideas about evolution, were raising very basic philosophical questions in social science.

More important, the positivists based their search for causes on empirical evidence. Lombroso himself studied and measured the facial features of hundreds of criminals and noncriminals. The results, he claimed, confirmed his ideas that about one-third of all criminals have atavistic features. But in response to criticism, he also gathered data on all sorts of factors that might be associated with crime: climate, economic factors, type of government, religion, alcoholism, education[11]—the same sorts of things a criminologist today might investigate.

Lombroso's approach far outlasted his ideas of atavism in one other important direction: his emphasis on the individual criminal. Lombroso was interested in how criminals differed from noncriminals. He also argued that since crime resulted from individual defects, then special treatment might help the criminal overcome his handicaps. Even atavistic tendencies might be channeled into noncriminal activities. It followed logically that prisons should be places of rehabilitation and treatment, not just punishment. This view, at least in principle, remained a dominant ideology of prisons through the 1960s, though in recent years it has been on the decline. The focus on individual deficiencies (rather than on social ills) influenced not only prison policy but also later criminological theory and research. The positivist legacy appears in the line of biological and psychological study on crime that continues to this day.

The Lombroso Legacy

The search for criminal features did not end with Lombroso. Early in this century an English researcher, Charles Goring, spent eight years measuring chins, foreheads and ears, as well as education, alcoholism, and standard of living. Goring had set out to prove that Lombroso's atavism theory was wrong and that his research methods were sloppy. So starting in 1901, Goring took his micrometer and other measuring instruments to English prisons and elsewhere, eventually compiling data on 3,000 prisoners and a comparison group of noncriminals. He spent another two years analyzing his data using modern statistical techniques, and in 1913 he published his conclusions: "There is no such thing as a physical criminal type."* He added, "The physical and mental constitution of both criminal and law-abiding persons of the same age, stature, class, and intelligence, are identical."[12]

Definitive as this statement sounds, Goring was rejecting only the idea of atavism. He did not abandon the biological approach to crime. On the contrary, his data showed that while English convicts were "normal," they were nevertheless marked by "defective physique" (i.e., they were smaller) and "defective mental capacity."[13] Goring also saw no relationship between crime and the environmental factors he had measured, and he went on to develop his own theory that crime was largely a genetically inherited tendency.

Mind and Body in America

In the United States, the search for a crime-body link was led by E.A. Hooton, a Harvard anthropologist. In the 1930s, Hooton conducted a large study of 17,000 people in 10 states. Hooton did not mention atavism, but in many other respects, his work echoes themes from Lombroso. American criminals came from "the physically inferior element of the population"; their inferiority was "principally hereditary" and led them to "gravitate into unfavorable environmental conditions," where the weakest turned to crime. Criminals were "inferior" to noncriminals on most measures of body and mind. The two groups differed on facial features—lips, ears, jaws, etc. Criminals were less likely to have purely dark eyes or blue eyes; instead, they usually had mixed-color eyes, a sign that criminals, instead of being "pure racial types," were more of the mixed type. They also more frequently had

---

* The research had grown out of Lombroso's challenge to his critics to set up an impartial committee to test his ideas. The atavism challenge never came off, since Lombroso's conditions for the committee were impossible to meet. And by the time Goring published his own findings, Lombroso had been dead for four years.

thin eyebrows, long, thin necks, sloping foreheads, and tattoos.* Their broader noses were evidence of "infantilism and primitivism." Like Lombroso, Hooton claimed he could distinguish between different types of criminals: Forgers, for example, were tall and heavy; robbers tall and thin.[14]

Policy and Ideology

When Hooton published his work in 1939, most criminologists disagreed with his ideas and criticized his research. But it is important to understand why his work caused such controversy. By 1939, Americans had already come to know something about racial theories and where such ideas had led under Nazism and Fascism. The Nazis had used biology and physical anthropology to support their claims to racial superiority, and American scientists feared the same ideas might be used against blacks, Jews, and others in America.† Hooton claimed that it was wrong to confuse his ideas with Hitler's, and that the Fascist misuse of biology was no reason to stop all research into the biological sources of human behavior. He felt that his innocent baby was being thrown out with Hitler's dirty bathwater.

But how different were they? Hooton wanted "to investigate seriously the racial anatomical characters which are the outward signs of inheritance"; in the case of crime, this meant the study of racially inherited inferiority. The same idea and practically the same vocabulary about "racial purity" lay at the heart of Nazi studies on racial inferiority. Moreover, Hitler's solution to the presence of low-grade, inferior humans was to exterminate them or to lock them away in concentration camps. How different was Hooton's solution? Let's let him speak for himself.

> Criminals are organically inferior. Crime is the resultant of the impact of the environment upon low-grade human organisms. It follows that the elimination of crime can be effected only by the extirpation of the physically, mentally, and morally unfit; or by their complete segregation in a socially aseptic environment.[15]

Body Types

The idea that physical features reflect personality took a somewhat different approach in the 1940s with the technique of **somatotyping**. William Sheldon, a doctor and something of a fan of Hooton's, developed a scheme for classifying people according to their body build. The theory of somatotyping

---

* Lombroso also noted criminals' tattoos. You might think that having tattoos is not so much a physical factor as it is a somewhat uncomfortable social custom or fashion—something like shaving or having pierced ears or wearing high heels. Lombroso and Hooton thought otherwise, and they are not the last in this line of thinking. Keep reading.

† Today, when prejudice is based largely on sociological data (e.g., that blacks in fact have higher rates of crime), we may have lost sight of the extent to which prejudice in the 1930s in this country relied on ideas about the biology of race.

holds that there are three basic body types—endomorphic, mesomorphic, and ectomorphic—each linked to a type of temperament.

Endomorphic: soft and round body; extroverted, easy-going temperament.
Mesomorphic: muscular, athletic body; active, aggressive temperament.
Ectomorphic: slender, small-boned body; introverted, sensitive temperament.

Each person contains a combination of the three characteristics. What is important is the proportion of each of the three basic ingredients. This proportion (or somatotype profile) varies from one person to another. In his research on crime, Sheldon compared the somatotype profiles of 200 delinquents against those of 200 college men and found that delinquents, on average, were much more mesomorphic and much less ectomorphic than the control group of students.

There may be some validity to Sheldon's results. The group of delinquents probably did have more of the mesomorphic "jock" types and fewer of the skinny, nervous types. However, some aspects of Sheldon's research muddy its implications for the study of crime. In the first place, Sheldon used an odd definition of delinquency. Rather than measure the amount of crime or the seriousness of crime, Sheldon defined delinquency as "behavior disappointing beyond reasonable expectation."[16] In addition, Sheldon recognized that this body type is far from unique to criminals. He found the same physical and psychological traits among salesmen and politicians.* Finally, Sheldon shared the belief of others going back to Lombroso that the criminal was an "inferior human organism," and that this inferiority lay in the person's basic physical being.[17] Obviously, a person does not acquire these physical characteristics by learning them; he or she is born with them. By implication, the "behavioral inferiority" that accompanies them also must be part of the person's basic biological makeup. In other words, more than 70 years after Lombroso's theory of atavism first appeared in print, some social scientists were still talking about born criminals.

Born to Be Bad? Doc: Some Are (Headline in *The New York Daily News*, 1979)
The question under discussion here is whether there is a biological basis for human behavior, especially criminal behavior. So far (we're up to about 1950), researchers have looked for evidence in physical features that are visible to the naked eye: ear shape, eye color, body type, etc. Although the researchers themselves claimed that their evidence supported their ideas, they met with a variety of criticisms: The theory was absurd, or the methodology was shoddy, or the ideas seemed too congenial to Fascist, racist politics. The idea that some babies were born with criminal tendencies and

* This similarity among salesmen, politicians, and criminals may no longer seem like an odd coincidence.

were morally inferior contradicted many of our most noble sentiments ("all men are created equal"). It also contradicted much evidence that showed the importance of environmental factors in crime.

Chromosome Abnormalities

The search for the born criminal was not abandoned entirely. Researchers in the latter half of the 20th century did, however, begin to take new approaches. One line of inquiry followed technological and scientific advances that made it possible to look for previously invisible biological factors that might be associated with crime. Instead of measuring the slope of a person's forehead, researchers could now measure hormones in the blood, Galvanic skin response, brain waves (EEGs), or chromosome structures.

In the 1960s there was a flurry of interest surrounding the possible link between crime and genetic abnormalities, specifically what was called the XYY syndrome. A person's sex is determined by one of the 23 pairs of chromosomes inherited from parents. Everybody inherits an X chromosome (so called because under a microscope it looks like an X) from the mother. Some people inherit a second X chromosome, also from the mother. These people (XX) are called women. Others inherit a Y chromosome from the father. These people (XY) are men. That takes care of almost everyone. However, about one person in every thousand inherits a third chromosome. Those with an extra X chromosome (XXY) are basically male but have some female characteristics—they may even develop breasts—and are often mentally retarded. Now if males with an added X chromosome are more feminine, what about males with an extra Y chromosome (XYY)? Will they be "supermales," exaggerating all those masculine tendencies that can lead to aggressive, violent crime?

Such speculation grew when research on inmates in a British maximum-security prison turned up a much greater frequency of XYY males (one or two in a hundred instead of one or two in a thousand), some of whose crimes "would supply material for a series of horror films."[18] It began to look as though indeed there was a genetic component to crime. However, as more research data on more XYY men accumulated, the "supermale" idea looked less and less plausible. The XYY males were different. They were generally taller and had lower IQ scores. They even were somewhat more likely to commit crimes than were normal (XY) males of similar IQ, social class, and other demographic traits. However, their crimes generally were *not* of the violent, "supermale" type. In addition, the XYY abnormality occurs so rarely that these findings are probably more relevant to the field of genetics than to criminology. XYY males account for very little of the total crime in our society.

The idea of linking crime to the "supermale" was based on the well-known fact that men commit far more crime than do women. It is also a well-known fact that men are biologically different from women. These two facts (biological differences, crime differences) led to the chromosome studies. The same line of thinking has also led to research on one of the key hormones that makes men different from women: testosterone. Since men have more testosterone than do women, would criminals have higher levels of testosterone than would noncriminals? The research findings are not extensive, though at least one study in the 1970s found that testosterone is related to violent crimes; that is, prisoners with higher testosterone levels were more likely to have committed violent offenses than were other prisoners.[19] A more recent study of 1,700 men showed that high testosterone levels were associated with traits like dominance and competitiveness. Some high-testosterone men had a history of crime, but for other men with similar levels of the hormone, these traits emerged as socially acceptable aggressiveness in athletics or business.[20] However, not all studies have supported this conclusion, and the issue remains in dispute.

All in the Family

By the 1950s, the behavioral sciences—sociology, psychology, anthropology—had swung far from the biological point of view. The dominant ideology held that all behavior was learned and that environmental factors played the largest part in determining behavior. Against this view, the biologists began to take a new tack. They set aside the search for specific biological elements (e.g., testosterone) that might be related to criminality. Instead, researchers tried merely to show that behavior and personality do have biological and hereditary bases, even though we may not know the specific genetic factors involved.

Researchers who take this approach look at degrees of similarity. If there is a genetic factor in crime, then the greater the biological similarity between two people, the greater will be their similarity in crime. For example, people in the same family are more similar biologically to each other than they are to nonfamily members. So we might look at the criminal records of brothers. If one brother has a criminal record, will the other brother have one also? Of course, you can immediately see the problem here. Even if the brothers are similar, the causes for that similarity could just as easily be environmental as hereditary. They inherited similar genetic material, but they probably also grew up in the same environment. How can we know which was causing the similarity?

Twins—Fraternal and Identical

There are two general research strategies for untangling the strands of environment and heredity. The first method studies twins. Twins, as you may know, can be created in two different ways. In some cases, two separate eggs are fertilized at the same time. These are called **dizygotic** (DZ) or fraternal twins, and genetically they are no more similar than two separate eggs fertilized at different times; that is, fraternal twins are no more similar genetically than ordinary brothers and sisters. They share about half their genes. However, in some cases, a single fertilized egg divides into two embryos. These embryos develop into identical or **monozygotic** (MZ) twins. They share all the same genetic material. That is why identical twins are always the same sex, while fraternal twins may be of opposite sexes.

Researchers, therefore, have looked at the degree of similarity (called "concordance") between twins of each type. Generally, they find greater similarities of crime between identical twins than between fraternal twins. For example, a Danish study of 3,500 sets of twins found that the concordance for MZ twins was more than twice that for DZ twins. If one MZ twin had a criminal record, the other twin had a record 52 percent of the time. For DZ twins, the figure was only 22 percent.[21] It is unlikely that MZ twins grow up in a more similar environment than DZ twins do. So the stronger similarity must come from the greater genetic similarity. Of course, other factors must play a part, since even among MZ identical twins, only about half the pairs were concordant.

Fathers and Sons

The second strategy has been to look at the criminal similarity of fathers and sons. After all, if there is a genetic component to crime, then it will be transmitted from parent to child along with other genetic material. Here again, we face the problem of untangling heredity from environment. If we find that sons resemble their fathers in criminality, the cause might be some genetically transmitted traits. But the cause might also be a variety of social factors. Kids might pick up their fathers' ways through imitation. Or fathers who are more criminal also may be very ineffective parents. How then can we know to what extent the similarity is biological and to what extent it is social?

One way of separating heredity and environment is to have two separate fathers, one for heredity and one for environment, and then see which one the son most resembles. Of course, we cannot deliberately perform such an experiment. But, as you may already have realized, something very close to this experimental design already exists: adoption. All we need to do is find out the criminality of the adoptive parents, the biological parents, and the son. Table 10–1 shows the results from one such study.

Look at just the left-hand column—children born to noncriminal parents. Does raising the child in a criminal home make a difference? Only very slightly—13.5 percent raised by noncriminals turned out criminal; only a slightly higher percentage (14.7 percent) of those raised by criminal parents

Table 10–1 ▪ Criminality of Sons

| Are adoptive parents criminal? | Are biological parents criminal? | |
	No	Yes
No	13.5% (of 2,492)	20.0% (of 1,226)
Yes	14.7% (of 204)	24.5% (of 143)

Source: Table derived from Mednick, et al. (1980).

became criminal.* In the right-hand column (children born to criminal parents) the effect of raising the adoptee with criminal parents makes a somewhat greater difference (24.5 percent vs. 20.0 percent).

Now look at the table the other way. Look at just the top row—boys raised by noncriminal parents. Does the criminality of the biological parents make a difference? Yes, it does. It raises the percentage of offenders from 13.5 percent to 20.0 percent. And for boys raised by criminal adoptive parents, the effect of biology appears even larger—24.5 percent criminal among those born to criminal parents; only 14.7 percent criminal among those born to noncriminal parents.

Biological Explanations of Crime: Methods, Usefulness, and Ideology

These twin studies and adoption studies, like the other biological research mentioned in this chapter, have come in for much criticism. Some of these criticisms are specific and technical; others are broad and ideological. The technical criticisms find flaws in the methods used. They point out that many of these studies use only a small number of cases; or that the definitions of "criminal" and "noncriminal" are misleading. But these flaws should make it harder, not easier, for researchers to discover biological links to crime.

More serious are the questions not about the accuracy of the heredity studies but about their usefulness. These studies might show that heredity makes a difference, but how much difference? How do the effects of biological and genetic factors compare with the effects of environmental factors? Sarnoff Mednick, one of the leading American biologists doing research on crime, had this to say on this question: "Social factors are much more important in the etiology [causes] of crime and everybody knows this,

---

* In this study, "criminal" meant having one or more criminal convictions. Criminal adoptive parents usually had only one conviction. Criminal biological parents often had two or more.

especially the biologists."[22] In addition, biological theories have a limited relevance; they can help explain individual differences. But they are all but useless in explaining the social facts about crime, such as large changes in crime *rates*. Remember, the biological and genetic makeup of the population does not change. The "gene pool" in the United States in 1970 was substantially the same as it was in 1960. Yet during that decade crime rates more than doubled. Something must have changed, but it wasn't biology.

Finally, biological theories are a political issue, with liberals and conservatives taking predictable positions.* The political objections to biological theories begin with the claim that biological ideas divert attention from the social sources of crime. If crime is a matter of biogenetic inheritance, then we need not worry about poverty, inequality, race relations, or other matters of social reform. The critics, generally on the left, would like to see the government do something about these other social problems. Second, critics fear that some people will take biological theories to mean that certain individuals and groups are inferior. The assumption of biology, whether in the latest studies or in the writing of Lombroso, is that people are different in their essential biological makeup and that these differences may be inherited. The person who is a criminal may be biologically and morally inferior. Now, what if we applied this idea not just to individual criminals but to crime rates? For example, if crime rates are higher among the poor, might that not mean that poor people are biologically inferior?

The question becomes even more controversial with racial differences in crime. Blacks in the United States today, Italians, in the United States 80 years ago, the Irish in Great Britain—all of these groups have higher rates of crime than do the majority of the society. Moreover, these racial or ethnic groups, unlike different social classes, are biologically different from the majority group. They have different physical features, which are transmitted genetically from parent to child. The question is whether behavioral or moral traits are also part of the biogenetic inheritance. Right now, no responsible biologist would claim that one racial group can be morally superior on the basis of its biological inheritance. But some biologists do claim that there may be a biogenetic component in criminality. The critics fear the abuses to which such an idea can lead. Some of the worst atrocities in history have resulted from ideas of racial inferiority.

Few people, even the most vigorous critics, really believe that biological theories of crime could lead to a revival of anything resembling Nazism or slavery. But some people do fear even the less extreme policies that could

---

* In the 1980s, if you knew a criminologist's opinion of biological explanations of crime, you could probably also have guessed his or her opinion on Nicaragua or nuclear disarmament. (At the time of this writing, I cannot even guess what the analogous issues of the 1990s will be.) I have no data to support this statement, and there is no obvious connection between biogenetic research and U.S. foreign policy. But it seems to me that among criminologists, biological theories find support among political conservatives and are opposed by those with more liberal or radical views. Criminologists' opinions on biology have not always divided this way. One of Lombroso's major followers was a socialist.

emerge from biological ideas. These policies might involve the use of biological information to determine what kind of treatment an offender will receive. An offender who has been biogenetically identified as a high risk would receive a sentence different from that given a low-risk offender convicted of the same offense. This policy, however, would be punishing someone for his biogenetic makeup rather than for the crime he has committed.

FROM BIOLOGY TO PSYCHOLOGY

Studies of twins and adopted children may show that there is some biological basis for crime. But they make no attempt to identify the precise physiological component that leads to crime. As a way of explaining crime, these more sophisticated studies are less satisfying than Sheldon's ideas about body types. At least Sheldon could link a specific physique to a higher rate of delinquency. Yet even Sheldon does not say exactly what it is about the mesomorph, athletic type that makes him more prone to delinquency. We have to go all the way back to Lombroso to find a theory, even a silly one, that explains why a particular type of body is linked to crime. Lombroso thought that criminals were less evolved in both body and mind; being more like savages or even animals, criminals naturally preyed on others without regard to modern law or morality.

Conscience and Conditioning

In the 1960s, some psychologists speculated that the connection between mind and body might be based on **conditioning**. The concept of conditioning originated with Pavlov, the Russian psychologist who conditioned a dog to salivate at the sound of a bell. Dogs generally salivate when they are fed, such salivation being a natural or "unconditioned" response to the "unconditioned stimulus" of the food. So Pavlov rang the bell each time he fed the dog. After a while, the sound of the bell, even without the food, would cause the dog to salivate. The bell, then, was a "conditioned stimulus" and the subsequent salivation was what is called a "conditioned response."

How do we get from drooling dogs to crime? First, let's ask why most people do *not* commit crimes. The answer is not for fear that they will be caught and punished. A quick look at "clearance rates" (the proportion of crimes that result in arrest) confirms what many people feel: The majority of crimes go unpunished. Why, then, do so many people not commit crime? One answer is conscience. Conscience is not just our sense of morality reminding us that something is wrong; conscience extends beyond mere knowing. It is also a feeling of guilt, an automatic reaction of fear or dread that keeps us from committing the forbidden act. Since conscience is an automatic and even physiological reaction to an abstract stimulus (i.e., to a thought), some psychologists argue that conscience is essentially a conditioned response. It develops in people through the same psychological mechanism that makes the dog drool: conditioning.

Psychologists who accept the idea that "conscience is a conditioned reflex"[23] may differ as to what kind of conditioning creates conscience. Besides the "classical" conditioning à la Pavlov, there is something called "instrumental" or "operant" conditioning. In operant conditioning, the person (or animal) can control the reinforcement by behaving one way or another. For example, a laboratory rat can avoid shocks and gain food by turning right in a maze instead of left. The distinction between classical and operant conditioning is not always clear, nor is the distinction essential here. The important part is that the learned reaction becomes automatic and internalized. Long after the original stimuli and reinforcements are gone, the conditioned responses remain.

Physiology and Psychology

What does any of this have to do with physiology, aside from the obvious fact that reinforcers—especially in the conditioning of laboratory animals—are often physical (e.g., food, electric shocks)? If you have ever tried to train an animal, you know that there are two sides to the process—the trainer and the trainee. From the trainer's side, if the rewards and punishments are not strong enough or do not come consistently or promptly, the conditioning will be less effective. For example, child-rearing manuals these days strongly condemn parental inconsistency. Imagine a parent who ignores the child's misbehavior much of the time or gives only threats that are never carried out; but every so often, long after the misbehavior, the parent blows up and punishes the child severely. A child raised in this way, say the manuals, is unlikely to learn to behave correctly.

The quality of training may vary from one trainer (or parent) to another. But the trainees may also differ. The exact same techniques that work with one breed of dog, for example, may not work so well with another. Children, too, differ from one another. Some may be harder to "condition" than others, and some may respond differently to different types of reward or punishment. Some of these differences are a matter of temperament or personality. But what if there were also physical differences that made some people less "conditionable"? For example, what if some people were less sensitive to pain? Since punishments would be less painful, they would have less effect. In fact, some psychologists claim that there are people who generally feel less physical sensation. These people can tolerate a greater level of stimulation; they may prefer or even need such heightened stimulation. They go in for contact sports and loud music. And of course, they are more likely to commit crimes. Their "greater immunity to pain . . . explains, in part, their inability to sympathize with the pain of others. This might underlie their greater involvement in accidents, their noisiness, and even [their] preference . . . for tattooing themselves."[24] Does this description (from a criminology textbook of 1984, written by a prominent criminologist) sound familiar? Go back and check Lombroso's inventory of criminal traits (p. 331).

Responsiveness and Sweaty Palms

A variation on this idea comes from studies of **skin conductance**; that is, how easily a person's skin will conduct electricity. Skin conductance is an indicator of the arousal of the "autonomic nervous system," the mechanism that controls reflex-like responses such as heart rate and breathing. When a person is nervous or afraid, the surface of the hands becomes more moist, and skin conductance increases. For this reason, it is one of the measures used in polygraph ("lie-detector") tests. Basically, this part of the polygraph is just a very sensitive device for detecting sweaty palms.

Researchers have found that criminals and noncriminals differ from each other in what is called **skin conductance recovery**. This is the length of time it takes for the skin conductance to return to its normal level following arousal. Typically, a person in such an experiment receives an "aversive stimulus"—is given a hypodermic injection or an electric shock; is told that such a stimulus will be given; or is shown someone apparently reacting to a painful shock or injection. In these conditions, people become nervous, their hands become more moist, and skin conductance increases. The question is how much it increases and how long it takes for it to return to normal. Generally, in these studies, criminals show less arousal and a longer recovery time.[25]

According to the theory, a person with low arousal and slow recovery time is less easily conditioned. Take the example of the child who starts to do something wrong, like hitting another child. The parent intervenes, scolding, threatening to withhold love or to punish the child; in any case, the parent presents an "aversive stimulus" that arouses the child's fear. The child stops hitting, the parent approves, and the child no longer feels fearful. In other words, the child feels fear when misbehaving, and relief upon ceasing the misbehavior. The child who will be most affected is the child who feels a great arousal of fear and then a quick and equally great reduction in fear. But what about the child who feels less fear-arousal and whose fear-reduction comes more slowly? That child will not feel such a big difference between punishment and relief, or between good and bad behavior. The "conditioned reflex" of conscience will not be as strong. That child will be more likely to misbehave and eventually to break the law.

Beyond Behaviorism

The research on the relationship between crime and the autonomic nervous system rests on two key assumptions: first, that people commit crime because of a weak conscience; and second, that people acquire a conscience in the same way that dogs can be conditioned to salivate at the sound of a bell or rats can be trained to turn right in a maze. The evidence is suggestive but certainly not conclusive, perhaps because conscience is such a difficult thing to define and measure.

The research cited so far falls within a tradition in American psychology known as *behaviorism*. Behaviorism dominated most university research on psychology in the mid-20th century. As its name implies, it concentrated on behavior rather than on thinking. According to behaviorism, it doesn't really matter what might be going through a dog's mind as long as you can train it to salivate at the sound of a bell (or not to mess up the carpet). In the same way, behaviorism saw human thought as secondary to behavior. And human behavior, so the theory went, was learned in the same way as animal behavior was—through conditioning. For behaviorists, the mind was merely a collection of conditioned reflexes.

The Freudian Perspective

Outside of the research labs, psychology came under the influence of a much different theory: psychoanalysis. Psychoanalytic theory and therapy were largely the creation of Sigmund Freud, whose ideas developed out of his treatment of middle-class patients suffering from neurotic symptoms like phobias, obsessive behavior, and "hysteria" (i.e., physical symptoms—paralysis, anesthesia, coughing—for which there was no physiological cause). Freud himself wrote little about crime or criminals, but his ideas do offer a very general explanation. Freud, like the behaviorists believed that what prevented people from committing crimes was conscience (and this may be the only thing these two schools of thought share). Freudian theory, however, offers a much different model of the psyche (i.e., "mind" or "soul"). It sees the mind not as a set of conditioned reflexes, but as a three-part structure. Without conscience, people would be ruled by the **id**—the part of the psyche that serves as a sort of reservoir of sexual and aggressive energy. The **ego**, the second component of the psyche, is the part we are most likely to think of as our "self." The ego deals with everyday reality, negotiating in the real world in order to get gratification for the instinctual desires of the id.

Conscience à la Freud

If the psyche consisted only of ego and id, then people would do anything they could in order to satisfy their impulses. However, most people do not commit crimes—even ones they could get away with. Either the thought does not even enter their (conscious) minds, or if it does, it is accompanied by feelings of fear or guilt—the pangs of conscience. This unconscious mechanism that automatically keeps people from doing the forbidden is called the **superego**. In Freud's theory, the superego is not part of a person's original mental makeup. It develops in early childhood as the child internalizes the demands of parents. The strength of the superego will depend on the relationship between child and parents.

Some crimes are the result of too weak a superego, when unconscious impulses from the id go unrestrained. But other crimes may arise when the superego is too strong; then it creates an unconscious sense of guilt that must also be satisfied. As one author/journalist (not a psychiatrist) observed,

> After talking to many [criminals] and reading an even larger number of case histories, I found it hard to avoid concluding that many criminals arrange for their own capture. It is equally hard to avoid concluding that they do so because, on some level, they feel they are 'bad' and should be punished, or because they want someone to stop them from doing the terrible things they keep doing.[26]

In this theory, crime, like symptoms of Freud's patients, is a symbolic way of dealing with unconscious wishes and conflicts. The motivation for crime is complicated and often unconscious.

The Freudian and Behaviorist Models—Are They Useful?

Discovering the particular unconscious ideas that are symbolically expressed in a crime may be very interesting. For example, a psychoanalytically trained psychiatrist may discover that a criminal's stealing was a symbolic compensation for the love he felt his mother had withheld from him in childhood. The difficulty with this kind of interpretation is not in its accuracy (though Freudian ideas have long come under attack, and prisoners treated with Freudian types of psychotherapy do not seem to do any better at keeping out of trouble than others). The real problem is that the interpretation cannot be generalized beyond the individual case. Psychoanalysis can tell us much about the individual criminal but very little about crime.

Both the Freudian model and the behaviorist model attempt to show how criminals fail to acquire conscience. Both theories also focus on development. This is a noble effort—the attempt to define the process of becoming a moral person—but one where conclusive evidence is hard to come by. Both theories would require careful, systematic observation of the daily interaction of children and parents. They would also require turning vague ideas like "internalization" or "reinforcement" into specific items of behavior that any observer could recognize.

Perhaps because developmental theories are so hard to prove, other psychological theories have placed less emphasis on *how* a child develops into a criminal and more emphasis on searching for common psychological or personality traits among criminals. Is there some identifiable collection of traits that distinguishes criminals from noncriminals? In essence, is there a criminal mind?

Psychopathy and Sociopathy—The Born Criminal Revisited

In the early 20th century, psychiatrists and social workers began to use the term **psychopath** to describe certain criminals. The term, derived from the Greek words for mind and disease, implies mental illness, and had been used to describe people who commit "senseless" crimes. Psychopaths act on no apparent purpose and seem to have no sense of guilt. But the term has been used to designate a wide variety of criminals. On the one hand, psychopaths were said to be impulsive, unable to control themselves. On the other hand, they have been described as cold people who manipulate others for their own ends. In either case, they are impervious to influence by others and feel little remorse for their crimes. In actual use, **psychopathy** was somewhat difficult to pin down, an understandable difficulty given that the label could be applied to both the impulsively violent criminal and the slick con artist. Often, it seemed that the diagnoses of psychopathy had more to do with the person doing the diagnosing than with the person being diagnosed. For example, in 1925, a clinic for troubled youths had been diagnosing as psychopathic about 1 percent of the cases brought to it. Suddenly, in one year, the clinic had six times that proportion of psychopaths. The children brought to the clinic were probably no different from those of previous years. What had changed was the fashion in psychiatric diagnosis.[27]

Because of the abuses of the term psychopathy, some psychiatrists and social workers substituted the term **sociopathy**, though the meaning was not much different. In either case, the concept of psychopathy or sociopathy explains antisocial behavior by seeing such behavior as a symptom of an underlying disease—a more or less permanent condition that makes someone unable to follow social rules.

Discovering Pathology

How can we know such a disease exists? We can't do lab tests as we would for a physical disease. The principal evidence must be the person's behavior. But how can we know that the behavior comes from the disease and is not simply a response to the pressures of the situation? One way is to see how the person behaves in a variety of situations and over a long period of time. In other words, we are asking two kinds of questions: Are criminals "bad" in most social areas? And do bad kids grow up to be bad adults? If so, then these consistencies would be evidence that the behavior was caused by something within the person, something like a permanent disease.

Probably the most extensive research on these questions is Lee Robins's 30-year follow-up of children* who had been brought to a child guidance clinic. Some had been referred by the juvenile court, others by parents or teachers. Robins had not been around in the 1920s for the original diagnoses of these children. However, she had salvaged the files and was able to get information on 524 of these problem children who had now grown up. In many cases, researchers were able to interview the people themselves or relatives who could fill them in on the course of the person's later life. For comparison purposes, the researchers also interviewed a control group whose members had not had serious behavior problems as children, but who otherwise matched the clinic children in age, race, IQ, and social class.

Did criminal children become adult criminals? Did kids who were diagnosed as psychopaths in the 1920s turn out be the worst adult criminals in later years? Unfortunately, Robins's book does not directly answer these questions. However, her report does give us some evidence relevant to the concept of misbehavior as a disease. Robins was more interested in sociopathy, a general pattern of antisocial or deviant behavior, rather than in just predatory crime or even crime in general. In fact, to be diagnosed a sociopath, the person had to be antisocial in several areas. So when Robins writes about sociopaths, it is not always clear whether she is referring to an armed robber or just someone with a poor work record, a series of unstable marriages, a drinking problem, bad health, and few friends. Nevertheless, a couple of things emerge from her study. First, compared with a control group of adults, the clinic children when grown up committed more crime and spent more time in prison. Second, there was some consistency from childhood to adulthood. Among the children with six or more "antisocial symptoms" (lying, stealing, running away, bed-wetting, truancy, etc.), 33 percent were diagnosed 30 years later as sociopathic, compared with 22 percent of all clinic children and only 3 percent of the control group. In other words, kids with a lot of problems were more like to become adults with a lot of problems.

When I see figures like this, I sometimes wonder about the other troubled kids, the 67 percent who did *not* wind up as "sociopaths." Let me give some rough figures based on this study and some other studies that focus just on crime. Suppose we take two groups, each with 100 children: One group has the most troubled and troublesome children; the other group shows no serious misbehavior. Among the "good kids," perhaps 20 will wind up in trouble with the law, and few of those will be serious or frequent offenders. In the other group, as many as half will be arrested, and of these, 20 will be serious offenders who wind up spending more than a year in prison.[28] Of course, these numbers mean that half the bad kids grow up having no

* More than one-fourth of these "children" were over 18.

further arrests, and that 20 percent of the good kids wind up being arrested as adults. So knowing whether a child misbehaves can help predict later criminality, but that prediction is far from perfect.

Crime as a Disease

Does this mean that there really is such a disease as psychopathy or sociopathy? And if so, does the disease contribute to crime? First, if sociopathy is a disease, it should turn up in several different types of situations. Unfortunately, Robins's study is of no use here, since she used trouble in several areas as her criterion for defining the disease. If we select as sociopaths those people who are deviant in several areas of life, we cannot also use that sample of people to prove that the disease *causes* deviance in several areas of life. It may be true that people in prisons are often general failures—with a history of bad marriages, unsteady and low-paying jobs, and drinking or drug problems—but there are two ways to interpret this fact. On the one hand, we can say that all these problems are symptoms of a single underlying disease, much in the same way that fever, chills, aches, tiredness, and sneezing are all symptoms of the influenza virus. On the other hand, it may be that a setback in one area makes it harder for a person to succeed in other areas. Losing a job puts greater pressure on a marriage; a broken marriage makes it hard to have a stable home life; moving around a lot makes it difficult to maintain friendships.

Second, if sociopathy is a disease, then unless it is cured, people will carry it from childhood through adulthood. But do they? Here, on the one hand, we have Robins's research: One-third of the kids who showed up at a child guidance clinic with several symptoms were diagnosed 30 years later as sociopathic. As adults, they had high rates of arrest (as well as other noncriminal problems—alcoholism, unemployment, etc.). On the other hand, two-thirds of the problem kids (those with six or more symptoms) did *not* become sociopaths. And even the sociopaths, while they may have led unenviable lives, were not all predatory criminals. If sociopathy is a disease, then it is one from which most of the diseased spontaneously recover.

It also might be worth noting that although the words psychopathy and sociopathy denote disease, these conditions are different from physical disease. They carry a heavy moral connotation. Unlike physical illness, a "moral disease" is an intrinsic part of the person. In fact, the person *is* the disease. Normally, we speak of someone as *having* a cold or *having* the measles. Putting it this way means that the disease is not a part of the person; it's just something he or she has. But even the most committed believers in the concept of psychological disease do not say that someone *has* sociopathy. Instead, they say that the person *is* a sociopath.

The "Criminal Mind"

Psychology assumes that a person's behavior often is an outward sign of some underlying mental condition. For example, Robins assumed that some crimes are a symptom of an underlying disease called sociopathy. All of Robins's evidence consisted of behavior, both in childhood and adulthood. Her diagnostic categories, for the most part, were very simple: sociopathy, present or absent. Other psychological approaches try to make finer distinctions among people and try to uncover underlying mental conditions through less direct means. Instead of looking only at what people do in the real world, psychologists also conduct diagnostic interviews and give people various paper-and-pencil tests. Their goal is to discover that more or less permanent set of traits called "personality."

Is there a special criminal personality? Behind this question are two crucial assumptions: first, that the "criminal mind" is different from the normal, noncriminal mind; and second, that these differences are rooted in largely unconscious ways of thinking and reacting that can be discovered only through subtle psychological tests. The brief answer to the question is "yes." Many studies using personality tests do find differences between groups of criminals and noncriminals. Looking only at the results of these tests, we might think that they had the ability to probe deeply into the mind and discover important psychological differences, to discover who is a criminal and who is not. However, when we look more closely at the tests themselves, these diagnoses sometimes appear to be the result of much less mysterious processes.

Minnesota, Hats Off to Thee

The most popular test in all of psychology is a personality test called the **Minnesota Multiphasic Personality Inventory** (usually referred to as the **MMPI**). It was developed in the 1940s at the University of Minnesota, and here's how it works.

If you take the MMPI, your results will give your score on 10 traits, among them schizophrenia, introversion, masculinity-femininity, hypochondria, and paranoia. The test itself consists of 556 true-or-false questions. Here are a few of them:

I refuse to play some games because I am not good at them.
I worry over money and business.
It takes a lot of argument to convince most people of the truth.

Did you say "true" on the first question, or "false" on the second? If so, your answers would increase your score on the schizophrenia scale.

You might wonder what not worrying about money has to do with schizophrenia. In fact, in the way that the MMPI was developed, there does not have to be any obvious, logical connection. The reason the money question counts toward a diagnosis of schizophrenia is that the testmakers, in trying out questions on people, discovered that schizophrenics tended to answer this question "false," while normal people tended to answer "true." Of course, one question is certainly not enough for a firm diagnosis. Instead, the MMPI diagnosis rests on a pattern of answers over the course of the 80 questions that make up the schizophrenia scale. The closer your pattern of answers resembles that of the schizophrenics, the more likely it is that you, too, are schizophrenic. A "false" on the third question listed above counts toward the masculinity-femininity scale—not because there is anything inherently masculine or feminine about argument but because women and homosexual men answered it "false."[29]

Can the MMPI diagnose crime? Can it trace a profile of the criminal personality? Researchers asking these questions have usually followed the strategy of giving the test to a group of noncriminals and to a group of prison inmates or juvenile delinquents, and then comparing scores. Researchers are especially interested in the **psychopathic-deviate** (Pd) scale, and here the MMPI confirms their suspicions. Offenders often (though by no means always) score higher on the Pd scale. The conclusion implied by this research is that lawbreakers have a different personality, one marked by psychopathic-deviate tendencies. The twisting and turning paths of their minds, formed long ago and now difficult to change, lead them to commit crimes.

But is that what the MMPI really tells us? When we look at the Pd scale itself, we find 50 questions. Because of the way the test is scored, a difference on only four questions will put you into the psychopathic deviate category.* One of the 50 questions is, "I have never been in trouble with the law." Another is, "I like school." Yet another is, "When I was a youngster I engaged in petty thievery."

Looking at the actual questions takes some of the mystery out of personality assessment. After all, it's one thing to say that delinquents suffer from a mental condition measurable on something called the psychopathic-deviate scale. It's quite another to say that they don't like school, commit petty theft, and get in trouble with the law.

Are these questions getting at personality, or do they merely reflect a set of attitudes and life experiences? To define the problem as personality implies that the criminal has a deeply ingrained set of psychological traits acquired early in life. However, to see the MMPI as measuring attitudes implies something less deep. Attitudes are ways of looking at the world, ways that a person learns from others. Anybody in the same position as the

---

* Of course, you would not know which items among the 556 counted on which scales; and in addition, some of the questions are there just to check on whether you are taking the test seriously and answering consistently. These questions count on the "validity" scales.

delinquent, anybody experiencing the same world, would tend to share the delinquent's typical point of view. And in fact, MMPI research confirms this idea. That is, we know that delinquents and "normals" score differently on the Pd scale of the MMPI. But what would happen if we compared delinquents with noncriminal youths from poor neighborhoods? In such comparisons, the differences are greatly reduced, and in some cases not significant.[30]

One final comment about criminal personality as shown by the MMPI: It is not just on the Pd scale that criminals score higher than normals. They score higher on every scale. This makes for somewhat confusing results. Most studies have painted criminals as impulsive, unrestrained, and aggressive. They lead a faster lifestyle, complete with liquor, drugs, and women.[31] But why then should criminals outscore normals on the masculinity-femininity scale, where high scores "often correlate with homosexuality"[32] and indicate more feminine interests and attitudes? Why should these extroverted, free-wheeling criminals score high on "tendency towards obsessive ruminations, guilty feelings, anxiety, indecision, and worrying" (the "psychasthenia" scale)? Or the "depression" scale? Criminals even scored slightly higher on the "social introversion" scale, though the difference was significant only for the most deviant group of prisoners. Still, unless all the other personality assessments are wrong, the scores should have gone the other way—toward extroversion, not introversion.

Other personality tests also show a difference between lawbreakers and other people. The California Personality Inventory (CPI), similar to the MMPI, has a "socialization" scale, specifically designed to detect antisocial people—the kind who do not form close attachments to others, who care too much for their own immediate desires and too little for the rights of others. Indeed, lawbreakers come out much lower than others. Here are some scores from sample groups, males only. The higher the score, the better socialized the person is.

Bank officers—39.06
High-school students—36.46
Psychology graduate students—34.24
Selective service inductees—32.83
County jail inmates—29.27
Prison inmates (New York)—28.28

As expected, the criminal groups score low on socialization. But it's also interesting to note that people studying for MAs and PhDs in psychology were about as close to jail inmates as they were to bank officers, and that the average guy drafted into the army to defend our country was more similar to the jail inmates than to the average high-school student.

The Criminal Personality

The MMPI and CPI are objective and empirical. A computer can score the tests and make the diagnoses. In fact, had a computer existed in 1940, it could, without any fancy programming, have come up with the original scales itself. In this way, the MMPI technique differs from the more "clinical" approaches based on observation and interviewing. A clinician diagnoses a patient by interpreting the thought processes and motivations that lie behind what a patient says and does. The MMPI is primarily a tool for putting the person into some diagnostic category.

For nearly three decades, the objective MMPI-style approach dominated the psychological study of crime. However, in 1978 two clinicians, Samuel Yochelson and Stanton Samenow, published a two-volume study called *The Criminal Personality*. It was based on long and repeated interviews with 240 male criminals, some of whom had been committed to a mental hospital as not guilty by reason of insanity.

Yochelson and Samenow concluded, first, that none of these men was insane. They did not hallucinate or hear voices. They were clearly in touch with the real world. Eventually, the clinicians also discarded several other conventional ideas. They had apparently started out with the notion that criminals were victims of deprived environments or bad child-rearing, and that with the insights gained in psychotherapy they could rehabilitate themselves to noncriminal life. After much effort at changing the criminals, the two clinicians gave up these notions. Most important, they abandoned the idea that the criminal was a victim of environment. Instead, they came to the conclusion that the causes of crime lay entirely inside the criminal's mind and were not much affected by the environment. In their book, Yochelson and Samenow do not speculate on what causes a person to arrive at a criminal mentality, but they do say that the process occurs very early in life. They even use the phrase "the criminal child" to refer to the criminal in his early years. He is not an innocent child led astray by bad companions. If he has bad companions, it's because he has sought out others like himself. If schools or parents reject him, it is only because he has first and repeatedly rejected them.

They go on to list 52 of the criminals' typical "thinking errors," though these also sound like personality characteristics that other researchers have noted.

Fearfulness—fear of rejection, of injury, of death

Superoptimism—the complete absence of fear that takes over when he commits a crime, even a very risky one

Zero state—a sense of worthlessness, hopelessness; however, unlike depression among noncriminals, this zero state is linked not to resignation but to anger

Anger—constant; sometimes expressed, often just under the surface

Pride—usually put in terms of manhood, independence, superiority to everyone else

Present-orientation—no thought to long-term consequences

If some of these seem contradictory (zero state vs. pride), it is merely a sign of the fleeting quality of the criminal's emotions. ("I can change from tears to ice in a minute.") The criminal constantly sizes up situations as to whether they can be exploited for crime, and he takes the same exploitative, manipulative view of other people. His thinking is dominated by self-centeredness and selfishness, so that while he demands that others treat him with respect and consideration, he shows no regard for the rights or feelings of others. He is incapable of anything resembling a close, trusting relationship with other people. Nevertheless, he also maintains a belief in himself as a good person, though he can commit brutal crimes without a twinge of conscience or remorse.

The problem with this description is not its accuracy. There must be something going on when we find such a striking similarity between the qualities described here and those found by observers over the course of a century, going back to Lombroso. The problem is representativeness. The criminals described by Yochelson and Samenow are only a small proportion of the criminal population, though they probably committed a substantial proportion of the crime (exactly how much we have no accurate way of knowing). In any case, they were not typical of all criminals. Very few criminals are judged not guilty by reason of insanity. These criminals, called psychopaths or sociopaths or chronic offenders, are the most serious 10 to 15 percent of the criminal population.*

Mind and Brain

The newest frontier in the search for a connection between the body, the mind, and criminal behavior is that of neuropsychology, a science which traces abnormal behavior to brain dysfunction or damage. In a way, neuropsychology brings us full circle back to phrenology, for we know now that the phrenologists were right about one thing: Some behaviors and functions are controlled by specific areas of the brain (though complex behavior requires the interrelation of various systems and pathways within the brain, not just a single localized area). We know that the left side of the brain controls most functions on the right side of the body, and conversely for the right hemisphere. The two hemispheres of the brain also contribute

---

* Mednick estimates these psychopaths (with low SCR) as 10 percent of the criminal population. Wolfgang's chronics were about 18 percent of all criminal youths. Of Robin's 524 criminals, 243 (45 percent) were referred for stealing; of these, 31 percent were diagnosed sociopathic—about 15 percent of the total.

differently to thought. The left brain contains the "speech center," which processes language; this hemisphere also dominates in logical, sequential reasoning. The right hemisphere is more dominant in "simultaneous-synthetic" thought—the kind of thought that doesn't really seem like "thinking," but instead seems like a spontaneous recognition of relationships between various elements. When we see someone, we know instantly who it is; we recognize the whole rather than logically and sequentially piecing together the components ("wide-spaced brown eyes, straight nose, narrow face, curly hair—it's George").

Much of the knowledge about these different brain functions in humans has come from studies of people whose brains have been damaged. For example, a person who suffers a stroke on the left side of the brain may suffer a loss of speech as well as some loss of function on the right side of the body. Other information has come from autopsies of people who exhibited unusual behavior. The electroencephalograph (EEG) and especially newer "imaging" technologies (the CAT scan and MRI are the best-known) have added to knowledge about the geography of the brain.[33]

For purposes of criminology, the most interesting research concerns what neuropsychologists refer to as "executive" functions, located in the frontal lobes. These executive functions include the capacity for abstract reasoning, planning and goal-setting, self-awareness, adaptability to change in circumstances, and inhibition of impulsive behavior. People who suffer brain disease which damages the frontal lobes often display

> lack of foresight, lack of insight . . . , absence of conscience, defective affect, inability to learn from experience, diminished sense of fear . . . , poor judgment, absence of anxiety, lies and fantasies . . . , aggressive behavior, and self-defeating behavior patterns.[34]

When a head injury damages the frontal lobes, the results are typically

> facetiousness, sexual and personal hedonism, disinhibition, lack of judgment, impulsivity, irritability, and absence of concern for others.[35]

These descriptions echo all the other descriptions of criminals from Lombroso through the latest version of psychopathy (e.g., Yochelson and Samenow). A tempting logic follows: People whose frontal lobes are damaged act like psychopaths, therefore people who act like psychopaths may have dysfunction or damage to the frontal lobes. Neuropsychologists do not quite jump to this conclusion, but they do suspect that some criminals have frontal lobes which function differently from those of other people.

Another area that to some extent distinguishes delinquents and nondelinquents is that of verbal intelligence. We have long known that on IQ tests, delinquents generally score about eight points below nondelinquents.[36] From the perspective of neuropsychology, it is especially interesting that the IQ differences are most noticeable in verbal ability. Delinquents and nondelinquents are indistinguishable in tests that measure "performance IQ" (i.e., ability in nonverbal, visual tasks like picture-sequencing, mazes, picture puzzles, and attention to detail). Some neuropsychologists take this difference as a reflection of a more general deficit in the left hemisphere (remember, verbal abilities are largely left-brain functions). They point to the finding in some (though not all) studies that criminals are more likely than noncriminals to be left-handed—that is, that the right hemisphere of the brain is dominant, and the left hemisphere (with the verbal ability) is comparatively less developed.

Much research supports the idea that those who become criminals are more likely to have verbal neuropsychological deficits. What remains at issue is why this deficit, which appears at a very early age, leads to delinquency and crime in later life. Some theorists believe that verbal ability is necessary for self-control; the abstract-reasoning quality of language enables us to think about a line of behavior and to imagine consequences before we act. Others believe that those who cannot deal with difficulties verbally are more likely to lash out impulsively. Some theorists focus on the ways in which other people respond to those with low verbal ability. Nonverbal children may find themselves more rejected by parents and peers, a response which makes it more difficult for the child to form the attachments which inhibit antisocial behavior.

CRITICISMS AND CONCLUSION

Biological and psychological theories of crime focus on two basic questions: In what ways are criminals different from noncriminals, and what accounts for those differences? The theories emphasize individual traits, and the research usually focuses on those characteristics which criminals have in common but which are much rarer among noncriminals. Rather than seeing crime as a possibly normal response to situational pressures, the individual-based perspective seeks essential, underlying differences or abnormalities within the person that predisposes him or her toward criminal behavior. Some theories have found the abnormality in the criminal's facial features or physique, others in the criminal's blood chemistry or brain paths. What is striking about all these studies, and what lends support to their assumption about essential differences, is that no matter how unscientific and wrongheaded the theory may now seem, the descriptions of criminals are remarkably similar. Nobody takes seriously Lombroso's theory of atavism, but many of his observations of criminals' social and psychological life sound much like those of more scientific observers more than a century later.

A generation ago, criminology textbooks tended to dismiss biological and psychological explanations of crime. After all, it was easy to chuckle at Lombroso; and most of the later studies, as I have tried to show in this chapter, had methodological flaws that left them open to question. By the 1950s, criminology had come to be dominated by a more sociological view that emphasized environmental factors and disparaged individual-based explanations for crime. The anti-individual approach was a response to the available evidence, but it was also a response to larger historical events. The horrors of Nazism lingered in the consciousness of social scientists, who remained sensitive to the political implications of theories about biological differences.

Today, individual-based theories have returned to mainstream criminology. The consistency of antisocial behavior from childhood to adulthood, the similarities between family members, even those raised in different environments, the link between delinquency and performance on physiological and neurological tests—these and other sources of evidence point to a place for psychological or biological factors in the explanation of crime. The environment cannot explain everything. Some criminals have fairly enduring biological and psychological characteristics which are different from those of the rest of the population.

The criticisms of biological and psychological theories focus mostly on what individual factors *cannot* explain. Most researchers in these areas acknowledge that environmental factors are more influential on criminal behavior. Individual factors may predispose a person toward selfish, antisocial behavior, but the social environment will determine whether that behavior takes the form of crime. Nor is it clear just what part of the criminal population is affected by the various biological or psychological factors that may influence crime. Lombroso put the ratio of "born criminals" at 33 percent. Later studies have estimated that "psychopaths" comprise about 10 percent of the criminal population. We must wonder about the other 90 percent.

A second problem with the psychological approach is that many people, not just the most extreme 5 percent or 10 percent of the population, can become capable of behavior that an observer would label cold-blooded or even psychopathic. This possibility—that normal people can commit pathological deeds—is now well established. One of the most frightening experiments in social science created a mock prison, with college students assigned to the roles of guard and prisoner. Although none of the students could have been diagnosed as anything near to psychopathic, within only a few days some of the guards were humiliating prisoners far beyond what the experimenters expected. Not all the guards did so, but even the ones who did not brutalize prisoners did nothing to restrain the brutality of their colleagues.[37] In real life, there are war atrocities and police brutality, but we needn't go so far afield for examples. College fraternity initiations often have featured psychological or physical torture (under the euphemism "hazing"), with the torturers showing no guilt or compassion.

If normal college students and others can behave pathologically, then we must question another basis of these theories. Psychology assumes that the personality traits precede and cause the criminal's behavior. But the process may also work the other way around. That is, criminal ways of thinking are part of the job. Just as people who join and stay on the football team often acquire a taste for violence (a "good hit"), at least on the field, criminals, too, may acquire their typical ways of thinking on the job. Or if they bring some of these psychological traits with them, their life as criminals tends to reinforce those traits. The same reversal may be present in biological and neurological factors as well. Higher testosterone levels may make a person more dominant, but behaving in a dominant way also can raise a person's testosterone levels.[38] Similarly, a criminal lifestyle may cause a neuro-psychological deficit.[39]

A third criticism, one I have already mentioned, is political; it looks at the policies that psychological theories might create. Such policies would ignore social factors like economic inequality. These policies might also use psychological tests to decide the fate of individuals—punishing them on the basis of their responses to psychological tests, rather than on the basis of the crime committed. Would society or the courts tolerate such policies? I hope not. However, when public fear and concern rise, people may accept any proposal that claims to offer a convenient solution. For example, in 1970, in the wake of the urban riots of the late 1960s, a national commission issued a report calling for social change. However, in response, President Nixon's personal physician offered

> another direct, immediate and . . . effective way of tackling the problem at its very origin by focusing on the criminal mind of the child.
>
> The government should have mass testing of 6- to 8-year-old children to help detect the children who have violent and homicidal tendencies. Corrective treatment* could begin at that time.[40]

This proposal never became policy. But given the influential position of its author, it did provide substance for fears about the misuse of psychological theories of crime.

The fourth criticism of psychological explanations of crime is the most critical: Psychological theories of crime, like biological theories, cannot account for the most important demographic facts about crime. If crime is the result of certain personality traits, why should those traits be more common to urban people than to those in the suburbs? Or to 15- to 20-year-olds rather than to 30-year-olds? Why should those traits be so much more prevalent in the United States than in Canada? And even in the United States, did the large increase in crime in the decade 1963 to 1973 mean that a greater proportion of psychopaths had been born into the population?

* From the perspective of the person sent to a special program or institution, it's often hard to tell the difference between "corrective treatment" and punishment. In fact, in many states, prisons still are officially known as "correctional institutions."

Psychological concepts may help us to understand the differences between serious criminals and those people who commit few or no crimes. But none of the psychological theories seems well-equipped to explain the important facts about the social distribution of crime. For this reason, we turn in Chapter 11 to sociological explanations of crime.

NOTES

1. David Harris Willson (1967), *A History of England*, New York: Holt, Rinehart, and Winston, p. 93.

2. Barbara W. Tuchman (1978), *A Distant Mirror: The Calamitous 14th Century*, New York: Knopf, p. 141.

3. Graeme Newman (1978), *The Punishment Response*, New York: J.B. Lippincott, pp. 89–94.

4. Newman, p. 126, 138.

5. Cesare Beccaria (1764, 1963), *On Crimes and Punishments*, translated, with an introduction by Henry Paolucci, Indianapolis, IN: Bobbs-Merrill.

6. Ibid., p. 12.

7. Ibid, p. xxii.

8. George B. Vold (1979), *Theoretical Criminology*, New York: Oxford University Press, p. 53-55.

9. Cesare Lombroso (1911), *Criminal Man*, reprinted 1972, Montclair, NJ: Patterson Smith, pp. 6–7.

10. Cesare Lombroso (1911), *Crime: Its Causes and Remedies*, reprinted 1968, Montclair, NJ: Patterson Smith, pp. 365–66.

11. Vold, op. cit., p. 37.

12. Charles Goring (1913), *The English Convict: A Statistical Study*, London: His Majesty's Stationery Office, quoted in Vold, op. cit., p. 61, and James Q. Wilson and Richard J. Herrnstein (1985), *Crime and Human Nature*, New York: Simon and Schuster, p. 76.

13. Goring, op. cit., quoted in Wilson and Herrnstein, op. cit.

14. E. A. Hooton (1939), *Crime and the Man*, Cambridge, MA: Harvard University Press, pp. 301–8, quoted in Wilson and Herrnstein, op. cit., p. 78, and Vold, op. cit. pp. 62–65.

15. Hooton, op. cit., quoted in Vold, op. cit., p. 62.

16. William H. Sheldon (1949), *Varieties of Delinquent Youth*, New York: Harper.

17. Sheldon, p. 752, quoted in Vold, op. cit., p. 68.

18. Sarnoff A. Mednick and Jan Volavka (1980), "Biology and Crime," in Norval Morris and Michael Tonry, eds., *Crime and Justice: An Annual Review of Research*, Chicago: University of Chicago Press, pp. 85–158.

19. L. E. Kreuz and R. M. Rose (1972), "Assessment of Aggressive Behavior and Plasma Testosterone in a Young Criminal Population," *Psychosomatic Medicine*, vol. 34, pp. 321–32, cited in ibid.

20. Daniel Goleman (1990), "Aggression in Men: Hormone Levels Are a Key," *The New York Times*, July 17, pp. C1, 6, reporting on research by Richard Udry and others.

21. K. O. Christiansen (1977), "A Preliminary Study of Criminality Among Twins," in Sarnoff A. Mednick and K.O. Christiansen, eds., *Biosocial Bases of Criminal Behavior*, New York: Gardner Press, cited in Mednick and Volavka, op. cit.

22. *The Trenton Times*, Aug. 9, 1982, p. C1.

23. Hans J. Eysenck (1977), *Crime and Personality*, London: Routledge and Kegan Paul.

24. Gwynn Netler (1984), *Explaining Crime*, 3rd ed., New York: McGraw-Hill, p. 302. See also A. Petrie (1967), *Individuality in Pain and Suffering*, Chicago: University of Chicago Press.

25. For a review of these studies, see Mednick and Volavka, op. cit., pp. 119–22.

26. Charles Silberman (1978), *Criminal Violence, Criminal Justice*, New York: Random House, p. 84.

27. Lee N. Robins (1966), *Deviant Children Grown Up: A Sociological and Psychiatric Study of Sociopathic Personality*, Baltimore: Williams and Wilkins, p. 16.

28. Lee N. Robins and K. S. Ratcliff (1979), "Risk Factors in the Continuation of Childhood Antisocial Behavior into Adulthood," *International Journal of Mental Health*, vol. 7, pp. 96–116, cited in R. Loeber and T. Dishion (1983), "Early Predictors of Male Delinquency: A Review," *Psychological Bulletin*, vol. 94, pp. 68–99. Also, Mark Peterson, Harriet Braiker, and Sue Polich (1980), *Doing Crime: A Survey of California Inmates*, Santa Monica, CA: The RAND Corporation.

29. Robert C. Colligan, David Osborne, Wendell M. Swenson, and Kenneth P. Gifford (1983), *The MMPI: A Contemporary Normative Study*, New York: Praeger.

30. Arthur Volkman (1959), "A Matched Group Personality Comparison of Delinquents and Non-Delinquent Juveniles," *Social Problems*, vol. 6, pp. 238–45.

31. Donald J. West and D. P. Farrington (1977), *The Delinquent Way of Life*, London: Heinemann.

32. Richard Herrnstein (1983), "Some Criminogenic Traits of Offenders," in James Q. Wilson, ed. (1983), *Crime and Public Policy*, San Francisco: ICS Press, pp. 31–49 (quote on p. 40).

33. Most of my information on neuropsychology comes from Terrie E. Moffitt (1990), "The Neuropsychology of Juvenile Delinquency," in Michael Tonry and Norval Morris, eds. (1990), *Crime and Justice: A Review of Research*, Chicago: University of Chicago Press, pp. 99–169.

34. Frank A. Elliott (1978), "Neurological Aspects of Antisocial Behavior," in W. H. Reid, ed. (1978), *The Psychopath*, New York: Bruner/Mazel, cited in Moffitt, op. cit., p. 111.

35. Dietrich Blumer and D. Frank Benson (1975), "Personality Changes with Frontal and Temporal Lobe Lesions," in D. Frank Benson and Deitrich Blumer, eds. (1975), *Psychiatric Aspects of Neurologic Disease*, New York: Grune & Stratton, cited in Moffitt, op. cit.

36. Travis Hirschi and Michael J. Hindenlang (1977), "Intelligence and Delinquency: A Revisionist Review," *American Sociological Review*, vol. 42, pp. 571–87.

37. Philip G. Zimbardo (1973), "A Pirandellian Prison," *The New York Times Magazine*, April 8, pp. 38–60.

38. Goleman, op. cit.

39. Moffitt, op. cit, p. 126.

40. *The New York Times*, April 11, 1970, p. 15.

Talking Heads: Sociological Theories, Part I

CHAPTER 11

THE SOCIOLOGICAL PERSPECTIVE

WHAT MAKES A THEORY SOCIOLOGICAL? OF COURSE, NO SIMPLE ANSWER COULD POSSIBLY satisfy all sociologists. But to oversimplify, we might say that if biological and psychological approaches try to show how criminals are different from you and me, sociological theories try to show how they are similar to us. Psychological theories see crime as the result of abnormal people doing abnormal things. Sociological theories tend to see crime as the product of normal people engaging in normal social processes in normal (though perhaps not ideal) social environments.

Psychological and biological theories look for the differences between individuals. According to these theories, the important causes of crime are to be found *within* the person. Deficiencies or defects inside the person make him or her different from other people and cause him or her to break society's rules. Sociological theories, in contrast, tend to emphasize causes found in the *environment*. Certain environments will produce more crime, regardless of the characteristics of the people living there. Individual differences hardly enter into these theories.

The sociological approach raises an important question: If sociologists believe that crime is largely a result of environmental causes, does this mean that sociologists also believe that criminals are not responsible for their crimes, since the causes lie not in the person but in the social environment? The answer is no, although many people have just such an image of sociology. I once spent a frustrating two weeks on jury duty—frustrating because the district attorneys prosecuting the cases always rejected me as a prospective juror after the voir-dire questioning. (In principle, you are not told which lawyer—prosecution or defense—rejected you, but it was not hard for me to guess.) One afternoon, in the hall, I ran into a district attorney who had kept me off a jury that morning. "Why did you toss me off your case?" I asked innocently.

"Are you kidding?" he said. "A sociologist? You people don't think anyone's responsible for what they do."

At the time, I didn't know just what to say, and the conversation ended there. But what I should have said is that he was confusing two separate questions. It's one thing to understand the social forces that may have caused a person to commit a crime. It is quite another matter to absolve that person of all blame for the crime. For a lawyer or a juror (even a juror who is also a sociologist), the question of guilt is paramount. But for the sociologist who is thinking about crime as a social problem, the issue of individual guilt or innocence is much less important. Sociological theory often dodges the problem of assigning moral or legal blame, just as it also avoids the issue of individual differences. In this way, sociological theorizing is different from everyday thinking about crime. Often, when we read about some horrible crime, our first thought is a moral one (this is a bad person), and our second response may be to look for individual differences and defects (what's wrong with him that made him so bad?). Sociological theory often sidesteps both these issues.

How can sociology, if it wishes to explain crime, ignore both the question of individual differences and the issue of moral guilt and blame? The answer is that sociologists look not just at individuals, but at groups.

Rates and Cases

If we are acting as jurors or psychologists, we must focus our attention on a single case, a single criminal. But if we are sociologists, we want to look for larger patterns. We look not at this or that crime, but at crime in general. One way of gaining this broader view is to step back from the individual crime or criminal and look instead at crime *rates*. When we do, we often notice something interesting: Although the rate is made up entirely of individual cases, it seems to have an existence of its own, apart from any individual case. To put it another way, while individuals may change their behavior unpredictably from day to day or year to year, the society's overall rates of behavior show a remarkable consistency; and when these rates do change, they do so gradually. For example, most people who commit murder do so only once. There is a great variation in the murderer's behavior: This year he killed; he had never done so before, and will probably never do so again. Yet, despite this great variation in each murderer's behavior, the overall murder *rate* every year is quite close to that of the previous year. So we can predict that next year in the United States, about 21,000 people will commit homicide. We also know that different societies or different sections of the country will have predictably different rates. And these rates are predictable on the basis of social, not psychological, factors.

Of course, knowing rates allows us only to predict other rates—not individual cases. We can roughly predict the number of homicides, or highway deaths, or births, or whatever, but we cannot specify which individuals will engage in these behaviors. Here's a useful analogy: Suppose that a casino spins a roulette wheel 38,000 times. I know that since there are 38 numbers in the wheel (counting the 0 and 00), my lucky number (26) will come up approximately 1,000 times. Unfortunately, I do not know exactly on which spins it will come up. (If I did, I would probably not be writing this book.) But I do know that the total will be very close to 1,000.

This is one of the basic and most important insights of the sociological perspective: We *can* predict the collective number or rate of these events in a given population even though each individual event may be unpredictable and unintended. For example, we can predict that the number of people who will die in traffic accidents next year will be roughly 50,000. This estimate is not exact, but we can be sure that the number will be closer to 50,000 than to 40,000 or 60,000. Probably the first use of this insight—

at least in the area of criminology—came over 150 years ago. In 1835, a French writer, Alfonse Quetelet, published a book called *A Treatise on Man and the Development of His Faculties.*" As the book's title implies, Quetelet wanted to explain how physical changes that happened as people grew older affected their moral or psychological life. But a funny thing happened on the way to the answer. While trying to find out the age at which human passions are strongest, Quetelet collected statistics on murder and on crime in general. When he had compiled these annual figures for several years, he discovered certain regular patterns: Numbers stayed remarkably stable from one year to the next. Differences among the various regions of France, differences between the sexes, differences among age groups—all showed consistent patterns. For example, year after year, women committed about 14 percent of all violent crimes and 21 percent of property crimes.[1]

Today, we take these consistencies for granted. But to Quetelet and other "moral statisticians," as they were called, these were discoveries that raised important questions. The statistics added a new element to the philosophical debate over free will. Today, most of us assume that, as individuals, we have free will. But if our behavior—even our seemingly impulsive, unpredictable behavior—falls into a consistent, predictable pattern, is our sense of free will merely an illusion? Are we perhaps merely parts in some larger design?

For purposes of criminology, the philosophical questions do not concern us as much as do the sociological ones. Quetelet and Guerry (a Belgian who lived during the same period and explored much of the same statistical territory)—along with others of this "cartographic" school of thought—mapped out the geographical and social distribution of crime rates (see Table 11–1). The data they gathered set what should have been the agenda for criminology. Unfortunately, their work was largely ignored. The dominant ideas in thinking about crime focused on the individual criminal, and it was nearly a century before sociologists began to pick up the trail blazed by the cartographic school.

Evil Effects, Evil Causes?

Besides emphasizing rates rather than cases, sociological theories take an interesting perspective on the moral issue. Individualistic theories usually assume that criminal behavior arises from some deficiency, from something wrong—bad genes, bad psychology, bad family, bad environment. Sometimes called the evil-causes-evil assumption, this way of thinking seems to come naturally. If something is wrong, we assume that it must have both evil causes and evil consequences. However, this assumption limits the kinds of questions we can ask and the kinds of perceptions we can have about the subject. For example, if we think that smoking marijuana is bad, when we study it we would ask, "What's wrong with this person that he or

Table 11–1 ■ **Crime in France, 1825 to 1830**

Crimes against the person

Region	1825	1826	1827	1828	1829	1830	Population	Percent of population
North	25	24	23	26	24	25	8,757,700	27.6
South	28	26	22	23	25	23	4,826,500	15.2
East	17	21	19	20	19	19	5,841,000	18.4
West	18	16	21	17	17	16	7,008,800	22.1
Center	12	13	15	14	18	14	5,238,900	16.5

Crimes against property

Region	1825	1826	1827	1828	1829	1830	Population	Percent of population
North	41	42	42	43	44	44	8,757,700	27.6
South	12	11	11	12	12	11	4,826,500	15.2
East	18	16	17	16	14	15	5,841,000	18.4
West	17	19	19	17	17	18	7,008,800	22.1
Center	12	12	11	12	13	13	5,238,900	16.5

Source: A.M. Guerry (1833) "Essai sur la statistique Morale de la France," in Terence Morris (1957), *The Criminal Area*, London: Routledge and Kegan Paul, p. 46.

she needs to use this drug?" Our question assumes that something bad (marijuana use) must be caused by something else bad (a psychological deficiency). We probably also assume that the drug also will have evil consequences. Therefore we also might do research on the harmful physical and psychological effects of marijuana. In fact, questions like this have shaped much marijuana research.[2] But go back a century and you will find the same kinds of assumptions regarding the causes and consequences of masturbation.[3] Only since the 1960s have researchers suggested that there might be benefits to "the solitary vice."

My point is not that one moral position is right and another is wrong. I merely want to show how a narrow moral viewpoint—the "corrective" approach—may limit our perceptions and understanding.[4]

Some of the theories we will be looking at directly challenge the evil-causes-evil assumption, even in the study of crime. Some theories find causes of crime in some of the most valued aspects of our society. One theory says that something good (an emphasis on success) causes something bad (crime). Other theories hold that something bad (crime) can cause something good (social cohesion). They argue that crime has positive consequences for society—that a society *needs* a certain amount of crime, and if the criminals fail to meet their production quotas, the society will create more crime. For example, people may "raise" their moral standards. Although people once accepted a behavior, they may later think of it as a problem to be corrected. In the end, they will have created whole new categories of crime and criminals.[5]

MERTON AND ANOMIE

In 1938, Robert Merton, an American sociologist, published an essay titled "Social Structure and Anomie."[6] It proved to be one of the most influential articles in sociology. Every sociologist has read it; it has appeared more often in the footnotes and references of other sociological articles than has any other title.[7] Nearly every criminology textbook outlines it (the book you are now holding is no exception). Merton has never been a criminologist, and he presented no new information about crime. Nevertheless, this article remains important because it explains something about crime by using purely sociological ideas.

Merton begins his essay by rejecting psychological and biological theories, since they cannot explain why different social groups consistently have different amounts of crime. As Merton puts it, "Our perspective is sociological. We look at variations in the *rates* of deviant behavior."

The basic fact Merton is trying to explain is the connection between social class and crime. He assumes that in America, poorer people commit more crime than do wealthier people. (Although many people now question this assumption, at the time it was widely accepted and supported by the available research.)* He set out to explain not individual differences (criminals vs. noncriminals) but rather the different crime rates of different social groups.

Means and Ends

Why, then, are poorer people more likely to commit crime? The obvious answer is: because they need the money. But the problem in that answer is the word *need*. After all, there are many populations in the world who by any objective standard are much needier than the lower classes of the United States; yet they commit far less crime—and not just because there is less available for them to steal.

The crucial factor is not how much money you have, but rather how you *feel* about what you have. Do you feel satisfied or frustrated? This feeling about the satisfaction of needs comes down to the match-up between ends and means—that is, between the goals and the means to achieve those

---

* For a review of the connection between crime and social class, see Chapter 4.

goals. If the available means allow you to move toward your goals, you will be satisfied; if those means are not sufficient for your goals, you will feel frustrated. All this is obvious. It is also fairly obvious that society does not distribute the same package of means to everybody. Children born to poor parents will not have the same opportunities as children born to middle-class or wealthy parents. Poor children's chances even of surviving the first few years of life are not as good; they will not get as good an education; they may not meet the "right" people or learn how to deal with them in the "right" way. They will more likely wind up in dead-end, low-paying jobs.*

Merton, however, reminds us of something less obvious: that goals, too, are socially distributed. We can easily see that the structure of society helps determine the means we will have available. But when we think about our goals—what we want, what is good—we usually see these goals as ideas that we have arrived at by ourselves. If we admit to being influenced by someone else, it is usually the kind of influence we can control, such as specific advice we can accept or reject. However, society influences us in a more general and subtle way. To take a trivial example, consider our ideas of beauty. If you look at movie stars of 70 years ago—or clothing of seven years ago—you may wonder how people could have thought them the pinnacle of attractiveness. Yet years from now, the same will be said of the bodies, faces, and clothes that are today's ideals. Obviously, in our ideas about what looks good, we have been influenced by other people, by "society." In the same way, society also teaches us our more abstract ideas of what is good or worth pursuing—our values and goals.

Conditions for the Class-Crime Connection

Crime rates are higher in the lower class, then, not merely because lower-class people have less money. For a society to have a strong connection between crime and lack of money, three other conditions must exist:

1. Poorer people must share the same goals as better-off people.
2. These goals—the things people want—must be easily transferrable.
3. The society must emphasize attaining goals rather than using approved means.

America meets these three conditions so well that we may have difficulty imagining a society where they do not hold true. However, not all societies resemble ours in these respects. Take, for example, the point about the poor

---

* If you think these environmental factors make no difference, imagine that you could choose the family you will be born into in your next life. Would you choose to be the child of poor, teenage, unwed parents?

sharing the same goals as other people. The important point to remember here is that *both* means and goals are "socially distributed." In other words, "society"—something over which the individual has little power—creates these goals and means and instills them in people. In some societies, different social groups may have different goals—different standards of success. Poor people there will not compare themselves enviously with better-off people. But in America, according to Merton, people on all rungs of the social ladder place a high value on financial success—or, in a word, money. Every child is taught—at home, in school, and later at work—that anyone can and should work hard and become wealthy. Even the poor adopt this ideology of individual success. They will compare themselves not just with each other but with those at a higher level, and they will feel that they are missing something. Although Merton does not identify this concept by name, he is using the idea of **relative deprivation**—the notion that how deprived you feel depends on with whom you compare yourself. Although the comparison will be more stressful for the poor, Americans at all economic levels, says Merton, tend to compare themselves with people who are somewhat more successful. And everybody measures success chiefly in terms of money.*

Money provides a very good means of comparison. Not only is it easily calculated, but it has the advantage of being easily transferred from person to person (point 2 listed above). Money is money, regardless of who is holding it, regardless even of how the person got it. Americans, in Merton's view, are rather tolerant of ill-gotten gain—especially if the amount is large enough and if it has been handed on to the next generation. A Mercedes-Benz costs $60,000 and looks classy no matter who is driving it. But it's not just that money can buy things; in America, "money has been consecrated as a value in itself." No matter how much we have, we always want just a little (or a lot) more.

Relative Deprivation and Social Structure

Not every society will have this correlation between poverty and crime. People with lesser means need not feel envious or deprived so long as they are in a society "where rigidified class structure is coupled with *differential class symbols of success*." Imagine a strict caste society, one where the caste you are born into largely determines your lot in life. Different castes will have different ideas and symbols of success, and the institutions of society—

---

* In 1986, investigations revealed that several high-paid members of the financial world had broken laws in order to make even more money. Soon after, a newspaper article about Wall Street traders carried the headline "Feeling Poor on $600,000 a Year." (*The New York Times*, April 26, 1987, sec. 3, p. 1.)

especially the family—will reinforce these differences. In each caste, the family will teach its particular goals to its children. Members of a lower, poorer caste would not necessarily feel deprived relative to someone in a higher caste. Instead, they would judge themselves by the unique standards of their particular caste. Even in some industrialized societies, the working class may have a strong class-consciousness; people may feel that the work-ing-class way of life is every bit as legitimate as middle-class life. In such a society, working-class parents might hope not that their children will move up into a "better" class, but that the position of all working-class people will become more comfortable—but with no basic changes in their way of life. In the United States, however, according to Merton, everyone shares the same basic goal.

When we think of money and the things it buys—houses, cars, vacations, furniture and other consumer items that are the staple of TV game shows—we may find it hard to believe that there are societies where some people would not want such desirable consumer goods while other people enjoyed them; or where the members of a lower caste do not constantly look with envy upon the goods of another caste. We can scarcely imagine such a sys-tem. The closest analogy I can think of in our own society is that of male-female differences. The sex division is perhaps the nearest thing we have to caste. What one sex might strive for (bulging biceps, hourglass propor-tions) members of the other sex might not find at all enviable for themselves.

More to the point, not all societies base the status of the individual on such impersonal, transferable things as money and the things it buys. In simple societies, people's positions in the world—their work, their rela-tionships with others, the respect others give them—may be determined almost entirely by their age, sex, and family. These sources of status are nontransferable. Things like age and position in a family structure cannot be acquired through hard work: If you are not born as the eldest child of a chief, no amount of talent and hard work will get you there. Consequently, in these societies, striving for success will not be so important.

Not just in small-scale, simple societies, but in those based on aristocracy as well, a person's place may be largely determined by the family he or she is born into. Even in modern European societies, the faint traces of an aristocratic tradition may make for somewhat less emphasis on money as a measure of who a person is. Modern Europeans visiting America today still seem surprised by our preoccupation with success.

America has much less of an aristocratic tradition. Our democratic, egal-itarian ideals extend from the political arena into the area of economics and society. We judge all people by the same standards. But at the same time that our society leads us all to want similar goals, we do not all have the same opportunities to achieve those goals. People with less opportunity will feel a certain amount of strain between their culturally prescribed goals and the socially structured means available to achieve those goals. Something will have to give. In the extreme case, the result will be **anomie**, a condition of normlessness where the rules of the game no longer make sense. Short of this kind of social chaos, there may be less drastic adaptations. When legitimate means and goals do not mesh, people may give up one or the other or both.

Adaptations to Anomie

Merton outlines five logical "modes of adaptation" to the means-ends conflict. A person can either accept (+) or reject (0) a culturally prescribed goal; he or she can respond likewise for taking legitimate means towards that goal. Or the person can both reject the means or goal and substitute a different one (0/+).

Modes of Adaptation	Cultural Goals	Institutionalized Means
Conformity	+	+
Innovation	+	0
Ritualism	0	+
Retreatism	0	0
Rebellion	(0/+)	(0/+)

Conformity—law-abiding behavior—is probably the most common adaptation and does not much concern us here. But innovation—keeping the goal of financial success while adopting illegitimate means to achieve it—obviously includes many forms of economic crime. Merton expects that this adaptation will be found most frequently in the lower class. But he also mentions upper-class crime—from the robber barons of the 19th century to contemporary white-collar criminals. The pressure toward innovation is characteristic of American society at all levels. When goals cannot be achieved by legitimate means, we keep the goal. Since the goal (producing goods, making a profit) is worthwhile, Americans tend to overlook some corner-cutting and questionable business practices. Break a few rules if you have to, but get the job done.

Other societies, even those with greater inequality, may stress means over ends. People will do things in the proper or traditional way—even though those means may not be the quickest way to the goal. At the extreme, this leads to what Merton calls ritualism. Ritualists, in Merton's scheme, are the people who abandon success goals while continuing to follow the rules of society, paring down their aspirations and not taking chances. The lower middle class is the most likely place to find ritualism, since these people discipline their children to conform, while their chances for real financial success remain small.

Retreatists have given up. They are "psychotics . . . outcasts . . . vagrants

. . . drunkards . . . addicts." They do not pursue success, nor do they conform to the approved ways of doing things. Surely, the skid-row wino, who moves from the street to drunk-court to jail and back to the street, is neither pursuing success nor following approved means.

Rebels, too, have become alienated from the goals and means of society, but unlike retreatists, they are organized, and they take collective action to bring about change in the values and laws of the society.

Criticisms of Merton

I have outlined Merton's essay at length here, primarily because it has had so much influence on criminological thinking but also because it presents a truly sociological view of the issue of crime. Merton begins not with criminals but with the structure of a society and its cultural ideas and ideals. He directs his attention not to the individual criminal but to the different rates among social classes. People at certain places in the class structure will experience a strain between the goals society has taught them and the means society has made available to them. In fact, Merton's theory and others like it are often referred to as **strain** theories.

Merton also refuses to take a condemning attitude toward criminals. Too often, we think of criminals as some sort of alien race that has invaded our basically noncriminal society. In Merton's view, criminals are just as much a part of society and just as much a product of it as anyone else. By suspending the usual moral condemnation of criminals, Merton also avoids the evil-causes-evil assumption. In fact, according to his theory, both the worst street crime and the greatest capitalist achievements flow from the same sources. By putting street thieves in the same category with the robber barons and calling it innovation, Merton is implying that both the burglar and the railroad builder are products of the same aspects of American culture: the value placed on economic success and the emphasis on goals rather than means.

Merton's views can be criticized at both the theoretical and empirical levels. For example, his theory does not include any explanation of violent, noneconomic crime. It might be possible to place murder, rape, and assault under the heading of innovation, but this classification would stretch that category considerably, and Merton himself never suggests that innovation should include these crimes. Nor do they fit into any of his other adaptations. In addition, even crimes which do have an economic goal may be motivated as much by the immediate experience of the crime itself as by a desire for money and what it buys.[8] As for the empirical evidence on social class and crime, it is not exactly overwhelming. The poor probably commit more crime than do the middle class, but the difference is not as large as Merton's theory would lead us to expect. Furthermore, the difference is probably greatest for crimes of violence—precisely those crimes which Merton's theory ignores.

In addition, Merton makes some assumptions about goals and means that are fairly difficult to prove. For example, how could we show that in the United States, compared with other countries, all social classes place a high value on financial success? Or that Americans are more likely than people of other cultures to let the ends justify the means? These perceptions may seem accurate; they may correspond well with what we think of ourselves, and visitors from other cultures may remark upon these same things. But it is difficult to measure these variables in any systematic way—especially for purposes of comparison between different countries.

Some studies do provide evidence that for Americans of every social class, money is the principal measure of social standing.[9] And there are many studies that show to what extent our class system limits a person's opportunities.[10] But in order to compare the United States with other countries, we need the same measures for these other societies. And, at least at present, these measures have not been made.

A final criticism of Merton's theory has to do with his picture of the relationship of the individual to society. Whenever I read this essay, I get the picture of the individual as isolated, not in contact with other people. If he finds his opportunities too limited, his path blocked, then all by himself he schemes some illegal method of getting money—what Merton calls innovation. However, we know that most crimes are not very "innovative" in the usual sense of that word. In fact innovation, as we usually think of it, would apply much more to upper-class, white-collar crime rather than to ordinary street crime: the frustrated computer programmer who, working alone, electronically and undetectably credits his own account; but not the lower-class car thief. Most burglars, robbers, and thieves today use techniques that have been around for hundreds of years.

This lack of real innovation and the tendency of street criminals to learn their crimes from other people bring up another gap in Merton's theory. Oddly enough, this weakness in Merton's theory is also its strength—its purely sociological approach. By drawing back from the individual, it allows us to discover patterns that we might have missed. But it cannot therefore very well explain *how* a person at whatever place in the social structure becomes a criminal. Because of its distance from actual behavior, this viewpoint also ignores the individual's capacity for thought and free will. As Howard Becker wrote several years later, "The people sociologists study often have trouble recognizing themselves in the sociological reports written about them" (his criticism was not directed specifically at Merton). Sociology often runs the risk of treating people as "conceptual boobs"; that is, as mere extensions of abstract social forces like "social class" or "values," rather than as people who can think and talk about what they do and why they do it.

CRIME AND CULTURE

During the same period that Merton was writing about the crime-causing strains in the American social structure, another sociologist, Edwin Sutherland, was creating what was to become the other dominant theory in American sociology—the theory of **differential association**.

Most social theories are elaborations of some common sense notion. As such, they can be summarized in a sentence or two in a way that makes them sound so obvious they're hardly worth writing about. For example, we might reduce Merton's theory to this: Poorer people commit more crime because they want more money. Of course, Merton's essay is valuable because it shows the conditions where this statement will and will not be true. In a similar way, Sutherland's theory of differential association boils down to the idea that a person becomes criminal because he or she falls in with the wrong crowd. However, to understand the importance of Sutherland's ideas, it helps to know the kinds of ideas about crime he was reacting against. Perhaps a little history is in order here.

Social Pathology, Social Disorganization

In the early 20th century, much writing about crime took a perspective known as **social pathology**. The word *pathology* means disease, and as the name "social pathology" implies, this school of thought saw society as something like a living organism. Social pathologists were concerned with crime, drunkenness, divorce, mental illness—what sociologists today call "social problems." But by calling them social pathology, these writers likened the deviant behavior to a disease in an otherwise healthy society. Of course, they were primarily concerned with "curing" the disease, and their writings, therefore, provided the intellectual basis for practical social work during this era. But whatever its good intentions, social pathology as a theory suffered from a major flaw: It assumed that there is an objective state of health for society, just as there is for a single organism. On closer inspection, this standard of health turned out to be American, small-town, middle-class values.[11]

To sociologists of that time, the idea of social pathology did not *explain* the origin or persistence of the behaviors it intended to correct; it merely labeled them, using an analogy (society as body) that had a basically conservative view of society. Sociologists, on the other hand, took a more tolerant view of things like drinking and divorce. They did not consider them forms of pathology. More important, they wanted a better explanation for crime and deviance. Therefore, in place of social pathology, sociologists of the 1920s developed the concept of **social disorganization**. In this view, society is not an organism; it is an organization. Just as formal organizations are based on rules, the basis of society lies in its rules, written and unwritten, which are called **norms**. Where people are closely tied to each other, as in small villages, they will be less likely to deviate from these rules. But where relationships become less personal and less permanent, an individual will feel more free to break the rules.

Although social disorganization theory does not have an explicit central metaphor as does the organism metaphor of social pathology, it does have its own unstated image of society. It reminds me of those pictures of iron filings in the presence of a magnet. Social norms are like a central magnet, keeping people in line. But some members of society are farther away, at the edges of the magnetic field, where the norms of society do not pull them as strongly. It is in these areas that deviance will flourish. Modern society, in contrast to a rural village, is particularly likely to develop pockets of disorganization, farther from the pull of social norms, where people (just like those iron filings) would get "out of line." The main causes of this breakdown, in this theory, were industrialization, urbanization, and immigration—processes that weaken personal ties and increase anonymity.*

The idea of social disorganization was particularly influential with sociologists at the University of Chicago in the early part of this century. Some of their research took the form of close observation and description of life in less respectable social areas—places and groups that outsiders might well have labeled as examples of "pathology" or "disorganization": the taxi-dance hall, "hobohemia," juvenile gangs, inexpensive rooming houses, and other disreputable settings. However, their research showed that far from being disorganized, social life in these areas also had its rules. These rules might have differed from those of conventional society, but they nevertheless provided a basis for social life.

Social Ecology and Natural Zones

Another style of research that emerged in Chicago was sometimes called **social ecology**. It was based on the idea that social life in cities, like plant and animal life in the wild, conformed to regular patterns that could be mapped by geographic area. Cities developed natural areas according to the functions that would be performed there. These zones tended to take the form of concentric circles radiating from the central business district

---

* Sociologist Robert Park included the automobile, movies, and newspapers in this list of "demoralizing" aspects of progress (he was writing in 1925, long before television): "Apparently, anything that makes life interesting is dangerous to the existing order."

(Zone I) to the better residential area farthest away (Zone V). In between lay the area of middle-class housing (Zone IV), that of working-class housing (Zone III), and an area of transition (Zone II). As the central industrial area expands, owners of buildings in this transitional zone expect to sell their property. Therefore, they do not invest much in maintenance or improvement, and buildings deteriorate. Rents are low. The residents tend to be recent immigrants, who move on as soon as they can. There is rapid population turnover, and few people feel any strong attachment to the area or to the people in it.

Zone II is the picture of social disorganization, and it is here that social problems are most likely to occur. The important point to remember is that the ecological view stresses the geographic and social area itself, more than the people who happen to live there, as a source of crime. This may not seem like a very unusual idea to us; we expect some neighborhoods to have predictably higher rates of crime and delinquency, mental and physical illness, poverty, marital breakup, etc. But at the time, some popular explanations of crime tended to emphasize ethnic factors, sometimes in a way that sounded downright racist. To show the superiority of the ecological approach, two sociologists, Clifford Shaw and Robert McKay, collected statistics on delinquency over a period of several decades. During these years, the ethnic makeup of the Zone II area in Chicago changed from predominantly German and Irish to Polish and Italian. Yet Shaw and McKay found that regardless of ethnicity, Zone II always had the highest rates of delinquency.

Why did crime and delinquency persist in the zone of transition despite the changing population? Shaw and McKay emphasized two factors. First, social disorganization means that conventional, noncriminal people cannot exert much control over those who break the law. Second, criminals can pass their ideas and way of life to others in the neighborhood. This idea of a "way of life," however, implies that social life, even in this most unstable zone, is not *dis*organized, but rather that it is organized on a different set of norms. What some people saw as social disorganization could be better seen as (in Sutherland's phrase) "differential social organization." Different geographic areas and different social groups have different sets of norms for conducting everyday life. In a word, they have different cultures.

This line of thinking laid the basis for cultural theories of crime. As opposed to Merton's view of America as a land with a single set of goals and means that individuals either accepted or rejected, cultural theories see America as a collection of different subcultures. In regard to crime, the essence of cultural theories is that while all subcultures have norms, the norms of some subcultures allow or even demand behavior which violates the law. For example, during Prohibition, a culture in which drinking was a basic part of social life would inevitably come into conflict with the law. It may not be purely coincidental that the theories we have been looking at were developed during the 1920s, the era of Prohibition. Not only did Prohibition mean that the pursuit of culturally approved activities would lead some people to violate the law or help others to violate it; Prohibition also gave rise to the first extensive organization of crime.

Probably more important than Prohibition in the development of sociological views of crime was the phenomenon of immigration. The vast numbers of immigrants who came to America in the period roughly between 1890 and 1920 transformed the social landscape. Earlier generations of immigrants had come largely from northern Europe and, except perhaps for the Irish, had tended to settle in rural areas. The new immigrants came in unprecedented numbers; they came from Southern and Eastern Europe (Italy, Poland, Russia, Slavic countries), and they settled in the large cities. It would have been difficult for anyone—especially sociologists studying cities at the University of Chicago—to ignore this cultural diversity.

Sutherland and Differential Association Theory

Of course, we cannot be sure to what extent these historical events influenced sociological theory. In any case, the ideas of differential social organization and cultural transmission came together in the work of Edwin Sutherland, sometimes referred to as the "dean" of American criminology. In the first edition of his *Principles of Criminology*, published in 1934, Sutherland stated, "The conflict of cultures is . . . the fundamental principle in the explanation of crime."*

Though neither Merton nor Sutherland intended it, their theories complement each other. Sutherland's theory focuses on an aspect of crime that Merton avoids—the social and psychological process of becoming a criminal. While Merton begins with the large-scale elements of society such as social class, Sutherland starts from the smallest element: a person who, in some specific situation, decides to break the law. That decision is based on a particular way of seeing that situation; people who commit crimes see the situation as an occasion for crime. To understand crime, therefore, we must understand why that person sees that situation as an occasion for crime. However, in saying that criminals see things differently from noncriminals, Sutherland does not mean that there is anything abnormal about them. Their thought processes have evolved in the same way as anyone else's. In other words, Sutherland, too, refuses to assume that the causes of crime must be evil or abnormal. Instead, crime, like any other form of behavior, is learned, and that criminals are socialized into criminal life, just as noncriminals are socialized into conventional ways of life.

---

* In the full formulation of the theory, Sutherland eventually dropped the explicit mention of culture and conflict.

SUTHERLAND'S THEORY OF DIFFERENTIAL ASSOCIATION

1. Criminal behavior is learned. Crime and deviance are learned in the same way as conventional behavior.
2. Criminal behavior is learned in interaction with other persons in a process of communication.
3. The principal part of the learning of criminal behavior occurs within intimate personal groups. Sutherland emphasized the primary group as the chief source of social learning. Impersonal agencies of communication (e.g., films, newspapers, and other media) play a relatively unimportant part in the specific process of deviant learning.
4. When criminal behavior is learned, the learning includes techniques of committing the crime (which are sometimes very complicated and sometimes very simple) and the specific direction of motives, drives, rationalizations, and attitudes. Deviant attitudes and motives prepare the way for the movement into a deviant career.
5. The specific direction of motives and drives is learned from definitions of legal codes as favorable and unfavorable. Values in modern society may be contradictory, conflicting, or ambiguous. Legal codes reflect value splits, and, for some groups, encourage positive attitudes toward breaking the law.
6. A person becomes deviant because of an excess of definitions favorable to violation of law over definitions unfavorable to violation of law. This is the principle of *differential association*. It refers to the "counteracting forces" between criminal and anticriminal association. Sutherland believed that the crucial conditions for entrance into deviance were contact with criminal persons and codes, and exclusion from conventional patterns.
7. Differential associations may vary in frequency, duration, priority, and intensity.
8. The process of learning criminal behavior by association with criminal and anticriminal patterns involves all of the mechanisms that are involved in other learning.
9. Although criminal behavior is an expression of general needs and values, it is not explained by those general needs and values, since noncriminal behavior is an expression of the same needs and values. This position runs counter to the poverty-causes-crime notion, which views criminality as an expression of economic want.

Source: Edwin H. Sutherland and Donald R. Cressey (1978). *Principles of Criminology.* Philadelphia: J.P. Lippincott.

This may seem rather obvious, but it goes against the idea, prominent since Lombroso, that criminals are essentially different from noncriminals. In fact, as late as the 1950s, a well-known criminologist, Sheldon Glueck, criticized Sutherland on just these grounds. According to Glueck, since criminal behavior was "antisocial," those who committed it had not been "socialized" to *any* culture. Consider Glueck's picture of the young criminal: "Unsocialized, untamed, and uninstructed, the child resorts to lying . . . hatred, theft, aggression, attack . . . in its early attempts of self-expression and ego formation."[12]

Sutherland took a sharply different view. He continued to reject the idea that criminals were somehow abnormal or deficient. Crime, according to Sutherland, is not some nearly instinctive, unsocialized act. It is learned behavior. Law-abiding behavior, street crime, "white-collar crime"*—they are all learned. It is here that Sutherland begins the nine-point statement of his theory (see box).

Learning and Meaning

By saying that behavior, even criminal behavior, is learned, Sutherland is saying quite a lot. From the sociological point of view, behavior is like language. It is not just an action; it also has a "meaning." When we learn a word, we learn not only how to make the sound—we also learn what the sound means. Similarly, when we learn some behavior, we learn more than just how to do it. We learn what that behavior "means"; that is, we learn the ideas that people in our society have about it. For example, the clothes we wear do more than just keep us warm. They are part of a meaning system. When people worry about being "overdressed" or "underdressed" for some event, they are not talking about how warm or cold they will be but whether their clothes will be appropriate in a symbolic sense. We don't wear a bathing suit to a job interview.

More important, part of the meaning for some item of behavior is not just how it is done but *why* it is done. We learn a set of ideas, attitudes, and even feelings that allow us to repeat the act. Other people play an important part in this process, even if they are not consciously "teaching." They explain, make suggestions, help us conquer doubts, and give encouragement. This function of other people applies to both conventional and law-breaking behavior. Why, for example, do you go to school now that it is no longer compulsory? As a child, you may even have complained about having to go; perhaps later in your career as a student you wondered why you were staying in school. At these times, the culture—in the form of parents, friends, teachers—explains the motives and attitudes that justify going to school. You have probably learned these ideas so well that if somebody were to ask you now why you are in school, you probably could give a convincing, and predictable, answer about the value of education.

In a similar way, people who commit crimes learn the "motives, drives, rationalizations, and attitudes" (Sutherland's point 4) that allow them to perform that behavior. Many studies of criminals—muggers, drug users, armed robbers, professional murderers—find that during their first crimes, the perpetrators felt afraid. However, they overcame their reluctance in the same way that students overcome their doubts about school. The crime and the decision to commit it usually occur in a group, with the more experienced members showing the novices how things are done and helping them

---

* Sutherland, incidentally, coined this phrase and was one of the first sociologists to study the topic.

over rough spots. Even so, the novices may still feel uneasy after the crime, and it takes the reassurances of others (and the absence of negative consequences) to convince them that the behavior was worthwhile. It is only after several crimes that they begin to become "hardened criminals," who have put aside conventional ideas about crime.[13]

This is not to suggest that school and crime are morally equivalent; only that the same normal social process—the same evolution of ideas, attitudes, and feelings—occurs in each. Of course, crime, by definition, is against the law. Schooling is required by law. Perhaps dating is a better example, since no written law requires it. Children of eight or nine may make fun of the kid who shows an attraction to the opposite sex. A few years a later, however, they must learn to reverse this attitude, and this learning resembles the way young criminals overcome their initial reluctance about crime. Social pressures cause people to do something (mugging, dating) that left alone they might prefer not to do. You may already be familiar with how it works. First dates (and first muggings) are frequently group events so that the others can keep the novice from making too many mistakes. Afterwards, others may discuss the date with the person, trying to convince him or her that what felt like a frightening and unnerving experience was really a lot of fun, or at least that it will be fun "once you get the hang of it."

In other words, people come to have different views of the same situation. One person may see it as a source of discomfort and even humiliation; another may see it as an opportunity for social and perhaps physical enjoyment. But in either case, they have *learned* their view with the help of others. This learning of different **definitions** of a situation is the key to Sutherland's theory of crime. Suppose you are in a store, waiting to buy something, but the clerk is out of sight in the back of the store. Although you realize that it might now be possible to shoplift an item or two, your principal reaction would probably be to define this situation as an inconvenience: having to wait to pay. But some people might define it primarily as a chance to steal. This is what Sutherland means in point 6 by "an excess of definitions favorable to violation of law over definitions unfavorable to violation of law."

Evaluating Differential Association Theory

Over the years, differential association theory has come in for its share of criticism, and in response, some criminologists influenced by Sutherland have made their own modifications while keeping some of the basic approach that Sutherland laid down. For example, **social learning theory** uses well-established psychological principles of conditioning to explain how criminal behavior is learned. According to this approach, people learn criminal behaviors and ideas through the same mechanisms that laboratory animals learn to press a bar or turn right in a maze—through "reinforcement." If a person's criminal behavior meets with the approval, affection, or respect of other people, these social rewards will reinforce the behavior.[14] Even with this modification, differential association theory has its shortcomings. For example, suppose that two brothers grow up in the same environment—same parents, same friends, etc.; yet one becomes a criminal, while the other does not. How can the theory of differential association explain these different outcomes?

One way of resolving the problem is to refer to the statement in point 7 that "associations may vary in their frequency, duration, priority and intensity." We might then say that the criminal associations of one brother had a greater "priority and intensity." If we probe into the criminal brother's past, we might find that he did feel more strongly tied to his criminal friends than did his brother. Their associations merely looked the same to an outsider; internally, one brother was giving his criminal associations much more intensity. One criminologist has developed this idea into a theory of **differential identification**; that is, who you *associate* with is not as important as who you *identify* yourself with. A boy growing up in a largely law-abiding area may still identify himself with Al Capone.[15] If we look closely enough, say these theorists, we can find the pattern of associations that lead to crime.

Putting the matter in these terms—that associations or reinforcements or identifications *lead to* crime—makes these ideas sound like theories of cause. Sutherland explicitly phrases it that way: "A person becomes delinquent *because* . . ." Yet speculation about the intensity of association or identification or the balance of definitions is frequently an after-the-fact explanation masquerading as a prediction. In fact, points 6 and 7 provide an escape clause, a heads-I-win-tails-you-lose gimmick, that allows the theory to "predict" or at least explain any outcome. If someone commits a crime, we can always say that he had an excess of criminal definitions; if he does not commit the crime, we can say that he had an excess of noncriminal definitions. Then we can search the person's history for the associations or reinforcements that led to those definitions. And of course, we will be able to find them.

However, these explanations point to the central weakness of the theory. Used this way, it is not "falsifiable", i.e., there is no way to prove it wrong. In principle, a theory should be testable. A theory says, given these conditions, I predict this specific outcome. If the prediction is right, the test supports the theory. If the prediction is wrong, the test serves to falsify the theory. But if a theory can—after the fact—"predict" *any* outcome, it can never be disproved.

A real test of Sutherland's theory would have to have a way of measuring beforehand the quantity of criminal and noncriminal definitions each person had, and then seeing whether people with more criminal definitions committed more crimes. But as yet, nobody has come up with any such measurement.[16]

A second sort of criticism of differential association theory centers on the more practical question of policy. Even if every word written by Sutherland and his colleagues were 100 percent accurate, would the theory still provide a basis for preventing or reducing crime?[17] Of course, a theory may be true even if it cannot be applied. But in fact, there have been attempts to put Sutherland's ideas to work.

Noble Experiments

Impossible though it may be to use the ideas of differential association on a grand scale to reduce the crime rates of a nation or city, the principles may still be used to change individual criminals. For example, from the standpoint of differential association theory, sending someone to prison is usually a good way to increase his criminality. In prison a person lives isolated from law-abiding ideas and in constant association with criminal ideas. For this reason, criminal justice systems have often tried to keep offenders out of the system. Many states have special facilities for first-time offenders to keep them away from "hardened criminals." These programs, however, merely try to reduce the offender's criminal associations; they do nothing to increase his "definitions unfavorable to violation of law."

A few programs have made the heroic effort to change delinquent ways of thinking. In the 1960s, two such programs were carried out, complete with control groups so that their results could be scientifically evaluated. The juvenile offenders in this program spent three hours a day in group discussions designed to change their ideas about crime. With one adult as a nondirective leader, the boys would discuss their lives. The aim was to get them to see that crime was not worth the risk and that brighter futures awaited those who stayed out of trouble. This sounds a bit corny. After all, these boys had committed such crimes as burglary, auto theft, and robbery. They would hardly be persuaded by sermons and rap groups. However, the authors assure us, the group discussions worked. After several weeks, the boys became convinced and even took an active part in passing these noncriminal ideas along to newcomers in the group. The control group, who resembled the others in age, background, criminal history, and so on, received probation—with no group obligations.

Here is a real test of differential association theory. The daily discussions had changed the boys' associations and their ideas about crime. If the theory is correct, the boys in the experiment should have become less criminal than the control group. The results were somewhat ambiguous: In the year after the program ended, 80 percent of the group boys had no recorded delinquency. However, the figure for the control group was the same. About 80 percent of the boys who had *not* gone to the special groups also had no further recorded delinquency. This result seems to contradict differential association theory. Or, to put it more bluntly, the theory (and the experiment derived from it) didn't work.

These studies did, however, turn up one fact which does support differential association theory: During the time that the boys were attending the groups, they committed fewer crimes than did the control group of boys on probation. It was only *after* the program ended that the differences between experimentals and controls faded.

So you can interpret the results of these programs either way. A critic of differential association theory could argue that despite their changed definitions and ideas, the experimental group turned out just as criminal as the control group. A supporter of the theory could respond that the theory worked: As long as the boys were in "intimate personal groups" that favored law-abiding behavior, they were less criminal. When they went back to their previous associations, they became no different from the control groups. This line of argument may save the theory. Unfortunately, it does little to turn the theory into an effective policy.

Even if Sutherland's theory has not led to any sure-fire method of rehabilitation or crime prevention, and even if it adds little to our ability to predict trends in crime rates, it has nevertheless laid the groundwork for *understanding* crime and criminals. Sutherland's theory urges researchers to understand the world the way the criminal sees it. Following Sutherland, researchers have gotten inside the world of a wide variety of criminals and have come to see them not as the inert objects of abstract social forces, nor as monsters gratifying their animal impulses, but as people who act on the basis of a certain view of the world. It may be true that this kind of understanding has not added much to our power to predict or change criminal behavior, but supporters of Sutherland would argue that crime policies that are not based on such understanding are doomed to failure.

To sum up: in the 1930s sociological thinking about crime had moved far away from the "social pathology" outlook of earlier decades. By looking at rates of crime rather than at individual criminals, sociologists had been able to apply ideas about social structure, social change, social organization, norms, and values to the study of crime. In addition, empirical evidence was confirming the notion that crime was more prevalent in the lower social classes. By the 1940s, two lines of thinking had developed to explain the class-crime link. Structural or strain theories (e.g. Merton's) emphasized the conflict between culturally prescribed goals and socially distributed means. Cultural theories focused on the ways in which people learn ideas that lead them to commit crime. In the next decade, sociological thinkers tried to combine the insights of these two points of view.

CLASS AND CULTURE

Although Sutherland and Merton have major differences in their approach to crime, they both wrote mainly about rational, economic crime. Merton—with his means-ends analysis—assumes that people break the law largely for economic reasons. And Sutherland's criminals—whether thieves or executives—usually have economic gain as their principal motive. "Senseless" crime does not figure heavily in either theory. Of course, when these theories appeared (the late 1930s and 1940s), violent crime and crime in general were at a relatively low ebb in America.

The next major contribution to criminological theory—at least in America—came in the mid- to late-1950s and had a slightly different focus. First, these theories stressed juvenile crime; and second, they gave the idea of "culture" a central place in their explanations.

There may be some historical reasons for this shift in emphasis. For one thing, the 1950s saw a reawakening of concern with juvenile gangs. American cities have always had gangs—young men who hang out together and sometimes break the law. But during the 1940s, World War II took many of these young men off the streets, and the trend away from gangs continued even in the immediate postwar years. But during the 1950s, juvenile delinquency once again began to attract public attention. There was nothing basically new about this concern. Parents in America have, since colonial days, felt threatened by their children's independence and seeming rejection of parental ways. But the 1950s may have exaggerated the usual anxieties, if only because of the sheer numbers of kids. Even in the early 1950s, when the kids at the leading edge of the baby boom were barely counting their ages in two digits, they nevertheless were making an impact on society. Products aimed at them began to occupy more of the culture; there was a lot of money to be made selling Davy Crockett hats and hula hoops. Before long, things took a more ominous tone. Movies like *Rebel Without a Cause* or *The Wild One* drew large audiences by depicting rebellious, destructive, sullen young men. The news media gave more attention to juvenile delinquency, and one of the most popular Broadway shows of the decade—*West Side Story*—was set in the context of juvenile gang warfare.

The Delinquent Subculture

Sociologists were not deaf to these cultural messages and responded with their analyses of this "new" old problem. In 1955, Albert K. Cohen published a book called *Delinquent Boys*. As the book's title implies, Cohen was looking not at career criminals or white-collar criminals or people who stole in order to get much-needed money, but at "boys," whose crimes consisted chiefly of vandalism or fighting or other low-profit activities. "Nonutilitarian, malicious, and negativistic" are the adjectives Cohen used to describe this behavior. Such seemingly senseless crime seriously challenges Merton's theory of crime. Bashing storefronts or school windows or other boys hardly fits with any of Merton's adaptations: There is no financial gain (innovation), and while the boys are not following accepted norms, their behavior does not look like retreatism or rebellion as Merton describes these adaptations.

More to the point are the ideas of differential association and cultural transmission introduced by Chicago sociologists like Sutherland. In fact, Cohen offers his theory as a fuller version of a well-known, everyday explanation for juvenile delinquency: "My Johnny is really a good boy but got to running around with the wrong bunch." The idea of a "wrong bunch" is at the heart of Cohen's theory. It is part of a more general phenomenon Cohen calls **the delinquent subculture**.

A subculture is a group of people within a society who share a set of ideas and ways of doing things that differs from the ways of the dominant society. A subculture provides its members not just with a sense of belonging but with solutions to certain problems. The delinquent subculture, as Cohen describes it, differs in at least two crucial ways from nondelinquent ways of life. For one thing, it is "negativistic." Delinquents enjoy activities which break rules or inconvenience other people. "There is an element of active spite and malice, contempt and ridicule, challenge and defiance." In addition, the subculture is based on "short-run hedonism" (i.e., pleasure-seeking). That is, "there is little interest in long-run goals" or anything that requires consistent practice or study.

How can a subculture based on nonutilitarian, malicious crime solve the problems of life? To answer this, Cohen reminds us of two facts in addition to the low-profit, negativistic quality of much juvenile crime. First, juveniles usually commit their crimes in groups, rather than alone. That is, delinquency is not merely a matter of individual maladjustment or psychological problems. And second, juvenile crime and the delinquent subculture are found primarily in "the lower socioeconomic strata of our society." But while he recognizes that social class is obviously a factor in delinquency, the lack of money, in Cohen's view, is not the basic problem. If it were, then lower-class boys would commit crimes that were more profitable. Instead, the delinquent subculture forms in order to provide a solution to the problems of *status*—"respect in the eyes of one's fellows."

Middle-Class and Lower-Class Culture

People gain the respect and recognition of others by living up to some set of standards. In America, the dominant standards of the society are middle-class values and norms. As these norms apply to teenagers, they emphasize ambition and success, academic achievement, responsibility for oneself, delay of gratification, control of physical aggression, and respect for property. While these norms are felt to some extent at all levels of society, the realities of life for people in the lower class often require them to live by a different set of norms. Ambition and planning must give way to the pressing needs of the moment. People must depend more on others. They will be less eager to leave the group to go off on their own, even if such a move might mean a step up the socioeconomic ladder. This group orientation also means that the middle-class ethic of responsibility gives way to an "ethic of reciprocity," or sharing.

In addition, working-class parents and middle-class parents raise their children differently. Working-class child-rearing is generally looser, less systematic. Other children are a more important part of the child's life, and the parents' control is less total. Where middle-class parents punish children by withholding love, working-class parents are more likely to use physical punishment, which does not create the same kind of constant striving found in the middle-class child.

In other words, there are subtle but important differences between the middle class and working class in the kinds of behavior that they encourage and reward in their children. These cultural differences pervade social life, and school is no exception. School, regardless of the social class of its students, is a thoroughly middle-class institution. The values of the school—enforced by middle-class teachers and administrators—are middle-class values: achievement, responsibility, control of physical aggression and activity ("Sit still!"). For middle-class boys, school merely repeats the values and norms of home life. But for working-class boys, school presents a culture different from the one where they live. Regardless of these children's native intelligence, the values they unconsciously live by are a barrier to gaining rewards in school. The message the school sends (intentionally or not) to the working-class or lower-class boy is that he is inferior. And it is a message he cannot ignore.

Adaptations

Faced with the daily problem of confronting an institution that defines him as inferior, the working-class boy can adapt in one of three ways. He can strive for middle-class goals (like college) or he can accept his lower status but not commit crimes, hanging out with his friends and eventually taking whatever kind of job comes along. Both of these solutions accept the superiority of middle-class norms. The delinquent solution, however, challenges the assumption that middle-class ways are better. By the "negativism" of their delinquency, these boys are saying that it is the middle-class norms and institutions that are inferior. "The delinquent subculture takes its norms from the larger (middle-class) culture, but it turns them upside down." If middle-class norms define something as good, the delinquent sub-culture defines it as bad, and the subculture reinforces the idea through words and actions. Since it is middle-class values that threaten their self-esteem, these delinquents reward and esteem each other for behavior that attacks the symbols of the middle class: vandalism (schools are a favorite target); terrorizing "good" kids; stealing things not for their value but "for the hell of it," because it is "wrong."

Walter Miller and Lower-Class Culture

Cohen's theory was only one of several influential theories that used the notion of subculture. However, not everyone agreed that the delinquent subculture was a reaction to middle-class standards or an inversion of them. In an article published in 1958—three years after Cohen's *Delinquent Boys*—Walter Miller challenged Cohen's idea that lower-class delinquents cared deeply about middle-class values and therefore had to act out their frustrations in negativistic crime. Yes, there was a delinquent subculture, Miller said, but it stood independent of middle-class culture. Instead, it drew its ideas and institutions from lower-class ways of life.

The title of Miller's essay, "Lower-Class Culture as a Generating Milieu of Gang Delinquency," sounds a bit awkward, but it concisely sums up his argument: first, that there is a distinct lower-class culture in America; second, that this culture is an environment (milieu) that causes gang delinquency to flourish.

Over the course of years of research, Miller and his co-workers spent many hours hanging around juvenile gangs in poor areas of cities, listening, observing, and talking with them. From this research, Miller concludes that poor people do not think about the world in the same way that middle-class people do. It is not a question of different "values," certainly not in the way that Cohen saw delinquents as reversing middle-class values; nor even in the sense of not valuing things like money or education or happiness. The differences lie not so much in what people think is good but in what people think *about*—the mental categories people used to perceive their world and themselves. To these categories Miller gives the name **focal concerns**.[18]

Focal Concerns

A focal concern of middle-class Americans is success or achievement. Obviously, they value success; they almost worship it. Miller's point, though, is not that for the middle-class, achievement is a value. Rather, it is a focal concern. It dominates their style of thinking. They tend to judge people and situations in terms of their potential for achievement. Middle-class people even see their personal lives in these terms: They talk about "working" on a marriage that "is going nowhere" in order to have a "successful" relationship. Lists of best-selling books always have a few titles on self-improvement and career advancement. Parents worry about their children's performance in similar terms: Is the child keeping up? Is the child behind or ahead?*

For lower-class Americans, according to Miller, achievement is not this kind of focal concern. "Trouble," on the other hand, is. " 'Getting into trouble' and 'staying out of trouble' represent major issues for male and female, adults and children." Trouble, for women, means "sexual involvement with disadvantageous consequences"; for men it often means fighting or criminal behavior. A mother, for instance, might want to know of her daughter's fiancé not how successful his career will be, but how much "trouble" he's likely to bring. Parents will ask of their schoolchildren not "Are you getting good grades?" but "Are you staying out of trouble?"

The other focal concerns of the lower class, as Miller outlines them, are:

—Toughness: "The almost obsessive lower-class concern with 'masculinity.' "
—Smartness: This is not scholarly achievement or knowledge, but rather "street smarts," the ability to outfox, outwit, or "con" others.
—Excitement: Lower-class culture has its own rhythm of life. Middle-class life runs on a regular rhythm, work alternating with home life or relaxation in a fairly even way. By contrast, the rhythm of lower-class life consists of long periods of boredom punctuated by brief periods of excitement. Lower-class people, especially men, spend a lot of time just "hanging out," waiting for the opportunity for some more risky adventure.
—Fate: Lower-class people have much less of the sense that they are ultimately in control of their lives. Middle-class people tend to believe that what happens to people in life depends on their own abilities and effort. Lower-class people see life more in terms of fate—either you're lucky or you're not.
—Autonomy: In lower-class life, there is a strong resentment of external controls ("No one's gonna push me around"). Autonomy also involves independence or a denial of dependence ("I can take care of myself").

Covert Commitment

Even if we accept this picture of lower-class culture, we must still ask how it promotes delinquency. Trouble may be a concern, but why should it lead

* The strength of this focal concern seems to be peculiarly American. European visitors to America (who are themselves middle-class and who meet mostly with middle-class Americans) have long been struck by this preoccupation with success, which apparently is not so strong in Europe.

to crime? Why not just stay out of trouble? As for gang delinquency, why not just demonstrate autonomy and stay out of gangs?

In response, Miller says that it was precisely to avoid this theoretical problem that he uses the idea of focal concern rather than the usual sociological concept of value. A value can have only one positive side. To talk of focal concerns, however, allows us to see the more complex reality: Either side of each dimension can be positive, depending on circumstances. Most of the time, it is rather obvious which side is positive. On the trouble dimension, getting into trouble is bad, staying out of trouble is good. Therefore, people usually maintain an "overt" (or open) commitment to law-abiding behavior. They say that they want to stay out of trouble. But, says Miller, they may also share a "covert commitment" to the other end of the dimension—that is, a hidden or even unconscious attraction to the negative side (law-breaking behavior).

The dimension of autonomy provides a good example. Lower-class males will voice strong commitment to independence and freedom from constraint. But what are we to make of the delinquent in "reform school" who, with only a week left to his sentence, tries to escape? He gets caught, of course, and receives an additional sentence of several months. In Miller's view, he is expressing an *overt* commitment to autonomy ("They can't keep me locked up here"), but a *covert* commitment to dependence, since his behavior has the predictable effect of keeping him even longer in a state of confinement and dependence.

The same is true of trouble. " 'Getting into trouble,' " says Miller, "achieves several sets of valued ends."[19] It demonstrates a boy's toughness, smartness, and autonomy, as well as his capacity for excitement. And getting caught need not be evidence of his lack of these qualities, since it was just "bad luck" (fate).

Lower-Class Institutions

A culture is more than just a set of ideas or ways of looking at the world. It also consists of institutions that organize people's behavior. Institutions differ from one society to another. For example, all societies must educate their youth, but the institutions for education vary widely from one time and place to another. Had you lived in America two centuries ago, you would probably have been apprenticed at an early age to learn some trade, rather than have gone to school for a minimum of 10 or 12 years as you do today. Even in our own day, different countries vary in the way they organize such institutions as education, religion, health care, and family.

Even within American society, there are differences in institutions from one social class to another. For the middle-class, the most important institutions are those of family, work, and—for the child—school. In the lower-class, there is another institution that plays a crucial part in people's lives: the one-sex peer group. In Miller's view, it is the principal institution of lower-class life. "Lower-class society may be pictured as comprising a set of age-graded one-sex peer groups which constitute the major psychic focus and reference group for those over 12 or 13." Lower-class people usually spend their free time (and often their work time) with groups of the same sex. For women and girls, this means friends or especially female relatives; for men, it means "hanging out with the guys"; for boys, it is the juvenile gang.

These groups are the heart of lower-class social life, more so than work or school or even family. Young men and women may get married (or as Miller puts it, "form temporary marital alliances"), but after trying out the more middle-class two-sex family arrangement, they "gravitate back to the more 'comfortable' one-sex grouping."

The gang has two important functions. First, it gives a sense of belonging; second, it awards status. For both of these, the boy must show that he possesses those qualities that are valued within his culture. The more a boy can show that he has the right stuff, the higher his status in the group. For the lower-class male, the right stuff consists of toughness, smartness, capacity for excitement and trouble, etc. Younger males—teenagers—share the additional concern of "adultness." For these boys, drinking, sex, driving, and ready cash take on a special importance, not just because they are pleasurable in themselves, but because they are the symbols of adult status.

It is easy to see how the focal concerns and the institutions of lower-class life foster delinquency. The crimes that gang members commit (gang fights, mugging, purse-snatching, shoplifting, auto theft) are ways of achieving status by living up to the standards of the peer group. And both this peer group and its standards are versions of institutions and focal concerns that exist throughout lower-class culture.

In understanding juvenile crime in this way, Miller is also arguing *against* two other views of delinquency. First, he is saying that delinquency is *not* a reaction against middle-class culture. Lower-class kids violate the law not for the sake of being bad. Rather, some of the things that they must do in following their own culture just happen to be illegal. (As Miller puts it, "The 'demanded' response to certain situations recurrently engendered within lower-class culture involves the commission of illegal acts.")

Second, delinquency is not the product of some kind of individual deficiency. These delinquents "are not psychopaths, nor physically or mentally 'defective'; in fact, since the corner group supports and enforces a rigorous set of standards which demand a high degree of fitness and personal competence, it tends to recruit from the most 'able' members of the community."

Opportunity Theory Revisited.   It is interesting to compare Miller's cultural theory with Merton's theory of anomie. Both seek to explain the prevalence of crime in the lower class, but the pictures these two sociologists offer of American society have some important differences. For example, in

Merton's terms, thieves are not just people who have learned their skills and ideas from others around them; they are "innovators." Merton's essay suggests an image of the isolated individual trying to make his way through life with some goals "society" has put in his head and with his opportunities severely limited (though Merton never shows exactly what life without those opportunities looks like). Miller, in contrast, paints a richly detailed and insightful portrait of lower-class culture. He pays attention, as Merton does not, to the face-to-face groups a person meets with every day—family and peers—which socialize him or her to their values. Merton, on the other hand, never makes it clear just how people acquire their culture's values. His picture of people moving individually through a great, unified, American culture seems almost simple-minded.

My point is not that Miller is "right" and Merton is "wrong," but rather that each essay leaves out something important. Miller, as you may have noticed, leaves out the question of money (or, as a sociologist would put it, of "socially structured inequality"). Most people would think that one big difference between lower-class and middle-class people is that lower-class people have far less money, but Miller does not find this fact important enough to bother mentioning. This omission is a major shortcoming in his theory, for most of the "focal concerns" are not just arbitrary beliefs chosen at random. They are grounded in reality. Lower-class people are concerned about "trouble" because trouble is an ever-present fact of lower-class life. The lower-class belief in "fate" is realistic in much the same way: Lower-class people do, in fact, have far less control over their lives than do middle-class people. To ignore this reality is to "blame the victim" by faulting poor people for choosing the wrong values. The fact is that middle-class values would be of little practical use in meeting the realities of lower-class life.

With all this emphasis on culture or subculture, the issue of opportunity seemed to have disappeared. In 1960, however, two years after Miller's essay, Richard Cloward and Lloyd Ohlin published a book, *Delinquency and Opportunity*, that helped bridge the gap between opportunity theories and cultural theories.

Subcultures and Opportunities

Cloward and Ohlin also start from the assumption that delinquency is primarily a lower-class phenomenon. Not only is delinquency more serious in the lower class, but it receives "support and approval" from various groups there. Since a subculture is a group that values (supports and approves of) particular forms of behavior, and since these groups (such as gangs) support and approve of delinquency, then we can talk about a **delinquent subculture**. Most delinquency, of course, takes place outside of delinquent subcultures. Most kids who break the law nevertheless believe that crime is wrong (just as most students who glance at someone else's paper during an exam probably also think that cheating is wrong). They have not substituted a set of criminal norms and values for the conventional ones. The delinquent subculture, on the other hand, is based on just such a rejection of conventional norms. Even though the delinquent subculture includes only a small proportion of juveniles, it is important to understand the delinquent subculture because these youths account for a disproportionate share of the most serious crime.

Cloward and Ohlin reject Miller's notion that the delinquent subculture is just one more version of lower-class culture. They argue that no large part of American society, not even the lower class, has a set of values which supports or approves of crimes like burglary, robbery, murder, or drug addiction. Cloward and Ohlin also reject the idea that members of delinquent subcultures are psychopathic or in any other way deficient or unable to meet middle-class standards. "The available data support the contention that the basic endowments of delinquents, such as intelligence, physical strength, and agility, are the equal of or greater than those of their nondelinquent peers."

Cloward and Ohlin instead start with the same ideas Merton proposed: first, that modern, industrial society—especially that of the United States—"emphasizes common or universal success goals"; second, that "structural barriers" come between lower-class youths and the pursuit of these goals. The most important means to success is education, but economic pressures force lower-class youths out of the educational system. They drop out not because they are less intelligent, but because they are poorer. "In a family that can scarcely afford food, shelter, and clothing, pressure is exerted on the young to leave school early in order to secure employment and thereby help the family." The result of this clash between goals and means is "intense frustration" that can lead to crime.

Opportunity—Legitimate and Illegitimate

So far, their analysis echoes Merton's. But while Merton gives the impression that the lower-class person *individually* chooses innovation or retreatism, Cloward and Ohlin recognize that deviant behavior, too, has its own social organization. That is, not only are there structures of legitimate opportunity (schools, colleges, jobs), there also are structures for *illegitimate* opportunity. And not all lower-class people will have the same access to those illegitimate opportunities.

Cloward and Ohlin identify three distinct types of delinquent subcultures that evolve as adaptations to the lack of legitimate opportunity:

> the criminal subculture, based on economic crime as a source of income
> the conflict subculture, based on fighting as a way of gaining status
> the retreatist subculture, based on drugs as a means of detachment from conventional society.

The fate of a lower-class boy with few chances for legitimate success will depend on the kind of subculture available in his neighborhood.

The Criminal Subculture. In some lower-class neighborhoods, there is a flourishing criminal subculture. Crime here is *organized* as a way of making money. Some forms of crime (e.g., gambling) are run almost like businesses. Even predatory crimes like burglary have an organization that coordinates different roles. A burglar who works alone, outside of a criminal subculture, runs great risks and is not always sure of a large haul. Much safer and more profitable is a system in which there are "fingermen," who tip off the thief to big "scores"; fences, who provide a safe place to convert stolen goods to cash; and, should anything unfortunate occur, bail bonds-men, lawyers, and perhaps corruptible police officers, district attorneys, or judges.

In a neighborhood with a well-developed criminal subculture, boys may see crime as a means to financial success. They may look up to successful criminals as role models. Boys may even serve the equivalent of an apprenticeship, with older criminals teaching them about the world of crime. In such an environment, say Cloward and Ohlin, even what looks like "malicious, negativistic, nonutilitarian" behavior may really be an attempt to catch the eye of adults in the criminal subculture.

The Conflict Subculture. The criminal subculture thrives mostly in neighborhoods that, although poor, also have a certain amount of stability. In less stable neighborhoods, crime, like the rest of life, tends to be less organized. The population is more transient, and people have fewer ties to each other or to the community as a whole. A person may turn to crime, but the kind of unorganized economic crime that he can commit will be less profitable and less protected. He will make less money, and he will spend more time in prison. In such neighborhoods, the young, according to Cloward, "are deprived of *both* conventional and criminal opportunity."

Cut off from both legitimate and illegitimate resources for economic gain, young men must fall back on the resources they do have—resources which are not part of any organization. They can win status primarily on the basis of personal qualities. Thus, interpersonal contests—from basketball to "the dozens" (a "rapping" game involving verbal ability, quick wit, and a repertoire of clever insults)—make up an important part of life in these groups. In interactions like these, income and "connections" count for nothing.

Obviously, there is another type of contest in which a youth can show his character and thereby gain status: fighting. Through violence, young men can demonstrate not just physical skill but courage or "heart"—a "willingness to risk injury or death in the search for 'rep.' " In some neighborhoods, violence becomes the primary basis of the status system for young men. This is what Cloward and Ohlin call the "conflict subculture."

In poor, disorganized neighborhoods dominated by the conflict subculture, adults can do little to restrain youth violence. In the more organized criminal subculture neighborhoods, the stability and organization of the community keep violence in check. The criminal subculture, which controls access to the resources for (illegitimate) success, has little use for gang violence. Since the youth here seek acceptance in this subculture, they refrain from excessive violence. However, in the disorganized neighborhood, adults do not control the resources to which youths might aspire. Consequently, neither in the family nor at the community level can adults control the violence of the conflict subculture.

The Retreatist Subculture.   In both of these delinquent subcultures (criminal and conflict), late adolescence is a crucial period. The criminal subculture does not have room for every boy who wants to join. Those who lack the necessary skill, character, or connections will find themselves excluded. In the conflict subculture also, some boys may not have what it takes, or they may just not like fighting and its sometimes unpleasant consequences. Older boys—even those who excel at fighting—face an additional problem: Violence may bring status among 15-year-olds, who think that they can prove their manhood in one-on-one or gang fights. But this attitude and behavior will be inappropriate for the older youth. After all, by virtue of being 18 or 19, he *is* a man; he should not need to resort to "kid stuff" like fighting in order to prove it.

What can become of the older teenagers who are rejected by the criminal world? Or those who have outgrown gang fighting? These young men have reached the point where they are "double failures," unable to make it in either the legitimate or the illegitimate world. Something has to change.

Many youths as they approach their 20s replace "youthful preoccupations" with "more individual concerns about work, future, a 'steady' girl, and the like." (Given their chances for success, we might classify them as ritualists, though Cloward and Ohlin do not mention this.) But some of these young men will join the retreatist subculture, a culture based on the use of drugs and on being "cool." Cloward and Ohlin, writing in 1960, identified addictive drugs as but one of the many sources of "kicks" (i.e., "ecstatic experiences") sought by retreatists. Other kicks included marijuana and alcohol, but also jazz music and "unusual sexual experiences" (Cloward and Ohlin do not go into detail). As for money, retreatists ("cats" as Cloward and Ohlin call them, using the lingo of that era) will do anything that does not resemble work. They hustle. They beg, borrow, steal, pimp, deal drugs, run petty con games. It's a way to get by, and it's a way to gain status. In the world of the retreatist subculture, kicks and hustling provide the bases for winning the admiration of others.

While Cloward and Ohlin's theory sounds plausible, empirical evidence was not overwhelming. It did offer an explanation for a fact that troubled other theories and popular notions about crime and drugs. According to the conventional wisdom, drug use led to crime. Yet most drug users had been stealing *before* they got involved with drugs. Cloward and Ohlin's the-ory also got some support in findings about the distribution of delinquency within the city. In some cities, neighborhoods with a criminal subculture may actually have fairly low rates of gang violence.[20]* But other evidence contradicts this theory. Most gangs do not specialize in one kind of crime. Boys in gangs drink and take drugs; they steal and vandalize; they fight and commit muggings.

Opportunity and Policy. Regardless of its lack of empirical support, *Delinquency and Opportunity* did have the advantage of offering recom-mendations for policy. The message was clear, just from the book's title. If boys move into delinquent subcultures because of barriers to legitimate opportunity, then we should remove those barriers and provide that op-portunity. If violent gangs arise because neighborhoods are disorganized, then we must organize those lower-class communities.

In fact, besides writing up their theory, Cloward and Ohlin also had de-signed a program for New York's Lower East Side, based on their ideas. Named Mobilization For Youth (MFY), it called for improved education, ex-panded job opportunities, community organization, and special social-work services for adolescents as well as for other individuals and families.

Their proposal came at the right time. The new President, John F. Ken-nedy, gave it his support, and eventually the federal government, New York City, and the Ford Foundation provided a three-year grant of $12.5 million (nearly $100 million in current dollars, and a lot of money at the time). At the ceremony launching the program in 1962, President Kennedy sounded very much like Cloward and Ohlin when he announced that "juvenile de-linquency is . . . really a question of young people and their opportunity."

By the time MFY went into effect, it had become part of the nationwide "War on Poverty." The most important idea in the various programs in this "war" was the Community Action Program, in which poor people themselves would help run the programs (as in the MFY plan for community-organiz-ing). Had it worked according to design, Community Action Programs would have shifted a significant amount of power from old entrenched politicians to poor people. Of course, the politicians were not going to give away their power easily. Consequently, MFY became snarled in political battles, and eventually it "sank in a sea of conflict."[21] To accommodate the various po-litical interests, MFY had to make several changes that took it further and further from the model designed by Cloward and Ohlin.

What was the outcome for crime? For whatever reasons, crime rates did not decrease; in fact, they increased. Critics see the failure of MFY as more evidence against opportunity theory. The problem, they say, is not in op-portunity structures but in the delinquents. Those who defend opportunity

---

* New Yorkers often claim that "Mafia neighborhoods" are safe neighborhoods.

theory say first of all that MFY, coming in the mid-1960s, was going against a tremendous rising tide of crime, especially juvenile crime. Given this nationwide trend, the MFY experience in New York was not so bad. In addition, because of all the changes that were forced upon it, MFY in practice was never a true test of opportunity theory. It was more like a case study in urban politics. With its more radical features compromised, MFY was also an example of the failure of halfway efforts. Unless there can be real change in the structures of power and opportunity, these critics say, piecemeal reforms will do little to reduce lower-class crime.

WHERE DO WE GO FROM HERE?

The influential criminology theories of the 1950s turned from the topic of crime in general to the more specific problem of juvenile delinquency, especially lower-class delinquency. There were probably good historical reasons for this shift in attention. For one thing, crime rates, which had fallen during the 1940s, remained fairly low (by U.S. standards) for nearly two decades following World War II. In addition, the usual candidates for causes of crime seemed to be things of the past. The great waves of immigration had ended in 1925. Urbanization had slowed as the population shifted out to the suburbs. The economy was thriving, and unemployment had decreased far below the prewar levels of the 1930s.

The apparent persistence of juvenile crime amid all this well-being called for an explanation. It was a sign of things still wrong in the society. For generally liberal sociologists, delinquency showed that not everybody was happy, that there was still a lower class, that the general affluence had bypassed many people. The poor continued to live a way of life that was all but hidden from public view, one that had its own problems and satisfactions, its own norms and values, and consequently its own high levels of crime and delinquency.

The 1960s was a decade of great turmoil and conflict. People who had previously been powerless and silent—women, blacks, youth—began to challenge the accepted authorities and the accepted truths. On a smaller scale, new viewpoints in criminology were questioning some of the certainties of sociological knowledge. Could we trust the official statistics on which theories were based? Could we even define crime, and could we study it while ignoring the officials who made and enforced the laws? Was crime really such a lower-class phenomenon as the official data claimed? Sociologists began to question basic concepts like *norm*, *value*, and *culture*. How did these ideas apply in real life? These questions, as we shall see in the next chapter, led to a radical critique of both society and conventional criminology. At the same time however, a more traditional, individual-based, and even conservative criminology was also in the making.

NOTES

1. Lambert Adolphe Jacques Quetelet (1842, 1968), *A Treatise on Man and the Development of His Faculties*, New York: B. Franklin.

2. Erich Goode (1973), *The Drug Phenomenon: Social Aspects of Drug Taking*, Indianapolis, IN: Bobbs-Merril.

3. H. R. Stout (1885), *Our Family Physician*, Peoria, IL: Henderson and Smith, pp. 333–34. Reprinted in John W. Petras (1975), *Sex: Male/Gender: Masculine*, Port Washington, NY: Alfred.

4. David Matza (1969), *Becoming Deviant*, Englewood Cliffs, NJ: Prentice-Hall.

5. Kai Erikson (1966), *Wayward Puritans*, New York: Wiley. Emile Durkheim (1895), *The Rules of Sociological Method*, trans. S. A. Solovay and J. H. Mueller (1957), Glencoe, IL: Free Press.

6. Robert Merton (1968), "Social Structure and Anomie," in *Social Theory and Social Structure*, NY; Free Press, pp. 185–214.

7. Stephen Cole (1975), "The Growth of Scientific Knowledge," in Lewis A. Coser, ed. (1975), *The Idea of Social Structure*, New York: Harcourt Brace Jovanovich, p. 175.

8. Jack Katz (1988), *Seductions of Crime: Moral and Sensual Attractions in Doing Evil*, New York: Basic Books, esp. pp. 313–17.

9. Richard A. Coleman and Lee Rainwater (1978), *Social Standing in America: New Dimensions of Class*, New York: Basic Books.

10. Peter M. Blau and Otis Dudley Duncan (1967), *The American Occupational Structure*, New York: Wiley. Robert Hauser and David L. Featherman (1978), *Opportunity and Change*, New York: Academic Press. Christopher M. Jencks, et al., *Who Gets Ahead? The Determinants of Income and Success in America*, New York: Basic Books.

11. C. Wright Mills (1943), "The Professional Ideology of Social Pathologists," *American Journal of Sociology*, vol. 69, pp. 165–80.

12. Sheldon Glueck (1956), "Theory and Fact in Criminology: A Criticism of Differential Association," *British Journal of Delinquency*, vol. 9, pp. 92–109.

13. Robert LeJeune (1977), "The Management of a Mugging," *Urban Life*, vol. 6, pp. 123–48.

14. Ronald L. Akers (1973), *Deviant Behavior: A Social Learning Approach*, Belmont, CA: Wadsworth.

15. Daniel Glaser (1956), "Criminality Theories and Behavioral Images," *American Journal of Sociology*, vol. 61, pp. 433–44.

16. Jack P. Gibbs (1987), "The State of Criminological Theory," *Criminology*, vol. 25, no. 4, pp. 821–40 (esp. p. 835).

17. James Q. Wilson (1975), *Thinking About Crime*, New York: Basic Books; Vintage Books ed. (1977), p. 53.

18. Walter B. Miller (1958), "Lower Class Culture as a Generation Milieu of Gang Delinquency," *Journal of Social Issues*, vol. 19, pp. 5–19.

19. Ibid., p. 8.

20. Irving Spergel (1964), *Racketville, Slumtown, Haulburg: An Exploratory Study of Delinquent Subcultures*, Chicago: University of Chicago Press.

21. Lamar Empey (1978), *American Delinquency: Its Meaning and Construction*, Homewood, IL: The Dorsey Press, pp. 294–300.

Sociological Theories, Part II

CHAPTER 12

CRIME AND CULTURE RECONSIDERED

THE PREVIOUS CHAPTER DISCUSSED VARIOUS CULTURAL THEORIES OF CRIME. THESE theories might disagree on exactly how the delinquent subculture is different, or the reasons that it forms, or its relationship to the conventional, law-abiding culture. Nonetheless, all these theories share the idea that crime arises and persists because group norms and values permit or encourage it. In other words, people who commit crimes believe in a different set of ideas, and these ideas precede and cause their criminal behavior.

The evidence for this conclusion comes mostly from "participant observation" research, where a researcher hangs around high-crime areas or groups and listens for people expressing ideas that tend to justify crime. Evidence gathered in this way suffers from some major flaws. First, it depends on the perceptions of the researcher. How can we know that another observer might not have heard different ideas being expressed? Second, it does not measure the two variables—culture and crime—separately. And third, even if people do voice "criminal" values and norms, does that necessarily mean that they have rejected conventional ideas?

A more convincing research study would first specify which values and norms should lead to crime; then it would discover people's values or norms; finally, it would see whether individuals, groups, or geographic areas with "pro-crime" ideas actually did commit more crime. Unfortunately, very few studies follow this pattern. In addition, it is difficult to measure such abstract notions as "values" or "norms" in a meaningful way. The studies that do try to measure values have gotten mixed results. They find that poor people, even gang members, share middle-class values and aspirations.

It shouldn't surprise us that poor people and criminals subscribe to conventional norms. After all, if cultural theories were absolutely accurate, if a significant portion of the population valued crime, and if people tried to live up to those values, then there would be far more crime than actually occurs. But in fact, most people at every social level, and even most juvenile gang members, spend most of their time in nondelinquent activity.

It is not just a question of how people spend their time. Even in the area of ideas, there is a strange mixture. Delinquents express support for conventional ideas. They look up to noncriminal culture heroes—astronauts, sports heroes, rock stars (even straight ones); they even resent being called criminals; they hope for noncriminal futures; and they admire such highly conventional qualities as honesty. Yet they can also behave and think in ways that seem to be solidly rooted in the criminal world.

"Drift" and "Neutralizations"

It was just this kind of apparent contradiction that led sociologist David Matza to the concept of "drift." Matza argues that the terms "criminal" and

Even the "worst" delinquents may share ideals and heroes from the conventional world—as one journalist discovered.

The most restrictive alternative for an under-sixteen who has been found to have committed an act which if committed by an adult would constitute a crime is one of the New York State Division for Youth's locked upstate facilities.

In one of those . . . secure facilities, Goshen, I talked with a tall, gangly boy who was sweeping the hallway between the resi-dents' rooms. Small rooms, they contain a bed, a chair, a locker for clothes and personal ef-fects, and pretty much whatever the boys want to put on their walls. Posters of basketball play-ers and rock stars mostly. A lot of Michael Jack-son.

Source: Rita Kramer (1988), *At a Tender Age: Violent Youth and Juvenile Justice,* New York: Henry Holt, p. 84.

"conventional" or "delinquent" and "nondelinquent" can be misleading when they are applied to people. We must recognize that these terms are abstract concepts that refer to sets of norms rather than to people. In the real world, most delinquents live at the border of the conventional and the criminal worlds. Delinquents exist in a state of "drift," not firmly committed to either set of norms.[1]

Since even delinquents support conventional norms, the question be-comes this: How can people violate norms which they themselves believe in? Matza's answer (contained in his book and in an earlier essay written with Gresham Sykes)[2] is that delinquents use **neutralizations** that allow exceptions to the norms. For example, if you believe that cheating on exams is not such a good thing, you might justify copying someone else's paper by saying that the professor is such a creep that he deserves to be cheated on. Thus, you have "neutralized" the norm against cheating and now feel free to steal a few answers.

Sykes and Matza identify this neutralization as "denial of victim"—the idea that certain people or institutions do not deserve the usual protection of the norms of society. This idea neutralizes norms against theft and even violence. By denial of victim, delinquents in their own minds turn stores that supposedly charge rip-off prices into fair game for theft, turn homo-sexuals into targets for assault, turn the phone company and its booths into objects of vandalism.

Sykes and Matza insist that these neutralizations are not mere ration-alizations that occur after the fact. These ideas *precede* the crime and make the crime possible. By the use of neutralizations, the person does not reject the conventional norm; he merely makes an exception in this particular case. Other neutralizations include:

Denial of responsibility: "The others made me do it"; or "I had to—it was self-defense."

Denial of injury: "Nobody was hurt"; or "It was a private quarrel"; or "The graffiti makes the building look better"; or "The store is insured."

Condemning the condemners: "The police are corrupt, so why shouldn't I steal, too?"

Appeal to higher loyalties: "I had to help my buddy in the fight."

Seeing delinquents in this way makes them seem more like you and me, since we, too, neutralize norms we believe in ("the 55-mph limit on this road is a good thing, but I have a one o'clock appointment"). Even the law recognizes these exceptions. For instance, both the law and juvenile delinquents recognize the principle of self-defense as a legitimate neutralization. It's just that the law accepts a much narrower version of this principle than do delinquents. In court, the boy pleading self-defense who says, "I had no choice: He called me a faggot so I had to beat the s--- out of him," is unlikely to win his case.

Two Kinds of Norms

People who hold conventional norms yet commit deviant behavior present us with what seems like a paradox. The concepts of drift and neutralization are only one explanation for this contradiction. Another way of explaining it is to distinguish between kinds of norms—namely norms of *pre*scription and norms of *pro*scription. **Prescriptive norms** define what a person *should* do; **proscriptive norms** define what a person should *not* do. Most people in this society follow the same prescriptive norms. But in the lower class, proscriptive norms are much looser. People tolerate a wider variety of behavior.[3]

The same idea is contained in the concept of the lower-class "value stretch," a phrase coined by Hyman Rodman.[4] Rodman was writing not about crime but about other aspects of lower-class life, like work and family; nevertheless, the concept is useful. It recognizes that while values are ideals and guidelines for action (they tell you in which general direction you want to go), they also are justifications for behavior. We appeal to values in order to justify what we have done. Therefore, we want as little discrepancy as possible between our values and our behavior. For the poor, this means that although they hold the same values as do middle-class people, they must reinterpret or "stretch" these values to fit the way they must live their lives. For example, in *Tally's Corner*, a classic study of poor, black, streetcorner men, Elliot Liebow mentions a man who at Christmastime went shoplifting for his children's presents.[5] Among middle-class parents, this shoplifting would clearly have fallen outside the norms. It would have been proscribed. In the lower class, however, traditional "family values" were stretched to include this obviously illegal behavior.

Norms and Enforcement

Just what are values and norms? How many different sets of values and norms are there in our society? How do people relate to them? These questions underlie most sociological theories about crime. Different views on norms and values are central to the debate between structural theories and cultural theories. This debate sometimes comes down to a single question: Do people who commit crimes share a different set of values and norms from the rest of society? To oversimplify, cultural theories say, "yes, lower-class people have different values"; structural theories say, "no, we all share in a single culture, and the real problem is unequal opportunity in the social structure." Other theories try to bridge the gap by arguing that "yes, there are different subcultures, but they have come into existence as adaptations to inequality that is built into the social structure."

The other way of answering the question, as we have just seen, is to recognize that values (ideas about what is good) and norms (rules for behavior) are only general guidelines. Even a single, unified culture will have competing and contradictory norms. Therefore, which rule is applied and how it is interpreted depends on the specific situation and the people involved in it. For example, there are laws against speeding, yet not everyone who breaks the law is stopped or fined. If a cop stops you for speeding, you probably will not question the general principle of speed limits, but you probably *will* wonder why you have been selected. As you can see from this example, values, norms, and even laws are abstract; they are different from rules in use.

This difference leads to a whole new set of questions: not, "Who breaks the rules, and why?" but instead, "Which rules get enforced; by whom; against whom; how; and with what effect?" In the hypothetical case just mentioned, you are unlikely to search for the sociological or psychological causes of your driving 75 mph. You are much more likely to ask, "Why is this cop picking on me instead of going after real criminals?"

Labeling Theory

The questions about rule enforcement are the basis for what is sometimes called **labeling theory**.* Labeling theory begins by recognizing that no act

---

* The term labeling "theory" may be incorrect. A theory, strictly speaking, is a set of logically connected propositions. It identifies important factors and predicts outcomes. A theory says, in effect, where such-and-such conditions exist, certain other results will occur. In this sense, labeling theory is not really a theory. It is not a tightly connected set of propositions, and it does not predict. Instead, it suggests outcomes that may possibly occur. It sensitizes us to possibilities that other theories ignore. It is not so much a theory as it is a way of looking at crime and deviance. For these reasons, some sociologists prefer to call it "the labeling perspective."

is inherently criminal; it is a crime only if there is a law against it. Crime, therefore, is not just a matter of rule breaking, but also of rule making and rule enforcement. To put it another way, crime is a joint product of the **interaction** of those who create and enforce the rules and those who break them. If we want the full picture, we have to look carefully not just at criminals but also at the criminal justice system and other forms of social control. Traditional criminology theories look at only one side of the interaction—the criminal. Labeling theory, on the other hand, usually has focused on law enforcers and law creators—the people that Howard Becker, whose *Outsiders* is one of the basic texts of the labeling approach, calls "moral entrepreneurs." They are in the business of making and enforcing morals—rules about what people should and should not do.[6]

By referring to the police, legislators, and reformers as moral entrepreneurs, Becker is taking an attitude of irony and skepticism toward the sorts of people and institutions that usually receive automatic and uncritical respect, not just from the public but from other criminological theories as well. Law creators and law enforcers usually present themselves as working for the general good, as motivated by abstract principles of right and wrong, without regard to the particular interests of any one group. But the term *entrepreneur* implies that this enterprise brings them some profit. The profit need not be financial; it may be more abstract, perhaps the confirmation of one moral position over another. In any case, labeling theory questions both the motives and effects of these moral entrepreneurs. It does not take them at face value. It looks for the discrepancies between what they do and what they say they do. For example, instead of looking at crime statistics as an objective measure of criminal behavior, labeling theorists see them as the outcome of police behavior. So official crime statistics would reflect not just crime but also the public relations interests of the police department, its routine procedures for handling complaints and arrests, and the general expectations and prejudices of police officers.*

This skepticism and irony are basic to much of labeling theory.[7] Even with law enforcement, labeling theory takes a somewhat ironical approach. It asks, "What does law enforcement really do?" The official position of law enforcers is, of course, that they prevent crime. Indeed, sometimes they do. But often, enforcing the law has unintended consequences—both for individuals and for crime in general. The criminal justice process is supposed to keep people from committing crimes. However, labeling theory argues that this process, by defining the person as criminal, may push him or her toward crime rather than away from it. Other people will respond to the label rather than to other facts about the person, and this response will

---

* See the Chapter 3 on statistics and Chapter 13 on the police for a fuller discussion of these problems.

make it more difficult for the labeled person to move easily into noncriminal society.[8]

Some people reduce this idea to the oversimplified notion that labeling a person a criminal or homosexual or whatever will inevitably make the person become that label. This process is called the **self-fulfilling prophecy** since the prophecy (X is a criminal) makes itself come true (X then becomes a criminal *because of the prophecy*). It *can* happen, but labeling theory does not claim that it *must* happen. Labeling theory merely suggests that researchers explore this as one of a number of possible outcomes. Labeling theorists want to see exactly *how* the labeling process can work and what other factors can also affect the outcome. For example, people with enough money, power, status, or organizational support may be better able to resist the negative effects of labeling.*

In any case, labeling theory—unlike most other theories—sees crime-control as a possible source of crime. Labeling research examines the unintended effects law enforcement can have, not just on individuals but on the broader organization of crime as well. For example, a labeling theorist might investigate how Prohibition helped organized crime to expand and consolidate its powers, or how making a drug like heroin or cocaine illegal has contributed to street crime. Since the drug's illegality drives up its price, users may turn to crime to get money for drugs. If they were cheap or free, nobody would need to steal to support a habit. (Of course, a free-drug policy might create other problems.)

Other research in the labeling tradition looks closely at the criminal justice system itself. Researchers look at police, lawyers, or prison workers as thoroughly as other research has looked at criminals. Rather than accept the statements of officials (that they just enforce the law), researchers investigate what people in the criminal justice system actually do. The police, for example, often do not arrest lawbreakers; officers have a great deal of discretion in responding to crimes. A labeling theorist would want to know just what determines whether a cop will make an arrest. The breaking of the law is only one of many factors influencing that decision. In fact, sometimes an officer may make an arrest even though the person has *not* broken the law (this occurs chiefly as a means of defusing a potentially explosive situation).[9]

Besides examining the enforcement of the law, labeling theory also has directed its attention to the creation of laws. If law enforcement is a process of human interaction, so is lawmaking. Laws do not write themselves. They are created by people with a particular interest in having such laws passed. In *Outsiders*, Becker devoted two chapters to the history of the federal law,

---

* For example, Richard Nixon's involvement in the Watergate scandal ended his presidency. However, not long after his resignation, he was being treated much more like a statesman than as an unindicted co-conspirator in a series of crimes.

finally passed in 1937, that outlawed marijuana. Becker traced the law to the efforts of only a few people in law enforcement agencies. They drafted legislation for Congress; but more important, they also managed, through an influx of stories in the popular press, to create an exaggerated image of marijuana and its dangers.* The point is not whether marijuana is more or less harmful than it was portrayed. The point is that moral entrepreneurs still try to work through the law, especially the criminal law. Each day's mail brings me their appeals. Handguns, abortion, the death penalty, pornography, drugs—whether for or against, the moral entrepreneurs are slugging it out to see whose version of morality and reality will be written into law.[10]

CONFLICT AND CONSENSUS

Conventional theories, in one way or another, all start from questions like, "Why do people commit crimes, and how can we get them to stop?" You may have had similar questions in mind when you signed up for a course in criminology. But if you put together some of the observations from the last several pages, you may arrive at a much different viewpoint. Take the idea, from neutralization theory and elsewhere, that the rules of society are not uniform and obvious; they are diverse and even contradictory. People select and interpret these rules in each situation. Which rule is enforced depends on the people involved in the situation. Add labeling theory's idea that the creation of laws and their enforcement is the product of human interaction, and that different groups may have different interests. Add the observation that the more power a person has, the better he or she will be able to resist being labeled, and the more power a group has, the better it will be able to have its morality enforced.

The conclusion from these propositions is that the enforcement of rules is not a matter of *consensus* or agreement, but rather that rule making and rule enforcement are matters of *conflict*.

Once you no longer assume that criminal laws and their enforcement are matters of consensus, you ask a much different set of questions. Instead of asking why some people break the law, you ask questions like, "Who has the power to create and enforce laws?" and "In whose interests are particular laws created and enforced?" and more crucially "In whose interests are particular laws *not* created or *not* enforced?"

---

* The 1936 movie *Reefer Madness* has provided cable TV and VCR viewers an opportunity to see a film version of the kinds of magazine articles that began appearing around the same time.

These kinds of questions are at the heart of a style of criminological theory that appeared in the 1970s. In the study of criminal justice, it turned its attention more toward questions about justice than questions about crime, more toward the actions of people with power than the actions of the poor and powerless. Its proponents had been influenced, even "radicalized," by the political events of the 1960s. After all, if you see police officers enforce the law by clubbing anti-war demonstrators or civil rights marchers, you might well come to question the basis of law enforcement and the law itself, rather than accept them automatically as legitimate—especially if you are among the clubees.

Some of these theorists called their approach the "conflict perspective" or "conflict theory." Others referred to their ideas as "critical theory," "Marxist criminology," "radical criminology," or "the new criminology." There are distinctions among some of these titles, and the criminologists involved address a variety of issues. They even differ with each other on some points. Nevertheless, I will try to sketch here the common ground they share.

The Marxist Legacy

One unifying theme in radical criminology is its critical view of the basic foundations of society. I mean critical here in both the neutral and the negative senses of that word. Radical criminologists call their theory "critical" because it proposes a critique, an evaluation, of the entire society. They seek the origins of crime in the basic economic, historical, and political arrangements of society. Traditional criminology, the "old" criminology, takes these arrangements for granted. In the opinion of the new criminologists, this a crucial omission: "The analysis of particular forms of crime, or particular types of criminal, outside their context in history and society, has been shown . . . to be a meaningless activity."[11]

Dismissing most criminology as "meaningless activity" is a fairly heavy charge, so let me offer a hypothetical example. Imagine that we are going to study crime in South Africa. If we use the models of conventional criminology, then we ask questions like, "Who commits crimes and why?" and "How can we get them to stop?" Our research might show us that young black males have high crime rates; that they commit most of their crime in their own towns against the persons or property of other blacks; that crime increased in the mid-1980s; that some townships have more crime than others. Our explanations for these findings might center on the culture of certain townships, or on the ethnic backgrounds of the criminals, or on rates of unemployment, or on the failure of the criminal justice system to catch and punish offenders, or on the family backgrounds of offenders.

What is missing here? You don't have to be a radical Marxist to see a glaring defect in all these explanations and in our basic research: They say nothing about apartheid. Apartheid is the basis of South Africa's legal, political, and economic systems. Under apartheid, the white minority (about 15 percent of the total population) controls the country. Blacks cannot vote, cannot move freely about the country, receive an inferior education, get the lowest paying jobs, and generally live in conditions of enforced inferiority. Do we really think that we can explain the *tsotsis* (muggers) of a black township like Soweto by looking at their differential associations or their probability of escaping punishment? These theories may have some relevance, they may even be supported by research data, but they are too shortsighted. They ignore or take for granted South Africa's basic economic and political arrangements.*

Radical criminology would not make this omission. Radical criminology generally tries to keep these basic structural factors near the center of attention. This focus is part of the Marxist orientation of most radical criminologists. Marx himself wrote little about crime, but he did hold that the basic economic structure of a society (its "social relations of production") provided the basis for all social (and antisocial) behavior. It is this fundamental idea, derived from Marx, that underlies much radical criminology. Radical (or critical) criminology makes the economic basis of society a major factor in the analysis of crime.

In principle, critical criminologists should take this approach whether they are analyzing crime and justice in South Africa or America or China; whether the system is capitalist, socialist, communist, or anything else. Their first task should be to relate the problem to the social relations of production. In practice, since most of these "new criminologists" are British or American, the societies on which they cast their critical eye are their own, the Western capitalist societies. And they have often found fault with what they see. Therefore, the writings of radical criminologists also have been critical in the negative meaning of that word. In explaining crime, they have pointed to some of the less attractive features of Western capitalism. They have focused far more on the faults of the system than on its virtues. Moreover, they argue that these faults are essential, fundamental parts of the capitalist system, not just a few flaws in a basically good society. Radical theories hold little hope that reforms will bring about real change. Therefore, only a transformation of the basis of the society will bring a large reduction in crime.

A Touch of Class

Another Marxian point central to radical criminology is the concept of social class. Other theories use the notion of social class only in seeking to explain

---

* Since 1988, South Africa has made many changes, and the future of apartheid is uncertain. Perhaps by the time you are reading this, the analogy will no longer be valid.

why the lower class does (or does not) have a higher rate of crime. Radical criminology starts from a different conception of class. For Marxists, class is not a matter of income or education, nor do terms like "upper-middle class" have much meaning for them. These all imply differences of "lifestyle" or patterns of consumption (i.e., how people spend their money). Marxists look instead at production. Marxists see two major classes: those who own or control the means of production and those who do not. Those who own the land, resources, machinery—what Marx called "capital"—are in a position to exploit those who have only their own labor. The interests of the two classes do not coincide. In fact, these interests are in conflict, and each class will use the tools at its disposal in order to further its own interests.

The law is an important tool in this conflict. One class will have a tremendous advantage if it can have laws passed against actions that harm its interests. The law adds to the power of the class by enlisting the machinery of the state; the class that can control the law now has the police and courts to do its work. Not only does the law then serve one class, but it drapes that class interest in the cloak of universal legitimacy. The law, since it applies to all people, has an air of neutrality and equality. Of course, in some cases, that neutrality barely hides the class bias of the law. As Anatole France said, "The law, in its majestic equality, forbids both the rich and the poor to sleep under bridges."

Radical criminologists are less interested in who *breaks* the laws and why than in who *makes* the laws and why. Much of the best research to emerge from radical criminology shows how particular criminal laws or patterns of law enforcement have fit into the conflict between social classes. A classic example is the anti-vagrancy law which appeared in the mid-1300s in England. The laws forbade begging and required that men or women without visible means of support should work for any one who needed workers ("shall be bounded to serve him which shall him require"). The question is, "Why this law at this time?" It helps if you remember that in 1348 the plague wiped out about 40 percent of the population of England. At the same time, the feudal system, which tied peasants to the manor estates of the lords, was beginning to break down. If laborers were free to refuse low wages and to wander about in search of the best wages, landowners would have to pay more. However, the new vagrancy laws, by forcing peasants to take work, provided landowners with a continued supply of affordable labor.[12] Obviously a law that prohibited idleness served the interest of the owners.*

Other historical research on the development of English law has shown how laws were changed to accommodate the interests of owners against the

---

* Even in the 20th century, when there are too many laborers rather than too few, vagrancy laws have served to control poor people who are not committing predatory crimes. Merchants might ask the police to clear vagrants from shopping areas, where their appearance might keep customers away.

interests of the common people. For example, by longstanding custom, common people had been able to take wood, game, and turf from the forests. But in the 18th century, much of this land was designated as the king's or was turned over to private owners, and Parliament passed anti-poaching laws to protect the rights of the landowners. For the landowners, these lands were now a source of greater income. But for ordinary people, the laws meant that what had once been a way of life was now a crime punishable in some cases by death.[13] In the United States, laws permitting slavery or restricting unions or prohibiting boycotts promoted the interests of those who control the means of production.

The relation between criminal law and economics is sometimes less direct. Drug laws, for example, would seem at first to have little to do with relations between labor and capital. We might assume that a drug becomes outlawed when it is shown to be harmful. However, one Marxist has argued that the passage of drug laws depends more on the economic position of the group that uses a particular drug, not the dangers of the drug itself. For example, anti-opium laws in America first appeared in the West in the late 1870s, not because opium was any more harmful than it had been 10 years earlier, but because the position of the Chinese had changed. Chinese workers had been brought to America to provide cheap labor, practically slave labor, for the building of the railroads. As long as this labor was needed, smoking opium was legal. However, when the railroads were largely completed and the country sank into economic depression, Chinese labor was no longer needed. In addition, some Chinese were opening businesses that competed with those of white merchants. The result was a flourishing of anti-Chinese prejudice and the criminalization of opium-smoking.* It is especially noteworthy that these laws did not ban opium itself. Liquid opium, widely drunk by whites in various patent medicines, remained legal. Only smoking, the form of opium ingestion preferred by the Chinese, was outlawed. Anti-drug legislation in the Southwest 50 years later followed a similar pattern, except that the laborers were Mexicans and the drug was marijuana.[14]

What About Street Crime?

Many nonradical criminologists have come to accept some of this historical research and its conclusions. Radical criminology must be credited for showing how powerful groups use the law in order to secure their own

---

* Of course, people urging anti-opium legislation said nothing about the economic position of the minority group (Chinese). Instead, their fears resembled those of the anti-cocaine panic of the 1980s: "Respectable" men and women were ruining their lives with a drug that had previously been confined to a minority group.

interests. But for most citizens, the crime problem is not vagrancy in the 14th century or poaching in the 18th century; it is mugging in the 20th century. What do radical criminologists say about the ordinary street crimes—the burglaries and robberies and rapes—that the majority of people see as "the crime problem"? Surely the laws against these crimes are meant to protect all people, not just the wealthy. Anyway, searching for the origins of laws is all very interesting, but how about explaining the origins of crime as well?

Radical criminologists respond to these questions in several ways. One of the most obvious answers is that street crime is a product of poverty, unemployment, and inequality. From the Marxist viewpoint, these economic problems are inherent in the capitalist economy. Radicals argue that the U.S. government could in fact ensure that all people had adequate income and employment. In that case, crime would drop dramatically. Why, then, does the government not take such action? Because, say the radicals, it would require a restructuring of the economy. The change would greatly benefit the poor and would reduce crime. But it would also diminish the position of the corporations and individuals that are now wealthy and powerful—the people radicals refer to as "the ruling class." In other words, those who have the power to eliminate unemployment and poverty have no reason to do so and many reasons not to.

As for the laws against street crime, radicals make a variety of observations. First, remember the epigram about sleeping under bridges. The law forbids both the rich and poor to commit burglary. But, say some radical criminologists, the law often does not criminalize many of the harmful acts committed by the wealthy in their pursuit of greater wealth. It was not criminal for Ford to build the flammable Pinto, even though the engineers and executives knew that the location of its gas tank would make rear-end collisions unusually dangerous.* It is not criminal for politicians to vote tax breaks for a business that contributes heavily to their campaign funds. It is not criminal for a defense contractor to charge the government $200 for a $5 hammer, or for a drug manufacturer to charge $40 for a bottle of pills that costs $0.10 to produce. The laws that do restrict business practices are usually regulations, not criminal laws. So even if these various profiteers are caught, they may be embarrassed, they may be sued, they may be fined; but they do not go to prison.[15]

This selective attention, focusing on the evils of the poor rather than those of the rich, continues well beyond the creation of laws. For those who do break the existing laws, each step of the criminal justice process—arrest, indictment, trial, conviction, incarceration—allows the wealthy to slip out. Those left to receive the full force of the system are the poor and powerless.

---

* The state of Indiana did bring criminal charges against Ford for reckless homicide after three teenage girls burned to death in a Pinto crash. The jury found Ford not guilty.

This bias in the criminal justice system provides a second reason that the wealthy would not want any real change. In fact, this bias drops an added benefit in the lap of the ruling class. From the creation of laws to the imprisonment of criminals, the system conveys an image that the crime problem consists of the crimes of the poor. Thus, in two ways, street crime is good for business. First, it is an inevitable result of the levels of poverty and unemployment that are necessary to our capitalist system. And second, it diverts public attention away from the much more harmful acts of the wealthy and allows them to continue with business as usual.

There is a third reason that the ruling class need not take drastic action to reduce crime: This crime rarely touches them. Street crime consists mostly of poor people ripping off other poor people. It does not affect corporations directly. And the people who run those corporations have been able to buy their way to safety. Their suburban homes or city apartments are well protected by police or private guards.

Criticisms of Radical Theory

Radical criminology has come in for a good deal of criticism. To talk about a ruling class in America offends many people, including some sociologists. After all, the United States is a democracy—a government of, by, and for the people—and our free enterprise economy, in principle, reinforces this democratic distribution of power. The argument between radical and mainstream criminologists, therefore, goes beyond questions of crime; it is about different pictures that people have of how society works. The most extreme radicals offer a model where a small ruling class runs nearly every part of the society in order to reinforce its position—a sort of collective J. R. Ewing.

Let's put it a bit more reasonably. First, power and wealth are not evenly distributed in society; some people and institutions have much more than others. Second, those who have power will use it to enhance their position. At a minimum, they will not do things that go against their economic or political interests; they will use the institutions they control in order to keep their positions of dominance. Third, this ruling class controls not only the economic institutions but also, ultimately, the institutions of justice. Therefore, the law and the criminal justice system, like other institutions in a society controlled by the powerful, will tend to reproduce these basic inequalities of wealth and power.

This model does not assume that the CEOs of corporations like General Motors and Citicorp necessarily get together with high-level politicians and scheme how they might get richer. Instead, it requires only that these people share a similar way of looking at the world and a similar set of interests. That is, the ruling class is not a closed conspiracy; rather, it is a set of powerful people whose interests are served by similar policies.

But is there really a ruling class? Granted that some people have far more power than do others, but do all those powerful people have the same goals? Is the state merely a tool of the ruling capitalist class, or does it represent other interests as well? Even some Marxist criminologists dismiss the idea that a unified and all-powerful ruling class is calling all the shots. Instead their model of society, though it still runs on power, sees that power as somewhat dispersed. They speak of "the partial autonomy of the state." The criminal justice system is not just one more instrument the ruling class can use for domination and exploitation. Instead, "law and law enforcement are . . . products of shifting alliances. The superior financial resources of capitalists naturally give them an advantage over other classes in conflicts over legislation and enforcement, but this advantage is not always decisive."[16]

Another criticism of radical criminologists is that they have not produced much empirical data to support their ideas. Marxist criminology may offer a perspective for viewing the historical development of laws. But does radical theory lead to propositions which can be tested with empirical evidence? If so, does the available evidence confirm the Marxists' statements?

There may be something to this criticism. Marx's ideas are not always easy to turn into measurable variables. But the same can be said of non-Marxian concepts as well, as we have seen with differential association theory.[17] Some sociologists have tried to show that the United States does in fact have a ruling class, but this research does not focus on crime.[18] Some criminologists have tried to show that the criminal justice system is used to oppress the poor. But despite many empirical studies, there is little conclusive evidence that, other things being equal, the courts treat the poor more harshly. It does appear, however, that the police (though probably not the courts) deal more harshly with blacks—especially in areas where there is a large black population.[19]

On the other hand, radical criminologists have sometimes used the empirical data from conventional criminology to support their ideas. For example, early research using self-report studies showed that middle-class youths were committing as much crime as were lower-class youths, while at the same time arrest data showed that more lower-class youths got arrested. Radicals interpreted the difference to mean that the police were biased against the lower class. One of the best examples of radical criminology is an essay by Marxist criminologist David Greenberg, titled "Delinquency and the Age Structure of Society." Greenberg uses data and ideas from mainstream sources, but he reaches a more Marxist conclusion: Delinquency is a result of the particular position of youth in the capitalist labor market.[20]

Finally, some critics have taken radical criminologists to task for their ideas on capitalism and crime. As with their ideas on the ruling class, radicals do not all agree on the specific connection between capitalism and crime. Again, the most romantic, extreme versions are the easiest to criticize. A handful of radical criminologists argue that crime is solely a product of capitalism. Some even go so far as to say that under socialism, crime as we know it will disappear. "As we engage in socialist struggle, we build a society that ceases to generate the crime found in capitalist society."[21] Statements like this fly in the face of reality. Societies like Cuba and the USSR have little or no private, capitalist ownership, yet they have crime. The USSR has one of the highest rates of imprisonment in the world (perhaps even higher than that bastion of capitalism, the United States).* At the same time, some vigorously capitalist countries have very low rates of crime (e.g., Japan, Switzerland). More flexible, less romantic Marxists recognize that socialist countries may have inequality, conflict between different classes of people, and alienation. In other words, they use Marxist concepts to understand crime in socialist countries, too.

CONTROL THEORY

Most of the sociological theories outlined here so far assume that individual differences play an insignificant part in crime rates. These theories locate important causes of crime in environmental factors such as the social structure or subcultural ideas, rather than individuals or families. If these theories point to any kind of policy, it is one of reforming society rather than punishing individuals. Some of these theories—labeling theory, for example—even question the assumptions on which the criminal justice system is based. In political terms, these theories are usually classified as "liberal," since they question or criticize society and hesitate to see individual criminals as the cause of the crime problem.

In recent years, some criminology theories have taken a more conservative turn. One of the most influential of these is control theory. Control theory rejects some important assumptions and strategies of the other sociological theories discussed here. First of all, when these theories begin by asking "Why do some people violate the rules of society?" they are making one important assumption: that the "natural" way of the world is for people to follow the rules. Control theory begins from a different assumption: namely, that people are by nature self-interested and antisocial, and unless this human nature is strongly controlled, we will have "the war of all against all."† So we must turn the crime question around and ask not why criminals commit crimes, but why other people do *not* commit crimes.

---

* The Marxists may have a point. Since the late 1980s, as the USSR has allowed more private enterprise and more personal freedom, crime rates have risen sharply.

† The phrase is from Thomas Hobbes, an 18th-century philosopher whose book *Leviathan* was an attempt to answer the question of why we do not have such chaos. "Why do [people] obey the laws of society?" is often referred to as "the Hobbesian question."

In this way, control theory resembles psychological theories of crime. Most psychological theories, too, start with the Hobbesian question. They assume that children come into the world with neither knowledge of society's rules nor an inclination to follow those rules. If society cannot install the necessary controls by the time these children begin to acquire the physical strength of adults, then society is facing an "invading army." The leading psychological theories—Freudian, conditioning, etc.—try to explain how the child is "socialized" into automatically and largely unconsciously controlling these "natural," antisocial, selfish impulses.

There is another important difference between control theory and other sociological theories (though perhaps Merton's is an exception). All of these other theories—to a greater or lesser extent—say that different groups have different concepts of the law and morality. Sutherland's statement that culture conflict is the basic cause of crime (see p. 377); Cohen's or Cloward and Ohlin's ideas that delinquent subcultures value certain law-breaking activities as a route to status within that group; labeling theory's idea that rules—both in the abstract and in actual use—depend on which group has the power to enforce its morality: All these see definitions of crime or morality as something shifting and flexible, a matter of conflict rather than consensus.

Nonsense, says control theory. Such ideas are either irrelevant or wrong. The simple truth is that for most crimes there is a clear morality of right and wrong, and some people choose to violate that morality. They know full well that what they are doing is wrong. In some special cases, there may be genuine disagreement over the legitimacy of a law (particularly with "victimless" crimes), but everyone, including criminals, agrees that predatory crimes like robbery, assault, theft, and burglary are wrong.

Travis Hirschi's Control Theory

Control theory comes in a variety of styles, and I cannot outline all of them here. Still, the one I will describe—that of Travis Hirschi—contains most of the basic ideas. Like many of the other theories, most control theories are trying to explain the behavior of younger criminals—i.e., delinquents. This is probably a legitimate strategy; first, because most adult criminals started as delinquents, and second, because juveniles commit such a disproportionate amount of crime.

Hirschi's book, *Causes of Delinquency* (1969), presents both a statement of the theory and empirical support based on a sample of some 2,000 high-school boys in the San Francisco–Oakland area. The boys filled out questionnaires covering a variety of attitudes and behavior, including, of course, crime.

Hirschi begins by rejecting "strain" theories (e.g., Merton's anomie theory) and cultural theories, challenging them on theoretical and, more important, empirical grounds. Crime and delinquency were confined neither to the lower economic levels nor to any one racial group. The self-report questions on crime showed very little difference between blacks and whites or among levels of socioeconomic status (though differences did turn up when he used arrests as the measure of crime).*

Since race and social class did not seem to be important factors in delinquency, was there anything else that might distinguish delinquents from nondelinquents? In answering this question, Hirschi went back to the original Hobbesian question: Why do people obey social rules? Hirschi's answer is that there is a "social bond" that ties us to society. As Hirschi puts it, "Control theory assumes that delinquent acts result when an individual's bond to society is weak or is broken."

This statement sounds logical. The trouble with it is that it is vague and difficult to prove. It runs the risk of being unfalsifiable—like Sutherland's "excess of definitions." If a boy does not become delinquent, we can say his bond to society is strong; if he becomes delinquent, we can "explain" his delinquency by saying that his bond to society was weak. Such after-the-fact explanation is not very impressive. For the idea of the social bond to be convincing, we must measure it independently of delinquency and then see if the two (social bond and delinquency) are correlated.

Hirschi rises to this challenge. First, he specifies the abstract concept of **social bond** by breaking it down into four elements. Then he measures each of these elements. Then he correlates the boys' scores on each element with their delinquency.

The four elements of the social bond correspond with four levels of analysis: feeling (called "affect"—accent on the first syllable); cognition (based on rational calculation); behavior; and belief or values.

Attachment to Parents

The first element Hirschi deals with is the affective (emotional) component of the social bond, which he calls "attachment." Of course, a person is attached not to society in general but to specific institutions and people. Hirschi, therefore, measured attachment to three distinct groups: family, school, and peers. His questionnaire had several items like these:

Do you like school?
Do you share your thoughts and feelings with your mother (father)?
Would you want to be the kind of person your father is?
Do you care what teachers think of you?

---

* Some later research has challenged Hirschi's statements about race and class. Even some self-report studies have found correlations between these factors and crime. For a fuller discussion, see Chapter 4.

The theory says that the closer a boy is attached to family, school, and peers—or, in fact, to anything—the less likely he will be to break society's norms. Taking family first,there is no theoretical problem for middle-class boys: The less attached they are to their parents, the more likely they are to become delinquent. And Hirschi's questionnaire results bear this out. Among sons of professionals and white-collar workers, those who score low on the attachment-to-parents questions are twice as likely to be delinquent as are those who are highly attached.

An interesting theoretical question arises in the case of lower-class boys. Among lower-class boys, who will be more delinquent—those strongly attached to parents or those less attached to parents? Imagine what a strict version of cultural theories would say. The values and norms of lower-class culture allow or even promote delinquency; therefore, the boy's attachment to parents is attachment to the representatives of a delinquency-generating culture. More attachment should lead to more delinquency. Control theory, on the other hand, predicts that the relation between attachment and delinquency will be the same as with middle-class boys: more attachment, less crime (and vice versa).

The actual results of Hirschi's survey confirm the prediction of control theory: Attachment to parents reduces crime for both middle-class and lower-class boys.

Attachment to Peers

It should not really come as a surprise that even among lower-class boys, those closer to their parents are less likely to be delinquent. To expect otherwise would require an exaggerated distortion of cultural theory. Attachment to peers, though, is a different story, for here the theory that contradicts common sense is control theory. Hirschi predicts that attachment to peers (like attachment to anything else) will dampen delinquency: The closer a boy feels toward his friends, the less likely he will be to commit crimes— *even if those friends are delinquents.*

For boys with nondelinquent friends, there is no argument. All theories would expect closer friendships to reduce delinquency. But what about those boys whose friends are delinquent—should strong attachment bring more delinquency or less? Common sense and most of the cultural theories (especially differential association theory) would predict that boys strongly attached to delinquent friends would be more delinquent than boys who were not so tight with their delinquent friends. Hirschi went out on a limb to challenge common sense. His control theory maintained that *any* social attachment—even to hoodlum friends—will act as a buffer against the urge to violate social norms.

Hirschi had to sift his data thoroughly to find any support for his idea. If it held true at all, it was only for those boys with the greatest number of delinquent friends; the more these boys wanted to "be the kind of person your best friend is," the less likely they were to have a police record. But the differences were very small, and for boys with one or two delinquent friends, attachment made no difference. Results from most other studies confirm differential association ideas: The closer a boy is to his delinquent friends, the more delinquent he will be.[22]

Nevertheless, there may be some validity to Hirschi's ideas about attachment among delinquents. We may especially need to correct the popular image of the juvenile gang. The media—both in fiction and in the news—like to portray these gangs as tight, supportive, highly organized, permanent groups, with special "colors" and a fairly regular schedule of confrontations with other gangs—something like a football team. This image may play well on the screen, but it rarely resembles reality. Instead, most research finds that gangs are fairly loose associations. It's true that delinquents commit most of their crimes in groups of two, three, or four. When several of these sets of friends hang around together, usually because they live in the same neighborhood, it's a gang. Sometimes these groups do develop more cohesiveness, but the army regiment type of organization depicted in movies is rare.[23] More important, relationships among gang boys are based not on warmth and respect, but on defensiveness, constant threat, insult, and aggression.[24]

Attachment to School

The results in this area are exactly what anyone would expect: There is a strong negative correlation between delinquency and attachment to school (more attachment, less delinquency). Or, stated simply, kids who like school commit fewer crimes. The question is, which is causing which? Other theorists (e.g., Cohen or Cloward and Ohlin) insist that delinquents are just as smart as nondelinquents. However, they say, school is culturally stacked against lower-class boys; they do poorly, and some of them withdraw into delinquent groups. In other words, the initial cause is the school's rejection of the lower-class boy. If only schools were more tolerant of lower-class kids; if somehow schools were run so that lower-class kids would feel more at home there; if teachers could reach their lower-class students rather than put them down; then there would be less pressure toward delinquency. In essence, delinquency is the school's fault.

Hirschi, in contrast, absolves the school of all blame and locates the cause in the individual. First, he denies that there is a correlation between crime and social class. Since middle-class boys are as delinquent as lower-class boys, the school's supposed anti–lower class bias cannot be to blame for delinquency. Second, Hirschi claims something that all of the other theories reject: that delinquents *are* less intelligent. This academic incompetence means that they will do poorly in school and therefore resent and reject the school and its authority. This rejection of authority will loosen the social bond and leave them free to commit crimes.

Commitment

In Hirschi's theory, commitment is that part of the social bond that involves the person's rational calculation of the costs and benefits of violating laws. The concept of commitment refers to the future, the continuation of some line of action. Commitment links choices in the present to goals in the future. For a boy who has high future goals, the costs of crime (if he is caught) are much greater. He has more to lose. He has a greater **stake in conformity**.

Hirschi is interested in two aspects of a boy's "commitment to conventional lines of action": What aspirations does he have regarding college and career? And how willing is he to give up adult privileges in the present in order to attain his future goals? Of course, Hirschi finds that boys with higher aspirations commit less crime. This result should not surprise us, except—as Hirschi reminds us—if we really believe theorists like Merton, Cohen, or Cloward and Ohlin. All of these theorists, you may recall, say that boys who become delinquent start out with the same aspirations, the same desire for success, as do nondelinquents. However, they lack legitimate means to these goals. The strain between means and goals creates frustration which in turn leads to crime. If these boys didn't have such high aspirations, they wouldn't become delinquent.

In fact, Hirschi's own evidence also gives some support to this idea. Apparently, how we measure "means" is crucial. Studies that use father's occupation as the measure of the boy's social status find no evidence for strain theory. Boys with high aspirations are less delinquent—at all social levels. But if we measure means in terms of the boys' realistic expectations, the results are different. Some of the boys who had high goals had little realistic expectation of achieving those goals—a classic goals-means strain. And these boys had higher rates of delinquency than did boys who felt no such strain.[25]

Hirschi sees commitment not just in large future goals like college and career, but in everyday choices like saying "no" to cigarettes, alcohol, and cars. Hirschi's data show a correlation between delinquency and boys' attitudes regarding smoking, drinking, and driving. The earlier a boy begins smoking, the more likely he is to become delinquent; the more important a boy thinks a car is, the more delinquent he will be. Of course, Hirschi is not saying that cigarettes cause delinquency, but rather that smoking signals a lack of commitment to conventional goals. Boys who become delinquents are those who think that adult pleasures in the present are more important than future goals.

Involvement

Involvement is the behavioral component of the social bond. The theory says that the more time a boy spends involved in conventional activities, the less likely he is to break the law. Hirschi's research study supports this idea up to a point. Boys who spent less time doing homework, and more time riding around in cars were more likely to have committed crimes. On the other hand, Hirschi's own data often did not support his general ideas about involvement. Other behaviors that show a lack of involvement in conventional activities—watching TV, reading comic books, playing games—were very poor predictors of delinquency. And having a part-time job was positively correlated with delinquency. That is, the boys with part-time jobs were somewhat *more* delinquent than those without jobs. This result, along with more recent research, deflates one bit of conventional wisdom—the idea that having a job somehow automatically makes kids more virtuous. Apparently, this popular notion is highly overrated.[26] Conventional activities per se do not reduce delinquency. Involvement works only when the activity also shows commitment to future goals.

Belief

Belief, the fourth part of the social bond, refers to abstract ideas people hold about conventional authority on the one hand and crime on the other. Conventional beliefs dampen the urge toward crime. Delinquency is "made possible by the absence of (effective) beliefs that forbid delinquency." Some of these delinquent beliefs resemble the "neutralizations" that Sykes and Matza defined. Boys were asked to agree or disagree with statements like, "Most things that people call delinquency don't really hurt anyone" (denial of injury); or "Policemen try to give all kids an even break" (disagreeing here would be condemning the condemners); or "I can't stay out of trouble no matter how hard I try" (denial of responsibility). As you would expect, those who took the neutralizing positions were more likely to have broken the law.

The problem with belief is that even if certain beliefs go hand-in-hand with delinquency, how can we know which is cause and which is effect? Hirschi says that lack of conventional belief "makes crime possible." But it is also possible that the boy who, for whatever reasons, commits crimes will come to adopt ideas that justify his breaking the law. In this case, the belief is a consequence of crime, not a cause.

The same criticism can be made about Hirschi's ideas on involvement or attachment to school, and perhaps even attachment to parents or commitment. Given that a boy has decided to commit crimes every so often, the rest will follow. He will not confide in his parents (attachment); he will not do his homework (involvement); he will do poorly in school and dislike it (attachment); having gotten a police record, he will give up on long-range goals (commitment) and adopt a set of beliefs about society that justify his behavior.[27]

In other words, it is very difficult to establish these elements of the social bond as causes of delinquency. Hirschi himself, after reviewing the results of the research, does not place much emphasis on belief or involvement. He rests his theory chiefly on attachment to parents and attachment to school.

Still, these two ideas mark a departure from other sociological theories. By stressing attachment to parents, Hirschi is pointing to the family as a cause of crime. This emphasis should not seem strange, since many people blame crime on "the breakdown of the family." However, for 50 years, sociologists had rejected this position, since it blamed the family rather than social inequality. But there also were empirical reasons, since the attempts to show a connection between delinquency and family had not been very convincing. Most of this research looked at the problem of "broken homes" (i.e., those with only one parent). A review of these broken-home studies found only a slight effect on delinquency. Of course, the number of parents living at home (which is fairly easy to measure) is not the same as the quality of parent-child relations (which is fairly hard to measure). More recent studies, however, that do try to measure conflict or unhappiness within the home have found more of the effects that we would expect. Happy families produce fewer delinquents. Also, when parents are emotionally distant and uninvolved, or when they exert little supervision, children are more likely to become delinquent.[28] Still, the family as a cause of delinquency remains a matter of much dispute among criminologists.

The second factor Hirschi identified as a cause of crime is that of individual differences. To suggest that there was any basic difference in ability or IQ between delinquents and nondelinquents was sociological heresy. Sociological theories had long insisted as an article of faith that delinquents were every bit as intelligent and competent. If delinquents did poorly in school, it was because the school treated them badly. Hirschi, however, says that the primary factor in the school-delinquency connection is the basic academic incompetence of those who eventually wind up breaking the law.

The Last Word

These last three chapters have offered an overview of theories of crime—biological theories, psychological theories, sociological theories, and a few others that don't quite fit in any one category. Theories which will come along in the future may try to combine some of the different approaches.[29] One recent approach, called the **routine activities** approach, is a variation on opportunity theory, though it addresses a slightly different set of questions from those examined by Merton or Cloward and Ohlin. Instead of

The human ecology approach that inspired the early sociological studies of crime in the United States fell into relative obscurity for nearly a half century. In a 1987 essay, Rodney Stark revived the idea of deviant places, offering a theory that also included elements of opportunity and control. Stark's essay took the form of 30 propositions. I have excerpted only 11 of these.

Norman Hayner, a stalwart of the old Chicago school of human ecology, noted that in the area of Seattle having by far the highest delinquency rate in 1934, "half the children are Italian." In vivid language, Hayner described the social and cultural shortcomings of these residents. . . . Today this district . . . remains the prime delinquency area. But there are virtually no Italians living there. Instead, this neighborhood is the heart of the Seattle black community.

How is it that neighborhoods can remain the site of high crime and deviance rates *despite a complete turnover in their populations?* If the Garfield district [of Seattle] was tough *because* Italians lived there, why did it stay tough after they left? Indeed, why didn't the neighborhoods the Italians departed to become tough? . . . The composition of neighborhoods, in terms of characteristics of their populations, cannot provide an adequate explanation of variations in deviance rates. Instead, *there must be something about places as such that sustains crime.* . .

There are five aspects of urban neighborhoods which characterize high deviance areas of cities . . . (1) density; (2) poverty; (3) mixed use; (4) transience; and (5) dilapidation.

These characteristics . . . [have] specific impacts . . . on the moral order as *people respond to them.* Four responses will be assessed: (1) moral cynicism among residents; (2) increased opportunities for crime and deviance; (3) increased motivation to deviate; (4) diminished social control.

Proposition 1. *The greater the density of a neighborhood, the more association between those most and least predisposed to deviance.*

In dense urban neighborhoods, the "bad" kids often live in the same building as the "good" ones, hang about close by, dominate the nearby playground, and are nearly unavoidable. Hence, peer groups in dense neighborhoods will tend to be inclusive, and all young people living there will face maximum peer pressure to deviate.

Proposition 2. *The greater the density of a neighborhood, the higher the level of moral cynicism.*

In dense neighborhoods it is much harder to keep up appearances—whatever morally discreditable information exists about us is likely to leak.

Proposition 4. *Where homes are more crowded, there will be a greater tendency to congregate outside the home in places and circumstances that raise levels of temptation and opportunity to deviate.*

Proposition 5. *Where homes are more crowded, there will be lower levels of supervision of children.*

Proposition 10. *Mixed use increases familiarity with and easy access to places offering the opportunity for deviance.*

Proposition 11. *Mixed-use neighborhoods offer increased opportunity for congregating outside the home in places conducive to deviance.*

Proposition 14. *Transience weakens voluntary organizations, thereby directly reducing both informal and formal sources of social control.*

Proposition 15. *Transience reduces levels of community surveillance.*

Proposition 22. *Stigmatized neighborhoods will tend to be overpopulated by the most demoralized people.*

Proposition 25. *Stigmatized neighborhoods will suffer from more lenient law enforcement.*

People in stigmatized neighborhoods complain less often . . . [and] are much less willing to testify when the police do act. . . . The police frequently come to share the outside community's view of stigmatized neighborhoods—as filled with morally disreputable people, who deserve what they get.

Proposition 28. *More lenient law enforcement draws people to a neighborhood on the basis of their involvement in crime and deviance.*	*Source:* Rodney Stark (1987), "Deviant Places: A Theory of the Ecology of Crime," *Criminology,* vol. 25, no. 4, pp. 893–909.

asking who commits crimes and why, the routine activities approach seeks to explain the amount and distribution of crime.[30] It focuses on the ways in which the routine activities of ordinary people offer opportunities for criminals.* Its mapping the location of crime takes us back to the ecological approach, though its explanations are different from those of the sociologists of the old Chicago school. Other ecological approaches try to incorporate ideas of control theory as well as those of differential association (see box).[31] Other theories may emerge from the study of white-collar crime or organized crime or drunken driving—the kinds of crime largely passed over by earlier theories. In any case, the theory will try to do what any good theory does—to bring together and explain different sets of facts. Nevertheless, if you come across other theories or if you've managed to read these chapters, you might be tempted to ask two questions: "So what?" and "Which of these theories is right?"

The first question, though it sounds much less sophisticated, is probably a better question. Certainly it is the more difficult question. To ask of each theory whether it is right or wrong misses the point. Theories in social science are not like theories in the "hard" sciences, where one theory gains ascendance and replaces another. In the hard sciences, old theories are like quaint objects gathering dust in an attic, interesting only for historical curiosity—much like the vintage automobile. The Model T Ford had a great impact in its field; it might even be elegant in its own way. But you wouldn't want to have to rely on one for your daily commute on the interstate. Similarly, no chemists today would pursue phlogiston theory, nor are there any physicists who base their research on Rutherford's model of the atom. These ideas are left to historians of science.

In social science, though, old theories never die. And if they fade away, they have a strange way of returning. For example, Beccaria's utilitarian ideas on crime (1764), while helping in the reform of courts and laws in the 18th century, had little influence on theories of crime in the 19th and early 20th centuries. But roughly two hundred years later, what were the "new" trends in criminology? Economic cost-benefit analyses of crime and sociological research on the deterrent effects of punishment.† Utilizarianism was back in fashion.

* For a fuller discussion, see Chapter 3 on crime rates.

† For a fuller discussion of deterrence, see Chapter 16.

In the natural sciences, new research may prove a theory wrong. Then, a new theory that can explain the new facts replaces the old theory entirely. With theories of human behavior, however, research seldom "proves" a theory wrong. When the results contradict a theory, supporters of the theory can (and frequently do) argue that the research was methodologically flawed. After all, rarely can research on human behavior (especially criminal behavior) approach the precision of experiments in the chemist's laboratory. In addition, the abstract concepts of a social theory are often difficult to define and measure in actual research. If a particular piece of research appears to contradict my theory, I can always argue that the researchers used a misleading definition of crime, or social class, or attachment, or identification. An idea in social science comes and goes, then, not so much because of its validity as demonstrated by research but because of its interest or usefulness.

Instead of a single theory dominating an entire field, as in the natural sciences, many social science theories may exist side by side at the same time. It looks as if these theories are competing with each other. Their proponents criticize each other, sometimes in the most caustic terms. They dismiss each other's research as methodologically shoddy, politically biased, or simply irrelevant. But this conflict may be more apparent than real. The different theorists are like the blind men discussing the elephant. They are not really talking about the same part of the subject. Or, to take a slightly closer analogy, imagine theories about the problem of highway accidents. Some theorists might come up with principles of automobile construction. Other theorists would concern themselves with the perceptions, reactions, and mental states of drivers. Still other theorists would point to the relationship between the powerful auto industry and the government's regulatory agencies. And each group would have research findings to support its ideas.

Is my analogy off the mark? Look at two of the more influential theoretical positions in criminology today—the two I have discussed at length in this chapter: conflict theory and control theory; one radical, the other conservative. Control theory concentrates on differences between criminals and noncriminals; it asks why some people commit crime while others do not. Conflict theory pretty much ignores questions about why people commit crime. Conflict theory does, however, question the political and economic structure and its effect on crime. Control theory, by comparison, accepts the status quo and all but ignores the effects of social institutions (including even the criminal justice system). In their disputes, Marxists and control theorists may not be able to speak to each other in any meaningful way, since they are addressing different questions. But an apparent dispute does not always mean that one side is right and the other wrong. Instead, each theory may be useful in understanding the questions it has selected. The real dispute is whether those questions are the right questions.

How do we decide whether a set of questions is worthwhile? Frequently, the answer depends not on the facts but on our values and general world view. In other words, instead of saying that a theory is wrong, those who disagree can merely say, "So what?" Even professional criminologists may take this approach. For some criminologists, the ultimate test of a theory is whether it leads to policies for reducing crime, especially street crime. If it doesn't, then so what?[32] But applicability is not the only test of a theory, nor even necessarily the best test. By this criterion, physicists should have dismissed Einstein's ideas when he proposed them in 1905, for at that time there were few useful applications for a theory of relativity. For other criminologists, a theory is worthwhile mostly insofar as it clarifies the economic and political structure of society. For still others, a theory must further our understanding of how people think; it must help us understand the subtle forces that influence the thoughts of criminals, police, judges, and others in the criminal justice area.

In other words, if a theory—a set of questions and answers—fits with our world view, if it is useful for clearing up some of the puzzles of that world view, then we tend to find it interesting and important. Otherwise, we tend to find it boring and irrelevant; we say, "So what?"

In discussing theory especially, this is the question I most fear, the question where my answer will be the least satisfactory, for if you do not already think that the facts or issues addressed by a theory are relevant or interesting, I probably have little hope of convincing you otherwise.

NOTES

1. David Matza (1964), *Delinquency and Drift*, New York: Wiley.

2. Gresham M. Sykes and David Matza (1957), "Techniques of Neutralization: A Theory of Delinquency," *American Sociological Review*, vol. 22, pp. 664–70.

3. John E. Conklin (1986), *Criminology* (2nd ed.), New York: Macmillan, pp. 191–92. James F. Short, Jr. and Fred L. Strodtbeck (1965), *Group Process and Gang Delinquency*, Chicago: University of Chicago Press.

4. Hyman Rodman (1963), "The Lower-Class Value Stretch," *Social Problems*, vol. 42, no. 2, pp. 205–15.

5. Elliot Liebow (1967), *Tally's Corner: A Study of Negro Streetcorner Men*, Boston: Little, Brown.

6. Howard Becker (1973), *Outsiders: Studies in the Sociology of Deviance*, New York: Free Press.

7. David Matza (1969), *Becoming Deviant*, Englewood Cliffs, NJ: Prentice-Hall.

8. For example, see Richard D. Schwartz and Jerome H. Skolnick (1962), "Two Studies of Legal Stigma," *Social Problems*, vol. 10, pp. 133–42. For a variety of studies in the labeling tradition, see Earl Rubington and Martin S. Weinberg (1987), *Deviance: The Interactionist Perspective*, New York: Macmillan.

9. Egon Bittner (1967), "The Police on Skid-Row: A Study of Peace Keeping," *American Sociological Review*, vol. 32, pp. 699–715.

10. Joseph R. Gusfield (1963), *Symbolic Crusade*, Urbana, IL: University of Illinois Press. Kristin Luker (1984), *Abortion and the Politics of Motherhood*, Berkeley, CA: University of California Press.

11. Ian Taylor, Paul Walton, and Jock Young, eds. (1975), *Critical Criminology*, London: Routledge and Kegan Paul, p. 44.

12. William J. Chambliss (1964), "A Sociological Analysis of the Law of Vagrancy," *Social Problems*, vol. 12, pp. 67–77.

13. Douglas Hay, Peter Linebaugh, John G. Rule, E. P. Thompson, and Cal Winslow (1975), *Albion's Fatal Tree*, London: Allen Lane.

14. John Helmer (1975), *Drugs and Minority Oppression*, New York: Seabury Press.

15. John E. Conklin (1977), *Illegal but Not Criminal*, Englewood Cliffs, NJ: Prentice-Hall, pp. 99–129.

16. David F. Greenberg, ed. (1981), *Crime and Capitalism: Readings in Marxist Criminology*, Palo Alto, CA: Mayfield, p. 193.

17. Ibid., p. 20.

18. C. Wright Mills (1956), *The Power Elite*, New York: Oxford University Press. G. William Domhoff (1983), *Who Rules America Now?*, Englewood Cliffs, NJ: Prentice-Hall. Michael Useem (1983), *The Inner Circle: Large Corporations and the Rise of Business Political Activities in the U.S. and U.K.*, New York: Oxford University Press.

19. Terence P. Thornberry (1973), "Race, Socioeconomic Status, and Sentencing in the Juvenile Justice System," *Journal of Criminal Law, Criminology and Police Science*, vol. 64, pp. 90–98. Dale Dannefer and Russel K. Schutt (1982), "Race and Juvenile Justice Processing in Court and Police Agencies," *American Journal of Sociology*, vol. 87, pp. 113–32. For a review, see Allen E. Liska (1987), *Perspectives on Deviance* (2nd ed), Englewood Cliffs, NJ: Prentice-Hall, pp. 175–210.

20. David F. Greenberg (1977), "Delinquency and the Age Structure of Society," *Contemporary Crisis*, vol. 1, pp. 189–223.

21. Richard Quinney (1977), *Class State and Crime: On the Theory and Practice of Criminal Justice*, New York: David McKay, p. 144.

22. Delbert S. Elliott, David Huizinga, and Suzanne S. Ageton (1985), *Explaining Delinquency and Drug Use*, Beverly Hills, CA: Sage.

23. Irving A. Spergel (1990), "Youth Gangs: Continuity and Change," in Michael Tonry and Norval Morris (1990), *Crime and Justice: An Annual Review*, vol. 12, Chicago: University of Chicago Press, pp. 171–276 (esp. pp. 199–208).

24. Lewis Yablonsky (1959), "The Delinquent Gang as a Near-Group," *Social Problems*, vol. 7. Walter B. Miller (1974), "American Youth Gangs: Past and Present," in Abraham S. Blumberg, ed. (1974), *Current Perspective on Criminal Behavior*, New York: Knopf, pp. 210–38.

25. Travis Hirschi (1969), *Causes of Delinquency*, Berkeley, CA: University of California Press, p. 173. Elliott, Huizinga, and Ageton, op. cit., pp. 23–24.

26. Ellen Greenberger and Lawrence Steinberg (1987), *When Teenagers Work: The Psychological and Social Cost of Adolescent Employment*, New York: Basic Books.

27. Terence P. Thornberry (1987), "Toward an Interactional Theory of Delinquency," *Criminology*, vol. 25, no. 4, pp. 863–91.

28. Rolf Loeber and Magda Stouthamer-Loeber (1986), "Family Factors as Correlates and Predictors of Juvenile Conduct Problems and Delinquency," in Michael Tonry and Norval Morris, eds. (1986), *Crime and Justice: An Annual Review*, vol. 7, Chicago: University of Chicago Press, pp. 151–88.

29. Elliott, Huizinga, and Ageton, op. cit.

30. Lawrence E. Cohen and Marcus Felson (1979), "Social Change and Crime Rate Trends: A Routine Activities Approach," *American Sociological Review*, vol. 44, pp. 588–608.

31. Rodney Stark (1987), "Deviant Places: A Theory of the Ecology of Crime," *Criminology*, vol. 25, no. 4, pp. 893–909.

32. James Q. Wilson (1965), *Thinking About Crime*, New York: Random House, p. 53.

Something Blue:
The Police

CHAPTER *13*

WHY POLICE?

IN THE UNITED STATES IN 1987, STREET CRIMINALS COST THE PUBLIC ABOUT $12 BILLION. That same year, the police cost the public $26 billion. [1] Not only do the police cost more than crime, they also cost more than the other parts of the criminal justice system (courts and corrections). Since $26 billion is a lot of money, maybe I ought to start this chapter by asking why: Why do we have police? Why not get rid of them and save the money?

Think about it for a moment, and try to come up with an answer before you read the next paragraph.

When I ask students this question, they sometimes look at me as if I were impossibly stupid. "What do you mean, 'Why do we have police?' " they say. "You gotta have police."

"But why?" I repeat.

"To enforce the law. To prevent crime. To catch criminals." These are the typical responses, and chances are your answer sounded like one of them.

However, to a great extent, the police do not enforce the law, do not prevent crime, and do not catch criminals.

Since this is a fairly provocative and unusual statement, I should explain it fully.

Enforcing—and Not Enforcing—the Law

Of course the police do enforce the law—sometimes. But think of all the times you have seen police officers. What were they doing? When I ask students this question, I get answers like

> riding around in their cars
> directing traffic
> giving me a ticket
> sitting in Dunkin' Donuts drinking coffee
> helping out after a traffic accident

Except for the speeding ticket (which was probably from a state trooper, not a city cop), none of these require the enforcement of laws. Of course, students had not intended to make most of these "observations" of police. Would we find something different if we looked at the things we specifically call on the police to do? In other words, have you ever called the police, and if so, why? When I ask students this question, most of the answers have little to do with enforcing the law, preventing crime, or catching criminals:

I locked myself out of my car.
There was a dead animal in the street somebody ran over.
My little brother got lost.
Someone broke into our house.

What the Police Do

These examples are not unusual. People call on the police for a wide variety of services. In poor neighborhoods especially, police may be called on for all sorts of social services—the kinds of things for which middle-class people call doctors or psychologists or social workers or lawyers. Of the calls that the police get, the large majority involve things other than crime. When crime does occur, people may call the police—sometimes. But as you may remember from the chapter on crime statistics, in over half of all crimes the victim does *not* call the police.

These images of the police present something of a paradox. We refer to police as "law enforcement officers"; we think of them as our defense against crime; and yet most of the things we call on them to do, and most of the things we see them doing, have very little to do with crime and law enforcement.

One possible way to explain the contradiction is to say that of course we—the good, law-abiding citizens—rarely see the police in their crime-fighting, law-enforcing roles because we stay on the right side of the law. We don't have a complete view of police work. For that, we would have to follow the police through an entire working day for a complete view of what they actually spent their time doing.

In fact, there have been just such studies. Here is the breakdown from one study of police in a city with a population of about 400,000.[2]

Activity	Percent of Time Consumed
Crimes against persons	2.96%
Crimes against property	14.82
Traffic	9.20
On-view	9.10
Social service	13.70
Administration	50.19

"On-view" refers to investigations initiated by the officer (rather than in response to a call)—checking the locks on buildings, stopping automobiles or people on foot if they seem suspicious. "Social service" calls were mostly for family crises, drunkenness, or mental illness. Under "administration" came everything from taking reports and serving warrants to going on coffee breaks.

Crime took up only about 18 percent of the police time. Other studies of police time, by using different definitions, have come up with different numbers, but the largest amount of time any study has found police devoting to crime is 50 percent. Most studies estimate that police spend 10 to 25 percent of their time in crime-related activity.[3] Whatever the exact figure, it's a far cry from the exciting, action-packed image of police we get from "Hunter" or *Lethal Weapon*. As one city cop put it, "Most of the time, this job is as boring as can be. You just sit behind the wheel and go where they tell you. . . . Your mind kinda wanders and some nights it's a bitch to stay awake."[4]

Police Discretion

To say that police enforce the law is misleading in still another way. This definition of the police as "law enforcement officers" implies that the police size up situations by asking what law is being broken and how can they enforce it. The officer in this definition becomes more or less a tool of the law. The legislature passes laws, and the police go out and enforce them.

Do you really believe that this is what the police do? Have you ever been confronted by the police for violating the law—a traffic violation, Halloween mischief, a loud party? Did you try to influence the police officer not to arrest you or give you the ticket or the summons? If so, then you were acting on the belief that the police often do not enforce the law, even when they come upon a violation. You intuitively recognized something that social scientists only recently began to pay attention to in their theories about police: **discretion**. Discretion means the power to decide: Rather than having to act in a prescribed way, the officers can exercise judgment over what to do. They can write the ticket, or they can let you go with a warning.

Time after time during their eight-hour shift, police officers come upon violations of laws and ordinances: public drunks, loitering teenagers, fights among acquaintances or family members, delivery trucks blocking the street, construction equipment blocking the sidewalk, and many others. Most of the time, the officers do *not* enforce the law as it appears written in the statute books. They do not arrest the drunk; they do not bring assault and battery charges against the guy who punched out his friend; they do not write a summons for every sidewalk violation. All this nonenforcement should make us revise our ideas about the relationship between the police and the law. Instead of seeing the officer's primary function as "enforcing the law," we might better think of it the way most police officers do—as "handling situations." The officer is not interested in applying all the available laws and ordinances. Instead, the law—the power to make an arrest—is just one tool the police have for achieving their primary goal of restoring *order.* Instead of the officer being an instrument of the law, it's the other way around: The law is an instrument used by the officer.

Police—A Definition

Recognizing this relationship between law and officer leads to a slightly different way of defining the term *police.* Suppose you had to give a concise definition of this word. One criminology professor, Carl Klockars, begins his course on police by asking students to write down a brief definition of "police." Answers range from the serious ("an agency of government which enforces the law and keeps the peace") to the cynical ("The police are a bunch of hotshots who get their kicks by hassling blacks, students, and most other people who are trying to have a good time.").[5] When I borrow this exercise for my own class, someone usually says that the police are the people you always see hanging out in doughnut shops. My favorite was, "The police are the people you call when you call the police." This is not as dumb as it sounds, as I will try to show.

The other definitions, the more typical ones, all define the police in terms of *goals*—what the police should do. Even definitions about hassling students or eating doughnuts have a "should" behind them. They imply that the cops *should* be doing something else, so even these sarcastic definitions still focus on the goals of policing. But no goal definition could possibly encompass all the things the police do or should do. What makes the police unique, what differentiates them from civilians, lies not in their goals but in the *means* they have at their disposal to accomplish those goals. Unlike anybody else, the police are allowed to use force.

Klockars gives a more elaborate definition based on this basic insight about means: "Police are institutions or individuals given the general right to use coercive force by the state within the state's domestic territory."[6]

When we define the police in terms of means—the legitimate use of force—we can see what all the different goals of police work have in common. Controlling crowds at parades or ball games; responding to reports of accidents or dog bites; driving drunks home; removing dead bodies from houses; intervening in arguments between landlord and tenant, customer and merchant, husband and wife; removing children from abusive or negligent parents; getting a reluctant but seriously ill person to go to the hospital . . .; the list is endless. What they all share is that somebody—a civilian, a social worker, a doctor—has called the cops because the situation may require coercive force. That's why I liked the idea that "the police are who you call when you call the police." Beneath this circular definition (or what philosophers call a tautology) is an intuitive recognition about who possesses the legitimate use of force. As another sociologist, Egon Bittner, has summarized this idea:

> Many puzzling aspects of police work fall into place when one ceases to consider it as principally concerned with law enforcement and crime control. . . . It makes much more sense to say that the police are nothing other than a mechanism for the distribution of situationally justified force in society.[7]

Bittner goes on to say that people call the police when a situation might require the legitimate use of force: situations in which "something ought not to be happening about which something ought to be done NOW."[8]

Obviously, one of these "somethings" that ought not to be happening is crime. But crime occupies only a small part of police time. Nevertheless, most people, including the police, see crime-fighting as the "core activity" of the police role in society. Accordingly, the next sections of this chapter will examine the two major parts of the crime-fighter image: preventing crime and catching criminals.

Preventing Crime

The idea that the police prevent crime is basically the idea of deterrence, and you can find a more thorough discussion of it in Chapter 16. The question is not simply whether the police prevent crime. Undoubtedly they do. The questions are, how much crime, what kinds of crime, under what conditions, and at what cost? Here is a somewhat oversimplified summary of the evidence on these questions:

> Ordinary police-car patrol deters little, if any, crime.[9]
>
> An officer on foot patrol deters more crime than no patrol at all. Further increases in the number of foot patrols add very little deterrent effect.[10]
>
> Greatly increased foot patrols may decrease crimes that would be visible from the street. For crimes that usually occur out of view of the street (murder, rape, assault), police patrol makes little difference.[11]
>
> Police may also deter crime in enclosed environments, like subway cars or subway stations.
>
> The cost of police, relative to the financial cost of the crimes they deter, is very high. In 1965, New York increased police patrol in subway trains and stations. Crime went down, but the cost of the patrol was such that each deterred felony cost the city $35,000.[12]

So to the question, "Do the police prevent crime?," the answer must be, "Yes, but. . . ." Or, as a Maryland police chief summarized the relationship between the police and crime, "We are not letting the public in on our era's dirty little secret: that there is little the police can do."[13]*

---

* Street cops, of course, may think otherwise. In their view, cops *could* do something about crime if only the courts or the police management "downtown" would let them.

Perhaps in recognition of the relative ineffectiveness of police patrol as a deterrent, some police departments have developed special teams often called "anti-crime" units. My first reaction on hearing of these was to ask, "Aren't *all* police anti-crime?" In fact, the name acknowledges the "dirty little secret" that most police on general patrol have little effect on crime. The idea behind these units is not deterrence but "incapacitation" (see Chapter 17)—getting the worst criminals off the streets. By going after "habitual offenders," "career criminals," or "dangerous offenders," the police would be getting the most crime reduction for each arrest. Here, at last, is something that matches our TV image of cops. ("We know Smith's a one-man crime wave, so we just stake out his usual places, wait for him to make his move, then we nail him.") The idea sounds good, but the results have not always been encouraging.

Making arrests is not the problem. The special units do arrest criminals, nearly all of them for felonies. But arrests do not keep criminals off the streets; convictions and sentences do. Yet only about a third of the arrests made by anti-crime units result in convictions. This seems paradoxical. The anti-crime unit is collaring the worst criminals—the ones that prosecutors and judges as well as police want to put away. Still, two out of every three of these criminals "walk." Why?

One reason is that while it's easy to arrest a criminal for *something*, it's much harder to catch him for a serious crime. Suppose that the police have identified Criminal Smith as a repeat offender and make him a target for arrest. Officers in the special unit may be so intent on arresting Smith that they are willing to bring him in for a less serious offense or for a crime where the evidence is flimsy. The district attorney looks at the case and either lets it drop or must bargain it down to a less serious charge.

Because of the small percentage of "quality" arrests, these special programs may have problems of cost-efficiency. The department winds up spending a lot of money for a few good arrests. For example, in Washington, D.C., 62 officers worked on a "repeat offender project" (ROP); by the end of the year, they had produced 66 convictions, or only about one per officer per year.[14] Even so, not all these convictions were for felonies. In 1981, only 19 percent of the arrests produced felony convictions. Even with "innovative" improvements in the next two years, the ROP still got felony convictions in only one of every four arrests. Thirty-eight percent of the repeat offenders got misdemeanor time, and 37 percent walked.[15] The ROP cops may have nabbed serious offenders, but they could not get them for serious crimes. In Kansas City, the police instituted a program that aimed specifically for quality arrests; the goal was to convict *career* criminals for *serious* crimes. But the special unit netted only six such convictions, and the police power spent on the project amounted to 240,000 hours. That is, each conviction cost an average of 40,000 officer hours—the equivalent of one officer working 20 years.[16]

Where special units appear to be more productive, it may turn out that many of the arrests are really the work of the regular police force. For example, the Miami Stop Robbery unit averaged four arrests per officer per month. However, in over 90 percent of these arrests, the officers were merely executing an existing warrant, accompanying another officer to make the arrest. Similarly, a Long Beach, California, anti-burglary unit produced a fair number of arrests, but only half of the arrests were for burglary or fencing; and of these, only half resulted from the unit's special work.[17]

Outside of such special units, the ordinary officers patrolling their beats rarely come upon a crime in progress. A 1967 study found that the average Los Angeles cop detected a robbery once every 14 years, though perhaps this means that the officer's presence does deter (or at least delay) the criminal.[18] But even if the police are something of a deterrent, this crime prevention is not readily visible to the naked eye. By definition, a prevented crime is one that would have taken place but didn't. And it's very hard to see something that didn't happen. The cynical student of a few pages ago saw cops sitting in the doughnut shop and concluded that they were loafing. He could not quite so easily see that just by sitting there the cops may also have been keeping the doughnut shop from being robbed or from being disrupted by rowdy customers. This insight, however, probably was not lost on the owner of the place, who was only too glad to provide the police with coffee and doughnuts at no charge.[19]

However, even the police may find it frustrating that most of their crime prevention is invisible. Aside from the doughnuts, it goes unrewarded and unrecognized even in departmental reports.

> You can't put down the number of times you prevented a burglary by parking the radio car in the right place and questioning a guy in the street. It's not on the radio. It's never known.[20]

Crime prevention, then, is the less dramatic component in the crime-fighting image of the police. It's certainly not good material for TV shows. Catching criminals, on the other hand, comes much closer to our idea of what "real" police work is all about. We want cops and robbers, where the police nab the bad guy. But do they?

Catching Criminals

When I said at the beginning of this chapter that the police do not catch criminals, I was, of course, exaggerating. The police do catch criminals. In 1988, police in the United States made 13.8 million arrests. The category with the highest total arrests was "driving under the influence" (1.8 million). Another 2.4 million arrests were for simple assault, disorderly conduct, and drunkenness, where arrest is often used as a means of handling a situation or keeping order.* The police did make 2.9 million arrests for Index crimes, but these still only produced a clearance rate of 21 percent. That is, of all Index offenses, "known to the police," one in five resulted in an arrest.[21] Whether .210 is a good batting average is a matter of opinion. But what lies behind these 2.9 million Index crime arrests? How do the police manage to catch criminals at all? Let's start by looking at how criminals were caught before cities had police forces.

Criminals Without Police

The first city police force that we might recognize as such did not come into existence until 1829 in London. By then, the population of London had grown to over 1 million, and street crime and riots occurred with alarming regularity. In the United States, Boston organized a small police force in 1837, patterned after that of London. Several other cities followed in the late 1840s. At that time, there were at least a dozen cities with population over 25,000, and they, too, could be fairly rough places. Still, up until then, cities had no regular police force. Who caught criminals? Who made arrests?

For the most part in 19th-century America, the responsibility for solving crimes fell upon the victim. There were constables, but they were really more like servants of the court than servants of the people. A person who had been wronged could go to court and swear out a warrant. The victim would take the warrant to the constable and tell him who had committed the offense and where that offender might be found. The constable would then make the arrest. The victim also had to pay the administrative fees for processing the case.

England had a similar system. However, because it was coupled with a reward system for catching felons, it gave rise to the specialized occupation of "thief-taker." Ideally, thief-takers would catch thieves and collect a reward from the government. Or they would deal directly with victims, catching the thief and, for a fee, returning the stolen property to the victim. If you think about it for a minute, you can see how such a system could easily become corrupt. In practice, it led to a very close link between thief-takers and thieves, to the point where it was often hard to tell the difference. In fact, one legendary thief-taker, Jonathan Wild, used the reward system to create a large criminal organization in 18th-century London.† Wild was a "fence." He bought stolen goods from thieves and resold them, frequently to the original owner. Impatient with such an unpredictable flow of loot for resale,

---

* Arrests for vagrancy and loitering also used to contribute to this category, but court decisions from the 1970s have greatly restricted the use of vagrancy and loitering laws.

† In *The Threepenny Opera*, the character Peachum (Mack the Knife's father-in-law), who runs the London underworld of beggars and thieves, was based on Wild.

he soon started arranging the thefts in advance, forcing thieves into working for him. If a thief refused, Wild could always turn him in, thereby both getting rid of the uncooperative thief and pocketing a handsome reward for catching a felon. Obviously, the reward system had its drawbacks.[22]

Arrests: Who Solves the Crime?

The modern system of catching criminals is, at least in principle, much different. The responsibility now belongs not to the victim or private thief-takers but to the agents of the state—namely, the police. The police are specialists in this enterprise, and are therefore presumably much better at it. TV shows provide endless examples. Most cop shows involve white-collar criminals, organized crime, or high-level drug deals—crimes that often really do require specialized police work. Some movies and TV cop shows do deal with street crimes like robbery, larceny, or burglary, but these shows, too, portray crime solving as clever criminals being outwitted by even more clever and hard-working cops. Through sophisticated techniques of "forensic science"—fingerprints, ballistics, etc.—the detectives manage to figure out the identity of the killer or burglar. Or they arrange to be in the right place at the right time to catch a robber in the act. Through it all, the citizens (victims, TV viewers) stand aside and watch with respect and gratitude as the police nail the bad guy. TV and movies reinforce this idea of the cop as specialist by having the plainclothes detectives do all the real police work, while the uniformed patrol officers come off second best.

How well does this picture reflect what goes on in the real world? Is this really the way the police solve crimes? To find out, researchers have looked not just at the most spectacular cases but at a more representative sample of the crimes reported to the police. The conclusion from these studies is that most arrests result from very routine and unexciting methods.

In real life, in contrast to the TV image, it is the citizen or the patrol cop, not the detective, who usually solves the crime. A RAND Corporation study of detectives found that in 30 percent of solved crimes, the officer arriving at the scene of the crime makes the arrest, either because citizens have stopped the criminal or because the criminal is still roaming the area. More to the point, in *half* of all crimes cleared by arrest, "the perpetrator is known when the crime report is first taken, and the main jobs for the investigator are to locate the perpetrator, take him or her into custody, and assemble the facts needed to present charges in court."[23] Think about what this means in terms of progress in the last 300 years. The most common way in which crimes are solved very much resembles the methods of the pre-police era: The victim or a witness tells the cop who did it; the cop goes and makes the arrest.

It may seem odd, especially if we cherish the image of crime depicted in the media, that citizens often know who the criminal is. In fact, in a surprising number of cases, the victim and offender already know each other—especially when the crime is murder. Most murders occur between acquaintances, friends, or family members. Only 18 percent of murders are clearly between strangers (in another 26 percent, the victim-offender relationship is unknown).[24] The same pattern is true of rapes and assaults; although, unlike murders, when these crimes occur between acquaintances or family members, they seldom get reported to the police. The people involved—both victim and offender—may see this violence as a personal matter rather than a legal one, especially in assaults, or even murders, where there is little to distinguish the victim from the criminal. However, when the crime is public enough or serious enough, the police arrive and make an arrest. Career criminal John Allen, in his autobiography *Assault With a Deadly Weapon*, describes the crime leading to his first conviction on that charge. It is typical, both in the circumstances of the crime and in the method of solution by the police. Hearing that his girlfriend was the next target for gang rape by a rival gang, Allen put a gun in his pocket and went to confront the leader. He found himself facing six or seven young men armed with bricks and knives. When the first bricks started flying, Allen started shooting. He shot the rival leader twice, not fatally. Allen maintains, "I was completely right and he [the victim] was completely wrong. . . . If I hadn't . . . shot him, I probably would have wound up in the hospital." The police easily learned who had done the shooting, and Allen, then a juvenile, was sentenced to six years.[25]

Even with robbery and burglary, a surprisingly large proportion of crimes occurs among family and acquaintances. A New York study found that about one-third of the arrests for burglary or robbery involved crimes between people who knew each other. (Of course, these were *arrests*, not total crimes or even reported crimes. Crimes between strangers are less likely to be solved.) Consider the following robbery:

> A woman reports that her sister and her sister's boyfriend assaulted her, threatened to kill her baby, and took her purse and $40. Later, she explains that it was a misunderstanding. Previously the boyfriend had bought the woman a baby carriage; she had thought it was a gift, but he did not. The crime was his attempt to get what he thought was rightfully his.[26]

Burglaries, too, may be ways to settle personal scores. An angry man breaks into his ex-wife's house, steals her clothes, and drives them to his new home several hundred miles away.[27] Even burglaries intended for profit may have this element of personal revenge. John Allen, the street criminal, says of his early burglaries, "We always tried to get the dude that the neighbors didn't like too much or the guy that was hard on people who lived in the neighborhood. . . . I like to think that all the places we . . . broke into was kind of like the bad guys."[28]

Other Crimes, Other Methods

In most burglaries and robberies, victims or witnesses cannot immediately identify the criminal. Many of these crimes are "cold"—i.e., the police arrive too late to arrest a suspect, and the victim cannot name the criminal—and most of them are not solved. In New York City, police manage to clear only 2 percent of these "cold" cases,[29] though other cities may have slightly more success. However, even when the police do solve these crimes, their investigations rarely resemble the glamorous or high-tech detective work that makes for exciting television. The methods are almost always routine.

In crimes where the victim has seen the criminal, if any procedure can lead to an arrest, it is the routine method of having the victim look through mug shots. For other crimes, the routine methods include tracing gun ownership or pawn shop slips, checking a person's identification against a list of persons wanted on outstanding warrants, and checking auto registrations against a "hot car" file. Many other reported auto thefts are "solved" by the officer asking the victim three questions: Did you lend the car to anyone? Might a relative or friend have borrowed it? Could it have been repossessed for nonpayment?[30] These rather unspectacular techniques resolve more cases and produce far more arrests than does intensive detective work. Sophisticated techniques like fingerprinting account for only about 2 percent of all crimes solved.[31] In fact, a police detective whose house has been burglarized probably would not want the fingerprint squad to come in. They rarely get a usable print, and they leave a big mess.[32] Even if the police do get a fingerprint, it becomes useful only *after* they have a suspect. They can then match the suspect's prints against the one found at the crime scene. But if they don't have a suspect, checking the fingerprint against all existing prints on file is a hopeless task. Only if the crime is particularly important will the police go to such extraordinary lengths (see box).

Today, fingerprinting brings results in one or two cases in a hundred. In the future, however, if computers can be programmed to read and match fingerprints, searching for this kind of physical evidence may become much more worthwhile. Computers also may speed up the tedious search through the mug shot books.[33] After all, similar technological advances have turned hot car checks, ID checks, and weapons tracing into routine procedures.[34] Even these advances probably will do little to make real crime solving more like TV, with its glamorized and fashionably dressed detectives. Detectives will have their place in the small minority of crimes that receive extraordinary attention. But for most crimes, if they are solved at all, the patrol officer who arrives first at the scene to interview the victims and witnesses will be the one who gets the valuable information. Patrick Murphy, who has been chief of police departments in Detroit, New York City, and Washington, D.C., puts it more bluntly. A *Newsweek* article quotes him as saying, "The truth about detectives is that . . . they are not likely to be effective police

BURGLARS' FINGERPRINTS: A LONG SHOT TO ARREST
BY TODD S. PURDUM

He has lifted fingerprints from windowsills and doorjambs, from lacquered jewel boxes and glass coffee tables—thousands of fingerprints from thousands of burglarized apartments in New York City in the last 11 years.

But in all that time, Officer William McNally, a fingerprint expert in the 20th Precinct on the Upper West Side of Manhattan, has handled only one case in which stolen property was found and returned to its owner. . . .

Last year . . . the police say, precinct fingerprint officers responded to 118,800 . . . burglaries and lifted fingerprints in 11,500 cases. . . .

In about 600 cases in which prints were lifted, the prints matched those of known crim-inals on file. As a result, about 300 arrests were made. . . .

Officer McNally . . . said he had success-fully identified 31 suspects in the 11 years he has been taking prints.

Source: Copyright © 1986 by *The New York Times Company*. Reprinted by permission.

Note: Six hundred identifications out of 11,500 prints is about 5 percent. On the other hand, if you look at how often the effort of dusting for prints produces an arrest, the figures are even less encouraging: 300 arrests in 118,800 burglaries is less than three-tenths of 1 percent.

---

officers." The article continues to paraphrase the chief: "They [detectives] spend much of their time in bars, supposedly seeking information, or but-tering up politicians and the press, which gives them strong allies when they need to resist reform."[35]

KEEPING THE PEACE

Let us return to the original question, "Why do we have police?" To enforce laws? To prevent crime? To catch criminals? The police do perform all these functions, but not to the extent that we might think.* Their enforcement of laws is very selective, their effectiveness in preventing crime is at best hard to demonstrate, and their ability to catch predatory criminals depends mostly on the help of civilians. Of course, *somebody* has to do these things,

---

* It's not exactly clear what we think of the police. Most people express support and approval of the police. Yet nearly four out of 10 Americans say that they have very little confidence or none at all in the ability of the police to solve crimes and catch criminals. (*Source*: ABC News poll reported in *Sourcebook—1984*, p. 212.) Edmund F. McGarrell and Timothy J. Flanagan, eds. (1985), *Sourcebook of Criminal Justice Statistics—1984*, U.S. Department of Justice, Bureau of Justice Statistics, Washington, D.C.: U.S. Government Printing Office.

even if imperfectly; but somebody also had to do them in the centuries before 1830. So why do we have police?

One way of answering the question is to look at the origins of the police. If we understand why this institution came into being, perhaps we also can understand something about why it continues to exist. Of course, we also must trace the evolution of the police to see what has changed and what has remained the same.

The New Police—London

The uniformed, patrolling police force is a relatively recent invention. As mentioned earlier, it was not until 1829 that London instituted the first police force resembling those that we now take for granted. The idea quickly caught on in America, and by the 1870s, most U.S. cities had police forces.[36] Obviously, the police force was an idea whose time had come. But why? Cities had existed for centuries, and as early as 1750, there had been proposals in England for an urban police force. But it was nearly another 100 years before the idea was put into practice. Why had people resisted the formation of police forces? What other institutions allowed cities to get by for so long without police? And what was happening in the 19th century to make police forces acceptable or even desirable?

To a great extent, the pre-police era depended on private means for doing the things that today are done by the police. Catching criminals was the responsibility either of the individual or of the community collectively. In London there were private detective agencies and thief-takers who, for a fee, would assist victims in recovering stolen property and would, perhaps, bring the thief to justice. In the countryside, the system more resembled that of the posse of the American West. When the parish constable needed help putting down a disturbance or chasing a criminal, he would "raise the hue and cry," and all men in the parish were required by law to come to his assistance.[37]

The job of catching criminals, then, did not belong to a single, specialized occupation; neither did the responsibility for crime prevention. That, too, was largely a matter for the individual or the community. The most common form of crime prevention—the precursor of the cop patrolling a beat—was the "watch." The person on watch walked about the town on the lookout for fires and other dangers, including disturbances and suspicious persons. In some towns, the watch had the power to arrest people and hold them until a hearing the next morning. He might also ring bells, or call the hour ("eleven o'clock and all's well"), or light the lamps. It was not an attractive job, and in some towns men were forced to serve by a sort of draft: Any male over 18 was liable to serve for a period of time—or pay someone to substitute for him. In most towns, the wage was low and, consequently, so was the quality of the watch. Elderly, sleepy, corrupt, or just incompetent, the night watch—since Shakespeare's time and before—has probably provided more comic relief than real security. In London, watchmen were routinely taunted and occasionally murdered by rich young men, who thought it great sport. As a result, the watchmen tended to spend much of their time out of sight—an understandable strategy, but hardly an effective deterrent to crime.[38] In Boston, the watch was so ineffective that merchants either paid for extra watchmen or hired their own private patrols.[39]

In any case, the system did little to reduce crime. By some accounts, London in the 1780s was a far more dangerous place than is any present-day American city although the actual amount of crime is a matter of dispute among historians and criminologists.[40] At the very least, many influential people at the time saw crime as a widespread problem. From time to time, "crime waves" would seize public attention and create a crisis atmosphere. One such crisis arose in the 1730s, when gin became widely available. Prior to then, the only liquors available (mostly brandy) were upper-class drinks, too expensive for the masses, who got by with less potent beverages like ale. But the availability of cheap gin democratized drinking, and the new drunkenness among the poor caused some alarm. In the view of the wealthy, gin had brought new levels of violence, crime, laziness, family disruption, and general moral and physical decay to great numbers of people. In response, the government passed anti-gin laws, which had little effect on the flow of gin but did add a new source of corruption for the constabulary.*[41]

In addition to the continual presence of crime, riots posed a danger periodically. Since the poor and even the middle class were largely powerless (they still did not have the right to vote), they made their position known by means of riots: riots over specific issues like wages or the price of bread; politically motivated riots, like the extremely violent, anti-Catholic "Gordon riots" of 1780; and riots based on vague, general feelings—"the belief in a rough sort of social justice, which prompts the poor to settle accounts with the rich by smashing their windows, or burning their property," as occurred in the 1760s and 1780s.[42]

Yet despite all this crime and riot, and despite several Royal Commissions on police and legal reform, London still did not replace the watch system with uniformed police until 1829. And the reason behind their reluctance is important: Upper and lower classes alike saw the police as a threat to political liberty.

Those who resisted the establishment of a police force believed that there was an inherent conflict between the power of the state and the freedom of

---

* You may have noticed that the gin crisis of London in the 1730s sounds a lot like the drug crisis of the United States in the 1980s: A drug of the wealthy (cocaine) becomes democratized in potent form ("crack"); the elites (lawmakers, et al., greatly aided by the media) declare a crisis and call for more severe penalties and more law enforcement. It is an open question whether the similarity lies more in the nature of the drugs and their effects or in the relations between social classes.

the people. If the state were granted more power—in the form of a police force that could, for purposes of controlling crime, intrude into people's lives—then freedom would be diminished. Their fears are well-grounded. In principle, a police force may be a neutral enforcer of the law, but it also can use its extraordinary power to keep tyrannical governments in power. The police have always been such a danger, and they still are. Look at any dictatorship today and you will see a regime that depends on its police, uniformed or secret, to suppress opposition. In Haiti under the Duvaliers, the most hated symbol of tyranny was the *tonton macoutes*, the secret police. In South Africa, it is against the police and their informers, white or black, that the blacks have directed most of their violence. In the relatively nonviolent revolutions in Eastern Europe in 1989–1990, the people were most vengeful toward the secret police—the *stasi* in East Germany, the *securitate* in Rumania. Similarly, in England and America in 1800, people feared the authoritarian use of police, and to confirm their fears they had only to look across to France, where the police acted as spies, informers, and *agents provocateurs*, brutally stifling political dissent. Americans wary of police could also look to their own recent history as colonies policed in part by the British army.*[43]

Overcoming such resistance required a combination of historical factors. The creation of the London police force, like any historical change, came about both because of large social forces and because of the efforts of individual people. The social changes had been building for a long time: As peasants were forced off the land, they came to the city; in the expanding and crowded city, traditional forms of social control broke down. These trends helped create an urban lower class. Upper classes felt threatened by the crime and riot they associated with the "dangerous classes"—i.e., the urban poor; a changing economy gave rise to a new middle class of merchants and professionals, whose business demanded a more regulated, coordinated, and orderly society.

As for the individuals involved, the person credited with creating the police was the young Home Secretary, Robert Peel. To win passage of the Police Act, Peel had to overcome popular fears about possible police repression. He had excellent credentials for the task. Previously, in his reform of the old criminal laws, he had taken a stand against arbitrary and cruel government power. Prior to Peel's efforts, a person could be hanged for crimes as minor as theft of much-needed food.[44] In his plan for the new police, Peel imposed three important limitations on police power.

---

* In America, these fears also caused the Founding Fathers to place strict limits on the use of the army in domestic, nomilitary affairs. Recently, this fear of government police power has emerged in controversies over the involvement of the CIA in domestic affairs, the use of the FBI to spy on political groups, and the use of the military to enforce drug laws.

The police were to be **unarmed**. They carried truncheons but no firearms. This meant that the officers would have to rely on their authority, not their power. Authority, unlike power, depends on its acceptance by the other person. Unarmed, the police cannot act unless the people accept their role as legitimate.

The police were to be **uniformed**. This obviously kept the police from being used as political spies or informers.

The police were to be confined to **preventive patrol**. They were there principally to keep order. Only to a much lesser extent were they criminal catchers or crime solvers. They were more like the watch, except that they would patrol both day and night, and, it was hoped, they would be more effective.[45]

In any case, thanks to Peel's good political sense in limiting police power, a police force was established. More important, from the very first, London police did their job in a "professional" manner—fair, impartial, impersonal, detached, and relatively incorrupt. After a short while, they won fairly wide approval. The people of London even invented two affectionate terms for the new police—nicknames derived from the name of their founder: "Peelers" or (the one that stuck) "bobbies."

The Police in America

The image of the London bobby—unarmed, impartial, restrained, doing things by the book—stands in contrast to the image of his American counterpart. Perhaps you know the picture I have in mind: the (usually) Irish cop who knows everybody in the neighborhood and runs his beat pretty much the way he wants to. He got his job through political patronage, carries a gun, deals out "street justice" with his nightstick, and takes payoffs from various crooks operating in the area. This image has much basis in reality, especially for the early years of policing in the United States.[46] As professional as the bobbies appeared, American police seemed the opposite. New York City police even wore street clothes rather than uniforms. Not until 10 years after the force was founded, and with the patrolmen still protesting, did the commissioners succeed in imposing the blue symbol of discipline. The police also became known for their tendencies toward brutality and corruption, which largely went unpunished.[47]

For all their differences, the London and New York police shared one important similarity—the reason for their existence. The police were needed in order to impose a more orderly existence on riotous sections of the population. As the economy and the urban society became more complex, the need for order increased. At this time, America, too, had its "dangerous classes," and respectable folk welcomed a police force to deal with this problem. In part, the dangerous class consisted of tramps and paupers (what today we call the homeless). For them, the police might provide lodging for a night or two and then force them to move on out of town.[48] But the dangerous classes also included the immigrant, urban poor. Their threat lay not just in their higher rates of predatory crime. It was more general than that—threat of disorder and riot and even somehow the threat that the dangerous classes might undermine the political system. In the early police years (1840–1870), these urban immigrants were the Irish, and the anti-Democratic, anti-Irish slogan "Rum, Romanism, and Rebellion" neatly summarizes these fears.* The issue for "nativist" Americans was not just different norms about drinking (rum), or a different religion (Romanism); it was rebellion, the stability of the whole society.

The police were a response to this threat. They were there to preserve the political status quo (things as they are). They wound up doing many other things—finding lost children, catching criminals, putting down labor strikes, and so on—but their original reason for existence was to preserve social order.

The Police and the Politics of Order

Preserving order or keeping the peace sounds like a politically neutral activity, hardly a matter for debate. But in reality, policing is "neutral" only when there is substantial agreement among all members of society. But what happens when some people think that current social arrangements are not right and that there is systematic injustice? What happens when these people agitate for social change?

Usually, when such conflict arises, the police find themselves protecting the status quo. The police ultimately are representatives of the state, the government. When people challenge the legitimacy of that government, the police naturally find themselves opposing the challenge. That is their job. They do that job not in the name of some political ideology—no cop sees himself as going out and oppressing minorities or stifling social progress. They do so in their traditional role as crime fighters, peacekeepers, and law enforcers. The police see themselves as neutral, enforcing the law and keeping order, but in effect they are conservative—"conservative" in the literal sense of conserving things as they are. This political function of the police usually is invisible to those who support the status quo, especially when there is little open, organized conflict in the society. For most citizens in the United States today, the role of the police seems neutral; there is nothing wrong with the order that the police maintain. If anything, these citizens

---

* By analogy, imagine Jesse Jackson winning the Democratic Presidential nomination and the Democrats being labeled the party of "Crack, Race, and Rap." The phrase is less alliterative than its 19th-century counterpart, but it does convey the combination of fear and resentment directed at the urban poor.

want more policing, more order, more law enforcement. For a view of the police as oppressive, as too vigorous in their law enforcement, we must ask those who stand somewhat outside of the status quo—the young, the poor, and the minorities, although even among these groups a majority still expresses general support of the police.[49]

The conservative nature of the police becomes more apparent in times of conflict, especially when we can look at that conflict from a distance. The political function of the police seems fairly clear in totalitarian societies, where they represent the interests of the government against those who seek change. To outsiders it may seem clear that they are repressing politically uncomfortable ideas and the people who express them. But there as elsewhere, the police probably believe sincerely that they are protecting society: controlling crime, maintaining order, and enforcing the law. Certainly, those in authority justify police work in the name of these legitimate and seemingly neutral goals.

In democracies also, conflict usually puts the police on the side of the establishment. In the United States of the mid-19th century, preserving order meant enforcing the position of the established Protestant groups against the threat posed by the immigrant, urban Irish. Later, it meant protecting the interests of the owners of factories and mines against union organizers and striking workers. In the 1950s and 1960s, police in the South enforced segregationist "Jim Crow" laws against civil rights workers. Also in the 1960s, during the Vietnam War, police confronted anti-war demonstrators—all in the name of maintaining order and enforcing the law.

Much has changed over the years. The police cultivated their image as crime fighters rather than peacekeepers, and they managed to separate themselves from the obvious politics of urban political machines.* However, regardless of party politics, the police, as an arm of the state, are a conservative political force. The bulk of police work still consists of preserving order, and when there is social conflict, that means preserving the status quo.

POLICE MISCONDUCT—GUARDING THE GUARDS

Any society must protect its members—from outside dangers and from each other. A small society, much like a family, keeps its members from doing what they shouldn't through very informal kinds of interaction. Consciously or not, people are always regulating each other's behavior. Larger, more

---

* In the 19th century, when policemen got their jobs through political patronage, they used to work on election day to get out the vote for the party.

complex societies may designate a special group to control and protect. If the society also grants that group extraordinary power, one crucial problem arises: *Quid custodiet ipso custodes?*, or Who will guard the guards themselves? (I've used the Latin original not just to show off, but to clue you in that this problem has been recognized for quite a long time.)

Vigilantism as a form of policing has always loomed as this kind of threat. Citizens may start vigilante groups to provide protection where the government does not. But once started, vigilantes may use their power beyond the intentions of the citizens who created them. In Aurora, a mining town in the Wild West, the "Citizens' Safety Committee" brought about what one newspaper called "a general skedaddling of murderers, gamblers and thieves." But a month later, because of "questionable arrests and banishments," citizens petitioned the governor to stop the vigilantes, and the local paper called on the vigilantes to disband.[50] In the cities, the Mafia, like vigilante groups, began in part as a protector of immigrant citizens who got little protection from the police. Of course, as the evolution of the Mafia shows, the big problem with vigilantism is how to prevent a protection scheme from becoming a protection racket.

A police force, at least in theory, is a solution to this problem. As an agency of the government, it is subject to democratic influence: If the citizens don't like it, they can change it. Moreover, since the police are officers of the law, they must also be ruled by that law. And while society grants the police a unique power (the right to use force), it also places legal restrictions on the use of that power.

Of course, merely writing laws that the police *should* not abuse their power does not automatically mean that they *will* not abuse it. There may still be good reason to ask, "*Quid custodiet?*" The police, because of their power and because of the tasks they must perform, occupy a position where certain types of misconduct become possible. Too often, that possibility becomes a reality.

Brutality and the Use of Force

When a society grants the police the right to use force, it creates also the possibility for the misuse or excessive use of force. In the United States, brutality apparently was a part of policing from the very beginning. Dispensing "street justice" always was simpler than going to the effort of making an arrest—especially before the police had call boxes and might have to walk a prisoner a mile to the station house. In Chicago of the 1880s, "it was not customary for a policeman to arrest anyone for a small matter. The hickory had to be used pretty freely."[51]

From time to time, reformers would investigate and find systematic brutality. In 1903, a former police commissioner spoke of a "procession of citizens with broken heads and bruised bodies. . . . Many of them had done nothing to deserve an arrest. . . . The police are practically above the law."[52] Yet for long periods of time, police brutality received little attention in the press and even among sociologists.* The general public may have been dimly aware of police brutality, but there was little demand to stop it. The people on the receiving end of the violence were generally poor and powerless: street criminals, drunks, homosexuals, juveniles, the mentally disturbed, the homeless—people who could not or would not make an issue of it.

In the 1960s, police violence came to public attention inescapably and in a way that often tarnished the image of the police. In the early 1960s, millions of Americans saw TV news film of Southern police using violence against civil rights workers—blacks and whites who wanted nothing more than to register to vote or eat a hamburger at Woolworth's. Against them, preserving the status quo and Jim Crow, were the police, using tear gas, fire hoses, cattle prods, attack dogs, and clubs. Later in the decade, the media brought pictures of urban riots. In some cases, riots began when police making an arrest in a black ghetto used more force than the people thought appropriate. In many other cases, previous patterns of police brutality were seen as an underlying condition that contributed to the riot.[53] Then in 1968, outside the Democratic presidential convention in Chicago, crowds of anti-war demonstrators (mostly peaceful and mostly white and middle-class) were attacked by the Chicago police in what some commentators called a "police riot." It was all on TV, and police brutality became a topic of much greater concern.

Important as these scenes were, they provided little information about violence in everyday police work. When do the police use force, in what situations, against whom, with what justification? Getting that kind of information requires more systematic observation, not just the spectacular events that make TV news. So in the 1960s, criminologists began to turn their attention not just to criminals but also to the police. In one 1968 study, a team of 36 researchers rode with police in high-crime neighborhoods of four large cities for a period of seven weeks. In that time, they saw 37 instances, involving 44 citizens, where the police used improper force. About 3 percent of all suspects encountered by police were unnecessarily brutalized. Half the victims suffered bruises but no major injuries. Three citizens had to be hospitalized.[54]

Why do the police abuse people? The reasons haven't changed much since cops first started patrolling. Some police still see street justice as more effective and less troublesome than arrest—especially if the officer believes that the punishments imposed by the courts are not certain enough or severe enough. Violence is particularly likely after a chase, fight, shootout, or anything else that might give the cop a "combat high" or "adrenalin

---

* A doctoral thesis published in the 1950s was practically the only scholarly research on the topic, and it was all but ignored for 15 years.

rush."[55] Cops may inflict severe brutality against people arrested for crimes that offend the officer's own morality: certain sex crimes, crimes against women and children, or assaults against the police.[56] Officers also may use force to get information from suspects. After all, solving crimes is the essence of the kind of "real police work" officers rarely get to do. Given the chance to get credit for an arrest, officers might be willing to break the rules (and a few heads).

Sometimes violence arises when the person arrested initially challenges the officer or resists arrest. Then, even after he is handcuffed and subdued he may be beaten by the police. In one such case, a boy was beaten after the police had taken him in to the station house. As one of the cops told the researcher, "On the street you can't beat them. But when you get to the station, you can instill some respect in them."[57]

R-E-S-P-E-C-T. Find Out What It Means to Me

This officer's comment provides a clue to some of the reasons for police brutality. First, by discussing the action, the cop shows that he thinks it was a legitimate thing to do. Second, he is also telling us that while civilians on the street would condemn his actions, the other officers in the station house would look on the beating as justifiable. It's not that the police approve of *all* violence done to prisoners. The police, like anyone else, have a moral code that distinguishes between legitimate and illegitimate violence, between "normal" force and excessive force. "But the police draw the lines in extremely different ways and at different points than do either the court system or the public."[58] (See box.) This means that most police brutality is *not* the result of the psychological quirks of a few isolated "rotten apples." It is a group phenomenon. The officer commits the brutality in the presence of other officers and sometimes with their assistance. In addition, the morality shared throughout the department not only justifies but sometimes demands excessive and illegal force. "For the street cop, it is often a graver error to use too little force and develop a 'shaky' reputation than it is to use too much force."[59]

Finally, the officer's emphasis on "respect" represents one of the most common police justifications for violence. By far the greatest number of brutality cases arise not from actual threats or attacks on the police or even resisting arrest, but from disrespect—the challenge to the cop's authority.[60] For a person stopped by the police, showing respect may mean the difference between a warning and an arrest or even a few blows with a nightstick. This preoccupation with respect does not mean that our cities are being patrolled by a bunch of Rodney Dangerfields in blue. There is good reason for it. Respect is an acknowledgment of the cop's **authority**, and authority is the most important tool the police have for doing their job.

Remember, people call the police when "something ought not to be happening, about which something ought to be done NOW." Frequently in these situations, the officer must persuade people to do something they would rather not do—and to do it quickly. Whether it's getting spouses to stop assaulting each other or kids to turn down their radio, putting an arrested person into a patrol car or keeping a crowd at bay; whatever the situation, the cop needs to be in control, to maintain his "edge,"[61] in order to do the job. Sometimes a cop may believe that he must use actual force to maintain his edge.

The following excerpt from an interview with a police officer illustrates the different perspectives on police violence—the citizen's view, the legal view, and the cop's view. It also touches on other topics such as lying, police solidarity, and the cop's sense of isolation, all as part of the police culture each cop learns.

Policemen are taught very early that truth rarely, if ever, can be helpful. . . .

They don't know how much force they can use, so they lie to protect themselves. Because they've been told by unions, by fraternal groups, by older cops, "Everybody out there is going to try to hurt you. You open your mouth and they'll use it against you. So you tell them s--- Don't tell them anything. You don't remember."

Of course you remember. Nineteen witnesses say that this guy got beat over the head by this cop with a nightstick. The cop gets called into a review board and they ask him, "Did you hit this guy?"

"No, I didn't hit him. I never hit him. Nope. He may have hit his head on the car when we were putting him in the radio car. Maybe he tripped and banged into something."

"There's 19 witnesses here who say you were doing a number on this guy in the street."

"Who you going to believe, those people there or me? f---ing creeps. You f---ing crazy? Is there a pro-cop among that whole bunch or what? They're just looking to hurt me."

His PBA lawyer and his PBA delegate are sitting there with him. Before they went in to talk to the investigators on the review board,

he spoke to these two guys and he said, "Look, I banged the guy. I didn't want to, but the guy was robbing an old lady and he gave me some s--- and I hit him."

"You can't tell them that," the lawyer and the delegate say. "No way. You can't punch him. You can't hit him with your nightstick."

"Then what have I got a nightstick for?"

"You got a nightstick so you can probe with the nightstick. You can't hit somebody over the head with it. Hit them over the head and—

. . . —you're trying to kill them. So just say he's lying."

But that cop has every right to use that nightstick. He has every right to hit someone in a situation where he feels threatened or the guy is threatening him. The cop has the right to say, "Hey, I'm forty-nine and I go 145 pounds. I got somebody here six-four and two-thirty or forty. He's going to take me apart. So, yeah, I beat him up. My partner grabbed him and I hit him. It was great." That's okay, that's not bad. You're allowed to do that. But they'll never admit it. Instead, they make up all sorts of stories.

Source: Mark Baker (1985), *Cops: Their Lives in Their Own Words,* New York, Simon & Schuster, p. 280.

In general, it's the cop who hits first. You say, 'Nah, cops react, they don't act first.' Not if they've been on the street for a while and they know how to handle the situation.[62]

The cop's ultimate weapon in staying on top of the situation is the gun. But the more important and more useful tool is authority—the agreement by the citizen that the cop is to be obeyed. Without authority on the street, suddenly the cop is vulnerable, for despite all the hours of boredom and tasks that are not "real police work," there is always the risk of danger. Police lore is full of stories of cops losing control of the situation and winding up at least embarrassed and sometimes seriously injured. But the issue of authority goes beyond the officer's own safety, for in the officer's mind, the authority is also that of the state. Respect confirms the cop's authority and the legitimacy of the state. Disrespect not only carries a threat of injury for the officer; it also resonates with undertones of potential chaos for the state. In the eyes of the officer, therefore, the citizen who challenges authority might just as well have made a grab for the officer's gun. Little wonder then that the police generally approve of using violence to "instill respect," even though the cop is no longer in danger and even though neither the law nor the public generally recognize this as a legitimate use of force.[63]

Police Corruption

Eskimos have 14 different words for snow. The police vocabulary for corruption is equally rich, and for much the same reason: It is part of the environment. Words meaning corruption include graft, the pad, taking, bribery, chiseling, mooching, paying with your badge, extortion, shakedown, scoring, and probably others I do not know. What they all share is that in one way or another, the officer receives something and, in return, agrees not to enforce the law.

It is impossible to get an accurate measure of police corruption. With police brutality, observational studies by sociologists or complaints from victims may provide at least a rough estimate of the extent of police misconduct. But corruption usually has no obvious "victim," certainly not one who will complain. Only when there is a full-scale investigation—such as the Knapp Commission in New York City in 1970—does the public get an idea of the amount and variety of police corruption. Even so, the measurable part—the dollar value of illegal payments—may be the least important aspect of corruption.

In economic terms, the total impact of police graft is insignificant. The real cost is the degradation of the job, the destruction of morale, the erosion of supervision, and the breakdown of clear standards of what constitutes "good work" which allows some policemen to become criminals in every sense of the word.[64]

As with crime, the least serious forms of police corruption are the most common—variations on the theme of the old cop on the beat who takes an apple from the sidewalk grocery as he walks by. A legitimate business is granting a small favor. In return, the merchant expects that the cop will help if the need arises and that the cop will not enforce petty laws and ordinances.

> I used to eat hamburgers and drink coffee in the sector for nothing. . . . Was it corruption? Yes. . . . There was a fire hydrant in front of the place . . . and we didn't hang tags on [illegally parked cars].[65]

Officers also learn which stores and movie theaters in their sector will allow them to "pay with the badge." At Christmastime cops may find the merchants in their sector giving them gifts, often cash. Large-scale legitimate businesses may have similar arrangements with the upper levels of the police department or even city government. A precinct captain who has his men start ticketing the illegally parked trucks at a large distribution center may get a call from "downtown" telling him to "lay off."[66]

Illegal businesses or those that operate on the fringes of the law invite more serious corruption. After-hours bars, gambling, prostitution, drug-dealing—all these victimless crimes that fall into the category called "vice" have long been sources of corruption. In New York, it's called the "pad," in Philadelphia, the "steady note"; other cities may have still other names, but the idea is always the same: People who sell illegal goods and services pay the police on a regular basis not to enforce the law. The Knapp Commission found the pad to be particularly pervasive among plainclothes divisions. Detectives on the pad would each get from $300 to $1,500 every month from gambling establishments. Uniformed cops on a pad generally got much smaller amounts—perhaps $20. In addition to a regular pad, detectives sometimes got one-time payoffs called "scores." For example, a narcotics dealer stopped by detectives might offer the cops a large amount of cash in exchange for retaining his freedom and his inventory. The largest such score uncovered by the Knapp Commission was $80,000; shakedowns for several thousand dollars also were common. Even when the detectives made an arrest, they would often would hold back some of the confiscated cash and drugs for themselves.[67]

Non-vice work also brings opportunities for acquiring goods cheaply. Cops arriving at the scene of a burglary might finish the job the burglar had begun. One cop told of a supermarket where

> there had been a legitimate break-in, and one particular detective had been so busy loading the back seat of his car full of hams and picking up sides of beef that he was stumbling and falling down back and forth from the cooler to the alley, and he didn't even know who was around him he was so busy carrying things out.[68]

Of the cops involved in corruption, most settle for the opportunities that come their way in the course of their work. In New York at the time of the Knapp Commission, they were referred to as "grass-eaters," and most of what they did was condoned by the other cops. However, the commission also found a smaller number of "meat-eaters," officers who aggressively sought out sources of illegal income or created their own opportunities. For these cops, it was short step from cleaning up after a burglary to planning and carrying out the whole operation, from making drug deals as undercover cops to doing the same thing for personal profit.[69]

Explaining Police Misconduct—Personality and Opportunity

The distinction between grass-eaters and meat-eaters implies that individual integrity is important in determining how corrupt, if at all, a cop will be. Certainly, individual character makes a difference, especially with the most corrupt and the most incorruptible. Sociological ideas are not much help in understanding a cop like Frank Serpico, who resisted taking payoffs himself and then risked his life helping to expose the widespread corruption among his fellow detectives. Nor can sociological ideas fully explain the cop who is unusually corrupt or sadistic.

However, explanations that look only at individual personality have some important shortcomings. First, these explanations offer little in the way of a solution. Aside from the screening that departments already use, no test yet developed can distinguish those who will make "good cops" from those who will go beyond the norm in brutality or corruption. Second, even successful screening will do nothing to reduce the payoffs and the use of force that the law and the public see as wrong but which the police accept as normal, acceptable, and even unavoidable. Police misconduct is more than just a few "bad apples" in an otherwise blemish-free barrel.

While it's true that some cops are more honest than others, it also is true, and perhaps more important, that some kinds of police work present far more opportunity for corruption than do others. As one Knapp Commission witness said, commenting on the honesty of officers in the Central Park precinct, "What are you going to do—shake down the squirrels?" At the other extreme are the plainclothes officers ("into clothes," in police jargon) who deal with vice. "There's no way you can go into clothes and be clean. The best you can do is avoid getting caught."[70]

Detective work is so corrupting for reasons of both morality and materialism. As with the everyday kinds of corruption that even uniformed cops commit, the payoffs for nonenforcement involve violations that most people would not object to. The crimes involved are nonpredatory, with no direct victim who demands police action. In many cases, it's not even clear that the public in general wants the crime stopped. It may be hard for the cop, as well as the citizen, to make a moral distinction between betting at the track and betting with a bookmaker, between serving a drink at 1:45 a.m. and serving a drink at 2:15 a.m.

Another obvious answer is that the amounts of money offered are just too tempting.* Certainly temptation plays a large part in the corruption of detectives who encounter high-level narcotics dealers. However, for the more common corruption involving street-level criminals and much smaller pay-offs, we must look to another aspect of detective work—namely, the relationship between cop and criminal. When a cop arrests a mugger or burglar, neither one has a stake in continuing the relationship, nor will the criminal have much to offer the cop. In narcotics work, however, even the poorest street junkie may be able to offer something the cop legitimately needs: information—information that will eventually lead to an arrest of top-level dealers. Since the detectives can never know just when the right bit of information may come along or who will have it, they must maintain their relationships with criminal informants. The informant can give the cops information or introductions to higher-level dealers; the cops can give the informant immunity from arrest. However, once the relationship is established, cop and criminal are no longer just adversaries; they are also partners, much in the manner of thief-takers and thieves in 18th-century London. They may then find other things to exchange. Cops can provide drugs to the addict; the addict, who also may be stealing to support his habit, can offer the cops free stolen merchandise.[71]

The combination of temptation and opportunity as an explanation of misconduct obviously carries some validity. As long as the police must regulate illegal commerce, the temptation will exist. But what kind of solution follows from this? To reduce these opportunities for corruption would require fairly drastic changes in the laws against immorality, and legislators generally do not rush to legalize sin. From time to time someone proposes decriminalizing one or another of the various forms of vice that the police are called on to regulate—especially gambling, prostitution, and drugs—usually to no avail. America's one large-scale experiment in decriminalization—the repeal of Prohibition—was immensely popular and probably reduced police corruption as well.[72] However, at least for now, the decriminalization of bookmaking, prostitution, and especially drug-dealing seems unlikely.

"Working Personality" and Police Culture

A few paragraphs ago, I downplayed the importance of the personality the cop brings to the job. Much more important, though, in understanding

---

* Some people think that the FBI managed to remain free of corruption because J. Edgar Hoover deliberately kept it out of those areas that were likely to tempt agents into corruption. During most of Hoover's tenure, the FBI concentrated on bank robbery and political subversion, not gambling, drugs, or organized crime.

police behavior (and misbehavior) is the personality the job brings to the cop. That is, police officers, because of their work, develop a particular way of looking at the world, a particular set of attitudes and beliefs, a particular way of thinking and responding. These components pretty well fit the psychology textbook definition of "personality." But this personality, this way of looking at the world, is too widely shared among police officers to be mainly a matter of individual psychology. Jerome Skolnick called it the officer's **working personality**.[73] It is a product of the experiences the cop has on the job and the understandings of those experiences that he or she learns from the other cops.

I have already mentioned the central place that **authority** has in this working personality, and we have seen how it can lead to the use of excessive force. Skolnick also says that police integrate the **conservatism** of the job into their working personality. Other types of misconduct can involve other aspects of the working personality. For example, when anti-vice work requires the police to enforce laws which they themselves violate, the result may be a type of **cynicism**. And this cynicism and disillusionment may be deepened by other aspects of police work. Police may become cynical about the criminal justice system when they see criminals they have arrested getting off lightly. They may become disillusioned by their own very limited ability to improve the world they patrol. Being a cop, perhaps more than any other role in society, brings one face to face with the darker side of human nature. Deceit, crime, insanity, misery, suffering, and cruelty are all part of the daily round.

> The job runs against every good impulse you ever had. . . . That's probably the greatest single tragedy that every cop faces. You find out that nothing is on the level. You find out that people die for nothing.[74]

The feeling that nothing is on the level combines with another important element—the sense of **danger**—to produce another facet of the police working personality: **suspiciousness**. Police are keenly sensitive to things that don't look quite right. Police also have a sense of **isolation** from the general public, the feeling that "nobody loves a cop." The feelings of danger, suspicion, and isolation produce one other characteristic—**solidarity** with other cops.[75]

Since cops generally share this view of the world, there is a considerable overlap between working personality and the norms (or unwritten rules) of police culture. To a great extent, the traits of the police working personality and the norms and values of police culture are indistinguishable from each other. For example, police solidarity is not just an individual feeling; it emerges as a set of norms, an unwritten code, that governs police behavior. A primary rule of this code expresses the norm of solidarity: "Watch out for your partner first, then for the rest of the guys working that tour."[76] Police solidarity grows out of the sense of danger and the need for mutual protection. On the street, protection can mean the difference between safety and injury, or even between life and death. But cops also are vulnerable administratively, since all of them have in some way or other violated the rules.

> How the f--- can I tell anyone who ain't a cop that I lie a little in court or that sometimes I won't do s--- on the street 'cause I'm tired. . . . The only people who can understand are people who've had to pull the same s--- . . . and there ain't nobody in this department from the Chief on down who hasn't pulled some tricks in their time on the street.[77]

Solidarity and the sense of isolation also make it almost impossible to get one cop to testify about another cop's misconduct. Even when an officer's brutality goes far beyond what other officers find acceptable, they still will do nothing to expose the wrongdoer to outside forces. They may avoid him, but they won't turn him in. This solution may be adequate for the problem of the cops in the precinct, but it is hardly ideal for the citizenry.

> I told the bosses . . . ," He's crazy. . . . Let the next guy who comes in work with him."
>
> That's what they did. The new guy would work with him for two months and then the next new guy would work with him for two months. I saw him years later. I was going into a precinct and he was coming out with a prisoner. His prisoner looked like he'd been through a meat grinder.[78]

In some departments, the cop who refuses to take payoffs, like the officer who is reluctant to use force, may become suspect in the eyes of others and get shunted off to some unattractive post. Rather than try to expose or change others, the honest cop will merely try to transfer to a different sector. Thus, besides the other reasons for police misconduct—individual, structural (temptation), and cultural—there is one final one: There is little effective way to combat it.

There is nothing new here. This combination of factors goes back to the earliest days of the police, and at its worst, it can resemble what a journalist wrote in 1869: The police, he said,

> are compelled to associate with vulgarians and scoundrels of all grades; are exposed to every species of temptation; act unfavorably on each other, and have no restraining influence beyond their own intelligence, which is not very great, and their fear of exposure, which is not probable.[79]

VARIETIES OF POLICING

Up to this point, I have been treating the police and police departments as though they were all the same. Obviously, they are not. I only wished to point out some of the problems inherent in the institution of police. Society hands over into police care a set of tasks and limitations, what is sometimes called the "police mandate."[80] At the heart of the police mandate is maintaining order, the essence of everyday police patrolling. It also includes crime fighting and the provision of certain social services. Yet the mandate often contains contradictions that make it impossible to fulfill. For example, police are supposed to follow and enforce "the rule of law" as well as to maintain order. But (at least according to one sociologist-lawyer), " 'law' and 'order' are frequently found to be in opposition."[81] Some things may be disorderly yet legal; other things may be illegal (certain kinds of police misconduct, for example) yet keep things more orderly. Contradictions also will arise when a police department serves a diverse community. The demands made on the police by one segment of that community may conflict with the demands of another segment.

Different departments serve different kinds of communities and adapt in different ways. What follows is a sketch of three different types of police departments, outlined by James Q. Wilson in his study of police departments in eight cities.

One style of patrol exists mostly in homogeneous, middle-class communities and does not have so much relevance for the problem of crime. Wilson calls it the **service** style, and it emphasizes community relations. Here is how one precinct commander summed it up:

> The wealthier people of Nassau County know we are servants and they demand service. The kind of service they expect is prompt appearance and frequent, high visibility of policemen on patrol in their areas.[82]

The department's concern is to patrol against burglaries. It also tries to handle the transgressions of its citizens (offenses involving too much drink, juvenile delinquency, etc.) in a discreet way that does not embarrass or damage them.[83]

The **watchman** style of policing represents a kind of holdover from previous eras. The department is closely tied to a political machine; getting a promotion depends on political connections. The pay is low (officers often moonlight), the training minimal, the turnover high. The patrolling style stresses order rather than law. The cop follows his own informal ways of getting things done rather than following formal procedures, especially in dealing with juveniles and with minor offenses. The cop might have one set of standards for whites, another for blacks. In disorderly situations, people are dealt with on the basis of what the officer thinks they "deserve," more than on what they have done. Aside from predatory crimes and serious disturbances, law enforcement is not vigorous; arrests are relatively infrequent. The department does not bother illegal businesses like gambling, except perhaps to take payoffs. The cop prefers to avoid trouble and "keep his nose clean." The department's preference, similarly, is not to rock the boat, since the department has strong ties to the locally dominant political party.[84]

Until the 1930s, most police departments in the United States followed the watchman pattern. Every so often, reformers would expose the abuses that occurred in these departments: the corruption at every level, the brutality of street justice or confessions produced by the "third degree," the dependence on political connections, the inconsistency of patrol and the unequal treatment of citizens according to the cop's personal whim, the general lack of discipline (e.g., drinking on the job), and other shortcomings.

The answer to these problems was "professionalism." Today, when people in all sorts of jobs call themselves professionals, the meaning of the word has become rather vague. However, the progressive reformers around the turn of the century had something fairly specific in mind.[85] The professional police department was to be a disciplined, military-like organization, with centralized authority, separated from politics, and focusing on the impartial enforcement of laws. The movement had some success, and gradually, police departments began to adopt some of these reforms. Then in the 1930s, the notion of police reform began to take a narrower focus: the control of crime through the application of scientific knowledge.[86] Several developments gave a boost to this idea. "Criminalistics" (fingerprinting and other crime detection techniques), telephones, radio-cars, the police academy, crime statistics—all these contributed to the image of the cop as a crime fighting technician.*[87] Of course, despite this image, even "professional" departments must deploy most of their officers in routine patrol.

The result is what Wilson calls the **legalistic** style. Legalistic departments operate by the book. Authority, both within the department and between the officer and the public, is formal, not personal. Police dealing with minor offenses are more likely to make an arrest rather than use some informal procedure. For example, the police will arrest a bad-check passer or shoplifter even when the wrongdoer has paid up and the merchant is willing to drop the charges. Compared with the casual style of watchman departments, the police in legalistic departments are neatly dressed, formal, and polite. The department keeps extensive records, and officers must fill out daily logs and a variety of reports. The department maintains its independence from local politics. It tries to recruit college-educated, middle-class officers who will seek a career in police work.[88]

The Dilemma of Professionalism

In practice, every department will be a combination of these styles. What will vary will be the proportions in the mixture. Given the mandate of police in a large and diverse city, no style of department or patrol will be perfect.

---

* Sergeant Joe Friday of the old "Dragnet" TV series was the perfect example of this image. He dealt only with serious crime, and he did so in a highly efficient, technical way ("Just the facts, Ma'am").

Each solution will create its own particular problems. The pitfalls of the watchman style are fairly easy to see, especially in light of the historical record. But the professional model, with its legalistic style, also has its short-comings. The most serious is that the professional model does not fit well with what the police are most often called upon to do. Remember, most police calls do not involve crime. They involve disorder, where frequently no crime has been committed—the sort of trouble where a "watchman" would intervene. But if the police take a purely legalistic approach, then they wind up shortchanging the traditional "watchman" tasks. And it is these peace-keeping tasks, not crime fighting, that make people feel safer.[89]

> There are no streetlamps to light anymore, but there are a large number of con-stabulary functions—maintaining order in public places (parks, buses, subway platforms), resolving marital disputes, disciplining noncriminal but harmful ju-venile behavior, preventing public drug and alcohol use—which no other public organizations have taken up since they were abandoned by the police. These jobs simply are not done.[90]

The above excerpt overstates the case. The police mandate still includes maintaining public order. The trouble is that the professional, legalistic style of policing is ill-suited to these tasks. Police professionalism works on a bureaucratic model, and bureaucracy means, among other things, playing it by the book. This phrase, playing by the book, implies a set of rules and procedures that the worker learns and then uses in dealing with the various cases that come up. The worker sees how the specifics of each case fit with the rules and then acts accordingly.

The principle involved here is called **universalism**, and it is the basis of "the rule of law" and of "fairness." It places the law above any particular individual. It applies the same set of rules equally to all people, regardless of race, social class, sex or other individual differences.

What's wrong with universalism, with playing it by the book? The first problem is that no book could possibly cover all the situations that the officer must handle. All the training in the police academy does little to prepare the new officer for the variety of situations that arise. In fact, many officers feel that the academy is useless for learning about street patrol. What the academy can and does teach well is the bureaucratic part of the job—how to fill out forms.

What everyday policing requires in practice is the opposite of universal-ism: **particularism**. This term means treating each situation as a special case and dealing with it according to its particular needs, rather than ac-cording to some abstract set of rules. Particularism places people or situ-ations above rules. It means recognizing all the special characteristics of a situation or person, not just those that fit with some set of rules. It allows for flexibility. Under the principle of particularism, if the rules don't fit the needs of the person, too bad for the rules. Under the principle of universalism, if the needs of the person don't fit the rule, too bad for the person.*

If policing really were a legalistic activity—the universalistic enforcement of the law—then any officer who has learned the rules of policing could be sent to any sector and do a good job. This was the idea behind the early reforms. Reformers saw that police corruption arose when the close ties between cops and the people in their areas led to the selective enforcement (or nonenforcement) of the law. Professionalism would defeat corruption by centralizing authority, so that the cop's major ties would be to the department. Officers might be moved from one beat to another to prevent corruption. After all, it's harder to offer a bribe to a perfect stranger than to someone you know—especially if the stranger is wearing a uniform. Professional policing, then, meant "stranger policing."

But good police work depends on a thorough and highly particularistic knowledge of an area and the people in it. Certainly this is true for the peacekeeping side of police work. Domestic disputes, drunkenness, juvenile delinquency, and other situations of disorder are probably better handled by an officer who knows the people involved. The cop may even be able to work out a decent solution that has nothing to do with the legal aspects of the situation. Crime fighting, too, requires the same particularistic knowledge. Knowing the streets and alleys that can give the quickest route to the scene of a crime, knowing which gang controls which turf, knowing people who can provide information about different sorts of crime—all these make the officer more effective in preventing and solving crimes.[91] Given also that the police generally depend on the citizens for the information that solves crimes, then the better the police know the people, the more effective they will be as crime fighters.

There is another way in which the professional model does not fit with the reality of police work. Professionalism assumes a military-like chain of command, where the most experienced and highest-ranking officers who give the commands have the most influence over what the force does. The army may work like this, but a city police force, despite its weapons and uniforms and military ranks, does not. In the first place, unlike officers in the army, police captains and lieutenants do not lead their troops into battle. The troops are out there alone—an arrangement that has crucial consequences as to where the real decision-making power lies. Remember discretion. Because of the wide variety of situations patrol officers must respond to, they have a great deal of discretion in deciding what to do. The police department, therefore, in actual practice, turns the army model upside down: The greatest amount of discretion flows to the people at the lowest rank.

---

* The professor who tells a student, "Gee, I'd like to help you, but if I gave you an extension on your term paper, then I'd have to do it for everybody," is invoking the principle of universalism.

The idea of professionalism in policing seems to have declined over the last two decades. Not that reformers now call for unprofessional police—instead, it seems that people have come to see the limits of the idea of police as primarily crime fighting technicians. The radio-patrol cars that can arrive at the scene of the crime within a few minutes had little impact on crime. How could they, when most citizens wait a half-hour before they call the cops, preferring to talk first with a friend or relative or someone they know, someone who can provide comfort? It also turns out that uniformed strangers riding around in glass-and-steel cages do not reduce crime and do not make the citizens feel safer.

Community Relations—Or Everything Old Is New Again

As study after study revealed the limits of the cop as crime-fighter idea, the reformers of the 1980s offered the idea of "community relations." The term itself is vague. It refers to the feeling the citizens have for the police. But there is no specific set of practices associated with "community relations." Nor is there any measure of it, just in case a department wanted to know if its community relations were better or worse and by how much.

A community relations approach requires that the department and its individual members pay more attention to the way the citizens will feel about the police—much like the service style of department. This means more than just the usual "community relations officer" who handles complaints. It means that the police themselves should take seriously the noncriminal aspects of their job—all the unglamorous peacekeeping and social services. The civilians, for their part, were to be encouraged to participate in everyday crime control with citizen patrols, crime watch programs, and the like.

Community Policing—The Beat Goes On

In practice, the major change to emerge from this phase of reform was the return of the foot-patrol officer. In a strategy called **community policing**, once again the cop on the beat was to belong to the community, not just to the police department. Community policing places more emphasis on the police officer as peacekeeper rather than crime fighter, and perhaps the revival of this strategy in the face of an upsurge of crime in the late 1980s was a recognition that ordinary patrolling could do little to reduce crime rates. Moreover, experiments like the Newark foot-patrol project (described in Chapter 2) showed that returning to this old style of patrolling was no more or less effective than modern methods in preventing crime. But in foot-patrolled areas people felt safer and liked the police more.

Community Relations—Mickey Mouse or Karl Marx?

Not everybody welcomes the community relations approach. Much resistance comes from the police themselves, especially the street cops. Managerial cops (the high-ranking, policymaking cops "downtown") may see a need for sensitivity to public opinion, but to street cops, community relations is "Mickey Mouse bulls---."[92] They cling to the idea that the essence of police work is crime-fighting. And they have a point. Press releases from "downtown" may extol community relations, but it is still crime work—catching criminals—that brings rewards. The cop who makes arrests for important crimes gains the admiration of the public and other police and wins the more tangible rewards of promotion. Therefore, the police often dislike changes that de-emphasize their own role as crime fighters. They also may dislike volunteer patrols sponsored by the department. As police themselves say, "Cops don't like civilians, and especially they don't like them inside the station house where they can get to know a cop's business."[93] Nor do the police care much for an independent group, like the Guardian Angels, that encroaches on the police department's crime-fighting turf.

A slightly different line of criticism comes from those who see the police as an instrument for repression of the lower class. From this point of view, community relations is "a cover behind which the actual practice of lower-class repression can persist."[94] In this view, the essence of policing in lower-class communities is an "iron fist" of crime control and repression hidden in the "velvet glove" of community relations programs.[95]

Of course, cops who work in lower-class neighborhoods would disagree. They see their work as saving or at least helping lower-class people, not repressing them. They provide a wide range of services to people too poor to afford specialists; the only people they try to repress are the criminals who prey upon the decent citizens of these neighborhoods.

The radical version of police as repressors of the lower class may have a certain validity to it. It is true to the extent that the state is based on social class. But the class basis of the government has little to do with the motives or politics of the police themselves. In any political system, the police are an arm of the state. If you see the state as a democratic representative of all groups in society, then you will see the police as fair and impartial. If you see the state as representing the interests of certain groups against the interests of other groups, then you will see the police as an agency whose ultimate purpose is the use of force for political repression.

> The ineluctable fact is that *the police deal in and dispense violence in protection of the interests of the state.* . . . They are inextricably linked to the status quo and are, in effect, duty bound to sustain and uphold it. The violence they exercise, given the present class nature of our society and the control of the police by local government, seems almost unavoidable.[emphasis in original][96]

SUMMARY AND CONCLUSION

In contrast to the excitement, clever crime solving, and glamorized violence of the police shown in the movies and on TV shows, the bulk of police time spent on the job has little to do with crime. In most cities, the police patrol in cars, waiting for the radio to dispatch them, usually in response to citizens' calls. People call on the police for a variety of services, especially when situations may require the use of legitimate force. Police work, therefore, is now and historically has always been more a matter of keeping the peace than of enforcing the law. Restoring peace and order is the goal, and enforcing the law is only one of several available tools to accomplish that task. As for crime, the police have some deterrent effect. Adding police can reduce only certain types of crime and only under certain conditions—usually at great financial cost. The police catch criminals; police clear by arrest about 20 percent of all Index crimes. The methods of catching criminals, however, are usually routine and depend much more on civilian cooperation than on sophisticated crime solving techniques.

Since the police are empowered to use force and the law in carrying out their work, the potential abuse of this great power is a constant problem. The most notable abuses are brutality and corruption. Brutality is most likely to occur when civilians challenge the officer's authority, for authority is the officer's primary tool. Without it, even the ordinary aspects of police work—directing traffic, controlling crowds at parades, settling family disputes—become difficult and dangerous. Ordinary corruption arises from the great amount of discretion built into the police role and the mandate of the police to enforce laws against victimless crimes. Severe corruption combines these two elements with the temptation of large amounts of money. Both brutality and corruption can continue unchecked because police solidarity—the blue wall of silence—makes prosecution difficult.

There is no ideal solution to all the dilemmas of police work. The long trend toward "professionalism" may reduce corruption and brutality, but it also makes for "stranger policing." The more recent trend toward community relations goes in the opposite direction. Putting the cop back on the beat and in touch with the people of the community may make the public feel better, but it also may be resisted by the police themselves, who prefer the "real" police work of crime-fighting over the Mickey Mouse of community relations—especially if it means more civilian knowledge or control over what the police do.

Finally, we should not forget that ultimately the police are an agency of the state and as such they are a political institution. In times of political consensus, this political role is almost invisible. However, when the consensus breaks down, when large numbers of people question the legitimacy of the government and the law, the police are on the front line defending the political status quo. Even in times of general consensus, dissenters who see the state as illegitimate or unjust will see the police as the enforcers of injustice.

NOTES

1. Katherine M. Jamieson and Timothy J. Flanagan, eds. (1989), *Sourcebook of Criminal Justice Statistics—1988*, U.S. Department of Justice, Bureau of Justice Statistics, Washington, DC: U.S. Government Printing Office, pp. 2, 445.

2. John A. Webster (1970), "Police Task and Time Study," *Journal of Criminal Law, Criminology, and Police Science*, vol. 61, no. 1, pp. 94–100.

3. Ruben G. Rumbaut and Egon Bittner (1979), "Changing Conceptions of the Police Role: A Sociological Review," in Norval Morris and Michael Tonry, eds. *Crime and Justice: An Annual Review*, vol. 1, Chicago: University of Chicago Press, pp. 239–88, esp. p. 246.

4. John Van Maanen (1974), "Working the Street: A Developmental View of Police Behavior," reprinted as "Kinsmen in Repose," in Peter K. Manning and John Van Maanen, eds. (1978), *Policing: A View From the Street*, Santa Monica, CA: Goodyear, pp. 115–28, esp. p. 116.

5. Carl B. Klockars (1985), *The Idea of Police*, Beverly Hills, CA: Sage.

6. Ibid., pp. 7–12.

7. Egon Bittner (1971), "The Functions of the Police in Modern Society," reprinted in Manning and Van Maanen, eds., op. cit., pp. 32–50.

8. Quoted in Klockars, op. cit., p. 16.

9. George L. Kelling, Tony Pate, Duane Dieckman, and Charles Brown (1974), *The Kansas City Preventive Patrol Experiment*, Washington, DC: The Police Foundation.

10. See evidence summarized in James Q. Wilson (1975), *Thinking About Crime*, New York: Basic Books, Chapter 5; and in Samuel Walker (1985), *Sense and Nonsense About Crime: A Policy Guide*, Monterey, CA: Brooks/Cole, Chapter 7.

11. Wilson, op. cit, p. 83. Lawrence W. Sherman (1990), "Police Crackdowns: Initial and Residual Deterrence," in Michael Tonry and Norval Morris, eds. (1990), *Crime and Justice: A Review of Research* , Chicago: University of Chicago Press, pp. 1–48.

12. Jan M. Chaiken, Michael W. Lawless, and Keith A. Stevenson (1975), "The Impact of Police Activity on Subway Crime," *Urban Analysis*, vol. 3, pp. 173–205.

13. Robert J. diGrazia (1976), "Police Leadership: Challenging Old Assumptions," *The Washington Post*, Nov. 10.

14. Walker, op. cit., p. 113.

15. Susan E. Martin (1986), "Policing Career Criminals: An Examination of an Innovative Crime-Control Program," *Journal of Criminal Law and Criminology*, vol. 77, no. 4, pp. 1159–82.

16. Tony Pate and Robert A. Bowers (1976), *Three Approaches to Criminal Apprehension in Kansas City*, Washington, DC: The Police Foundation. Also cited in Walker, op. cit., p. 114.

17. Jan Chaiken, Peter Greenwood, and Joan Petersilia (1977), "The Criminal Investigation Process: A Summary Report," *Policy Analysis*, vol. 3, no. 2, pp. 187–217.

18. Charles Silberman (1978) *Criminal Violence, Criminal Justice*, New York: Random House, p. 207.

19. I am grateful to Jennifer Hunt (personal communication) for this insight.

20. Mark Baker (1985), *Cops: Their Lives in Their Own Words*, New York: Simon & Schuster, p. 249.

21. UCR, 1984, pp. 152, 163.

22. J. A. Sharpe (1984), *Crime in Early Modern England, 1550–1750*, Essex, U.K.: Longman, p. 112.

23. Chaiken, et al., op. cit.

24. UCR, 1984, p. 11.

25. John Allen (1977), *Assault With a Deadly Weapon: The Autobiography of a Street Criminal*, Diane Hall Kelly and Philip Heymann, eds., New York: McGraw-Hill, p. 62–70.

26. Vera Institute of Justice (1977), *Felony Arrests: Their Prosecution and Disposition in New York City's Courts*, New York: Vera Institute of Justice.

27. Donald Black (1983), "Crime as Social Control," *American Sociological Review*, vol. 48, no. 1 (February), pp. 34–45.

28. Allen, op. cit., p. 38.

29. Silberman, op. cit., p. 220.

30. Webster, op. cit.

31. Chaiken, et al., op. cit.

32. Walker (1985), op. cit., p. 112.

33. *The Boston Globe*, Aug. 17, 1987 ("Computerized Mug Shots Help Nab Suspects," Jim Gomez).

34. Chaiken, et al., op. cit.

35. Jerrold K. Footlick (1978), "Police Myths," *Newsweek*, Feb. 6, p. 71.

36. Eric H. Monkkonen (1981), *Police in Urban America, 1860–1920*, Cambridge, U.K.: Cambridge University Press, p. 54.

37. Klockars, op. cit., p. 26.

38. Walter Besant (1903), *London in the Eighteenth Century*, cited in Jonathan Rubinstein (1973), *City Police*, New York: Farrar, Strauss, Giroux, p. 5.

39. Roger Lane (1967), *Policing the City: Boston 1822–1885*, Cambridge, MA: Harvard University Press, pp. 10–12.

40. See Manning, *Police Work*, p. 44.

41. Rubinstein, op. cit., pp. 5–7.

42. George Rude (1973), *Paris and London in the Eighteenth Century: Studies in Popular Protest*, New York: Viking, pp. 31–32, 268–318.

43. Miller, op. cit., p. 4.

44. David Harris Wilson (1967), *A History of England*, New York: Holt, Rinehart, and Winston, p. 629.

45. Klockars, op. cit.

46. Miller, op. cit., p. 29. Mark Haller (1976), "Historical Roots of Police Behavior, Chicago 1890–1925," *Law and Society Review*, vol. 10, no. 2, pp. 303–23.

47. Miller, op. cit., p. 43.

48. Monkkonen, op. cit., pp. 86–128.

49. James Q. Wilson (1983), *Thinking About Crime (rev. ed.)*, New York: Vintage, pp. 91–92.

50. Roger McGrath (1981), *Gunfighters, Highwaymen, and Vigilantes: Violence on the Frontier*, Berkeley, CA: University of California Press, pp. 97–98.

51. Quoted in Haller, op. cit.

52. Frank Moss (1901), "National Danger From Police Corruption," *North American Review*, vol. 173, pp. 470–80, quoted in Albert J. Reiss, Jr. (1971), *The Police and the Public*, New Haven, CT: Yale University Press, p. 152.

53. National Advisory Commission on Civil Disorders (1968), *Report of the National Advisory Commission on Civil Disorders*, New York: Bantam Books, pp. 6, 149, et passim.

54. Albert Reiss, Jr., (1968), "Police Brutality—Answers to Key Questions," *Trans-action*, vol. 5, pp. 10–19.

55. Jennifer Hunt (1985), "Police Accounts of Normal Force," *Urban Life*, vol. 13, no. 4, pp. 315–41.

56. For some graphic examples, see Hunt, op. cit., p. 332; also Baker, op. cit., pp. 233–36; Rubinstein, op. cit., p. 183.

57. Reiss (1968), op. cit.

58. Hunt, op. cit., p. 317.

59. Ibid., p. 321. Also Rubinstein, op. cit., p. 319.

60. Reiss (1968), op. cit. Paul Chevigny (1969), *Police Power: Police Abuses in New York City*, New York: Pantheon, p. 70.

61. John Van Maanen (1978), "The Asshole," in Peter K. Manning and John Van Maanen, eds., *Policing: A View From the Street*, Santa Monica, CA: Goodyear Publishing, pp. 221–38.

62. Baker, op. cit., p. 81.

63. William A. Westley (1953), "Violence and the Police," *American Journal of Sociology*, vol. 59, pp. 34–41. Jamieson and Flanagan, op. cit. (*Sourcebook*), p. 199.

64. Rubinstein, op. cit., p. 420.

65. Baker, op. cit., p. 252.

66. Rubinstein, op. cit., p. 411.

67. *The Knapp Commission Report on Police Corruption* (1972), New York: Braziller.

68. Ellwyn R. Stoddard (1968), "The Informal 'Code' of Police Deviancy: A Group Approach to Blue-Coat Crime," *Journal of Criminal Law, Criminology and Police Science*, vol. 59, pp. 201–13.

69. *The Knapp Commission Report*, op. cit.

70. Rubinstein, op. cit., p. 399.

71. See Peter K. Manning and Lawrence J. Redlinger, "Invitational Edges of Corruption: Some Consequences of Narcotic Law Enforcement," in Manning and Von Maanen, op. cit., pp. 147–66.

72. Rubinstein, op. cit., p. 375.

73. Jerome H. Skolnick (1966), *Justice Without Trial: Law Enforcement in a Democratic Society*, New York: Wiley.

74. Baker, op. cit., p. 244.

75. Skolnick (1966), op. cit.

76. Elizabeth Reuss-Ianni (1983), *Two Cultures of Policing*, New Brunswick, NJ: Transaction Books, p. 14.

77. Von Maanen (1974), op. cit., p. 119.

78. Baker, op. cit., p. 243.

79. Junius Henri Browne (1869), *The Great Metropolis: A Mirror of New York*, quoted in Miller, op. cit., p. 43.

80. Peter K. Manning (1977), *Police Work: The Social Organization of Policing*, Cambridge, MA: MIT Press, pp. 89–126.

81. Skolnick, op. cit., pp. 7–9.

82. Ibid., p. 206.

83. James Q. Wilson (1968), *Varieties of Police Behavior: The Management of Law and Order in Eight Communities*, New York: Atheneum, pp. 200–226.

84. Ibid., pp. 140–71.

85. For an account of the Progressive movement, see Richard Hofstadter (1955), *The Age of Reform*, New York: Vintage, especially pp. 164–76.

86. Mark H. Moore and George L. Kelling, (1983), " 'To Serve and Protect': Learning From Police History," *The Public Interest*, no. 70, pp. 49–65.

87. David R. Johnson (1981), *American Law Enforcement: A History*, excerpted as "The Triumph of Reform: Police Professionalism 1920–1965," in Abraham S. Blumberg and Elaine Niederhoffer (1985), *The Ambivalent Force: Perspectives on the Police* (3rd ed.), New York: Holt, Rinehart, and Winston, pp. 27–36.

88. Ibid., pp. 172–200.

89. See Chapter 2 of this book.

90. Moore and Kelling, op. cit.

91. Rubinstein, op. cit., pp. 129–48.

92. Reuss-Ianni, op. cit., p. 121.

93. Ibid., p. 100.

94. Center for Research on Criminal Justice (1976), *The Iron Fist in the Velvet Glove: An Analysis of the U.S. Police*, Berkeley, CA: Center for Research on Criminal Justice.

95. Ibid.

96. Manning, *Police Work*, p. 361.

Courts and Rights

CHAPTER **14**

A DAY IN COURT

COURTS, MORE THAN ANY OTHER TOPIC IN THIS BOOK, PRESENT THE BIGGEST CONTRAST between the ideal and the reality. I didn't appreciate how large the difference was until I spent a day in court just watching what went on. I had been there before, on jury duty or to meet a friend who worked there. But I hadn't really noticed my surroundings. I had to take another look.

From the outside, the court building looks just like a courthouse in the movies, with its broad, stone steps rising to the entrance, the stone columns a hundred feet tall, the sculpted facade carved with noble quotations. Several movies have in fact used this exterior for courthouse scenes. It conveys the majesty of law and justice.

Inside, it was a different story. What I saw reminded me of what you see at other city agencies. The floors were dirty, the walls scarred. In some rooms, the cushioned theater-style seats for jurors were ripped or broken. But what most reminded me of other city agencies were the people. What you see in the criminal court building is what you see at the public hospital or the welfare department: poor people waiting. They sit on long, wooden benches. Most of them are relatives of accused people scheduled for court that day. They do not know when their son or daughter, husband or wife, will be brought from the holding pen into the court. By the afternoon session, some of them will have been waiting six or seven hours. A court officer walks through the room waking up people who have fallen asleep.

At the front of the room, things are busier. Defendants are brought to the courtroom in groups of four or five, handcuffed, and wait on a bench off to the right of the judge. The clerk calls a name. The prisoner is unshackled and led before the judge, district attorney on one side, defense attorney on the other. The clerk reads numbers that indicate the charge. The people who have been waiting cannot get close enough to the judge's bench to hear what is happening. The lawyers, judge, and clerk often speak in what sounds like a code anyway. "Charged with one-six-five-four-oh," "waive the reading," "vacate the warrant," "deponent is informed by complainant," and so on.

The defendants themselves often seem to have little grasp of what is going on. The attorneys make very brief statements about the case. Sometimes the judge sets bail; sometimes there is a plea of guilty and a sentence. Five days. Time served. Papers are shuffled. A cop leads the defendant out the door, and the next defendant is brought forward. The whole process takes only a few minutes. Lower courts that deal with less serious crimes—misdemeanors—work in a still more impersonal way. There, a judge may dispose of dozens of cases, at the rate of a few seconds each, rarely spending more than a minute on a case.[1]

The whole scene is far removed from the image of courts that we see on television—no prosecutors cleverly cross-examining witnesses, no defense lawyers jumping up and shouting, "objection." Nevertheless, there is a logical and sometimes real connection between these two pictures of justice—the ideal, civics-book version of the criminal process, and the everyday reality of a big-city court.

THE ADVERSARIAL SYSTEM

Criminal justice in the United States is based on what is called the **adversarial** model. According to this model, the court is an arena for a conflict between two adversaries. Obviously, civil cases, as opposed to criminal cases, must be adversarial. For example, if Jones beats up Smith and injures him, Smith may sue in **civil** court. The case will be *Smith v. Jones*, naming the two adversaries. Smith is the plaintiff (the one who brings the complaint), Jones the defendant. If Smith wins, the court will require Jones to give Smith some **compensation**, usually money. Of course, beating up somebody also violates criminal laws against assault. But in **criminal** cases, the plaintiff is always the state (i.e., the government). The state, not the victim, brings charges against the defendant. The case will be called *State of New Jersey v. Jones*, and if Jones loses, the court will impose some **punishment**.

In criminal cases, the state charges a person with breaking a particular law, and in front of a jury (or impartial judge), the state produces whatever evidence it can legally find to establish guilt; the defense tries its best to discredit the state's evidence and testimony. The **burden of proof** is on the state. The state must prove guilt beyond a reasonable doubt. The defense does not have to prove innocence. It has only to show that the state's case does not prove guilt beyond a reasonable doubt. A verdict for the defendant, therefore, is not "innocent"; it is "not guilty."*

Since most of us have not been exposed to other models of justice, we might assume that the adversarial model is the best, if not the only, model for determining guilt. But think about it for a minute. Is this really the best way to find out if a person has broken the law? A trial, at least in theory, is a truth-finding process. Is the adversarial system the best way to discover the truth? How can it be, when neither side has truth as its primary goal? The primary goal of each side is to win. In this respect the system resembles

---

* The news media almost invariably miss this distinction. They report that "the defendant pleaded innocent," or that "the jury found the defendant innocent of all charges." Wrong. As a lawyer guest-lecturing in my class told a student who had asked him about winning a verdict of innocent: "In the entire history of this country, not one person in a criminal trial has ever been found innocent."

the medieval practice of trial by combat. Six hundred years ago, in legal disputes between nobles, the adversaries would fight to determine the verdict. Often the nobles themselves would not fight; instead they would have "champions" represent them in battle. In cases where one person brought criminal charges against another, the accuser and accused themselves would fight it out, usually to the death. (If the loser was not already dead, he would be immediately hanged on the gallows.)[2] In either case, trial by combat meant that the outcome depended on fighting ability, not on truth. Our adversarial system runs the same risk: The winner may be merely the side with the ablest champion (i.e., lawyer), not necessarily the side with truth.

Adding to this danger, the adversarial model puts the final decision in the hands of a jury of ordinary people. Jurors are not lawyers. They do not know the law, nor do they have any special knowledge that makes them the best people to judge the evidence. In fact, in order to become jurors, they must be completely ignorant of any of the evidence. Nor do they even have to be very intelligent. It is possible that a jury may decide a defendant's fate on the basis of irrationality, prejudice, faulty logic, or misunderstanding of the facts or the law. Since juries deliberate in secret and keep no records, we do not know how often jurors make these errors.

For these reasons, some societies have based their trial process on a more **inquisitorial** model. The inquisitorial system is designed not as a battle but as a cooperative effort, an inquiry to discover the truth. In the ideal of the inquisitorial model, the investigators do not take sides. They merely assemble the relevant facts of the case. In France, for example, the presiding judge (*juge*) is a person trained both in the law and in criminal investigation. She or he has broad powers of inquiry to ask any questions of anyone—the police, the defendant, and witnesses. The defense lawyer may present witnesses, but it is the *juge* who asks the questions. The *juge* also sits with the judges (professional judges or ordinary citizens) who deliberate and return a verdict.[3]

The inquisitorial model may sound more reasonable than the adversarial model—a direct quest for the truth by skilled and trained persons rather than the wrangling of two competitors trying to convince 12 untrained people. However, the inquisitorial model has one large flaw: It places an immense amount of power in the hands of a single person, the investigator. In any social system, large or small, centralized power may allow for speed and efficiency in reaching decisions. But the system works well only so long as the person in power is both very capable and very fair. If that person is incompetent, then the system does not accomplish its task; if that person is not fair, the result is tyranny. For this reason, trial by a jury of one's peers, for all its inefficiency and possible error, may be the most important institution we have to prevent tyranny—more important even than the vote.[4]

The Rules of the Game

The founders of the United States recognized the potential for tyranny. They created a constitution that structured the government on the separation of powers, thereby limiting the concentration of power. In their desire to prevent tyranny, the Founding Fathers also continued the English adversarial system—with its diffusion of power among state, defendant, judge, and jury. But the framers of the Constitution recognized something else about the adversarial system of criminal justice. It turns the justice process into a contest, and in contests, the rules of the game become very important. These rules are called **procedural law**, as distinguished from **substantive law**. Substantive law refers to laws that specify what people may not do. These laws define and set penalties for things like robbery, fraud, and conspiracy. Procedural law refers to those laws that specify the procedures the government must follow in prosecuting people. For example, procedural law forbids the government from torturing people in order to get evidence.*

Some of these rules of U.S. procedural law are descended from English **common law**. Common law is not law created by legislation; rather, it is a body of judicial precedents and principles which has accumulated over the centuries, ever since King Henry II, in the 12th century, instituted a system of law common to all people in England. Many of the principles of English common law were incorporated into principles of law in the United States, including some restrictions on the government that are written into the U.S. Constitution.

When we look at courts, we must also distinguish between **factual guilt** and **legal guilt**. A person may be factually guilty—that is, he or she committed the crime. But for the person to be legally guilty, the prosecution must present evidence to prove that guilt, it must gather and present this evidence in accordance with the procedural law, and it must prove the guilt beyond a reasonable doubt.

The Bill of Rights and Due Process

Because of their concern about tyranny or at least about the dangers of a too-powerful government, the first Congress elected under the new constitution proposed a set of constitutional amendments specifically designed to limit the powers of the government. In 1791, the states ratified ten amendments, known as the Bill of Rights. The First Amendment, as most

---

* This does not necessarily mean that agents of the state always follow procedural law. As recently as 1986, a New York City police officer was found to be using electric shocks from a "stun gun" to force a confession from a person accused of selling $10 worth of marijuana.

people know, concerns freedom of speech and of the press. But what does it say about these freedoms? That they are good things? That people should have them? No. The specific language of the amendment is important. It says, "*Congress shall pass no law* . . . abridging the freedom of speech, or of the press" [emphasis added]. In other words, it strictly limits the power of the legislative branch of the government. Four of the amendments, however, deal with the rules for criminal cases, and they are similarly concerned with limiting the power of the government. Remember, a criminal case is contested between the government and the individual (unlike civil cases, where both sides are private parties). So the Founding Fathers stressed that the government must follow correct procedures in bringing criminal cases against persons. The cornerstone of procedural law is the Fifth Amendment:

> No person shall be held to answer for a capital, or otherwise infamous crime, unless on presentment or indictment of a Grand Jury . . . nor shall any person be subject for the same offence twice to be put in jeopardy of life or limb; nor shall be compelled in any criminal case to be a witness against himself, nor be deprived of life, liberty, or property without due process of law. . . .

This amendment contains many familiar ideas; you have probably heard phrases like "double jeopardy" or "taking the fifth" (refusing to testify about oneself). But it is the last phrase that is crucial: **due process of law**. Due process means procedure. The government must follow the correct procedures in proving a person guilty.

The due process clause serves the same function as the ideal of "innocent until proven guilty," a phrase which, by the way, does not appear anywhere in the Constitution, though it was part of English common law. But the Fifth Amendment goes beyond "innocent until proven guilty." It says that in order to deprive a person of life (i.e., to execute), liberty (i.e., to imprison), or property (i.e., to fine), the government must follow due process. If the government does not follow the correct procedures, it cannot punish. So if someone asks, "Where does it say that a criminal should go free just because of a technicality?," the answer is there in the Fifth Amendment. No matter how vicious the person, no matter how clear the guilt—if the government doesn't follow procedure, if it doesn't observe due process, then it cannot fine, imprison, or execute that criminal.

Crime Control and Due Process

The Constitution has built a basic contradiction into the role of the courts. On the one hand, the justice system is supposed to protect the community from criminals. On the other, the Constitution spells out specific protections for people accused of crimes. This contradiction is at the heart of many current debates about the role of the courts. In the view of Herbert L. Packer, a prominent legal authority, these debates often come down to a choice of two "models" of how courts are supposed to work: the **crime-control model** and the **due-process model**. The crime-control model sees the main purpose of the courts as doing something about crime—i.e., preventing crime by punishing criminals. The due-process model sees the main purpose of courts as the protection of constitutional rights, making sure that the government respects the rights of all individuals, even those accused of crimes. If you are arrested and demand your right to an attorney, or if you ask the judge to throw out the confession you made because the police forced you to talk, you are invoking the due-process model. On the other hand, if you demand that the courts pay more attention to the rights of victims or the right of people to be safe from muggers, you are invoking the crime-control model.

Of course, the rights of victims or potential victims are not of the same order as the rights of the accused. The rights of the accused are constitutional rights, spelled out in the various amendments. Nowhere in the Constitution is there any mention of the rights of victims or the public, rights that are the province of substantive criminal law and civil law. The Constitution says nothing about substantive criminal law, probably because the Founding Fathers did not consider substantive criminal law basic to the structure of government. They left such law for later legislation by the states and the federal government. However, the Constitution does speak to issues of procedural law. It says specifically what must happen if the government fails to follow the rules. The framers of the Constitution apparently were much more worried about protecting citizens against the government than about protecting citizens from each other.

BAIL

"Let the jury consider their verdict," the King said. . . .
"No, no!" said the Queen. "Sentence first—verdict afterwards."
"Stuff and nonsense," said Alice. "The idea of having the sentence first!"

—from *Alice's Adventures in Wonderland*
by Lewis Carroll.

Would the Queen of Hearts be at home in an American court today? In theory, no. That's what due process is all about: no punishment without a guilty verdict arrived at according to all the rules of procedure. However, "due process" and "innocent until proven guilty" are concepts whose purity is often muddied in the reality of the court system. For example, on an average day, U.S. municipal and county jails hold about 350,000 people.* More than half of these people have not been convicted of a crime.[5] Still, they are locked up, unable to go to work and earn their daily bread. These people, deprived of liberty and property without having been convicted, are those who have been arrested and are awaiting trial.

Bail: Origins and Uses

What can the criminal justice system do with the people it arrests? To lock them up before trial seems to be a denial of due process—punishment before conviction—but to let them go runs the risk that some of them may flee rather than stand trial when the time comes. One solution to the problem is **bail**.

The practice of bail developed in medieval England, when judges traveled from one town to another, and the interval between arrest and the trial might be quite long. Jails were wretched places, and it was expensive to keep people there. In addition, the accused, still not convicted of any crime, would need to feed his family and prepare his defense. Originally (that is, over 1,000 years ago) the accused was released into the care of another person—his bailor, usually a relative. If the accused did not return for trial, than the bailor was tried and punished in his place. Over the years, the concept changed so that property, rather than another person, became the basis of the bail. The accused posts a **bond**, an amount of money set by the judge. When the defendant returns for trial, the court returns the money; if the defendant fails to show up for trial, the court keeps the money.

From the beginning, the only purpose of bail was to ensure that the accused return for trial. To use bail as a means of punishing the accused would have violated the principle of innocent until proven guilty. Of course, by setting a high bail, a judge could in effect punish a person without having to go to the trouble of proving guilt. Recognizing the possibility for this abuse, the framers of the U.S. Constitution included in the Bill of Rights the Eighth Amendment, which says in part, "excessive bail shall not be required." Supreme Court decisions in the early 1800s reaffirmed the limited purpose of bail.[6] Of course, there is still the question of what is excessive. But a 1951 decision by the Supreme Court defined as excessive any

---

* **Jails** are municipal or county institutions. They hold people awaiting trial and people convicted of misdemeanors (i.e., crimes punishable by less than one year). **Prisons** are state or federal institutions and hold only those convicted of felonies (i.e., crimes punishable by more than one year).

amount higher than the amount that should reasonably make sure that the defendant will show up for trial.[7]*

Although these court rulings have defined the use of bail in principle, in actual practice, judges have used bail to accomplish two other goals that are not so clearly legitimate: first, the punishment of the accused; and second, the protection of the community. Consider the following from a New York City court judge setting bail for two juveniles.

> Maybe a couple of days in jail may solve the problem. I'm going to set $5,000 bail on each. Now, I'm leaving word that if a bond is presented, the matter is to be sent back to me, and I'll tell you right now, if they put up $5,000 bail, I'll make it $10,000, and if they put up $10,000 I'll make it $25,000. I want these boys to spend one or two nights in jail. Maybe that is the answer.[8]

The judge may be right. Maybe a couple of days in jail will deter the boys from further crime. But that is not the point. The point is that the judge's action is a denial of due process. His intent here is clearly to punish the boys (i.e., send them to jail) by setting high bail, even though they have not been convicted of any crime. The judge seems to share the Wonderland legal philosophy offered by the Queen of Hearts: sentence first, verdict afterwards.

Using bail for reasons other than assuring that the accused appear for trial seems especially likely in cases of political conflict. In the 1960s, for example, during civil rights protests in the South, local police would arrest demonstrators for breaking segregation laws or marching without a permit. It was highly unlikely that the protestors would flee in order to escape trial. A court hearing was exactly what they wanted, since in court they could challenge the legality of segregation laws. Nor did these demonstrators pose any criminal threat to the community. In fact, they made a point of practicing nonviolence. Nevertheless, Southern judges would set bail at thousands of dollars, and the jails would fill up with people like Martin Luther King Jr. and his followers awaiting trial.

Preventive Detention

> "He's in prison now being punished: and the trial doesn't even begin till next Wednesday: and of course the crime comes last of all."
> "Suppose he never commits the crime?" said Alice.
> "That would be all the better, wouldn't it?" the Queen said.
>
> —from *Through the Looking Glass,*
> by Lewis Carroll

---

* By the same logic, the Supreme Court allowed judges to deny bail for capital crimes (i.e., those punishable by death). After all, if a defendant stands to lose his life if he returns for trial, no amount of bail money will surely prevent him from skipping trial.

Blocking political protests seems an obvious abuse of bail. But what about denying bail entirely in order to keep a dangerous person off the streets? This practice is called **preventive detention**, and it remains a controversial topic. As with many other conflicts in the legal process, on one side is the defendant's right to due process; on the other, the need of the wider community to be protected from crime. The defendant could argue that he is being punished without due process; he has not been convicted of any crime, yet he is being locked up. Can it be legal to lock someone up for what he *might* do rather than for a crime he has been convicted of? The community, for its part, would just as soon keep a dangerous person in jail until trial. The argument comes down to this: Can the purposes of jail and bail be widened to include more than just assuring that the accused appears for trial? Can bail be used to try to protect the community?

In practice, the answer has usually been yes. If judges can get away with using bail to punish—a clear violation of the Constitution—certainly they can use it to keep dangerous but unconvicted people in jail, regardless of what the Supreme Court might have said. And in fact, most judges when setting bail often consider the dangerousness of the defendant. As for the constitutional question, that too seems to have been settled, at least for the foreseeable future. In 1987, the Court upheld the preventive detention section of the federal Bail Reform Act of 1984. Chief Justice Rehnquist, writing the majority opinion, ruled that the defendant's right to liberty may "be subordinated to the greater needs of society." Does jail before trial deny due process? The Court said, "The pretrial detention of the Bail Reform Act is regulatory . . . and does not constitute punishment before trial in violation of the Due Process Clause."[9] This is a fairly subtle distinction, more easily seen from the Supreme Court bench than from inside a jail cell. The detained prisoner may find it difficult to see the difference between his own condition of being "regulated," and that of his convicted cellmate who is being punished. Moreover, the Due Process Clause says nothing about "punishment"; it refers to being "deprived of . . . liberty or property."

Nevertheless, preventive detention is now legal, and several states have adopted preventive detention provisions. Most of these allow preventive detention only for those who have been arrested for a violent crime and who have prior records of violence. It's hard to say what effect these statutes will have. With jails already overcrowded, judges may be reluctant to make extensive use of preventive detention. Of course, in most cases, judges do not really need to use these new laws to keep defendants in jail. Most defendants have little money, so judges can do what they have always done: set high bail.

There remain the practical questions: Does preventive detention work? Does it in fact prevent crime? And if so, at what cost? These are not easy questions to answer. They require us to estimate the number of crimes a defendant *would have* committed *if* he or she had been out on bail.

Here is a rough summary of the data relevant to this issue. First, some criminals are more likely than others to commit crimes while free on bail. Defendants arrested for robbery seem to be the worst risks. About 30 percent of them are rearrested while out on bail. Nevertheless, this means that as many of 70 percent of even the worst risks can safely be released.[10]

Second, to use preventive detention on a broad scale—i.e., to lock up large numbers of defendants—would be very inefficient. Most preventive detention laws are concerned with violent crimes. Their purpose is to prevent violent crime, and usually only those arrested for violent crimes can be detained.* Under preventive detention, 95 percent of the arrestees who might legally be denied bail would not commit violent crimes if released. In other words, applying preventive detention across the board would result in locking up 19 safe defendants for every one who would commit another violent crime.[11]

Third, if preventive detention is to be efficient, judges must be able to guess accurately who would commit a crime while out on bail and who would not.† However, to use preventive detention selectively would not be very efficient either. Judges are not very good at picking out the one defendant in 20 who constitutes a dangerous risk. A judge's selections for preventive detention might turn out to include a few people who would commit further crimes, but the judge would still wind up locking up many more who were safe risks. And keeping "safe" defendants in jail is not a harmless error. It has its costs.

The most easily calculated cost is money. Currently, a jailed defendant costs the state between $50 and $100 per day. (This is a large range and a conservative estimate. In New York City in 1987, the cost was $119 per day.) If the average time between arrest and verdict is 100 days (and 200 days for cases that go to trial instead of being plea-bargained),[12] then each person preventively detained costs the taxpayers, on the average, $5,000 to $10,000.

The other cost is incalculable. Suppose that a person must stay in jail until trial because the judge has either denied bail or set a bail far beyond the person's means. Now suppose also that the person is acquitted of the crime. He is found not guilty; nevertheless he has already served several months in jail. This in itself is quite severe punishment, since in most cities the conditions in jails are worse than those in the prisons where convicted criminals are sent. In addition, the defendant may have lost his job and will almost certainly have lost the income that goes with it. He also may have

---

* Judges have also used preventive detention in order to keep organized crime bosses from continuing "business as usual" while awaiting trial, even though they were not on trial for violent crimes.

† These problems in preventive detention are identical to those in "selective incapacitation," and are discussed more fully in Chapter 16.

lost a car or household appliances he could not make payments on, and his marriage also may suffer.[13]* So even if the Supreme Court approves of more types of preventive detention, we still must ask whether its benefits outweigh the costs.

The Question of Money

The second problem in the bail system is its potential for discriminating against the poor. In effect, bail allows wealthy defendants to await trial in freedom, while poor defendants must await trial in jail. The difference is not merely one of comfort. Making bail has more important consequences, as a landmark study in the 1960s demonstrated. The study followed two groups of defendants matched as nearly as possible for crimes, past records, and other sociological factors. One group had been out on bail (or on personal recognizance); the other group awaited trial in jail. The results were clear: The defendant who enters court a free person is less likely to be convicted than is the defendant who comes in from the jail. And even among those convicted, those who have been free on bail receive more lenient sentences than do those who have been waiting in jail.

Until the 1960s, defendants who could not afford bail usually had three choices: plead guilty; stay in jail until trial; or find a **bail bondsman**. A bail bondsman is someone who posts bond for the defendant. His fee for this service is typically 10 percent of the bond. Suppose you are arrested and the judge sets bail at $5,000, a sum which you do not have in either cash or property. If a bail bondsman is willing to take you as a client, you pay him $500 immediately and walk out of jail. The bail bondsman's risk, in theory, is that if you skip town and fail to show up for trial, he must pay the court $5,000. But to you, the defendant, the bail bondsman can say in effect, "Pay me $500 or stay in jail."

Understandably, the bail bondsman throughout history has had a reputation as a sleazy character, a necessary but detestable part of the criminal justice system. Bail bondsmen make their money off of other people's misery. They hold the key to the jail and will sell it at a price. And if the accused skips trial, bail bondsmen can use methods that even the police cannot legally use—they can search without warrants, extradite without a court order, and even hire modern-day bounty hunters (called "skip-tracers"). To this already unpalatable basis of their profession, they sometimes add outright corruption. A bail bondsman might bribe jailers, police, and court clerks to steer defendants his way. He might bribe a magistrate at the original bail hearing to set a high bail. Or he might take bribes from a lawyer

* Nearly all people jailed under preventive detention laws are men. Women may suffer all these consequences, plus the disruption of their ties to their children.

hungry for any clients the bail bondsman might send him. The bondsman's close association with criminals might even lead him to aid his clients in their illegal work, such as by fencing the goods that his clients steal.[14] With so many glaring flaws, the system was long overdue for reform. But it was not until 1961 that social science finally offered evidence that something else might work.

As a test of alternatives to bail, a wealthy philanthropist in New York City sponsored the Manhattan Bail Project, in which many young defendants who usually spent their pre-trial days in jail were instead "released on recognizance" (ROR)—that is, released on no money bail. The defendants were selected on the basis of their ties to the community—family, length of residence, jobs, prior criminal record, and general character (the same information bail bondsmen often use in deciding whether to take a client). The study was a great success: Less than 1 percent of the ROR defendants failed to show up for trial, and only 2 percent committed further crimes while on bail.[15]

The success of the Manhattan Bail Project spurred other courts in New York and elsewhere to reform their bail procedures. Many more defendants were released on recognizance. The state of Kentucky outlawed bail bondsmen entirely. Other jurisdictions adopted a practice where defendants could post "cash alternative"—usually 10 percent of bail (equivalent to the cash they would have paid to a bail bondsman); when they showed up for trial, the court would return 90 percent of this cash. Thus bail set at $5,000 would in the end cost the defendant only $50. As a result of these measures, bail bondsmen have all but disappeared in many jurisdictions. However, the problems that gave rise to the bail bondsman in the first place will not go away—that is, the problem of what to do with the many people arrested for crimes.

Bail reform was largely a liberal policy, initiated during the 1960s. In the 1980s, public opinion and court policies swung back to a more conservative, crime-control perspective. In 1984, a federal law that carried the title of "Bail Reform Act" called for increased use of preventive detention. More arrests, fewer RORs, and very few bail bondsmen added up to a large increase in the jail population, so much so that the news media regularly carry stories about overcrowding in the jails. The solution to this problem remains elusive. Speedier trials would help, especially since the longer a defendant is out on bail, the greater the chances that he will commit a crime. But with courts, like jails, already overloaded, speedier trials seem unlikely.

The link between crime and jails illustrates a more general point. We often think of the criminal justice system—the police, the courts, the jails and prisons—as our primary force for controlling crime. In fact, if there is any cause-effect relationship, it probably runs the other direction: The system has little effect on the overall amount of crime, but crime rates can have a noticeable effect on the criminal justice system.

The problems of bail also illustrate the theme I mentioned in the first sentence of this chapter—the contrast between everyday courtroom reality and the lofty principles of the law. A bail hearing may look like a trivial, routine matter (go visit a court and watch a few of them). But the issues underlying bail are far from simple or trivial. They involve matters of highest principle: the conflict between due process and crime control; the protection of the individual against the government; the protection of people against criminals; the historical legacy of British common law and of the U.S. Constitution, a document born out of anti-government revolution.

Bail also raises practical questions: Does it really protect rights? Does it really control crime? These questions arise at other points in the criminal justice process—that long sequence of events from arrest to sentencing. Bail is neither the beginning nor the end of that process, and to start this chapter with a discussion of bail was somewhat arbitrary. So let's move back a step and see how some of these same general themes appear at earlier stages—during arrest and the taking of evidence.

SEARCH AND SEIZURE

The Writs of Assistance and the Fourth Amendment

Before the American revolution, the colonists found many policies of English rule intolerable, especially taxation. The English prime minister, as a way of making sure that the colonists were not avoiding taxes, empowered customs agents with "writs of assistance." A writ of assistance gave the officer the power to search anyone, anywhere, for anything. The English government also had used such writs and "general warrants" to allow officers, both in England and in the colonies, to ransack people's houses looking for anti-government literature.

The American Revolutionary War was fought at least in part over issues like the writs of assistance. Such legal practices gave the government far too much power to intrude into the lives of citizens. They were part of a style of government that we call totalitarian or authoritarian today and that the colonists more bluntly called tyranny. When it came time for the Founding Fathers to create a government for their own new nation, they were still most sensitive to the possibility for tyranny. They feared the concentrated power of government and therefore designed the Constitution based on the separation of powers. But more important for the individual, they attached to the Constitution a Bill of Rights—10 amendments that sought to protect the rights of citizens against the government. One of the most important and controversial of these is the Fourth Amendment:

> The right of the people to be secure in their persons, houses, papers, and effects, against unreasonable searches and seizures shall not be violated, and no warrants shall issue but upon probable cause, supported by oath or affirmation, and particularly describing the place to be searched and the persons or things to be seized.

The amendment in itself is not controversial. Nobody favors unreasonable searches. But just what makes a search "unreasonable?" What constitutes "probable cause?" More important, what should the courts do when the police make an unreasonable search? Take the following example:

> On the night of April 23, 1973, Herbert Joseph Giglotto, a hardworking boiler-maker, and his wife, Louise, were sleeping soundly in their suburban house in Collinsville, Illinois. Suddenly, and without warning, armed men broke into their house and rushed up the stairs to the Giglottos' bedroom. Giglotto later recalled, "I [saw] men . . . dressed like hippies with pistols, yelling and screeching." The night intruders threw Giglotto down on his bed and tied his hands behind his back. Holding a loaded gun at his head, one of the men pointed to his wife and asked, "Who is that bitch lying there?" . . . The men refused to allow the terrified couple to move from the bed or put on any clothes while they proceeded to search the residence. As books were swept from the shelves and clothes were ripped from hangers, one man said, "You're going to die unless you tell us where the stuff is." Then the intrusion ended as suddenly as it began when the leader of the raiders concluded, "We made a mistake."

The raiders were from a federal anti-drug agency set up under President Nixon. That same night, another group from the same agency

> kicked in the door of the home of Donald and Virginia Askew. . . . Virginia Askew, who was then crippled from a back injury, fainted as the men rushed into the frame house. While she lay on the floor, agents kept her husband . . . from going to her aid. Another agent kept their 16-year-old son . . . from telephoning for help by pointing a rifle at him. After the house was searched, the agents admitted they had made another mistake and disappeared. (Virginia Askew the next day was rushed to a mental hospital for emergency psychiatric therapy.)[16]

The police had no warrant to search either of these houses. The searches were clearly unreasonable. We find them especially offensive since the victims were innocent. But since everyone is presumed innocent until proven guilty, such searches would have been just as unreasonable if the houses had contained illegal drugs. It was exactly such government invasion of people's homes that the Fourth Amendment sought to prevent, and the authors of that amendment knew full well that in order to protect the innocent, the right to be secure against unreasonable government searches had to extend to *all* persons. That's why the amendment does not say, "The right of good, innocent, law-abiding people who don't possess illegal materials to be secure in their persons, houses, etc., shall not be violated; but other people, it's o.k. for the government to violate their rights." It says, "The right of the people to be secure in their houses . . . shall not be violated."

But what if the police do conduct an unreasonable search like the ones in Collinsville and find illegal drugs? Suppose, for example, that the agents had found a gram of cocaine in Mr. Giglotto's drawer. The search was illegal, but the government now has evidence of a crime. What should happen? Here the language of the Fourth Amendment offers no explicit instructions. It says only that the government should not conduct unreasonable searches; it does not say what should happen if the government does violate a person's Fourth Amendment rights.

Common law had few provisions on the matter. Under English common law, the victim of a search could sue for trespass or for the return of stolen property. But the evidence, however the police obtained it, could be used in court. After all, evidence is evidence. The defendant could argue that the evidence was irrelevant or insufficient, but he could hardly claim that it didn't exist.[17]

Critics of the common-law view argued that if courts continued to allow such evidence, then the Fourth Amendment was meaningless. It could not keep the police from making unreasonable searches, since they had nothing to lose and might gain a conviction. In 1914, the Supreme Court agreed. In a unanimous decision in the case of *Weeks v. U.S.*, the Court established the **exclusionary rule**: evidence seized in violation of the Fourth Amendment could not be used against the defendant.[18]

Although law enforcement officials criticized the Court's decision, *Weeks* did not revolutionize police procedure. The reason was simple. *Weeks* was a federal case. The evidence against Weeks was seized by a U.S. marshal, and the case was tried in federal court. However, most criminal cases— typical street crimes like burglary and robbery—are violations of state laws. In 1914, the Supreme Court's decisions on criminal procedure applied only in federal courts. States were still largely free to establish their own versions of due process. In other words, local police could still make illegal searches and use the evidence.

The federal/state distinction raises a central constitutional question. The language of the Bill of Rights clearly restricts what the *federal* government can do. But to what extent do the protections in the Bill of Rights apply to the *states*? Advocates of "states rights" argued that these constitutional restrictions applied only to federal cases. They based their argument on the 10th Amendment: All powers not specifically granted to the federal government belong to the states. For example, the First Amendment says only that "Congress shall make no law . . . abridging freedom of speech, or of the press." The amendment says nothing about the state legislatures; it restricts only the Congress. For over a hundred years, therefore, the Court refused to extend the protection of the First Amendment to people prosecuted in state courts.[19]

In criminal cases, too, like the *Weeks* case, the Court applied constitutional guarantees only in federal courts. In the years following *Weeks*, the Court stood by this state-federal distinction. Occasionally, a particularly offensive police action would be appealed to the Court. For example, in 1952 the Court reviewed the case of a man named Rochin who had been convicted of a drug offense in state court. How had the police obtained the evidence? They entered Rochin's house illegally and, having seen him swallow some capsules, they arrested him and forcibly pumped his stomach.

Rochin was *factually* guilty since the capsules had contained illegal drugs. The local court had convicted him, and the California Supreme Court had upheld the conviction. But the U.S. Supreme Court ruled that even though this was a state case, the search was so outrageous that the evidence must be excluded despite state-federal differences.[20] Still, the Court refused to make any general policy binding on all states.

The stage was set for one of the most important and controversial cases in criminal law: *Mapp v. Ohio.* In 1957, in Cleveland, Ohio, the police received a tip that a suspect in a recent bombing was hiding out in the home of Mrs. Dolree Mapp and that the house also held illegal gambling equipment. The police went to the house, but Mrs. Mapp, on the advice of her lawyer, refused to admit them without a search warrant. The police kept the house under surveillance and returned to the door three hours later, this time forcing their way in. When Mrs. Mapp demanded to see a search warrant, one of the officers waved a piece of paper which Mrs. Mapp grabbed and stuffed in her bosom. The officers, with some struggle, retrieved the paper (at the trial, no warrant was ever produced). They then handcuffed Mrs. Mapp to a railing and continued to search the entire house. They found no bombers and no gambling equipment. However, in the basement of the building, they found some pornography. Mrs. Mapp was eventually convicted of possession of obscene materials, and the Ohio Supreme Court upheld the conviction. She appealed the case to the U.S. Supreme Court.

In a 5-3 decision, the Court reversed the conviction. The constitutional reasoning in this decision is crucial because it had implications far beyond the fate of Dolree Mapp. Obviously, the Fourth Amendment had a central place in the Court's reasoning since this warrantless search was illegal.* The question was whether the evidence could be excluded. By 1960, nearly half the states in the country had adopted some kind of exclusionary rule, but Ohio was not one of them.[21] The search, while illegal, was not so unusual or repulsive—nothing like the stomach-pumping case where the Supreme Court had stepped in before. So if the Court were to overrule, if it were to make sure that the Fourth Amendment protected Ohio residents, it would

---

* Ohio argued that the search was legal since it was incident to Mrs. Mapp's arrest. However, as the defense pointed out, the original arrest was itself illegal since the police did not have probable cause.

have to extend the exclusionary rule to state courts as well. Was there any constitutional basis for such a broadening of Court rulings?

The answer lay in the 14th Amendment. The 14th Amendment, along with the 13th and 15th, was passed in the aftermath of the Civil War—a war whose major aim and justification had been the preservation of the Union. If the 10th Amendment meant to guarantee the rights of individual states, then the 13th, 14th and 15th amendments meant to enforce certain minimum, uniform standards upon all the states in the Union. The 13th Amendment banned slavery in all states. The 15th Amendment guaranteed that in all states, all races would have the right to vote.

The 14th Amendment is far longer and broader in scope than the other two. Its first section says in part, "No State shall make or enforce any law which abridges the privileges and immunities of the citizens of the United States." This phrase seems to say that no state can deny the basic rights of a citizen of the United States.

The next phrase of the amendment seems to extend the "due process" clause of the Fifth Amendment to all states. This section reads, "Nor shall any State deprive any person of life, liberty, or property, without due process of law; nor deny to any person within its jurisdiction equal protection of the laws."

So if the Bill of Rights protects the people's rights against the federal government, then the 14th Amendment seems to protect those same rights against state governments.[22] I say "seems to" here because for nearly a century the Supreme Court had interpreted the amendment very narrowly. In effect, the Court allowed each state to make up its own version of due process.[23] Only when particularly ugly procedures came to light did the Supreme Court step in.

However, by 1960 the membership and philosophy of the Court had changed. Under Chief Justice Earl Warren, the Court had already used the "equal protection" clause of the 14th Amendment to ban segregation in public schools. The school decision had two other notable features: It imposed a national standard on a state, and it protected the rights of individuals against discrimination by a state. Similarly, in the *Mapp* decision in 1961, the "Warren Court" extended a federal standard in order to protect the individual's rights against the state. The Court ruled in effect that the exclusionary rule would apply not just in the federal courts but in all *state* criminal procedures as well.

The Effects of *Mapp v. Ohio*

The reaction to *Mapp* was immediate and predictable. It was a classic example of conservative vs. liberal, crime control vs. due process. Police and other "hard-liners" spoke out vigorously against it. They claimed that the Supreme Court had handcuffed the police. Criminals would be freer to commit crimes; they would be released on these technicalities and return to the streets to commit more crimes. Civil libertarians, on the other hand, applauded the decision as a step toward preserving the right to privacy and as a way to ensure that the police, too, abide by the law of the land, the Constitution.

Who was right? Did the new restrictions change the way in which the police gathered evidence? Did *Mapp* decrease police violations of citizens' Fourth Amendment rights? And did it allow criminals to go free?

It is difficult, if not impossible, to know the answers to all these questions. We could easily find anecdotal evidence to support either side—stories of criminals getting off on search-and-seizure technicalities, or stories of police continuing to make illegal searches. What we need here, however, is good, systematic evidence. Unfortunately, such evidence is not always easy to find.

On the issue of whether *Mapp* changed the nature of police work, the answer is probably this: not immediately, not universally, and not for most arrests for street crimes. Arrests of thieves or robbers or burglars rarely involve questionable searches. The police either are lucky enough to catch the criminal in the act or they rely on information from other people. Search warrants are not so important in these cases, and where warrants are required, the police can get them easily enough—as they could and did before *Mapp*. On the other hand, we shouldn't ignore the strength of police reaction against *Mapp*. Perhaps they were reacting to the symbolism of the Court's decision, since it seemed to side with the criminal and against the cop. But perhaps police also objected to *Mapp* because it forced them to change the way they conducted themselves. All this is speculation, however, not proof. In any case, police departments did begin to set up new programs to teach officers how to conduct everyday searches so that the evidence would stand up in court.

For illegal possession of drugs, the effects of *Mapp* are less clear. In New York, in the aftermath of *Mapp*, police continued to arrest drug users on the streets. However, the content of the police reports changed. Where before officers would report that they searched the suspect and found drugs, now the reports said that the officer had seen the suspect drop a glassine envelope which the officer then picked up and which was later found to contain heroin. Had the police really changed their behavior to comply with the law? Had the drug users of New York suddenly turned into the clumsiest group in history? Or had the police gone on with business as usual and merely changed what they wrote in their reports?[24] This is only one area in one department, and nobody has done any systematic survey of police behavior in general before and after *Mapp*. Still, some observers believe that *Mapp* did have its intended effect, and that to some extent police departments have become more professional in the way they carry out searches.

Now, did *Mapp* reduce the number of illegal searches? This question is even harder to answer. To do so, we would have had to count the illegal

Under the "plain view" doctrine, the Supreme Court has ruled that while police officers may not search a car that they have stopped for an ordinary traffic violation, they may seize evidence that is in plain view. As with the clumsy drug users on the streets of New York in the 1960s, the careless drivers in the 1990s may exist more in the police write-ups than in reality.

COPS TALK, JURIES BALK
BY WILLIAM MURPHY

While police brutality was being debated in public last month, I was sitting on a grand jury, listening to secret testimony—much of it from police officers—and weighing its credibility.

It became clearer with each passing case that cops on the street did whatever was necessary to arrest the bad guys, and figured out later how to make it legal.

According to the collective testimony of law enforcement agents, people in vans who happen to have drugs in plain sight are also remarkably bad drivers. They don't use their turn signals, giving police a reason to stop them and observe the drugs inside.

And it would appear that people who have illegal guns in their vehicles usually stick them under the seat when the police approach. They always leave the butt of the gun protruding in plain sight, however, giving the officers the justification and the right to search the vehicle.

Source: New York Newsday, Apr. 11, 1991, p. 114. Copyright Times Mirror Company.

searches that occurred before and after 1961. As we saw in the chapter on crime statistics, it's hard enough to get an accurate count of criminal behavior committed by civilians. To count illegal acts by the police is almost impossible. The fact is that few illegal searches ever become known. Therefore, in the absence of good evidence, we have to fall back on common sense, on what seems reasonable.

People who believe that the exclusionary rule will deter the police from making illegal searches argue that the police, like most people, hate to see a guilty person go free. That's why they make the illegal search in the first place—in order to get the goods on a criminal. It follows logically that if their illegal searches result not in conviction but in acquittal, the police will soon give up their unconstitutional ways and start observing the Fourth Amendment. They will feel pressure from their superiors and from fellow officers to play by the book in order to ensure that the guilty are punished. Due process will become synonymous with good police work.

This logic ignores one important limitation: The exclusionary rule affects only those searches where the police want to convict a criminal in court. If the police aren't interested in getting a conviction, court policy can do little to keep them from violating the Fourth Amendment. For example, sometimes the police use illegal searches to harass rather than to gather evidence for a trial. They may use their power of search and arrest to relieve a drug dealer of his cash and inventory, or to show potential criminals (and the public) that the police are getting tough on crime.* These searches may be illegal, but since they do not lead to the filing of criminal charges, the exclusionary rule is irrelevant. The same is true if the police make an illegal search of a truly innocent person. Suppose that the police illegally search a house or person, find no evidence, and let their victim go. With no arrest, no charges, and no trial, such misconduct cannot be deterred by the exclusionary rule.

Finally, the police officer who makes the illegal search rarely suffers the direct consequences. To begin with, nobody prosecutes the cop for making an illegal search. Second, once the case gets past the arrest stage, the police play a secondary role. The case becomes the district attorney's to win or lose (or more likely to win or dismiss). The DA may blame the cop for bad police work, but police are little influenced by the opinions of anyone except fellow officers. Even if an officer does care about the case, the illegal search issue might not be decided for months or even years. Any deterrent effect of the exclusionary rule will have been dissipated over such a long time.[25]

The final question is a bit easier to answer and it is the one that is of greatest concern to most people who are speaking up about the exclusionary rule these days. How many criminals go free because of *Mapp*? Here are the results of one study of felony cases in California, 1976 to 1979.[26]

Total number of cases	520,993
Cases rejected before filing of charges	86,033
Cases rejected for search-and-seizure technicalities	4,130

Of all cases (520,993), less than 1 percent were rejected for Fourth Amendment reasons. Most of the more than 4,000 rejected cases were for a single category of crime: drugs. Drug arrests accounted for nearly three-quarters of the rejected cases. Therefore, jurisdictions that handle a large proportion of drug arrests may have somewhat higher rates of search-and-seizure rejections. What impact did the exclusionary rule have on violent crime? Table 14–1 shows the number of violent crimes and arrests for violent crime in San Diego. It also shows the number of cases dropped (either screened out by the prosecutor or dismissed in court) and the reason for this decision. The last column shows the number of cases dropped because of due-process problems.

---

* Do the police really make such arrests? In 1987, a Chicago judge ordered that city to "erase from the record 800,000 to 1 million disorderly conduct arrests, mainly involving blacks and Hispanic people, over the last five years." The judge ruled that "the arrests were unconstitutional because no prosecution was intended." (*The New York Times*, April 1, 1987, p. 22.)

Table 14–1 ▪ Index Crime in San Diego, 1987

	Reported crimes	Arrests	Reject & dismiss	Reasons for rejections/dismissal		
				Evidence	Witness	Due process
Murder	176	132	20	12	1	0
Rape	801	482	219	64	113	1
Robbery	5,421	1,137	365	124	104	7
Agg. Asslt	9,886	1,684	799	187	332	10
Burglary	35,214	4,123	1,006	344	93	53
Larceny and MVT	106,263	2,374	746	245	61	20
Violent Crime	16,284	3,435	1,403	387	550	18
TOTAL	157,761	9,932	3,155	976	704	91

Source: Barbara Boland, Catherine H. Conly, Paul Mahanna, Lynn Warner, and Ronald Sones (1990), *The Prosecution of Felony Arrests, 1987*, Washington, DC: Abt Associates. *UCR,* 1987.

As you can see, most violent crimes (nearly 80 percent) do not end in arrest. Prosecutors reject or dismiss about 40 percent of these arrests. But only a handful (18 out of the original 16,284 arrests) are rejected on due-process "technicalities." Even assuming that all the cases in the last column were search-and-seizure problems, it is obvious that the exclusionary rule does not hamper the state's ability to prosecute violent crime. It accounts for much less than 1 percent of all reported crimes or arrests and only about $1\frac{1}{4}$ percent of all cases dropped.

If the exclusionary rule affects any area of crime, it should be crimes of possession—of stolen property, drugs, weapons, or gambling materials. In San Diego, about 10 percent of all drug arrests were dropped because of due-process problems; for stolen property and weapons offenses, the proportion was much smaller. In many other cities, even the proportion of drug offense affected by due process is small. In Seattle, for example, in the same year (1987), police filed over 1,800 drug arrests. Prosecutors screened out or dismissed nearly 45 percent of these, but only two cases were dropped because of due-process problems.[27]

If a case does get to court, the defendant may still try to have evidence excluded (or in legal terms, "suppressed"). But the judge does not automatically go along with these requests. A Boston study of drug and gambling cases found that only 13 percent of defendants moved to suppress evidence, and the court denied 80 percent of these motions. Of the 512 cases, only 11 defendants (about 2 percent) were able to have evidence excluded.[28]

These studies and others point to some general conclusions about the

effects of *Mapp*. First, the exclusionary rule affects relatively few cases.*
Second, the cases in which the exclusionary rule makes a difference are *not*
predatory crimes in which innocent citizens are victimized. They are, like
the *Mapp* case itself, crimes of illegal possession (most of them drug possession). If the Supreme Court were to abolish the exclusionary rule completely, it would have very little effect on street crimes like robbery or burglary, much less on the most serious violent crimes of murder and rape.

Beyond Mapp: Other Issues in Search and Seizure

While the *Mapp* decision settled the question of how to enforce the Fourth
Amendment, it raised a host of other questions over how to interpret its
language. Just what makes a search "unreasonable," and what constitutes
"probable cause"? When may a police officer "stop and frisk" someone in
the street? In the years following *Mapp*, the Supreme Court has had to settle
borderline cases and establish the boundary between legal and illegal
searches. However, although the Court may have shifted that boundary over
the course of time, it still has held to the principle of the exclusionary rule:
If a search is defined as unreasonable, then the evidence may not be used.
That position, however, has changed.

In 1984, the Court began to move toward allowing **good faith** exceptions
to the exclusionary rule. This exception means that if a police officer acts
in good faith, then the evidence may be used, *even if the search warrant
is not valid*. In one case, the police had used the wrong form and had filled
it out incorrectly.[29] In another case, the police seized evidence on the basis
of a warrant, but it later turned out that the information the police used
to get the warrant in the first place was not sufficient to establish probable
cause. Had a lawyer challenged either of these warrants *before* the search,
a judge would probably not have allowed the search. Nevertheless, the Supreme Court ruled that the exclusionary rule did not apply because the
police had acted in good faith—that is, they had thought that the warrants
were valid.

The reasoning of the Court was especially interesting. Instead of holding
the police to strict procedures, the Court adopted a "balancing approach."
It weighed the defendant's right to due process against the "truth-finding"
functions of a trial. It weighed the benefits of deterring unreasonable

---

* Some observers take a different view. They look, for instance, at the California study cited
earlier, in which less than 1 percent of all cases were rejected for due process problems. To
them, these numbers mean that 4,000 criminals, mostly drug criminals, went free because of
the exclusionary rule. Whether 4,000 in a four-year period, out of a total of 520,000, is a lot
or a little is, apparently, a matter of opinion. The Supreme Court, in a later decision (*U.S. v.
Leon*), thought it was a lot. (Caleb Nelson (1989), "The Paradox of the Exclusionary Rule," *The
Public Interest*, no. 96, pp. 117–30.)

searches against the cost of letting a guilty person go free.[30] In effect, the Court was asking a different set of questions. Instead of asking, "Was this search legal?," it asked, "What will be the effect of excluding the evidence? Will it greatly deter police misconduct? Will a guilty person go free?"

Police Misconduct—Other Remedies

The exclusionary rule has long been a favorite target of conservative politicians. In the 1980s, they began to propose legislation against it. During the Reagan administration, the attorney general, Edwin L. Meese, also took a similar stand. His argument was nothing new: that the exclusionary rule excludes the truth and lets guilty people go free. Here again, we have a conflict between the crime control model of criminal justice and the due process model. To restate the conflict in extreme terms: Due process advocates argue that in order to protect all people from the excesses of the police, the Constitution must protect the rights of even the most wicked, regardless of the consequences. Crime-control advocates argue that anything which helps put bad people behind bars is justified. Due process protects only the guilty; if such protections are abolished, law-abiding citizens will still have nothing to fear.

But without the exclusionary rule, what protection do people have from illegal police searches? In theory at least, people are protected by both criminal and civil law. Police officers who violate people's rights may be subject to criminal prosecution. Some states, but by no means all, have criminal laws against warrantless searches, and there are federal laws as well. But except in the most extreme and publicized cases, prosecutors rarely file criminal charges against the police, and juries are often reluctant to convict.

Some opponents of the exclusionary rule propose civil remedies for those who have been victims of illegal police searches. Let the evidence be used, they say, but if the police have violated a person's rights, let that person sue in civil court. In reality, such suits are rarities. To begin with, most victims of illegal search are criminals. Even if the police have violated the criminal's rights, a jury may tend to make its decision more on the basis of general character rather than on a strict application of the law. Second, the victim may be risking further harassment by the police. Third, even the truly innocent people who become victims of illegal police searches are not likely to sue the police. These victims usually are not the middle-class, suburban people of the Collinsville raid. Instead, they are the poor and powerless—people unable to afford lawyers (if they can even find a lawyer willing to sue the police), unable to afford the time for a long court case that may drag on for years.* Finally, the amount of money the victim can collect may

---

* Cities, like people, prefer to postpone paying out money which can otherwise be accumulating interest.

not be enough to make it worthwhile to pursue the case. As one constitutional expert has summed it up, "When the police violate the Fourth Amendment, their victim has no effective legal redress."[31]

In the closing years of this century, we can probably expect further eroding of *Mapp*. As the good-faith rulings show, the current Supreme Court (the "Rehnquist Court" or "Reagan Court") appears to be more tolerant of police misconduct in the interests of crime-fighting. In its 1986 to 1987 term, the court reversed 16 of 19 decisions where lower courts had upheld the rights of the accused.[32] For example, in a 1987 case, the police had a warrant and thought they were executing it, but they made a mistake and searched the wrong apartment, one on the same floor but not named in the warrant. They found illegal drugs. Despite the explicit language of the Fourth Amendment ("particularly describing the place to be searched . . ."), the Court ruled that since the police had acted in good faith, the evidence could be used.[33]*

But giving the police a freer hand in searches will have little effect on crime, especially street crime and violent crime. Search and seizure issues arise mostly in drug cases, so perhaps the police will win more drug convictions and confiscate more drugs. More drug dealers or users may go to prison. However, the drug trade in general remains remarkably unaffected by arrests, convictions, or confiscations.[34] It will be harder to know how easing the exclusionary rule affects police violations of people's rights. At the least, it seems logical to conclude that there will be no decrease in such violations.

MORE RIGHTS

The *Mapp* decision was only one of the historic and controversial rulings on criminal law made in the 1960s by the Warren Court. Two others which have become well known are *Gideon* and *Miranda*. As with *Mapp*, these later decisions also involved a conflict between two different models of the criminal justice system—the due-process model and the crime-control model. But as we shall see, the Gideon case also brought to light a third view of the criminal justice system—what might be called the "administrative model." As with *Mapp*, the case hinged on the conflict between federal standards and state standards, and therefore the decision also involved new interpretations of the Bill of Rights and the 14th Amendment.

---

* Apply this same logic to the Collinsville raids described earlier in this section. The federal agents probably had warrants, but they raided the wrong houses. If, by chance, they had found anything illegal, they would argue that they had made the search in good faith and that the evidence should be admissible.

Gideon and the Right to Counsel

In the early hours of June 3, 1961, in the small town of Bay Harbor, Florida, somebody smashed the window of the poolroom, entered, took some wine and beer, and broke into the coin boxes of the cigarette machine and juke-box. Following a lead from an eyewitness who happened to be there, the police arrested Clarence Earl Gideon, a drifter who sometimes ran poker games and who had a record of crimes and prison terms dating back to his youth in the 1920s. Gideon pleaded not guilty to the break-in. At his trial that August, he requested that the court appoint a lawyer for his defense. The judge refused, telling Gideon, "Under the laws of the state of Florida, the only time a court can appoint a counsel to represent a Defendant is when that person is charged with a capital offense."

Gideon, with little choice in the matter, acted as his own lawyer. Considering that he had never had much formal education of any kind, let alone legal training, Gideon did about as well as could be expected. He lost. The case against him came chiefly from the eyewitness testimony of the young man who claimed to have seen Gideon inside the poolroom at 5:30 a.m. He said that Gideon came out with a bottle of wine in his hand, phoned for a cab, and left in the cab. Acting as his own lawyer, Gideon called eight witnesses, but his questioning of them seemed rambling and inconclusive. The jury found Gideon guilty, and the judge imposed the maximum sentence—five years.

Gideon appealed to the Supreme Court. The Court receives many such letters—handwritten in pencil on prison stationery—and it rejects most of them. But the Court decided to hear Gideon's case. And the Court appointed as his attorneys one of the best Washington law firms.

Gideon's appeal rested on the Sixth Amendment, which says in part, "In all criminal prosecutions, the accused shall enjoy the right . . . to have the assistance of counsel for his defense." But what did this mean? In Florida, it meant that if Gideon wanted to go out and hire a lawyer for his defense, he had every right to do so. If he did not have the money, well, that was no concern of the state.

By the time the Supreme Court decided to hear Gideon's case, an earlier decision (1938) had already ruled that the Sixth Amendment required a court-appointed counsel when the defendant was too poor to afford one.[35] However, the Court limited this policy to federal courts. State courts were still not required to provide lawyers for poor defendants. As in the development of search-and-seizure standards, the Supreme Court had overturned some convictions in state courts when the denial of counsel had been "fundamentally unfair"; for example, when the defendants were mentally unfit to conduct their defense, either because the defendant was feeble-minded, illiterate, or too ignorant, or because the case was too complex.

The Court had also required free counsel in state trials for capital offenses (i.e., those carrying the death penalty). The poolroom break-in was not a capital crime; Gideon was mentally competent; the case was not legally complicated; and there were no special circumstances. So at the time of Gideon's trial in Florida, the judge's denial of Gideon's request for a lawyer was perfectly in accord with the law of the land.

Gideon's attorneys, therefore, were asking the Supreme Court to change its previous interpretations of the Sixth Amendment. They argued that if the right to counsel meant a court-appointed lawyer in federal courts, then it should mean the same thing in state courts. They based this argument on the due process clause of the 14th Amendment ("nor shall any state deprive . . . without due process of law").

The state of Florida argued that the Constitution provided for diversity among the states and that the Court should not change the policy which had guided it for nearly 200 years. Florida also made an argument on practical as well as constitutional grounds: If Gideon and thousands of other poor defendants like him were given the right to counsel, there would be a flood of not-guilty pleas requiring court time for jury trials even in minor cases. "The entire undertaking would result in an unnecessary expense to taxpayers."[36]

This practical argument is not a very strong one from a moral or a constitutional point of view. Imagine yourself in the position of a poor defendant being told, in effect, "No justice for you because we want to keep taxes down." However, the argument does reveal something else about the criminal justice system: that in reality courts operate along the lines of neither the due-process model nor the crime-control model. Instead, most of the time they run on what might be called the **administrative model**.[37] Regardless of ideological statements about justice and crime, the primary goal of the courts is not to implement due process, nor is it to control crime. Instead, a court is like any other public bureaucracy—the department of motor vehicles or the welfare department. Its principal goal is to process a large number of cases rapidly. It accomplishes this goal by establishing a routine procedure. The routine procedure for handling criminal cases requires that defendants plead guilty rather than go to trial.

This system has come in for a good deal of criticism. Liberals insist that it shortchanges the poor, who are pressured to plead guilty rather than have their day in court. Conservatives grumble that the criminals who plead guilty are rewarded with sentences that are far too short. However, for at least 70 years, most criminal cases have been settled by guilty pleas. To do otherwise, some argue, would clog the courts and bring the machinery of justice to a grinding halt so that it could neither protect the rights of the accused nor punish the guilty.

The Supreme Court ignored Florida's argument and sided with Gideon. In its historic 1963 decision of *Gideon v. Wainwright* (Wainwright was the

Florida district attorney at the time Gideon submitted his appeal), the Court remanded Gideon's case to Florida to be retried, this time with a court-appointed attorney. But the Court's decision had implications far beyond the fate of Gideon. The Court's ruling meant that in all state proceedings for felonies (i.e., crimes punishable by a year or more in the state prison), poor defendants would have the right to a court-appointed lawyer.*

The constitutional history of the right to counsel resembles that of the exclusionary rule: First the Court sets a standard for federal courts; then it extends that standard to state trials involving unusual circumstances; finally the Court imposes the standard in all state trials. In *Gideon*, as in *Mapp*, the Court did not say that *all* aspects of the Bill of Rights would now hold in state courts as well as federal courts. Instead, it held that the right to counsel was so "fundamental and essential to a fair trial" that it was to be "absorbed" into the 14th Amendment.[38]

The Sixth Amendment (and Gideon) Vindicated

What happened to Clarence Earl Gideon? He was tried again for the Bay Harbor Poolroom break-in, and the difference between the first and second trials offers an excellent illustration of the basis of the Supreme Court's decision: "In our adversary system of criminal justice, any person haled into court, who is too poor to hire a lawyer, cannot be assured a fair trial unless counsel is provided for him."

There is a made-for-TV movie (now available on videocassette) of the *Gideon* case, based on Anthony Lewis's excellent book *Gideon's Trumpet*, and starring Henry Fonda in the title role. The movie opens with Gideon's arrest and first trial. When I saw it, it left little doubt in my mind of two things: first, that Gideon was not much of a lawyer; but second, and more important, that he was factually and legally guilty. The eyewitness knew him, so there was little doubt of misidentification. The prosecution presented another witness, a cab driver who drove Gideon from the poolroom into town early that morning. And there was circumstantial evidence as well: when Gideon was arrested the morning after the break-in, he had more than $25 worth of change in his pockets. Moreover, Gideon could not present any relevant evidence in his own defense to throw doubt on the prosecution's case.†

---

* Nine years later, in *Argersinger v. Hamlin*, the Court extended this right to all cases that carry any jail sentence.

† My students, when I show them this video, are far less willing to be convinced of Gideon's guilt. Perhaps they have seen too many other TV movies in which the hero, despite all the evidence available at the start of the film, really is innocent.

The second trial, this time with an experienced defense lawyer, leads to two other conclusions. First, it is clear that Gideon is not *legally* guilty. That is, the prosecution cannot prove its case beyond a reasonable doubt. Gideon's lawyer suggests that the eyewitness himself may have committed the crime (after all, what was this young man doing outside the poolroom at 5 a.m.?). And for every other bit of evidence the prosecution offers, the defense has a reasonable explanation. Establishing reasonable doubt should have been enough for the jury, and it was. After an hour's deliberation, they found Gideon not guilty. But if you see this movie (and perhaps if you had seen the trial itself) you will think that Gideon is more than legally not guilty of the break-in. You will think that he was probably *factually* not guilty as well—that is, that he didn't do it. The trial is an example of our adversary system of justice operating at its ideal.

But did the *Gideon* decision create a return to the adversary ideal in all cases, or even most cases? Remember, the state of Florida argued that it could not afford this ideal. Was this argument correct? Did run-of-the-mill street criminals, thinking that they would get a free F. Lee Bailey, suddenly start pleading not guilty? The answer is clear: no. In the first place, by the time of the *Gideon* decision, most states already had some kind of arrangement to provide free counsel. In fact, only five states (Florida, Alabama, Mississippi, North Carolina, and South Carolina) did not provide attorneys for poor defendants.[39] Many jurisdictions provide **public defenders**. These are lawyers who, like the prosecuting attorneys, draw a regular salary from the government. Some jurisdictions have **legal aid** societies—foundations that hire lawyers to defend the poor. These foundations get their money from private contributions or from the government. The oldest and most common method of providing lawyers for the poor is the system of **assigned counsel**. Here, the court may appoint regular private lawyers to handle the cases of the poor. Either the court pays a modest legal fee or the lawyers contribute their services free (*pro bono publico*).

Providing free lawyers for the poor made very little difference in everyday court proceedings. The vast majority of defendants plead guilty. Both before and after *Gideon* and *Argersinger*, about nine out of 10 cases that wind up in court are settled by guilty pleas. The percentage may vary from city to city, but the average is about 85 percent, and the figure rarely falls below 75 percent.[40]

Why do so many defendants plead guilty even though they have a lawyer? There are two answers. First, pleading guilty usually is more convenient and less painful than going to trial. Second, most defendants plead guilty because they are guilty—both factually and legally. If they went to trial, even with a good lawyer, they would lose. These are "open and shut" cases, or as they are known informally among public defenders in Los Angeles (and perhaps elsewhere), "deadbang" cases.[41] The reason that these public defenders get mostly deadbang cases is that the prosecutor already has screened out the other cases.

Discretion: The Better Part of Prosecution

Prosecutors have a great deal of discretion in deciding what happens to people who have been arrested, and there are several points along the way from arrest to trial where the prosecutor can exercise that discretion and drop a case. Soon after an arrest, the arrested person must appear before a magistrate for an **initial hearing** to be formally notified of the charge and to have bail set. Many jurisdictions have done away with the initial hearing to save time. Instead, the accused goes directly to the **preliminary hearing**, where a magistrate determines whether there is probable cause to charge the suspect.

The next step is the determination of formal charges. The prosecutor presents evidence to a grand jury, which either returns an **indictment** (a "true bill") specifying the charges, or returns a "no bill," freeing the accused. In some states, and especially for less serious crimes, instead of a grand jury indictment, the prosecutor presents evidence in an **information** before the magistrate. The magistrate then decides whether the evidence is sufficient to "bind over" the defendant for trial.

At any point in this process the prosecutor may drop the case. If the prosecutor lacks the evidence or witnesses to win a conviction, or if it appears that the arrested person is really innocent, then the prosecutor may enter a ***nolle prosequi***, a statement that the case will not be further prosecuted. For example, in New Orleans (a jurisdiction that screens cases very carefully at the initial stage), about half of all felony arrests are "nolled out."[42] If the case is a felony, the prosecutor may also decide to reduce the charge to a misdemeanor, or to divert the case to juvenile court if the offender is a juvenile.

Once formal charges have been filed, the prosecutor (or a defense lawyer) may still file for **dismissal** of the case, usually for the same reasons that cases are rejected earlier in the process—lack of witnesses or evidence. Manhattan (New York) prosecutors reject only 3 percent of cases at the initial screening. But 32 percent of the cases are later dismissed. In New Orleans, where most weak cases don't make it past the initial screening, only 5 percent of cases are dismissed.[43] In other words, at some point early in the process, prosecutors drop about half of all felony arrests. As a result of this weeding out, prosecutors ensure that they are left with only the strongest cases. As one prosecutor put it,

> We have them cold-cocked. They plead guilty because they are guilty. That's something that people don't understand. Basically the people that are brought here are believed very definitely to be guilty or we wouldn't go on with the prosecution. We would *nolle* the case.[44]

Given such a strong position, prosecutors do not really have to bargain. In fact, most of the time, the defendant pleads guilty to the top charge.[45] Contrary to popular images, for most defendants the plea bargain isn't much of a bargain.

Why shouldn't the defendant fight the case anyway in hopes of persuading a jury? For people charged with relatively minor offenses—misdemeanors—defending their innocence just might not be worth it. Going to trial imposes costs on the defendant—even if he or she is represented by a free, court-appointed lawyer. To begin with, there is the question of bail. If the defendant pleads not guilty, the judge sets bail. Unless the judge grants release on recognizance, the defendant must put up money for bail—a significant decision for defendants who are poor. Even though the bail money will be returned to them at trial, they might need the money right now for other expenses. Otherwise, he or she or whatever (see box) must wait in jail.

For most persons charged with misdemeanors, the costs of waiting in jail or having to leave work to make further court appearances far outweigh the costs of pleading guilty and receiving a fine or a short sentence. A defendant considering whether to exercise his rights might be asked by the judge, "Do you want a lawyer, or do you want to settle this today?"[46] For many less serious offenses, the defendant is sentenced to "time served"; that is, the time that he or she has already spent waiting for the initial hearing of the case. The title of one book on the lower courts sums it up fairly well: *The Process Is the Punishment.*[47] This system, so far from our ideal model of courts, allows for the rapid disposal of large numbers of cases.

Seven women charged as prostitutes have been brought from jail, where they have been held since being arrested, to the holding pens of the court, and finally into the courtroom.

Shirley Dillard, dressed in tight yellow slacks, a white blouse and a yellow sun visor, reached the bench at midmorning, charged with loitering for the purpose of prostitution. A Legal Aid lawyer . . . repeated the familiar line: "My client has authorized me to enter a plea of guilty."

[The] judge was confused, but only momentarily. He addressed the defendant first as "madam," then as "sir." The defendant was a man.

"Would you like to say anything in your behalf?" the judge asked.

Mr. Dillard said yes, he was not guilty. He said he had only been out taking a walk, getting some sun.

Why, then, had he pleaded guilty?

"Because," he replied with an exaggerated sigh, "I can't stay in jail forever."

"Then I won't accept the plea," the judge said. He set bail and a trial date.

If Mr. Dillard could not make bail, defending his innocence would likely cost him more time in jail than a guilty plea.

Source: Copyright © 1983 by *The New York Times Company.* Reprinted by permission.

This incident illustrates one other important point: The judge has the final word. In this case, the judge refused to accept a guilty plea from a person who appeared to be factually not guilty. In most cases, the judge almost automatically ratifies whatever deal the district attorney and defense have worked out. Still, judges do not always accept the bargain—unless, as is the case in some courts, the judge plays an active part in the plea bargain.

For more serious crimes, the defendant who insists on a trial incurs additional risks and costs. In a plea bargain, defendants are offered fairly specific sentences. If they accept, they know how much time they are facing. If they choose instead to go to trial and are found guilty, they will probably receive a much longer sentence. One study found that for the same crime, defendants who lost in jury trials received sentences twice as long as those who pleaded guilty.[48]

Some people have argued that such a system is unfair to defendants, since they are being penalized for exercising their Sixth Amendment right to trial. Nevertheless, the Supreme Court has given its approval to the prosecutor's use of this bargaining chip.

There are many criticisms of the current system. Conservatives argue that plea-bargaining allows wicked people to get off too lightly. This lenience both denies justice to the public and encourages crime. In the good old days, they argue, people who were arrested went to trial; if they were found guilty, they received sentences appropriate to their crimes. Critics from another perspective argue that too often plea-bargaining denies justice to the defendant. The administrative style of justice means that the defense lawyer is less interested in providing the best defense for the defendant than in handling a large volume of cases.

Look at the following transcript from a New York City courtroom.

Judge: But the offer is 90 days, only 90 days.
Defendant: I said I won't take more than 60.
J: My God, this is arrogance. A Class A felony drug sale, punishable by a sentence of 15 years to life, and they are offering you a plea to a misdemeanor and 90 days. That's very generous, sir.
D: You offer me 90 days because you ain't got no case. And if you ain't got no case, why can't I go home right now?
Legal Aid lawyer: They are not offering to send you home.
D: Hey, you my lawyer, ain't you?
LAL: Yes.
D: Then how come you never talk to me?
LAL: I am trying to determine your circumstances. What you say doesn't mean s___. What matters is what's on the court papers and the record.
[The defendant continues to protest.]
J: The matter will have to be litigated. Is the district attorney asking for any bail?
District attorney: $500.
J: $500 bail.
D: I'll take the 90 days. I'm guilty.[49]

This small case, typical of hundreds that come through city courts every month, illustrates several points. First, the defendant's final statement tells us that this is probably a "deadbang" case. Second, the transcript shows the way in which the prosecutor—with the judge's cooperation—can use bail to force a reluctant defendant to cooperate. Third, as the judge points out, there is a large difference between the penalty the defendant would risk in a trial and the penalty he receives for a guilty plea.

But how are we to interpret this discrepancy? From one side, it looks as though a serious criminal—one guilty of a 15-year-to-life felony—is getting off very lightly. On the other hand, a mere $500 bail—which he will get back—is sufficient to persuade this drug dealer, this "serious felon," to accept a sentence 50 percent longer than his original demand.

Finally, notice the relationship between the defendant and his lawyer. The lawyer all but ignores the defendant; instead he is interested in the factors that will determine the outcome of the case: the prosecutor and the court papers. More important, the lawyer seems to have no interest in helping his client bargain for a shorter sentence. If the DA has, with no explicit bargaining, already reduced a 180-month sentence to three months (15 years down to 90 days), why does the defense lawyer not join his client in trying to get the DA to knock off another 30 days? Why does this defense lawyer seem to abandon his adversarial role? Whatever happened to *Gideon v. Wainwright*?

As for the DA and the judge, why should they resist the defendant's counteroffer of 60 days? Do they really think that the extra month the defendant will spend in jail will accomplish any goal? Will a three-month stay in a crowded New York jail rehabilitate him significantly more than will a two-month stay? Will that 30-day difference deter him or others from future drug deals? Will keeping him in jail an extra month reduce the amount of drug sales in Manhattan at all? Is it a question of justice—that 90 days for a 15-year felony is a just sentence, while 60 days is not? If the answer to these questions is no (as it almost certainly is), why should the DA and judge insist on 90 days?

"Normal Crimes" and the Courtroom Work Group

In the 1960s, just as research on the police had provided evidence of sharp contrast between the ideal role of the police and what they actually do, research on courts also offered some sobering views of what really goes on in court. Two of the most famous sociological articles from this period analyzed the role of the defense lawyer. In "Normal Crimes,"[50] David Sudnow argued that the pressure of having to handle a large volume of cases forced the district attorney (DA) and the public defender (PD) to create a kind of shorthand—a set of categories into which most cases would fit. "Over the course of their interaction and repeated 'bargaining' discussion, the PD and DA have developed a set of unstated recipes for reducing original charges to lesser offenses." These recipes include not only the crime itself, but also the motives and the characteristics of the offender and victim—Sudnow notes, "most ADWs (assault with a deadly weapon) start with fights over some girl." This system allows for a quick disposal of those cases that fit into the typical categories. " 'Typical' burglaries are reduced to petty theft, 'typical' ADWs to simple assault, 'typical' child molestation to loitering around a schoolyard, etc." The burglary might not actually have involved petty theft, and the child molestation might have happened far from any schoolyard; nevertheless, if the accused seems to be a "typical" burglar or "typical" child molester, that's the way the charge gets bargained out.[51] The classifications of the law as written in the statute books take a secondary place to the set of categories that the DA and the PD have worked out.

Sometimes, the crime does not fit into the "normal" category. The deadly weapon was not a knife or handgun but a machine gun. The burglary took place in a wealthy neighborhood or involved much property damage. These distinctions may not make the crime any different in terms of the written law. But for the prosecutor and defender, these special circumstances mean that the usual plea bargain cannot automatically go forward. The case requires its own special bargaining or, especially if the crime is more serious, perhaps even a trial.

When the court works this way, the relationship between prosecution and defense changes from adversarial to cooperative. The public defender's role is no longer to fight tooth and nail for his or her client. Instead, "the major job of the public defender, who mediates between the district attorney and the defendant, [is] to convince his 'client' that the chances of acquittal are too slight to warrant this risk [of trial]." The PD does not really try to determine if the facts of the case fit the law the defendant is accused of violating; instead, the PD tries to determine if the crime fits into the profile of a "normal" crime. Instead of a courtroom in which the defense attorney and the prosecutor are adversaries and the judge a referee, we now have the three working together. They constitute what some observers call the **courtroom work group**.

Let's go back to the questions I posed about the drug trial cited earlier. To understand what is going on, we would do better if we stop thinking in terms of justice and adversarial bargaining and think instead in terms of "normal" crimes and the courtroom work group. To plead this case out at anything other than 90 days would upset the established routine for this kind of case. It would be a violation of the unspoken understanding between prosecutor and defense as to what this case was worth. The defense lawyer argues so forcefully against his own client ("What you say doesn't mean s---") because he knows that the prosecutor would never settle for a 60-day sentence. On the other hand, if the prosecutor had asked for six months instead of three, the defense attorney might have taken a more adversarial stance. He probably would not have gone to trial (assuming that this was a "deadbang" case), but he could use various legal devices to cause delays and generally give the prosecutor a hard time—if not in this case, then in one of the many other cases in which he would be confronting the same prosecutor.

The bargain between DA and PD goes beyond the classification of cases. It extends to those rare cases where a defendant insists on a trial. The DA and PD have worked out a set of ground rules that allows them to handle not just guilty pleas but trials as well in a routine fashion. According to Sudnow, "The district attorney, and the county which employs them both, can rely on the PD . . . not to make an issue of the moral character of the . . . local courts, the community or the police."[52] While private attorneys might try to trick up the state's witnesses or to point to community factors (like "the racial prejudice that produces our criminals"), the PD "is part of the team." In return, the DA also acts as less than a fierce adversary but instead treats the typical case routinely, without becoming hostile towards the defendant, without insisting that the judge or jury "throw the book at" the defendant.

In the courtroom work group, the DA and PD share a common language and a common knowledge of the law, both the ideal and the way it works in their particular court. They also share an interest in disposing of a great number of cases. In other words, the defense attorney has much more in common with the DA than with the defendant—the client whose interest the PD is representing.

A similar irony or contradiction is built into the role of prosecutor. Remember, the DA represents the state, the people. The view of the people about what sentence a crime deserves is, presumably, expressed in the penal code (i.e., in the laws written by the legislators the people elect). But prosecutors soon acquire a courtroom perspective different from that of their "clients," the people.

> It's like nurses in emergency rooms. You get so used to armed robbery that you treat it as routine, not as morally upsetting. . . . The nature of the offense doesn't cause the reaction in me that it would in the average citizen.[53]

Prosecutors may enter the job with the same perspective as the public, but they soon adapt to the system. The influence can come from other prosecutors, from defense attorneys, or from a superior. For example, here is a prosecutor talking about "a serious crime . . . a crime that I thought was serious at one time, anyway":

> He . . . is charged with aggravated assault. One guy got 25 stitches, the other 15. And the [defense] attorneys would want me to reduce it. I'd go talk to [the chief prosecutor]. He'd say, 'They both are drunk, and both got head wounds. Let them plead to breach of peace, and the judge will give them a money fine.' Things like that I didn't feel right about doing, since, to me, right out of law school, middle-class, you figure 25 stitches in the head, Jesus Christ.[54]

The Going Rate

This "insider's" view of the courtroom offers an interesting contrast to the criticisms that come largely from outside the court. Those criticisms frequently claim that the justice system does not do justice, especially in the sentences courts hand down. Conservatives often complain that the courts are too lenient; liberals may see the courts as unjustly severe. And critics from both camps argue that the courts are inconsistent: The same crime can receive widely different sentences.

In reality, when a court disposes of cases in a routine, administrative fashion, then it should achieve a high degree of consistency. Similar crimes or criminals will receive a similar sentence—the **going rate**. The sentences in a court may not conform strictly to the law, but they will conform to the sense of justice of the members of the courtroom work group. That sense of justice, however, is influenced much less by the law than by experience and by the number of crimes and the kinds of crimes that they must deal with every day. Prosecutors and defense lawyers in high-crime jurisdictions get used to knife wounds and muggings. In low-crime areas, the going rate for these crimes might be much stiffer.[55]

In recent years, some states have tried to reduce the disparity in sentences by reducing the discretion of prosecutors and judges. Some jurisdictions have placed limits on the prosecutor's discretion in plea-bargaining. More commonly, states have reduced judges' discretion by moving away from **indeterminate** sentences and toward **mandatory, determinate**, or **presumptive** sentencing.* The loss of discretion over sentencing may be more apparent than real. By using their discretion at an earlier stage in the game (for example, by deciding which charges, if any, to file against the defendant), prosecutors have often been able to maintain control over their courts. Judges, prosecutors, and even defense attorneys have cooperated in order to protect "their" courtrooms from the intrusion of the legislature and in order to continue coping with a large volume of cases while dispensing justice as they see it.

Private Attorneys: Perry Mason as Con Man

Sudnow portrays public defenders as compliant when they should be combative, accommodating when they should be adversarial. Why have they become such pushovers? In Sudnow's view, the reason is not just that the

---

* For a slightly fuller definition of these terms, see p. 543.

PD is on the county payroll. More important, the PD spends much time with the DA and very little time with any one defendant. As a result, the PD and DA come to share the same view of the world, including their views of defendants. Sudnow contrasts the PDs with private defense lawyers: "While it is common to overhear private attorneys call judges 'bastards,' policemen 'hoodlums,' and prosecutors 'sadists,' the PD, in the presence of such talk, remains silent."[56]

This assessment of private attorneys may have been too charitable. Two years after Sudnow's article appeared, Abraham Blumberg published an even more cynical view of defense lawyers: "The Practice of Law as a Confidence Game."[57] In most con games, the con artist deceives you into believing that he's on your side, when he is only out to get your money and is in fact teamed up with someone else. Defense lawyers, says Blumberg, are no different. He argues that private attorneys, much like public defenders and Legal Aid lawyers, are much more in league with the court system than with the defendant. "The accused's lawyer has far greater professional economic, intellectual and other ties to the various elements of the court system than he does to his own client." Like any confidence man, the lawyer must keep these ties hidden from the client and appear to be doing his or her all to help the client. Like the public defender, the private lawyer makes a more or less standard going-rate deal with the district attorney and then tries to sell that deal to the defendant. Of course, when he talks to his client, the lawyer makes it appear that the deal is an extraordinarily attractive, attainable only through the lawyer's particular craftiness and connections.

True, in court private defense attorneys may deliver ringing defenses of their clients or condemnations of the police or community, but these rhetorical exercises may be mostly a show put on to convince clients that they are getting what they paid for. And pay they must, for the private attorney, unlike the public defender or Legal Aid lawyer, must also make sure to collect whatever fee he or she is charging—"a sum which bears an uncanny relationship to that of the net proceeds of the particular offense involved."

Perhaps these studies paint too bleak a picture of criminal defense. Not all private defense attorneys are "cop-out" lawyers, incompetents who know only how to plead a client guilty. Not all public defenders go along with the prosecutor. Generally speaking, defense attorneys are more willing to go to trial than are prosecutors. In some cities, relationships between public defenders and prosecutors really do remain adversarial, even hostile.[58] However, the system creates pressures so that even the most able and committed public defenders may not be able to give their clients the best defense. The caseload is high; most clients are guilty, factually and legally; and the lawyer has neither the time nor the money to make an independent investigation of every case.

Gideon was an important case. It was an example of how our system of justice works in its ideal version. It vindicated the adversarial system and the necessity for the presumption of innocence. It pointed out the importance of having a lawyer, and by guaranteeing lawyers even to the poor, it gave substance to our ideal of equality before the law. In practice, however, it did little to change the reality of how courts operate. Most cases continued to be handled in an administrative rather than an adversarial way.

The *Gideon* decision was important in one other way. It provided a basis for some much more controversial Supreme Court rulings in criminal law.

The *Miranda* Decision—"You Have the Right to Remain Silent. . . ."

Probably the most famous decision in criminal procedure that the Warren Court handed down came in the case of *Miranda v. Arizona*. We have all seen TV cops reciting the Miranda warnings to people they arrest, "reading them their rights." In the 1980s the decision began to come under increasing attack. President Reagan's attorney general, Edwin L. Meese spoke out vigorously against it, calling it "an infamous decision," and sought to overturn it. It remains to be seen whether the Justice Department in the Bush administration will continue on this path. *Miranda* concerns, among other things, a suspect's right to remain silent. The Fifth Amendment explicitly provides this privilege against self-incrimination. And the U.S. Constitution is not unique in this regard. British common law, Catholic canon law, and ancient Hebrew Talmudic law also include this principle, though they have not always enforced it vigorously.

Critics with a crime-control perspective argue that *Miranda* is not just a misinterpretation of the Constitution but that it is impractical; it throws roadblocks in the path to justice and allows the guilty to go free. According to Attorney General Meese, it has led to "all these ridiculous situations in which police are precluded from asking the one person who knows the most about the crime."[59] The irony in all this debate is that *Miranda* was not really a turning point in the Court's philosophy. It was more a natural continuation of two earlier decisions—*Gideon* and *Escobedo*.

The history of the right not to self-incriminate in the United States resembles that of other aspects of due process. The framers of the Constitution were aware of the history of forced testimony. It was a useful tool for convicting criminals, but it increased the power of the government at the expense of liberty. The "Star Chamber" of 16th-century England, for example, was basically a way of enforcing the law without bothering with the inconveniences of the usual procedures—inconveniences like defendants who refused to testify and juries which did not always convict.[60] The Star Chamber, with its forced testimony and secret, nonjury trials, may have been swift and effective, but the framers of the Constitution were less concerned with the efficiency of government than with the liberty of the people.

By the time of cases like *Escobedo* and *Miranda*, the Supreme Court had overturned convictions based on forced confessions. In 1936, in *Brown v. Mississippi*, it reversed a murder conviction that had been based on confessions. One suspect had confessed after being hung twice by the neck to a tree (being let down each time before he died), tied to the tree and whipped, and two days later being arrested and severely whipped again. Other defendants in the case also were whipped in the jail; the deputies used leather belts with buckles that cut the men's backs to pieces. (The deputy in charge testified that such whipping was "not too much for a Negro; not as much as I would have done if it were left to me.") These defendants were persuaded when told that the whipping would continue until they confessed.[61]

In later years, the Court rejected confessions extracted by psychological pressure, lying, and deceit. As with other provisions in the Bill of Rights, the Warren Court in the 1960s broadened the Fifth Amendment protection to include state courts, not just federal courts.[62] And, as with some of the other constitutional protections, the Supreme Court in the 1980s began to allow some exceptions.[63]

Confessions and the Court

One objection to forced confessions is that they are unreliable. A person being tortured might say anything, regardless of whether it is true. Some people have argued, therefore, that a confession should be allowed in court if it is "voluntary." The Supreme Court, however, in its landmark decisions in the 1960s, went beyond this narrow, practical reasoning. It enforced the Fifth Amendment not because the confession might be unreliable but because the police must not be allowed to deny people their constitutional rights, including the right against self-incrimination. This right, combined with the Sixth Amendment right to counsel, formed the basis of the *Escobedo* and *Miranda* decisions.

A year before the Court decided *Escobedo*, it had already decided in *Gideon* that everyone had the right to counsel. The question the Court faced in *Escobedo* was this: When does that right begin? The police arrested Danny Escobedo in connection with a murder and questioned him for 15 hours, releasing him only after his lawyer, who had not been present, had gotten a writ of *habeas corpus*. Eleven days later, the police again brought in Escobedo for questioning after another suspect in the case had identified him as the murderer. Escobedo asked for his lawyer to be present, and the lawyer himself asked to be present, but the police refused these requests.

After more questioning, a Spanish-speaking officer told Escobedo that if he pinned the murder on one of the other defendants, he could go home. So in a confrontation at the police station, Escobedo said to the other defendant, "I didn't shoot Manuel. You did it." But by saying this, Escobedo was admitting his own part in the murder, and under Illinois law, this complicity made him as guilty as the actual killer. Obviously, if Escobedo's lawyer had been there, he would have told Escobedo to keep his mouth shut under any circumstances. However, by the time Escobedo was allowed to see his lawyer, he had already incriminated himself. He was convicted of murder and sentenced to 22 years.[64]

In a 5-4 decision in 1964, the Supreme Court reversed Escobedo's conviction, ruling that the police had violated due process. Specifically, the police had denied the Sixth Amendment right to counsel, a right which was "made obligatory on the states by the 14th Amendment." This right to a lawyer, the Court said, begins when the inquiry into a crime "has begun to focus on a particular suspect" and that suspect has been taken into custody. Furthermore, if the police deny a suspect's request for a lawyer or fail to warn the suspect of the right to remain silent, then they have violated the Sixth Amendment.

Two years later, the Court heard the case of Ernesto Miranda. Miranda was a suspect in the kidnapping and rape of an 18-year-old woman in Phoenix, Arizona. The victim had identified him in a lineup. The police questioned him without telling him of his right to an attorney. After two hours, they emerged with Miranda's written confession, which stated, among other things, that the confession was voluntary and made in full knowledge of his legal rights. The confession was used at his trial, and Miranda was convicted and sentenced to 20 to 30 years. The Supreme Court, however, overturned the conviction, holding that the government must get evidence against a defendant "by its own independent labors, rather than by the cruel, simple expedient of compelling it from his mouth." In addition, the Court, in this now famous (or infamous) decision, outlined specific procedures that the police must follow when they take a suspect into custody:

> Prior to any questioning, the person must be warned that he has a right to remain silent, that any statement he does make may be used as evidence against him, and that he has a right to the presence of an attorney, either retained or appointed. The defendant may waive effectuation of these rights, provided the waiver is made voluntarily, knowingly and intelligently. If, however, he indicates that he wishes to consult with an attorney before speaking, there can be no questioning. Likewise, if the individual is alone and indicates in any manner that he does not wish to be interrogated, the police may not question him.[65]

Nobody, not even the toughest crime-control proponents, advocates scrapping the Fifth and Sixth amendments. However, the constitutional right to a lawyer and the constitutional right to remain silent can be real only if the people know about them and can exercise them. What *Miranda* did was to ensure that people arrested by the police be informed of these rights and allowed to use them. Apparently, what bothers the critics of *Miranda* is that suspects may actually become aware of and assert their constitutional rights and that the police must respect those rights.

The Effects of *Miranda*

Apart from the legal basis of *Miranda*, we must also ask what practical effects the decision had. Did it change the way police operate? Did it allow more suspects to go free?

Like many of the other cases we have looked at in this chapter, *Miranda* overturned the conviction of a person who was factually guilty. Rochin did indeed possess the illegal drugs the police pumped out of his stomach; Dolree Mapp had been in possession of obscene materials; Danny Escobedo had been guilty of murder under Illinois law. And Ernesto Miranda had committed the crimes he confessed to.* The Court has reversed convictions in crimes even more horrible than the kidnap and rape Miranda committed.[66] In all these decisions, the Court has placed procedure ahead of results, an emphasis based on the due-process clause of the Constitution (no person shall be punished without due process of law).

Undoubtedly, in some of these celebrated cases, the guilty have gone free. But the Supreme Court rarely gets cases where the police have violated the rights of the truly innocent—not necessarily because the police do not make such violations, but because such abuses, like the outrageous search that produces no valid evidence, rarely result in arrest, much less in a court appearance. There is no conviction to overturn.

However, these due-process considerations count for very few of the cases where criminals go free. As the data in Table 14–1 show, in San Diego in 1986, of 9000 arrests for Index crimes, 44 (or less than one-half of 1 percent) were dropped because of due-process problems. In Manhattan the proportion was even smaller: Four cases out of 21,000 arrests or less than two one-hundredths of one percent.

A Final Word: Justice For All?

This chapter has focused on two large questions: What is the constitutional basis for criminal courts in the United States; and how do the courts actually deal with criminals? One way of reviewing it all is to look at the question of whether the system does justice—especially in light of the many criticisms leveled at it. Let's look at the complaints from liberals and conservatives and try to estimate the extent to which they are valid.

Liberals.   The courts still offer one system of justice for the rich, another for the poor. Free lawyers—whether public defenders, legal aid lawyers, or

---

* The Court, by the way, did not free Miranda. It merely ordered that Arizona retry him, this time without his confession as evidence. At his second trial, on the basis of other evidence, Miranda was again found guilty of the same rape and kidnap charges and sentenced to 20 to 30 years. He was paroled after a few years, arrested a couple of times—weapons, drugs, parole violation. In 1976, at the age of 34, he was killed in an argument over a card game in a Phoenix skid-row bar.

appointed counsel—sell out their clients, forcing them into plea-bargains rather than vigorously defending them.

How adversarial are defense lawyers? Much of their work appears to be helping things along rather than fighting for their clients at all cost. And, as Sudnow and Blumberg point out, even what looks adversarial may be merely a show meant to impress the client. But these lawyers do fight for their clients, though much of the adversarial work may be invisible. Some of it occurs in the early stages following arrest, when charges are dropped or greatly reduced. If defense lawyers were less vigorous, prosecutors might *nolle* out far fewer cases. Remember also that the "going rate," which looks like assembly-line justice rather than a vigorous defense, is the outcome of adversarial bargaining on similar cases that came before. Finally, the defense lawyer is usually playing a losing hand. The DA has eliminated all but the "deadbang" cases. The defendant is guilty factually and legally, and it is doubtful whether anyone, Perry Mason or Alan Dershowitz, could get a better deal.

Conservatives.   The courts are too lenient. Bad people who commit bad crimes are allowed to go free.

At first glance, the raw data on this question seem to support this very popular notion. Picture the criminal justice system as a corridor or a sequence of branching corridors with the crime at one end, the prison door at the other, and many other doors along the way. For 100 serious crimes like burglary and robbery at the beginning of corridor, more than 90 never make it to that final steel-barred door. Of course, it's important to understand why these cases exit the system, and it turns out that these reasons do not conform to the image of a criminal justice system "soft" on crime and hamstrung by the restrictions of due process.

To begin with, most of the crimes never really make it into the corridor as actual people. Only 20 percent of Index crimes result in someone being arrested; the other 80 percent exist only as uncleared crimes on police records. Still, of those arrested, half exit the system fairly quickly. The prosecutor holds open the door marked "reject" or "dismiss," or "divert to juvenile court," and out they go. But these rejections occur largely in the interests of justice. Remember the most frequent problems that cause rejection and dismissal of cases: evidence and witnesses. The lack of evidence may mean that the crime was not very serious to begin with. And witness problems usually arise when the victim, and perhaps other witnesses, know the defendant. After tempers cool, they may wish to settle the matter privately rather than pursue it in court. Or witnesses may feel that the crime is too unimportant to bother with. In other words, the cases that disappear are likely to be those whose dismissal would not upset even most conservative critics. And, as we have seen, the constitutional restrictions of due process, those infamous "technicalities," account for only the tiniest percentage of cases being dropped.

Who is still left in the corridor? People who commit the more serious offenses, those who commit crimes against strangers, or those who have a long criminal history. They are the people who must actually face charges and either plead guilty or go to trial. This brings us to the next criticism.

Conservatives: Plea-bargaining allows people who have committed serious crimes to get lenient sentences—a few months or even probation, the proverbial slap on the wrist.

Again, there is some truth to this criticism. Certainly, those who plead guilty get shorter sentences than do those who go to trial. But the serious criminals, repeat offenders who commit serious crimes, do receive stiff sentences. New policies that "close the loopholes," eliminate plea-bargaining, institute mandatory or determinate sentencing, or generally "get tough" seldom change the fate of these criminals. The courts are already dealing with them severely. The defendants most affected by these tough policies are the less serious offenders.[67] Prosecutors and judges use their discretion to differentiate between more serious and less serious defendants whose crimes nevertheless look the same on paper. Consider the following case, a man charged with grand larceny who nevertheless walks out of court free.

Bridgeman: Charged with 155.30, grand larceny and 165.40, criminal possession of stolen property. . . .

Legal Aid lawyer: (turning to the prosecutor) Petit larceny and time served?

DA: Fine. Let's go.

LAL: Okay, Mr. Abramson. If you admit you did it, they're willing to let you go home.

Defendant: I did it, but I ain't got no home.

LAL: Well, do you want to go to jail?

D: No. . . .

DA: Mr. Adamson,* is that your lawyer standing next to you?

LAL: Say yes.

D: Yes.

DA: Did you discuss the case with him adequately?

D: Yes.

DA: Do you understand that a plea of guilty is the same as a conviction after trial, and that by pleading guilty you give up your right to trial, your right to call witnesses on your own behalf, and your right to cross-examine witnesses brought against you? Do you understand that you are giving up all those rights?

D: Yes.

---

* The confusion over the defendant's name is perhaps not such a rarity, especially in a case like this where, as the transcript makes clear, everyone (except perhaps the defendant) is concerned mostly with bringing the case to a rapid conclusion.

DA: It is charged that on the night of April 23, on the corner of Broadway, you acted disorderly and took a purse from Viola Simpson. Are the facts true as stated?

D: Your honor, I didn't have nothing to eat for two days, and she was coming out of a restaurant, so I know she just ate. I snatched her purse.

Judge: And no one threatened you or made any promises to get you to enter this plea?

D: He told me I could go.

Judge: That's right. The plea is acceptable to the court. Sentence of the court: time served.[68]

Imagine what might have happened under a system that did not allow the prosecutor the flexibility to reduce the charges and did not allow the judge such discretion over the sentence.

The basic function of criminal courts is to determine guilt and then decide what punishment to assign the guilty. This chapter has focused on how the people in the court reach those decisions. The next chapters will try to answer a question which has been strangely absent in the discussion so far: What effect does that punishment have on crime?

NOTES

1. Jacqueline P. Wiseman (1979), *Stations of the Lost: The Treatment of Skid Row Alcoholics*, Chicago: University of Chicago Press, p. 47. Also Malcolm M. Feeley (1979), *The Process Is the Punishment: Handling Cases in a Lower Criminal Court*, New York: Russell Sage, p. 11.

2. Theodore F. T. Plucknett (1956), *A Concise History of the Common Law* (5th ed.), Boston, MA: Little, Brown, pp. 116–17.

3. Thomas Weigend (1983), "Criminal Procedure: Comparative Aspects," in Sanford Kadish, ed., *Encyclopedia of Crime and Justice*, vol. 2, New York: Macmillan, pp. 537–46.

4. Roger Brown (1986) *Social Psychology: The Second Edition*, New York: Free Press, p. 282. ("It is even possible to argue that, as a social institution, trial by jury is more diagnostic of the real state of freedom and justice in a nation than is democratic election of political leaders.")

5. Bureau of Justice Statistics Bulletin (1986), "Jail Inmates 1984." Washington, DC.

6. Wayne LeFave (1983), "The Right to Bail," in Kadish, ed., op. cit., pp. 99–107.

7. *Stack v. Boyle*, 342 U.S. 1, 5 (1951), cited in Sue Titus Reid (1985), *Crime and Criminology* (4th ed.), New York: Holt, Rinehart, Winston, p. 408.

8. Ronald Goldfarb (1965), *Ransom: A Critique of the American Bail System*, New York: Harper & Row, p. 47, quoted in James Inciardi (1987), *Criminal Justice*, New York: Harcourt, Brace, Jovanovich, p. 404.

9. Quoted in *The New York Times*, May 27, 1987, p. A20.

10. Wayne Thomas (1976), *Bail Reform in America*, Berkeley, CA: University of California Press.

11. Samuel Walker (1985), *Sense and Nonsense About Crime: A Policy Guide*, Monterey, CA: Brooks/Cole, p. 51.

12. Barbara Boland and Ronald Sones (1986), *The Prosecution of Felony Arrests*, Washington, DC: INSLAW, p. 33.

13. James A. Inciardi (1987), *Criminal Justice* (2nd ed.), New York: Harcourt, Brace Jovanovich, p. 401. Also Jonathan D. Casper (1972), *American Criminal Justice: The Defendant's Perspective*, Englewood Cliffs, NJ: Prentice-Hall, p. 68.

14. Dave Davis (1983), "The Bail Bondsman," paper given at the Eastern Sociological Society.

15. Charles E. Ares, Anne Rankin, and Herbert Sturz (1963), "The Manhattan Bail Project," *New York University Law Review*, vol. 38, p. 68. Also Inciardi, op. cit., p. 406.

16. Edward Jay Epstein (1977), *Agency of Fear*, New York: Putnam, pp. 18–19.

17. Inciardi, op. cit., p. 237.

18. *Weeks v. United States*, 232 U.S. 383 (1914).

19. *Prudential Insurance Co. v. Cheek*, 259 U.S. 530 (1922), which refused to extend First Amendment protections; *Gitlow v. New York*, 268 U.S. 652 (1925), *Near v. Minnesota* and *Stromberg v. California*, 1931), cited in Anthony Lewis (1964), *Gideon's Trumpet*, New York: Vintage, p. 244.

20. *Rochin v. California*, 342 U.S. 165 (1952).

21. Lewis, op. cit., p. 163.

22. Michael Kent Curtis (1986), *No State Shall Abridge: The Fourteenth Amendment and the Bill of Rights*, Durham, NC: Duke University Press.

23. "Any legal proceeding . . . in furtherance of the general public good which regards and preserves those principles of liberty and justice, must be held to be due process of law." Justice Matthews in *Hurtado*, 110 U.S. 535, 1884.

24. Paul Chevigny (1969), *Police Power: Abuses in New York City*, New York: Vintage.

25. Leonard W. Levy (1974), *Against the Law: The Nixon Court and Criminal Justice*, New York: Harper & Row, pp. 68–74.

26. U.S. Department of Justice (1982), *The Effects of the Exclusionary Rule: A Study in California*, Washington, DC: U.S. Government Printing Office.

27. Barbara Boland, Catherine H. Conly, Paul Mahanna, Lynn Warner, and Ronald Sones (1990), *The Prosecution of Felony Arrests, 1987*, Washing, DC: Abt Associates. *UCR*, 1987.

28. Sheldon Krantz, Bernard Gilman, Charles G. Benda, Carol Rogoff Hallstrom, and Gail J. Nadworny (1979), *Police Policymaking*, Lexington, MA: Lexington Books, cited in Walker, op. cit., p. 114.

29. *Massachusetts v. Sheppard* (1984), US SupCt 35 Crl 3296.

30. *U.S. v. Leon*, US SupCt 35 CrL 3273 (1984), in *The New York Times*, July 6, 1984, p. B6.

31. Levy, op. cit., p. 64.

32. *The New York Times*, May 31, 1987, sec. IV, p. 1.

33. *Maryland v. Garrison*, in *The New York Times*, Feb. 25, 1987, p. B6.

34. Peter Reuter and Mark A.R. Kleiman, "Risks and Prices: An Economic Analysis of Drug Enforcement," in Michael Tonry and Norval Morris, eds. (1986), *Crime and Justice: An Annual Review*, Chicago: University of Chicago Press, pp. 289–340.

35. *Johnson v. Zerbst*, 304 U.S. 458 (1938).

36. Quoted in Lewis, op. cit., p. 158.

37. Walker, op. cit., p. 22.

38. Quoted in Lewis, op. cit., p. 188.

39. Lewis, op. cit., p. 133.

40. Boland and Sones (1986), op. cit., p. 20.

41. Lynn A. Mather (1973), "Some Determinants of the Method of Case Disposition: Decision-making by Public Defenders in Los Angeles," *Law and Society Review*, vol. 8, 187–216.

42. Boland and Sones (1986), op. cit., pp. 5, 40.

43. Ibid.

44. Milton Heumann (1978), *Plea Bargaining*, Chicago: University of Chicago Press.

45. Barbara Boland and Brian Forst (1985), "Prosecutors Don't Always Aim to Pleas," *Federal Probation*, vol. 49, pp. 10–15.

46. Feeley, op. cit., p. 178.

47. Ibid.

48. Thomas M. Uhlman and N. Darlene Walker (1980), "He Takes Some of My Time; I Take Some of His: An Analysis of Sentencing Patterns in Jury Cases," *Law and Society Review*, vol. 14, no. 2.

49. Howard Senzel (1982), *Cases*, New York: Viking, p. 66.

50. David Sudnow (1965), "Normal Crimes: Sociological Features of the Penal Code in a Public Defender Office," *Social Problems*, vol. 12, pp. 255–76. reprinted in William Chambliss, ed. (1969), *Crime and the Legal Process*, New York: McGraw-Hill, pp. 237–61.

51. Ibid., p. 245.

52. Ibid., p. 258.

53. Heumann, op. cit.

54. Ibid.

55. James W. Meeker and Henry N. Pontell (1985), "Court Caseloads, Plea Bargains, and Criminal Sanctions: The Effects of Section 17 P.C. in California," *Criminology*, vol. 23, pp. 119–43.

56. Sudnow, op. cit., p. 256.

57. Abraham S. Blumberg (1967), "The Practice of Law as a Confidence Game: Organizational Cooptation of a Profession," *Law and Society Review*, vol. 1, pp. 15–39.

58. Herbert S. Miller, William F. McDonald, and James A. Cramer (1978), *Plea Bargaining in the United States*, National Institute of Law Enforcement and Criminal Justice, Washington, DC: U.S. Government Printing Office, p. 177.

59. *The New York Times*, Jan. 9, 1986, p. A13.

60. David Harris Willson (1967), *A History of England*, New York: Holt, Rinehart, Winston, p. 228.

61. *Brown v. Mississippi*, 297 U.S. 278 (1936), cited in Smith and Pollack, op. cit., p. 175.

62. *Malloy v. Hogan*, 378 U.S. 1 (1964).

63. *New York v. Quarles* (1984), U.S. SupCt 35 CrL 3135. *Nix v. Williams*, U.S. SupCt 35 CrL 3192 (1984).

64. *Escobedo v. Illinois*, 378 U.S. 478 (1964). Alexander B. Smith and Harriet Pollack (1980), *Criminal Justice: An Overview*, New York: Holt, Rinehart and Winston, pp. 176–77.

65. *Miranda v. Arizona*, 384 U.S. 436 (1966).

66. *Brewer v. Williams*, 430 U.S. 387 (1977).

67. Michael L. Rubinstein, Stevens H. Clarke, and Teresa J. White (1980), *Alaska Bans Plea Bargaining*, Washington, DC: U.S. Government Printing Office. Walker, op. cit., p. 31.

68. Senzel, op. cit., pp. 64–66.

Rehabilitation

CHAPTER **15**

PUNISHING CRIMINALS

PEOPLE CONVICTED OF CRIMES RECEIVE SOME PUNISHMENT. THAT IS HOW WE KNOW IT'S a crime. If the misdeed were a "tort" (or civil wrong), the defendant would make some sort of **restitution** to the plaintiff. But when a defendant loses in a criminal case, the state imposes a punishment. The U.S. Constitution specifically mentions three types of punishment: deprivation of "life, liberty, or property"—in other words, execution, prison, and fines.

At the time of the writing of the Constitution, courts could impose several other types of punishment, including whipping, branding, and mutilation. These are forms of **corporal punishment**, (i.e., punishment done to the body of the convicted person). Some Moslem countries and others still impose whipping and even (though rarely) mutilation as a form of punishment. All modern industrialized countries, East and West, have abolished these corporal punishments.* Most Western democracies have also abolished *capital punishment* (i.e., the death penalty). The United States, of course, is the main exception, though Japan has executed a handful of criminals over the last 40 years. Capital punishment is much more likely to be found in countries like Iran or South Africa—countries with authoritarian, totalitarian, or otherwise oppressive forms of government.

Today in the United States, the most common forms of punishment are **fines** (money paid to the state, not to the victim) and **incarceration** (i.e., being locked up) or some other form of supervision. The United States currently has 750,000 people in prisons and jails, but an additional 2 million convicted criminals are on **probation** and **parole**.[1] Probation and its close cousin **suspended sentence** do not involve any incarceration at all. **Parole** is a form of early release for those in prison. Probation and parole are forms of **conditional release**. That is, instead of spending time in prison or jail, the offender must fulfill certain conditions. The courts may impose a wide variety of conditions, especially with probation: reporting to a probation officer, participating in a drug or alcohol rehabilitation program, working a specified number of hours in "community service," avoiding certain places or people, holding a job. More recently, courts have begun to make restitution a condition of probation. If the convict violates the conditions of probation or parole, the court may impose a prison sentence.

Practical Matters—Rehabilitation, Deterrence, Incapacitation

Why impose any of these punishments that cost so much money? Why shouldn't we just let criminals go?

The chances are that your first answer to this question was a practical

---

* The state of Delaware did not abolish whipping until 1973. In 1963, the law was challenged, but the state court ruled in favor of flogging. The state legislature finally repealed the law in 1973. In 1968, a federal court ruled that whipping of prisoners was unconstitutional.

one: We punish criminals to reduce crime. If we didn't punish them, crime rates would increase. This is an empirical proposition—one that can be tested against evidence. Accordingly, this section of the book will try to present the reasoning and evidence on how punishment affects crime. Here is a brief preview.

The practical effects of punishment fall into three categories. One justification for punishment is **rehabilitation**. This reason for prison rests on the idea that prisons can rehabilitate or improve convicts and turn them into people who will not commit crimes. For more than a century, rehabilitation provided the dominant ideology of prisons. In recent years, this ideology has lost much support, and for good reason: There was precious little evidence to prove that prisons could in fact rehabilitate criminals or correct their behavior. Nevertheless, governments still place prisons under the heading of "corrections"; prisons are still officially known as "correctional facilities," and they still offer a variety of rehabilitation programs. In the next section, I try to trace the history of rehabilitation—the long road to its ascendancy and the shorter path of its decline.

A second justification for punishment is **deterrence**. The idea of deterrence is that the pain or threatened pain of punishment will prevent people from committing crimes. Probably the best-known arguments about deterrence revolve around the issue of capital punishment, with supporters of the death penalty maintaining that if people knew they would be executed for murder, murder rates would not be so high. They also apply this same logic to other crimes and penalties, arguing that if punishments were more certain and more severe, crime rates would drop. In the last 25 years, public support for deterrence, and especially for the death penalty, has risen steadily. However, the evidence on deterrence, like the evidence on rehabilitation, is not so clear or encouraging.

Finally, even if prisons do not rehabilitate, and even if they do not deter, they still may reduce crime by keeping criminals off the streets. This function, known as **incapacitation**, has been the topic of much recent research in criminology. The logic of incapacitation is irrefutable: As long as criminals are in prison, they cannot be on the streets committing crimes. Incapacitation as a policy, however depends on two questions that are not so easily answered: How much crime can prisons prevent? And at what cost?

Justice—The Moral Dimension

Punishment is not just a matter of practical effects. For example, several years ago, Jean Harris, a prep-school administrator, shot and killed her lover, who was a physician and the author of a best-selling diet book. A jury convicted Ms. Harris of murder. What sentence should the judge have given her? Assume that if released, Ms. Harris would never commit another crime; and assume also that her immediate release would not affect anyone else's behavior; it would not inspire anyone else to commit a murder. In other words, locking her up would have no effect on crime; letting her go would not increase the danger to anyone at all. Should the judge have let her walk out of court free?

If you said no, you could not be basing your answer on any of the practical reasons for punishment. I already stipulated that rehabilitation, deterrence, and incapacitation were not at issue. Instead, you were basing your decision on the morality of sentencing rather than on its practical effects. It just would not be "right" to let a convicted murderer go. Much of the debate over capital punishment concerns concepts of right and wrong. Opponents of the death penalty argue that it is not right for the state to be in the business of killing people—especially in the absence of evidence that execution is a deterrent that saves other people's lives. Supporters of the death penalty argue that even if capital punishment is not a deterrent, a person who commits an exceptionally brutal or cold-blooded murder deserves to die.

A few years ago, as I wrote the first draft of this section of the book, demonstrators outside a New York court were carrying signs saying, "Justice for Jennifer." Jennifer Levin was killed by a young man named Robert Chambers, who was then on trial for murder. The prosecution called the incident murder; the defense called it accidental death. The demonstrators wanted to see Chambers punished not because the punishment would affect crime or safety, but because anything else would not do "justice." It is worth noting that the justice demanded by the demonstrators was not really for Jennifer, since Jennifer was no longer around to appreciate any possible verdict or sentence. Instead, it was for the demonstrators themselves. Most demands for justice have this sort of goal; it is to make us, the noncriminals, feel better, secure in the knowledge that the world we live in is a just place.

This fourth reason for punishment usually is called **retribution**. It resembles revenge, but ideally it is based less on personal feelings than on general principles. Criminals should receive the punishment that they justly deserve; they should get their **just deserts**. Although the concept of justice plays a large role in people's views of crime and punishment, it is also the area where social science and empirical evidence are the least relevant. When we talk about "justice" and what people "deserve," we are no longer in the world of factual information, of cause and effect. We are no longer in the world of science, where we ask, "What is?" We are in the world of philosophy and ethics, where we ask, "What ought to be?"

Can prisons rehabilitate robbers? Can punishment deter robbers? How much robbery can we prevent through incapacitating robbers? These are empirical questions; they can be answered by research and evidence. There may be problems with the quality of the actual data, but at least we can design research that brings in relevant data, and we can imagine data that would answer the question one way or the other. If I say prison rehabilitates robbers and you say it doesn't, we can get evidence on the success of robbers who enrolled in various rehabilitation programs. Ideally, the evidence would settle the argument.

But when we ask, "What sentence does a robber deserve?," we are asking for a moral judgment. If I say 50 years and you say two years, I cannot imagine any data that would prove either of us correct.

The following sections, therefore, will contain no attempt to answer questions of justice, which is not a concern of this book. It is important that we examine our notions of justice, for too often we take them for granted and assume that everyone agrees, as though justice were a matter of fact rather than a matter of philosophy. However, in this text, I try to stay closer to matters of fact. If you wish to wrestle with the question, "What is just?" (and I certainly hope you do wish to question your own thinking on this matter), take a course in philosophy.

REHABILITATION: THE EVOLUTION OF AN IDEAL

Over 150 years ago, a young Frenchman wrote what is still probably the best book ever written about the United States—its people, its culture, its government, and its problems. But Alexis de Tocqueville had not set out to write *Democracy in America*. He had sailed to America in 1831 for much narrower purposes: to study its prisons. Nor was he the only one. In that same decade, England and Prussia also sent experts to look at U.S. prisons; even nonexpert tourists made prisons a part of their travels.[2] What was it about American prisons that drew such international attention?

America had not always had such exemplary forms of justice. Punishments in colonial times resembled those of England, since America was still under English rule. The most frequent punishments were fines and whipping. But colonial justice included other punishments, some that may now seem quaint, others brutal. The *ducking stool* was a chair in which the offender was repeatedly lowered into a pond or river. Other offenders were sentenced to sit in the *stocks*—a wooden board with holes for immobilizing the hands and feet. The *pillory* was similar to the stocks, except that the offender stood rather than sat. Here is a description from Boston, 1771.

> A little further up State Street was to be seen the pillory with three or four fellows fastened by the head and hands, and standing for an hour in that helpless posture, exposed to gross and cruel jeers from the multitude, who pelted them constantly with rotten eggs and every other kind of repulsive garbage.[3]

Punishments could also be quite brutal by modern standards. A pilloried offender might have his ears or tongue nailed to the board or cut off entirely.

Others might be branded on the forehead, cheek, shoulder or hand—T for theft, M for manslaughter, SL for seditious libel; B might mean burglar or blasphemer, depending on the jurisdiction.[4] In other cases, the offender was not branded but had to wear a letter sewn onto the clothing to indicate the crime. Fiction has given us the best-known example: Hester Prynne's scarlet A for adultery (though Ds for drunkenness were far more common).

Finally, and frequently, there was the gallows. In the 1700s, both in England and America, criminals were put to death for crimes like burglary, theft, and counterfeiting as well as for more serious crimes like murder. Many of those executed were third-time offenders. A first offense would bring a fine and whipping. A second-time offender would be sentenced to more whipping and perhaps a few hours sitting in the gallows with a rope about his or her neck, presumably as a warning against a third offense.[5] In any case, capital punishment occurred far more often than it does today. And America was, if anything, more tolerant than Europe, where in the 17th century those accused of witchcraft were executed by the tens of thousands.[6] As late as 1805 in England, about 13 percent of all convictions (7.6 percent of all indictments) resulted in the death sentence.*[7] At that rate, the United States today would be putting 750,000 people onto death row each year.†　Executions were public events. In England, crowds of people turned out, giving the event a riotous, almost festive atmosphere. In America, too, hangings were public, though the atmosphere was usually more solemn.

England did have recourse to one other form of punishment—transportation. Some countries today occasionally deport a few criminals (especially

Table 15–1 ■ Sentences for Property Crimes in Surrey, England, 1740–48

Punishment	Percentage of total sentence
Hanging	9.8
Transportation	49.3
Whipping	31.0
Discharging	8.8
Imprisonment	1.0

Source: J. M. Beattie (1977), "Crime and the Courts in Surrey, 1736–1753," in J. S. Cockburn, ed., *Crime in England, 1550–1800,* Princeton, NJ: Princeton University Press, pp. 155–86.

* Of those sentenced to die, many were granted reprieves. Only about one in four actually went to the gallows.

† In 1983, 10,500,000 criminal cases were filed in state courts. If 7.6 percent were executed, that would be 750,000.

noncitizens). But from the time of the first American settlement up until 1776, England shipped tens of thousands of convicts to America. After American independence, Australia became the favored destination. As for prison, it was not widely used in colonial America. In England, prison terms became fairly common by 1800, though most sentences were for less than a year (see Table 15–1).

Different Societies, Different Punishments

If you had walked into a town square in 18th-century America or England, you would have seen the focal points of community life—the courthouse and the church. But you also would have noticed the stocks, the whipping post, and the pillory. Many colonies had laws requiring each town to build these devices. Probably you would not have seen a jail. And if the town did have a jail, it would have looked much like any other house, rather than like a secure lockup for hardened criminals. Today, by contrast, we have no pillory, no ducking stool, no tongue-piercing, no branding. Even whipping is outlawed.* Instead, we spend billions of dollars to build prisons.

Why did these other punishments disappear, and how did incarceration become the preferred way of punishing criminals? First, look at the differences between punishment 250 years ago and punishment now. The older punishments were physical, and they were public. Today, punishment is private. The stocks and pillory exposed offenders to the rest of the community. Prison deliberately removes them from public view. Even capital punishment, where it exists today, is a far more private event—execution behind prison walls with only a handful of witnesses rather than a public hanging preceded by an uplifting sermon.

One reason for the change may be that the stocks, the pillory, and other public punishments are best suited to small, stable communities—towns where everyone knows everyone else and where people depend on each other in a variety of daily interactions. Public punishments depend on shame—shaming the offender in the eyes of the community. Corporal punishments also took place in public, literally adding insult to injury. Flogging was done either at the whipping post or with the offender tied to a cart and pulled through the town. These punishments, in one important way, resemble the punishments school teachers inflict on pupils (though, of course, Puritan punishment of criminals was more severe): The punishment is public, and it involves the entire community. The dunce cap may have disappeared from classrooms, but teachers still respond to misbehavior with open criticism, sarcasm, and even name-calling—all forms of humiliation in the eyes of the

---

* The ban on corporal punishment often applies only to adults; many states still allow authorities (schoolteachers, "reform school" guards) to beat children.

community (i.e., the other fourth-graders). Some teachers still make the gum-chewing child stand in front of the class with the chewing gum stuck on his or her nose. In many schools teachers are still allowed to use corporal punishment, sometimes carried out in front of other children.

What is the point of such humiliation? Its effect on the offender is at best questionable. Nevertheless, public punishment serves an important function for the rest of the community. It marks the boundaries of proper behavior, and it enlists the entire community in supporting those boundaries.[8] However, this form of punishment can work only in a small community where everyone generally shares the same values and beliefs. If opinion is already divided, then the punishment may make those divisions even sharper. If the criminal is something of a hero to many members of the community, it does little good for authorities to punish him publicly. Such an event, instead of uniting people in support of the laws, is more likely to cause an outpouring of support for the criminal and resentment against the authorities.*

Public shaming worked in colonial America because towns were usually stable, uniform communities. People knew each other's business and shared a fairly narrow range of ideas and opinions.[9] This uniformity was no accident. To prevent diversity, towns enacted laws to restrict the flow of outsiders into the community, and they closely monitored people's daily behavior. People with unorthodox ideas might find themselves banished from the town. "Right to privacy" and "freedom of expression" as we know them today were alien concepts in early America. However, by the 19th century, this small-town uniformity was falling victim to historical demographic changes. The population was growing rapidly, and Americans were becoming a "people on the move."[10]

Demographic change often brings social change. As societies become larger, the division of labor becomes more complex. What had been a task for the whole community becomes the province of specialized people or institutions. In the 1800s, as the population became more mobile and as communities grew larger and less unified, towns developed special agencies to perform the tasks once performed by the community at large. Where once citizens patrolled on the watch, now police walked a beat. Where once the shaming of offenders had been a task for the whole community, now punishment became the province of a specialized institution, the prison.[11] (Similarly, when pupils graduate from the grammar school where they spend all day in the company of the same 25 children, to the more individualistic, mobile, and diverse society of the high school, shaming punishments give way to the school equivalent of prison—detention.)

---

* In London (already a large city by 1700), when Daniel Defoe was pilloried for writing an anti-church satire, crowds pelted him not with rotten food but with flowers. (Newman, p. 117.)

Punishment and Patriotism

There is another source of the change in America from public punishments and executions to incarceration: the American Revolution—its underlying philosophy and sentiment. In the aftermath of the Revolution, both leaders and the general public were filled with feelings of optimism for their new nation. Philosophically, America was a product of the Enlightenment, the Age of Reason. Politically and emotionally the Revolution represented a rejection of things British—including the English system of punishment. The Bill of Rights, with its prohibition of "cruel and unusual punishments," is one result of the spirit of those times. The Americans felt that the extensive use of capital and corporal punishment was the mark of a government and a society based on privilege, tradition, and tyranny rather than equality, reason, and freedom.[12]

The Enlightenment ideas that inspired the Revolution and the new republic also provided the philosophical basis for criminal reform. In the area of crime, the most important Enlightenment document was Beccaria's essay, "On Crimes and Punishments." Beccaria criticized extreme punishments, torture, and execution; they were irrational, out of all proportion to their utility as deterrents to crime. Instead he advocated that lawmakers see the law more as a matter of prevention than as one of punishment; he also recommended more use of incarceration and less use of corporal punishment. One of the colonies, Pennsylvania, had taken this direction much earlier, in 1682, owing to the Quaker influence of its founder, William Penn. The Pennsylvania criminal code abolished capital punishment for all crimes but murder, and it replaced corporal punishments with incarceration or other more humane punishments. The experiment did not last long, however. Pennsylvania still was a colony dominated by England, and 25 years later, a political conflict between the colony and the crown resulted in the instatement of the English criminal code, with its long list of capital crimes.[13]

Reforming the Criminal

Besides rejecting the older English criminal codes, Enlightenment ideas of punishment also contradicted earlier ideas of crime and justice that had prevailed in America as well. The Puritans who founded the New England colonies in the 1600s saw crime as the outcome of the devil's temptations and the natural sinfulness of humans. Theirs was a pessimistic view, for it saw little hope for reform. A century later, however, the dominant philosophy held not only that society could prevent crime but that it could reform individual criminals. The principal instrument of this reform would be the prison.

Jails, prisons, and other houses of correction already existed in the 18th century but they were not widely used in colonial America.[14] Some prisons looked like houses, and were about as easy to escape from. Others resembled those in England—horrid places where men and women, children and hardened adults, were all kept together under inhumane conditions.[15] However, in the 1790s, the prevailing spirit of optimism led many states to revise their criminal codes and to build new houses of detention based on new philosophical principles. It was these new institutions that drew observers like de Tocqueville to visit America.

Prisons—Ideology and Architecture

At the time of de Tocqueville's visit, the United States was the site of two different models of prison, both of them new: the Pennsylvania model and the Auburn model. It may be difficult for us, looking back across nearly two centuries, to appreciate the differences. And perhaps these differences don't really matter. What is important to note about both systems is that they were attempts to design a prison specifically for the purpose of rehabilitation.

The Pennsylvania system, in its theory and its architecture, relied on one basic idea—separating the prisoner from evil influence. Pennsylvania had two main prisons, the Eastern Penitentiary near Philadelphia and the Western Penitentiary near Pittsburgh, both built in the 1820s. Each prison housed several hundred prisoners, but the prisons were designed so that the inmates never saw each other. For his entire term, a prisoner was isolated in an 8′ × 12′ cell. In that cell, a prisoner would eat, sleep, and work at some kind of craft. His only human contact would be with guards or clergy; the only book permitted was the Bible. For exercise, each cell had an equally small yard adjoining it.

This system may seem cruel to us, but it has a certain logic—especially for rehabilitation purposes. First, the solitude allowed the prisoner, uninfluenced by any other forces, to reflect upon his sins. The isolation was also intended to prevent contamination by other prisoners. A prisoner could not learn criminal techniques and ideas from other prisoners, nor could he establish criminal contacts that might influence him after his release. (Incoming prisoners were even blindfolded on the way to their cells so that they would not be able to glimpse other prisoners.) The isolation also made it easier for staff to control inmates and made the prisoner an eager worker when he was finally allowed some kind of handicrafts in his cell.[16]

Pennsylvania's **separate** or **solitary** system offered one way of reforming the criminal and preventing his being contaminated by communication with other prisoners. However, it was not the only model for accomplishing these goals. In Auburn, New York, a prison built in 1823 offered a different solution. As in Pennsylvania, the New York prison tried to reform the criminals through religious instruction, work, and isolation from evil influences. And as in Pennsylvania, the New York prison permitted no contact with the outside world and no books except the Bible. However, at Auburn, prisoners worked and ate together; they moved from cell to dining hall to workplace together. What prevented the spread of evil ideas from one prisoner to another was Auburn's **silent** system. Prisoners were absolutely forbidden to speak to each other. New York prisoners also introduced the "lockstep" (a tight-formation shuffle in which prisoners marched from place to place), and prison stripes, the uniform that remained part of prison life into the next century.

Experts debated which system was better. Supporters of the Pennsylvania system pointed out that the New York model tempted prisoners to speak to each other by packing them together, and then punished them cruelly for breaking silence. And in fact, Auburn guards did resort to a variety of punishments for those who spoke: flogging with rawhide or wire whips, sudden drenching with icy water, and other tortures.*[17] Supporters of the New York system criticized Pennsylvania's isolation as inhuman; but more important, they pointed out the economic advantages of the New York prison. It was far cheaper to construct a block of small, inside cells ($7' \times 3\frac{1}{2}'$) than the outside cells of the Eastern Penitentiary. Eventually, with the rise in prison populations in the 1840s and 1850s, more and more states followed the Auburn model. Even Pennsylvania finally abandoned its solitary system.

Rehabilitation, Round Two—The Indeterminate Sentence

The reform movements of the 1790s had culminated in the widespread construction of prisons. By the 1820s, capital and corporal punishments had all but disappeared. Instead of these pessimistic versions of justice, state governments turned to the prison, with its potential for rehabilitating criminals. Before too long, however, both the Pennsylvania model and the Auburn model eventually had their ideals compromised by the pressure of numbers. In a pattern that by now has become all too familiar, the practical problems of running a prison soon undermined the lofty goal of rehabilitation. To prison authorities faced with problems of overcrowding, underfunding, poor discipline, and the possibility of riot and escape, it didn't make much difference whether the prison had been designed to rehabilitate prisoners through silence or through separation. Their first goal was the smooth running of the prison. So rehabilitation gave way to discipline, and

---

* In one form of "water cure," drops of water, one at a time, would be dripped onto the prisoner's head, sometimes for days at a stretch. Though today this method is sometimes called the "Chinese water torture," it was in use (if not devised) in America nearly 200 years ago.

the new prisons came quickly to resemble the old—complete with degraded living conditions and brutal punishments.

The stage was set for the next round of reform, which came in the 1870s. Like the reformers of the previous century, prison experts of the 1870s saw prison as a place for rehabilitation rather than punishment. Toward this goal, they emphasized two new ideas: first, that prisons should provide decent living conditions and a variety of rehabilitation programs; second, that instead of **determinate** or fixed sentences, courts should impose **indeterminate** sentences. Instead of a sentence of five years (no more, no less), a prisoner might be sentenced to three to 10 years. The actual date of release would depend on the prisoner's own individual progress.

This kind of sentence may seem unfair, but from the standpoint of rehabilitation, indeterminate sentencing was the most logical policy. If the purpose of punishment was rehabilitation, then it made little sense to keep a person in prison after he or she was reformed. Similarly, releasing a prisoner too early (i.e., before complete rehabilitation) was harmful both to the prisoner and to society. Since different criminals would take different lengths of time to reform, determinate sentences were inappropriate. Instead, what was required was a system of indeterminate sentences coupled with **parole**.

Parole is a conditional release from prison. The parolee agrees to a set of conditions. Today these conditions usually include reporting regularly to a parole officer, keeping a job, avoiding use or possession of guns or illegal drugs, and generally leading a respectable, law-abiding life. A prisoner becomes eligible for parole after having served a certain proportion of the maximum sentence. This proportion varies from state to state; one-quarter and one-third are commonly used formulas. A prisoner sentenced to five to 10 years may be eligible for parole after three-and-a-half years (the eligibility date may be earlier, since inmates can also reduce their sentences by earning **good time**; i.e., time off for good behavior while in prison). In some states, prisoners must serve the minimum term specified in the sentence, so that the person sentenced to five to 10 years would have to serve at least five years before being paroled. Of course, eligibility is no guarantee that parole will be granted. The prisoner must convince a parole board that if released, he or she will be a good citizen.

The U.S. reformers of the 1870s were not the first to propose or even to try out these ideas. In 1840, the British government assigned a reformer, Captain Alexander Maconochie, to run its Norfolk Island penal colony off the coast of Australia. An earlier investigation by Maconochie had made the British aware of the degraded conditions in its Australian prisons, and Norfolk Island was the most extreme. Inmates sentenced to death would drop to their knees and praise Jesus for their deliverance. Catholic prisoners, whose religion strongly prohibited suicide, would sometimes draw straws, the winner being killed immediately; the runner-up would do the killing, thereby assuring his own conviction and execution.[18] Maconochie tried to humanize the prison and institute rehabilitation programs. Under Maconochie's new system, prisoners would earn "marks" through their labor and good behavior; when a prisoner accumulated the required number of marks, he would be given a "ticket of leave" equivalent to parole. Unfortunately, Maconochie governed only a short time at Norfolk Island, and when he left, the prison reverted to its old brutal ways.

Maconochie's ideas received a warmer welcome in the United States, where reformers of the 1870s proposed similar changes in prisons. By that time, the failure of prisons was not exactly a secret. A New York Prison Commission report in 1852 concluded that long-term imprisonment "destroys the faculties of the soul"; long-term prisoners were "distinguished by a stupor of both the moral and intellectual facilities. . . . Reformation is then out of the question."[19] Here again was the idea that the principal goal of prison should be rehabilitation. Nearly 20 years later this idea was echoed at a convention in Cincinnati which set the agenda in prison reform for nearly a century. Prisons were to achieve the goal of protecting society by means of rehabilitating prisoners. Zebulon Brockway, an influential prison administrator, said, "The supreme aim of prison discipline is the reformation of criminals, not the infliction of vindictive suffering."[20] Brockway also held that reformation could be brought about by education, religious instruction, and "industrial training" (which is probably better understood as hard work rather than job training).

In 1876, Brockway had a chance to put his ideas into practice. He was appointed superintendent of a new prison in Elmira, New York. His plans for the prison embodied the principles announced at the Cincinnati conference six years earlier: indeterminate sentences, education, job training, better living conditions, and a "mark system" where inmates earned marks towards greater privileges and eventually release. Elmira became a shining example to prison reformers, even though the reality of prison life rarely matched the ideal. In 1894, an investigation at Elmira revealed that prisoners were regularly whipped, thrown into solitary confinement, or shackled to the cell door.[21] Apparently, even in a reformer's prison, ideals took second place to the pressures of maintaining order and security.

While actual conditions at Elmira may have degenerated, the rehabilitative ideal continued to gather support. By the early 20th century, most states had some form of parole and indeterminate sentencing. The ideology of rehabilitation fit well with two typically American traits—optimism and the belief in progress through science. This was the era during which psychology and sociology were becoming popular. These new social sciences held out the same hope for social problems that the "hard" sciences offered for technological problems. Reformers of this period (the late 19th century) could also look to medicine as an example. Recent discoveries in germ theory had led to the birth of scientific medicine and to real hopes for curing and preventing many diseases. Reformers, therefore, tended to see the problem of crime and criminals in terms of a "medical model." That is, the criminal, rather than being evil or sinful, was "sick." Prisons could be most useful if they tried to cure rather than punish. Psychology and sociology would provide the scientific basis for this cure, especially through individualized treatment. So instead of talking about punishment, prison reformers began to talk about treatment and about the "needs" of different kinds of prisoners. By the 1920s, the idea of psychiatry was a well-established part of prisons, and many prisons had at least part-time psychiatrists.

The greatest success of the reformers seems to have been not a practical one but an ideological one: They convinced legislators, prison administrators, and the general public that prisons should be and could be places for rehabilitation. Reformers also succeeded in getting prisons to expand rehabilitation programs. In practice, however, the new programs were often not really new. Even in the 18th century, proposals for prison reform had included work, religion, and education. More important, the reformers' programs often turned out far different from the shining ideals set forth at the 1870 conference in Cincinnati. For example, prisons have always tried to provide work for prisoners. Usually, however, the prison work experience fell far short of any rehabilitative ideal. Many Southern states, especially after the Civil War, contracted out inmate labor to private companies. The prisons got money, and the private companies got cheap, slave-like labor. Obviously, the purpose of this arrangement was economic rather than rehabilitative, and after investigations revealed the cruelty and high rates of death, states began to outlaw this form of prison work. In Northern states, where reformers had more influence, prisons set up prison industries. But before long, these came to suffer from inadequate (or nonexistent) machinery, lack of supervision or training, and various other problems. Investigations in the 1920s found that work programs existed mostly on paper. For much of the day, prisoners had nothing to do. Education programs followed a similar pattern. The reform movement of the 1870s had inspired many prison systems to offer some sort of teaching. But by the 1920s, most prison education programs had inadequate classrooms, too few books, too few teachers, and too few students.[22]

Rehabilitation—One More Time

In the 1950s, new kinds of rehabilitation programs were introduced into prisons. Some of them, like religious programs, education, and job training, merely broadened old ideas. Religion had been part of even the earliest U.S. prisons. Prisons in the early 1800s might have forbidden prisoners from speaking to one another, but each prisoner could have a Bible. Today, most prisons have a variety of religious programs. Anyone, from low-key, pastoral-style clergy to intense evangelicals to Black Muslims, can get a crack at saving criminals. Prisons have also tried different kinds of classroom instruction and vocational education. If the 1950s brought any real change in rehabilitation, it was the increased emphasis on psychological counseling.

The rehabilitative ideal came to dominate thinking about prisons, both among those who worked in the criminal justice system and among the public as well. In 1970, nearly three-quarters of the public thought that the main emphasis of prisons should be rehabilitation. Less than 20 percent wanted punishment or protecting society as the main emphasis of prisons.[23]

By the time that poll was taken, prisoners had a variety of rehabilitation programs available to them. Depending on the prison and state, a prisoner might be able to choose from a variety of psychotherapies, both individual and group. Newer therapies like transcendental meditation and behavior modification recently have been added to the list. Drug and alcohol counseling and religious programs were also available. Education programs offered basic education, GED studies, and even college courses. Job-training programs included instruction in trades like baking, TV repair, sheet-metal work, printing, and many others. And in recent years, prisoners have been able to sign up for training in more modern areas like computers.

Rehabilitation Programs—"What Works?"

The big question about all these programs is do they work? Do they rehabilitate criminals? Perhaps the most noteworthy attempt to answer these questions began in 1966. A New York State commission hired a team of researchers, headed by Robert Martinson, to find out what works. This seems like a logical thing for the state to do. After all, it is spending money on several different types of rehabilitation programs. If it could find out which ones were most successful, then it could expand those programs and let the unsuccessful programs wither away.

But how do we measure the success of a program? Education programs might give tests to find out how well their students had learned. Psychotherapy programs could try to measure personality change or general adjustment inside prison and out. Job training programs could evaluate specific skills. But the most important question, one that cuts across all programs and gets at the basic idea of rehabilitation, is this: Did a program help prisoners keep out of trouble once they were released?

The usual way to answer this question is to measure **recidivism**. How many released prisoners were rearrested or reconvicted, and for what kinds of crimes? How many were returned for parole violations?*

* Parole violations are not necessarily crimes; they are merely violations of the conditions of parole and may include nothing more serious than getting drunk, hanging around with old acquaintances, losing a job, or failing to meet with the parole officer. In New York, more than half the parolees who had their parole revoked were returned to prison for these kinds of technical violations. In other states, the figure might be less than 25 percent. (John Wallerstedt (1984), "Returning to Prison," Bureau of Justice Statistics Special Report, Washington, DC: U.S. Government Printing Office.)

Martinson looked at every study he could find published in English from 1945 to 1967 which evaluated a rehabilitation program. It turned out that many of these "evaluations" had no scientific validity. Some did not adequately describe the treatment program; others did not bother to include data on recidivism or used unreliable measures of success. Still others made a crucial omission by failing to use a **control group**—a group of similar prisoners who did *not* go through the particular program. Suppose a treatment program claims a 75 percent success rate (i.e., that only 25 percent of released prisoners who had completed the program were subsequently convicted of a crime). If a control group also had a 75 percent success rate, then we might as well scrap the program and use the money for something else; we would still have a 75 percent success rate. Only a study using a control group can really tell us whether having a program is effective.

After Martinson had thrown out all the evaluation studies marred by shoddy research methods, he was left with 231 acceptable studies. Here is what he found:

> With few and isolated exceptions, the rehabilitative efforts that have been reported so far have had no appreciable effect on recidivism.[24]

This finding was only the beginning. Or perhaps it was *not* even the beginning, for the New York State planning agency refused to publish Martinson's study. They even tried to prevent Martinson from publishing it on his own. Apparently the results threatened more than just current theories about prison; Martinson's conclusion also threatened the vested interests of people involved in the planning and operation of rehabilitation programs.

Eventually Martinson, with the help of a lawyer, was able to publish his results in a 1974 article called "What Works?" Although Martinson's article carried the title "What Works?" and although he strongly implied that the answer was "nothing works," the truth is a little more complicated. What he found was "no clear pattern to indicate the efficacy of any particular method of treatment." In other words, if 10 job training programs reduced recidivism but 10 others did not, then Martinson could not say that job training "works," since there was no clear pattern of positive results.

Although other researchers had previously reached similar conclusions, Martinson's article created quite a stir. It appeared in a widely read journal, and the history of the research itself showed the seamier side of prison politics. Besides, the rehabilitative ideal was already beginning to fade, and Martinson's article added scientific support for those who wanted to abandon rehabilitation. Indeed, by 1978, four years after Martinson's article, the Harris poll asked, "What should be the main emphasis in most prisons?" support for rehabilitation had declined to 48 percent, while punishment and protecting society had risen to 46 percent. In 1970 (four years before "What Works?") the figures had been rehabilitation—73 percent, punishment and protect society—20 percent. By 1982, the figures had changed further: rehabilitation—44 percent; punishment and protect society—51 percent (see Figure 15–1).

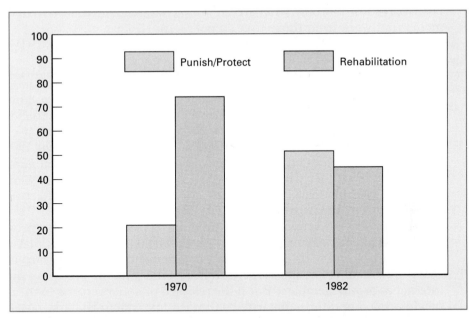

Figure 15–1   What Do You Think *Should* Be the Main Emphasis in Most Prisons?

Source: Louis Harris (1982), The Harris Survey, New York: Tribune Media Services, p. 4. In Edmund F. McGarrell and Timothy J. Flanagan, eds. (1985), Sourcebook of Criminal Justice Statistics—1984, U.S. Department of Justice; Bureau of Justice Statistics, Washington, DC: U.S. Government Printing Office.
   * Punish/protect: 1970, 8% said punish the guilty, 12% supported protecting the innocent; 1982, 19% polled voted to punish the guilty, 32% voted to protect the innocent. Percentages do not add up to 100 because those saying "Not Sure" were not included.

I do not mean to imply that Martinson's article caused this shift in public opinion, only that in both social science and public opinion the terms of the debate had changed. The shoe was on the other foot. At mid-century, rehabilitation had been taken for granted, and the burden of proof lay upon those who doubted. Twenty-five years later, the burden of proof had shifted. Proponents of rehabilitation would now have to prove that the idea was still valid.

Critics did attack Martinson's methods and conclusions—so much so that five years later, Martinson himself revised his views. He took into account the variability of different programs, both for better and for worse.

Some programs are indeed beneficial; of equal or greater significance, some programs are harmful.[25]

Why Rehabilitation Fails

Perhaps "what works?" was not quite the right question to ask. In any case, it should not have been the only question. Instead, two related questions immediately arise. First, why did no one type of program show consistently positive results? Second, what are the characteristics that distinguish treatments that work from those that do not?

Cures and Causes

One general answer to the first question is that the cure (rehabilitation) may have little to do with the disease (crime). Treatment assumes that crime arises because of a defect, a curable defect, in the person. But if crime instead is caused largely by environmental factors, treatment will be ineffective. Suppose, for example, that lack of a job leads to crime. Rehabilitation programs, even if they work, can create only job skills, not jobs. If there are no decent jobs for released prisoners, the program will be ineffective, no matter how well the prisoners have learned.

In the same way, a psychotherapy program in prison may help a prisoner to understand his or her problems, but psychological problems may have had nothing to do with that person's involvement in crime. Group counseling may help prisoners learn to talk to others about problems and to interact as group members. But if the released prisoner returns to the same neighborhood and the same friends that led to crime in the first place, the effects of group counseling will quickly dwindle to nothing.

It Ain't What You Do, It's the Way That You Do It

There is another reason why rehabilitation programs fail. A program as it actually takes shape in prison may look very different from the program as it was originally drawn up on paper. Sometimes the actual program differs from the planned version because of the people who run it. After all, prisoners are probably not an easy group to work with, and rehabilitation programs will require a most dedicated staff—teachers, counselors, psychologists, administrators. If these people do not have the proper training or the motivation, if they are merely going through the motions, then the program has little chance of success.

Even when the staff members are competent and dedicated, they may find that they cannot run the program as it was intended. The prison may lack sufficient space or facilities. The lack of money can become a problem. The prison may not have money for the necessary equipment, supplies, or books. Job-training programs may have to make do with outdated, secondhand equipment. Some job-training programs will wind up training inmates in outdated skills for jobs that no longer exist. Also, if some part of the rehabilitation program conflicts with the security needs of the prison, the program will be the loser. Suppose, for example, that an idealistic welding shop outside the prison proposes to train inmates and to give them jobs upon their release. The warden looks over the equipment—acetylene torches, masks, and a lot of plate steel—and realizes that while this program may provide job training, it is also furnishing material that prisoners can easily convert to weapons. I suspect that few wardens would allow such a program into their prisons.

Another possible reason for the failure is that most rehabilitation programs occupy only a small part of a prisoner's time. If a program teaches specific job skills or basic education, then it might work, at least in the sense of educating prisoners. But if a program aims to win prisoners over to a different set of attitudes and ideas about crime, it is competing with most of the rest of prison life. A prisoner may spend at most a few hours a day in some rehabilitation program. He lives the rest of his life in the inmate world. There, the "inmate culture" that dominates most prisons does not place a high value on staying out of crime.[26]

Different Strokes—Programs and Prisoners

High rates of recidivism, Martinson's research, and a constant media supply of anecdotal evidence ("Paroled Robber Shoots Storeowner") all contributed to a general disillusionment with rehabilitation. However, as even Martinson later admitted, *some* programs did work for *some* prisoners. Perhaps underneath the overall impression of failure lies some modest hope for success. The basis of this new hope is that a program may work better with some types of prisoners than with others. Prisons have a variety of rehabilitation programs and a variety of criminals. If the program could be matched with the criminal, then there might be a better chance for success.

Accordingly, psychologists have tried to develop ways of classifying prisoners. Many prisons classify prisoners on the basis of the MMPI* (a well-known personality test).[27] There have also been several systems for classifying juveniles. One popular system, for example, classifies delinquents according to the causes of their delinquency—immaturity, neuroses, psychopathy, or subcultural involvement.[28]

Unfortunately, classifying criminals or delinquents seems to have little effect in reducing recidivism. It's not that criminals cannot be classified—they can. Many of these tests differentiate consistently between different types of personality or different motivations for crime. But rarely does a prison have a rehabilitation program tailored to each classification. Instead, prisoners, whatever their classification, choose from the same programs. And it is still difficult to show any consistent effect of these programs in reducing recidivism. This does not mean we should stop trying to classify prisoners. But at present these classification systems are useful only within the prison itself. On the basis of criminals' life histories and psychological tests, prison administrators can more confidently assign them to minimum or maximum security settings.[29] For example, in the first four years of Cal-

---

* See Chapter 10.

ifornia's classification system, low-risk inmates were moved to lower-security prisons. As a result, the rate of violent deaths dropped, as did the rate of escapes—despite a 66 percent increase in the total inmate population.[30] But while classification systems may make for less dangerous prisons, they have not yet been able to reduce recidivism.

We should not be surprised at the failure of rehabilitation programs. The conditions in most U.S. prisons range from brutal and inhumane at worst to boring and monotonous at best. Prisons are overcrowded and understaffed; prisoner culture is dominated by resentment toward both the legitimate world in general and prison authorities in particular. In addition, few rehabilitation programs, if any, extend beyond prison. Prisoners who leave are on their own, frequently back in their old environments. Perhaps we should be surprised that recidivism rates are not even higher than they are.

Despite these conditions, some rehabilitation programs do work. But what makes them work, I suspect, has little to do with the content or design of the program. The key factor is probably the quality of the people involved. People who are good at working with prisoners have some chance of success, even in a program that on paper looks quite ordinary. On the other hand, people who are less dedicated will have no success even in better funded and well-designed programs.

PAROLE

As belief in rehabilitation waned, so did the idea of indeterminate sentences. Remember, indeterminate sentencing rests on two assumptions: first, that prison can rehabilitate criminals; and second, that parole boards can tell when a prisoner is rehabilitated. The first assumption, as we have seen, was much too optimistic. Prisons and rehabilitation programs, as they are currently run, do little to reduce recidivism. The second assumption is equally shaky. To some extent, social science can identify factors that make a prisoner a greater risk: a history of alcohol and drug abuse, a crime career that begins at an early age, a record that includes very serious offenses. These factors, however, are unchangeable parts of the prisoner's biography and have nothing to do with rehabilitation or anything else that goes on in prison. If these biographical factors are our best predictors of parole success, then it makes little sense to talk of granting parole when the prisoner is "ready"—that is, when he will no longer return to a life of crime. Using these predictors, a parole board could just as easily make the decision at the time the prisoner is admitted.

Parole Under Attack

The policy of indeterminate sentencing and parole has come in for criticism from both the public and the prisoners, from conservatives and liberals. Conservatives argue that parole undermines the purposes of punishment by making the actual punishment too lenient. A sentence may appear severe (e.g., 15 years) yet allow the criminal to be paroled after a much shorter stay in prison (five years). This reduction undermines the purposes of punishment. First, it does not do justice. If a crime "deserves" a 15-year sentence, then the criminal paroled after five years is not getting his "just deserts." Second, lenient sentences, conservatives argue, will not deter as effectively as will longer terms. And, most tellingly, the prisoner released after five years instead of 15 will have 10 more years in which to commit crimes. The media sometimes provide anecdotal evidence for these ideas. If a parolee commits a newsworthy crime, the media will almost always mention that the perpetrator was on parole, creating the impression that the parole board had done a bad job in granting release.* If it had not paroled the prisoner, the crime would not have happened. (Of course, parole board successes—the parolees who never commit crimes—never make the newspapers.)

Some liberals and prisoners themselves also object to parole. Prisoners, too, argue on the basis of just deserts. Parole in effect punishes a person on the basis of what the parole board predicts he will do in the future, not on the basis of what he has done. Just deserts should be based on deeds, not on predictions. Other objections to parole focus not on its lenience but on its unfairness. The system, which grants so much discretion to a handful of people on a parole board, carries a great potential for inequity—a potential many prisoners are aware of. Two prisoners with identical records sentenced for the same crime might wind up serving very different lengths of time. Prisoners also say that the uncertainty about parole is demoralizing; a prisoner never really knows when he will be released. Prisoners may become even more cynical than they were to begin with; they may conclude that the system depends not on principles of justice but upon how well you can "con" a parole board.

Despite these attacks from both sides, parole has remained a part of the criminal justice system. Some states have reduced judicial and parole board discretion. Many states have narrowed the ranges of their indeterminate sentences. Some states have tightened parole guidelines by specifying the items that parole boards must consider in their decisions. And a very few states have abolished parole boards entirely; the prisoner's date of release depends on his sentence, minus good time. Nevertheless, the number of

---

* In the 1988 presidential election, George Bush made a similar criticism, implying that Michael Dukakis was responsible for granting a weekend furlough to Willie Horton, a criminal who escaped and committed a serious crime.

prisoners on parole continues to grow and currently stands at more than 250,000.³¹ The chief supporters of parole are the people who run the prisons. They see parole, like good time, as a useful tool for controlling prisoners. If a prisoner's release depends on his good conduct in prison, then he will do what the prison administration wants him to do. Prison officials fear that without the reward of parole or the threat of withholding it, they would find prisoners less easy to control.

Given the conditions in prisons today, parole may even be a necessity. As prisons become more and more overcrowded, some prisoners must be released to make room for new ones. Parole acts as a safety valve for dangerously overcrowded prisons. In some cases, courts have ruled that prison conditions constituted "cruel and unusual punishment," and have ordered prisons to start releasing convicts as a matter of law. As inexact as parole board hearings may be, they at least provide some semblance of rationality in deciding which prisoners to release.

Parole—Costs and Effectiveness

From the state's point of view, parole has a distinct advantage over prison: It is much cheaper. It costs about $15,000 a year to keep a person in prison. To keep a person on parole costs only about $1,500 per year. Both figures vary according to jurisdiction; in some states, the cost of parole is less than $300 per parolee.³² Of course, we must ask what we get for our money. Could we just as easily abolish parole? Is parole effective? Do paroled criminals refrain from committing crime? Obviously, parolees commit more crimes than do prisoners who are still locked up. But how many more crimes do they commit?

As with rehabilitation, the principal measure of parole success or failure is recidivism. And as with rehabilitation, the different ways of measuring recidivism give different answers. Some studies estimate that two-thirds of released prisoners eventually return. However, one study of parole found an overall success rate varying from a high of 90 percent for paroled murderers to a low of 65 percent for paroled car thieves. Put another way, that's a recidivism rate of only 10 percent to 35 percent. Generally the more serious the crime, the greater the success rate; those paroled from manslaughter and rape convictions did far better than did those paroled from burglary or check-passing convictions.³³

Parole has two aspects—early release and subsequent supervision. Abolishing parole, therefore, can mean two highly different things: having prisoners serve their full term without hope of parole, or letting prisoners go at an earlier date but without requiring them to report to parole officers.

Keeping everyone in prison is, of course, a very costly proposition. It would reduce crime—somewhat. For example, a 1985 study looked at about 150,000 people sent to prison. One-third of these were ex-convicts who had served out their terms. They had "max'd out" of prison and then gone on to commit other crimes for which they were convicted. But another 28 percent (about 43,000 prisoners) were parolees. About 15 percent of them were sent back to prison for technical parole violations. But 36,000 were sentenced for real crimes they committed while still on parole. These recidivists were not model citizens; most of them had four or more prior convictions. Nevertheless, compared with the other convicts, they were less likely to be entering prison for violent crimes. Instead, they were being returned to prison for property crimes like check-passing and possession of stolen property.[34] So abolishing early release would have prevented the crimes and technical parole violations of these 43,000 people—at a cost of $645,000,000 per year.*

These numbers tell us only what parole does compared with what prison does. Obviously, prison prevents more crime, but at great financial cost. But how effective is parole compared with doing nothing? Does parole supervision make a difference? To find out, criminologists compared parolees with criminals who were released without any supervision (in most cases because they had served out their terms). The study found two important things. First, recidivism rates for both groups were much higher than in other studies; second, parolees did somewhat better than did those who left prison unsupervised (see Table 15–2).

According to the figures in Table 15–2, three years of parole supervision lowered recidivism from 85 percent to 77 percent. Assume that parole costs $1,500 per parolee, per year. If we release 100 convicts unconditionally, we spend nothing, and in three years 85 of them will have been reconvicted. If instead, we grant the 100 convicts parole, in three years 77 of them will have been reconvicted, and we will have spent $450,000 ($1,500 × 100 convicts × three years). Are those eight convictions we prevented worth $450,000? Calculations like this, combined with the other arguments against parole, have led some people to call for its abolition, except as a way of reducing sentences.[35] Others argue that parole would be more effective

Table 15–2 ▪ Recidivism Rates

	After two years	*After three years*
Paroled	70%	77%
Released	82%	85%

Source: Howard Sacks and Charles Logan (1980), *Parole: Crime Prevention or Crime Postponement?*, Storrs, CT: University of Connecticut School of Law Press.

* This is a low estimate, based only on maintenance costs. In reality, without early release, prisons would quickly run out of space, and governments would have to build new prisons— at the cost of $75,000 per cell.

if parole officers' caseloads were smaller. Current caseloads allow very little time for any real supervision or help. The average amount of face-to-face interaction between parole officers and parolees can average as little as three minutes a week.[36] However, even cutting caseloads by more than half— from 75 to 30—has little effect on recidivism.[37]

SUMMARY AND CONCLUSION

For about 150 years, the idea of rehabilitation dominated the ideology of imprisonment in the United States and in other industrialized countries. Before the 1800s, prisons had been used to house people awaiting trial; prisons also served as workhouses where those arrested for vagrancy or begging were forced to work. In England, jails (spelled then and now "gaols") were also used as punishment for criminals, though only a fraction of those convicted went to prison. Other punishments included whipping, public humiliation, banishment, and death.

In the 19th century, reformers spread the idea that prisons could rehabilitate criminals. Rehabilitation, they said, required decent living conditions and effective programs. Toward this goal, prisons over the years have instituted everything from silent religious meditation to computer programming. Unfortunately, there is little evidence that any of these programs consistently reduce recidivism. This is not to say that criminals are never reformed. But whether a criminal "goes straight" depends more on the criminal than on any program he or she might have taken in prison. And if a program is effective, the reason is more likely to be found in the quality of the staff than in the program itself.

Reformers were only slightly more successful in changing living conditions than in rehabilitating prisoners. Discipline, economy, and security usually take precedence over humanity and idealism. There seems to be a never-ending cycle of exposé and reform. Periodically, reformers or reporters will expose the degraded conditions that exist in the jails and prisons. Prisons then will be cleaned up, only to disappear from public view. The old conditions will return, and the cycle will begin again. Doubtless the prisons in the United States today are vastly more humane than the bridewells of two centuries ago. Still, many of them remain places of boredom and violence.

The idea of rehabilitation also affected other aspects of the criminal justice system. Rehabilitation provided the ideological basis for the current system of indeterminate sentences and parole. The evidence on the effectiveness of parole is no more encouraging than the evidence on rehabilitation. Parole boards are not very good at predicting who will commit further crimes if released. Nor does supervised parole reduce crime much more than does unconditional release.

The ideology of rehabilitation has been declining since about 1970. This change is probably linked to the rise in crime rates of the 1960s. As crime rates rose and remained high, people became more cynical about the ability of the prisons to reform criminals. Public attitudes, including support for capital punishment, became more punitive. Almost nobody called for restoration of the pillory and whipping post,* but more people began to demand that prisons punish criminals, isolate them from society, or execute them. If crime rates ever return to their low levels of the 1940s and 1950s, perhaps we will see a revival of interest in rehabilitation. For the moment, the public, the policymakers, and many criminologists seem more interested in two other functions of punishment: deterrence and incapacitation (which, coincidentally, are the topics of the last two chapters of this book).

NOTES

1. "Probation and Parole 1985" (1987), Bureau of Justice Statistics Bulletin, Washington, DC: U.S. Government Printing Office.

2. David J. Rothman (1971), *The Discovery of the Asylum: Social Order and Disorder in the New Republic*, Boston: Little, Brown, p. 81.

3. Alice M. Earle (1792), *Curious Punishments of Bygone Days*, Rutland, Charles E. Tuttle, quoted in Graeme Newman (1978), *The Punishment Response*, New York: J.B. Lippincott, p. 118.

4. Newman, op. cit., p. 118.

5. Rothman, p. 52.

6. Newman, op. cit., p. 145.

7. Ibid., p. 141.

8. Kai Erikson (1966), *Wayward Puritans: A Study in the Sociology of Deviance*, New York: Wiley. Also Newman, op. cit., p. 114.

9. Michael Zuckerman (1970), *Peaceable Kingdoms: New England Towns in the Eighteenth Century*, New York: Knopf.

10. Ray Ginger (1975), *People on the Move: A United States History*, Boston: Allyn and Bacon.

11. Samuel Walker (1980), *Popular Justice: A History of American Criminal Justice*, New York: Oxford University Press, p. 113.

12. Rothman, *Discovery of the Asylum*, p. 59.

13. Walker, p. 32–33.

* In the late 1980s, amid the panic over illegal drugs, some state legislators proposed the reinstatement of whipping as a punishment for drug crimes.

14. Rothman (1971), p. 56.

15. James A. Inciardi (1987), *Criminal Justice* (2nd ed.), New York: Harcourt Brace Jovanovich, p. 529. Rothman, op. cit, pp. 53–56.

16. Rothman (1971), op. cit., pp. 82–88.

17. Inciardi, op. cit., p. 517.

18. Robert Hughes (1987), *The Fatal Shore*, New York: Knopf.

19. George Underwood, et. al. (1852), "Report of the Committee Appointed to Examine the Several State Prisons," *New York Assembly Documents*, no. 20, p. 14. Quoted in Rothman (1971), op. cit.

20. Zebulon R. Brockway (1870), "The Ideal of a True Prison System for a State," in *Transactions of the National Congress on Penitentiary and Reformatory Discipline* (reprinted Washington, DC: American Correctional Association, 1970). Quoted in Walker, p. 85.

21. *In the Matter of the Charges Preferred Against the Managers of the New York State Reformatory at Elmira*, 1894. Quoted in David Rothman (1980), *Conscience and Convenience: The Asylum and Its Alternatives in Progressive America*, Boston: Little, Brown, p. 36.

22. David J. Rothman (1980), *Conscience and Convenience*, pp. 135–43.

23. Louis Harris (1982), *The Harris Survey*, New York: Tribune Media Services. Reprinted in Edmund F. McGarrell and Timothy J. Flanagan, eds. (1985), *Sourcebook of Criminal Justice Statistics—1984*, U.S. Department of Justice, Bureau of Justice Statistics, Washington, DC: U.S. Government Printing Office, p. 233.

24. Robert Martinson (1974), "What Works? Questions and Answers about Prison Reform," *The Public Interest*, no. 35, pp. 22–54.

25. Robert Martinson (1979), "New Findings, New Views: A Note of Caution Regarding Sentencing Reform," *Hofstra Law Review*, vol. 7, p. 244. Cited in Clemens Bartollas (1985), *Correctional Treatment: Theory and Practice*, Englewood Cliffs, NJ: Prentice-Hall, p. 13.

26. Gresham Sykes (1958), *The Society of Captives*, Princeton, NJ: Princeton University Press. John Irwin and Donald Cressey (1962), "Thieves, Convicts, and the Inmate Culture," *Social Problems*, vol. 10, pp. 142–55.

27. E. I. Megargee and M. J. Bohn (1979), *Classifying Criminal Offenders: A New System Based on the MMPI*, Beverly Hills, CA: Sage.

28. H. C. Quay and L. B. Parsons (1971), *The Differential Behavioral Classification of the Juvenile Offender*, Washington, DC: U.S. Bureau of Prisons.

29. Tim Brennan (1987), "Classification for Control in Jails and Prisons," in Don M. Gottfredson and Michael Tonry, eds., *Prediction and Classification: Criminal Justice Decision Making*, Chicago: University of Chicago Press, pp. 323–66.

30. Norman Holt and Daniel Glaser (1985), "Statistical Guidelines for Custodial Classification Decisions," in Robert M. Carter, Daniel Glaser, and Leslie T. Wilkins, eds., *Correctional Institutions* (3rd ed.) New York: Harper & Row.

31. "Probation and Parole 1985" (1987), Bureau of Justice Statistics Bulletin, Washington, DC: U.S. Government Printing Office.

32. U.S. Department of Justice, Bureau of Justice Statistics (1983), *Report to the Nation on Crime and Justice: The Data*, Washington, DC: U.S. Government Printing Office, p. 92.

33. Don M. Gottfredson, Mark G. Neithercutt, Joan Nuffield, and Vincent O'Leary (1973), *Four Thousand Lifetimes: A Study of Time Served and Parole Outcome*, Hackensack, NJ: National Council on Crime and Delinquency.

34. Lawrence Greenfeld (1985), "Examining Recidivism," Bureau of Justice Statistics, Washington, DC: U.S. Government Printing Office.

35. Andrew von Hirsch and Kathleen Hanrahan (1978), *Abolish Parole?*, Washington, DC: U.S. Government Printing Office.

36. Andrew von Hirsch and Kathleen Hanrahan (1978), *The Question of Parole: Retention, Reform, or Abolition*, Cambridge, MA: Ballinger. Cited in James R. Davis (1986), *The Science of Criminal Justice*, Jefferson, NC: McFarland, p. 103.

37. Mark G. Neithercutt and Don M. Gottfredson (1973), "Case Load Size Variation and Difference in Probation and Parole Performance," Washington, DC: Federal Judicial Center. Also, Davis, op. cit., p. 103.

Deterrence

CHAPTER **16**

AS THE PUBLIC'S BELIEF IN REHABILITATION OF PRISONERS DECLINED, STATE LEGISLA-tures and the federal government as well began to move toward fixed or **determinate** sentences. Determinate sentencing takes various forms, some more determinate than others. The strictest version does away with min-imum and maximum terms (e.g., four to 10 years). Instead, anyone con-victed of the crime receives the same fixed sentence (e.g., five years), with no parole or early release. Sometimes this policy is called **flat sentencing**. Along similar lines, a state legislature may impose **mandatory sentences** for some crimes. When a sentence is mandatory, the criminal must spend a certain amount of time in prison; nobody convicted of the crime may receive probation or a suspended sentence. Various states have instituted mandatory sentences for crimes like drug offenses, gun crimes, violent crimes, and kidnapping.

Fixed sentences and mandatory sentences remove all discretion from judges and parole boards. These sentences have the apparent virtue of fair-ness and impartiality: People convicted of the same crime serve the same sentence. The weakness of this system is its inflexibility. It may wind up lumping together the hoodlum who robs a stranger at gunpoint with the teenager who takes another kid's pocket money by threatening him with a stick; technically, they are both armed robbers. Some jurisdictions, there-fore, combine determinate sentencing with devices that bring discretion back into the system. In some states with "fixed" sentencing, a prisoner may become eligible for parole after serving some percentage of the sen-tence—usually one-third to one-half. Some states have **presumptive sent-encing**, which resembles determinate sentencing except that judges have some discretion to increase or decrease the presumptive sentence by a few months, depending on the circumstances of the crime and the criminal.

Determinate sentencing has several justifications. It seems fairer: A pri-soner's sentence depends on the crimes committed, not on the ability to win approval from a judge or parole board. Probably more important, at least from the viewpoint of the public, determinate sentencing promises to eliminate leniency. It lets criminals know that they won't be able to get away with crime. A person convicted of a crime will receive the sentence narrowly specified in the law, no matter what.

Determinate sentencing is a popular idea, since many people blame high crime rates on the lenience of the courts. The logic of this widely held, commonsense notion of crime and punishment goes something like this:

> People commit crimes because crime is an easy way to get money—easier, for instance, than working. The way to keep people from committing crimes is to punish them. If criminals are not punished, they will commit more crimes. Worse still, the lack of punishment encourages other potential criminals to join the criminal ranks. The trouble is that criminals are seldom caught; when caught, they are seldom punished; when punished, they get off too lightly. Insofar as crime rates rise or remain high, the criminal justice system (the police, courts, and prisons) is not doing its job. It is not catching and punishing criminals.

Like other commonsense ideas, this one is perfectly logical and corresponds well with the picture many people have of street crime today. The media regularly provide us with stories that confirm this picture: Citizens complain that the police neglected to try to solve a crime ("They didn't even look for fingerprints"); demoralized police officers complain about the futility of arresting criminals when no punishment follows; perpetrators of terrible crimes plea-bargain for light sentences; other criminals are found to have spent little or no time in prison despite a long record of prior arrests; crimes are committed by people who are out on bail or parole. Judged only on this kind of information, the truth of this theory appears obvious. But, as with other seemingly obvious truths, we must test these ideas by more systematic evidence. So in the following pages, I will try to take the ideas in this theory one by one and see what evidence exists to support or contradict them.

The underlying idea of the theory is that of **deterrence**. You can probably find this idea in the earliest writings on human behavior. The first formal statement of it, for criminological purposes, is Cesare Beccaria's essay "On Crimes and Punishments," first published in 1764. Beccaria emphasized that the purpose of punishment is not to demonstrate the evil of the criminal, but prevent crime. The penalty for a crime should be just severe enough to offset the possible gain from the crime. His "utilitarian" theory takes an essentially economic approach. Basically, it is the idea that crime pays. The theory assumes that criminals rationally calculate their costs and benefits. If the benefits outweigh the costs, people will commit crimes. Punishment (time in prison) is one such cost.

Beccaria also outlined the variables which are still considered the basis for research on deterrence: the **certainty, severity**, and **swiftness** of punishment. Research on deterrence asks this: If criminals' chances of getting caught increase, or if their punishment is more severe, or if the punishment more quickly follows the crime, will crime decrease? To give a preview of the results: not much (an oversimplified answer to a complicated question). The research provides only modest support for the theory. It seems that although the notion of deterrence is simple and straightforward, conclusive evidence for it in the criminal justice system is hard to find. Therefore, besides reviewing the results of the various studies, I also will try to outline some of the reasons deterrence is so difficult to prove.

Some of these reasons are methodological. There are many variables besides punishment which may affect crime, and it is very difficult to isolate a single variable and assess its impact apart from the others. It's a little like asking how much difference the manager of a baseball team makes in the team's success. There are many factors (hitting, pitching, fielding) over which the manager has little control but which affect the team's performance. Yet after a bad season, it's the manager who gets fired (especially if he is the manager of the New York Yankees). This may satisfy the general manager or the fans, but how much better will the team do next year? And more important, even if the team improves the next year, how can we be sure it was the new manager who made the difference?

In the same way, different thinkers about crime have their favorite targets to blame as the cause of crime. Whatever the emotional satisfaction of pointing a finger at police or courts or schools or unemployment or . . . (the list is endless), it is the job of social scientists to measure those causes and determine how much difference each one contributes. Unfortunately, even the most advanced statistical techniques cannot give us rock-solid answers, especially when several causes are operating at the same time, and when we do not have the luxury of performing tightly controlled experiments.

In discussing this research, I will sometimes mention methodological problems or suggest other possible explanations for the findings. These points may seem "merely technical," but they are often crucial to understanding not just the piece of research at hand, but the real world that the research is trying to describe. Usually, that world is not the scientific laboratory; it is the real world of crime and criminals, of cops and courts.

SPECIFIC DETERRENCE

In considering the effects of punishment, criminologists distinguish between **specific deterrence** and **general deterrence**. The idea of specific deterrence is that punishing a person for a crime will deter that person from committing crime again. The idea of general deterrence is that punishment will affect the general population, not just the individuals who are caught and punished.

Specific deterrence seems especially simple and logical; it is essentially what psychologists call "operant conditioning"—punishing undesirable behavior, rewarding good behavior. And it works—at least with laboratory animals. Psychologists in the United States have devoted great amounts of laboratory time to experiments which confirm the basic hypotheses of deterrence: The greater the certainty, severity, and swiftness of punishment, the more cooperative a little white rat will be. If you have ever tried to housebreak a dog, your goal was a form of specific deterrence, and the principles you used were those of operant conditioning.

Some psychological experiments with human volunteers have supported the basic ideas of operant conditioning, but these experiments usually occur in the controlled and artificial setting of the laboratory and deal with relatively trivial kinds of behavior. Ideally, in studying deterrence as applied to crime we would experimentally change the certainty, severity, or swiftness of punishment for each person and see how changing these variables affected the person's subsequent crime. But in the real world, criminologists can rarely exercise this kind of control over the relevant variables (though in a few frightening instances, researchers have performed highly unethical experiments on unsuspecting human beings, usually prisoners).[1] Instead of manipulating the important variables, criminology researchers must be satisfied with trying to measure these variables as they occur in the real world, while trying to control statistically for all the other factors that might influence a person's criminal behavior.*

To know whether punishment is a good specific deterrent, we need to measure two variables—the punishment and subsequent crime—and look for a correlation between them. We look for an increase or decrease in the severity of the punishment, the certainty of the punishment, or the swiftness of the punishment, and then see whether that change led to a change in crime. Measuring severity of punishment is fairly easy. Researchers usually measure severity in the same way that courts and criminals do: by sentence length. A criminal's further crime, called **recidivism**, presents a tougher problem. Ideally, we would measure the frequency and seriousness of all crimes committed by released prisoners, whether or not they get caught. Getting this information would require extensive self-report interviews with people who are sometimes very hard to find, and who, for one reason or another, may not be too accurate in their self-reporting. So researchers usually wind up measuring recidivism by arrest or even return to prison. These measures may not be perfect indicators of crime, but they are far more easily available.

Prison as a Specific Deterrent

The data on recidivism do not give much cause for believing that prison is a good specific deterrent. Most criminals (about 60 percent) going to prison have been there before.[2] Most released prisoners are rearrested, and about 40 percent of released prisoners wind up back in prison.†[3] These data are not quite a test of deterrence. We must take a closer look. According to our commonsense theory, the more severe the punishment, the more effective it will be. A light sentence—the proverbial "slap on the wrist"—will do little to deter a criminal from further crime. So, other things being equal, prisoners serving longer sentences should have less recidivism than do those serving shorter terms. However, most research on this question has failed to find any connection between time served and recidivism.[4] Parolees are no more likely to commit further crimes than are prisoners who serve out their full terms.[5] A Wisconsin study of three juvenile "cohorts" (a cohort is a group of people all born in the same year—in this case, groups born in

---

* For more on statistical controls, see Chapter 2.

† The difference between these two statistics (60 percent and 40 percent) is not a contradiction. They represent different ways of measuring recidivism. By analogy, if I wanted to measure "academic recidivism," I might measure the percentage of students getting a D or F on the final exam who also got a D or F on the midterm. To measure it another way, I might take the percentage of students who got a low grade on the mid-term and then went on to get a low grade on the final. The two percentages will not necessarily be the same.

1942, 1948, and 1955) concluded: "What we found, in a variety of analyses and with considerable regularity, was an increase in frequency and severity of misbehavior in the periods following those in which sanctions were administered."[6] In other words, kids were more delinquent after being punished than they had been before. This "reverse deterrence effect" of prison may hold for adults as well. One study of 4,000 released prisoners showed that among those locked up for the same crime (e.g., robbery), those who served longer sentences were if anything more criminal after release than were those who served shorter terms.[7]

Why doesn't punishment deter? Why might it even increase recidivism? The most obvious answers are those from differential association theory and labeling theory: Punishment usually takes the form of imprisonment, and prisons are "schools for crime." In prison, inmates learn the techniques, attitudes, and values of the criminal world. Then, once they are released, they may also find that other people are less willing to accept them into the straight world. In fact, one labeling theorist looking at the results of recidivism research has recommended "radical nonintervention" with juvenile delinquents: "*leave kids alone wherever possible*"[8] (emphasis in original).

Politically, the call for less punishment is obviously part of a generally liberal position on crime, a position which would concentrate on changing society rather than punishing individual criminals. Conservatives, on the other hand, see the answer to crime in "getting tough" with lawbreakers. Accordingly, one study of deterrence conducted by political conservatives did find evidence for the deterrent effect of punishment. Instead of just asking whether a person was ever rearrested, these researchers measured the number of rearrests. They reasoned that even if punishment did not reform a boy entirely, it might still reduce the amount of crime he will commit. Their sample was a group of 317 boys classified as "serious delinquents." (How serious? Although the average age was 16, their combined arrest records included 14 homicides, nearly 200 armed robberies, and over 700 burglaries. And those were only arrests. The actual number of crimes probably was much higher.)[9]

Under the program studied, a boy could be sentenced to one of five alternatives—anything from group homes to wilderness experience to intensive counseling. Boys who did poorly in these might be sent to ordinary juvenile prisons. Comparing the boys' arrest rates before sentencing with their arrest rates after release, researchers found a surprising result. Everything "worked." Boys averaged fewer arrests after release, no matter what type of institution they had been sent to. Some programs were more effective than others. Prison was more effective than "in-home" supervision, but rural camps were more effective than prisons.

Apparently, the reduction in crime shows that arrest, sentencing, and punishment—any sort of punishment—act as a specific deterrent. However, some critics have questioned this conclusion. There may be other reasons the boys committed less crime after serving whatever type of sentence they received. Suppose that delinquents who commit crimes are something like "streak hitters" in baseball. Sometimes, for reasons we do not understand, they commit crimes fairly frequently; at other times they go into a "slump" and commit fewer crimes. Since delinquents are much more likely to get caught during a high-frequency period, the boys coming into the program were probably on a streak. They might have cooled off afterward, no matter what. It was time, more than imprisonment or wilderness, that caused the decrease in their crime. As one critic puts it, "Why should . . . three months of counseling at a community center cause a long-time, repeat offender to cut his crime rate in half?"[10]

My own conclusion is that prison is not much of a specific deterrent. A high proportion of released prisoners, despite their best intentions (or at least their statements to parole boards), return to crime.*

GENERAL DETERRENCE

Societies create laws and punishments not just to punish, and perhaps reform, those who are caught. The criminal justice system may also reduce crime through the "general deterrent" effects of punishment. This phrase means that the mere possibility of being caught and punished should have some deterrent effect. Even people who have never been caught will refrain from crime because they fear the possible punishment.

To assess general deterrence, criminologists use the same basic ideas as for specific deterrence, except that instead of measuring the effect of punishment on individuals, they look at its effect on the general population. Instead of measuring the crime of each individual (i.e., recidivism), studies of general deterrence measure the crime of the general population; that is, these studies look at crime rates.

To take a simple example, suppose that in order to reduce illegal parking on campus, a university raises the fines for violations, instructs the campus police to ticket more frequently, and even tows away illegally parked cars. The administration has increased both the severity and the certainty of punishment. To see if the "crime rate" has changed, all we have to do is check the parking lots before and after the new policy and count the number of illegally parked cars. The chances are that more people—even those who have not been ticketed or towed—will obey the parking rules.

General deterrence of "real" crime can be far more complicated. Some of the problems involved can be seen in the research on one special topic—one that is not a typical example of general deterrence, but which is worth exploring since it is the subject of so much controversy: the death penalty.

---

* Many people believe that prison is more of a deterrent to white-collar criminals. However, white-collar crimes are discovered so infrequently that measuring recidivism accurately or even usefully is practically impossible. The same technical problem also makes it hard to assess the impact of punishment on drunk drivers.

Capital Punishment as a General Deterrent

As fear of crime and concern over crime have risen in the past two decades, so has support for the death penalty. The debate over capital punishment raises several questions. Is it effective? Is it fair and just? Is it moral? Is it legal? Most people taking sides on the issue make their decision on the basis of morality; legislatures and courts must consider additional questions of legality. On these moral and legal questions, scientific research counts for little. Social science cannot tell us whether capital punishment is morally right or wrong; whether a criminal "deserves" to die, or whether the state has a moral right to kill people. Nor can social science settle legal questions. The Supreme Court has considered sociological evidence in death penalty cases, but such evidence plays only a small part in the Court's decisions.*

The debate over capital punishment also involves the question of general deterrence. Proponents of the death penalty often claim that potential killers would be less likely to kill if they knew they were risking execution. Opponents argue that the death penalty is no more a deterrent than are long prison terms. Both sides are making statements of cause and effect, not morality. In theory at least, these statements about deterrence can be tested by empirical evidence. Ideally, a research study would conclude that, other things being equal, the death penalty does (or does not) reduce the rates of those crimes to which it applies. Unfortunately, actual research is not so simple, for—especially in the case of the death penalty—other things are seldom equal.

How can we know whether the death penalty deters the crime to which it applies—murder? One of the first systematic studies on the subject compared murder rates of states with the death penalty and states without it. If the death penalty is a deterrent, then (other things being equal) states with the death penalty should have lower rates of murder. In fact, it turned out to be the other way round.[11] The murder rates in non–death penalty states were lower than the national rate and lower than the average rate for their respective regions. Table 16–1 is based on data from 1988, when only 11 states had no death penalty. Still, of those 11 states, only two had murder rates higher than the national average of 8.4. Among death penalty states, 14 of 39 (35 percent) had murder rates above the national average. The positive correlation (more death penalty, more murder) was even stronger 10 or 15 years ago when fewer states had the death penalty. If the correlation had been negative (more death penalty, less murder), we would have taken it as evidence that the death penalty reduces murder. Does the actual pos-

---

* In *Furman v. Georgia* (1972), the decision which invalidated all existing death penalty laws, the Court made use of social science data on deterrence. The Court has also used sociological data on the racially biased application of the death penalty for rape. However, the Court chose to discount similar information in *McClesky v. Kemp* (1987).

Table 16–1 ▪ **Murder Rates in States with and without the Death Penalty, 1988 (by region)**

States with death penalty		States without death penalty	
Connecticut	5.4	Maine	3.1
New Hampshire	2.3	Massachusetts	3.5
Vermont	2.0	Rhode Island	4.1
New Jersey	5.3	New York	12.5
Pennsylvania	5.5		
Illinois	8.6	Michigan	10.8
Indiana	6.4	Wisconsin	3.0
Ohio	5.4		
Missouri	8.0	Iowa	1.7
Nebraska	3.6	Minnesota	2.9
South Dakota	3.1	North Dakota	1.8
		Kansas	3.4
Delaware	5.2	West Virginia	4.9
Maryland	9.7		
Virginia	7.8		
North Carolina	7.8		
South Carolina	9.3		
Georgia	11.7		
Florida	11.4		
Alabama	9.9		
Kentucky	6.2		
Mississippi	8.6		
Tennessee	9.4		
Arkansas	8.7		
Louisiana	11.6		
Oklahoma	7.4		
Texas	12.1		
Arizona	6.6		
Colorado	8.5		
Idaho	5.7		
Montana	3.6		
Nevada	2.6		
New Mexico	10.5		
Utah	11.5		
Wyoming	2.5		
Alaska	5.7		
California	10.4		
Hawaii	4.0		
Oregon	5.1		
Washington	5.7		

Source: UCR, 1988. "Capital Punishment, 1988," Bureau of Justice Statistics Bulletin, 1989. Washington, DC: U.S. Government Printing Office.

itive correlation mean then that the death penalty causes higher murder rates? Probably not. It may also logically mean that murder causes the death penalty. Look again at the table. Many of the states contributing to the positive correlation (high murder rates accompanying the death penalty) are in the South. Most Southern states have the death penalty, and most also have above-average murder rates. It may be that these states have the death penalty because they have had high murder rates—just as the increase in murder rates in Northern states has led to a demand for the death penalty there.

Does the death penalty affect the murder rate? Or does the murder rate affect the death penalty? Perhaps, both effects are occurring at the same time, creating a tangle known as **simultaneity**. Or perhaps there is a third explanation. When A and B are correlated, there are at least three possible explanations: A causes B (death penalty causes higher murder rates); B causes A (higher murder rates cause the death penalty); or a third factor, C, is causing both A and B (high murder rates and the death penalty). Theorists who favor the idea of the "subculture of violence" might argue that this third factor is culture. In Southern culture, according to this view, people see death as a more acceptable means of resolving conflicts. Individuals will more readily use deadly violence to settle personal matters, and the state will more readily use deadly violence to settle criminal matters. Therefore, the South will have both more murders and more executions.

The national figures on murder and capital punishment may not be a fair test of deterrence theory, for they are really comparing the South with other regions. A good test would control for geographical region and for other factors that might be associated with murder rates: poverty, economic inequality, percentages of blacks and whites, or urban and rural populations. A better study would compare states similar in all respects except the death penalty—some with, some without. Or a study might trace murder rates in a single state when that state changes its death penalty laws. Some states have abolished their death penalties; other states have instituted the death penalty where there had previously been none. Of course, a state's decisions on the death penalty may depend on changes in its murder rate—again, the simultaneity problem. But conveniently for social scientists, in 1967 the federal courts ordered a moratorium in all states on all executions. The court, facing several death penalty cases, ruled that until the Supreme Court resolved the constitutionality of the death penalty, nobody would be executed.

Raymond Bowers took advantage of this moratorium on executions to assess the deterrent effects of capital punishment. Figure 16–1 shows his graph of the murder rates in neighboring (and presumably similar) states with and without the death penalty. If the death penalty is a deterrent, we should find that in non–death penalty states, 1967 should not mark any change in murder rates. Rhode Island, for instance, had no death penalty before 1967 and no death penalty after then. On the other hand, neigh-

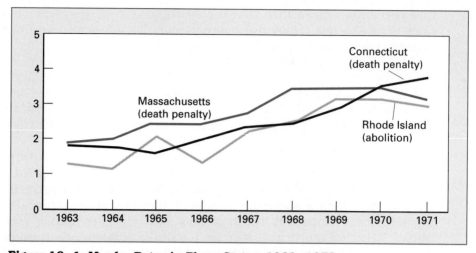

Figure 16–1 Murder Rates in Three States, 1963–1972
Source: Raymond Bowers (1974), Executions in America, Lexington, MA; D. C. Heath.

boring Massachusetts and Connecticut had the death penalty up until 1967, when it was suspended by the moratorium. If the death penalty had been deterring murders in Massachusetts and Connecticut, then we should see an increase in murder after its removal in 1967.

As you can see from Figure 16–1, no such change occurred. Murder rates rose gradually before 1967 in all three states, and continued to rise at about the same rate after 1967. There was no difference between the death penalty

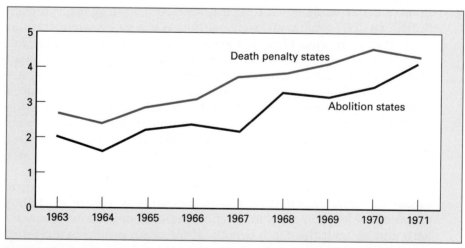

Figure 16–2 Murder Rates in Death-Penalty and Non-Death Penalty States, 1963–1972
Source: Raymond Bowers (1974), Executions in America, Lexington, MA: D. C. Heath.

states and the non–death penalty states attributable to the moratorium. Bowers compared other sets of states, and none of the comparisons showed evidence for a deterrent effect (see Figure 16–2).

The Death Penalty—Severity or Certainty

Some critics (generally those who favor the death penalty) point out that this kind of research focuses only on severity; it completely ignores the question of certainty. Suppose a state has the death penalty but never actually applies it, or applies it only very rarely. The penalty is severe, to be sure, but its certainty is very low. Such an uncertain penalty will lose all its possible deterrent effect. In fact, during the years covered in Bowers's research, many of the death penalty states executed the same number of people as non–death penalty states: zero. The other states executed only one or two each. Even for murderers in the South, execution was hardly a certainty.

In 1972, in the case of *Furman v. Georgia*, the Supreme Court ruled that the death penalty, as it was then administered in the various states, was unconstitutional. The Court based its decision partly on the lack of deterrence. The Court reasoned, in part, that the death penalty was so extreme that if it provided society no more protection than did long prison terms, then it constituted "cruel and unusual punishment" and was therefore in violation of the Eighth Amendment of the Constitution.[12]

Soon after this decision, Isaac Ehrlich, an economist, published an article claiming a deterrent effect for the death penalty. Proponents of the death penalty quickly seized upon this research as support for their position. Controlling for other variables, Ehrlich looked at executions and homicide rates in the United States between 1932 and 1969. He estimated that "an additional execution per year . . . may have resulted in . . . seven or eight fewer murders."[13] Subsequently, however, other economists and sociologists have reanalyzed Ehrlich's data and methods and found cause to question his conclusions.[14] Most of this analysis is too technical to summarize here, but to cite one criticism, the (negative) correlation between executions and murder rates occurred only in the years from 1962 to 1969.

Figure 16–3 shows both the murder rate and the number of executions for 1932 to 1969. As you can see, beginning in about 1940, the number of executions dropped steadily—from nearly 200 in 1938 to fewer than 60 in 1960, and only two in 1966. At the same time, murder rates declined slightly until the late 1950s but increased sharply beginning in the early 1960s.

Cover up the left part of the graph, leaving visible only the years after 1960. The effect looks impressive: Executions drop off to nothing, and the murder rate rises drastically. Now cover up the last 10 years of the graph and look only at 1932 to 1960. As executions decreased, so did the murder rate. What happened to the deterrent effect? If the death penalty is a de-

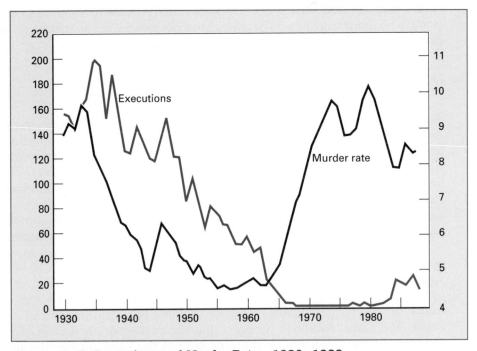

Figure 16–3 Executions and Murder Rates, 1930–1988
Source: U.S. Bureau of the Census (1985), Historical Statistics of the United States, Washington DC:
U.S. Government Printing Office. Sourcebook—1988.

terrent, it should have deterred in the 1930s, 1940s, and 1950s, not just the 1960s. And a similar study using data from Canada in the years 1926 to 1960 also failed to find any deterrent effect.[15] If the death penalty is a deterrent, it should deter Canadians as well as Americans.

Even in the 1960s, the decrease in executions was probably not the cause of the increase in murder. This was, after all, a decade in which all crimes were increasing dramatically. Since the death penalty does not apply to robbery, larceny, or auto theft, the rise in these crimes must have been caused by some combination of factors other than the decline in executions. It is likely that these other factors, and not the decrease of executions, also caused the increase in homicide.

Can we conclude then that the death penalty has no deterrent effect? Not quite. Most social scientists state their conclusions more cautiously, saying instead that if there is a deterrent effect, nobody has yet demonstrated it. In any case, research on the death penalty will continue, and the next few years may be quite important. Beginning in 1977, the Supreme Court began to uphold several death penalty statutes, and although the 600 prisoners on death row at the time of the Furman decision were released from death row (though not from prison), many others have been sentenced under new laws. As of 1990, over 2,000 inmates are on death row. As their appeals run out (especially since many government officials, including the Chief Justice of the United States, wish to limit death penalty appeals), the number of executions will rise, though it is doubtful it will ever reach the three-per-week average of 1935. Nevertheless, if more executions deter, then murder rates should drop dramatically. The evidence as of this writing is hardly convincing. In the first seven years after the Supreme Court began allowing executions (1977 to 1983), only 11 people were executed and the murder rate went from 8.8 to 8.3 per 100,000. In the next six years, 110 people were executed, and the murder rate rose from 8.3 to 8.7. Four states—Florida, Georgia, Louisiana, and Texas—accounted for 70 percent of these executions. In the heavy-execution period (1983 to 1989), murder rates decreased in Texas, increased in Georgia, increased slightly in Louisiana, and remained essentially unchanged in Florida.[16]

General Deterrence and Other Crimes

Even if capital punishment were a sure deterrent, it would have little impact on the overall crime rate. Capital crimes constitute only a small fraction of all crime. Moreover, while the Supreme Court in recent years has upheld a number of death penalty statutes, it has also restricted the crimes punishable by the death penalty. In effect, the death penalty applies only to crimes which involve the taking of life in a particularly horrible or cold-blooded manner. Rape, which—especially in the South—used to carry the death penalty, is no longer subject to capital punishment. Even the typical homicide—an argument leading to a fight in which someone gets killed—is not sufficiently aggravated to warrant the death penalty.

Penalties exist for all crimes. Periodically, politicians and other public voices call for stiffening these penalties on the grounds that "getting tough" will reduce crime. Their proposals are based on the idea of general deterrence, and again the questions are the same: Will increased penalties or increased certainty of punishment for a crime keep more people from committing that crime?

Research on the general deterrence of noncapital crimes runs into the same kinds of problems that complicate death penalty research. First, it is hard to measure punishments and crimes accurately. Second, it is very difficult to isolate the variables we want to examine—certainty or severity of punishment—from other factors which may affect crime rates: factors like poverty, inequality, geography, age, and culture. Third, even when we find a correlation, it will not always be clear what is causing what.

The Police as a Deterrent

The police represent the first step in deterring crime. Citizens look to the police to prevent crime, and the police, too, may think of themselves as a "thin blue line" separating civilization from chaos or at least from crime. Police represent the "certainty" factor in deterrence: In theory, the more police there are, the more likely a criminal will be caught; the greater the certainty of being caught, the less crime. This logical idea—more police, less crime—may be highly overrated.

To begin with, the ratio of police to population varies among U.S. cities. Some cities have fewer than two officers per 1,000 people; other cities have as many as 7 per 1,000. If nothing but deterrence were involved, then the higher the ratio of cops to people, the lower the crime rate should be. But in fact, there is no such correlation.[17] Of course, these intercity (or "cross-sectional") comparisons run into the simultaneity problem: Higher crime may cause cities to hire more police. The question might better be answered by "time-series" data that trace crime rates when a single locality receives extra police.

Kansas City Streets, New York Subways

Two well-known experiments on this question have demonstrated the limits of police deterrence. One took place in Kansas City, where, as in most U.S. cities, preventive police patrolling took the form of squad cars cruising the streets. Five of the 15 "beats" studied continued this practice. Another five beats, similar to the first five in other respects, received "proactive patrol"—that is, the number of squad cars patrolling the area was doubled or tripled. The remaining five beats, also matched for similarity to the others, received only "reactive" patrol: Police cars entered the area only in response to calls; there was no routine cruising. The experiment stayed in effect for a year.

At the end of the year, researchers could find no conclusive evidence of deterrence. Neither intensifying nor eliminating routine patrols significantly affected the crime rate one way or another. And researchers measured crime both by official police statistics and by victimization surveys.*[18]

The other experiment involved a different type of police patrol. In 1965, in response to an increase in subway crimes, New York City put special

---

* In reality, there were some differences in crime rates, but they were not large enough to be "statistically significant." Some criminologists think that if the experiment had used more than 15 sectors, the results would have passed the statistician's criteria.

It also turned out that for the reactive (no-patrol) areas, the police patrolling around the borders or responding to a call did so in a highly visible way. So, ironically, in the interests of preventing crime (or doing what they thought would prevent crime), the police may have helped prove that they do not prevent crime.

patrols on subways during the high-crime nighttime hours—the 8 p.m to 4 a.m. shift. Police statistics soon showed a substantial reduction in crime during these hours of beefed-up patrolling. (Some of this decrease occurred on paper only; police administrators subtly encouraged patrolling officers writing up crime reports to downgrade the seriousness of the crime or even to change the time of occurrence so that serious crime would fall outside the target hours.[19]) Even so, crime really did decrease on the 8-to-4 shift; for a short while crime even decreased during the hours when patrols had not been increased. However, the cost was enormous. It was estimated that each deterred felony cost an additional $35,000 (and that was in 1965 dollars; allowing for inflation, that sum would be equal to more than $100,000 today).[20]

These two studies illustrate several points about deterrence. They show first that in actual practice, experiments in the field don't always go exactly the way sociologists draw them up on paper. People in the criminal justice system may muddy the scientific purity of experimental design and data-gathering. The studies also demonstrate the difficulty of generalizing about deterrence. Increased policing reduced crime in the New York subways, but not in the streets of Kansas City. These contradictory results mean that we need to be more specific in the way we ask questions. Instead of asking the broad question, "Do the police deter crime?," we must specify the type of patrolling, the setting, and the type of crime. Subway cars and stations offer criminals opportunities different from those offered by city streets. Cops on foot pose one kind of threat to potential criminals, patrol cars another.

The Economics of Deterrence

Policymakers also must ask the very practical question: How much does it cost? How much deterrence does each cop bring? In Kansas City, adding a second or third patrol car did not bring significant reductions in crime, but perhaps quadrupling the patrols would have. Perhaps there was some **threshold** level that had to be reached before police became a deterrent. On the other hand, there may be a "law of diminishing returns"—a decrease in what economists call the **marginal** effect of each extra cop. For example, a study done in Great Britain found that increasing the number of bobbies on a beat from zero to one reduced the number of reported crimes. Increasing patrols thereafter from one to two or three or four brought no further reductions.[21] That is, the marginal effect of the first cop was very large; the marginal effect of each cop added after that was very small.

This result suggests the commonsense conclusion that having no police at all in the streets would bring a large increase in crime. But how can we know? As it turns out, the police on occasion voluntarily provide an experiment in zero-policing: They go on strike. Sometimes crime rises dramatically in response. For example, during a 17-hour police strike in Montreal in 1968, bank robberies occurred at 12 times their normal level.[22] But the results of these "experiments" are not always what we expect. In the 1970s, there were police strikes in at least 11 U.S. cities, strikes lasting anywhere from three days to a month. Deterrence would predict that crime would go up during the strike and then decrease when the police came back on the job. In some cities, for some crimes, that is what happened. But in many more cases, there was no such consistent pattern of increase and decrease.[23]

Explaining the Weakness of Police Deterrence

What started out as a simple question—do the police prevent crime?—has become quite complicated, and the "obvious" answer now seems in doubt. The deterrent effect of the thin blue line is, apparently, fairly weak. It is not hard to think of reasons the police might not be such an overwhelming deterrent. For one thing, police can deter only those crimes that they might see. Indoor crimes—especially assaults, rapes, murders, and other nonutilitarian crimes between acquaintances—will not be affected by more cops in the street. Second, police cannot be everywhere at once. Even the most impulsive, opportunistic criminals can wait to find a time or place with no blue uniforms in sight. The subway study, for example, found evidence for this **displacement** of crime. Subway crime diminished, but crime on city buses increased. Criminals who are more professional may be especially likely to displace their work to other times or places or to switch to lower-risk crimes. A special program to reduce robbery, for example, may merely drive criminals into other lines of work (e.g., burglary).[24] The evidence from police "crackdowns" on specific areas or types of crime shows that a massive police effort does have a deterrent effect, but that much crime is merely displaced (depending on the type of crime) and that the economic cost is considerable.[25]

Another possible explanation is that mere police presence does not necessarily increase the certainty of punishment. For punishment to be certain, police must actually catch the criminals. Therefore, we ought to count not the number of police but the number or proportion of arrests.

Arrest Rates and Crime Rates

When the police arrest someone for a reported crime, the crime is said to be "cleared by arrest." The clearance rate is the percentage of "crimes known to the police" which are "cleared by arrest." Researchers have sometimes used this rate as a measure of certainty of punishment. If criminals think they can easily avoid arrest, they will be bolder about committing crimes. Deterrence theory would predict that when the police clear a greater percentage of crimes, the crime rate will decrease. And in fact, research has generally found an inverse correlation between the two: The higher the clearance rate, the lower the crime rate. The obvious conclusion is that arrests by the police deter criminals.

Such a conclusion, while obvious and logical, might not be the only explanation for the correlation. For one thing, these figures (clearance rates and crime rates) come from police sources and are highly vulnerable to inaccuracies in police bookkeeping.* To take a hypothetical example, suppose our city has a population of 100,000; in 1990 it had 5,000 burglaries. Of these 5,000 burglaries, 500 were cleared by arrest. Suppose that in the next year (1991) the actual number of burglaries committed and cleared remains the same, but we decide not to record 2,000 of the unsolvable ones. The figures will look like those in Table 16–2.

Through a little artful record keeping, we have improved our city's image; we have lowered crime and raised police effectiveness. But more than that, someone looking at these figures might take them as evidence for deterrence: As the clearance rate rose from 10.0 percent to 16.7 percent (i.e., as criminals faced a higher risk of arrest), people committed fewer crimes. (The numbers in this hypothetical example—40 percent of crimes kept off the books—are not so farfetched. Prior to 1965, New York City police kept about 30 percent of reported robberies off the records, thereby maintaining clearance rates for robbery at more than double what they actually were.[26])

Simultaneity

Even if the police faithfully record every crime, the cause-and-effect relationship between clearance rates and crime rates may not be so clear. The data for most of this research comes from the 1960s, when clearance rates were falling and crime rates were rising. One plausible explanation is that the lower risk of getting caught encouraged more people to commit more crimes: A causes B. What about the possibility that B causes A, i.e., that

Table 16–2 ■ **Clearance Rates and Crime Rates (Hypothetical Figures)**

	1990	*1991*
Clearance rate	$\dfrac{500}{5,000} = 10.0\%$	$\dfrac{500}{5,000} = 16.7\%$
Crime rate	$\dfrac{5,000}{100,000} = 5,000$	$\dfrac{3,000}{100,000} = 3,000$

* For more on the police and crime statistics, see Chapter 3.

Table 16–3 ▪ Deterence Factors and Robbery Rates, 1959–1971

A Year	B Robbery rate	C Robbery clearance rate	D Robbery conviction rate	E Clearance per 100,000 population	F Conviction per 100,000 population
1959	40.3	42.5	64.8	17.1	11.1
1962	51.3	40.5	54.4	20.8	11.0
1965	61.4	38.4	46.7	23.6	11.0
1968	131.0	27.3	41.1	35.7	14.6
1971	187.1	24.6	31.5	46.0	14.5

Source: Lee R. McPheters (1976) "Criminal Behavior and the Gains from Crime," *Criminology,* vol. 14, no. 1, pp. 137–52.

rising crime rates lead to lower clearance rates? Look at the figures in Table 16–3.

First, look just at the first four columns. They seem to support the idea of deterrence: as smaller proportions of robbers were arrested (column C) and convicted (column D), the robbery rate (column B) increased. The same data from these columns are presented graphically in Figure 16–4. A deterrence theorist would conclude that the decrease in certainty of punishment encouraged robbers to commit more crime.

Before we accept this conclusion, we must consider the problem of simultaneity. It is equally logical to argue that the increase in robberies caused

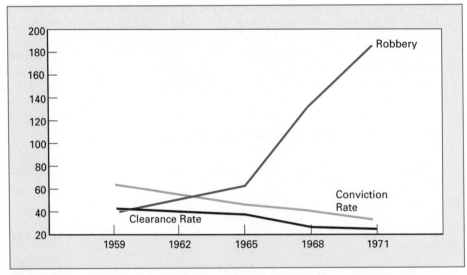

Figure 16–4 Robbery, Robbery Clearance Rates, and Robbery Conviction Rates, 1959–1972

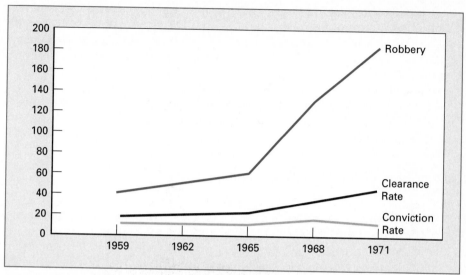

Figure 16–5 Robbery, Robbery Clearance Rates, and Robbery Conviction Rates per 100,000 Population, 1959–1972

the decrease in clearance rates and conviction rates. Look at the last two columns of Table 16–3, or their graphed version in Figure 16–5.

Column E shows that as robbery increased, the police were arresting more people for robbery. Column F shows that eventually the courts were convicting more people of robbery. But the volume of robbery was increasing much more rapidly than was the capacity of the criminal justice system. Although this capacity gradually grew, it could not keep up with the increase in robberies. So instead of a decrease in arrest and conviction rates causing an increase in robbery, it was the other way around: An increase in robbery caused a decrease in the rates (but not the absolute numbers) of robbers arrested and convicted.

One method of resolving this "simultaneity" problem is to allow for a certain time lag between a change in arrest rates and a change in robbery rates. Will a change in this year's clearance rate affect next year's crime rate? Will a change in this year's crime rate affect next year's clearance rate? This kind of research requires statistical techniques too complicated to review here, but the answer from at least one study is that "arrest rates have no measurable effect on reported crime rates."[27]

The Police and Crime—A Summary

These conclusions are tentative, and there are probably criminologists who would disagree with some of them. First, it is likely that without police our cities would eventually see large increases in crime. Second, increasing police patrols beyond present levels can deter some crime that patrol officers might happen upon, such as auto theft or street robbery. But more foot patrols or more squad cars cruising the streets do little to decrease crime in more private or indoor places. Some studies suggest that more police effort and more arrests may reduce crime, but methodological issues make this conclusion uncertain. In addition, the number of crimes deterred may be relatively small, while the cost of added police will be large. Massive police crackdowns deter crime in the areas where they occur but displace some crime to other areas.

Conviction and Imprisonment as Deterrents

Some proponents of deterrence argue that the police can deter crime only if the arrests they make lead to real punishment. If the courts do not convict and imprison criminals, the lack of punishment will undermine the deterrent value of arrest (and also undermine the morale of the police). If the courts "get tough" on criminals, so the argument goes, crime will decrease.

Getting tough usually means increasing the severity of punishment. Legislatures rewrite the criminal statutes, raising minimum sentences and allowing for harsher sentences, including the death penalty. Increasing the certainty of punishment is more difficult, since legislatures cannot increase the ability of the police to catch criminals. Lawmakers can, however, make punishment more certain by requiring mandatory sentences and by calling for the abolition or restriction of plea-bargaining.

(I should note here that prison terms in the United States—both official sentences and actual time served—are already longer than those in other Western industrialized countries. Most of these other industrialized democracies have also abolished capital punishment. Nor is punishment in those countries more certain than in the United States. The ratio of imprisonment to the number of reported crimes is about the same in England or Germany as it is in the United States.[28] But European countries have much lower crime rates. These facts themselves should throw some doubt on the notion that crime control is mostly a matter of deterrence.)

What results do these legal changes bring? Unfortunately, the way courts actually work makes it difficult to evaluate most of the evidence. In general, the few available research studies point to a deterrent effect: Higher rates of conviction and imprisonment accompany lower crime rates.[29] But as with other deterrence research, these studies have problems of simultaneity—of what is causing what. This chapter's tables and graphs showing an inverse relation between arrests and crime during the 1960s also showed a similar pattern for rates of conviction and imprisonment. During these years, a smaller percentage of criminals were sent to prison, and crime rates rose. Does this correlation mean that criminals became bolder because they knew their chances of imprisonment were smaller? Or does it mean that the courts and prisons could not keep up with the rapid increase in crime?

Passing "get tough" laws is fairly easy. Implementing the law and reducing crime, however, are quite different matters. The history of New York's 1973 drug law provides a typical example. Governor Rockefeller, responding to public concern over crime and drugs (mostly heroin), proposed a very strict drug law, which the legislature promptly enacted. Known around Albany (the state capital) as the "Attila-the-Hun Law," it called for mandatory prison terms for convicted drug dealers, eliminated plea-bargaining in drug cases, and set up additional courts to deal with drug cases.

Six days after the law went into effect, the governor was quoted as saying, "Heroin seems to be disappearing, drying up in the city."[30] He did not specify the data on which he based this conclusion. Five years later, a study by the New York Bar Association concluded that the law had not had any effect on drug use in New York. Estimating changes in drug-related crime, number of addicts, and quantity of drugs, the study concluded that these changes were no different from those that occurred in other cities in states that had not passed such punitive laws.[31] The governor's assessment was a bit premature and a bit too optimistic.*

Deterring Gun Crimes

In later years, some states have tried to enact similar laws to reduce gun crimes. However, the laws do not always have the desired effect—either in the courts or in the streets. In the 1970s, as Detroit was becoming known as the murder capital of the United States, the Michigan state legislature passed a law which added an automatic two years to the sentence of anyone possessing firearms while committing a felony. An armed robber, instead of getting a five-year sentence, would now get five for the robbery plus two for the gun. The two-year supplement was automatic and could not be plea-bargained. The law went into effect amid much publicity in the news, on billboards, and on bumper stickers ("One with a Gun Gets You Two").

A follow-up study three years later found two major results. First, the law did not greatly affect the length of sentences. Second, the law did not affect gun crimes. To understand why the law had not really made sentences longer, remember the concept of judicial discretion. Judges could alter sentences on the original felony to keep total time, as one judge explained,

---

* Cynics pointed out that the law was by no means a total loss. It had allowed Rockefeller to increase his political capital, both with the public and with local politicians. Then, as now, being four-square against drugs was good public relations. As for real politics, to handle the predicted increase in drug trials, the law provided for 40 additional judges. Forty judgeships to dispense is a hefty piece of political patronage.

pretty much the same. So you didn't say this is an armed robber, a five-year armed robber and now he is a five-year armed robber plus the two-year gun. . . . No, I'd do two plus three, for sure.[32]

So the only sentences actually changed by the law were those that previously would have been less than two years.

As for crime, there were no decreases attributable to the new law. Armed robbers did not switch from guns to less lethal weapons. Firearm homicides declined slightly, but firearm assaults increased. That is, people were shooting at each other just as much, but for some reason (probably chance) their shots were not as accurate.

Proponents of deterrence argue that crime did not change because judges refused to increase the severity of punishment.[33] However, this explanation seems unlikely. The media campaign had created an impression of increased severity, and it would have taken some time for contrary information, sentence by sentence, to become known. More likely, robbers continued to use guns for their own safety and convenience in carrying out their crimes. Given the risk of confronting a victim who might well be packing his own gun, robbers would just as soon risk the extra two years and carry their own firearms.[34]

In Massachusetts, a similar gun law—called Bartley-Fox, after its two authors—required a one-year minimum sentence in some gun offenses. A follow-up study of the law's first year showed that Massachusetts judges, unlike those in Michigan, had followed the spirit of the law in sentencing offenders. The report also found that the law had caused "a small but demonstrable reduction of violent crime."

Even so, the law was not necessarily a cure-all. True, gun robberies decreased, but non–gun robberies increased; gun and nongun assaults followed a similar pattern. It looked as if criminals were responding to the new law—by changing their weapons rather than closing up shop. Then, in the third year that Bartley-Fox was in effect, gun robberies increased.[35] Perhaps the publicity effects that accompanied the early stages of the law had worn off. But where do potential robbers get their information about what's really going on in the courts—from the media or from other robbers they know? If they do rely mostly on the criminal grapevine, then as more and more robbers went to prison for gun robberies, the effects of deterrence should have increased, and gun robbery incidence should have gone down. But that is not what happened.

Why Deterrence Is Hard to Find

Deterrence, which at first seems so obvious a factor in crime, has turned out to be very difficult to demonstrate conclusively. No wonder people become so frustrated with social scientists. Instead of being able to confirm an obvious idea, researchers bring back little more than uncertainty and tentative conclusions.

The absence of solid evidence of deterrence may be more than just a matter of research difficulties. Perhaps criminals cannot be deterred. Or, to put it more accurately, perhaps our criminal justice system cannot increase certainty and severity sufficiently to have any impact on crime rates. This is a controversial view. After all, if a change in the system could deter even one additional criminal out of 10 potential criminals, or deter a criminal so that he commits nine crimes where he might have committed 10, the crime rate would drop by 10 percent. That would mean a reduction of over 1 million "serious" crimes in the United States each year. But consider why criminal justice policies may not deter criminals.

Deterrence, Knowledge, and Perception

Most research on deterrence tries to find correlations between certainty and severity of punishment on the one hand, and crime rates on the other. Usually, the correlations are very weak. One reason for the lack of deterrence might be that criminals are just not aware of clearance rates, conviction rates, or sentence length. Think of this in terms of yourself. Suppose you are thinking of committing a burglary. Do you know what your chances of getting caught are; and if caught, your probability of being convicted and sentenced; and if sentenced, the minimum, maximum, and average terms for burglary? Do you know whether your local clearance rates for burglary have increased or decreased recently? Most likely, you have no knowledge of the actual statistics on these crucial questions.

According to deterrence theory, if increased certainty or severity is to deter criminals, the criminals must know about these factors. Or, more precisely, criminals should be deterred if they *perceive* a high probability of being caught and punished, regardless of the reality of these risks. For example, many juvenile delinquents reduce their crimes or cease altogether as they get to be 17 or 18, and one reason may be that they know that they face adult courts and prisons rather than the juvenile system. The same goes for adult criminals with prior convictions. As one "serious" (though not professional) thief put it, "I know I'll grab big time if I go up again." (He also listed other, nondeterrence reasons for his early retirement from crime.)[36]

On the other hand, knowledge of harsh penalties may have little effect on those who commit crimes. Criminals generally have a more accurate knowledge of criminal penalties than does the general, noncriminal public. Most straight people tend to err on the low side; they think sentences are more lenient than they actually are. Now, according to deterrence theory, who should be more likely to commit crimes—those who think penalties are lenient or those who think penalties are harsh? In fact, contrary to what deterrence would predict, those who think penalties are harsh (i.e., criminals) commit crimes, while those who think penalties lenient (i.e., the public) are more deterred.[37] So while the public and politicians call for more severe sentences, criminals themselves discount the effectiveness of such changes. A questionnaire given to California prisoners included the following item: "If prison time were a lot harder, most men who've done time would go straight when they got out." Only 13 percent agreed; 83 percent disagreed (and most of these checked "strongly disagree").[38]

Nor do criminals think that certainty of punishment has much effect on their decisions. The same questionnaire had the following statement: "It's possible to get so good at crime you'll never get caught." Nearly 80 percent disagreed.[39] Criminals know they are going to get caught and go to prison. As a common saying in the criminal world advises, "If you can't do the time, don't do the crime."[40] Of course, criminals do not ignore the problem completely. They try to minimize the chance of getting caught; they commit their crimes when nobody else (especially a police officer) will notice. But they rarely make a careful assessment of their actual chances.

If criminals think that getting caught is so certain, why do they commit the crimes? If asked later about the contradiction, a criminal might say, "If you thought about getting caught, you'd never do the crime." Opportunistic criminals may be too impulsive to think about consequences. But even older, more professional criminals say that they use this psychological tactic on themselves. Putting aside all negative thoughts is one way to neutralize the fatalistic view that prison is an eventual certainty. Not that it makes a difference; the California study found that criminals who thought that arrest was likely committed just as much crime as did those who estimated a low probability of arrest. That is, perceptions of certainty of punishment had no effect on actual levels of crime.

A second psychological process insulates criminals from their own knowledge that eventually everyone gets caught and goes to prison. Despite the odds, criminals often develop a belief in their own invulnerability. In part, this belief, this confidence, develops as the criminal commits more and more crimes successfully. A young mugger may approach his first crimes with a feeling of fear and with an assessment of his chances as only 50-50. By the time he has committed several muggings with no trouble, he may come to feel nearly certain of his safety from the law.[41]

In any case, the long-range statistical probabilities indicated by clearance rates have a very weak influence over people's moment-to-moment decisions to commit crimes. In the first place, criminals do not have an accurate knowledge of these probabilities. Second, criminals, like most people, make decisions on the basis of information available in the situation at hand rather than on abstract statistical information. To take a noncriminal example, students choosing courses pay less attention to the results of a student survey ("Professor X got an 80 percent positive rating") than to the in-person advice of two or three students ("Don't take Professor X; he's awful"), or their first impressions of the professor on the first day of class.

For criminals, the most important deterrent factors are those in the visible present. In fact, one possible interpretation of all the studies we have looked at is that the closer some element of deterrence is to the crime, the greater its power to deter. People in a house deter burglars, and cops on the subway deter subway criminals, more effectively than do increased clearance rates, conviction rates, or imprisonment rates. If I am a criminal in search of an opportunity, police or even civilians in the area will affect me directly. I can see them; they can see me. But an increased imprisonment rate in my city will have touched only other criminals, not me (at least not yet). Some theorists think that "each arrest . . . has a relatively large effect on the perceptions of a small number of potential criminals,"[42] implying that if my criminal friend is arrested, I will be deterred. However, most criminals do in fact know others who have gone to prison; and despite the fate of their friends, they go on committing crimes. Why? My hunch is that the possible deterrent elements of the criminal justice system just do not seem as real, especially compared with other pressures on a person—direct economic and social pressures in the immediate situation.

Scared Straight?

In recent years, some law enforcement agencies have tried deterrence policies aimed at first offenders and juveniles on the theory that these people are not yet "hardened" criminals and that they may have committed their crimes out of a mistaken perception of the realities of crime and punishment. Some youths, if arrested early enough, will reduce or stop their crime.[43] The deterrence probably affects the less serious juvenile delinquents, and even for these first offenders, the evidence is not clear. One federal program instituted the practice of **split sentences**—a short term in jail followed by probation. Follow-up studies found that "a taste of the bars" had no extra deterrent effect. A similar program of **shock probation** in Kentucky had the same lack of effect: Offenders who received a brief "shocking" term in jail followed by probation were no more successful than were offenders sentenced only to straight probation.[44]

A more widely known type of program has been used on juveniles—even those who have not been in trouble with the law. These programs try to change juveniles' perceptions of the certainty and severity of punishment by exposing them to real criminals in real prisons. In the late 1970s, a television documentary entitled "Scared Straight!" presented one such program—the Juvenile Awareness Project at Rahway State Prison in New Jersey, now probably the best-known of these programs, but certainly not the only one. Typically in these programs, kids are taken inside prison, where a select group of convicts graphically explains the horrors of prison. As the TV film shows, the convicts are indeed frightening as they depict, and to a certain extent enact, the humiliation and abuse many prisoners endure at the hands of guards and other prisoners. From the point of view of deterrence, the prisoners' message emphasizes the severity of punishment (prison is not a vacation; it is a physically and psychologically horrible experience). Their message also conveys the certainty of punishment (I was a smarter criminal than you'll ever be, and I got caught; therefore, if you don't straighten up, you will certainly wind up in here, too).

The original TV show and a sequel five years later gave mostly glowing reports on the 13 juveniles it followed through the Rahway program. Unfortunately, the show did not have a control group (i.e., a group of similar kids who did not undergo the experiment). However, since not all adolescents in New Jersey had participated, there was a ready-made experiment waiting to be done: Match a group of scared straight kids with a control group i.e., kids who had not undergone the program, and see who stays out of trouble. Compared with the control group, kids who have been "scared straight" should be less likely to commit crimes.

Systematic Evidence vs. TV

To test this idea, James Finckenauer followed two groups—one experimental (scared straight) and one control—for six months after the experimentals had visited the prison. He counted as "successes" youths who had no recorded offenses in that six-month period. "Failures" were those who had one or more offenses. Table 16–4 compares only nondelinquents— youths who had no record of offenses prior to the study. Table 16–5 compares those who did have prior records of delinquency.

Clearly, the "scared straight" kids did worse. Among the "good kids" (no previous offenses), 31.6 percent of the "scared straight" group had offenses in the six-month follow-up period, compared with only 4.8 percent of the unscared control group. For kids with prior offenses the failure rate was

Table 16–4 ▪ Outcomes for Nondelinquent Experimentals and Controls

	Successes	Failures	Total
Nondelinquent experimental	13 (68.4%)	6 (31.6%)	19
Nondelinquent control	20 (95.2%)	1 (4.8%)	21
Total	33	7	40

Source: James Finckenauer, SCARED STRAIGHT! and the Panacea Phenomenon, © 1982, pp. 137, 152. Adapted by permission of Prentice-Hall, Inc., Englewood Cliffs, NJ: 07632.

Table 16–5 ■ Outcomes for Delinquent Experimentals and Controls

	Successes	*Failures*	*Total*
Delinquent experimental	14 (51.8%)	13 (48.2%)	27
Delinquent control	11 (78.6%)	3 (21.4%)	14
Total	25	16	41

Source: James Finckenauer, *SCARED STRAIGHT! and the Panacea Phenomenon,* © 1982, pp. 137, 152. Adapted by permission of Prentice-Hall, Inc., Englewood Cliffs, NJ: 07632.

experimentals 48.2 percent, controls 21.4 percent. The "scared straight" kids had proportionally more than twice as many failures.

These results surprised and in some cases angered the people who ran the Juvenile Awareness Project. Even some people without a vested interest in the project—perhaps those who had seen the TV show—had similar reactions. The results are upsetting because they disprove two very appealing notions. First, these results strongly question the "obvious," commonsense view of crime and punishment that began this chapter. Second, if the results had shown the Juvenile Awareness Project to have the 80 to 90 percent success rate it claimed, we would be looking at a very cheap solution to the crime problem. "Scared Straight!" suggested that for the mere cost of a bus trip to the nearest state prison, we could significantly reduce crime. Such a solution sounds too good to be true. It was.*

The results of this systematic research on "Scared Straight!" may have been disappointing. However, the findings probably did not surprise people familiar with research on similar programs.[45] None of this research has found a deterrent effect. Nor should this surprise us, if we recall the results of other studies of specific deterrence, which have consistently failed to show large deterrent effects. Juvenile awareness programs differ from these other studies only in that they do not allow the people being punished to become part of the inmate culture with its criminal values. Apparently, however, even when kids are kept apart from inmate culture, the brief exposure to prison wears off quickly and has far less influence than do other factors in the day-to-day life of youths. Here is a typical example—a boy with a prior record of delinquency who went through the Rahway project but later committed a crime.

> Sixteen . . . , black, and in the county youth home. He was referred [to the project] by his probation officer for stealing and for a breaking and entering . . . He said

* Finckenauer's finding that experimentals did worse may have been caused by methodological problems. There had originally been 50 subjects in each group. During the experiment and follow-up period, four experimentals and 15 controls disappeared from the data. They moved out of state or in some other way became impossible to trace. But at the very least, even if all the missing data had gone in the direction predicted by deterrence theory, the two groups would have had identical success rates.

[referring to the prisoners at Rahway], "I thought they might kill me—some of the things they said scared me." He thought the visit helped him stay straight for a while; but asked why he got in trouble again, he said, "Some things just happen."[46]

Modifying Deterrence Theory

The failure of these projects and the limited success of other forms of deterrence do not necessarily mean that we must throw out the idea entirely. The ideas behind deterrence are theoretically valid. Making those ideas work is a completely different matter. The certainty and severity of punishment are only two among several factors that influence crime, and it is unlikely that in reality the criminal justice system can raise these deterrent factors enough to offset the weight of other forces. If the criminal justice system could raise real rates of punishment so that a criminal might commit only three or four crimes before being locked up, crime rates would probably fall significantly. But the system cannot approach such effectiveness, and I suspect that the small increases that police, courts, and prisons can bring about are too small to have noticeable deterrent effects.

Another reason for the failure of deterrence efforts may be that some crimes and criminals are less easily deterred than others. For example, we would expect that increased risk or increased cost would be more effective in deterring "instrumental," rational crimes (i.e., crimes planned for economic gain). "Expressive" crimes, on the other hand should be less susceptible to an increased risk of punishment. In such crimes, the pressures of the immediate situation make cost-benefit calculation difficult if not impossible. Small wonder that the death penalty has proven an ineffective deterrent to murder. Most murders are expressive crimes, conflicts which escalate quickly into violence. There is some evidence to suggest (though not enough to demonstrate convincingly) that harsher penalties may have some effect on the more "instrumental" murders such as those committed during robberies.[47] The Supreme Court used this commonsense notion—though without any evidence—in its first decisions upholding a new death penalty statute in 1976.[48]

Perhaps we expect too much of deterrence because we overestimate the long-term rationality of criminals. We mistakenly expect that criminals will calculate the long-term outcomes of their actions. But obviously they do not. Opportunities or group pressure can force a person's attention away from long-range costs and benefits and focus it on the immediate situation. Juvenile awareness projects fail probably because juveniles are especially vulnerable to group pressures. So even property crimes like auto theft and larceny may derive from psychological and social "expressive" causes, rather than from economic, "instrumental" causes.

The lives of adult criminals too—except for the professionals—are not marked by a great deal of rational planning. Criminals generally feel that they have little control over their lives. They usually do not have the resources to leave the types of neighborhoods they know and feel comfortable in. They may try to stay out of trouble, but given the pressures of the moment, and perhaps the effects of alcohol or drugs, they may forget these long-range plans. They may drift to the opportunities offered by the world they live in, and sometimes those opportunities will be criminal. In their lives too, as in that of the boy quoted above, "Some things just happen."

NOTES

1. Richard M. Restak (1975), *Pre-meditated Man*, New York: Viking, p. 32. Jessica Mitford (1973), *Kind and Usual Punishment: The Prison Business*, New York: Knopf, p. 123.

2. Lawrence Greenfield (1985), "Examining Recidivism," *Bureau of Justice Statistics Special Report*, Washington, DC: U.S. Government Printing Office.

3. Allen J. Beck and Bernard Shipley (1987), "Recidivism of Young Parolees," *Bureau of Justice Statistics Special Report*, Washington, DC: U.S. Government Printing Office.

4. For a more complete review of this research, see Philip J. Cook (1980), "Research in Criminal Deterrence: Laying the Groundwork for the Second Decade," in Norval Morris and Michael Tonry, eds., *Crime and Justice: An Annual Review of Research*, vol. 2, Chicago: University of Chicago Press, pp. 211–68.

5. David Greenberg (1975), "The Incapacitative Effects of Imprisonment: Some Estimates," *Law and Society Review*, vol. 9, pp. 541–80.

6. Lyle Shannon (1982), "Reassessing the Relationship of Adult Criminal Careers to Juvenile Careers: A Summary," *Report for U.S. Department of Justice*, Washington, DC.

7. Daniel Gottfredson, Mark G. Neithercutt, Joan Nuffield, and Vincent O'Leary (1973), "Four Thousand Lifetimes: A Study of Time Served and Parole Outcomes," *Law and Contemporary Problems*, vol. 41.

8. Edwin Schur (1973), *Radical Non-Intervention: Rethinking the Delinquency Problem*, Englewood Cliffs, NJ: Prentice-Hall, p. 155.

9. Charles A. Murray and Louis A. Cox (1979), *Beyond Probation: Juvenile Corrections and the Chronic Offender*, Beverly Hills, CA: Sage.

10. Elliott Currie (1985), *Confronting Crime: An American Challenge*, New York: Pantheon, p. 74.

11. Thorsten Sellin (1959), *The Death Penalty*, Philadelphia: American Law Institute.

12. *Furman v. Georgia* (1972), 408 U.S. 238.

13. Isaac Ehrlich (1975), "The Deterrent Effect of Capital Punishment: A Question of Life and Death," *American Economic Review*, vol. 81, no. 3, pp. 521–65.

14. Hans Zeisel (1976), "The Deterrent Effect of the Death Penalty: Facts vs. Faith," in Philip B. Kurland, ed. (1976), *The Supreme Court Review 1976*, pp. 317–43. Also in Hugo Adam Bedau, ed. (1982), *The Death Penalty in America*, New York: Oxford University Press, pp. 116–38. See also Lawrence R. Klein, Brian Forst, and Victor Filatov, "The Deterrent Effect

of Capital Punishment: An Assessment of the Estimates," in Alfred Blumstein, Jacqueline Cohen, and Daniel Nagin, eds. (1978), *Deterrence and Incapacitation: Estimating the Effects of Sanctions on Crime Rates*. Washington, DC: National Academy of Sciences, pp. 336–60.

15. Kenneth L. Avis (1976), *Capital Punishment in Canada: A Time Series Analysis of the Deterrent Hypothesis*, cited in Zeisel, op. cit., p. 129.

16. UCR, 1983; UCR, 1989.

17. U.S. Department of Justice, Bureau of Justice Statistics (1983), *Report to the Nation on Crime and Justice—the Data*, Washington, DC: U.S. Government Printing Office.

18. George L. Kelling, Tony Pate, Duane Dieckman, and Charles E. Brown (1974), *The Kansas City Preventive Patrol Experiment: A Summary Report*, Washington, DC: Police Foundation. Richard C. Larson (1975), "What Happened to Patrol Operations in Kansas City? A Review of the Kansas City Preventive Experiment," *Journal of Criminal Justice*, vol. 3, pp. 267–97.

19. Jan Chaiken (1975), "What's Known About the Deterrent Effects of Police Activities," Santa Monica, CA: The RAND Corporation.

20. James Q. Wilson (1975), *Thinking About Crime*, New York: Basic Books, p. 96.

21. Ibid., p. 93.

22. Gerald R. Clark (1969), "What Happens When the Police Strike?" *The New York Times Magazine*, Nov. 16. In Donald R. Cressey, ed. (1971), *Crime and Criminal Justice*, Chicago: Quadrangle Books, pp. 58–76.

23. Edwin H. Pfuhl Jr. (1983), "Police Strikes and Conventional Crime: A Look at the Data," *Criminology*, vol. 21, no. 4, pp. 489–503.

24. Cook, op. cit, p. 234. Simon A. Hakim and George F. Rengert (1981), *Crime Spillover*, Beverly Hills, CA: Sage.

25. Lawrence W. Sherman (1990), "Police Crackdowns: Initial and Residual Deterrence," in Michael Tonry and Norval Morris, eds. (1990), *Crime and Justice: A Review of Research*, Chicago: University of Chicago Press, pp. 1–48.

26. Blumstein, Cohen, and Nagin, op. cit., pp. 114–115.

27. David F. Greenberg and Ronald C. Kessler (1982), "The Effect of Arrests on Crime: A Multivariate Panel Analysis," *Social Forces*, vol. 60, no. 3, pp. 771–90. Scott H. Decker and Carol W. Kohfeld (1985), "Crimes, Crime Rates, Arrests, and Arrest Ratios: Implications for Deterrence Theory," *Criminology*, vol. 23, no. 3, pp. 437–50.

28. James P. Lynch (1987), "Imprisonment in Four Countries," *Bureau of Justice Statistics Special Report*, Washington, DC: U.S. Government Printing Office.

29. Blumstein, Cohen, and Nagin, op. cit., pp. 42–44.

30. *The New York Times*, Jan. 26, 1973, p. 1. Quoted in Franklin Zimring (1978), "Policy Experiments in General Deterrence: 1970–1975," in Blumstein, Cohen, and Nagin, op. cit., pp. 140–86.

31. Zimring, op. cit., p. 159.

32. Milton Heumann and Colin Loftin (1979), "Mandatory Sentencing and the Abolition of Plea Bargaining: The Michigan Felony Firearm Statute," *Law and Society Review*, vol. 13, pp. 393–430.

33. James Q. Wilson (1983), *Thinking About Crime*, New York: Basic Books, p. 136.

34. Heumann and Loftin, op. cit.

35. Glenn Pierce and William Bowers (1979), *The Impact of the Bartley-Fox Gun Law on Crime in Massachusetts*, Boston: Center for Applied Social Research, Northeastern University.

36. W. Gordon West (1978), "The Short-term Careers of Serious Thieves," *Canadian Journal of Criminology*, vol. 20, no. 2, pp. 169–90.

37. Assembly Committee on Criminal Procedures (1968), "Public Knowledge of Criminal Penalties," in R. L. Henshel and R. A. Silverman, eds. (1975), *Perception in Criminology*, New York: Columbia University Press, pp. 74–90.

38. Mark Peterson and Harriet Braiker (1981), *Who Commits Crimes: A Survey of Prison Inmates*, Cambridge, MA: Oelschlager, Gunn, and Hain, p. 113.

39. Ibid.

40. Charles Silberman (1978), *Criminal Violence, Criminal Justice*, New York: Random House, pp. 75–76.

41. Robert LeJeune (1977), "The Management of a Mugging," *Urban Life*, vol. 6, no. 2, pp. 123–48.

42. Cook, op. cit., p. 225.

43. Douglas A. Smith and Patrick R. Gartin (1989), "Specifying Specific Deterrence: The Influence of Arrest on Future Criminal Activity," *American Sociological Review*, vol. 54, no. 1, pp. 94–106.

44. Nicolette Parisi (1981), "A Taste of the Bars," *Journal of Criminal Law and Criminology*, vol. 72, no. 3, pp. 1109–23.

45. James A. Finckenauer, *SCARED STRAIGHT! and the Panacea Phenomenon*, © 1982, pp. 137, 152. Adapted by permission of Prentice-Hall, Inc., Englewood Cliffs, NJ 07632.

46. Ibid., p. 52.

47. Colin Loftin and Robert H. Hill (1974), "Regional Subculture and Homicide: An Examination of the Gastil-Hackney Thesis," *American Sociological Review*, vol. 39, pp. 714–24.

48. *Gregg v. Georgia* 428 U.S. 153 (1976).

Incapacitation

CHAPTER *17*

WHY DO WE HAVE PRISONS? SO FAR WE HAVE LOOKED AT REHABILITATION AND deterrence as possible functions of prison. Let us oversimplify for a moment and suppose that the evidence is clear: that prison does not deter people from crime, nor does it rehabilitate those who spend time there. Of course, the evidence does not speak quite so boldly. But it certainly should be enough to dampen both the liberal's enthusiasm for prison as rehabilitation and the conservative's enthusiasm for prison as a deterrent. Even so, there is a third practical use for prison: to keep criminals off the streets. This purpose is known in criminology as **incapacitation**: literally taking away the criminal's capacity to commit crimes.

In the 1970s, ideas about the purpose of prison were changing. This change in focus may have been a response to the discouraging evidence on rehabilitation and deterrence. It may also have been part of a disillusionment with efforts to get at the social causes of crime. In any case, incapacitation began to attract more attention, both from the public and from criminologists. The idea of incapacitation holds a great advantage over deterrence or rehabilitation: It is indisputable. You don't have to do fancy research to show that it works. As long as criminals are behind bars, they cannot be victimizing the public.

Here was the basis for a policy to fight crime: Keep criminals in prison for longer terms. It was the obvious solution to the problem of high crime rates. Or was it?

As with deterrence—specific and general—so with incapacitation: We must distinguish between two types of effect—on the one hand, the effect on the individual; on the other, the more general effect on crime rates. Obviously prison keeps each individual inmate from victimizing the public. But will locking up more people for longer periods of time substantially reduce the overall crime rate? A lock-'em-up policy will undoubtedly prevent some crimes. The real question is how many crimes it will prevent and at what cost.

COLLECTIVE INCAPACITATION—LOCK 'EM ALL UP

Some rough evidence on incapacitation comes from policy changes that took place in the 1970s. As faith in rehabilitation faded, many states turned to policies based on incapacitation (and possibly retribution). Legislators passed laws requiring stiffer sentencing, and judges sentenced more criminals to prison. As a result, a greater proportion of criminals were going to prison. In 1971, state and federal prisons held about 200,000 people, an "incarceration rate" of 95 per 100,000; that is, for every 100,000 people in the country, 95 were in prison. (This number does not include those in county and municipal jails or juvenile detention centers.) Ten years later, the prison population had risen to 300,000, and the rate had gone from 95 to 153 per 100,000 (see Figure 17–1).

Unfortunately, during the same decade, crime rates did not go down. Victimization surveys showed very little change in crime, and police statistics showed an increase. Why did crime rates remain high despite the great increase in imprisonment? Was the strategy of incapacitation a failure? And if so, is incapacitation a worthless idea?

Of course, many other changes could have been affecting crime in the United States in the 1970s. A more localized example will offer a better idea of how incapacitation does or doesn't work. Yet even in narrower studies, incapacitation research is a tricky business. When we ask, "How much crime can we prevent by increasing the prison time of people convicted of crime?" we are really asking, "How much crime would these criminals commit if we let them go?" The answer requires predicting the future. This is a difficult task at best, and often we have no way of finding out whether the prediction was correct.

A different way of asking the question is to look back and ask, "How much crime was committed by people who were arrested but not locked up?" This question is a bit easier to investigate. It also addresses the popular version of the incapacitation argument: that many crimes are committed by criminals who get arrested but not punished; that criminals walk out of court and go right back to crime, crime which could have been prevented had they instead gone to prison.

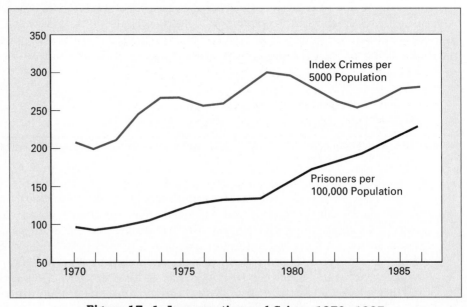

Figure 17–1 Incarceration and Crime, 1970–1987

To test the accuracy of this popular view, one team of researchers looked just at violent crime (murder, rape, robbery, and assault) in a single year (1973) in a single county (Franklin County, Ohio, which includes the state capital, Columbus). That year, roughly 3,000 violent crimes were reported to the police. The researchers asked, "How many of these crimes could have been prevented if the courts had been tougher on crime?" Suppose that beginning in 1968, every person convicted of a felony had been locked up for five years. How many criminals would be affected, and how much crime would be prevented? Suppose that Criminal Smith had been convicted of a felony in 1970, but had served only one year, and that he had then committed a violent crime in 1973. Under the hypothetical five-year policy, he is a "preventable recidivist"; that is, his repeat offense could have been averted by a five-year sentence, since he still would have been in prison in 1973. His violent offense was a preventable crime. The researchers wanted to know how many of the 2,892 violent crimes in 1973 were this type of preventable crime.

Unfortunately, they could not find out what they needed to know for all of those 2,892 crimes. They could know only about the 638 where someone was arrested (or in police terms, crimes that were "cleared by arrest"). That meant that 2,254 violent crimes remained unsolved. Not knowing who committed these crimes presents a serious problem in estimating incapacitation; but in criminology, researchers often must make do with the available information, even when it is incomplete, and make their best estimates about the rest. In this case, the information consisted of the 638 violent crimes cleared by arrest. The researchers looked at the records of all persons arrested for these crimes to see how many of them had convictions for any felony (violent or not) in the past five years. There were 342 people arrested in all. (It is important to keep in mind the distinction between crimes and criminals. The 342 arrested criminals* accounted for the 638 crimes cleared by arrest.)

Of the 342 people arrested, only 63 (less than 20 percent) had been convicted of a felony in the last five years. Therefore, a five-year sentence would have prevented the crimes of these 63 people. The violent crimes of the other 279 arrestees would have occurred anyway. Some of these 63 people committed more than one violent crime each. In fact, the 63 "preventable recidivists" were arrested for a total of 111 violent crimes. Since there were 2,892 violent crimes reported to the police, these 111 arrests constitute 4 percent of the total. In other words, the five-year sentence that would have kept these 63 criminals off the streets would have reduced violent crime by *at least* 4 percent. I say "at least" 4 percent because these 63 people may have committed still other violent crimes beyond the 111 they were arrested for. Remember, 2,254 (nearly 80 percent of the violent crimes were un-

---

* For purposes of estimating incapacitation, we are assuming that each person arrested really did commit the crime for which he or she was arrested.

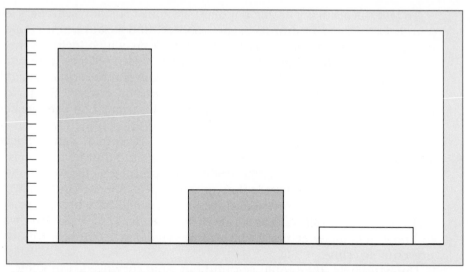

Figure 17–2 Violent Crimes: Reported, Cleared by Arrest, Cleared by Arrest and Committed by Preventable Recidivists
Source: Derived from Van Dine, et al (1979).

cleared. The 63 freed convicts probably committed some of these uncleared crimes. But how many?

One of the great problems with this study (and others like it) is trying to estimate that number. To make the estimate, you have to make a model. The term "model" here has something of its everyday meaning—a scaled-down representation of some larger thing in the real world. In science, it is more useful to think of a model as a set of assumptions—assumptions about the relationships between things we know and things we don't know,[1] in this case between crimes we know about and crimes we don't know about. If we are creating a model to estimate the incapacitation effect of different sentencing policies, we have to make assumptions as to how many un-cleared violent crimes the criminal commits for every one violent crime he gets caught for. In the Ohio study, the researchers plugged in some as-sumptions that they thought would give them the largest reasonable in-capacitation effect. First, they assumed that for every violent crime arrest, the person arrested had gotten away with four other violent crimes (the Ohio researchers thought this was a rather high estimate, but they used it anyway in order to give a maximum incapacitation effect). Second, they included juveniles in their five-year sentence policy. Using this model, they estimated that if *everyone*, juvenile or adult, convicted of *any felony*, violent or nonviolent, had been locked up for five years, violent crime would have been reduced by 28 percent.

A 28 percent reduction in violent crime is good news. However, the ques-tion remains whether the five-year policy would be practical. Most states, for reasons of justice if nothing else, are unlikely to lock up most juveniles or nonviolent criminals for five years. In addition, the policy would be extremely wasteful and costly. In order to imprison those 63 people who committed later violent crimes, the state of Ohio would also have had to lock up many hundreds of people who did not go on to commit any violent crimes. As a statewide policy, it would mean an increase of 500 percent in an already overcrowded prison system. Ohio would be spending quite a bit of money to lock up a lot of people in order to achieve a 28 percent reduction in crime. And even if all these people had been locked up beginning in 1968, about three-quarters of the violent offenses of 1973 would have occurred anyway.

This high percentage of unpreventable crime is not unique to Franklin County, Ohio. In New York State, for example, of all people convicted of felonies in 1982, 76 percent had no prior felony convictions, and the proportion was even higher for the more serious crimes. For "A felonies," 94 percent of those convicted had no prior felony convictions. For "B felonies," it was 80 percent. Similarly in Maryland, incapacitation would have failed to prevent 77 percent of the major crimes. Of felons convicted in 1981 and 1982, 33 percent had only minor prior convictions, and 44 percent had no prior convictions of any sort.[2] A national study estimated that of all those admitted to prison, only about one-quarter were "preventable recidivists" (i.e., offenders on parole or probation). The others were either first offenders or recidivists who had served out their terms. Violent crimes were even less preventable than were property crimes. Nearly half of the violent offenses were committed by first offenders; a third were committed by previous offenders who had served their full terms. Only one violent offense in five could have been prevented by keeping all offenders in prison till the expiration of their full sentences.[3]

Does all this mean that we should give up on incapacitation as a goal (perhaps the major goal) of prisons? One answer—the answer given by proponents of incapacitation—is that doubling or even quintupling (as in the Ohio study) the number of people in prison is using the wrong idea of incapacitation. In this view, the crucial part of incapacitation is not *how many* people go to prison; it's *who* goes to prison.

The Ohio study proposes an indiscriminate policy of putting all felons in prison—a policy called **collective incapacitation**. You may be more familiar with a different example of it. When a state tries to reduce drunken driving by raising the drinking age (say from 19 to 21), it is using a policy of collective incapacitation. Just as imprisoning all felons for five years removes them from the possible crime-committing population, raising the legal drinking age (assuming that the law is effective) removes all 19- and 20-year-olds from the possible drunken-driving population. Since they cannot drink, they cannot commit the crime of drunken driving. Of course, some people (especially 19- and 20-year-olds) may argue that this policy is wasteful. Even if it incapacitates the relative handful of unsafe drinkers, it also incapacitates a large number of safe drinkers.

A similar controversy runs through the debate over gun control. Everyone agrees that too many crimes are committed with guns. Proposals for gun control are really a type of collective incapacitation: Make it harder (or in some proposals impossible) for *everyone* to get guns. If nobody has a gun, nobody can commit a crime with a gun. Opponents of gun control propose policies based on *deterrence*: Let people have all the guns they want, but severely punish those who use them in crimes. With gun control, they argue, too many noncriminals will be incapacitated, and law-abiding sportsmen will be unnecessarily deprived of their guns.*

The same argument holds for imprisoning all offenders. And unlike raising the drinking age or restricting the sale of guns, imprisonment brings direct costs to the taxpayers. Collective incapacitation—lock 'em all up—may be emotionally appealing, but as a policy it is very expensive. However, there may be a more efficient use of our limited prison space.

SELECTIVE INCAPACITATION—LOCK SOME OF 'EM UP

We know that some offenders commit only a few crimes; others commit many crimes. It makes no sense, from the standpoint of incapacitation, to fill our prisons with infrequent offenders. Instead, we should concentrate on those who commit the worst crimes and commit them most frequently. For incapacitation to be most effective, we must select the worst criminals for prison—a policy known as **selective incapacitation**. Proponents of this policy argue that the huge increases in the prison population in the 1970s were not a good test of incapacitation. If most of the additional prisoners were low-rate offenders, then persistent high rates of crime should have come as no surprise.

Selective incapacitation, even more than collective incapacitation, sounds very tempting. Its proponents promise reductions in crime without large increases in the prison population. Recall the relevant fact from the various cohort studies: A fairly small number of people commits a large proportion of the crime. In Wolfgang's study of all Philadelphia teenage boys born in 1945, the 627 "chronic offenders," out of 10,000 boys, accounted for over half of all arrests. These arrests included nearly two-thirds of all serious (Index) crimes and over four-fifths of all robberies.[4] The tempting conclusion is this: If somehow we could have incapacitated those 627 boys, we could have greatly reduced serious crime. As a police chief in another city said, "If I could just get 200 guys off my streets . . . I could cut the crime rate in half."[5] Criminal justice bureaucrats, using less blunt language, talk

---

* They make other arguments as well—that gun restrictions are unconstitutional, that criminals will get guns anyway—but for purposes of this chapter, I am interested only in the underlying principle of incapacitation, not the practical problems of putting policies into effect.

about focusing on the "career criminal" or "habitual offender." They are all talking about selective incapacitation as a means of reducing crime.

Selecting Career Criminals—the RAND Study

The crucial and difficult part of selective incapacitation is the selection. Since we want to select those criminals who will commit the most crimes unless we lock them up, we are once again in the prediction business. For selective incapacitation to work, we must predict what a criminal would do if he or she were set free. In actual practice, people in the criminal justice system make this prediction every day. When a district attorney decides to charge an arrested person with a lesser crime, when a judge decides to sentence a criminal to a shorter term or to probation, when a parole board decides to grant a prisoner an early release, they are all predicting that the offender will not commit further crimes. Unfortunately, these predictions have, on the whole, been no more accurate than guessing.

Ever since Lombroso, criminologists studying individual criminals have tried to predict criminal behavior. Often, the prediction is disguised as a backward-looking explanation rather than a forward-looking prediction. But the implication is that if we had known about the important explanatory factors earlier—if we had seen the particular skull shape or the telltale signs of psychopathy or sociopathy—we could have predicted the criminality. In the last decade or so, criminologists have tried to devise scientific and more accurate ways of predicting future criminal behavior, not just of children but of those already convicted of crimes. In 1982, researchers from the RAND Corporation published the results of a study claiming that selective incapacitation used as a basis for sentencing criminals could reduce robbery by 20 percent with no increase in the prison population.[6] A 20 percent reduction in robbery with no additional cost to the taxpayers is a rather attractive proposal. It even caught the attention of the popular press (e.g., *Newsweek* magazine). Since this study remains influential, I will go into it in some detail here.

What distinguishes selective incapacitation from collective incapacitation is that selective incapacitation recognizes that criminals are not all alike. The number of crimes prevented by locking up Criminal A will be different from the number prevented by locking up Criminal B. A policy of selective incapacitation aims at efficiency—the use of scarce prison cells to achieve the maximum crime reduction. According to principles of selective incapacitation, judges should sentence low-rate offenders to shorter terms and high-rate offenders to longer terms. But faced with a person convicted of robbery, how can we know whether he is in the low, medium, or high category? We cannot very well ask him, since no criminal, knowing that his future depends on the answer, will go on record as being likely to commit several stickups every month.

In order to estimate the incapacitation effect of locking up a criminal, we must estimate how much crime he would commit if out on the streets. In the Ohio study, researchers just assumed that, on the average, a criminal commits four violent crimes for each violent crime arrest. But the RAND researchers wanted more than "on the average." They wanted to be able to predict which criminals would be below that average and which would be far above it.

Peter Greenwood, who headed the study, and his colleagues interviewed inmates of jails and prisons in California, Texas, and Michigan. The researchers had information on the inmates' official criminal history (arrests, convictions, imprisonment). But in the interview, they would ask an inmate not just about the crime he'd gotten locked up for, but about all the other crimes that he had committed in the two years prior to getting caught.

On the basis of these self-reports, the researchers divided the inmates into three groups according to their recent amounts of crime. For example, among robbers, the low-rate group reported an average of two robberies per year; the high-rate robbers averaged 31 robberies per year (and hundreds of other crimes as well). Once they discovered these ranges of criminal activity, the researchers put this information out of sight and pretended they did not know the offense rate of any individual inmate. Instead, they made this one fact the thing they were trying to predict. In terms of statistics, this amount of crime—low, medium, or high—became the **dependent variable**; that is, the thing to be predicted.

The researchers' problem then was to find some useful **independent variables**—that is, other information which would allow them to make better guesses as to whether a person was a high-, medium-, or low-rate offender. Therefore, Greenwood also asked inmates about their juvenile crime, their employment and marital histories, their use of drugs, their education, and other social factors. Information on race and age also was readily available. If a variable turned out to be correlated with an individual's rate of crime, then using that variable would allow better prediction for sentencing purposes.

Greenwood and his colleagues discovered that by using seven items from their interviews, they could create a formula that did a fairly good job of measuring how serious a criminal each inmate was. (That is, they could use this combination of independent variables to make a better prediction about the dependent variable.) The seven items were:

Prior conviction for robbery or burglary,
Being incarcerated for more than half of the preceding two years,
Juvenile conviction prior to age 16,
Commitment to a state or federal juvenile institution,
Current heroin or barbiturate use,
Heroin or barbiturate use as a juvenile,
Employed less than half of the preceding two years (excluding jail time).

Remember, Greenwood claimed that the use of this scale in sentencing robbers "could reduce the robbery rate by 20 percent with no increase in the total number of robbers incarcerated."[7]

Does the scale really work? Yes and no. On the one hand, it is an improvement over random guessing; on the other, it still misclassifies a great many people. Whether these mistakes outweigh the benefits is a matter of debate, so let's see why some people object to Greenwood's seven item scale.

Beware of False Positives

No formula for predicting human behavior is perfect. In any prediction scheme, there will be two kinds of errors: false positives and false negatives. A diagnosis of "positive" means that the person has what we are looking for—in this case, a high rate of crime. But we could just as easily use pregnancy as an example. If you take a test for pregnancy and it comes out "positive," it is predicting that you are pregnant. If you are in fact pregnant, then the test result is valid—a **true positive**. But if you are not really pregnant, then this prediction is a **false positive**. Similarly, if the test says that you are not pregnant, the prediction is "negative." If you really are not pregnant, the test is a **true negative**. But if six months later you give birth to a bouncing baby, the test was a **false negative**. These scientific terms have become more familiar in recent years as a result of the increased concern over illegal drugs. As more businesses and agencies want to test their workers for drugs, some people have raised the question of false positives: The test says the person is using illegal drugs, when in fact he or she has been taking a prescription drug or even nothing stronger than an over-the-counter cold medicine.*

There is one important difference, however. The pregnancy tests and drug tests try to determine whether a person has some condition right now. The test for criminality is trying to predict what someone will do in the future. Perhaps automobile insurance premiums provide a better analogy. An insurance company finds out which variables correlate with accidents; then it assigns rates accordingly. If you have an accident, your rates go up not because the company is punishing you for making them pay out a claim, but because people who have had an accident are more likely than others to be in another accident. In the same way, if you are under 25, your rates are higher not because insurance companies are anti-youth, but because young drivers are more likely than older ones to get into accidents. Of course, even in the higher-risk groups, most people are false positives—that is, they do not have accidents. But the number of true positives is higher than in low-risk groups.

---

* The drug testing controversy involves much more important issues—questions of constitutional law, ethics, privacy, individual rights, and public safety. But for purposes of this chapter I am concerned only with the issue of false positives.

Table 17–1 ■ **Predictions and Outcomes**

		Actual offense rate			
		Low	Medium	High	Total
Predicted	Low	**159**	33	17	209
offence	Medium	174	**89**	73	336
rate	High	59	71	**106**	236
	Total	392	193	196	

Source: Derived from Greenwood and Abrahams (1982). Santa Monica, CA., RAND.

Each type of error has its own costs. In predicting high-rate offenders, a false negative means that we predict someone as a safe risk and release him from prison; the cost of our error is the further crimes he commits. The cost of a false positive is all the money we spend to imprison a relatively harmless person.

How well did the RAND study do in avoiding these errors in classifying criminals? In Greenwood's seven-item test, anybody who had four or more of the seven characteristics was a "positive" (i.e., predicted to be a high-rate offender). Those who had only one or none of the seven characteristics were predicted to be low-rate offenders; those scoring two or three were predicted to be medium-rate offenders. Table 17–1 shows how well the predictions worked. (Correct predictions are in boldface.)

The scale works fairly well in identifying the less serious criminals. Better than 75 percent of these predictions were correct (159 out of 209). And less than one in 12 (17 of 209) of these people diagnosed as good risks were actually high-rate offenders. These would have been false negatives, since they were predicted, mistakenly, *not* to be high-rate offenders.

But the scale is far less efficient in picking out the serious criminals. Of the 236 people predicted to be high-rate offenders, only 106 (45 percent) were actually in that category. The other 55 percent were false positives. This means that if we were using this scale for actual sentencing, more than half the people receiving stiff sentences would be serving unnecessarily long terms.

Since selective incapacitation requires accurate prediction, all those false positives weaken the argument for selective incapacitation, even on its own terms. But in addition, there are other problems—technical, practical, legal, ethical—that may undermine the use of this scale and others like it.

Selective Incapacitation vs. Due Process

The technical problems, which challenge the accuracy of the results, involve statistical matters too complex for me to describe in detail here. But to give one example, it may not be accurate to use data from incarcerated people (presumably the most serious offenders) to make predictions about criminals in general who will be coming through the courts. Also, the "predictions" were tested against the same group of people used in deriving the scale. In classifying a new group of offenders, the scale would be less accurate. It would yield even more false positives than 55 percent, and we would have to reduce Greenwood's optimistic estimates. The reduction in robbery would probably be less than 20 percent, and the prison population would probably increase.

The legal and practical problems arise from the nature of the items in the scale. For the last three items, which involve drug use and employment, we must rely on the criminal's self-reports. Of the remaining four items, two deal with juvenile records. But in states where juvenile records are sealed, the criminal will again be the only source of information. If the scale were actually used for sentencing, it is unlikely that courts could require criminals to give this damaging information about themselves. In fact, for most practical purposes, the only items readily available to the court will be the first two: prior convictions and prison time. Since judges already give these factors great weight in their sentencing decisions, the RAND scale could probably do little to change the real world of criminal justice.

Regardless of its practical effect, the RAND study raises an important question: "Even if we could know all the information, should we use it to determine a criminal's sentence?" A principle of our system of justice is that a person should be punished for what he has done, not for what he is and not for what someone predicts he will do. To take an obvious example, suppose Greenwood had found that on the average, whites were more likely than blacks to be high-rate offenders. Should we give whites longer sentences? Purely from the standpoint of incapacitation, yes; from the standpoint of justice and fairness, no. In principle, we do not punish people for being white.* Given two people convicted of the same crime, can we give a long term to one because he has been unemployed? Or because he used drugs when he was young? Such a policy seems to violate the constitutional principle of "due process of law." The problem is especially troubling given the large percentage of false positives. Over half the people receiving long terms will have been sentenced on the basis of predictions that were incorrect.

Of course, under the current system, the same kinds of inequities exist. People convicted of the same crime and with the same criminal history may receive quite different sentences. Judges, too, like the RAND scale, may take into account drug use and employment, as well as other factors like family status and perhaps even (unconsciously) race. Moreover, the current system—and this is the whole point of the RAND study—already imprisons

---

* In fact, Greenwood did look at race and found that it made little or no difference in predicting rates of crime.

many people who could safely be released. The RAND study does not claim to make sentencing any fairer; it merely claims to make it more efficient and more systematic.

WHY INCAPACITATION FAILS

Why has incapacitation not turned out to be the magic bullet that will stop crime? One answer is that even using the best scientific information (much of which would be legally excluded in court), we would still not be very good at identifying the worst criminals. In order to make sure that we catch most of the big fish, we have to cast a wide net and haul in a lot of smaller fish as well.

Of course these other criminals are not exactly small fry, and that's part of the problem. The courts already let the obviously good risks go with probation or perhaps a short jail term. The convicts in the RAND study were criminals who had committed enough serious crimes to wind up in state prisons. These were the tough customers. However, even within this group of convicts there was considerable variation. The worst 10 percent averaged 87 robberies a year; the rest of the prisoners averaged only five per year. In other words, even among the prison population, it is still only a handful who have committed most of the violent crimes. Locking up one of these high-rate robbers would prevent as many robberies as locking up 17 or 18 of the others. Selective incapacitation would work if—and this is the big if—we could pick out this handful from the other convicts. It would be easy to separate the bad guys from the boy scouts. What selective incapacitation requires, however, is an instrument sensitive enough to separate the really heavy dudes from criminals who demand people's money at knifepoint only two or three times a year. Unfortunately, as matters now stand, it is unrealistic to expect that we can develop a simple set of questions that will allow us to identify the very worst 25 percent or so in this group of serious criminals.

If we are already incapacitating the most serious criminals, why do crime rates remain high? This question quickly brings us back to the different theoretical explanations for crime. For example, both liberals and conservatives may argue that incapacitation as a strategy does nothing to change the *causes* of crime. Liberal versions of this idea focus on unemployment, poverty, inadequate schools, violent families, etc. Unfortunately, these theories do not explain why these causes should produce *more* criminals to replace those swept into prison.

Incapacitation vs. Supply and Demand

The conservative version does try to answer this question by taking a purely economic approach. This argument assumes that a person chooses crime for the same kinds of reasons that he might choose any other work—because it's the best job he can get. Will reducing the number of people in that job make it less attractive? For example, if you were deciding whether to go into accounting as an occupation, you would consider the difficulty of this field relative to your own talents. You would also consider the job market, or the "demand" for accountants. This demand would be reflected in the pay compared with other careers a person with your talents might consider: The greater the demand, the higher the pay. Suppose now that for some reason many accountants started to leave their jobs (perhaps they made so much money that they could retire comfortably by age 55). Would their departure lower the demand for accountants?

In a similar way, economists talk about the "demand" for robbery or burglary or other crimes. Of course, we usually don't think of anyone demanding crime in the way people with complicated finances demand accounting services. But economists think of demand as a function of income compared with cost. Anything that raises income or lowers cost contributes to the demand. If you or I buy stolen merchandise, we are obviously contributing to the overall demand for theft by bidding up the profit. In a less obvious way, we may lower the costs of crime by making ourselves more attractive as targets—by not locking doors, by putting stereos in our cars and not just in our homes, or by stocking our houses with easily resold consumer goods.[8] In this way, too, we are contributing to the "demand" for crime. According to this demand-and-supply model, retiring more criminals does nothing to change the demand for crime, any more than retiring more accountants changes the demand for accounting (see box).

There is another fact to consider, one which incapacitation studies often seem to ignore: Many criminals work in groups of two or three or even more. Suppose that we catch a robber who, along with two others, has been committing 50 robberies a year. If we lock him up, will next year's robberies decrease by 50? Or will his two uncaught friends continue their work in his absence, perhaps recruiting someone to take his place? In this example as well, incapacitation cannot decrease the "supply" or "demand" for robbery.

Of course, this economic line of thinking, with its emphasis on the criminal's benefits and costs (i.e., the profit from the crime and the risk of going to prison), is basically the deterrence model, a model whose use as a crime-control strategy is quite limited. Nevertheless, it may help explain why locking up criminals may have little or no effect on certain types of crime. For example, incapacitation will probably not affect crimes involving

The following item contains an example of one of the more questionable assumptions of incapacitation. By Mr. Greenleaf's logic, locking up two dozen car thieves would completely eliminate auto theft from Newark.

NEWARK LEADERS URGE ACTION ON CAR THEFTS
BY FREDERICK W. BYRD

The Newark City Council yesterday urged increased efforts to combat car theft in the city, with Councilman Earl Harris commenting, "The story is getting around that it is not safe to drive your car into our city."

During hearings on the municipal police budget yesterday, Police Director Louis Greenleaf said the problem is not the number of arrests being made but the fact that many of the offenders captured are not incarcerated. . . .

"The trouble is there is no strong enforcement after we arrest people," he said. . . .

"A juvenile may be arrested 10 times in six months, steal three or four cars a day, and in court he gets probation, probation, probation.

"If they would put one kid away, that would mean 600 less stolen cars," the director asserted.

Source: The Star Ledger (Newark), March 15, 1988, p. 1.

---

the sale of illegal goods or services. What happens, for instance, when the government wages a "war on drugs" by locking up more drug dealers? Public concern over heroin in the 1960s and cocaine in the 1980s led to stricter laws. More drug dealers went to prison. Yet the get-tough policies did not affect the drug business. In the 1980s, prison sentences for drug crimes pushed many prison systems well beyond capacity. Between 1984 and 1988, New York State tripled the number of drug dealers sent to prison—from 1,376 to 4,089. In addition, several dealers were put out of business permanently by their competitors. Yet during the same period, cocaine became even cheaper and easier to buy.[9] As with drugs, so with other illegal businesses like gambling and prostitution. Taking suppliers out of the market will have only a temporary effect, if any, on the total amount of business. But what about less businesslike crimes?

Incapacitation and Predatory Crime

It would seem, for example, that incapacitation should work well for the crime of rape. Locking up a rapist will prevent him from committing further rapes; in addition, it is hard to imagine a "demand for rape" that would lead others to take his place. But despite this logic, the evidence on incapacitation of rapists is disappointing. For example, Jacqueline Cohen, in her study of criminals in Washington, D.C., estimated that if every man convicted of rape were imprisoned for life, the rate of rape in Washington would decrease by only 3.6 percent. Life sentences for other noneconomic, "expressive" crimes would bring greater reductions—7.9 percent for murder, 13.7 percent for aggravated assault. But of course, no judge can hand down a life sentence on a first conviction for aggravated assault. Cohen therefore also estimated the reduction for repeat offenses. She concluded that if the life sentence were imposed after only a second assault conviction (also unlikely in the real world), aggravated assault would decrease by 3.3 percent.[10]

A life sentence policy for first offenders will never happen. The laws would not permit it. Nevertheless, suppose for a minute that courts could and did hand down such sentences. What would happen? It would bring a modest decrease in crime levels; if every Index-offense conviction brought a life term, the reduction might be as great as 25 percent. But this policy would also create a much larger prison population, and a much older one. After a while, newcomer teenage convicts would be jostling Grey Panthers for elbow room in prisons.

Age and Sentencing

The image of old folks taking up valuable prison space suggests one more important factor in incapacitation: criminal careers. We know that age is important in crime. Forty-year-olds, on the whole, commit only one-tenth as much crime as 18-year-olds. Even serious criminals become less active as they get older.

The facts about age and crime have led some criminologists to criticize current policies regarding the sentencing of juveniles. Many states still have a different set of institutions and procedures for juvenile offenders; along with these goes a different, and usually more lenient, sentencing policy. The criticism of this separate system has usually emphasized retribution (or justice or morality): A person who commits adultlike crimes should suffer adultlike penalties. A 16-year-old who robs people should receive a stiff sentence for robbery, not a shorter sentence for juvenile delinquency. In the early 1980s, many states changed their laws to allow juveniles to be tried as adults for certain crimes, and in 1986, the first death sentence was carried out for a murder committed by a juvenile.

But some criminologists, notably James Q. Wilson, have also argued for the same policy not because it is morally right, but because it will help reduce crime by incapacitating high-rate offenders.

The two-track system (one for juveniles, one for adults) tends to allot punishment according to the criminal's "debt to society." The more crimes a person has committed, the greater his social debt, and therefore the greater his punishment. Imagine two people, one age 35, the other age 18; each is arrested for burglary. The 35-year-old, with his long record of arrests and convictions and perhaps some previous time in prison, has "used up society's hospitality"; he owes a large social debt. The judge sentences him to a long term. On the other hand, a younger criminal, whose record shows only a few arrests, will receive a lighter sentence, perhaps probation.

But, Wilson argues, these sentences based on debt to society make no sense for purposes of preventing crime. The older criminal is probably near the end of his criminal career, while the youngster may be just moving into his most intense criminal phase. Wilson suggests that for "serious repeat offenders" courts should do away with the two-track (juvenile/adult) system. These offenders, whatever their age, should be sentenced to incarceration or "close supervision" in order to protect society.[11]

This proposal is really selective incapacitation all over again, with the age factor added in. How much crime would such a plan prevent? Remember the estimates from the Ohio study: Of the 342 adults arrested for violent crimes, 63 had felony convictions as adults in the previous five years, and an additional 30 had felony arrests as juveniles in that period. Had these 93 been locked up after their first offense, violent crime (according to the researchers' estimates) would have been reduced by 28 percent—but at the cost of a vastly increased prison population.

In addition to these adults with juvenile records, 126 juveniles were arrested for violent crimes. But only 26 percent had previous felony convictions. Therefore, with juveniles, as with adults, even the most severe policy—five years for a first offense—will not affect the crimes of nearly three-quarters of the violent offenders. Of course, even the most conservative thinkers on crime would not want to lock up all first offenders. But if we limit the five-year sentence to repeat offenders, the incapacitation effect would become even smaller.[12]

There is one other problem in Wilson's proposal. It may be a mistake to think that the 35-year-old criminal is slowing down and nearing the end of his career. Other research on criminal careers suggests just the opposite. Most criminal careers are short. The majority of those who commit crimes, even of those who get arrested, end their careers by their late teens. Others taper off gradually, perhaps after a prison term, and have pretty much gotten out of crime by age 25.[13] The younger criminals who turn up in court will probably be out of crime in two or three years. However, the few who do stay in crime into their 30s are likely to be fairly active in crime even into their 40s.[14] For these offenders—older, with long rap sheets, and likely to continue in crime—sentences based on debt to society will also serve the purposes of incapacitation.

SUMMARY AND CONCLUSION

The problems with incapacitation are not theoretical. They are practical and technical. Deterrence and rehabilitation each have central theoretical questions that are still unresolved: Under what conditions—if any—can prisons be a deterrent to crime? What kinds of programs—if any—can rehabilitate prisoners? But incapacitation is a fact. Locking up people prevents them from committing crimes.

The practical problems are financial. It costs money to lock people up. Building new prisons is an especially expensive proposition. Construction costs vary from one part of the country to another, but current estimates range from $50,000 to $100,000 per cell. Adding in the cost of land and interest payments can double this figure.[15] Running prisons also costs money; each prisoner costs the state between $10,000 and $50,000 a year.[16] It is the public, the taxpayers, who must eventually foot the bill, and despite the popularity of the idea of locking up more and more criminals, voters have not always been willing to endorse the expense required by that policy.

Since cost prohibits locking up all lawbeakers for maximum terms, people at various places in the criminal justice system must decide who to lock up for longer or for shorter terms. What selective incapacitation research has tried to do is discover ways of using valuable prison space most efficiently. Efficiency, in this case, means using that space to prevent the greatest amount of crime. This efficiency requires predictions about what a criminal will do if released. Unfortunately, some prediction schemes require information that courts would exclude; and even when this information is allowed, many of these predictions turn out to be false positives.

NOTES

1. S. A. Livingston, personal communication.

2. Herbert Koppel (1984), "Sentencing Practices in 13 States," *Bureau of Justice Statistics Special Report*, October, Washington, DC: U.S. Government Printing Offices.

3. Lawrence Greenfeld (1985), "Examining Recidivism," *Bureau of Justice Statistics Special Report*, Washington, DC: U.S. Government Printing Offices.

4. Marvin E. Wolfgang, Robert M. Figlio, and Thorsten Sellin (1972), *Delinquency in a Birth Cohort*, Chicago: University of Chicago Press.

5. Steve Van Dine, John P. Conrad, and Simon Dinitz (1979), "The Incapacitation of the Chronic Thug," *Journal of Criminal Law and Criminology*, vol. 70, pp. 125–35.

6. Peter W. Greenwood, with Allan Abrahamse (1982), *Selective Incapacitation*, Santa Monica, CA: RAND.

7. Peter W. Greenwood (1984) "Selective Incapacitation: A Method of Using Our Prisons More Effectively," *NIJ Reports*, no.183, p.6.

8. Philip J. Cook, "The Demand and Supply of Criminal Opportunities," in Michael Tonry and Norval Morris, eds. (1986), *Crime and Justice: An Annual Review of Research*, Chicago: University of Chicago Press, pp. 1–27.

9. Robert M. Morgenthau (1988), "We Are Losing the War on Drugs," *The New York Times*, Feb. 16, p. A21.

10. Jacqueline Cohen, "Incapacitation as a Strategy for Crime Control: Possibilities and Pitfalls," in Michael Tonry and Norval Morris, eds. (1983), *Crime and Justice: An Annual Review of Research*, vol. 5, p. 67.

11. Barbara Boland and James Q. Wilson (1978), "Age, Crime, and Punishment," *The Public Interest*, no. 51, pp. 22–34.

12. Cohen, op. cit., p. 27.

13. David P. Farrington, "Age and Crime," in Michael Tonry and Norval Morris, eds. (1986), *Crime and Justice: An Annual Review of Research*, Chicago: University of Chicago Press, pp. 189–250. Alfred Blumstein, Jacqueline Cohen, Jeffrey A. Roth, and Christy A. Visher, eds. (1986), *Criminal Careers and "Career Criminals"*, vol. 1, Washington, DC: National Academy Press.

14. Cohen, op. cit., p. 65.

15. Sue Titus Reid (1985), *Crime and Criminology* (4th ed.), New York: Holt, Rinehart and Winston, p. 692, notes 15–16.

16. Samuel Walker (1985), *Sense and Nonsense About Crime: A Policy Guide*, Monterey, CA: Brooks/Cole, p. 60.

Name Index

Subject Index